More titles from Visible 🖐 W9-BZC-816
to keep the juices flowing

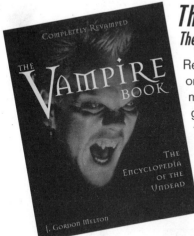
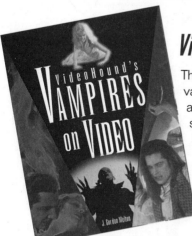

ABOUT THE AUTHOR

J. Gordon Melton is a longtime collector of vampire lore and paraphernalia and is the author of the critically acclaimed *Vampire Book: Encyclopedia of the Undead*, which in 1997 was named Nonfiction Vampire Book of the Century at the Dracula '97 Centennial Celebration. Dr. Melton is also the author of *Video-Hound's Vampires on Video* and is a nationally recognized author, lecturer, and scholar best known for his reference works in the field of religion. He often serves as a consultant to the mass media on religion and cults, and has appeared on several programs on The Learning Channel and other networks as a vampire expert. Dr. Melton founded the Institute for the Study of American Religion, which is now housed at the University of California at Santa Barbara.

THE VAMPIRE GALLERY

A

WHO'S

WHO

OF THE

UNDEAD

J. GORDON MELTON

VISIBLE
INK
PRESS

DETROIT • LONDON

THE VAMPIRE GALLERY
A WHO'S WHO OF THE UNDEAD

Published by Visible Ink Press
a division of Gale Research
27500 Drake Rd.
Farmington Hills, MI 48331-3535

Visible Ink Press is a trademark of Gale Research.

Most Visible Ink Press books are available at special quantity discounts when purchased in bulk by corporations, organizations, or groups. Customized printings, special imprints, messages, and excerpts can be produced to meet your needs. For more information, contact Special Markets Manager, Gale Research, 27500 Drake Rd., Farmington Hills, MI 48331-3535.

Cover Designers: Mark Howell and Cindy Baldwin
Page Designer: Michelle DiMercurio
Typesetting: LM Design

Library of Congress Cataloging in Publication Data has been applied for.
ISBN: 1-57859-053-1

TABLE OF CONTENTS

des Essientes, M. • Desire • Desnoirs • Diego y Rey, Lord Eduardo • Dieudonné, Genevieve Sandrine de l'Isle • Dominguez, Don Sebastian Juan • Donna Mia • Doran • Draculina • Dracutwig • Dragosani, Boris • Drake, Mr. • Drayven • DuCharme, Janette • Duckula, Count • Duncan, Fred • Dupah • Durward, Lady

E [155]

Edward • The Elder • Ely, Duncan • Enkil • Eramus • Evans, Hugh

F [163]

Fallon, Webb • Feodorovna, Tatiana • Ferenczy, Thibor • Ferguson, Carlotta • Fern • Fionguala, Ethelind • Fitzroy, Henry • Fleming, Jack • Ford, Alexander Algernon • Frene, Frank • Frost, Deacon • Fury, Michael • Futaine, The Cevalier Pierre

G [179]

Gabrielle • Geraldine • Gilcrease, Murphy • Gilda • Gordell, Belec • Green, Dr. Hess • Gregory • Greystone, Christina • Griffin, Dierdre • Grimes, Crispen • Grimwald, Lady Vanessa • Grinder

H [193]

Harker, R. B. • Harrison, Dr. • Hart, Josie • Harte, Dennis • Heather • Henzig, Lord of • Hitler, Adolf • Hofnstyne, Baron Hegyi Lipzig • Howler

I [203]

Illyana

J [205]

Jacula • James, Raglan • Jeepers, Mrs. • Jerry See: Nero, Jerry • Jesse • Jonas, Father • Jordan, Lily • Jorge, Count • Judge Axel • Julian, Damon

K [215]

Karnstein, Carmilla • Katani, Baroness Clarimonde • Katrina • Kenyon, Countess Sarah • Keogh, Harry • Khayman • Killer • Kimble, Grace • King of the Vampires • Klopotkin, Count Yorgi • Knight, Nick

L [235]

LaCroix, Lucien • Lake Fujimi, Vampire of • Latham, Benjamin • Lavud, Count • Lazaro Ruiz Cortinez, Don • Lee, Count Magnus • Lemachard, Philip • Lestat See: de Lioncourt, Lestat • Levé, Ralph • Lichtenstein, Dr. • Lilith • Lilith, The Daughter of Count Dracula • Little Dracula • Lodovico • Lothos • Louis See: de Pointe du Lac, Louis • Lucard, Adam • Luna • Luxura • Lyall, Andrew

M [259]

Mackenzie, Nathaniel • Madeleine • Mae • Mael • Magnus • Maharet • Malt Liquela, Count Demonte • Man-Bat • Marie • Marius • Marks, Chastity • Marlowe, Dr. Wendall • Martin • Mastenbrook, Miranda • The Master of Rampling Gate • Maximillian • Meinster, Baron • Mekare • Metternich, Paul • Mezgar, Bela • Mikhailovich, Count • Mink • Miriam • Miyu, Vampire Princess • Modoc • Molloy, Daniel • The Monk • Mora, Count • Morbius, Michael • Morgan, Michelle • Mornay, Edward • Morrisey, Max • Mortella • Murray, Cousin

N [301]

Nadja • Nero, Jerry • Nocturna • Nothing

O [309]

Opoltscheska, Duchess • Orlock, Graf • Orlok, Byron

P [315]

Pandemonium, Santanico • Pandora • Parker, David • Pasteur, Louis • Perkins, Nancy • Peron, Eva • Perne, Alisa • Principal's Wife • Purgatori

Q [327]

Quay, Sabella • Quesne, Marshall

R [333]

Radkoff, Dr. Victor • Radu • Rakosi, Bela • Rampling, Julie • Randy • Ravna, Dr. • Ravnos, Countess Tanya • Redfern, Delos • Reed, Richmond • Regine • Renauld, Thurman • Rentlow, Jeremy • Robespiere • Robey, Drake • Roissey, Nicole • Rollins, Katherine • Rose • Rozokov, Dimitri • Ruthven, Lord

S [353]

Sackville-Bagg, Rudolph • St. Clair, Adrienne • St. Germain • Sanders, Count Damien Vincent • Santiago • Santino • Sarah • Screech • Seth • Shade, Scarlett • Sinistre, Count Armand • Skeeter • Skorzeny, Janos • Steelgate, Jack • Stockton, John Sinclair • Stone, John Alucard

T [373]

Talbot, David • Talbot, Jane • Tasha • The Temptress • Tesla, Armand • Thompson, Edward "Evil" • Tibor, Baron • Trapp, Philip • Tsepes, Stephen • Tummelier, Peter Augustus

V [385]

Vampire • The Vampire (*The Dance of the Damned*) • Vampirella • Vampré, Lady • Vanthor, Pontius • Vardelek, Count • Varney, Sir Francis • Velcro, Vincent • Venessa • Venisette, Rovena • Victor, Son of Dracula • Viroslav, Count Alexander • von Beethoven, Ludwig • von Kaldenstein, Count Ludwig • von Klatka, Count Azzo • von Krolock, Count • von Lock, Adam • Voytek, Anton

W [407]

Warram, Robert • Westenra, Lucy • Weyland, Dr. Edward • Whipsnake • Wingate, Simon • Winters, Jeff • Wulfe, Klaus Johann

Y [417]

Yaksha • Yorga, Count • York, Captain Joshua Anton

Z [423]

Zachery • Zaleska, Countess Marya • Zane Ziska, Baron Alexis

Vampire Groups and Clans [429]

The Brotherhood • The Cadre • The Camarilla • Church of Eternal Life • Clans, Vampire • The Conclave • Deadbeats • Knight Club • Nightstalkers • Societas Argenti Viae Eternitata (S.A.V.E.) • Southern Coalition Against Vampires • Theatre des Vampires

Vampire Hunters and Associates [445]

Adam • Ambronsius, Professor • Blade the Vampire Slayer • Blake, Anita • Blood Hunter • D • Drake, Frank • Giles, Rupert

İNTRODVCTİON

J. Gordon Melton

Why vampires? Sitting down to write *The Vampire Gallery*, I paused to think about my interest in these creatures of the night. Since taking my involvement with vampires to a new level in the 1990s, both in my studies and writing, I have been continually asked, and have asked myself, "Why vampires?" To discover an adequate answer, I broke the big question into a number of relatively simple questions: Where did vampires come from? Why has belief in them survived over the centuries? Are there, or were there ever, real vampires? What is the significance of vampire mythology and why does it have such a hold on us? Where does Count Dracula come from, and how is he related to Prince Vlad the Impaler? All very important questions when examining vampire mythology from an academic standpoint.

However, in asking all these questions, it dawned on me that what makes the serious study of vampires so appealing was actually personal: the hundreds of fictional vampires that I have encountered through the years. Vampires who came to life on the silver screen, in the pages of a horror novel, or in the vivid artwork of a comic book. These characters became animated and alive, drawing me to them even as they terrified me. Watching a vampire prepare to pounce on his next victim onscreen or having one seemingly jump out of the pages of a novel has fueled my interest in the undead and complimented my serious study of this fascinating subject area. In the last three decades, I have had the opportunity to see hundreds of vampire movies and read several times that many novels, stories, and comic books. It is this passion for the vampire as an epic character of fiction that fuels *The Vampire Gallery*.

After finishing *The Vampire Book: The Encyclopedia of the Undead* (Visible Ink Press) five years ago, I realized that the characters I enjoyed so much had been largely neglected by my colleagues in vampire studies. Thus I began to envision a survey of vampire characters, a sort of "Vampires Who's Who" that evolved into the book you are holding right now: *The Vampire Gallery: A Who's Who of the Undead*. By writing biographies of popular vampires characters in fiction, vampire myths are explored, advances in the genre are highlighted, and the unique contributions of important authors, screenwriters, and directors are covered.

The *Gallery* contains the biographies of nearly 350 vampire characters brought to life on the silver screen and in print. It also provides the biographies of significant vampire hunters, those hardy souls who have made a living out of tracking and dispatching the undead. And to complete the characters who have played an important part in vampire fiction, the *Gallery* also covers certain mortals who have been brave enough to befriend a vampire (such as Dr. Natalie Lambert from the television show *Forever Knight*) and important groups of vampires, both ancient and modern, such as the Theatre des Vampires from Anne Rice's *Vampire Chronicles* and The Camarilla from the popular role-playing game *Vampire: The Masquerade*.

The *Vampire Gallery* was assembled with two very different, but hopefully complementary, purposes. The first is the sheer enjoyment I hope you gain from seeing all these different vampires and related characters brought together in one volume for the first time. Compiling the book was hard work, but at the same time, I can't imagine working on a project that was more fun. As I reread favorite books and watched classic movies to prepare each biography, I was delighted by every shiver and scream, and I hope the *Gallery* will stir your own memories of favorite vampire characters. The second, and related, purpose of this book is to introduce you to new vampires that you may not have encountered in the past. This book will have done its job if it motivates you to read the books of Chelsea Quinn Yarbro for the first time, or leads you to finally rent that vampire film you've been meaning to bring home for weeks.

The *Vampire Gallery* also has a more serious purpose: it serves to further document the rise and evolution of the contemporary vampire myth. A vampire is defined by a series of characteristics that sets him or her apart from humanity. For example, human beings are normally thought of as the product of evolution or the creation of God. Not vampires— they are the undead, the unholy. They were created by Satan or are the product of some natural aberration, a vampire disease, if you will. Like most nineteenth century vampires, Count Dracula's origin was supposedly a product of Satanism, which author Bram Stoker brought to light during a speech by vampire hunter Abraham Van Helsing:

> The Draculas were, says Arminius, a great and noble race, though now and again were scions who were held by their coevals to have dealings with the Evil One. They learned his secrets in the Scholomance, amongst the mountains over Lake Hermanstadt, where the devil claims the tenth scholar as his due.

Similarly, Anne Rice traced her vampires to an incident of demonic possession that occurred in ancient Egypt. Others, seeking a more naturalistic explanation, have traced vampires to an extraterrestrial species (for example, the *Vampirella* comic books) or to a medical condition, i.e. a germ or genetic flaw. Each of the origin myths seems to impart its own unique set of characteristics to the vampires it creates. For example, vampires of supernatural origin tend to have extensive powers, from enormous strength to the ability to shape-shift or fly. Non-supernatural vampires tend to lack these powers, and are sometimes nothing more than ordinary humans who suffer from a horrible blood lust. Once a vampire's "type" has been determined, a whole laundry list of characteristics can usually be associated with that creature.

Van Helsing himself made this point in *Dracula*. As mentioned, he believed that vampires were the devil's work and were supernatural in nature. According to him, all vampires possess a set of fangs, have a pale complexion, sleep in coffins, are associated with bats, and only come out at night. Indeed, fangs, which are used to suck blood out of the victims, have become the single most recognizable feature of the vampire. The presence of fangs immediately marks a person as a vampire to motion picture audience and signals that any humans who are close to the vampire are now in imminent danger.

The other most common vampire trait is that almost all vampires are creatures of the night who spend each day in a coma-like sleep. Many have red eyes and are cold to the touch. They cannot enter a room until invited. In addition to these nearly universal vampire traits, supernatural vampires also possess other attributes: they have great strength, they can fly (or at least levitate), they possess some hypnotic power (which forces victims to submit or makes them forget that the vampire is present), they have acute night vision, and they can undergo a transformation into a variety of animals (usually a bat or possibly a wolf). Vampires avoid garlic, sunlight, sacred symbols (such as crucifixes and holy water), and they may need to sleep on their native soil. They may be killed by a wooden stake thrust in their heart, or consumed by fire. Sunlight is a relatively new weapon against vampires—it wasn't until the twentieth century that death by sunlight became a common part of the vampire myth.

Twentieth-century writers have tended either to follow the vampire as defined by Van Helsing, or to create a character that completely challenges the Dracula stereotype. The former has led to the creation of many, many vampires who seem to be from European nobility, while the latter has allowed the vampire myth to grow and change as characters with new powers and weaknesses appear.

Since there are literally thousands of vampires throughout the worlds of film and fiction, the nearly 350 we have chosen for the *Gallery* are a representative sample. We began with those who were undoubtedly the most popular and influential since the beginning of vampire literature in the late eighteenth century. This list includes Count Dracula, Lord Ruthven, Sir Francis Varney, Carmilla Karnstein, and more. From those early vampires, the list moved forward through the years until it encompassed more recent additions to vampire lore, including Lestat de Lioncourt, Barnabas Collins, St. Germain, Nick Knight, Stephen Austra, Jack Fleming, Angel, and many more.

I also tried to sample the wide variety of media in which vampires have appeared, from poems to novels, from television to feature-length movies, from comic books to juvenile literature. In compiling the list, I must admit a certain partiality to comic books, a media which has been significantly transformed since the days of my childhood. Comic books are the most neglected medium in which vampires are prominently featured, although they are one of the most important. Many fans who now devour vampire novels were first introduced to vampires through the colorful comic books of the past, including such classics as *Tomb of Dracula*. In fact, more than 4.000 English-language vampire comic books have been issued in recent decades. Today's comic books, or graphic novels as they are often called, feature some of the finest and most exciting vampire art ever produced, as well as fascinating characters and well-developed storylines. Many of today's comic books are aimed squarely at adult audiences and include healthy doses of sexuality and bloody mayhem, two themes that are common throughout the vampire world.

When sampling the vampires, I found that there was no way I could write about all these popular vampires without also writing about their archrivals, the vampire hunters. After all, the name Van Helsing has become as common as Dracula in the world of vampire fiction, and a number of members of that famous family are covered in the chapter on Vampire Hunters and Vampire Associates. And, perhaps the most dominant character in vampire fiction today is not a vampire at all, but rather a vampire slayer. Buffy Summers, star of the Warner Brothers television show, *Buffy the Vampire Slayer*, has made vampires popular with a whole new audience of young viewers. Additionally, while vampires have traditionally been loners, today's vampires also live in communities. *The Vampire Gallery* would have been incomplete without mentioning some of the most popular of these communal structures, such as The Camarilla, so the chapter on Vampire Groups and Clans is devoted to them.

Finally, *The Vampire Gallery* has attempted to locate some of the famous (and not so famous) firsts in vampire fiction, such as the first screen vampire to actually sink his fangs into a victim (it was Count Lavud, not Bela Lugosi's Dracula). It has also tracked those vampires who were a little different from the norm—extraterrestrial vampires, natural vampires, and even pseudovampires. With such broad coverage, I hope that, in addition to pleasing vampire fans, *The Vampire Gallery* will become a useful tool for people conducting research on the genre.

The Vampire Gallery begins at the logical starting point when considering fictional vampires—with Count Dracula. A special chapter on the king of vampires opens the text and provides an in-depth examination of the most important vampire ever. Prominent vampires are then covered in A to Z fashion, followed by the separate chapters on hunters and groups, which are also in alphabetical order. Vampires known popularly under one name but who are listed under their full names in this book have see references directing readers to the correct name. In addition, all entries are extensively cross-referenced—a name appearing in boldface type in any entry indicates that a separate entry on that character exists in the *Gallery*. *The Vampire Gallery* contains a comprehensive index that lists all vampire names, all book and film names, all author and director names, and all the names of actors and actresses who starred in vampire films. Photos from popular vampire movies, as well as cover art and other prints from comic books and novels are included to enhance your reading pleasure and bring to life some of the characters discussed in the *Gallery*. Finally, sidebars on various topics related to vampires in fiction should increase your knowledge of the genre.

I have enjoyed preparing this work for you, and as you begin your journey, I close this introduction by hoping that you gain as much enjoyment from it as I did.

Count Dracula:
King of the Vampires

C ount Dracula is unquestionably the most influential vampire of the twentieth century, perhaps of all-time. His debut came as the title character in Bram Stoker's 1897 novel, which celebrated its centennial in 1997 and is still as popular as ever. That novel and the subsequent numerous incarnations of the Count (especially in the 1931 film adaptation of the novel starring Bela Lugosi) fully established the image of the vampire as he appeared in popular culture. There had been a variety of vampires prior to Dracula, several of whom had rather extensive character development that differed drastically from Dracula, but none caught the public imagination like the infamous Count from Transylvania did. He effectively combined the elements of power, sexuality, and sensuality that lifted the vampire head and shoulders above other literary monsters and helped to make vampires the rich subject of modern horror fantasy that they are today.

Dracula is written as if it were a collection of documents, the first being the diary of Jonathan Harker as he travels from England to Eastern Europe. Harker unknowingly introduces the reader to Dracula in that first chapter, although neither Harker nor the reader realize they are meeting the Count at the time. The meeting occurs on Harker's carriage ride from Borgo Pass to Castle Dracula. Harker notes that the carriage driver has a "grip of steel," and later it is revealed that the driver was actually Dracula. It seems that he lived a rather lonely existence in his castle and had no staff or servants, so he had to drive Harker himself.

It is the evening of May 5 (now determined to be 1893) when Harker reaches the castle. Upon his entrance, Dracula, in perfect English but with a strange accent, speaks his first words, "Welcome to my house! Enter freely and of your own will!" Harker notes that Dracula is "a tall man, clean shaven save for a long white moustache, and clad in black from head to foot, without a single speck of color about him anywhere." After Harker enters, Dracula steps forward to shake hands with him; the Englishman notes that his host has "a strength which made me wince, an effect which was not lessened by the fact that it seemed as cold as ice—more like the hand of a dead than a living man."

After dining, Harker has a chance to reflect on his arrival and record the impressions of his first evening with his host. He offers a more complete description of the Count, the first of several crucial passages in which Dracula's nature is uncovered:

> His face was a strong—a very strong—aquiline with high bridge of the thin nose and peculiarly arched nostrils; with lofty domed forehead, and hair growing scantily round the temples, but profusely elsewhere. His eyebrows were very massive, almost meeting over the nose, and with bushy hair that seemed to curl in its own profusion. The mouth, so far as I could see it under the heavy moustache, was fixed and rather cruel looking, with peculiarly sharp white teeth; these protruded over the lips, whose remarkable ruddiness showed astonishing vitality in a man of his years. For the rest, his ears were pale and the tops extremely pointed; the chin was broad and strong, and the cheeks firm though thin. The general effect was one of extraordinary pallor.
>
> Hitherto I had noticed the backs of his hands as they lay on his knees in the firelight, and they had seemed rather white and fine; but seeing them now close to me, I could not but notice that they were rather coarse—broad, with squat fingers. Strange to say, there were hairs at the center of the palm. The nails were long and fine, and cut to a sharp point. As the Count leaned over me and his hands touched me, I could not repress a shudder. It may have been that his breath was rank, but a horrible feeling of nausea came over me, which, do what I would, I could not conceal. The Count, evidently noticing it, drew back; and with a grim sort of smile, which showed more than he had yet done his protuberant teeth, set himself down again on his own side of the fireplace. We were both silent for a while; and as I looked towards the window I saw the first dim streak of the coming dawn. There seemed a strange stillness over everything....

Thus, in his first encounter with Dracula, Harker noted a number of characteristics that would constantly reappear in literature and in film as basic elements of a vampire's image. He had unusual strength. He had a prominent set of fangs—extended canine teeth. His skin was very pale, and his body was cold to the touch. He had a noticeable case of bad breath that emulated the stench of death. Harker's description also noted elements that would not survive in the popular vampire myth, such as the hairy palms of his hands and his sharp fingernails. It should be noted, however, that in the 1950s or early 1960s, the sharp fingernails did return when some movies included the scene from the book in which Dracula used his nails to cut his skin so the heroine, Mina Murray, could drink his blood.

The following evening Harker makes even more observations about the oddness of his situation, especially noticing the lack of mirrors in the castle. Dracula's long teeth are again evident that evening, but more importantly, Harker observes:

> ...I had hung my shaving glass by the window, and was just beginning to shave....This time there could be no error, for the man was close to me, and I could see him over my shoulder. But there was no reflection of him in the mirror!.... but at that instant I saw that the cut had bled a little, and the blood was trickling over my chin. I laid down the razor, turning as I did so half-round to look for some sticking plaster. When the Count saw my face, his eyes blazed with a sort of demonic fury, and he suddenly made a grab at my throat. I drew away, and his hand touched the string of beads which held the crucifix. It made an instant change in him, for the fury passed so quickly that I could hardly believe that it was ever there.

Bela Lugosi (with Dwight Frye in 1931's *Dracula*) is the most famous Dracula ever.

Gradually Harker begins to catalog Dracula's stranger characteristics, those that he feels are far beyond expected foreign eccentricities. With a growing sense of dread, Harker dutifully notes:

> I have yet to see the Count eat or drink.... And in light of the bizarre situation in which he had been entrapped, he wondered, "...How was it that all the people at Bistritz and on the coach had some terrible fear for me? What meant the giving of the crucifix, of the garlic, of the wild rose, of the mountain ash? Bless that good, good woman who hung the crucifix round my neck."

While Harker notices the lack of servants and staff, he learns that Dracula does not live alone. Also residing in the castle are three women, the so-called brides of Dracula. The three are vampires, but their exact relationship to Dracula is never clearly defined. This vagueness in regards to the female characters gave later writers room to interpret the women's role in the Dracula myth as they saw fit, a fact that was especially important when the feminist movement of the late twentieth century redefined women's roles throughout literature. Watching Dracula interact with the women, Harker notes yet another detail about the Count—his eyes are normally blue, but when he becomes enraged, they become red and appear to have the flames

Original poster art for the 1931 release of *Dracula*.

of hell behind them. This important observation would become the basis of contemporary vampires taking on bestial features when they were about to feed or became angry.

DRACULA'S BACKGROUND: On May 7, Harker learns a little bit about Dracula's history when the Count offers a spirited discourse on Transylvania. Dracula's castle is located in the mountainous borderland of Transylvania. Centuries earlier, the area had been turned over to the Szekelys tribes, who were known for their fierceness and effectiveness in warfare. Their land served as the initial barrier should any people to the east attempt an invasion of Hungary. Dracula is a member of the Szekelys. In fact, he is a boyar, or feudal lord, and is a member of Hungarian royalty, "We Szekelys have a right to be proud, for in our veins flows the blood of many brave races who fought as the lion fights, for Lordship," he tells Harker.

This glimpse into Dracula's past is really a subplot to Stoker. His main focus is on how, with each encounter with Dracula and his increasingly strange behavior, Harker's conventional understanding of the world is shattered a little further. The most mind-boggling event occurs as Harker peers out of the window in his room and observes Dracula literally climbing outside on the castle wall. "I saw the whole man slowly emerge from the window and begin to crawl down the castle wall over that dreadful abyss, face down, with his cloak spreading out around him like great wings..."

Increasingly concerned with what is happening to him, Harker realizes that he sees the Count only at night. "I have not yet seen the Count in the daylight. Can it be that he sleeps when others wake, that he may be awake whilst they sleep!" Finally, on June 25, he discovers the final piece of the puzzle that convinces him Dracula is a vampire—he discovered Dracula deep in the daytime sleep of the vampire:

> There, in one of the great boxes, of which there were fifty in all, on a pile of newly dug earth, lay the Count! He was either dead or asleep, but I could not say which, for the eyes were open and stony, but without the glassiness of death- and the cheeks had the warmth of life through all their pallor, and the lips were as red as ever. But there was no sign of movement, no pulse, no breath, no beating of the heart. I bent over him, and tried to find any sign of life, but in vain....

> There lay the Count, but looking as if his youth had been half-renewed, for the white hair and moustache were changed to dark iron-grey; the cheeks were fuller, and the white skin seemed ruby-red underneath; the mouth was redder than ever, for on the lips were gouts of fresh blood, which trickled from the corners of the mouth and ran over the chin and neck. Even the deep, burning eyes seemed set amongst swollen flesh, for the lids and pouches underneath were bloated. It seemed as if the whole awful creature were simply gorged with blood; he lay like a filthy leech, exhausted in his repletion.

DRACULA IN ENGLAND: At the end of June, Dracula leaves Harker at the castle with the three female vampires and travels to England to take up residence at the estate he had purchased. Carrying with him the 50 boxes of his native soil, he travels to the Black Sea and secretly boards the *Demeter*, the ship that will take him to his new home. Aboard the *Demeter*, he quietly arises from his box each night and feeds on the sailors. One by one, the men grew weaker and weaker before eventually dying. When the ship reaches the shore of Whitby, a small town in northern England,

Dracula uses his power to conjure a sudden storm that blows the ship aground. Dracula transforms into a wolf and leaves the now deserted ship.

While this is happening, another portion of the plot is unfolding in Whitby, where Mina Murray and **Lucy Westenra** are vacationing. The novel temporarily shifts away from Dracula to Mina and Lucy and the various men in their lives. Dracula is relegated to the background, but the menace he represents is never far removed from the central story. Upon landing in Whitby, Dracula attacks Lucy. He lures her out of her apartment to a seat on the banks of the river that runs through Whitby, where earlier a suicide had occurred (making the ground unhallowed). He bites her on the neck and drinks her blood. He next appears outside of her room in the form of another animal, this time a bat. In the meantime, he retrieved his boxes of earth from the *Demeter* and had them shipped into London, where the novel then shifts. Dracula distributes the boxes at his main Carfax estate and in various locations around the city.

He continues his attacks upon Lucy, which leads her doctor to call upon the well-known **Abraham Van Helsing** to assist with the situation. Van Helsing orders a series of blood transfusions after each attack, although he and the other men soon realize that they are only prolonging Lucy's ordeal—she is sure to join the undead and become a vampire. At first, the men do not believe that Lucy is becoming a vampire— it takes a demonstration by Van Helsing of Lucy's vampiric powers to convince them that they must kill her and unite to fight Dracula. First they kill Lucy using a stake, garlic, and decapitation. Then, Van Helsing trains the men to be vampire hunters. In doing so, he describes Dracula to the men, explaining his powers and his weaknesses. He explains how a vampire commands the dead and the animals, especially the "meaner things"—rats, bats, owls, and foxes. He can disappear at will, reappear in many forms (especially a wolf, a bat, and as a mist), and can alter the weather. Dracula casts no shadow, he does not reflect in mirrors, he can see in the dark, and he cannot enter anywhere without first being invited. Folklore concerning vampires said that they preyed on the people they loved the most, but Van Helsing changes this slightly, telling the men that Dracula preys upon the ones *they* loved best.

Dracula has grown strong through his centuries of existence, but his strength is severely limited during the day. He can move around during the day, and he can only transform himself into another creature or mist at the moments of sunrise, high noon, and sunset. He can only pass over a running tide at high or low tide. He is not invulnerable. He can be rendered powerless by garlic, various sacred objects (crucifix, the Eucharist), and the wild rose. He can be destroyed by attacking him in his coffin with a bullet fired into the body, a stake through his body (not necessarily the heart), and then decapitation. Van Helsing's (i.e., Stoker's) understanding of Dracula was derived primarily from the folklore of vampires in Transylvania/Romania as described by Emily Gerard in her popular travelogue book, *The Land Beyond the Forest* (1885).

Soon after the training session, Dracula attacks and kills R. N. Renfield, a madman who had been trying to become Dracula's faithful servant. Dracula then attacks Mina. The men break into her bedroom only to find her drinking Dracula's blood, presumably the crucial step in someone becoming a vampire. Those who were merely drained of blood by a vampire simply died. The men drive away Dracula and launch a counterattack. Their first step is to sanitize Dracula's boxes of native soil. They find 49 of the 50 boxes and place a piece of the Eucharist in each. As the men are doing this at Dracula's home in Picadilly, the vampire arrives and confronts them but quickly flees because it is still daylight.

With only one box of the needed soil left, Dracula flees back to his homeland. Van Helsing and the others pursue him, bringing Mina with them. Dracula travels by ship, while the others take the train. The final destination is Dracula's castle. Van Helsing arrives there first and sanitizes the castle, including Dracula's tomb. Dracula arrives at his now desecrated home with the other men in hot pursuit. Just as sunset approaches and Dracula is about to regain his full powers, Jonathan Harker and Quincey P. Morris kill him by simultaneously decapitating him (Harker) and plunging a Bowie knife into his heart (Morris). The centuries-old Dracula crumbles to dust.

DRACULA IN FILMS, DRAMA, AND BOOKS: While Dracula may have been destroyed in the book, it was actually just the beginning of his literary and commercial appeal. Almost immediately after the book appeared, Stoker moved to assert his rights to any dramatic productions by staging a single public performance of *Dracula* in London. While the novel was well received by the reading public, that one stage appearance was the last for Dracula until after Stoker's death.

Records exist claiming that Dracula appeared in two Eastern European silent movies (one Russian and one Hungarian), but, if they ever existed, they have been lost. The first screen portrayal based on the character of Dracula was the 1922 silent classic *Nosferatu*, which featured the vampire **Graf Orlock**. Orlock was modeled on Dracula but was even more monstrous to look at—he had a rodent-like appearance with pointed ears, a bald head, and a pair of fangs in the front of his mouth, rather than extended canines. He was Dracula at his most repugnant, but he was still recognizable as Dracula, and Florence Stoker asserted her ownership of the film rights to her late husband's novel. Her successful lawsuit against Prana Films not only bankrupted the company but kept the film from being shown in public for 25 years. Once it became public property, however, the several copies that had survived were reproduced and widely distributed. Orlock would become the direct influence for a number of other vampires, most notably **Kurt Barlow** (*Salem's Lot*) and **Radu** (*Subspecies*).

Shortly after the end of the *Nosferatu* case, Dracula found his way to the stage in a play written and produced by Hamilton Deane. The play opened in 1924 and was extremely influential in the development of the modern popular image of the vampire. In the original novel, Dracula dressed completely in black. He was an aristocrat with arrogant manners and an extreme case of halitosis. In contrast, Deane made Dracula (as portrayed by Raymond Huntley) a much more dashing figure, outfitting him in formal evening wear, complete with an opera cloak that would further the identification of Dracula with the bat. A cape had been mentioned by Stoker, most dramatically when it spread out as Dracula was crawling on the outside wall of Castle Dracula. In the novel, Dracula rarely appeared in the chapters set in London, but in Deane's play, he freely entered scenes ready to match wits with the other characters, especially Abraham Van Helsing. Deane, in his negotiations with Florence Stoker, seemed to have consciously moved away from the image of the film *Nosferatu*, in which Dracula was portrayed as a monster with a truly odd and frightening appearance. The Huntley Dracula would be further transformed by Bela Lugosi, who appeared in a revised version of Deane's play prepared by John L. Balderston.

Dracula made the jump to the silver screen in the 1931 Universal film *Dracula*, which featured a screenplay revised from the play by Louis Bloomfield. Bela Lugosi's portrayal of the Count stands beside the book as the most influential vampire image ever in popular culture. The first vampire film with sound, Lugosi's portrayal reached millions who had never seen the stage play. His suave aristocratic European manner and pronounced Hungarian accent still define the character of Dracula.

The film was able to do many things that the play could not. An opening sequence was added to show Jonathan Harker's trips to Transylvania and has his initial encounter with Dracula and his three vampire brides. This was an important addition, since these scenes from the opening chapter of the book are considered to be among the most dramatic moments in the novel. Some dramatic license was taken with the trip—instead of Harker traveling to the castle, it is Renfield who makes the trip, which accounts for his insane behavior following his return to England. An elaborate set was developed for the memorable scenes in the castle, but it was poorly utilized. Director Tod Browning has been justly criticized for the restricted and flat manner in which he shot Dracula's encounter with his English guest. In spite of Browning's failures, the scenes (which began with Lugosi's famous opening line, "I am...Dracula.") are among the most memorable, powerful, and influential in horror film history. It is interesting to note that the film also included a brief scene aboard the *Demeter*, the ship that brought Dracula to England.

Given the rules of film making in Hollywood at the time, it is often forgotten that Lugosi's Dracula did not have fangs and never actually bit anyone on-screen, although the bite marks on his victims' necks were shown. He was true to Stoker's character in most ways. He did not reflect in mirrors, was repelled by the cross, and slept on his native soil in a coffin. His bite itself did not automatically infect the victim with vampirism, nor did one bite automatically kill—instead, victims withered away over a period of time. The best way to kill Dracula was with a stake in the heart delivered while he was deep in his vampiric sleep. Dracula was nocturnal, but only in later movies would his abhorrence of the sun be made a more permanent part of the vampire myth. Lugosi also stamped the character with his own personal flair—hypnotic eyes, an aristocratic bearing, and the now-famous widow's peak.

Dracula, of course, did double duty in 1931. Not only did he appear in Browning's *Dracula*, but also in a Spanish-language version of the film using the same set and script and starring Carlos Villarias (also know as Carlos Villar) in the lead role of Dracula. Though the film continued to be shown in Latin American countries for several decades after its release and is considered by critics to be superior to the better-known Browning version, it was largely ignored and quickly forgotten in the English-speaking world. Fortunately, thanks in large part to the efforts of David J. Skal, the

1931 Spanish *Dracula* was recovered and is now readily available.

During the next two decades, Lugosi portrayed several different Dracula-like characters—most notably **Armand Tesla** and pseudovampire **Count Mora**. Other famous actors—most notably Lon Chaney Jr., and John Carradine—also portrayed the Count on the screen. While none of these portrayals approached the success of the original, they kept Dracula alive in the public consciousness until Christopher Lee gave vampire fans the next great screen version of Dracula in 1958.

While Lugosi's portrayal of the legendary vampire is certainly the most famous, Lee's has perhaps been even more influential in setting the image of Dracula in contemporary popular culture. In 1958's *Dracula* (subsequently released in the United States as *Horror of Dracula*), Lee attempted to reinterpret Lugosi's Dracula while also returning to the Stoker novel at various points. Jimmy Sangster's screenplay opens with Jonathan Harker's arrival at Castle Dracula, not as a real estate agent, but as Dracula's new librarian. Secretly, though, he is

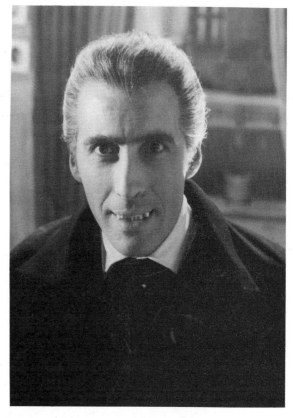

Christopher Lee, star of several Dracula films for Hammer Studios.

working undercover as Abraham Van Helsing's assistant. His goal is to kill Dracula, but he is unable to realize his objective. Instead he is attacked and bitten by one of Dracula's brides, whom he in turn kills. In the process, he becomes a vampire himself. For this reason, *Horror of Dracula* is responsible for popularizing the assumption that a single bite by a vampire is all that is necessary for one to become a vampire. This assumption of course differs from Stoker's novel. Dracula escapes before Van Helsing (played by Peter Cushing in a role he was famous for) arrives at Castle Dracula to check on his assistant. Discovering that Harker has been turned into a vampire, Van Helsing is forced to stake and kill him. He then returns to England to begin his one-on-one confrontation with Dracula that is the true subject of the film.

Dracula reaches England before Van Helsing. In England, the audience is introduced to a different cast of characters than the ones found in Stoker's novel. Gone are Dr. John Seward, Renfield, and Quincey P. Morris. Arthur Holmwood, the dominant male in the book, is married to Mina, and Lucy has been recast as Holmwood's sister (and Harker's fiance). Lucy is the primary object of Dracula's interest, he having taken her picture from Harker before leaving his castle. When he arrived in England, Van Helsing discovers that Lucy has already been bitten and is vampirizing

YOU'VE COME A LONG WAY, DRAC BABY!

In the novel *Dracula*, the title character is described as a sinister character, dressed in black with protruding fangs. He changes little throughout the novel except to grow younger as he feeds off of his victims in London. Bram Stoker's *Dracula* is not likable in the least—he is evil personified who survives by attacking people.

Then, without really meaning too, Bela Lugosi revolutionized the character and made him a sex symbol. Lugosi received thousands of fan letters from females who responded to his sensual screen portrayal of Dracula in 1931. When Frank Langella revived the part in 1979, he played to the romantic appeal of the well-dressed aristocratic vampire even more than Lugosi had.

Lugosi and Langella paved the way for Gary Oldman in Francis Ford Coppola's *Bram Stoker's Dracula* (1992), the full-blown sexual predator who attempted to seduce Winona Ryder's Mina Murray more than he tried to attack her. As they sipped absinthe in a cafe, she sucked erotically on a sugar cube, obviously enjoying the attention of the handsome young Prince. He emphasized that she was safe in his presence, and as he sang the praises of his long lost love, he moved in for the kill. Such a scene, unthinkable to Stoker, was readily accepted by a movie audience already conditioned to accept Dracula as a highly sexual being.

others. He takes the lead in killing her. An angry Dracula then attacks Mina.

Two elements seem to have contributed to the success of *Horror of Dracula*. First, it was the first Dracula movie in Technicolor, and it made full use of red, red blood throughout the picture. The arrival of Technicolor coincided with relaxed censorship standards that allowed greater freedom in the amount of blood and gore that could be shown on-screen. In 1931, Lugosi never showed his teeth nor bit anyone on camera. Lee regularly showed his fangs and had no problem offering his victims, especially the women, his special kiss. He was the second vampire to actually bite his victims on-screen. The year before *Horror of Dracula*, German Robles, portraying a Dracula-like vampire named **Count Lavud**, had become the first.

Second, whether on purpose or accidentally, *Horror of Dracula* presented a new level of sexuality for vampires in which Lee seemed to revel. He seduced women with his kisses and gained their affection before he sunk his teeth in their neck. As David Hogan notes, "When he bites a young lovely's throat he is not merely feeding, but experiencing (and inducing) a moment of orgasmic ecstasy." Lee would go on from *Horror of Dracula* to become an international star and, like Lugosi, he developed a large and loyal female following.

In the final scene of *Horror of Dracula*, Van Helsing confronts Dracula in his castle. Dracula has all but defeated Van Helsing, when, as so many villains before him have done, he pauses for just a moment to savor his triumph. In that moment, Van Helsing recovers and pushes the vampire away. He rushes across the room and pulls the drapes from the window, allowing the sunlight to stream into the room. (Earlier, Van Helsing had emphatically informed the movie audience that sunlight is fatal to vampires.) Grabbing a cross, Van Helsing pushes Dracula completely into the sunlight, which completely consumes him. Dracula's ashes blow away in the wind leaving behind only his large ring. Lee himself would rise from the dead and go on to star in numerous other Dracula vehicles, including *Dracula Has Risen from His Grave* (1969), *Taste the Blood of Dracula* (1970), *The Scars of Dracula* (1970), *Dracula A.D. 1972 (1972)*, and *The Satanic Rites of Dracula* (1973).

Lee's portrayal of Dracula in those and other films would provide the most significant landmark in the development of the Dracula image since Lugosi. His image of Dracula held center stage in the vampire community for many years, until two historians mining the rather obscure field of Eastern European history would provide the next stage in the development of Dracula's image. In their 1972 book, *In Search of Dracula*, Dr. Raymond McNally and Dr. Radu Florescu tracked down Prince Vlad the Impaler, the original Dracula. Vlad was a fifteenth-century Wallachian ruler and apparently served as the historical figure used as a model by Bram Stoker when creating Dracula. The following year, the pair published a more complete study of Vlad in *Dracula: A Biography of Vlad the Impaler, 1431–1476* .

These two books provided a new depth to the myth of Count Dracula and inspired a new generation of fiction writers to further push the limits of the genre. For example, working with Dan Curtis, Richard Matheson authored a screenplay for a new adaptation of *Dracula* first shown on television in 1973. Dracula was portrayed by Jack Palance and for the first time was identified with Prince Vlad. That connection with Vlad answered one of several unanswered questions in the original novel: Why did Dracula concentrate on Lucy and Mina when all of London was available to him? Matheson speculated that Mina was identical to the woman who was the lost love of Vlad's life in the fifteenth century, a theme that would be revived by Francis Ford Coppola in his film *Bram Stoker's Dracula* (1992)

Soon afterward, novelist Gail Kimberly picked up on the Prince Vlad/Count Dracula connection and integrated Transylvanian geography and a surviving Prince Dracula in her 1976 volume, *Dracula Began* in which some Americans encounter Dracula. Interestingly enough, in her book, Castle Dracula is located not far from Sighasora (rather than in the northeast corner of Transylvania, beyond Bistritz). Since the 1970s, Vlad and Dracula have been closely identified in vampire fiction, and the reign of Prince Vlad the Impaler had been used to supply depth to modern fictional vampires.

The new level of interest in Dracula through the 1970s culminated in two very different appearances by the now well-known Count. In the late 1970s, Frank Langella portrayed the most sensual Dracula to date, first in a new version of the Deane-Balderston stage drama and then a new film version of *Dracula* done by Universal. The play and movie explored the relation of sexuality and horror. Dracula as portrayed by Lugosi and Lee was essentially the object of horror, the undead. Yet as Langella's Dracula entered the Steward household, he had little need of brute force. After falling in love with Mina and then Lucy, he did not so much attack them as seduce them. Dracula's complete triumph occurs when he invades Lucy's bedroom and she takes his blood (body fluids) as he had hers—as sensual a scene as is found in any vampire movie. Subsequently Lucy, completely captivated by Dracula's magnetism, rushes off to join him at Carfax.

Frank Langella created a sensual Dracula when he played the vampire on stage in the late 1970s.

The same year that the Langella movie appeared, *Love at First Bite* gave us a comic Dracula as George Hamilton romped across the screen looking for his true love, who turned out to be a New York fashion model. Holding nothing sacred, Hamilton's Dracula lampooned Lugosi and Lee and put the Count in some ludicrous situations: a funeral in Harlem (as the guest of honor), a drunken ordeal after taking blood from a wino, and a confrontation in a nightclub with an incompetent Van Helsing. The film is still recognized as the best of the vampire comedies in spite of Mel Brooks' more recent *Dracula: Dead and Loving It* (1995).

Dracula's appearances on the screen were crowned in 1992 with *Bram Stoker's Dracula*, the elaborate production directed by Francis Ford Coppola. The movie was noteworthy for its close adherence to the original plot and for keeping all of the major characters from the original novel in the same relationships they originally enjoyed, the first screen production to accomplish that difficult task. Dracula was portrayed by Gary Oldman and was consciously identified with Vlad the Impaler and the frustration he carried forward from the fifteenth century to modern times. Oldman synthesized the horrific Dracula of Lugosi and Lee with the fifteenth-century warrior (Palance) and the sensuous lover (Langella). In fact, his seduction of Mina rivaled Langella's.

Ever since Hammer Studio's Dracula films initiated a comeback of the vampire genre in the 1960s and interest was rekindled in the Vlad/Dracula connection in the 1970s, Dracula has been a popular subject in film and books. Over 150 films have featured Dracula and other vampires who are nothing but thinly veiled imitations of the Count. Dracula has now become the fictional character most often brought to the screen, with the possible exception of Sherlock Holmes.

DRACULA IN PRINT: Stoker's novel has been reprinted frequently in the century since its initial publication. Doubleday published the first American edition in 1899. Since entering the public domain, several hundred reprints have appeared, from cheap paperbacks to fine limited boxed editions. There are also numerous condensed versions and adaptations for juvenile audiences. As early as 1972, an abridged version for children by Nora Kramer was published by Scholastic Book Services.

The first foreign translation, into Icelandic, of all things, appeared in 1899. It was the only one published during Stoker's lifetime. Two decades later, the publication of a French translation (1920) signaled the move of Dracula into the various European languages. Today, it can be found in more than 20 languages, including Finnish, Chinese, Korean, and Japanese.

Authors have also taken to coming up with new ways to play with the Dracula myth and create new interpretations of this highly intriguing literary figure. Prior to 1960, Dracula seems to have appeared in only one novel, 1928's *Kasigli Voyvode* (*The Impaling Vampire*) by Turkish writer Ali Riga Seifi. He also was the subject of several short stories, such as Ralph Milne Fraley's "Another Dracula," which appeared in the September and October 1930 issues of *Weird Tales*. In 1960 two new Dracula novels—Otto Frederick's *Count Dracula's Canadian Affair* and Dean Owen's *The Brides of Dracula*, were to be the first of more than 100 Dracula novels published over the last four decades. Memorable in these novels are the several series of Dracula novels

Gary Oldman in Francis Ford Coppola's *Bram Stoker's Dracula*.

by Robert Lory (nine action stories), Fred Saberhagen (nine novels), and Peter Tremayne (three novels).

DRACULA IN OTHER MEDIA: Dracula made his first television appearances in the 1960s. Bela Lugosi made a brief appearance as Dracula on the popular television series *You Asked for It*, and John Carradine appeared in an NBC production of the play *Dracula*. Other television adaptations of *Dracula* featured Denholm Eliott (1971), Jack Palance (1973, in the Dan Curtis made-for-television movie), and Louis Jourdan (1977). A comic contemporary Count Dracula (originally portrayed by Al Lewis) was a regular character in the 1964 to 1966 series *The Munsters* , which is still seen regularly in syndication. During the 1990–1991 season, a more serious and sinister Count appeared briefly in his own show called *Dracula: The Series* .

As early as 1953, Dracula first appeared in a comic book in Eerie's (Avon Periodicals) adaptation of the novel. Dracula made several additional appearances before vampires were banished in 1954 under the conditions of the Comics Code. During the period of banishment, Dell (which did not adhere to the code) brought out one issue of a *Dracula* comic, but most of his appearances were limited to guest shots in various humorous comics such as *The Adventures of Jerry Lewis* (July-August 1964), and *The Adventures of Bob Hope* (October-November 1965) and *Herbie* (September 1966). Dracula did appear in several European and South American comic books, but it was not until the 1970s that he made his comeback in one of the most successful comics of the decade, *The Tomb of Dracula* . In that series, Marvel Comics brought Dracula into the contemporary world and placed him in conflict with the descendants of his antagonists in the Stoker novel. He soon got a second Marvel series, *Dracula Lives!*, and has made numerous appearances in different Marvel comics as a guest villain ever since. Most recently he also was the subject of two comic books from Topps that grew out of the latest attempt to bring Dracula to the screen in Francis Ford Coppola's *Bram Stoker's Dracula* .

Dracula has even been celebrated in music. A tune called "Dinner with Drac" (Cameo, 1957) appeared on a hit record by John Zacherle. A 1950s humor album, *Dracula's Greatest Hits*, had parodies of popular hit tunes that had been transformed into songs about Dracula. Dracula made a number of musical appearances through the 1960s and 1970s, primarily in comic situations, but a whole new environment arose in 1979 with the emergence of what would become known as the gothic subculture. That musical community was launched by the rock band Bauhaus, whose first hit was an eerie piece, "Bela Lugosi's Dead." The gothic world found the vampire an apt symbol of the dark world they were creating and Bela Lugosi's Dracula served them well as a starting point for costumes. Vlad, leader of one gothic band, the Dark Theater, is a Lugosi/Dracula fan who not only has adopted aspects of Lugosi's persona into his own, but created a shrine to Lugosi in the living room of his home.

The image of Dracula made popular by Lugosi has appeared in a number of additional places from candy labels to ads selling different products. Each October, his face graces numerous greeting cards, posters, buttons, party favors, and miscellaneous paraphernalia made for Halloween. There have also been Dracula statues and dolls, in almost every medium, from the artistic to the cute, produced over the last two or three decades.

So powerful and pervasive is the image of Dracula that it is not a gross exaggeration to say that all of the vampires created in the last half of the twentieth century have been either Dracula clones or creatures developed in conscious reaction to him.

As writers develop their characters, they draw from a genre, at the fountainhead of which stands the Transylvanian Count, always casting his shadow over their work.

SOURCES:

Dresser, Norine. *American Vampires: Fans, Victims, Practitioners.* NewYork: W. W. Norton & Company, 1989.

Glut, Donald F. *The Dracula Book.* Metuchen, NJ: Scarecrow Press, 1975.

Ludlam, Harry. *A Biography of Dracula: The Life Story of Bram Stoker.* London: Fireside Press/W. Foulsham & Co., 1962.

Skal, David J., ed.,*Dracula: The Ultimate, Illustrated Edition of the World-Famous Vampire Play.* New York: St. Martin's Press, 1993.

———. *Hollywood Gothic: The Tangled Web of Dracula from Novel to Stage to Screen.* New York: W. W. Norton & Company, 1990.

Stoker, Bram. *Dracula.* Westminster, London: A. Constable & Co., 1897.

Waller, Gregory A. *The Living and the Undead: From Stoker's Dracula to Romero's Dawn of the Dead.* Urbana: University of Illinois Press, 1986.

The Further Adventures of Dracula: A Select List of Novels

Aldiss, Brian W. *Dracula Unbound.* New York: HarperCollins Publishers, 1991.

Andersson, Dean. *I Am Dracula.* New York: Zebra Books, 1993.

Aubin, Etienne. *Dracula and the Virgins of the Undead.* London: New English Library, 1974.

Augustyn, Michael. *Vlad Dracula, the Dragon Prince: A Historical Novel.* Philadelphia: Vasso, 1995.

Davies, David Stuart. *The Tangled Skein.* Wymouth, Dorset, UK: Theme, 1992. Reprint, Penyffordd, Chester, UK: Calabash Press, 1995.

Doherty, P. C. *The Lord Count Drakulya.* London: Hale, 1986.

———. *The Prince Drakulya.* London: Hale, 1986.

Estleman, Loren. *Sherlock Holmes vs. Dracula.* New York: Doubleday & Company, 1978. Reprint, New York: Penguin, 1979.

Kalogridis, Jeanne. *Children of the Vampire: The Diaries of the Family Dracula.* New York: Delacorte Press, 1995.

———. *Covenant with the Vampire: The Diaries of the Family Dracula.* New York: Delacorte Press, 1994.

———. *Lord of the Vampires.* New York: Delacorte Press, 1996.

Knight, Amarantha [Nancy Kilpatrick]. *The Darker Passions: Dracula.* New York: Masquerade Books, 1993.

Lee, Earl. *Drakulya.* Tuscon: See Sharp Press, 1994.

Lory, Robert. *Challenge to Dracula.* New York: Pinnacle Books, 1975.

———. *Dracula Returns.* New York: Pinnacle Books, 1973.

———. *Dracula's Brothers.* New York: Pinnacle Books, 1973.

———. *Dracula's Disciple.* New York: Pinnacle Books, 1975.

———. *Dracula's Gold.* New York: Pinnacle Books, 1973.

———. *Dracula's Lost World.* New York: Pinnacle Books, 1975.

———. *The Drums of Dracula.* New York: Pinnacle Books, 1974.

———. *The Hand of Dracula.* New York: Pinnacle Books, 1973.

———. *The Witching of Dracula.* New York: Pinnacle Books, 1974.

Love at First Bite. Los Angeles: Fotonovel Publications, 1979.

Myles, Douglas. *Prince Dracula, Son of the Devil.* New York: McGraw-Hill Book Company, 1988.

Newman, Kim. *Anno-Dracula.* London: Simon and Schuster, 1992.

———. *The Bloody Red Baron.* New York: Carroll & Graf, 1995.

Rudorff, Raymond. *The Dracula Archives.* London: David, Bruce & Watson, 1971.

Saberhagen, Fred. *Dominion.* New York: Pinnacle, 1982. Reprint, New York: Tor Books, 1982.

———. *The Dracula Tape.* New York: Warner, 1975. Reprint, New York: Tor Books, 1989.

———. *The Holmes-Dracula File.* New York: Ace Books, 1978. Reprint, New York: Tor Books, 1990.

———. *A Matter of Taste.* New York: Tor Books, 1990.

———. *An Old Friend of the Family.* New York: Ace Books, 1979. Reprint, New York: Tor Books, 1987.

———. *A Question of Time.* New York: Tor Books, 1992.

———. *Seance for a Vampire.* New York: Tor Books, 1994

———. *A Sharpness in the Neck.* New York: Tor Books, 1996.

———. *Thorn.* New York: Ace Books, 1980. Reprint, New York: Tor Books, 1990.

The Further Adventures of Dracula: A Select List of

Shirley, John. *Dracula in Love.* New York: Zebra Books/Kensington, 1979.

Tremayne, Peter. *Dracula Lives!* London: Signet, 1993.

———. *Dracula My Love.* Folkstone, UK: Bailey Brothers and Swinfen, 1980.

———. *Dracula Unborn.* Folksone, UK: Bailey Brothers and Swinfen, 1977. Reprint as, *Bloodright.* New York: Dell, 1980.

———. *The Revenge of Dracula.* Folkstone: Bailey Brothers and Swiften, 1978.

Warrington, Freda. *Dracula the Undead.* New York: Penguin Books,

A.J.

A.J., the college kid who bites off more than he can chew, becomes a vampire in the film *Vamp* (1986). A.J. is a traditional vampire. He has no reflection in mirrors, is vulnerable to sunlight and fire, and grows fangs when getting ready to feed. He also assumes a bestial appearance when the blood lust arises.

The story begins with A.J. as a freshman at an unnamed university who wants to join a fraternity merely to get out of the chaos of dormitory life. He and his friend Keith want to avoid the hazing rituals associated with the frat initiation, so A.J. cuts a deal with the frat house. He and Keith will supply the fraternity with the things it needs, beginning with the party that same evening, and the fraternity will let them join, sans initiation.

With wheels supplied by Duncan, the wealthy nerd on campus, the three kids leave for the city in search of a stripper for the party. They wind up at the After Dark Club, a strip joint. A.J. ventures inside to hire a dancer while Keith and Duncan sit down to enjoy the show. A.J. likes **Katrina**, the sensual African-American dancer, who is also the owner of the club. He is taken back to her room after she finishes dancing, where he tries to engage her for a performance at the fraternity house. She says nothing, but begins to seduce A.J. before suddenly transforming herself into a bestial bloodsucker.

A.J. is drained and his body thrown in the trash. However, Keith finds his body and calls the police. In the face of the alarm, Katrina's minions recover A.J.'s body and suddenly he reappears very much alive. After telling Keith what had happened, Keith stakes him, but A.J. does not die. It seems that Keith stabbed him with Formica, and it just did not take. As Keith struggles to escape Katrina, he realizes that a waitress at the club is an old friend of his and tries to save her too. A.J. returns in the nick of time to help Keith, who survives the night and returns to campus life as usual. Keith and A.J. are still best friends, but A.J. accepts the reality of his new life as a vampire who must keep his distance from the mortal world.

Barbara Steele portrayes Princess Ada in *Black Sunday*.

Ada, Princess

Princess Ada, as played by Barbara Steele, is a Moldavian witch/vampire who is the central figure in Mario Bava's 1960 film, *Black Sunday*. A princess of the house of Vida, she is condemned as a servant of Satan by her own brother, who is the local Grand Inquisitor. Before she dies, the youthful princess curses her brother and his descendants and vows that she will return. Ignoring her words, her brother orders that she be branded and a spiked mask placed on her face. Her body (and that of her servant) is supposed to be cremated, but a hard rain comes down just as the bonfire is started, and she is instead buried in a crypt in the family castle. Her servant is not so lucky—he is buried in unconsecrated ground near the local village.

One hundred years later, to the day, an earthquake shook the area and created an opening in Ada's crypt. For only one day, Ada, in spirit form, returns. She kills 20-year-old Princess Marsha, who looks a great deal like Ada. After killing Marsha, Ada returns to her crypt.

The movie then jumps to 200 years after the execution. Ada's story is well known and has become part of the local folklore, but a professor of medicine and his youthful assistant traveling near Ada's castle know nothing of the tale. The coach they are riding in breaks down, and while waiting for it to be fixed, the two enter the castle and find Princess Ada's crypt. Thinking that the castle must be deserted, the professor gives in to his curiosity and removes the spiked mask covering Ada's face. In the process he cuts himself and several drops of blood fall on the body, which appears to be amazingly well preserved considering it is two centuries old. The drops of blood revive Ada, who was in a state of vampiric sleep.

Ada awakens intent upon seeking her revenge. She hopes to attack Princess Katia, the daughter of current ruler Prince Vida, and merge her spirit with the young girl's body so that she truly return to the land of the living. Ada calls her servant out of his grave and orders him to attack the prince, but Vida uses a cross to drive the servant away. The servant then tricks the professor into coming to the castle, where Ada vampirizes him and turns him into her thrall. At Ada's bidding, the professor then arrives at the front door of the castle to care for the Prince. Over the evening, however, the Prince and his son are killed, as are several of the villagers. Ada's long-time servant delivers Katia to Ada's side so that Ada can merge with her and become human again.

With Katia in her possession, all seemed to be going just as Ada had planned. However, unknown to Ada, the professor has found an icon that contains instructions on how to destroy Ada and her minions. The professor, who has fallen in love with Katia, finds Ada just as she is about to kiss Katia and merge with her; he uses the icon to destroy Ada.

Black Sunday (originally released in Italy as *La Maschera del Demonio*) though portraying an Eastern European vampire, represents a distinct break with the **Count Dracula** legend while retaining the supernatural context of the traditional vampire story.

Akasha

In Anne Rice's *Vampire Chronicles*, Akasha is said to be the original vampire. She first appears in *The Vampire Lestat* (1985) and is the main subject of *The Queen of the Damned* (1988) which recounts her origin and ultimate fate.

Her story is a complicated one. Before becoming a vampire, she was a queen in ancient Egypt more than six millennia ago. She was born into royalty in the city of Uruk in the Tigeris and Euphrates Valleys (now Iraq) and was a worshiper of the goddess Inanna. When she becomes queen of old Egypt, she rules beside her weaker husband **Enkil**. She is most known for her lack of tolerance for those who hold beliefs different than her own. Early in her rule, she issues edicts ordering the end of cannibalism and the addition of more grain in her people's diet. While she seems to be a reasonable ruler, Akasha also has a dark side that leads her on a search to experience the supernatural. To help her reach that goal, she brings two young female witches—**Maharet** and **Mekare**—to her court. She orders them to demonstrate their connection to the spirit world, and reluctantly they obey. They make contact with a spirit known as **Amel** and are severely punished when Amel turns out to be a troublemaker.

An original illustration by Daerick Gross of Akasha from the comic book version of *Queen of the Damned*.

Seeing the two women punished by Akasha's Chief Steward **Khayman** for his actions makes Amel angry. His anger changes the course of Akasha's life forever. He attacks Khayman for his role in the punishment. Priests try to exorcise Khayman's dwelling but are unsuccessful. The unrest gives those who oppose Akasha the chance they have been waiting for. There are many who want to return to the old tradition of cannibalism. To help make this happen, they assassinate Akasha and Enkil. As Akasha lays bleeding and dying, her soul seeks its escape from her body. Amel seizes it and merges his being with her soul before entering her body, thus creating the first vampire. Once she is a vampire, Akasha heals quickly and she shares her blood (and, as it turns out, the presence of Amel) with Enkil. He also heals miraculously and the two of them begin their new life as vampires.

Akasha and Enkil have no desire to remain vampires, so they immediately begin seeking a way out of their dilemma. The witches inform them that the only way they can end Amel's possession is to destroy their bodies. Upon learning this, Akasha tries to rationalize her situation, reasoning that either her body has become the host for a demon or that she and Enkil are young gods. She chooses the latter, insisting that she is a young diety who needs to learn the designs of heaven. Akasha again attempts to kill the two witches, but this time they are saved by Khayman, who was the first vampire created by Akasha. He offers the women the "Dark Gift" by vampirizing them.

She and Enkil soon discover that Amel has a tremendous thirst for blood, which causes them to kill many people to assuage it. They also create additional vampires as time passes. Interestingly, as the number of vampires increases, Akasha and Enkil's hunger decreases. Eventually, they no longer need blood at all. Since reaching that state, they have remained together and have become living statues while attaining legendary status in the vampire community as "Those who must be kept." They are preserved and protected by vampire guardians who are aware that somehow the existence of all vampires is dependent upon the two.

That dependency is made abundantly clear one year when vampires everywhere are mysteriously burned. A vampire named **Marius** is dispatched to Egypt to determine the problem. When he arrives, he finds that the current guardian has grown tired of his job and placed Akasha and her husband in the sun. Akasha and Enkil survive that ordeal, and Akasha urges Marius to take her to Europe. He then becomes the new guardian. She becomes an impersonal observer of the world, projecting her consciousness from her body and utilizing the eyes of others, both vampires and mortals.

Over the years, Akasha receives a number of visitors. The witch Maharet approaches Akasha and strikes her. Akasha does not move when struck, so Maharet takes a dagger and stabs her in the heart. As she sinks the blade in, Maharet feels an amazing thing—because she too is a vampire, she "feels" Akasha's heart stop beating and feels her own imminent death as well. She quickly pulls the knife out. Akasha's body quickly heals itself. From that moment, Maharet understands that the very core of Amel is within Akasha and that somehow the life of all vampires resides within her.

On another occasion, while visiting Marius, **Lestat de Lioncourt** makes his way to the underground shrine room where Akasha and Enkil are located. He awakens Akasha and they embrace and exchange blood. Suddenly Enkil awakens and separates them. Only the appearance of Marius saves Lestat from certain death.

Some years later, in 1985, Akasha is awakened by Lestat's music. She then sucks the life out of Enkil and initiates a plan of world domination. She sets out to destroy most of the males (both mortal and vampire) in the entire world so she can establish a new Eden in which women, especially Akasha, would reign. Along the way, she invites Lestat to join her and takes him on one of her killing sprees (this time in the Himalayas), as a demonstration of her power. She kills an old vampire named **Azim** who had lived as a god in his isolated region. She informs Lestat that he can either help her achieve her goal or he can die, the choice is his.

Akasha is foiled by her real enemies, however—the witches Maharet and Mekare, who have survived through the centuries. They are present at a gathering of surviving vampires in Sonoma, California, when Akasha appears. Before she can act, however, Mekare pushes her through a glass wall, decapitating her. Maharet immediately isolates the heart and brain of the fallen queen and passes both to Mekare who quickly devours them. When she eats Akasha's organs, the essence of Amel passed to her and she becomes the new life for the entire vampire community. With Akasha destroyed, undead life returns to some degree of normalcy.

SOURCES:

Ramsland, Katherine. *The Vampire Companion: The Official Guide to Anne Rice's The Vampire Chronicles.* New York: Ballantine Books, 1993.

Rice, Anne. *The Queen of the Damned.* New York: Alfred A. Knopf, 1988. Reprint, New York: Ballantine Books, 1989.

———. *The Vampire Lestat.* New York: Alfred A. Knopf, 1985. Reprint, New York: Ballantine Books, 1986.

Alcore, Dr. John

Dr. John Alcore, the wealthy director of the Life Reach Foundation in the 1990 movie *Red Blooded American Girl*, is, in fact, a vampire. More properly stated, he is a man infected with vampirism. Through his research on aging, Alcore inadvertently discovered that vampires actually do exist, but that they are not the supernatural creatures of folklore and popular superstition. They are not affected by garlic, they do not grow fangs, and they do not sleep in coffins. Rather, they are normal human beings who have been victimized by a very real, if rare, disease.

Alcore (portrayed by Christopher Plummer) has been experimenting with various rare viruses in his quest to overcome aging and extend life indefinitely. In the process he becomes infected with the vampire virus. Although it offers some life-enhancing qualities, the virus has its dark side. For example, it inflicts its victims with a powerful thirst for blood. Fortunately for Alcore and several of his infected staff, they are able to sustain a continuous supply of fresh blood by pretending to engage in AIDS research. In the meantime, Alcore embarks upon new research to find a cure for the vampire disease.

Along the way, Alcore infects his assistant, Dennis, an unstable young man who is unable to control his blood cravings. Dennis bites and infects a young woman, Rebecca, who Alcore imprisons in the basement of the Foundation. In the meantime, Alcore hires Dr. Owen Urban, a brilliant and unorthodox researcher, to complete the research toward a cure for Alcore's disease. Initially unaware of the Foundation's true purpose, Urban begins to investigate the strange events at his workplace with the assistance of a former staff member, Paula Bukowsky. Although they soon find Rebecca, Paula is bitten and infected while trying to interview the bloodthirsty young woman.

Paula's vampire condition soon emerges and Alcore orders her confined as well. During an attempted escape, Paula kills Dennis by draining him of blood. Having by this time fallen in love with Paula, Urban concentrates fully on completing the work on a cure that he believes he has discovered. To test it, however, Urban must mingle his blood with Paula's and thus risk infection. He goes through with the transfusion and Paula is cured. Alcore watches their interaction on the Foundation's closed circuit television system. After Paula manifests her freedom from the vampire virus, Alcore enters the scene and makes peace with his young researchers. Science has triumphed, and the world is forever saved from vampirism.

Alex

Alex is the featured character in the 1992 film *A Tale of a Vampire*, which is set in contemporary London. His age is unknown, although his body is young and handsome. He is at least two centuries old, as the first event he can remember involves an encounter in the early nineteenth century with a five-year old child, Virginia. Alex has just finished feeding when Virginia, who is lost in the woods, stumbles upon him. Virginia makes a lasting impression on Alex—years later, he reenters her life and falls in love with her, even though she is married to a man named Edgar. She also falls in love with Alex, and when he offers to turn her into a vampire, she accepts. Alex shares his blood with her to consummate their love.

Alex vows to be with Virginia forever, but it is not to be. Nearby villagers suspect Virginia of murdering one of their townspeople, and they give chase to her and Alex. The pair separates, but Virginia is doomed when her ex-husband, Edgar, catches her. Enraged by her betrayal, Edgar realizes he cannot kill her, so he places her in an iron coffin and drops the coffin into the ocean, where supposedly she remains when the movie jumps to modern-day England.

Since Virginia's death, Alex has lived in a state of despair, mourning the loss of his one true love. In his modern life, he spends a period each day reading old books at the local library, which has a specialized collection of occult and mystical literature. Alex's world is rocked when a new librarian arrives who looks just like his lost Virginia. Anne, the librarian, has recently lost her boyfriend in an automobile accident and finds herself inexplicably drawn to Alex in spite of his strange ways.

The plot takes a sudden twist when Edgar, Alex's long-time rival, appears on the scene. It seems that he too is an immortal and that his hatred of Alex has remained strong through the years. He accosts Anne and tells her that Alex is a vampire, and while she is shocked at first, she begins to accepts his condition. In fact, she asks Alex to turn her into a vampire, but he refuses. It proves to be a fatal mistake by Alex. Edgar continues to punish him by killing Anne and leaving her body in Alex's lair. Since Alex and Edgar are both immortal, there is no resolution to their conflict.

Alexander, Ardeth

Ardeth Alexander, a young female vampire living in Toronto, first appears in Nancy Baker's 1993 novel, *The Night Inside*. A 28-year-old graduate student, her life is suddenly disrupted when she is kidnaped off the street while out for her morning walk. Blindfolded, she is taken to a house some distance from the city. Still groggy, she is struggling to orient herself when she realizes that someone is sucking blood from her arm. That someone is **Dimitri Rozokov**, a 400-year-old vampire who is also a prisoner at the house. Rozokov had been captured by a group of men who are forcing him to star in pornographic vampire snuff films—Ardeth is supposed to be his next meal.

Alexander is initially repulsed, but she overcomes that and concludes that the only way to get out of the house alive is to cooperate. She allows Rozokov to drain her to the point that her captors think she is dead. In reality, she has become a vampire, and, when the men fail to put a stake in her heart when they bury her, she is able to rise from the dead. Her first order of business is to return to the house to kill her former captives and free Rozokov. He is grateful and provides her with basic information on what it means to be a vampire, but he is a loner and wants nothing to do with her long-term. The two part ways when they reach Toronto.

Alexander returns to her apartment and contemplates her new existence as she bathes. She realizes that she has entered a new life and that she has to make a clean break from her old existence. She knows instinctively that she must not take any items from her past with her, leaving her apartment forever with only her sunglasses and some money. She changes her look, getting her hair dyed and restyled. A strong woman, she dedicates all her energy to learning how to live in her new state. Things are just starting to go well when Rozokov returns to her life. He needs her help because he is being tracked by a wealthy woman named Althea Dale. Ms. Dale is dying from AIDS and believes that a bit of Rozokov's blood will save her. This encounter with Dale becomes the first in a series of adventures that the two vampires share.

It is interesting to note that Alexander is a contemporary vampire. She is nocturnal, but has no need for a coffin or native soil for sleeping. Her image reflects in mirrors and sacred symbols have no negative effect on her. Her skin is pale. She needs blood once or twice a week, under normal conditions. She cannot transform into other life forms, but she is very strong.

SOURCES:

Baker, Nancy. *Blood and Chrysanthemums: A Vampire Novel.* New York: Viking, 1994.
———. *The Night Inside: A Vampire Thriller.* New York: Viking, 1993. Reprint. *Kiss of the Vampire.* Greenwich, CT: Fawcett Columbine, 1995.

Alucard, Count

Count Alucard is the vampire featured in a number of juvenile books by Willis Hall, beginning with *The Last Vampire* in 1982. In this initial story, Alucard is discovered by the vacationing Hollins family, who winds up camping near the Count's castle while touring Europe on holiday from England. Alucard has been living alone for many years as the last surviving member of his family, who are direct descendants of the Draculas. A tall, thin man with pale skin and swept-back black hair, Alucard wears a black suit, a starched white shirt with a black bow tie, a gold medallion around his neck, and a cape lined with scarlet material. Alucard retains some traditional vampire supernatural powers. For example, he can change into a bat and fly. However, he also possesses some peculiar characteristics for a vampire. He never drinks blood because he is a vegetarian. Although he can transform into a bat, he changes into a fruit bat, rather than a vampire bat.

While the Hollinses camp out near the count's castle on the outskirts of a small village, Alucard hides, as he does when anyone comes around, fearful of being discovered by the superstitious villagers. True to Alucard's fears, the villagers come to believe that the Hollinses are vampires themselves, in league with the castle's notorious resident, and take steps to rid their town of these evil influences. The villagers' actions push the family and the vampire into common cause as they struggle to avoid being killed by the ignorant townsfolk.

Just before the villagers burn down the count's castle with him and the Hollinses inside, the Hollinses escape with Alucard and set out to return with their new friend to their home in England. En route, the group encounters a problem: Alucard has neither a passport nor any other legal papers. He cannot board the ferry to cross the Channel. As a result, he is separated from his friends. Not to be defeated, Alucard stows away in a coffin that is placed aboard a Belgian freighter headed for Great Britain. As the ship approaches the British coast, a storm arises. Angry crew members, believing that the Count caused the storm, push his coffin overboard. When the storm subsides, the coffin washes ashore on the Yorkshire coast. Alucard emerges, free to be reunited with the Hollinses and to make a new life for himself in England. As it turns out, the worlds of stage magic and the circus are well suited to the count's particular talents.

Following his introduction in *The Last Vampire*, Alucard has reappeared in a continuing series of books that recount his adventures in England and, eventually, in America.

SOURCES:

Hall, Willis. *The Last Vampire*. London: The Bodley Head, 1982.
————. *The Vampire Vanishes*. London: The Bodley Head, 1995.
————. *The Vampire's Christmas*. London: The Bodley Head, 1994.
————. *The Vampire's Holiday*. London: The Bodley Head, 1992.
————. *The Vampire's Revenge*. London: Red Fox, 1993.

Alucard, Vic

Vic Alucard, also known as Vic the Vampire, is the new kid in the fourth grade. He makes his appearance in Hanna Bloom's young adult novel, *School Ghoul* (1990), although he and his school chums return for three sequels that deal with the problems of fourth graders in their own unique manner. Vic has slicked-back hair with a prominent widow's peak, his lips are bright red, and his skin is pale. His eyes glow, and two fangs appear when he smiles. Along with his black jeans and purple sweater, he has a black opera cape. Vic's folks come from Transylvania. They had lived in a castle but the upkeep was too expensive, so they moved to a house left to the family by Vic's great grandfather, Vito. According to Vic, Vito was 448 years old. He is not dead, just "hanging around some place."

Vic sits next to Mike Morgan, who finds him somewhat weird, but soon becomes his good friend. Mike covers for Vic when he fails to show up in the class picture. He visits Vic's home and meets his older sister, Viveca. Besides his parents, Vic's Uncle Vlad lives with the family. He has a large pet spider and hound dog, and his sister has a pet bat. Large hamburgers are served for dinner—raw.

Some kids at school think Vic is a vampire. One particularly obnoxious kid, Missy Thompson, calls him Dracula and is always trying to get the definitive proof. She even buys a book, *Vampires and How to Get Rid of Them*. She tries garlic (the class teacher is allergic), water (Mike steps in the way), and searches through his house when he hosts the school carnival. In the end, she and the class corner Mike and are about to beat him up for the truth when a bat flies out of nowhere and chases them off. After they run away, Vic appears. Mike realizes that his best friend really is a vampire, but it doesn't matter to him anymore.

Vic becomes accepted by the class, none of whom really believe he is a vampire, except for Missy. In the sequels to follow, Vic is most challenged to keep his cover when three vampire cousins with behavior problems show up for a visit.

SOURCES:
Bloom, Hanna. *Friendly Fangs*. Vic the Vampire, No. 4. New York: HarperCollins,

Amel

Amel, the timeless vampiric spirit in Anne Rice's *Vampire Chronicles*, makes his primary appearance in *The Queen of the Damned* (1988), where the ultimate origins of modern vampirism are traced to ancient Egypt. Amel is a spirit/soul from Shoel, the abode of the dead. As he watches humans through the years, he grows envious of their embodied existence and tries to find a way to once again possess a body. He makes himself known to the witches **Mekare** and **Maharet**, who are well known for being mediums who can talk to the spirit world. When **Akasha,** the queen of old Egypt learns of their talents, she summons them to come visit her. When they appear before her, Amel's spirit is nearby and stirs up trouble, which angers the queen. She orders the public rape and banishment of the two witches. Akasha's Chief Steward, **Khayman,** is responsible for raping the two women.

Amel responds by causing havoc in the house of Khayman. When the priests sent to exorcise the spirit from Khayman's house are unable to do so, they turn against Akasha and her husband **Enkil.** Followers of the priests, who believe in the old way of life before Akasha took power, kill Akasha and Enkil and leave them bleeding and near death. Amel seizes the opportunity to take human form by wedding himself to Akasha's soul and then fusing with her body, thereby creating a new creature that is the very first vampire. When the merger is complete, Akasha's wounds heal immediately. She then shares her blood with Enkil and he also heals miraculously and becomes a vampire. Inside his new hosts, Amel has an insatiable thirst for blood.

Amel's appetite requires that Akasha and Enkil demand numerous blood sacrifices; each victim they drain becomes a vampire. Although Amel is fused to Akasha, a little "piece" of him is present in every vampire that Akasha and Enkil create. His spirit somehow ties all vampires together, and as their number increases, they all share in the burden of feeding Amel. As the number of vampires grow and Amel gets blood from more and more sources, Akasha and Enkil begin to change until they no longer need to take blood to survive. However, since Amel's core resides within Akasha, the life of every vampire is dependent upon her well-being. The other vampires realize this connection and begin to guard Akasha and Enkil as, "Those who must be kept."

Amel also makes lesser appearances in *The Vampire Lestat* and *Memnoch the Devil.*

SOURCES:

Ramsland, Katherine. *The Vampire Companion: The Official Guide to Anne Rice's The Vampire Chronicles.* New York: Ballantine Books, 1993.

Rice, Anne. *Memnoch the Devil.* New York: Alfred A. Knopf, 1994. Reprint, New York: Ballantine Books, 1995.

———. *The Queen of the Damned.* New York: Alfred A. Knopf, 1988. Rept.: New York: Ballantine Books, 1989.

———. *The Vampire Lestat.* New York: Alfred A. Knopf, 1985. Rept.: New York: Ballantine Books, 1986.

Angel

Angel (portrayed by David Boreanaz) is one of the main vampires in the popular television series *Buffy the Vampire Slayer.* However, he is a vampire with a difference. Also known as Angelus, he is 240 years old. He was born on a Greek island, but spent most of his early years as a vampire in Europe. He appears to be in his 20s and is quite good-looking, with an innocent appearance. However, in his youth, Angelus is one of the most vicious vampires around—he feels no qualms in killing anyone, including his family, his friends, and his friends' children. His search for new victims leads him to Budapest at the beginning of this century, at which time there is a major earthquake.

In Budapest, he meets a young Gypsy girl, whom he seduces and kills. Her family takes its revenge on him when they, as Angelus tells it, "conjured the perfect punishment." To forever torment Angel, they let him remain a vampire but they restore his soul, which all vampires lose when they are first transformed. With no soul, vampires are able to kill without remorse. Angelus no longer has that luxury. He must have blood to survive, but now that he has a conscience and a soul, he is too tortured to kill humans. Since his encounter with the Gypsies, he has not fed on a human being even once. He changes his name from Angelus to Angel and moves to the United States as World War I is about to start in Europe. He becomes a loner in the U.S., shunning the company of other vampires.

Kate Nelligan in the 1979 version of *Dracula*.

In the mid-1990s, Angel lives in the town of Sunnydale, California, where he meets some of his old vampire friends, Darla and the Master. The Master invites him back into the vampire fold and Darla invites him back into her life, as they had shared a relationship in the past. He turns them down. While this is happening, he has become aware of **Buffy Summers,** a Sunnydale high school student who he recognizes as the person known as a the Vampire Slayer. One evening, as three vampires sent by the Master attack Buffy, he appears at her side and helps her defeat the creatures, thereby choosing sides against the Master. He makes Buffy aware that The Master is in Sunnydale and that he hopes to take advantage of a once-in-a-century phenomena known as a the Harvest to take over the world. Buffy defeats the Master in that initial battle, and as time passes, Angel begins to show up more frequently to help her fight the vampires in Sunnydale. The plot thickens during one of those fights. Angel is injured, and as Buffy helps him and bandages his wounds, she begins to fall in love with him. He is helpless to stop his own strong feelings for her. Over the course of the next few episodes, their relationship grows.

Although the Master has been defeated, Sunnydale is soon visited by two more powerful vampires, Spike and Drusilla, who were Angel's friends at the height of his vampiric killing sprees. Even though they used to be his friends (in fact, Drusilla may have been much more than a friend), Angel readily helps Buffy battle the twosome and their minions. At the same time, he continues to fall deeper and deeper in love with Buffy, until one night they consummate their passion and make love. That one night of passion sets off a horrible chain of events. It seems that there was another part to the Gypsy curse—if Angel ever experiences a true moment of happiness in his lifetime, he will instantly become a full-fledged vampire once again. Of course, his one night with Buffy is that happy moment. Angel wakes in his bed and realizes that he has lost his soul once again. He reverts to the vampire Angelus, and reunites with Spike and Drusilla. Buffy is shattered by the turn of events. She realizes that Angel is now her enemy and that she must destroy the very vampire with whom she has fallen so deeply in love. Angel torments Buffy and stalks her, but even he still remembers some of the feelings he once had for Buffy. As a the second season of the show drew to a close, it appeared that Buffy had killed Angel, but he is expected to survive the encounter.

SOURCES:
"Buffy the Vampire Slayer." *Spectrum.* 13 (May 1998): 8-23.

Anna

Anna, the young vampire of the 1997 movie *Habits*, lives quietly in the after-dark world of contemporary New York City, where her all-black outfits are never questioned. A sexually aggressive person, she chooses male victims and bites them when in a state of intense arousal, usually in the midst of the sex act. Her bite does not kill, at least initially, but her act becomes deadly as she returns night after night to take additional blood from her victim, sometimes manifesting as a succubus while her victim sleeps.

Anna possesses several traditional vampire attributes. Although she cannot transform into an animal or vaporize into mist, she has fangs when she feeds and is repelled by garlic and mirrors. Her hearing is acute and she enjoys the sounds of the night. Animals are attuned to her. She does not consume real food.

Anna finds her latest victim, Sam, at a party she has crashed. Sam likes Anna in spite of her strange ways. Anna refuses to share with Sam anything about her life, apart from her relationship with him, and mysteriously shows herself only at night, disappearing before dawn. As they meet evening after evening, however, Sam gradually becomes fatigued and begins to take on some of Anna's strange traits. One night, Sam resists Anna and, as dawn is approaching, they fight. Anna is killed when she falls out of his apartment window into the first light of morning.

Anubus

Anubus, an ancient vampire of unknown age and origin, appeared in the 1992 Canadian comic book, *Vampire Rock*. As the story opens in 1932, Anubus has emerged out of obscurity and is working as a stage magician for a member of the British royalty. After insulting the man's wife, he is impaled on a large sword and assumed dead. His body and all his possessions are shipped to Canada aboard a ship called the *Demeter* (the same name as the ship that brought **Count Dracula** to Whitby, England from Eastern Europe). In 1932, the *Demeter* wrecks and eventually sinks near the coastal town of Mount Hope. Before the boat sinks completely, however, two men salvage the ship's cargo, including a number of medieval artifacts and a coffin. The coffin—which contains Anubus's body—is interred in the local cemetery.

Shortly after the coffin is buried, the room that the artifacts from the ship are housed in is broken into. Arthur Gemor, one of the men who took the possessions from the ship, records the robbery in his diary, noting that the only item taken is a cup decorated with a set of fangs. A short time later, Gemor is mysteriously killed.

The murderer is Anubus, who since the time of the shipwreck, has lived in the cemetery, feeding off unwary victims who happen to pass by the cemetery at night. Anubus is a traditional vampire—nocturnal, with one prominent set of fangs and a second set recessed in his jaw. He is eight feet tall and very strong, with wild, unkempt hair and a bestial appearance. He has the power to shapeshift into a wolf as the situation dictates. He fears only one thing— the sword that he had originally been impaled upon. He knows that if he is impaled a second time, he would die, permanently. Ironically, the sword is missing because Arthur Gemor hid it and took its hiding place to his grave.

Anubus soon has a nemesis—Gemor's grandson, who often hung around the cemetery. One night, just before Halloween, the grandson happens to be in the cemetery when a naive musician wanders through the grounds on his way to a rehearsal. Anubus overtakes the musician and is about to collect some of his blood in the fanged cup when the younger Gemor interrupts the encounter and shoots Anubus. The grandson knows Anubus's wound is only temporary, so he quickly rescues the musician and gives him the fanged cup as a souvenir of his brush with death.

Anubus is enraged and knows he must get his cup back. He finds Michael, the musician, who still has the cup. He forces Michael to share blood from the cup and then merges with him. Anubus is now ready for his shining moment—a Halloween concert at the cemetery. His plan is to kill all the concert goers and then use his cup to feast on the seemingly endless supply of blood. Again, he is foiled by Gemor's grandson, who has found the deadly sword hidden in his grandfather's roll-top desk. Armed with the sword, he faces the ancient vampire in a final confrontation.

SOURCES:

Rehkopf, Mark. *Vampire Rock*. Canada: Undead Graphics, 1992.

Armand

Armand, a 400-year-old with a very youthful appearance, is a major continuing character in Anne Rice's *Vampire Chronicles*. He first appears in *Interview with the Vampire*, but his story is told in *The Vampire Lestat*. He was born in Southern Russia, but as a child his family was taken prisoner by Tartars and sold into slavery in Constantinople. He ends up in Venice after he is purchased by a vampire named **Marius,** who uses him as a model for a painting called *The Temptation of Amadeo*. He is just 17 when Marius turns him into a vampire. He is strikingly attractive, with auburn hair, brown eyes, and a beautiful face.

When Marius's home is invaded by a group of Satanists, Armand is inducted into their coven and goes on to become an accomplished leader. He moves out across Europe, gathering potential Satanists into new covens. Eventually he settles in Paris as the head of a coven. As a vampire, he needs to feed regularly, and through the years he has perfected a technique that somehow attracts people who have a death wish to him. He has never created another vampire. He also has either lost or never even possessed any belief in God or the Devil.

Armand had lived in Paris for nearly a century when he meets the young actor **Lestat de Lioncourt** for the first time. Lestat has just recently been turned into a vampire by the older vampire **Magnus,** who fell in love with Lestat and offered the 20-year-old the "Dark Gift" of immortality. Magnus commits suicide soon after he creates Lestat, leaving the young vampire a fortune but no mentor in the ways of the vampire. Seeking information, Lestat travels to Paris, where he meets Armand and his coven, who follow an old set of rules passed on from a similar coven in Rome. Armand and his coven resent Lestat's free lifestyle and believe it is not fit for a vampire. However, the coven fails to convert Lestat and in fact, dissolves after its encounter with Rice's most important vampire.

Armand next appears in Paris after learning that the vampires **Louis de Pointe du Lac** and **Claudia** have arrived in the city. He breaks up a fight between Louis and **Santiago,** whom he had sent to give an invitation to the **Theatre des Vampires.** Louis and Claudia attend the performance, and afterwards, meet with Armand. Louis and Armand are strongly attracted to each other and have a lengthy conversation concerning God and the meaning of existence. According to Armand (who is the oldest vampire either of them have ever met), no vampire has had any experience of God or the Devil. Louis has difficulty grappling with the meaninglessness of life.

Louis knows that his infatuation with Armand is causing Claudia a great deal of anxiety, since she views Louis as her father-figure and is afraid to lose him. To calm her, he turns a woman named **Madeleine** into a vampire to serve as Claudia's "mother." Armand lets all this happen, but he knows that Louis, Claudia, and Madeleine are in grave danger because the other vampires in the Theatre des Vampires wish to kill the three outsiders because they violated the vampire code by killing another vampire (Lestat, as told in *Interview with the Vampire*). When the three are taken captive, Armand allows Claudia and Madeleine to be executed but saves Louis from the coffin in which he had been confined. In return, Louis warns Armand that he should leave the theater because he is about to vent his anger and seek vengeance against those who killed his beloved Claudia. Thus Armand escapes when Louis burns the theater, killing many of the vampires caught in its confines.

Afterwards, Armand and Louis travel the world together—Egypt, across Europe, and on to New York. They live together in New York City for many years, only returning to New Orleans in the mid-1970s after Armand finally tells Louis that Lestat had not really died in the fire that Louis set in New Orleans decades ago. Louis confronts Lestat and has a final conversation with Armand, after which they go their separate ways.

Armand's next major adventure is with **Daniel Molloy**, the man that Louis allowed to interview him for the book *Interview with the Vampire*. After Louis gave the interview to Molloy, the writer came to New Orleans seeking Lestat but found Armand instead. They develop a relationship, but Armand comes and goes at will, leaving Molloy alone. Molloy begs Armand to give him the Dark Gift, but Armand refuses. Daniel serves as Armand's teacher, showing him how things work in the twentieth century. Armand is fascinated with modern technology—from food processors to television—and decides to leave his old ways behind. His vast knowledge helps him succeed when he becomes a businessman, and he quickly amasses a fortune, which he generously shares with Daniel. He builds a fantastic shopping/entertainment complex near Miami called Night Island, where he prepares a luxury apartment for Molloy.

While he repeatedly refuses to make Daniel a vampire, Armand does give him an amulet that contains a vial of his vampire blood. If Daniel is ever in danger and threatened by other vampires, all he has to do is break the vial and drink it. The attacking vampires would then feel Armand's power and leave Daniel alone. This appeases Daniel a little bit, but Armand's refusal to offer the Dark Gift remains a constant source of conflict. Daniel gets tired of waiting and leaves Armand, quickly allowing his quality of life to degenerate. Finally, in 1985, Armand locates his disconsolate young lover and realizes that turning him into a vampire is the only way to prevent his death. Besides, the vampire community is in crisis because vampires around the world are being killed off. The deaths are the work of the ancient vampire **Akasha,** although Armand does not realize this yet. To save Daniel's life and to help stop the threat to all vampires, Armand finally breaks down and makes Daniel a vampire, the first and only time that Armand transforms anyone into a vampire.

Armand and others win a bloody final confrontation with Akasha, after which the surviving vampires gather at Night Island to regroup before going their separate ways. Several years later, Armand travels to New Orleans to meet with Lestat, about whom he has become concerned. He meets his old friend as Lestat is about to embark on his adventure into heaven and hell (as told in *Memnoch the Devil*). He waits for Lestat to return from his journey and has his lack of faith in God and the Devil shaken when Lestat arrives and tells of his journey beyond death. He is so disturbed by Lestat's tale that he actually commits suicide by walking out into the sun and dying in a blaze of glory.

SOURCES:

Ramsland, Katherine. *The Vampire Companion: The Official Guide to Anne Rice's The Vampire Chronicles*. New York: Ballantine Books, 1993.

Rice, Anne. *Memnoch the Devil*. New York: Alfred A. Knopf, 1994. Reprint, New York: Ballantine Books, 1995.

————. *The Queen of the Damned*. New York: Alfred A. Knopf, 1988. Reprint, New York: Ballantine Books, 1989.

————. *The Vampire Lestat*. New York: Alfred A. Knopf, 1985. Reprint, New York: Ballantine Books, 1986.

Ash

Ash, the ancient master vampire of the 1996 movie *Vampire Journals*, was the spawn of **Radu** of Transylvania, the evil vampire from the *Subspecies* series. In *Vampire Journals*, Ash has emerged in post-Ceausescu Romania as the leader of a group of vampires who own a Bucharest nightclub, Club Muse. Many of Bucharest's social elite patronize the club, unaware of its true nature and of the labyrinth of rooms that exists some eighty feet below them, providing many entrances and exits for Ash's illicit activities. Ash is master of the vampires at the club and rules them as an autocratic monarch.

Ash (portrayed by Jonathan Morris) is a nocturnal being with pale skin, hypnotic eyes, and prominent fangs. He wears all-black clothing of a bygone era, complete with a long black topcoat typical of the eighteenth century. He can transform into a bat and fly. He is strong and quick, but vulnerable to sunlight. He shows his age when he sleeps, but quickly returns to a youthful appearance as he awakens. He is weakest in the throes of passion. His two passions—women and music—are united in his attraction to a beautiful young American pianist, Sofia Christopher, who is currently performing in Bucharest with the local orchestra. However, Ash's usual powers of attraction over the young woman are diffused by another vampire, **Zachery**, who harbors a vendetta against all vampires, and especially against those, like Ash, directly responsible for transforming him into a creature of the night. Zachery is not strong enough to face Ash directly. His plan is to catch Ash in a vulnerable moment.

Ash circumvents Zachery's tinkering by inviting Sofia to his club for an exclusive, private performance. After the concert, Ash begins his work to transform Sofia into a vampire. He delays her transformation, however, until Sofia agrees to acknowledge him as her master. Meanwhile, Ash has invited Zachery to the club to negotiate a deal. Claiming that it once belonged to him, Ash takes from Zachery the Blade of Laertes, the sword that Zachery has been using to decapitate the vampires he kills. Then, in order to consummate his passion for Sofia and rid himself of Zachery's meddling, Ash offers Zachery three things: sanctuary for the evening, a fresh victim for food, and a brief meeting with Sofia before she is transformed. In return, Zachery must leave Bucharest and never come back. Zachery accepts Ash's offer. The deal goes awry, however, when Ash brings Sofia into Zachery's room as he is feeding off another young woman. Despairing of any rescue, Sofia gives into Ash and allows him to transform her. Zachery, believing that Ash has betrayed him, finds the couple, wounds Ash with the sword, and heads out of the building with Sofia as dawn is approaching.

The ensuing chase sets up the final confrontation. In the end, Zachery is able to maneuver Ash into the sunlight, where he is weakened and quickly destroyed. Zachery now has the responsibility of teaching Sofia how to survive as a vampire.

Austra, Charles

Charles Austra, the twin brother of **Stephen Austra**, appears in Elaine Bergstrom's 1989 novel, *Shattered Glass*. He and his brother were born in A.D. 718, descendants of an ancient vampire race (possibly extraterrestrial) that was founded by their father. The twins' mother died in childbirth. As detailed in the separate entry on Stephen, the brothers invent a type of glass that protects vampires from the sun and form a business to place the special stained glass in the great cathedrals of Europe.

Charles was relatively happy and stable until the eighteenth century. His daughter, Anna Louise, had been betrayed by the escorts who were seeing her out of the country. Charles becomes a recluse for many years until he meets Claudia, whom he marries, and has two children. Unlike most vampire women, Claudia did not die during childbirth. Tragedy strikes, however, when she is involved in a shipwreck and dies trying to save her children, who survive. Charles is driven into a state of despair and refuses to see or even acknowledge the children. The loss of Claudia eventually drives him to madness.

In 1955, Charles travels to Cleveland, Ohio, where Stephen is busy restoring a cathedral. Still insane, he goes on a killing spree designed to get his brother's attention so that his brother will kill him and end his misery. He kills a priest at the church and then sets his sights on Helen Wells, a woman with whom Stephen has developed a relationship. He attempts to kill Stephen, and almost succeeds, but in the end he comes to his senses long enough to commit a selfless act so that Helen Wells might live. His final act costs him his life, and his body is burned.

SOURCES:
Bergstrom, Elaine. *Shattered Glass.* New York: Jove Books, 1989. Reprint. New York: Ace Books, 1994.

Austra, Stephen

Stephen Austra, a centuries old vampire, is the featured character in a series of novels by Elaine Bergstrom, the first of which is *Shattered Glass*. In that novel, Austra is introduced as a manufacturer of an exclusive type of stained glass found in churches and cathedrals around the world. In reality, he is a member of an ancient race, possibly extraterrestrial. He was born in A.D. 718 in northeast Romania. His father was the original vampire on earth—all members of the vampire race trace their lineage back to him. His mother, as was often the case, died during childbirth when she had Stephen and his twin brother **Charles Austra.** At the time of Stephen's birth, his family had just moved from to a sparsely populated area of the Carpathian Mountains, an area that figures prominently in many vampire legends, of course.

Stephen's family excelled in art, and he was no different. Early in his life, Stephen had discovered a form of glass that filtered out the harmful element in sunlight. The special glass, when used in windows, allowed vampires to come out of their underground residences during the day. Austra takes this a step further by leaving the Carpathians in 1123 and starting a family business (with his brother Charles) that uses his glass to create beautiful stained glass windows that are used in many of the great cathedrals of Europe—this allows vampires to seek sanctuary in the cathedrals during the day. The first major building he works on is St. Dennis Abbey, the original gothic cathedral in France. In 1910, the company moves its headquarters to Portugal. To minimize threats to the vampire community caused by shifting world political climates, Austra forms an international research division that projects world trends.

Through the years, Austra regularly creates new identities which allow him to keep coming back as one of his descendants, a necessary step since he remains forever young in appearance. In *Shattered Glass*, he claims to have been born in Czechoslovakia in 1916, and in 1934 he "replaces" the former Stephen Austra as head of the Austra company.

In the mid-1950s, Austra travels to the United States to work on St. John's Church in Cleveland, Ohio. His visit is marred by his brother Charles, who is in a state of despair over the death of his wife. Charles goes on a killing spree in an attempt to force Stephen to kill him, thereby breaking the family law against killing their own kind. Stephen survives this battle, but Charles does not.

Stephen Austra returns in Bergstrom's sequels, *Blood Alone* (1990) and *Blood Rites* (1991), which brings Austra's tale into the 1990s

SOURCES:

Bergstrom, Elaine. *Blood Alone*. New York: Jove Books, 1990. Reprint. New York: Ace Books, 1994.

———. *Blood Rites*. New York: Jove Books, 1991.

———. *Shattered Glass*. New York: Jove Books, 1989. Reprint. New York: Ace Books, 1994.

Azim

Azim is an old vampire who appears in Anne Rice's *The Queen of the Damned* (1988). For 1,000 years he rules as a God in an isolated area of the Himalayan Mountains where the fast-paced modern world has yet to penetrate. His ceremonies are conducted at a fever pitch of emotion. In them, he allows his believers to slash him and then he drinks their blood to the point of their death. A stream of pilgrims comes to his temple even though no one has ever returned from a trip there.

In 1985, his timeless world is disturbed by an intrusion from the outside world. Like many other vampires and mortals around the world he begins having mysterious dreams about red-headed twins. He also "hears" cries for help from the ancient vampire **Marius,** but he is unaware that those cries have been triggered by the awakening of **Akasha,** the original vampire. Akasha has undertaken a campaign of world domination. The vampire **Pandora** comes to Azim looking for Marius; she too has been having the disturbing dreams and does not understand their meaning. When she encounters Azim, he appears almost regal in black turban and gold slippers, his golden skin shining in the light. He tells her where Marius is and she departs to rescue him.

Azim has a special place in Akasha's evil plans. She brings **Lestat de Lioncourt** with her when she invades Azim's private domain. She intends to show Lestat how powerful she is. She designates Azim as her first martyr and causes him to burst into flames in front of his followers. She then directs Lestat to slaughter all the males in Azim's group. She tells the women of the group that they have been freed and that the bloody reign of their God has come to an end.

SOURCES:

Ramsland, Katherine. *The Vampire Companion: The Official Guide to Anne Rice's The Vampire Chronicles*. New York: Ballantine Books, 1993.

Rice, Anne. *The Queen of the Damned*. New York: Alfred A. Knopf, 1988. Reprint, New York: Ballantine Books, 1989.

Baby Jenks

Baby Jenks is a young vampire whose story is told in Anne Rice's *The Queen of the Damned* (1988). Born in the early 1970s and raised in the small community of Gun Barrel City, Texas, she is barely past puberty when she turns to prostitution. She becomes pregnant and is almost killed during an abortion attempt. Another vampire, **Killer,** gives her the "Dark Gift" and turns her into a vampire to prevent her death. Killer is a member of a nomadic vampire group called the Fang Gang. He teaches Baby Jenks about what it means to be a vampire and gives her a copy of the album by **Lestat de Lioncourt**'s rock band, The Vampire Lestat. Killer and Baby Jenks and the rest of the gang plan on going to San Francisco to hear Lestat in concert, but before they leave, she pays a visit to her parents and kills them both.

Baby Jenks never makes it to San Francisco. She is burned to death during the purge of the vampire community by **Akasha,** the primal vampire who is on a mission to take over the world. As she dies, she has a vision of someone who looks like the Virgin Mary.

SOURCES:

Ramsland, Katherine. *The Vampire Companion: The Official Guide to Anne Rice's The Vampire Chronicles.* New York: Ballantine Books, 1993.

Rice, Anne. *The Queen of the Damned,* New York: Alfred A. Knopf, 1988. Reprint, New York: Ballantine Books, 1989.

Baelbrow, The Vampire of

The unnamed vampire who in the 1890s invades Baelbrow, the old stone mansion on the coast of East Anglia, is among the most unusual in all of vampire writing. The story of the Vampire of Baelbrow originally published in 1898 in a popular British periodical, *The Strand,* focuses on the Swaffam family, who report that their 300-year-old house has, as long as anyone can remember, been the residence of a ghost, a perfectly harmless fellow who never bothered anyone.

Things begin to change after the Swaffams rent the house to Professor Jungvort, and his daughter, who is engaged to Harold Swaffam. Some weeks after their settling in for the summer season, a ghostly entity begins to appear who seems to be far more solid and malevolent than the ghost about whom they had been duly informed before they moved in. After a maid is found dead, Jungvort calls his friend, psychic detective Flaxman Low, to help investigate.

The creature, of whom only passing glimpses have been obtained, is humanlike with black hair. He is seen in the passageway that connects the two wings of the house. One person who was attacked from behind reports seeing shiny fingernails and a bandaged arm. The attacker is quite solid and quite strong. Another account reports a bony neck, dull-eyed face, and teeth stained with blood. The several women in the household who had been attacked, fainted and awoke fatigued with a small wound on their neck. When Low finally sees him, he shoots the creature in the foot as it runs away.

Low finally puts a complete enough description of the creature together to connect it to a mummy that Jungvort had shipped to the house. Upon closer examination, they find the mummy's foot has been shot off. They proceed to destroy the mummy by burning it, and the vampire attacks cease. Low later speculates that the vampire had been produced by the old ghost of the manor which had gained increasing strength through the attention paid to it over the years. He hypothesizes that the ghost animated the mummy's body.

SOURCES:

Heron, E., and H. Heron. "The Story of Baelbrow." *The Strand*, 1898. Reprinted in Parry, Michel, ed. *The Rivals of Dracula*. London: Corgi, 1977.

Barlow, Kurt

Kurt Barlow is the ancient vampire who settles in a small town in mid-1970s Maine in Stephen King's monumental vampire book, *Salem's Lot* (1976). According to the modern records, Barlow was German-born Kurt Breichen early in this century. He left Germany in 1938 and settled in England where he engaged in the import/export business. His business associate, human Richard T. Straker, claims to have worked with Barlow in Hamburg and London. However, as Barlow himself reveals, he is an ancient vampire who was already an old creature when the Catholic Church, his enemy through the centuries, was just coming into existence.

As the story takes place, Barlow and Straker move to Salem's Lot and open a furniture and antique shop. While Straker is the visible owner/manager, Barlow never seems to be available, and no one ever sees him, except the people he begins to turn into vampires. His initial victim is a young boy.

When Barlow finally appears, he has white skin, long sharp fangs, and red eyes. His eyes can hold a victim in a hypnotic spell and any who would oppose him work to keep their focus away from him. His hands are long and clawlike, with blue blotches on them. He has a deep, rich, and powerful voice. His face is handsome, but in a forbidding sort of way. He is very strong, but not inordinately so. He is repelled

Reggie Nader portrayed the horrifying vampire Kurt Barlow in Stephen King's *Salem's Lot*.

by sacred objects, but only if they are backed up by the faith of the one wielding them, as Friar Callahan, the local priest in Salem's Lot discovers when Barlow grabs the cross out of his hand. Barlow is completely nocturnal and sleeps in a coffin which he carries around the world with him. He keeps it in the basement of his residence in Salem's Lot, the old Marsten House on the edge of town. He is vulnerable to daylight, fire, and the traditional stake in the heart.

Barlow's bite is highly infectious. Those from whom he sucks blood soon rise as vampires and pass their condition on in a similar fashion. Many of the vampires in the book sleep in the root cellar at Barlow's house, but do not have their own coffins. As the number of vampires tend to double nightly when Barlow begins to feed in a new location, his ability to remain in one place for any length of time is somewhat limited.

In the movie adaptation of *Salem's Lot*, Barlow is portrayed as a hideous figure reminiscent of **Graf Orlock** in the film *Nosferatu* (1922), not a creature with enough human attributes to survive for a minute in human society. In the movie, he does not speak, his lines from the book being given to Straker. His nemeses are a young boy, Mark Petrie, who has an interest in horror books and movies, and writer Ben Means, who is fascinated with the Marsten House. As in the book, Barlow is finally destroyed by a stake in the heart. He immediately disintegrates as death overtakes him.

SOURCES:

King, Stephen. *Salem's Lot*. New York: Doubleday, 1975. Reprint, New York: New American Library, 1976.

Barrett, Jonathan

Jonathan Barrett was first introduced as a minor character in P.N. Elrod's 1990 novel, *Bloodcircle,* and then became the main character in a series of novels that started with *Red Death* in 1993. Red Death is set in colonial times in both the United States and England. Barrett is the eldest son of Samuel and Marie Fonteyn Barrett, who live on Long Island in New York state. As the American Revolution approaches, they send their son to Cambridge University to study law. Not the best of students, he spends more time on his social life than he does on his studies, initiating an affair with a Miss Nora Jones. During their sexual liaison, Jones drinks Barrett's blood and opens a wound in her own neck and invites Barrett to drink. He does not realize at the time that he has just been turned into a vampire.

In 1776, after three years at Cambridge, Barrett returns home, still unaware of his condition. However, a short time after his return, he is shot and killed and then buried in the local cemetery. He awakens in his coffin, alive but trapped. Somehow, he struggles to free himself and emerges from the ground in the graveyard. He still does not fully understand his condition, but he knows that somehow he has cheated death. He finally makes the connection between his current state and his liaison with Nora Jones and knows that somehow she changed him into the creature he had become. Once out of his grave, he grows fangs and realizes that he can no longer hold down real food. Instead, he feeds on the blood of a horse and discovers that the blood is like nectar to him, better than the finest food he had ever tasted.

As a vampire, Barrett is fully nocturnal—the sun hurts his eyes. His strength and senses have improved, especially a new ability to see in the dark. He does not have to breathe at all, except when he talks or is hiding his true identity from mere mortals. He has the power to influence humans and force them to do and believe whatever he wants. He also has the ability to change form, to become insubstantial, and to fly or move through seemingly solid walls. He still does not fully comprehend his nature, but he remembers a time when Nora told him that when something inexplicable or supernatural happened, he should just accept it. He decides to follow her advice and see where his new condition takes him.

He makes his way back to his parents' home and, beginning with his sister Elizabeth and his valet Jericho, begins to reveal himself to his family and servants, showing them that he is not dead. His family accepts him in his new state, and, with the Revolutionary War at its height, help him resume his life by preparing a dark room at the house in which he can live.

Desperate for more information about his condition he writes to Nora. After a year has passed and he has received no answer, he returns to England in 1777 and eventually locates and resumes his relationship with her. It seems that Nora is more than 100 years old, but that she has little understanding of their condition. She confirms much of what Barrett has already been able to determine about their abilities, but has little new to offer.

The remaining novels in Elrod's series— *Death and the Maiden, Death Masque,* and *Dance of Death*—cover more of Barrett's adventures in the 1700s. While there is little information about Barrett's life over the ensuing centuries, it is known that he survives into the twentieth century. This is due to the fact that *Bloodcircle,* the novel that Barrett first appears in, is set in the twentieth century. There, Barrett is an acquaintance of detective **Jack Fleming**, who is the protagonist in another Elrod series.

SOURCES:

Elrod, P. N. *Bloodcircle*. New York: Ace Books, 1990.
———. *Dance of Death*. New York: Ace Books, 1996.
———. *Death and the Maiden*. New York: Ace Books, 1994.
———. *Death Masque*. New York: Ace Books, 1995.
———. *Jonathan Barrett, Gentleman Vampire*. N.p.: Guild America Books, [1996]. Anthology that includes *Red Death, Death and the Maiden, Death Masque,* and *Dance of Death*.
———. *Red Death*. New York: Ace Books, 1993.

Bat, Mr.

Mr. Bat, the substitute teacher for Miss Candy, the best teacher in all of Critterville, is a vampire. At least that is the opinion of the more imaginative among the Critter kids, featured characters in the 1994 juvenile text *My Teacher Is a Vampire* by Erica Farber and J. R. Sansevere. Critterville is a fantasy town in which all the inhabitants are humanized animals—from tigers and bears to hippos and alligators. After L.C. Critter tells a story about being scared while watching a vampire movie the night before, his girlfriend, Gabby, expresses her belief about Mr. Bat being a vampire.

After doing some research on vampires, the kids decide that Mr. Bat not only replaced their favorite teacher, but that he displays all the identifying characteristics of a vampire: he wears a black cape, hates sunlight, and has two prominent fangs. In order to find out the truth about Mr. Bat, several of the kids follow him from school. They follow him past the edge of town, through the cemetery, and watch him go into a house. As he settles down to work in the basement, the kids watch him through a window. Suddenly, he disappears from their sight, and, seconds later, a bat comes swooping around the house straight for them. Now the kids are certain about the true nature of their new teacher.

The next day, Mr. Bat walks into his classroom and faces a desk covered with strands of garlic. Accompanying him is Miss Candy. She had missed school because she had taken the day off to become Mrs. Candy. She explains that Mr. Bat had set aside his research on bats in order to substitute in her class. Mr. Bat goes on to dispel the kids other notions about his vampirism, saying he had pulled down the shade to block the sunlight because he had a headache. He had been to the dentist, who fitted him with new teeth. Unfortunately, the teeth were the wrong size and made him appear to have fangs. He explains that he does not live in the cemetery, but merely walks through as a short cut to his home. And the previous night, while working on his research, one of his bats escaped. That was what had scared the kids.

Everyone relaxes and the class proceeds. However, after school that day, one of the kids reports on the final test they had set up to prove whether or not Mr. Bat is a vampire. The kids had taken a photograph of Mr. Bat walking through the school hallway. When the picture is developed, it shows only an empty hallway. Is Mr. Bat a vampire after all? In the end, that question remains unanswered.

SOURCES:

Farber, Erica, and J. R. Sansevere. *My Teacher Is a Vampire*. Racine, Wis.: Western Publishing Company, 1994.

Bathory, David

David Bathory is a descendant of Eastern European royalty, most notably Vlad Dracula and **Elizabeth Bathory.** He is the subject of Scott Baker's 1982 novel, *Dhampire* (revised in 1995 as *Ancestral Hungers*). Raised in Illinois, Bathory's mother died when he was two. He lived with his father, who was a money manager. He attended St. George Academy and then moved to California, where he went to Stanford for a year and then to the University of California (Berkeley) for one term before dropping out. He is a tall man, with green eyes and brown hair, and he wears a mustache.

In California, he develops an interest in snakes, which he attributes in part to his ancestry, since Dracula has been translated as "son of the dragon". After he inherits some property from an aunt, he opens the Big Sur Snake Farm. He marries a woman named Alexandria, and together they manage the prosperous business. Along with the exotic snakes that he sells, Bathory also deals cocaine, which provides a large part of his income.

His life changes dramatically when he is 29. First, his wife is killed by a poisonous snake. He decides to liquidate his business and sells off most of his animals. He then heads east to deliver several remaining specimens and to dispose of the last of his cocaine. Along the way, he is notified that his father has died. He returns to the family home, where he encounters the surviving members of his family, most importantly his uncle Stephen and brother Michael. He is startled to learn that a woman he met on his recent sojourn across the country is actually his half-sister Dara.

At home in Illinois, he learns his family's dark secret—the Bathorys are vampires. Each assumes his or her vampiric identity after death. The living members of the younger generation can become dhampires, a person capable of ruling the family vampires of all of the previous generations. (It should be noted that this use of the term is quite different from the more common definition of a dhampire as the child of a vampire with his widow.) As vampires, the Bathorys take life from humans, but that life is passed on to the dhampire, thus leaving the vampire unsatisfied and never satiated.

In each generation there can be only one ruling dhampire. That person must defeat his/her undead parents and then defeat the undead ancestors of previous generations to earn the title. The dhampire can control only the vampires from previous generations. He is powerless over vampires of his own generation. If a sibling of a dhampire dies, there is a period of 40 days before he or she rises as a vampire. A skilled dhampire can prolong 40 forty days into a longer period.

At the time David inherited the land in Big Sur, his father's sister had just died and was on her way to becoming a vampire. However, his father, who was a dhampire, had kept her in a suspended state until Michael found a way to release her. She subsequently became the agent of the older vampires and attacked David's father, driving him to his death. He was the object of the vampires' hatred because he was systematically destroying them.

Vampires in Baker's novel cannot be killed, but they can be transformed so that they are no longer vampires. To exist as vampires, they must make a pact with Satan; if they can be convinced that their pact with Satan is null and void, then they lose their vampiric powers. Satan never fulfills his part of the contract to satisfy their hunger.

David had moved to California to escape his family, but suddenly he finds himself unwillingly caught at the center of the family's problems. His Uncle Stephen is a Satanist who hopes to gain power through David and spread vampirism beyond the family. Michael wants to become the ruling dhampire of his generation; his sister Dara is largely under his will. David decides he has to act and first aligns himself with Stephen, though he knows that trusting his uncle is impossible. The elements of their deal calls for their union through a magical ceremony. The ceremony causes David to become possessed by a demon creature that lives inside him. On command from Stephen, the demon can cause David great pain. David's only ally is his half-sister Dara.

To escape, David must free Dara from Michael's control, defeat Michael, deal with the demon that Stephen had placed inside him, and move forward with his father's plan of destroying all the vampires in the family.

SOURCES:

Baker, Scott. *Dhampire*. New York: Pocket Books, 1982. Reprint as: *Ancestral Hungers*. New York: Tor Books, 1995.

Bathory, Elizabeth

The tale of Elizabeth Bathory (1560-1614) is one of the more interesting ones in vampire lore. A very real historical figure, Bathory became the star of many fictional vampire novels and movies. She is one of the most popular female vampires.

In real life, Bathory is best known for her torture and killing of numerous young women who worked as servants in her castle in what today is the Slovak Republic. Most of her adult life was spent at Castle Cachtice, near the town of Vishine, northeast of present-day Bratslava, where Austria, Hungary, and the Slovak Republic come together.

She was raised at the Bathory family estate at Ecsed in Transylvania. As a child she was subject to seizures accompanied by intense rage and uncontrollable behav-

Ingrid Pitt portrayed the infamous Elizabeth Bathory in the film *Countess Dracula*.

ior. In 1574 Elizabeth became pregnant from a brief affair with a peasant man. When her condition became evident she was sequestered until the baby arrived, as she had in the meantime been engaged to be married to Count Ferenc Nadasdy. The marriage took place in May 1575. Count Nadasdy was a soldier and frequently away from home for long periods. Meanwhile, Elizabeth assumed the duties of managing the affairs at Castle Sarvar, the Nadasdy family estate. It was here that her life of evil really began when she started disciplining of the large household staff, particularly the young girls.

In that day and age, cruel and arbitrary behavior by those in power toward their servants was common. Elizabeth, however, stood out for her level of cruelty. She did not just punish those who broke her rules, but also found excuses to inflict random punishments and delighted in the torture and death of her victims. This behavior went far beyond what her contemporaries could accept. For example, she would stick pins in various sensitive body parts, such as under the fingernails. In the winter she would execute victims by having them stripped, led out into the snow, and doused with water until they froze.

Elizabeth's husband joined in some of the sadistic behavior and actually taught his wife some new variations. For example, he showed her a summertime form of her freezing exercise by having a woman stripped and covered with honey and left outside to be bitten by the numerous insects. He died in 1604, however, and she moved to Vienna soon after his burial. She also began to spend time at her estate at Beckov and at a manor house at Cachtice, both locations in the present-day country of Slovakia. These were the scenes of her most renowned vicious acts.

In the years after her husband's death, Elizabeth's main cohort in crime was a woman named Anna Darvulia, about whom little is known. After Darvulia's death in 1610, Elizabeth turned to Erzsi Majorova, the widow of a local tenant farmer. It was Majorova who seems to have brought about Bathory's downfall by encouraging her to include a few women of noble birth among the people she tortured and killed. As early as the summer of 1610, an initial inquiry had begun into Elizabeth's crimes. Underlying the inquiry, quite apart from the number of victims (which was steadily growing), was the vested interest the crown had in bringing about Bathory's downfall. The state hoped to confiscate Bathory's large landholding and default on the large loan that Bathory's husband had made to the king. She was arrested on December 29, 1610.

Bathory was placed on trial a few days later. It was conducted by Count Thurzo as an agent of the king. The trial, rightly characterized as a show trial by Bathory's biographer Raymond T. McNally, was set up to obtain a conviction, but also to keep her lands from being confiscated. A week after the first trial, a second trial was convened on January 7, 1611. At this trial, a register found in Bathory's living quarters was introduced. It noted the names of 650 victims, all recorded in her handwriting. Bathory's accomplices were sentenced to be executed, the manner being determined by their roles in the tortures. Bathory was sentenced to life imprisonment in solitary confinement. She was placed in a room in her castle at Cachtice without windows or doors and only a small opening for food and a few slits for air. There she remained for the next three years until her death on August 21, 1614. She was buried on the Bathory estate at Ecsed.

Above and beyond Bathory's reputation as a sadistic killer, she has been accused of being both a werewolf and a vampire. During her trials, testimony was presented that on occasion Bathory bit the flesh of the girls during the process of otherwise torturing them. These accusations became the basis of her connection with werewolfism. The Countess's connection with vampirism is somewhat more tenuous. Of course, it was a popular belief in Slavic lands that a person who was a werewolf in life would become a vampire in death, but such was not the accusation leveled at Bathory. Rather, she was accused of draining the blood of her victims and bathing in it in order to retain her youthful beauty, and she was by all accounts a most attractive woman.

Bathory has not been accused of being a tradition blood-drinking or blood-sucking vampire, though her attempts to take and use the blood to make herself more youthful would certainly qualify her as at least a vampire by metaphor. Not well known at first, she was rediscovered when interest in vampires rose sharply in the 1970s. Since that time she has repeatedly been tied to vampirism in popular culture. Noticeable interest in Bathory was evident in the publication of a series of books in the early 1970s beginning with Valentine Penrose's *Erzsebet Bathory, La Comtesse Sanglante*, a 1962 French volume whose English translation, *The Bloody Countess*, appeared in 1970. It has been followed by a set of biographies and biographical sketches, the most authoritative volume being Raymond McNally's *Dracula was a Woman: In Search of the Blood Countess of Transylvania* (1984).

THE FICTIONAL BATHORY: Once she was associated with the vampire genre, Bathory became the subject of numerous novels, comic books, and films, some of which rewrote history and some of which turned Bathory into a modern-day character. Elaine Bergstrom's novel, *Daughter of the Night* (1992) drew its inspiration from McNally's study.

One graphic art adaptation of the Bathory legend by Brad Moore pictured Elizabeth as the product of a sadistic mother-in-law who forced her to submit to a harsh discipline of bondage and punishment. Upon inheriting authority when her husband died, she turned on her mother-in-law and then upon those around her, especially the servant girls.

BATHORY ON FILM: The first movie inspired by the Bathory legend was the now largely forgotten *I Vampiri* (1956—also known as *The Devil's Commandment*) notable today because of the work of soon-to-be director Mario Bava as the film's cameraman. A decade later, as part of its vampire cycle, Hammer Films released what is possibly the best of the several movies based upon the Countess's career, *Countess Dracula* (1970) with Ingrid Pitt starring in the title role. Having been widowed, Bathory is told that she will have to share her inheritance equally with her daughter, Ilona. Before Ilona can return from her boarding school where she has been for many years, Elizabeth discovers the amazing power of blood to take 20 years off her life. She has Ilona kidnaped, assumes her identity, and even takes a young lover. She fools all but a few who are in on her plot. Gradually, however, the power of the blood fails her and she begins to change back into the aging countess without warning. After Ilona escapes and makes her way to the castle, and the countess changes during her wedding ceremony, her plans are foiled and her actions become public.

Daughters of Darkness (1971), one of the most artistic of all vampire films, brought the Countess into the twentieth century in a tale with strong lesbian overtones. Bathory and her companion Iona, check in to an almost empty hotel, where they meet a couple of newlyweds. Thus the scene is set for the two vampire women to move in on the couple, the husband's violent streak providing the opening. One by one, the encounters lead to deaths until the new vampire, the wife, emerges as the only survivor. Bathory (or a character modeled on her) also appeared in *Legend of Blood Castle* (1972), *Curse of the Devil* (1973), and *Immoral Tales* (1974), all films of lesser note. In 1981, a full-length animated version of the Bathory story was released in Czechoslovakia. More recent Bathory-inspired films include *Thirst* (1980) and *The Mysterious Death of Nina Chereau* (1987).

SOURCES:

The Historical Bathory:

McNally, Raymond T. *Dracula was a Woman: In Search of the Blood Countess of Transylvania*. New York: McGraw-Hill, 1983. Reprint, London: Hamlyn, 1984.

Penrose, Valentine. *The Bloody Countess*. (London: Calder & Boyars, 1970); originally published as *Erzsebet Bathory, La Comtesse Sanglante*. (Paris: Mercure du Paris, 1962).

Ronay, Gabriel. *The Truth about Dracula*. London: Gallancz, 1972. Reprint, New York: Stein and Day, 1972.

The Fictional Bathory:

Andersson, Dean. *Raw Pain Max*. New York: Popular Library, 1988.

Baker, Scott. *Dhampire*. New York: Pocket Books, 1982. Reprint, New York: Tor Books, 1997.

Bergstrom, Elaine. *Daughter of the Night*. New York: Berkley, 1992. Reprint, New York: Ace Books, 1994.

Codrescu, Andreri. *The Blood Countess*. New York: Simon & Schuster, 1995.

Gordon, Francis. *Blood Ritual*. London: Headline, 1994.

Moore, Brad. *Bathory: Countess of Blood*. Carbondale, IL: Boneyard Press, 1993.

Robeson, Kenneth [Ron Goulart]. *The Blood Countess*. Avenger, No. 33. New York: Warner Books, 1975.

Parry, Michel. *Countess Dracula*. London: Sphere Books, 1971. Reprint, New York: Beagle Books, 1971.

Batman

DC Comics superhero Batman is one of the most famous comic book characters of all time, and while he is not a vampire, certainly his persona borrows from vampire legends and evokes certain vampiric images. One part of his image—that of a creature of the night with astonishing powers—can be traced back to the image of **Count Dracula** first made popular by Bela Lugosi in his 1931 movie. Over his lengthy crimefighting career, which is approaching six decades, Batman has primarily used his skills and intellect to battle human criminals, but he has occasionally been called upon to defeat some real vampires (including his continuing relationship with **Man-Bat**). Additionally, on several occasions he has himself slipped into the world of the vampire.

BATMAN AS VAMPIRE HUNTER: Batman first appears in *Detective Comics* No. 27 in 1939. The story is a well-known one thanks to the popular *Batman* films: Dr. Thomas

Wayne and his wife are killed in a mugging that is witnessed by their son, Bruce. In his grief, Bruce decides that he will grow up to be a policeman so he can avenge their death and fight crime. He studies criminology and at the same time develops his physical skills to an amazing level. After much thought, he decides that he can do more good if he becomes a vigilante. As he is trying to choose a uniform that will strike fear into the hearts of criminals, a bat flies into his window, giving him the idea for his costume. Later, the independently wealthy Wayne falls through a weak spot in the floor of his mansion and discovers that he lives about a bat-infested cavern. The Bat Cave is born.

Clad in his dark-blue uniform with signature mask and cape, Batman begins to fight crime in Gotham City. His first adventure as a vampire hunter occurrs a scant four months after his initial appearance. He encounters a vampire in a two-part story in issues 31 and 32 of *Detective Comics* in September and October 1939. A vampire named **The Monk** tries to take control of Bruce Wayne's girlfriend, unaware that Wayne is Batman. Batman tracks The Monk to Hungary, where the vampire lives with his allies, the werewolves . Batman eventually finds The Monk and his vampire bride, Dala, asleep in their coffins and kills them with silver bullets fired into their coffins. Despite their apparent deaths, The Monk and Dala will reappear in the 1980s to battle Batman again.

After that early first encounter, it would be many years before Batman encountered another vampire. That was due in part to the Comics Code, a series of regulations passed to police the comics industry, which had become a little gory in the years leading up to the adoption of the code in 1954. Part of the code, which was enforced until 1971, banned vampires altogether.

Once the code was lifted, Batman was free to fight vampires again. In the January 1976 issue of *Detective Comics* (No. 455), he battles a bloodsucker named **Gustav DeCobra**. Bruce Wayne and his butler, Alfred, are traveling together when their car breaks down. Seeking help, they enter a seemingly deserted house only to find a coffin in the center of the living room. As they search the house, DeCobra emerges from the coffin. Wayne immediately transforms into Batman to battle the creature. In the ensuing fight, Batman rams a stake into the vampire's chest, but it does no good—it seems that DeCobra has the ability to remove his heart from his body and hide it elsewhere. Batman withdraws to reevaluate how to best combat the vampire. By the time of his next confrontation with DeCobra, Batman has solved the riddle and realized that the vampire must be hiding his heart in the grandfather clock that was in the old house. Armed with that knowledge, Batman kills the vampire by impaling his heart with an arrow.

Batman encounters another vampire two years later. Bruce Wayne is acting as host to an ambassador from a foreign country, taking him on a camping trip into the Rocky Mountains. The trip takes a turn for the worst when the bus they are travelling in takes a wrong turn on a road that is not on the map. As soon as the bus crosses a bridge, there is an explosion that destroys the bridge.

Trapped on the wrong side of the bridge, Batman has two problems. First, he has to protect the ambassador, since one of the members of the camping party is supposed to be an assassin sent to kill the ambassador. Second, he learns that the area they are stranded in is supposedly protected by a white vampire bat (at least that's the tale the locals tell). It seems that 100 years ago, a wagon train heading west got snowed in. By the time spring arrived, five members of the party were dead, each drained of their blood. A survivor went into a trance and said that the deaths were punishment for trespassing in the area, but that if the survivors kept others away, they could live there in peace. Batman does not really believe the story, but in the end, he finds the assassin dead and drained of blood. As he discovers the body, he hears the sound of bat wings flying away.

Batman also has recurring encounters with the vampire-like creature known as **Man-Bat**. Batman is first introduced to Kirk Langstrom in 1970. Langstrom develops a serum that turns him into the giant bat creature known as Man-Bat. Langstrom becomes a crimefighter like Batman, and there paths cross several times during the 1970s and 1980s. Although Man-Bat is not a vampire bat, it was to be expected that he would eventually encounter vampires; it was also no surprise when Batman occasionally assisted him in his battles with vampires. Both Man-Bat's and Batman's encounter with vampires were facilitated by writer Gerry Conway, the first writer for Marvel's *The Tomb of Dracula*, and artist Gene Colan, who had worked throughout the 1970s on that groundbreaking comic book. Both were working for DC during the early 1980s.

In 1993, Batman encounters another vampire when he wanders onto an old movie lot and is taken prisoner by Mina DeMille, a former silent movie actress who had been turned into a vampire in the 1950s. DeMille has big plans to make her comeback in a new movie, and she intends to have Batman serve as her costar. She takes him prisoner and drinks a little more of his blood each night, sapping his strength. Just when it seems as if Batman will not escape, faithful butler Alfred discovers his predicament and ventures into the movie lot with a set of stakes. DeMille is a formidable foe who is finally undone by the glare of the spotlight, her own vanity proving her undoing.

BATMAN AS VAMPIRE: In 1982, with the Batman comics safely in the hands of Conway and Colan, Batman squares off against vampires again. The difference this time is that he himself is turned into a vampire for the first time.

The story begins when an unsuspecting Robin is captured by the woman he thought was his girlfriend. Dala it turns out, is really the girlfriend of The Monk, and is really a vampire, as is The Monk. The vampires fought Batman once before in 1939 and were thought to be dead. In an attempt to escape, Robin is bitten by the Monk, who allows Robin to flee back to the Bat Cave, supposedly to lure Batman back to Dala and The Monk. The plan works. Batman knows the only way to save Robin is with a serum made from the vampire's blood, so he goes after the vampires himself. His first confrontation ends poorly—he fails to get the serum and is actually infected himself and turned into a vampire. He manages to set up a second confrontation that is more successful; he obtains the blood and returns himself and Robin to normalcy.

In the 1990s, the character of Batman took a drastic turn when he was essentially reinvented in large-format, artistic comic books known as graphic novels. Instead of the almost cheerful crimefighter that people were used to from earlier comic books and Saturday morning cartoons, the Batman introduced in *The Dark Knight* was a brooding, troubled man who did not wear the mantle of hero very comfortably.

It was in this graphic novel format that Batman had his next encounter with vampires, and again he is turned into a vampire himself. In *Batman and Dracula: Red Rain*, the story occurs in what is described in the introduction as an "alternative future," and features a Batman who is "an altogether different Batman than we're used to." Gotham is under attack from a group of vampires led by **Count Dracula**, and Batman (without Robin) is drawn into the fray. Busy tracking what he thinks is a serial killer, he meets Tanya, a "good" vampire. Tanya is the leader of a group fighting Dracula, who is responsible for all the killings. She has developed a methadone-like substance for vampires to take instead of drinking blood. Tanya and Batman unite to fight Dracula, and they do defeat him. However, in the process, Batman becomes a vampire. In the closing lines of the story, he repeats words he heard Tanya say earlier: "Vampires are real...but not all of them are evil."

The same storyline is continued in *Batman Bloodstorm*. Batman has two problems. Tanya's serum is having less and less effect with each passing day. To make things worse, The Joker has reappeared and has organized the remaining vampires who were left leaderless by Dracula's death. The Joker wants to enlarge the small community of vampires by converting some of Gotham's more established criminals into vampires. Batman is intent on stopping him and begins a campaign to eliminate the remaining vampires. His butler, Alfred, creates a special weapon for him to use, a set of wooden knives not unlike those used by **Blade the Vampire Slayer**. He hunts down the vampires one-by-one and stakes them and then decapitates them. Though continually tempted, he refuses to take blood from his victims.

Batman's friends try to help the hero any way they can. He is befriended by Selina Kyle, a woman bitten by a vampire who attacked her in the form of a wolf. She manages to escape the vampire by swimming across a river, but later, in the light of the full moon, she transforms into a werecat. (Batman fans should recognize the name Selina Kyle: it is the name Michelle Pfeiffer used when portraying Catwoman in the movie *Batman Returns*.) Also, once it becomes obvious what The Joker's plan is, Alfred and Police Commissioner Gordon enter the homes of Gotham's crime bosses during the day and dispatch any vampires they find.

The Joker strikes out at Batman by killing Kyle. This only increases Batman's resolve, and he tracks The Joker down and kills him. However, in his rage, he is unable to resist temptation any longer and drinks The Joker's blood after he kills him. In his own mind, he is now no better than Dracula. He leaves a note for Alfred and Commissioner Gordon, telling them that he is the only remaining vampire. They treat him as he had all the other vampires—they kill him.

SOURCES:

Batman. No. 348-51. New York: DC Comics, 1982. *Batman Family*. No. 19. New York: DC Comics, 1984.

Detective Comics. No. 455. New York: DC Comics, 1982.

The Greatest Batman Stories Ever Told. New York: DC Comics, 1988.

Legends of the Dark Knight. No. 41. New York: DC Comics, 1995.

A scene from *Fright Night II,* which also featured the cross-dressing vampire Belle.

Moench, Doug, Kelley Jones, and Malcolm Jones III. *Batman and Dracula: Red Rain.* New York: DC Comics, 1991.

Moench, Doug, Kelley Jones, and John Beatty. *Batman Bloodstorm.* New York: DC Comics, 1994.

Rovin, Jeff. *The Encyclopedia of Superheroes.* New York: Facts on File, 1986.

Belle

Belle is the cross-dressing vampire minion of **Regine**, the ancient vampire of the film *Fright Night II* (1988). An African-American vampire with a huge head of hair and a nasty temper, Belle is of unknown age and origin. He assists Regine as she seeks revenge for the killing of her brother, **Jerry Dandridge**, at the hands of high schooler Charlie Brewster and vampire hunter and television-horror-movie-host **Peter Vincent**. He and Regine move into the Hotel Elegante, where Vincent resides, and their first night in town he kills one of the classmates of Charlie and his current girlfriend. He also attacks Charlie's friend Ritchie whom Regine brings to their hotel room.

Like the other *Fright Night* vampires, Belle changes when enraged or about to feed. He shows no reflection in mirrors, and crosses and holy water repel him. He sleeps in a coffin in the basement of the hotel.

DRACULA'S SONS

In some traditional folklore, and even many modern fictional works (among the prominent examples being the novels of Chelsea Quinn Yarbro) vampires are incapable of normal sexual relations. The undead don't have children. However, in scanning the literature, it appears that Dracula has, in fact, had a number of consorts and left behind several sons in his own image. Among the most well-known:

- The original *Son of Dracula*, the 1943 sequel to Dracula *(1931)*, in which the "Son" is really just another incarnation of Dracula himself.

- Victor, from the 1976 film *Dracula and Son* (originally *Dracula Pere et Fils*). Dracula finally has a son after four centuries, but he disappoints his father as children often do.

Victor actually kills his father (portrayed by Christopher Lee) and goes to live among the mortals.

- Adam Lucard (an anagram of Dracula), born after Dracula had a liaison with his own cousin in the comic book *Fright*. Adam becomes the first college educated member of the family.

- Little Dracula, the son who stays at home with Dracula and his wife. Little Drac saves his parents from being staked and learns how to live as an adult vampire.

- Count Vasily Vladovitch Bledinoff (the name's better than Alucard), whom Dracula can really be proud of. Bledinoff tried to create a vampire homeland in the Yukon but is foiled by a pesky female writer...and a fire that ruins his business...and those darn Canadian Mounties.

Belle is present when Charlie, Vincent, and Charlie's girlfriend enter their hotel apartment to kill Regine. In the pitch battle with her minions, Belle changes into a panther and launches himself at Charlie. He is finally killed by Vincent who traps the panther in an altar cloth borrowed from the local church.

Bender, Angus

Angus Bender is a child vampire who appears as a character in the graphic novels featuring vampire **Max Morrissey**, collectively known as "Citizen Nocturne." Reminiscent of **Claudia**, the child vampire of Anne Rice's *Interview with the Vampire*, Angus was six years old when he was transformed into a vampire in the early 1930s by the 200-year-old **Rovena Venisette**, the dominant vampire in Southern Germany and Austria through most of the twentieth century. Since that time he has aged mentally, but not physically. Angus is a traditional vampire, who uses his childlike appearance to draw his food to him. When there are no human victims, he also takes blood from cats and other small animals. He is nocturnal, repelled by garlic and crosses, and manifests no ability to transform into other life forms. He hopes that if Rovena can be killed, he can begin aging again.

To track Rovena, he makes common cause with Morrissey who in turn is forced to ally himself with **Dr. Lichtenstein**, a fanatical vampire hunter. Together with Morrissey's wife, the band enters Rovena's castle in Austria, and Morrissey kills her. However, Lichtenstein, believing that Morrissey has double-crossed him, decapitates the vampire and leaves his body in the castle to rot away. He is with Morrissey's wife, who has been freed from the semi-vampiric state occasioned by being bit one time, but, for some reason, he does not take Angus. After Lichtenstein departs, Angus places Morrissey's head back in place and pushes him into the pool of blood that Rovena has accumulated over the years. As Lichtenstein disappears over the horizon, Morrissey seems to be pulling himself back together.

SOURCES:

Allred, M. Dalton, and Laura Allred.*Graphique Musique.* Nos. 1-3. Eugene, OR: Slave Labor Graphics, 1988–90. Reprinted, *Citizen Nocturne.* Brave New Words, 1992.

Bennett, Lord Andrew

Lord Andrew Bennett, a 400-year-old vampire, emerged in the a series of stories collectively known as a "I ... Vampire" that appeared in the *The House of Mystery,* a horror anthology comic book published by DC Comics during the early 1980s. Bennett was raised during the Elizabethan Era in the England of the late sixteenth century. He became a hero during the Spanish War and afterwards a well-known figure at court. His life changes in 1591. While out one evening for a ride he is bitten by a *dearg-dul,* a type of vampire found in Ireland, and as a result becomes a vampire himself.

Bennett is in love with Mary Seward, personal handmaiden to the queen. Unexpectedly, after discovering his condition, she wants to spend eternity with him. She demands he make her a vampire also. Once she awakens as a a vampire, Bennett sees a very different side of his love. She expresses her belief that vampires are superior to the human race and that she and Andrew could rule over humans if they so desired. Bennett flatly rejects the idea. She leaves him, and he vows to find her and save her soul, which he had despoiled.

Bennett emerges as a fairly traditional vampire. He is nocturnal, and can be killed by sunlight. He needs to regularly ingest blood, but has sworn off human blood.

Bennett's attempts to deal with Mary continue into the late twentieth century. Mary seeks control of the planet and to that end has built an expansive international organization called The Blood Red Moon. The group commands a large number of vampires who operate as Mary's agents and function through a number of front groups. Bennett has a difficult time killing the vampires, as most of the things to which they are vulnerable can also hurt him.

Their conflict climaxes in the rush to gain what is termed the Russian Formula. The Russians have discovered that vampirism is caused by a virus. Taking the formula will make one a new kind of vampire, with all the vampiric powers (strength, transformation, etc.) but free from the limitations of the undead and able to live on common human food rather than blood. After Bennett secures and takes some of the formula he is able to walk in the sunlight. He discovers Mary's headquarters and prepares to destroy her and her sleeping vampire cohorts. But then he discovers that he is immobile. Too late he learns that the formula is to make new vampires but is not meant for existing vampires to consume. Now, though alive and conscious, his body experiences *rigor mortis.*

As Bennett lays dying, Mary bites Bennett's human girlfriend, Deborah Dancer. His final damnation is to know that she has become Mary's willing servant. However, Deborah had previously taken the Russian Formula, and had become a vampire through it. She fights Mary and drags her body into the sunlight, where she perishes. She returns to the dying Bennett to inform him of Mary's death and of her love. Thus Bennett can die in peace. Mary lives on as the new kind of vampire.

"I... Vampire" began in the March 1981 issue (No. 290) and appeared periodically through the August 1983 issue (No. 319).

SOURCES:

The House of Mystery. No. 290-319. New York: DC Comics, 1981-1983.

Bessenyei, Prince Lóránd

Prince Lóránd Bessenyei is the father of the title character in Frederick Cowles' 1940 short story "A Princess of Darkness." In the late fifteenth century the prince had become the head of the Bessenyei family and ruled their Transylvanian land from his castle. In his leisure time he dabbled in black magic and became a Satanist. Eventually, his occult practices caused him to become a vampire. He passed his vampirism to his daughter, **Princess Gizella Bessenyei.** According to state records, the branch of the Bessenyei family that owned the castle died out in the eighteenth century, and in the next century, the Hungarian government assumed ownership of the castle. But in fact, the prince has survived, existing quietly in a coffin in a family crypt beneath the chapel.

The possible existence of the prince in the 1930s is called to the attention of Professor Otto Nemetz in Budapest when Princess Bessenyei appears in the city and begins moving in the elite circles of the Hungarian capital. Her sudden appearances and disappearances from her Transylvanian home cause rumor to spread throughout Budapest. Nemetz possesses a picture painted in 1503 of the Princess Gizella Bessenyei. It appears to be the same Princess Bessenyei who is now in Budapest. A student of Hungarian history and folklore, Nemetz comes to believe that the princess and possibly her father have survived the centuries as vampires. He shares his belief with Harvey Groton, a member of the British Diplomatic Service, who is in Budapest to investigate rumors that the princess is involved in international espionage.

Together they visit the remote Bessenyei castle. There, they are met by a caretaker who invites them in with the ominous words, "Enter, gentlemen, enter of your own free will and become the guests of Castle Bessenyei." The next day they explore the chapel, where they find evidence of Satanic rituals and the body of the prince, who turns out to be the person who had greeted them the day before as the caretaker. Professor Nemetz ends the prince's 500 years of vampire existence with a dagger plunged into his heart.

While dispatching the prince is accomplished with relative ease, such is not the case with the princess, who vows revenge. Professor Nemetz dies a short time later.

SOURCES:

Cowles, Frederick. "A Princess of Darkness." In *Dracula's Brood*, edited by Richard Dalby. New York: Dorset Press, 1987.

Bessenyei, Princess Gizella

Princess Gizella Bessenyei, the title character in Frederick Cowles' 1940 short story "A Princess of Darkness," was born late in the fifteenth century in Transylvania. Her father, **Prince Lóránd Bessenyei**, had become a Satanist and, as a result of his dabbling in the black arts, a vampire. He passed his blood thirst to his daughter. During that time, the princess gained a reputation as a murderess and in 1506 was tried and executed. She was buried in the chapel of the Bessenyei castle. She also survived the ordeal and continues to live as a vampire. Over the centuries, her existence alternates between periods of rest in her grave and periods—as long as six months—during which she feeds on blood and otherwise lives a somewhat normal human life. She is repelled by garlic and crosses but unaffected by bullets.

In the twentieth century, during the 1920s and 1930s, the princess begins to circulate within Budapest society, though her mysterious nature, including her sudden appearances and disappearances, become fodder for the high society gossip mill. In 1938, while on one of her periodic visits, she encounters Harvey Groton, a member of the British Diplomatic Service, who has been sent to Budapest to check on reports that the princess is involved in international espionage. Groton reports that the princess is a slim woman with auburn hair and green eyes that often appear black in the right light. She has pale skin and her hand is cold to the touch. Her appearance is marked by a set of canine-like fangs that show themselves when she opens her mouth. Groton finds that she looks to be about 30 years old but radiates an aura of great age. She is reported to eat little, even at formal dinners.

One evening, as Groton is seeing the princess home, he kisses her. She bites his lip. They part with her telling him, "Now you are mine forever." That night he dreams of her. She comes to his room and bends over him with her mouth above his neck. Inadvertently, she brushes against the crucifix he always wears and immediately draws back, her mouth a gaping hole. The next day, the princess has a fresh scar on her mouth.

Groton refers the case to Professor Otto Nemetz, a scholar who has become convinced that the princess is a vampire and that her father, Prince Bessenyei, also survives as a vampire. Nemetz shows Groton a portrait of the princess painted in 1503 as evidence. Together the two make a trip to the Bessenyei castle to further confirm the professor's hypothesis and destroy the vampires. The professor carries holy water, garlic, a crucifix and a dagger. The two dine well on their sojourn, but their meal is vegetarian, since Nemetz believes it best to avoid meat when dealing with the occult. At the castle, they find the body of the sleeping Prince Bessenyei and destroy him by plunging the dagger into his heart. He turns to dust.

Destroying the princess proves more difficult, however. After her father is killed, the princess appears in the doorway, promises revenge on Nemetz, and reminds Groton that he is still hers. She disappears and the two return to Budapest. The princess is not seen again, but later that evening Nemetz is brutally killed. Police speculate that a wild animal must have gotten loose in his apartment. Groton subsequently ends up in a mental hospital. Shortly thereafter he is found dead, the only marks on his body being two small puncture wounds on his neck.

Cover art from an issue of Brainstorm Comics' *Bethany the Vampfire.*

Cowles wrote this story in 1940 but died before it was published. The story did not appear until anthologized by Richard Dalby in 1987.

SOURCES:

Cowles, Frederick. "A Princess of Darkness." In *Dracula's Brood*, edited by Richard Dalby. New York: Dorset Press, 1987.

Bethany

Bethany is a *vampfire*, a unique being in the vampire universe of Brainstorm Comics. She was born June 6, 1966, the product of the mating of her mother Salome, a vampire, and Belgratl, a demon. With Bethany, Salome hopes to launch a new family tree through which she will acquire the power of the underworld. However, Bethany refuses to cooperate. Bethany is neither vampire nor demon and finds herself alienated from and unaccepted in both the earthly plane and the fiery underworld. Wherever she goes, she is hunted. Her mother, resentful of Bethany's lack of cooperation with her scheme, also continually interferes with her daughter's longing for peace.

Bethany appears as a young adult with a full head of blond hair. She is passionate and full of love. She is also very strong and has access to the demonic underworld. Since she is not a vampire, she refrains from drinking blood. In fact, she prefers honey. Her single friend is the Angel of Death, the only lover she has taken in her century-long existence.

Now, as the twentieth century comes to a close, Bethany is informed that Salome has found a new way to forge the demon key and gain the power for which she hungers. Using Bethany's half sister, Echo, Salome plans a magical blood ritual to create a second vampfire. This new being will be her instrument to launch a new family tree. Bethany intervenes to stop the ritual and, in the process, kills her mother and inherits the guardianship of Echo.

Bethany and Echo come to live in the relative safety of the home of Professor Orcastle, who owns an old mansion in the city. One evening they visit Studio V, the nightclub owned by **Luxura**, an ancient vampire (and keystone of the Brainstorm Comics universe). When Bethany is separated from Echo and her friends, she goes looking for them and accidentally discovers the entrance to Luxura's underground world. Alerted to the intrusion, Luxura visits the club to investigate. Although discovered, Bethany is spared because Luxura senses the vampfire's relationship to Salome. Bethany tells Luxura the history of her strange creation, and Luxura informs Bethany that she is the one who originally transformed Salome into a vampire. Thus, it is revealed that Luxura is Bethany's grandmother. Luxura takes an immediate liking to Bethany and lets her know that she is now a recognized member of the House of Luxura.

Bethany, the creation of graphic artist Holly Golightly, is the lead character in a continuing series of comic books from Brainstorm Comics.

SOURCES:

Golightly, Holly. *Vampfire*, Nos. 1–2. Fayetteville, N.C.: Brainstorm Comics, 1996.

———. *Vampfire Erotic Echo*, Nos. 1–2. Fayetteville, N.C.: Brainstorm Comics, 1996.

———. *Vampfire Necromantique*, Nos. 1–2. Fayetteville, N.C.: Brainstorm Comics, 1997.

———. *Luxura & Vampfire*. Fayetteville, N.C.: Brainstorm Comics, 1997.

Biffi, Teresa

Among the earliest literary vampires, Teresa Biffi is the subject of "The Last Lords of Gardonal," an 1867 short story by British writer William Gilbert. Teresa is a beautiful young woman, the daughter of a well-to-do farmer in northern Italy. The valley in which she resides happens to be just over the mountains from the valley of the Engadin, ruled by Conrad, the Baron of Gardonal. One day, while in the neighboring valley, Conrad sees the young girl and decides he must have her. However, knowing of his cruel nature, her father turns down Conrad's proposal of marriage. In revenge, Conrad sends his men to Teresa's home, where, unable to gain entrance, the men burn down the house, killing both Teresa and her father. She later appears to the men in an apparition, and they report to Conrad that she has survived the fire.

Conrad demands that the men produce Teresa immediately and holds one of them hostage to encourage their success. Thus it is that a short time later Teresa, as lovely as when he first saw her, arrives at Conrad's castle willing to become his bride. They are quickly married, and, after a feast, as dusk approaches, they proceed to the castle terrace to take in the sunset. Conrad notices that Teresa is cold, and they return inside. As the last rays of the sun disappear, Teresa tells her new husband that she loves him and adds, "My very existence hangs on your life. When that ceases my existence ends." Conrad bends over to kiss her, only to discover his beautiful bride has transformed into a moldy corpse. Before he can run or cry out, the corpse grabs him, throws him to the floor, and begins to suck the blood from his neck.

When Conrad awakes the next day, he finds his beautiful wife playing with the village children. The notion that he has simply experienced a horrible dream is dispelled by the real wound on his neck. Though weakened by loss of blood, Conrad flees the castle and arrives at a house owned by his brother at the seashore near Genoa. He wishes only to rest and recuperate. However, the enjoyment of the ocean and the feeling of security he feels are disrupted at dusk, when his wife appears before him. She tells him that rather than try to kill him, she has come to offer him an indefinite extension of his life. Her continued existence, she explains, depends upon his life's blood.

Teresa presents Conrad with a goblet of blood, which she instructs him to drink. She tells him it will cure the negative effects of their first encounter. But Conrad cannot bring himself to drink. He realizes that Teresa did, in fact, perish that day in the fire at her home. He realizes that his wife, who was standing before him, is not the Teresa he longed for but only her body. It had been called forth from the grave and can survive only by regularly taking his blood.

When the last ray of sunlight disappears, Conrad still has not drunk from the goblet. Teresa attacks him and finishes draining his blood. Conrad dies and Teresa is never seen again.

SOURCES:

Gilbert, William. "The Last Lords of Gardonal." *Argosy,* 1967. Reprinted in *Dracula's Brood,* edited by Richard Dalby, 13–42. New York: Dorset Press, 1987.

Bitesky, C.D.

When Danny Keegan arrives to begin classes at P. S. 13 in Brooklyn, New York, he discovers four new kids in his fifth grade class. Elisa and Frankie Stein, sister and brother, who resemble a diminutive Frankenstein and his bride; Howie Wolfner, a wolf boy; and C.D. Bitesky, formally attired in a tuxedo and a satin-lined cape. Bitesky comes from a first-generation Transylvanian family. His father runs the Stitch in Time Tailoring Service in Brooklyn. While the new kids are a little weird, they soon become Danny's close friends. They are especially valuable when he has to deal with class bully Stevie Brickwald. Author Mel Gilden dubbed the group the "Fifth Grade Monsters" in the first of his fifteen juvenile novels, *M Is for Monster* (1987).

In the story, C.D. Bitesky is a traditional vampire whose attributes are adapted for a younger audience. This juvenile Dracula speaks with a strong Eastern European accent, has a prominent widow's peak, and sports a set of fangs. Fortunately, C.D. has no need to bite his classmates—an unacceptable behavior pattern for the average American fifth-grader—as he carries a thermos, filled with the "fluid of life," from which he regularly sips a red liquid. He eats most foods but refuses to partake of pizza with garlic sauce. He has a pet bat, Spike, and on occasion transforms into a bat himself.

While each volume in the Fifth Grade Monsters series offers new insights into C.D., he becomes the focus of the story in volume ten, *How to Be a Vampire in One Easy Lesson*. In this novel, C.D. introduces his friends to his kinsman, the Count, who resides in the catacombs under the Carfax Palace Theater. When bully Stevie Brickwald asks C.D. how to become a vampire, C.D. refers him to his father, who, like C.D., wears a tuxedo every day. As a start, C.D.'s parents dress Stevie in a tuxedo and slick back his hair before introducing him to the Count. The tall, pale count agrees to teach Stevie, warning him that learning to become a vampire is a serious and long matter. After his first session with the Count, however, Stevie takes matters into his own hands. He shows up at school looking somewhat disheveled and claiming to be a freelance vampire, first class. He refuses to tell C.D. more than that or to let him inspect his thermos to see if the red liquid really is the mysterious fluid of life.

The next day, his tuxedo in greater disarray, Stevie appears outside the school building to announce that he is now Baron Stevie von Brickwald, that his will is stronger than that of any who approach him, and that he no longer needs to go to school. Ms. Gunderson, the principal, proves Stevie wrong and has the custodian pick up the small vampire pretender and carry him into the school building. In the process, Stevie drops his thermos, which C.D. picks up and discovers to contain cherry soda. Stevie is mad, but C.D. reminds him that he had been warned. One cannot simply decide to become a vampire.

In each of the Fifth Grade Monsters adventures, one or two typical pre-teen problems and solutions are dramatized. For example, in the only series volume not authored by Gilden— *There's a Batwing in My Lunchbox* by Ann Hodgson —C.D.'s Transylvanian background becomes the occasion for the class to discuss how people from different cultures often feel alienated by the events described in the story of the Pilgrims' first Thanksgiving. Also, by interacting with a world of scary creatures—

zombies, dinosaurs, and witches—in non-threatening ways, C.D. shows youthful readers that there's nothing to fear but fear itself.

SOURCES:

Gilden, Mel. *Born to Howl.* (Fifth Grade Monsters, No. 2) New York: Avon, 1987.

———. *How to Be a Vampire in One Easy Lesson.* (Fifth Grade Monsters, No. 10) New York: Avon, 1990.

———. *Island of the Weird.* (Fifth Grade Monsters, No. 11) New York: Avon, 1990.

———. *M Is for Monster.* (Fifth Grade Monsters, No. 1) New York: Avon, 1987.

———. *Monster Boy.* (Fifth Grade Monsters, No. 13) New York: Avon, 1991.

———. *Yuckers!* (Fifth Grade Monsters, No. 8) New York: Avon, 1989.

———. *Z Is for Zombie.* (Fifth Grade Monsters, No. 5) New York: Avon, 1988.

Hodgman, Ann. *There's a Batwing in My Lunchbox.* (Fifth Grade Monsters, No. 3) New York: Avon, 1988.

Black, Captain Paul

Captain Paul Black, an American tank commander during World War II, appears in a short story in the comic book *Weird War Tales* (1973). During a lull in the fighting after the invasion of Italy, he is headquartered at Castello Nero. A painting of one Guiseppe Nero who looks very much like him hangs on the castle wall, and the village priest informs him that the Italian equivalent of his name, Black, is Nero.

Black finally meets his hostess, who immediately ushers the priest out of the castle under the excuse that 500 years ago the family and the church had a split that had never been healed. After he witnesses her jump back from the priest's cross, Black gradually learns that she is a fairly traditional vampire. Nocturnal, she has fangs, and does not show a reflection in the mirror. Bullets have no effect on her. Unfortunately, before Black can kill her, she bites him.

Black becomes a vampire from her bite. Turning his condition (he must feed each evening) into a positive experience, Black utilizes his new vampire abilities while leading nightly patrols into the German lines. When night patrols are discontinued as the Americans prepare for a new push, Black kills one of his own comrades. Seen and pursued, he cannot be brought down by rifle fire. However, as he is about to make his escape into the countryside, he slips on the rotting castle wall and plunges to his death, impaled on a wooden structure below.

SOURCES:

Drake, Arnold, and Tony de Zuniga. "Captain Dracula." *Weird War Tales.* No. 18. **City: Publisher,** Oct. 1973.

Blacula

Blacula, the most successful African American vampire of the "blaxploitation" film era of the late 1960s, is the name given to African Prince Mamuwalde after his transformation into a bloodsucker by **Count Dracula**.

Before his transformation, Prince Mamuwalde (portrayed by William Marshall) is an African leader, who, during the 1780s, is trying to find a way to stop the slave trade that plagues Africa's West Coast. In desperation, he seeks out the help of Count Dracula (portrayed by Charles Macaulay), who merely laughs at the idea. As the prince and his wife, Luva, prepare to leave the count, they are attacked by Drac-

William Marshall as Blacula, the most well-known African-American vampire.

ula and his vampire minions. Mamuwalde is vampirized and sealed in a tomb, while Luva is left to die of starvation, unable to help her husband. Dracula curses Mamuwalde to become Blacula, his African counterpart.

Almost two centuries later, in 1965, an American collector purchases the antique furnishings of the Castle Dracula and ships them to California. He is unaware that an ornate coffin included in the shipment houses Blacula's slumbering body. After arriving in Los Angeles, Blacula awakens and discovers a new love, Tina, who is the exact image of his lost Luva. Unfortunately, Tina falls victim to a shooting incident, and Blacula must turn her into a vampire to save her. He still loses her, however, when she is killed by a stake through her heart. In his grief, Blacula commits suicide by walking into the sunlight.

Blacula first appeared in the 1972 film that bears his name. He returned a year later through the magic of voodoo in the sequel movie, *Scream, Blacula Scream.* Aligning himself with Lisa, a voodoo priestess, he searches for a way to rid himself of his vampire condition but is thwarted by the police. In an unusual but entirely appropriate twist of the story line, Blacula is killed when a voodoo doll is impaled through its heart with a pin.

Charles Macauley as Dracula in the film *Blacula*. It was the Count himself who turned Prince Mamuwalde into Blacula.

The *Blacula* movies have enjoyed new life on video and join the small list of blaxploitation films that have found a broad audience beyond the African American community.

SOURCES:

Flynn, John L. *Cinematic Vampires*. Jefferson, N.C.: McFarland and Company, 1992.

Gross, Edward, and Marc Shapiro. *The Vampire Interview Book: Conversations with the Undead*. East Meadow, N.Y.: Image Publishing, 1991.

Blaylock, Miriam

Miriam Blaylock is the beautiful vampire featured in Whitley Strieber's 1981 novel *The Hunger*. In the 1983 film version of the novel, she was portrayed by Catherine Deneuve. Of unknown origin, Blaylock is one of five children in her family, all vampires. Her mother died when she was giving birth to her triplet sisters. She also has a brother.

Over the centuries, Blaylock has taken mortal lovers and turned them into long-term companions by sharing her blood with them. By A.D. 71, when she shows up in Rome, she has already lived several centuries, if not millennia. In Rome, she saves

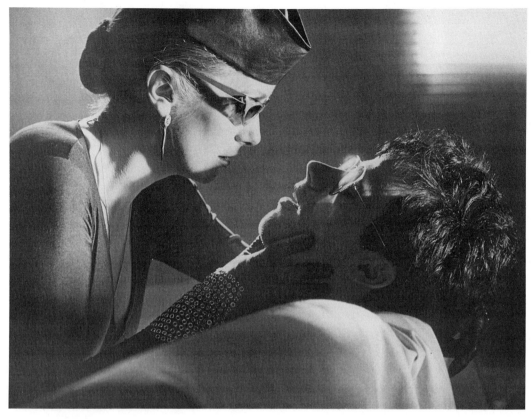

The beautiful Catherine Deneuve shows that it can be glamourous to be a vampire in the film adaptation of Whitley Strieber's novel *The Hunger.*

Eumenes from execution by crucifixion, nurses him back to health, and takes him as a lover.

Blaylock is a nontraditional vampire. She has no fangs and carries a knife shaped like a Egyptian *ankh* that she uses to cut open an artery in her victims. She needs to feed only once a week, but her feeding generally causes her victim to die. She sleeps six hours every day, which she has to do to keep her vampiric cycles stable. She is not bothered at all by sunlight. Miriam has few supernatural skills and instead must rely on her cunning to survive and thrive. She cannot change shapes and is not blessed with superhuman strength. She does have acute hearing and some clairvoyant hypnotic abilities, which initially helps her seduce her lovers. She never ages. Her companions, on the other hand, eventually do age, although they remain young for many years. Since she lured each man (or woman) in by promising them eternal life, she keeps her promise. Even after they age and die, she does not abandon them. At some sacrifice to herself, she arranges for them to be preserved in boxes that she takes with her on her travels throughout the centuries.

Her longest companion is Lollia, a women she meets in Ravenna, where she is a weaver of linen. Lollia stays with Miriam for a millennia, remaining at her side

Vampire Miriam Blaylock (Catherine Deneuve) tries to keep her aging lover David (David Bowie) alive in *The Hunger*.

through transitions from Rome to Constantinople to London. She comes to a horrible end in 1430 as she begins to age rapidly and take victims (she is a vampire also) with alarming frequency.

One of the most traumatic events in Miriam's long life occurs in 1740 when she travels with her brother and three sisters to Swabia. According to rumors, their kind can seek safe haven there. The rumors prove false. Her brother dies on the trip and her three sisters are captured and tortured to death. With no supernatural powers to help her, there is nothing Miriam can do to save her sisters from the mob that captures them. Miriam then settles in England, where she meets David (portrayed by David Bowie). He becomes her next companion, and they eventually move to America and make their home in New York City. By this time, she and all the other vampires in the world have become loners, so she rarely meets another of her kind.

In the early 1980s, after a long life, David begins to show the inevitable signs of aging. Miriam has become interested in the role modern science can play in preventing aging and is particularly interested in the work of Dr. Sarah Roberts, a researcher at nearby Riverside Medical Research Center. Miriam hopes that Roberts might be able to slow the aging process in David, but in case she can't, she plans to make Roberts her next companion.

It proves to be too late to help David, so Miriam is forced to help him make his final transition and place him in his box. She then begins an affair with Roberts, which angers Roberts' boyfriend. When Roberts realizes what is happening to her, she turns on Miriam and the two strong-willed women have a violent confrontation. In the novel, Miriam wins this confrontation, but the movie has an alternate ending.

SOURCES:
Strieber, Whitley. *The Hunger*. New York: William Morrow, 1981. Reprint, New York: Pocket Books, 1982.

Bledinoff, Vasily Vladovitch

Vasily Vladovitch Bledinoff, the son of **Count Dracula,** established himself in Dawson, Alaska, in the 1890s where, in Elizabeth Scarborough's 1989 novel, he became *The Goldcamp Vampire*. His family originated in Romania but moved to Russia, where they took a Russian (and appropriate) surname, Bledinoff. The family were descendants of a European dragon priest and may ultimately have been extraterrestrials.

Bledinoff was born in Russia and raised on the steppes in princely fashion, a second cousin to the infamous **Elizabeth Bathory.** Once grown, he moves in the royal circles in Moscow and Berlin, but gradually develops the vision of an isolated vampire utopia in the far north. Thus, he becomes one of the first settlers in the Klondike. He makes friends with the Eskimos and over a period of years builds a richly furnished house with treasures brought from his homeland.

Bledinoff enjoys the six months without sunlight and travels south as the summer approaches. He makes his fortune in furs, and after gold is discovered and the population begins to grow, he settles first in Circle City and later in Dawson, where he owns the Gold Vein, a popular saloon and entertainment establishment.

Bledinoff appears as a handsome young man with a white streak setting off his black hair. He tends to dress formally with a black cape, gold accessories, and black boots. He has dark eyes. He is a traditional vampire, his nocturnal nature being the cause of his coming to the Yukon. He sleeps in a coffin. He is repelled by garlic and holy objects. He can transform into a wolf and the claw marks he occasionally leaves on a victim cover the true nature of his crime. He also has an ability to hypnotically control people.

In 1897, the year that *Dracula* is published, Dawson is visited by authoress Pelegra Harper, who writes popular novels under the name Valentine Lovelace. From reading parts of Stoker's novel, she figures out that Bledinoff is a vampire and is responsible for a series of deaths that had begun in San Francisco even before her journey to Canada had begun. The fact that she has been accused of one of the murders and is being sought by the Royal Canadian Mounted Police motivates her to stop Bledinoff.

Eventually, Bledinoff confirms the nature of his existence and invites her to join him. She refuses. In 1897, the Gold Vein burns in a fire that consumes most of Dawson, and Bledinoff disappears. His present whereabouts are unknown. Lovelace would later write down her memories and leave the only real record of his vampiric existence.

SOURCES:

Scarborough, Elizabeth. *The Goldcamp Vampire.* New York: Bantam Books, 1989.

Blood, Baron

The vampire Baron Blood first appeared in 1976 in a series of stories by Roy Thomas in the Marvel comic book *The Invaders.* The Baron is one of a host of super villains created to be a worthy adversary of Marvel's super heroes.

Baron Blood is born late in the nineteenth century as John Falsworth, the younger son of Lord William Falsworth, British nobleman. Shortly after the turn of the century, when his older brother inherits control of the family fortune, Falsworth hatches a plan to obtain power of his own. He goes to Romania in search of **Count Dracula**, whom he intends to control for his purposes. However, Falsworth fails to reckon with the power of the count, who attacks Falsworth and turns him into a vampire minion. Falsworth returns to England as Dracula's servant/agent to create havoc in England. Dracula makes Falsworth his instrument of revenge for the defeat he suffered in London, recounted in Bram Stoker's novel.

During World War I, Falsworth becomes a German agent and assumes the identity Baron Blood. After the war, he disappears, only to reemerge in the 1930s as a supporter of Adolph Hitler. He returns to England as his own grandson and takes up residence at Falsworth Manor. He attacks his own family but is defeated by the Invaders, the super team that was assembled to defeat the Third Reich. The Baron is killed by a stalactite that is threaded with silver. He is entombed in a chapel with a stake through his heart, his casket surrounded by garlic.

Baron Blood is confined until 1981, when Captain America —one of the original Invaders—is summoned to England. The now-aged Lord Falsworth believes that Baron Blood is responsible for a recent rash of "slasher" murders. After Captain America discovers that Baron Blood is not in his tomb, he learns that the Baron was resurrected years before by Dr. Charles Cromwell, an agent sent by Dracula. After awakening, Blood killed Cromwell and assumed his identity. He has lived for many years, quietly taking blood from his patients. When Captain America tracks down the fraudulent Dr. Cromwell, he kills him, decapitates him, and burns his body.

Captain America finally disposes of Baron Blood, but he is too worthy a villain to leave in ashes. The Baron reappears yet again in the form of Victor Strange, the brother of Marvel's sorcerer hero, Dr. Steven Strange. Strange's brother had died and was cryogenically frozen. Strange tried to revive him with magical spells. Apparently, one of the spells worked, but also turned him into a vampire. So, in 1989, when the machine was turned off, Victor awoke as a vampire. He donned a costume like Baron Blood, a name given him by Marie Laveau, the New Orleans voodoo priestess that Strange was at the moment fighting. The new Baron Blood settled in Greenwich Village and like Marvel's other vampire, **Morbius**, satisfied his craving for blood by attacking Manhattan's low life. He reappears occasionally in *Dr. Strange* episodes until August 1993, when he commits suicide by plunging a knife into his midsection. Dr. Strange buries him, but there is no reason to believe that Baron Blood has finally been destroyed. In fact, later in 1993, he finds his way back via the British Marvel series *Knights of Pendragon*.

SOURCES:

Abnett, Dan, and John Tomlinson. "Blood Lines, Part 1." *Knights of Pendragon,* No. 9 (April 1993).
———. "Blood Lines, Part 2." *Knights of Pendragon,* No. 10 (May 1993).
David, Alan. "Baron Blood." *Official Handbook of the Marvel Universe 2,* No. 16 (June 1987).
Glut, Don, and Alan Kupperburg. "Back from the Grave!" *The Invaders,* No. 39 (April 1979).
———. "V Is for Vampire." *The Invaders,* No. 40 (May 1979).
———. "Beware the Super-Axis!" *The Invaders,* No. 41 (September 1979).
Rovin, Jeff. *The Encyclopedia of Super Villains.* New York: Facts on File, 1987.
Thomas, Roy, and Frank Robbins. "The Blackout Murders of Baron Blood!" *The Invaders,* No. 7 (July 1976).
———. "Union Jack Is Back." *The Invaders,* No. 8 (September 1976).
———. "An Invader No More." *The Invaders,* No. 9 (December 1976).

Blue, Sonja

Sonja Blue is the name assumed by Denise Thorne after she becomes a vampire in Nancy A. Collins' novel, *Sunglasses After Dark* (1989). Denise is the 17-year-old daughter of industrialist Jacob Thorne when she mysteriously disappears on August 3, 1969. Her disappearance occurs in London, where she meets Sir Morgan, a middle-aged man who invites her for a ride in his Rolls Royce. Sir Morgan rapes Denise and bites her before leaving her in the gutter.

Thorne awakens in a hospital, where she has partial amnesia. The hospital is unable to determine her identity, because the first change her body underwent when Morgan bit her was that her fingerprints changed. She escapes from the hospital but winds up in the hands of a pimp, who gives her the name Sonja Blue. A year later her vampiric nature blossoms and she kills her pimp. Uncertain as to what is happening to her as her powers develop, she finally finds a description of her condition in a book called *Die Rasse Vorgabe* (*The Pretending Race*). She later finds a more detailed volume, *Aegrisomnia*, which further describes the habits of the Pretender race. The Pretenders are preternatural beings who live on the fringe of reality (as most humans know it). They include ogres, succubi, vampires, and other creatures. The idea of the existence of the Pretenders race is closely related to the Cthulu mythos that was popularized by H. P. Lovecraft.

In the world of the Pretenders, vampires are the undead. An individual who is infected with vampirism dies and his or her body restructures. A demon forms in the vampires body. The new vampire is created by the injection of the attacking vampire's body fluids, usually saliva and sperm. As a vampire, Blue finds sunlight painful, but not fatal. She wears sunglasses and dresses in protective clothing if she goes out during the day. Though basically nocturnal, she can remain active during the daytime if necessary. Neither garlic, silver, crosses, nor holy water has any effect on her. Her spine is the most vulnerable point in her new body. If damaged, it cannot be repaired. Severed, death will occur. Traditional folklore about killing a vampire by decapitation is true for the Pretenders.

Blue has growing hypnotic and telepathic powers. She does not cast reflections in mirrors, only a reddish aura. She continues to age until 1976, when she is 23 years old. She befriends an occultist who wants to document her existence, and when he dies, she inherits his sizable fortune. This is fortunate for her, since she no longer has access to the fortune she was due as Denise Thorne.

Blue makes locating the vampire who bit her the major goal in her life (a new vampire is considered part of the brood of the one who transformed her). She learns that there is a vampire elite consisting of vampires whose brains have evolved and are more "complete" than other vampires. Early in her quest to find her attacker, she meets Pangloss, the vampire who made Morgan. He enlists Blue to kill Morgan, because the elite, ruling vampires feel that Morgan has gone mad and is trying to revolutionize Pretender society by creating an army of vampires to do his bidding.

After her initial appearance in *Sunglasses after Dark*, Sonia Blue's adventures have continued in subsequent novels, including *In the Blood* (1992), *Paint It Black* (1995), and *A Dozen Black Roses* (1996). A graphic art version appeared in 1995.

SOURCES:

Collins, Nancy A. *A Dozen Black Roses*. Clarkston, GA: White Wolf, 1996.

———. *In the Blood*. New York: ROC, 1992.

———. *Midnight Blue: The Sonia Blue Collection*. Stone Mountain, GA: White Wolf Publishers, 1995.

———. *Paint It Black*. London: New English Library, 1995.

———. *Sunglasses After Dark*. New York: Penguin Books, 1989. Reprint, London: Futura, 1990.

Collins, Nancy A., and Stan Shaw. *Sunglasses After Dark*. No. 1–6. Verotik, 1995.

Bolescu, Count Boris

Count Boris Bolescu is the aristocratic Transylvanian vampire given life in a series of juvenile books by Ann Jungman. The first of these books, *Count Boris Bolescu and the Black Pudding*, appeared in 1989.

Believed to have died many years ago, Count Bolescu and his wife, Countess Caroline, have survived into the present and live in an otherwise abandoned castle in a remote corner of Transylvania. In his prime, more than a century ago, the count had terrorized the countryside and was feared by its villagers. Now, there are no villagers nearby, and so his food supply has disappeared. Aging and dependent on his false teeth, glasses, and hearing aid, he is now but a parody of his once fearsome self.

Not realizing that the count and countess are still alive, the Tourist Board decides to market the count's home as an authentic vampire's castle and bring visitors to tour. During the day, workers install modern conveniences. When the first tour arrives, they finish and leave before nightfall. The nocturnal count and countess never see who is remodeling their castle and miss all the excitement of the first tour. However, following that first tour, a child— Mandy Bottomly — stays behind after everyone else has left. As darkness falls, she explores the fascinating castle. Alert to Mandy's presence, the count comes upstairs to attack the intruder. At last, he thinks, he can be a real vampire again. Having left his glasses in the basement, however, he hurts himself trying to capture his diminutive victim. Finally, the countess arrives and convinces the count to abandon his efforts. Grateful to be spared, but sympathetic to the count's dilemma, Mandy offers him some black pudding, explaining that it is prepared from animal blood and is often eaten in the north of England, where she lives. The count loves the pudding and stuffs it into his fanged mouth. Feeling energized, he flies around the room. Mandy agrees to send him a supply of pudding each week. Although he does not have anyone to bite, the count receives a regular supply of pudding from Mandy. Each evening, after the tourists leave, he and the countess dance and sing and eat the bloody dish.

Back in England, Mandy convinces the principal of her school to hold a black pudding contest and invite the count and countess as judges. The event is a great success, and, for entertainment, the count flies over the heads of the attendees and teaches them to dance the Transylvanian Tango. The people are so taken with the aristocratic, fun-loving vampire couple that they decide to organize a trip to Transylvania for a masquerade ball on Midsummer's Eve.

There is one problem for the count and his wife, however: all the publicity surrounding the school event attracts the attention of Baron Von Helsing, the famed vampire hunter. Von Helsing shows up at the ball with a stake and garlic ready to kill the count and his wife. The countess pleads with Von Helsing that her husband has not been a practicing vampire for many years and that all his evil deeds are many years in the past. Von Helsing is unmoved. The crowd surges to protect their host, grabs Von Helsing, and locks him in the count's crypt until he agrees to leave the count and countess alone. In the end, Von Helsing agrees, realizing that it will serve

The cover art from *Count Boris Bolescu and the Transylvanian Tango.*

his goals to accept the count's invitation to return and listen to his stories of life as a vampire. In fact, Von Helsing decides that he will come back often and expand his knowledge of vampires. One day, he might even move in.

As the crowd leaves, the count is thrilled: He has not been pursued by a vampire hunter in years; he has a new acquaintance to whom he can tell his stories; and he still receives his weekly packages of black pudding from Mandy in northern England.

SOURCES:

Jungman, Ann. *Count Boris Bolescu and the Black Pudding.* London: Young Corgi Books, 1989.
————. *Count Boris Bolescu and the Midsummer Madness.* London: Young Corgi Books, 1994.
————. *Count Boris Bolescu and the Transylvanian Tango.* London: Young Corgi Books, 1993.

Bouchard, Angelique

Angelique Bouchard (portrayed by Lara Parker) is a vampire in the *Dark Shadows* television series. She is introduced during a 1795 flashback which relates the origin of **Barnabas Collins** (portrayed by Jonathan Frid). Angelique is initially a witch, and she is very attracted to Barnabas, who was engaged to Josette du Prés. Angelique vows to stop the wedding and casts a spell on Josette, causing her to fall in the love with Barnabas' uncle, Jeremiah Collins. While Angelique moves to marry Barnabas, he kills his uncle in a duel. Barnabas is able to withstand Angelique's advances, and the frustrated witch then curses him. Shortly thereafter a bat attacks Barnabas and turns him into a vampire. Ironically, upon awakening, Angelique is the first person upon whom he satiates his thirst. Barnabas' problem soon leads to his confinement in a crypt for almost two centuries, but at the end of the 1960s he is awakened.

In 1969, Angelique again enters Barnabas' life as Cassandra Collins, the wife of Roger Collins. At this point, Barnabas has been cured of his vampirism. His brief return to mortality is interrupted by the arrival of warlock Nicolas Blair, who claims to be Cassandra's brother. In their first encounter, Barnabas is again attacked by a bat and thus placed under Nicolas' power, and Cassandra is killed. Nicolas raises her as a vampire, and she eventually bites Barnabas—both facilitating his return to the vampiric state and temporarily transferring his allegiance away from Nicolas to her.

Like Barnabas, the vampire Angelique is a nocturnal creature with prominent fangs. Both daylight and a stake to the heart are her enemies.

SOURCES:

Scott, Kathryn Leigh, ed. *The Dark Shadows Companion: 25th Anniversary Collection.* Los Angeles: Pomegranate Press, 1990.

Boya

Boya is a vampire of indeterminate age who, for a short time, became involved with several donut shop locals in Toronto in the film *Blood and Donuts* (1996). Boya appears as a young man in his twenties although he has been around for many decades—if not centuries—as a creature of the night. In 1969 he had gone to sleep underground, only to awaken 25 years later. He digs up his few possessions, including a scrapbook, and

In the television show *Dark Shadows*, Barnabas Collins (Jonathan Frid) was doomed to spend his life as a vampire after being cursed by the witch Angelique Bouchard.

rents a room in a cheap hotel just down the street from the donut shop. As a result of his lengthy rest, his fingernails have grown to an inordinate length. He clips his nails, but not his long brown hair that gives him a somewhat unkempt look.

THE VAMPIRE GALLERY

Boya is a nocturnal creature. While he can be awake during the day, direct sunlight burns him. He sleeps in the closet of his hotel room. He is strong, with acute hearing. He can be hurt by direct physical attacks, from bullets, or by stakes, but recovers quickly. When he attacks, he takes on a bestial appearance. He views vampirism as an addiction. He believes one can submit to its demands, such as the regular feeding off of humans, or one can choose to fight the urge. Boya chooses to live off of small animals such as rats and birds, refusing to partake in his "addiction."

On his first visit to the donut shop, Boya involves himself with Molly, the young waitress to whom he is strongly attracted, and Earl, an uncouth but loveable cab driver, whose weaknesses the local hoodlums are trying to exploit. Boya uses his supernatural powers to protect Earl from the hoods, but in the process both the cabbie and the waitress slowly become aware that he is a vampire. After some initial inner struggle, they both accept him for what he is.

Boya has a relationship issue with Rita, a young woman he left behind when he went underground. She knew when he awoke, and began to search for him. When she found him, she unloaded all her anger because 25 years ago he would not make her a vampire. If only he had changed her, she argues, she would not have had to age while Boya remained young. Confronting him, Rita tries to kill him with a stake, but he simply pulls it out and walks away. With all of the negatives associated with living with vampirism, he refuses the responsibility of passing it on.

Contemplating the nature of his impermanent relationships so dramatically illustrated by Rita's anger, Molly's unrequited love, and Earl's brush with death, Boya decides to end it all. He commits suicide by staying out in the morning light, which burns him to a crisp.

Braille

Braille is a reluctant vampire who is the featured character in Patrick Whalen's novel, *Night Thirst* (1991). He lives in Washington state, an orphan raised by a Japanese couple. They pass on to him a knowledge of the martial arts, which helps him a great deal when he serves as a Green Beret in Vietnam. He specializes in assassinating key enemy personnel until he is captured and spends three years in a prisoner of war camp. Since the war, he has worked as a professional hit man.

After the war he moves to Chinook Island, which is 20 miles off the Washington coast. As a cover for his work as an assassin, he operates a business raising and selling rare ferns and begins restoring an old lighthouse. He is unaware that a group of vampires who have been captured and immobilized are being held on the island. It seems that several vampires were brought to the island soon after World War I and entombed in the basement of a monastery. They were the last of the European vampires who had been trapped in the Ural Mountains, immobilized, and buried by agents of the Church. They had been kept in France, but after the war it was felt that a more secure resting place was needed. Chinook Island was chosen.

In 1981, the two priests assigned to guard the vampires died suddenly and the monastery was left untended. After several years, some college students exploring the island discovered the tombs and in their ignorance released the ancient vampires. The students became the first of the New Ones. Within a few nights, vampirism began to spread across the island. Realizing what was happening and hoping to stop the rampant spread of vampirism, **Gregory,** one of the older vampires attempts to isolate the creatures on the island by burning all the boats on the island.

Braille is on the island when the vampires escape. He is initially able to save a group of humans in his lighthouse. They make their escape in one of the last remaining boats, leaving one person behind to destroy the island by causing a nuclear reaction at a power plant on the island. Braille and three others escape, but in the process he is bitten by one of the vampires and realizes that he is beginning to transform. He is eventually rescued by the authorities and sent to a secret research facility where researchers conduct experiments upon him. He learns that, in the process of escaping, the other survivors were killed.

As he recovers and learns how to live as a vampire, he discovers that two other vampires have survived the nuclear blast on Chinook. One is Gregory, the Ancient One who attempted to stop the phenomena from leaving the island, and the other is a New One, a new vampire who lives only to quell his tremendous thirst for blood. Most of the New Ones either died in the blast or went mad after a short time. Braille, because of his martial arts training and self-discipline, has passed beyond the New One stage and, like Gregory, become an Ancient One. He needs blood every few days. He is largely nocturnal, but can survive in the sun. When he is about to feed or becomes enraged, his fangs extend, his eyes glow red, and his face takes on a bestial appearance.

The surviving New One finds his way to Seattle and establishes himself in the Seattle Underground. From there, a plague of vampirism grows and takes over a part of the central city. The New Ones, unable to control their thirst, reproduce freely as they show no concern for killing their victims. Braille travels to Seattle, where he joins forces with Gregory to convince the Army and the Vice-President of the United States of the nature of the problem they face. They argue that a nuclear explosion is the only way to get rid of the vampires. They finally convince both men, and a nuclear bomb is dropped on the city. Both Braille and Gregory try to commit suicide by going into the blast area, but their bodies are found after the blast and they are revived by transfusions of fresh blood.

SOURCES:
Whalen, Patrick. *Night Thirst.* New York: Pocket Books, 1991.

Brandt, Harriet

Harriet Brandt, a psychic vampire, invades Victorian society in Florence Marryat's novel, *The Blood of the Vampire* (1897). She is born in the mid-1870s in Jamaica, the daughter of Henry Brandt, a wealthy, but evil, man. He had been expelled from medical school in Switzerland before moving to Jamaica. On the island, he takes advantage of the black population upon whom he carries out torturous experiments that generally cause the death of his human guinea pigs. Harriet's mother was an Obeah woman, a witch, who was known for her taste for blood. At one point she had been bitten by a vampire bat. She died giving birth to Harriet.

Harriet is still a child when her father is killed by a group of blacks who revolt against his cruelties. She is handed over to a Mr. Trawler, a trustee who places her in a convent school where she stays for 10 years, until she reaches adulthood. At that time she receives her inheritance and leaves the convent and the island. She is tall and striking, with pale skin that does not reflect the African side of her lineage. Her lips are red, her hair black, and her dark eyes rest under thick black lashes.

After leaving Jamaica, accompanied by a friend from the convent school, Harriet travels to England and then to Belgium for a brief stay at the Hotel Lion d'Or in Heyst. A beautiful young woman, she attracts people and quickly makes friends with Margaret Pullin, a young mother. She is soon babysitting Margaret's child. She also keeps company with Margaret's brother, an army officer, much to the chagrin of Captain Pullin's fiancé.

Beginning with the Pullin baby, people begin to turn pale, and following a period of gradual decline and fatigue, die. Harriet eventually meets author Anthony Pennell, who has been asked to intervene in her troubled relationship with Captain Pullin. Pennell sees in Harriet a woman with a magnetic personality, with the unconscious ability to attract some people. He marries Harriet, and Harriet slowly comes to realize what she is. Unfortunately, her realization comes too late to save her husband, who dies in his sleep, just as the others did. Harriet, in her grief at what she has wrought, writes a will leaving her wealth to Margaret Pullin and then commits suicide.

SOURCES:
Marryat, Florence. *The Blood of the Vampire*. London: Hutchinson & Co., 1897.

Brides of Dracula

The "Brides of Dracula" is a name given to the three women who appear in the early chapters of Bram Stoker's *Dracula* (1897). They live as vampires at Castle Dracula, but their origin is unknown, as is the exact nature of their relationship with the Count. When Jonathan Harker arrives at the castle, he sees no one but **Count Dracula** and is not informed that the three women also live in the castle. He first encounters the women about a week after he arrives when he is walking around the castle one evening. The women are young and well dressed and carry themselves as individuals of culture. Harker immediately notices that they are unusual in that they throw no shadow in the moonlight.

Two of the women are dark with red eyes and seem to be ethnically similar to the Count; the third is fair skinned and blonde, with eyes like sapphires. They all have brilliant white teeth and red lips. They arouse Harker's passions in such a way that he feels he is betraying his fiancé, Mina Murray, just by looking at them. Their breath is sweet, but with an underlying odor that is bitterly offensive and hints of blood. The blonde is about to bite Harker when an enraged Dracula intervenes and pulls her away. They complain that he never loved them and that he doesn't love them now. He refutes their observation and promises that they may have their way with Harker as soon as he is finished with him. When they tell the Count that they are hungry, he produces an infant that he has brought home for their nightly meal of blood.

Harker does not see the women again for over a month. Then one evening, he overhears Dracula telling them to return to their own place. "Wait! Have patience! Tonight is mine. Tomorrow night is yours!" (This passage is one of the most controversial in the entire novel. In the American edition it was changed to read "Tomorrow night, tomorrow night is yours!" Modern scholars have suggested that the alteration occurred in an attempt to delete any hint of homosexuality.) When Harker opens the door separating him from the four, he sees them all enjoying a hearty laugh.

Dracula leaves the castle and Harker knows that he is now fair game for the women, that Dracula is no longer there to protect him. He manages to escape from the castle and makes his way to Budapest, and from there, to England (with Mina's help). His knowledge of the three "sisters" as they would later be called by **Abraham Van Helsing,** later helps the vampire hunter when he cleanses Dracula's castle at the end of the novel. The cleansing occurs when the Count is racing back to his home but is beaten there by Van Helsing. Soon after arriving at the castle, Van Helsing enters the chapel and finds the three women sleeping in their tombs; he dispatches each of them with a stake to the heart, garlic in the mouth, and decapitation. As soon as he severs each woman's head, her body crumbles into dust, indicating just how old the women were.

The idea of calling the three women "brides" as opposed to "sisters" as Van Helsing does seems to derive from the conversation following the death of **Lucy Westenra.** Lucy's disappointed fiancé tells the others how he feels as if he and Lucy became husband and wife because of the intimacy involved in sharing blood (he donated blood to give Lucy a transfusion after she was bitten by Dracula). The "bride" idea has been further strengthened in various vampire movies that frequently picture a male vampire biting women and building a harem of female vampires. In fact, in most novels and movies, vampires only attack humans of the opposite sex; thus, having a group of vampire brides ensures that a male vampire has a powerful weapon to use against his male enemies.

While not included in *Nosferatu*, vampire brides play a prominent role in *Dracula* (1931) and in the Hammer vampire films, where women share stardom with Dracula (portrayed by Christopher Lee). They were portrayed as completely sensuous vampire brides in the 1992 adaptation of Bram Stoker's *Dracula* by Francis Ford Coppola. Among the additional vampires who gathered multiple brides in harem-like arrangements were **Count Yorga** and **Richmond Reed.**

ELAINE BERGSTROM'S *MINA*: Perhaps the most detailed account of the brides of Dracula is the book *Mina* (1994), written by Elaine Bergstrom under the pseudonym Marie Kiraly.

In her ambitious novel, Bergstrom retells the final chapters of Stoker's *Dracula* in which Mina, Jonathan Harker, and Dr. Van Helsing track the Count to his castle and finally dispatch him. The book tells the story from Mina's perspective. Bergstrom chose to do this because in Stoker's original, Mina suddenly disappears from Stoker's text near the end of the book after playing a prominent role throughout. In *Mina*, the young woman explains her thoughts on Dracula and the vampire women, whom she feels a kinship with since she too has shared Dracula's blood. Mina knows she could have easily become Dracula's fourth bride.

After she and Van Helsing arrive at Castle Dracula, the three women appear to her. She is entranced by their beauty, their prominent fangs, and their allure. The three recognize that Mina was nearly one of them and call to her to come out of the protective circle created by Van Helsing. She cannot resist sticking her hand outside the circle, and when she does, the darkest of the three takes her by the hand. Telepathically, Mina knows the woman's name is Illona —her life story seems to play like a movie in Mina's head. In the fifteenth century, she had been Dracula's (Vlad's) child bride. When it appeared that he was about to be defeated on the battlefield, she made a pact with Satan. The next day, with the Turkish forces surrounding the castle, she did a dramatic dive off the castle walls but lived. When the battle ended, she found Vlad's badly injured body on the battlefield and brought it back to the castle. The pair recovered from their wounds, but their world was changed. Illona's pact had made them both vampires. Thus, because she in essence created Dracula, Illona always had a certain power over him that was constantly at war with his own, dominant male power.

As Mina's connection with Illona was fading, she learned that Illona was soon joined by Joanna, Vlad's sister. The two lived alone with Dracula for several centuries until they were joined by the blonde Karina Aliczni in the 1770s. That is the last thing that Mina learns from Illona. The very next day, Van Helsing enters the castle and kills Illona, Joanna, and Karina. Mina sees the ghostlike forms of the women and watches as blood gushes forth from them when they are staked.

When she leaves the castle, Mina takes with her a book she discovered in the castle and has it translated upon her return to England. The book tells the entire life story of the last of the vampire brides, Karina Liczni. She was born in Bratslava in 1753, although her family home was in Targoviste, the old capital of Wallachia (Romania). When she was old enough, her parents arranged a trip to Sibiu in Transylvania to find a husband. Instead she encountered Dracula. Over the course of several evenings, the Count drank from her. After this had happened several times, Illona appeared in her bedroom one evening. She came to take her to Dracula's castle. There the two women fed until days later when Dracula returned. The night that the Count returned, Illona forced Karen to drink from her neck. Dracula then pulled her to his side and made her also drink his blood; she thrilled at his touch and drank willingly. Later, as her uncertainty about what was happening grew, she tried to leave the castle but found that she HAD to be back by dawn—something seemed to draw her back. That something, of course, was her native soil, the soil on which she had been born as a vampire. In this case, the soil of the castle. Illona, in turn, was her master, since it was her blood that Karina drank first.

In England, Mina confides in her friend, Lord Gance, that all is not finished with the brides of Dracula. The two of them return to Dracula's Castle for a final confrontation with the three women, who had returned to a state of undeath even after Van Helsing's attack upon them. Illona develops a plan to bring the spirit of Dracula back in Gance's body, but her plot is foiled by Mina in a final confrontation.

SOURCES:

Stoker, Bram. *Dracula*. Westminster (London): Constable & Co., 1897. First (British) edition. Reprint, New York: Doubleday & McClure, 1899. First American edition. Both editions reprinted frequently.

Kiraly, Marie [Elaine Bergstrom]. *Mina*. New York: Berkley Books, 1994.

Brunnel, Adriadne

Adriadne Brunnel, the reclusive vampire in Hume Nisbet's 1900 short story "The Vampire Maid," lives in a cottage on the Moors near Westmoreland in rural England. She lives with her mother, who occasionally rents the spare rooms in their house to people wishing to spend some time in the relaxing atmosphere of the area. Adriadne is not considered a beautiful girl, but she has a magnetic appeal to the young men who have found their way to the isolated cottage. She has a livid white complexion, red lips, and black hair and eyes.

Seemingly typical of many men before him, the unnamed young male narrator of Nisbet's story finds, after he has rented two rooms at the cottage from the older woman and been introduced to her daughter, that he is completely captivated by Adriadne. Emotionally, he soon feels as if the fateful reason for his coming to the Moors was to meet her. He experiences love at first sight and each evening dreams of her. Throughout the days he wants nothing but to be in her company. However, he notices that as the days pass, she grows lively and her skin takes on color, while he languishes. He also develops a strange wound on his arm.

Several weeks pass, until one evening he dreams that a bat with the face of Adriadne flies into his room and attaches itself to his arm. It bites him and sucks his blood. At the same time he has a vision of the bodies of a number of young men not unlike himself dead as a result of the bat's attack. He then wakes up to find Adriadne sucking at his arm. He pushes her away and flees the cottage. Nothing further is heard of Adriadne and her mother. Perhaps they are still on the Moors or possibly in some other quiet location ready to offer a spare room to a passing stranger.

SOURCES:

Nisbet, Hume. "The Vampire Maid." In his *Stories Weird and Wonderful*, 1900. Reprinted in *Dracula's Brood*, edited by Richard Dalby, . New York: Dorset Press, 1987.

Buddha Dak

The ancient vampire Buddha Dak is the key personage in the Juvita-ta, a rejuvenation ceremony for Itsu, the evil criminal mind better known as the Sinister Hand in Flint Dille's and David Marconi's spy novel, *Acolytes of Darkness*. Buddha Dak resides deep in a cave somewhere in the desert near Machaerus, the site of the biblical King Herod's fortress, where John the Baptist was executed. In the twentieth century, during the Stalinist era, Buddha Dak is summoned by the Hand, the leader of a vast international sinister network, the Brotherhood, that manipulates many of the world's leaders and causes large-scale evil. His agents are under his control, even to the point of accepting his order to commit suicide. Itsu was a Lemurian who left the fabled continent 5,000 years ago and started the Brotherhood. He is virtually immortal, although he occasionally needs to undergo a rejuvenation.

Itsu sends one of his leading agents, Jinga-Gaa, to awaken the slumbering vampire. Jinga-Gaa takes with him a young woman who travels in a state resembling suspended animation. As they approached the cave, Jinga-Gaa pours a quantity of liquid down her throat. She is then able to walk into the cave with him, though she is still in a trance-like state. After an hour's walk, they arrive at a chamber and find Buddha Dak floating in a pool of blood. Jinga-Gaa wades in to the vampire's side and gives him some of the same liquid he had given the girl. The pale creature awakens and immediately satiates his thirst on the young woman. Jinga-Gaa then informs the vampire that it is time for the Juvita-ta.

As Buddha Dak makes his way to the site of the Juvita-ta, he signals his coming to those watching with a trail of bodies whose necks have been slashed and whose blood has been drained. The first victim is a prostitute in Tangiers. The clerk at the hotel where Buddha Dak is registered describes him as a handsome Egyptian with white skin and hands noticeably cold to the touch.

As the complicated ceremony proceeds, staged in various discrete steps over several days, Buddha Dak decides to improvise and satiate his seemingly constant thirst on one of the designated victims, secret agent Maggie Darr. As he is about to bite her, he suddenly faces Agent 13, the nemesis of the Brotherhood who has arrived to disrupt the Juvita-ta. The two fight, and Agent 13 is outclassed by Buddha Dak's strength. As a last disparate act, however, he is able to pull the vampire into a pit of water. The water dissolves the vampire just as a vat of acid would dissolve a human. Thus, the Sinister Hand loses a vital element in the rejuvenation ceremony, and Agent 13 can pursue him knowing that, at best, the ceremony could only partially be successful in restoring the Hand's youthful vigor. With luck, Agent 13 could get rid of the Hand altogether.

SOURCES:

Dille, Flint, and David Marcom. *Acolytes of Darkness*. (Bound together with *Web of Danger* by Aaron Allston.) New York: Double Agent Books/Tor Books, 1988

BUFFY THE VAMPIRE SLAYER *see:* SUMMERS, BUFFY IN VAMPIRE HUNTERS CHAPTER

Bunnicula

Vampires have become more and more popular in children's fiction in recent years, and none is more popular than Bunnicula, the cute little rabbit that lives a happy existence as a vegetarian vampire. Bunnicula is owned by Pete and Toby Monroe, who found him at the theater when they were seeing a **Count Dracula** movie. They take him home and introduce him to their other two pets, Chester the cat and Harold the dog.

Bunnicula does not suck blood, but he is a vampire nonetheless. His target of choice is vegetables, such as carrots and tomatoes, which he bites and sucks the juice out of, leaving only a husk. Instead of two prominent front teeth like those featured by Bugs Bunny, Bunnicula has two fangs. Like all good vampires, he sleeps all day.

Chester and Harold learn that Bunnicula is a vampire soon after his arrival. One night, after sleeping all day, Bunnicula sneaks into the kitchen and raids the refrigerator. He finds a nice, juicy tomato and drains it of all its juice and color, leaving behind only a white husk. Chester the cat, watches all this with wonder. When Mrs. Monroe finds the husk, she is baffled. Chester, however, is quite the educated cat who spends most of his spare time reading books. In one of those books, he learns about vampires and realizes that that is exactly what Bunnicula is. From his books, Chester also knows how to stop a vampire—he places garlic on the floor to prevent Bunnicula from reaching the kitchen. That's all well and good until Harold the dog realizes that Chester's actions are starving Bunnicula. Harold intervenes, seeing no good reason why the rabbit shouldn't be allowed to feed since he wasn't harming anyone. He smuggles the thirsty Bunnicula into the kitchen and then convinces Chester that they should all try to get along.

Eventually Chester, Harold, and Bunnicula become close friends and share a number of adventures together, all of which are chronicled in a series of books by James Howe and his wife Deborah.

SOURCES:

Howe, Deborah, and James Howe. *Bunnicula*. New York: Atheneum Publishers, 1979. Reprint, New York: Avon, 1980.

Howe, James. *Bunnicula Escapes*. New York: Tupelo Books, 1994.

———. *Bunnicula Fun Book*. New York: Morrow Junior Books, 1993.

———. *The Celery Stalks at Midnight*. New York: Macmillan Company, 1983. Reprint, New York: Avon, 1984.

———. *Creepy-Crawly Birthday*. New York: William Morrow and Company, 1991.

———. *The Fright Before Christmas*. New York: William Morrow and Company, 1988.

———. *Hot Fudge*. New York: William Morrow and Company, 1990. Reprint, New York: Avon, 1991.

———. *Nighty-Nightmare*. New York: Macmillan Company, 1987.

———. *Rabbit-Cadabra*. New York: Morrow, 1993.

———. *Scared Silly: A Halloween Treat*. New York: Morrow, 1989.

Burton, John

Vampire John Burton is the subject of the comic book story "Burton's Blood!" (1953). A traditional nocturnal creature with pale skin, Burton sleeps in a coffin and can easily transform into a bat. In this futuristic story, the formally dressed vampire survives the atomic war that occurs in 1998. He has an orgy of blood from the dying. In fact, he drinks so much blood he decides to find a safe place to sleep and not wake up until the world had been rebuilt. He settles in an unused coffin in a brand-new undamaged crypt.

His idea appears successful. He awakes to find a newly constructed city inhabited by many people walking its streets. Thirsty, he flies into a dark alley and changes into a half-man/half-bat form to attack his first victim. Unfortunately, his victim is unmoved by the horror before him, and simply returns the attack with a stake he holds in his hand. As Burton joins the truly dead, the would-be victim informs the vampire there are no more humans. Only robots have survived the atomic holocaust to build the new world.

SOURCES:

"Burton's Blood!" *Menace.* No. 2. 1953. Reprinted in *Vault of Evil.* No 11. June 1974.

Cabanel, Fanny Campbell

Jules Cabanel is the major land owner and principal holder of public office in the small community of Pieuvot in the Britanny region of France in Eliza Lynn Linton's 1880 short story, "The Fate of Madam Cabanel." For the first fifty years of his life, Jules resisted marriage, until one day, when he returns to his small town from Paris with a new bride: Fanny Campbell Cabanel. Blue-eyed Fanny is a foreigner—from England—with red lips and hair, rosy cheeks, and plump shoulders, which leads the cemetery gravedigger immediately and authoritatively to brand her a vampire. An orphan, Fanny worked as a governess in Paris but had been left stranded and penniless by a former employer.

Fanny is enjoying her new life and seeming to thrive, but the town is suffering. No one can remember such a concentrated number of illnesses and deaths in Pieuvot. In the meantime, Fanny has taken to frequently visiting the local graveyard, although she knows no one buried there. With little encouragement, the villagers decide Fanny is a vampire, and a mob gathers to throw her into a pit outside of town. Leading the mob is Adèle, the Cabanel's housekeeper, whose son Adolf had recently died of unknown causes. When the mob arrives at the pit having been unable to find Fanny, they discover that Fanny is already dead. Confronted with the reality of mob arrest and humiliation, she threw herself into the pit and died. The villagers have rid themselves of their vampire, and Jules Cabanel is once more alone.

SOURCES:

Linton, Eliza Lynn. "The Fate of Madame Cabanel." In her *Within a Silken Thread*, 1880. Reprinted in *Dracula's Brood,* edited by Richard Dalby. New York: Dorset Press, 1987.

Caine

In the mythological world of the popular role-playing game *Vampire: The Masquerade,* the biblical character Caine (commonly spelled Cain in English-language Bible translations) is the original vampire. According to the biblical story, the farmer

Caine made an offering of the fruits of his work to God as did his shepherd brother, Abel. God rejected Caine's offering while accepting Abel's. The resentful Caine murdered his brother, for which he was cast into the outer darkness. *Vampire* suggests that the curse was eternal life and a craving for blood, and that the curse has been passed to all present-day vampires.

In the darkness he met Lilith, the reputed first wife of Caine's father Adam. She shared her blood with Caine. Her blood awakened him to his Power. After wandering in the wilderness for many years, he once again lived among mortals and created a city. During his years there he created three vampires, who together were known as the Second Generation. They in turn created the Third Generation, and as it grew in number (the exact size being unknown), Caine forbade the further creation of additional vampires.

The stable situation of Caine's city was disrupted by a great flood. Reiterating his command not to create more vampires, he left his children on their own and began wandering the land again. His vampires ignored his admonitions and created a Fourth Generation, who rose up and slew most of the Elders of the Third Generation. Meanwhile, over the millennia, a person claiming to be Caine occasionally appears. He usually comes and goes very quickly. None of the older leaders of the present vampire community now organized as **The Camarilla** claim to have met Caine, and no one seems to know if the Caine myth concerning the creation of vampires is even true.

SOURCES:

Chupp, Sam, and Andrew Greenberg. *The Book of Nod.* Stone Mountain, GA: White Wolf, 1993.
Rein-Hagen, Mark, et al. *Book of the Damned.* Stone Mountain, GA: White Wolf, 1993.
———. *Vampire: The Masquerade.* Stone Mountain, GA: White Wolf, 1991.

Capello, Jeremy

Jeremy Capello (portrayed by Robert Sean Leonard) is the Houston, Texas, high school student and featured vampire in the 1988 movie *My Best Friend Is a Vampire.* One day after school, Jeremy, a grocery delivery boy, is sent to the old Gardner Mansion. The groceries are for Nora, a beautiful woman, whom he has already met in a recurring dream. That evening he returns to the mansion for a late night encounter with Nora that includes the bite that slowly turns him into a vampire. Over the next few days, dogs gather outside Jeremy's window, he loses his appetite, and he is no longer able to see his reflection in mirrors. His mother notices his paleness and fatigue. He is unable to eat pizza while out on a date, and as he is about to kiss his new girlfriend, fangs instantly grow out of his mouth.

No one, least of all Jeremy, understands these changes. His parents believe that he is gay. However, **Modoc**, a 200-year-old vampire mentor, insinuates himself into Jeremy's life and tells the teenager that the changes he is experiencing are a result of his being a vampire. Modoc also informs Jeremy of an all-night butcher where he can get blood (pig's blood is the best) that will allow him to feed without constantly attacking people. And, of course, he points out that vampirism has its good points, such as the fact that he will age only one year for each decade of human life, and thus, he now has time to enjoy life thoroughly and master whatever he chooses.

The real problem for this generation of vampires is getting the respect they are due as a beleaguered minority group. Jeremy's particular nemesis is **Professor Leopold McCarthy**, a self-appointed vampire hunter. He and his bungling assistant, Grimsdyke, had stormed in on Jeremy and Nora during their late-night tryst and attempted to kill her. They have been chasing Jeremy ever since. They also mistake Jeremy's best friend, Ralph, as a vampire.

Once Jeremy accepts who he has become, his situation seems more than tolerable: He has a book of vampire instructions, a pretty girl friend, and a new BMW car given to him by Modoc. One evening, however, McCarthy captures Ralph, and the chase is on. McCarthy and his sidekick take Ralph to a chapel next to the local cemetery and are about to stake him when Jeremy arrives and convinces them that Ralph is not a vampire. Of course, in the process Jeremy becomes the target. Jeremy and Ralph head for the graveyard, where fortunately they are joined by Modoc, Nora, and a bevy of beautiful young vampires. They have decided to take care of McCarthy in the most humane way: they allow him to join the night life.

Jeremy is not entirely ready for total nocturnal existence. It turns out that there are two kinds of vampires: the living vampire and the dead vampire. Jeremy has never died and, like Modoc, is of the former variety. He can go out in the daytime, though he needs to wear shades and a carry few sun protectors. He can, in fact, lead a somewhat normal life. His parents, now mentally and emotionally braced to accept his being gay, are overjoyed that he has a girlfriend and can learn to cope with having a vampire in the family.

Carnifax, Nathan

Nathan Carnifax is the vampire antagonist of werewolf Desiree Cupio in *Dream Wolves*, two comic book series by Daniel Presedo. He is a modern vampire: young, handsome, with long dark hair and prominent fangs. He is not bound by the night, though he prefers it, and is unaffected by holy symbols. However, between the two *Dream Wolves* series, his story changes considerably.

In the first *Dream Wolves* series, Carnifax, the king of vampires, enters the scene in the early 1990s as a Republican candidate for governor of Louisiana. Only Desiree recognizes him as a vampire. Desiree has reason to remember Carnifax and his true identity. In the mid-1970s, after many years alone as a vampire, Carnifax had finally fallen in love, but Simone Cupio, Desiree's mother, refused his offer of eternal life. Not knowing that Simone's young child was watching from a hiding place, the enraged Carnifax killed Simone, the only human he had loved since attaining his vampiric state.

Carnifax has his first encounter with the adult Desiree in a New Orleans cemetery. Their battle results in a draw; however, through their encounter Carnifax learns of Desiree's relationship to Simone and she of her possible relationship to Carnifax. Also, Desiree consumes some of Carnifax's blood and momentarily becomes enraptured with him. They both then head for Bayou Goula, where Simone's sister, Ellen, lives. Carnifax arrives first and learns the truth that Desiree is his daughter. He kills Ellen just as Desiree arrives. Her aunt's death prompts a second fight with Carnifax, resulting in her staking him.

In the second series, Carnifax is reborn in a slightly changed story line as a werewolf living in Louisiana. Cast out of his pack, he meets Desiree as a young woman living in Bayou Goula. He bites her and turns her into a werewolf. After their initial encounter, he moves to New Orleans. She follows as soon as she recovers from their meeting. While Desiree is trying to establish herself in an apartment in the French quarter, Carnifax has an unfortunate encounter with a vampire who bites him and transforms him into a vampire. Carnifax becomes bound to the night, living off of the small quantities of blood he now requires. The rest of his evenings are spent spying on Desiree, to whom he is strongly attracted.

Desiree is initially enraged at Carnifax's interference in her life, most recently attacking some of her friends. Carnifax desires Desiree and intrudes to the point of calling attention to the amoral nature of their new lives as creatures of the night. As the story ends, the possibility of their future interaction remains open.

SOURCES:

Presedo, Daniel. *Dream Wolves*. First series. Nos. 1–3. London: Night Studios, 1993–94.

———. *Dream Wolves*. Second series. Nos. 1–8. Baton Rouge, LA: Drameon Studios, 1994–95.

Caroline

Caroline (portrayed by Ghetty Chasum) is a young female vampire with a variety of body piercings who lives in contemporary New York City. She is the star of the low-budget film, *Red Lips* (1994). Broke, Caroline decides to donate blood to earn a few dollars. The doctor who takes her blood tells her that more money is available if she will cooperate in testing a new vaccine. Caroline agrees, but has a most unexpected reaction to the vaccine. She develops such intense stomach pains that she is overcome with pain and falls while walking down the street, cutting herself. When she tastes the blood from the cut, she finds that it relieves her pain. It also causes her to lose her appetite for normal food and drink. It seems that Caroline has somehow become a vampire. Her body metamorphoses quickly and a craving for blood overcomes her. Her first victim is a salesman in a cheap motel. She also returns to the clinic and kills the doctor who gave her the vaccine.

After killing several people, Caroline meets Lisa (portrayed by noted film scream queen Michelle Bauer), a lesbian who has just left her girlfriend. Lisa is distraught and on her own, and like Caroline, just needs someone to talk to. The two hit it off and soon after meet Gina, who invites the two women to stay at her apartment for a few days. Caroline repays this kindness by killing Gina so that she and Lisa can live in the apartment. Lisa realizes that her new friend is a vampire, but she decides to stick with Caroline and serve as her protector, at least until the two of them can find a way to reverse Caroline's condition. Her first act is to get rid of Gina's body.

Their growing relationship is interrupted when a gun-toting man breaks into the apartment looking for Gina. It seems that Gina was a hooker who had not been turning in enough cash before her death. He tried to threaten the girls, but Caroline knows her next meal when she sees it and attacks him. As she is slowly draining his blood, his gun goes off and kills Lisa. Suddenly, Caroline is left to face the future without her lover.

Caroline is a very nontraditional vampire. She was created accidentally in the medical experiment and had never actually died. She had none of the supernatural attributes usually associated with vampires and could move about in the daytime with no problem. She not only developed fangs, but as she went to feed, a whole mouth of sharpened teeth appeared. These teeth were not visible under normal circumstances. They also left a large hole in the victim's neck rather than two tiny puncture wounds.

Cassidy

The vampire Cassidy, one of the continuing characters in the popular comic book *Preacher*, emerged in the 1990s as the friend of Jesse Custer and his girlfriend Tulip. It is the premise of this supernatural series that major changes have occurred in heaven, partially the result of the mating of an angel and a demonic. The resulting child, Genesis, is a new kind of being, possessed of great power, but lacking strength of will. Genesis comes to earth and possesses Jesse, who now has the power to speak the Word and bend those who listen to his desire. In the meantime, he learns that God has retired and is no longer running heaven. Jesse begins a quest to find God and call him to account for the new state of affairs.

Cassidy accompanies Jesse on his adventures, which have taken them, among other places, to a hideaway fortress in southern France where a small group of followers has, for the past two thousand years, protected the descendants of Jesus. They assert that Jesus did not die on the cross but survived, married, and produced children whose bloodline continues to this day.

The story of Cassidy begins in 1900. Named Proinsas Cassidy, he is born and grows up in Ireland. He and his older brother, Billy, join the Irish freedom fighters attempting to throw off British rule during Easter week of 1916. At one point in the battle, Billy pulls his brother out of the battle, and together they head for home. On their way, as they stop to rest, a bog monster vampire attacks Proinsas. Before Billy can fight it off, the vampire bites Proinsas and drags him into the water. The date is April 27, 1916. Cassidy awakes the next day and struggles out of the water only to have his skin begin burning in the sunlight. He soon decides to wait in the water until after sunset.

Cassidy has no mentor, so he learns what he is and the nature of his powers slowly. While seeking some food, he attacks a sheep but is shot by its owner. Although the gunshot hurts, Cassidy not only survives, but quickly gets up and runs away. He learns to be active in the evening hours and decides neither to return home nor to let his family know what has happened to him. In Ireland, being a small country, Cassidy finds it difficult to develop a life—even a nocturnal one— that does not involve occasionally running into someone he knows. He decides to travel to the United States.

In Manhattan he finds a city that never sleeps. He finds a place in the late night pub crowd. He discovers Bram Stoker's *Dracula* and begins to understand his condition. Unlike Dracula, however, Cassidy has no fangs and is weakened by sunlight. During the ensuing decades, he has numerous adventures and many girlfriends, a few enduring as long-term relationships, though he hates to watch the women age while he remains young. He is able to live a somewhat normal life, though necessarily after dark. Although he needs a regular intake of blood, he also enjoys other foods. He consumes alcohol and drugs and is typically portrayed with a cigarette in his mouth.

Cassidy is almost completely invulnerable. The sun burns him and is probably his greatest enemy. At one point, he puts a knife through his neck to appear dead during a police raid. Taken to the morgue, he revives and leaves. Another time, he is shot numerous times, one arm and his penis being severed. He survives and his severed body parts soon grew back. Most severe, he is decapitated, generally the end of a vampire, but his friends see that his head is surgically reattached, and after a period of healing Cassidy is as good as new.

Although a continuing character, Cassidy's story is the special focus of *Preacher*, nos. 30–33 and the recent *Preacher Special: Cassidy: Blood & Whiskey*.

SOURCES:

Ennis, Garth, & Steve Dillon. *Preacher*. New York: DC Comics, 1995–present

———. *Preacher Special: Cassidy: Blood & Whiskey*. New York: DC Comics, 1998.

Cavalanti, Niccolo

Niccolo Cavalanti, an old vampire and leader among the vampire community, was featured in Michael Talbot's novel, *The Delicate Dependency* (1982). His appearance was that of a beautiful young man with reddish gold curls and a pale angular face. In his human life, he was a contemporary of Leonardo da Vinci and in 1476 modeled for him. He was a model for da Vinci's "Madonna of the Rocks." He was also accused of having a homosexual relationship with the artist. During a festival, he met the ancient vampire **Lodovico** and was turned into a vampire. He was only 17 years old at the time.

In Talbot's novel, the process of becoming a vampire is not a matter of dying and returning so much as it is receiving a "virus." Thus, Niccolo possesses some of the traditional characteristics associated with vampires, but he lacks many, especially those associated with death and the supernatural. He has fangs and is cold to the touch. Under normal conditions he feeds infrequently, perhaps once or twice a week. He is not bothered by garlic or holy symbols. His image shows in mirrors. He is nocturnal, but he does not sleep in a coffin and has no need of native soil. If wounded, he heals relatively quickly. He does not turn into either animal forms or a mist.

Cavalanti is a member of a vast international vampire community that lives inconspicuously within the human community. As one of the older vampires, he spends time contemplating philosophical questions such as the nature of a universe that could produce a vampire. On a more mundane level, he also occasionally serves as an agent for a group known as The Illuminati. While working for that group, he travels to London in the 1890s and becomes involved in the life of research physician John Gladstone. Niccolo suffers an accident that causes Gladstone to admit him to the hospital, where he slowly reveals his vampire nature to the doctor. Gladstone whisks him away from the hospital before he can come to harm at the hands of a fearful staff. He takes the vampire to his home and allows him to recover there.

Gladstone is unaware that Niccolo is part of an elaborate plot by Lodovico to win Gladstone's cooperation with some of his long-term goals. To that end, Niccolo kidnaps Gladstone's young daughter and takes her to a location elsewhere in Europe. Gladstone's attempt to track Niccolo leads him to a climatic confrontation at Lodovico's Italian estate.

SOURCES:

Talbot, Michael. *The Delicate Dependency*. New York: Avon, 1982.

Cedrin

Cedrin, an extraterrestrial vampire who, like **Vampirella,** comes from Drakulon, appears in the 1977 short story "The Mad King of Drakulon," by Bill DuBay. The story was published in graphic art form in the comic magazine, *Vampirella*. The story begins when Vampirella, early on in her stay on Earth, is visited by a strange extraterrestrial named Starpatch, who offers her the opportunity to return to Drakulon aboard his starship. Curious, she agrees, and when she arrives, she meets Cedrin, who introduces himself as the sole remaining citizen of the devastated planet. Its once fertile surface was baked dry by one of the planet's suns as the sun died.

Cedrin had been a member of the planet's Eastern Seas Science Council at the time that the sun began to go nova. He conceived of a planet evacuation plan, but because there were no space transports to carry out the evacuation, an alternate plan was adopted. Scientists on Drakulon began contacting passing space ships with radio

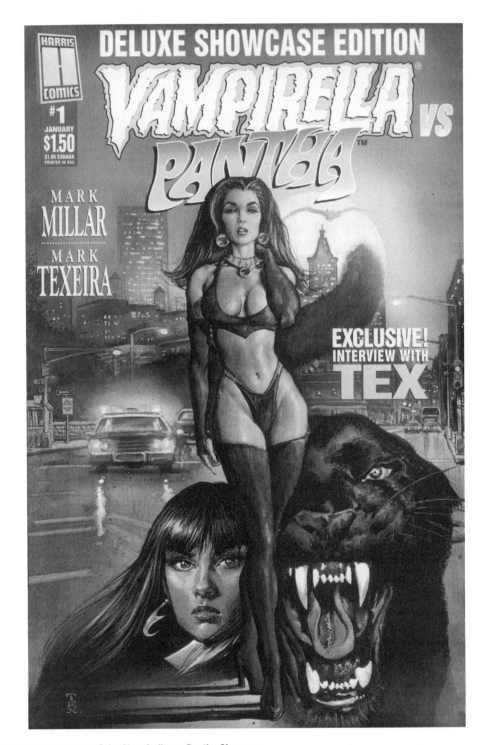

Shown here is the cover of the *Vampirella vs. Pantha Showcase*.

distress signals in hope that the ships would stop and rescue people. (Interesting side note: The signal was heard by NASA in the United States, which sent a space probe to the planet. The probe crashed on Drakulon, but it eventually served as the means via which Vampirella traveled to Earth.)

Cedrin takes his plan a step further by developing a "trap" for ships that he calls Starcatcher. The device harnesses the abundant magnetic energy of the universe to build a magnetic ring around Drakulon that pulls in any spacecraft passing the planet. He travels to the ring in his own ship to greet the other ships as they arrive, but he is unable to control his now insatiable thirst and drinks the blood of the first crew to arrive. By this point, the planet is beyond help anyway. As other ships arrive, he rescues any that survive their crash into the magnetic ring and sends the crew members off to a blood factory that he has created to process his victims. This ensures a continuous supply of blood. When Vampirella arrives, he hopes she will join with him in creating a new race of vampires.

Vampirella is tempted by his offer, but in the end, she decides that the price is too high. She turns down his offer and dismantles the blood factory. Cedrin is left behind as Starpatch tends to the surviving victims. Vampirella takes a quick tour of her planet before returning to face new dangers on Earth.

SOURCES:
DuBay, Bill and José Gonzales. "The Mad King of Drakulon." *Vampirella* No. 65. New York: Harris Comics, Dec. 1977. Reprinted in the: *Vampirella and the Blood Red Queen of Hearts*. New York: Harris Comics, 1996.

Chapman, Merrick

Merrick Chapman, a 900 year-old "vampire," first appears in Steven Spruill's novel, *Rulers of Darkness* (1995). Though most would think of him as a vampire, he defines himself as a "hemophage," human, but possessed of a unique gene. (Hemophage is simply author Spruill's term for his particular type of vampire.) The oldest hemophage is approximately 1,500 years old. Chapman has great strength and heals quickly from any wound, but he does not have any of the supernatural powers associated with traditional vampires (revulsion to religious symbols, ability to transform into an animal, etc.). His primary ability is that he can regulate the flow of blood in humans, which allows him to put a potential victim to sleep and take blood without either harming the person or making his activities known. Hemophages are nocturnal.

Because he does not age, Chapman is forced to move about frequently in his life. He tends to seek employment in law enforcement, first working as a law officer in Berkshire, England in 1680. In the 1880s, he worked on the metropolitan police force in London and had tracked the famous killer Jack the Ripper, who was a hemophage. At one point, 10 hemophages had united and tried to kill Chapman because he was a rogue who wouldn't follow tradition. He destroyed all but one whom he left to spread the word should others attempt it.

Through the years he had 16 lovers and fathered 43 children. Only one of the children, **Zane,** had become a hemophage. Some 500 years ago, when Zane was 12

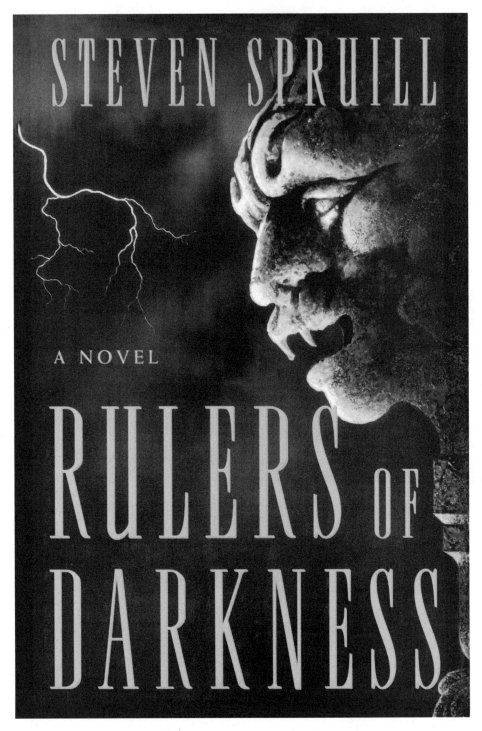

Cover art from Steven Spruill's novel *Rulers of Darkness*, which features Merrick Chapman.

years old, he developed leukemia. Chapman gave him some of his blood to save him. As a result, Zane became a hemophage.

Throughout the 20th century, Champman worked on a number of different police departments in different countries, most recently in San Francisco. In the late 1980s he moves to Washington, D.C., and, as the 1990s begin, is confronted with a serial killer. The first body is found next to a cathedral with all the blood drained. The case is even more puzzling because some of the victim's blood is smeared on a gargoyle high above the cathedral wall and because some blood found on the victim demonstrates some unusual properties. Chapman takes the case and has to track his own son while trying to conceal his life as a hemophage.

Chapman's adventures were continued in *Daughter of Darkness*.

SOURCES:

Spruill Steven. *Rulers of Darkness*. New York: St. Martin's Press, 1995.
————. *Daughter of Darkness*. New York: Doubleday, 1997.

Charlene

Charlene, the singing vampire, appears in the ultimate spoof of monster movies, *Saturday the 14th Strikes Back* (1988). Charlene is the first of a host of monsters to arrive out of a mist percolating through the floor of the basement of the Baxter house. She is a blonde whose body movements, dress, and hairstyle bear a faint resemblance to Marilyn Monroe. She, like her cousin Gregor who hangs around most of the time in his bat form, has prominent fangs. She makes her home in Eddie's room, and although he has a large family, only his mother is concerned. He learns that the mist is the means by which Charlene and other monsters come back in a new way to planet Earth.

Charlene often communicates in song, accompanied by additional vampires who join her to sing backup. She and the other monsters tell Eddie that a dark force is about to be released on the upcoming Saturday the 14th, which also happens to be his sixteenth birthday. On that day, astrological forces will align in a unique manner and as the energy builds, evil will erupt. Eddie has been selected as the new Master of the World. According to Charlene, Eddie really is one of them, and Eddie has to admit to himself that he likes the idea of being able to rise above his teenage powerlessness. Meanwhile, his familiar environment is disintegrating around him, as he confronts the fact that, even though powerful, he does not want to hurt anyone.

Finally, Eddie's grandfather comes to his assistance. Gramps turns out to be an ancient wizard, and Charlene (and her monster friends) are turned back and vanquished with the magical implement Eddie's grandfather assembles for him.

Chopin, Marguerite

Marguerite Chopin (portrayed by Harriet Gerard) is an elderly woman who is the main vampire in Carl T. Dreyer's film masterpiece, *Vampyr* (1932). Born in the village of Courtempierre in 1809, she had died there in 1867. She was buried in the local graveyard even though the church denied her the last rites because many people thought she was responsible for a vampire outbreak some years earlier when 11 people were killed. As a member of the undead, she appears in the movie as a heavy-set old woman with white hair. She walks with the aid of a cane.

As the movie opens, Chopin is on the prowl again and has chosen two young girls—Leoné and Giselle—as her next victims. The two girls are the daughters of a local resident named Bernard, who is aware that the vampire is stalking his daughters but is unsure how to stop her. Bernard enlists the help of a young man named David Gray who takes a room at the local inn. (Note: Dreyer filmed four versions of this film, and in some versions, David Gray is known as Nicolas.) He tells Gray of his suspicions and asks him to take action if he (Bernard) should die. Gray follows Bernard from his hotel and soon finds himself in a nightmarish, supernatural world seemingly created by Chopin. Things become even stranger when Bernard is shot and killed, leaving Gray to act, as he had promised he would. Gray and one of Bernard's servants begin to read a book on vampires that Bernard had left behind. From it they learn that vampires are the servants of Satan and are aided by the detached shadows of executed criminals (which appear to Gray throughout the film). Vampires rise at the full moon to attack their victims. They also try to drive their victims to commit suicide, since suicide victims can never enter God's presence in Heaven. Though Chopin never shows her fangs, she does leave two puncture wounds on the neck of her victims.

By the time Gray reads the book, Chopin has already attacked Leone, calling the young girl to her and feeding off of her. The bloodletting is interrupted by Gray, who volunteers to give Leoné a transplant. While he is giving blood, he has a horrible hallucination in which he imagines himself to be buried alive. Through a window in the coffin, he sees Chopin's face and realizes that the woman must be a vampire. After the hallucination, he awakens in the local cemetery. Gray gets one of Bernard's servants to assist him and travels to the cemetery where Chopin is buried. Together, the two men stake Chopin and end her reign of vampiric terror. It was easy for the two men to track her to the cemetery because they knew what she was and because they had the will to destroy her.

Vampyr was made just as sound was starting to be used in films. While remembered by movie historians as a memorable effort by a great cinematic artist and by vampire fans as an early classic, it had little commercial success. It was received as a silent film with occasional pieces of dialogue added. Emphasizing atmosphere over plot, it moved at a slow pace (compared, for example, to *Nosferatu* or *Dracula*) and had but slight influence upon the genre.

SOURCES:
Dreyer, Carl Theodore. *Four Screen Plays*. Translated by. Oliver Stallybrass. Bloomington: University of Indiana Press, 1970.

Clarimonde

Clarimonde, one of the earliest literary vampires, appears in Theophile Gautier's 1836 short story, "La Morte Amoureuse" ("The Beautiful Vampire"). Clarimonde is a notorious harlot in late eighteenth-century France. A young priest named Romauld, who does not know of Clarimonde's checkered past, sees her at his ordination and immediately falls in love with her. She is the most beautiful woman he has ever seen. She is tall, with golden hair, fair white skin, and green eyes. Her eyes are her most prominent feature, shining with a liquid brightness unlike anything Romauld had ever seen.

Though he does not see her after the ordination ceremony, Romauld is totally infatuated. Unfortunately, the next time he sees her is over a year later when he is asked to attend her in death. Her death proves false, however. As he leans over her "corpse" to leave her one last kiss, Romauld is startled when she responds to his touch—she is alive! He knows he cannot let anyone else know she is alive, so for the next few years, he leads a double life: priest by day, and Clarimonde's lover by night.

A short time after they begin this unusual relationship, the usually vivacious Clarimonde begins to appear sick and fatigued. Then one evening, Romauld cuts himself and she kisses his wound, drinking his blood. Immediately she feels better. It seems the key to her vitality is the priest's blood. Each night, she puts him to sleep and steals a few drops from him. Eventually, Romauld tires of his double life and he confesses to an older priest about what has been happening. Together they visit Clarimonde's grave and there they find her body, preserved as she was the day she died, with a drop of fresh blood on her lips. The older priest pours holy water on her and her body quickly turns to dust.

Clarimonde makes one last appearance. Her spirit visits Romauld the next evening to say good-bye to her lover. Romauld is left to his priestly life forever.

SOURCES:

"Clarimonde." Translated by Lefcadio Hearn. New York: Brentano's, 1899. Reprint, New York: R. M. McBride, 1927.

Gautier, Theophile. "La Morte Amoureuse." 1836.

Claudia

More than three years into his life as a vampire, **Louis de Pointe du Lac,** the vampire who tells his story in Anne Rice's *Interview with the Vampire,* has tried his best to avoid taking a human life. His high morals from his former life prevent him from thinking of humans as nothing more than food. He hates being a vampire and becomes despondent, even making a half-hearted attempt at suicide by refusing to drink the animal blood he survives on. He ponders his existence from a theological expression, wondering if he is damned for being a vampire. One night, while wandering the streets deep in thought, he encounters a five-year-old child sitting next to her dead mother and trying to get her to wake up. In that moment, his resolve breaks and his hunger overpowers him and he feeds from the little girl, whose name is Claudia. Louis's maker, **Lestat de Lioncourt,** watches Louis drink from the small child and almost laughs at the internal conflict he feels over taking human life. Louis drinks enough to satisfy his hunger but does not kill Claudia or turn her into a vampire.

Claudia is found on the street and taken to a hospital. The next evening, Lestat finds her there and brings her to the hotel where he and Louis are staying. Louis

Kirsten Dunst played the innocent-yet-deadly child vampire Claudia to perfection in the film version of *Interview with the Vampire.*

drinks from her again, and then Lestat takes over and makes her a vampire. Lestat announces that Claudia is now their child, but in reality, Louis adopts her and they become as brother and sister in the years ahead. Louis describes her as his only companion in immortality and for many years they sleep together in the same coffin.

As time passes, Claudia remains a child. Louis and Lestat always see her that way. They dress her as a child and bring her dolls and other things that are appropriate for children. Claudia learns to use her appearance as a child in her hunting and feeding. She appears on the street as a needy child and then turns on the people who are kind enough to take her in. Like Lestat, she cruelly toys with her food.

Claudia is trapped forever in the body of a five-year-old, but she matures mentally. Louis provides her education and begins to read deep works of philosophy to her. She also delves into the study of witchcraft and the occult. Finally, Claudia grows to resent being stuck in the body of a child so much that she forces Louis to tell her the story of her origin. She demands to know who had turned her into a vampire.

From Louis, then she learns that it was Lestat who had actually made her. She decides to kill Lestat and poisons him with absinthe and persuades Louis to help her dispose of his body in a swamp. She then proposes that she and Louis travel to central Europe, where vampires are more common, meaning it might be easier for them to learn more about their condition. However, before they can leave, Lestat returns from his swampy grave. Acting in haste, Louis sets Lestat and their residence on fire and he and Claudia immediately depart for the ship that will take them to Europe. They first visit Transylvania, which is a disappointment, then travel to Paris.

In Paris they make contact with a group known as the **Theatre des Vampires,** which is a group of vampires playing humans playing vampires. Claudia senses danger from the other vampires should they discover that she killed Lestat. She also senses that Louis is drawn to **Armand,** one of the Parisian vampires, and would leave her if he beckoned. While she can do little about the former, she turns to Madeleine, a doll-maker, to ease her loneliness and demands that Louis make her a vampire. After much pleading, he consents.

The pleasure of her new life with Madeleine is short-lived. Lestat arrives in Paris and tells the other vampires how Claudia tried to kill him. They decide that she must die and move against her. It should be noted here that this part of the plot in the book is carried out in a different sequence in the film *Interview with the Vampire*. In the end, however, Claudia and Madeleine are placed in an open air shaft and allowed to burn as the rays of the morning sun overtake them.

Having been killed in the first volume of the *Vampire Chronicles*, Claudia does not reappear in the later volumes except in a passing vision of Lestat's in *Tale of the Body Thief* (1992).

SOURCES:

Ramsland, Katherine. *The Vampire Companion: The Official Guide to Anne Rice's The Vampire Chronicles.* New York: Ballantine Books, 1993.

Rice, Anne. *Interview with the Vampire.* New York: Alfred A. Knopf, 1976. Reprint, New York: Ballantine, 1979.

Clemens, Atta Olivia

Atta Olivia Clemens, the friend of the ancient vampire **St. Germain,** makes her initial appearance in Chelsea Quinn Yarbro's 1979 novel *Blood Games.* Clemens was born in Rome and grows up during the reign of the Emperor Nero. At the age of 20, with her family in debt, she is forced to marry Cornelius Justus Silius, an ambitious man very much her senior who hopes to one day be emperor. She is his third wife. Silius is a sadistic man who gains pleasure by watching his wife be raped and brutalized by gladiators. Olivia is forced to bear her situation in silence as Justus threatens to harm her family if she refuses.

St. Germain befriends her and secretly becomes her lover, though their affair is difficult to keep secret as the years pass. As a vampire, St. Germain cannot have normal intercourse but he does have oral sex that includes drinking a small amount of Olivia's blood. Over a five-year period, Olivia and St. Germain meet on 30 different occasions, more than enough to ensure that Olivia will become a vampire unless her spine is severed or damaged. St. Germain begins to instruct her on the changes that will occur when the change is complete. She will need to stay close to her native soil,

Atta Olivia Clemens had received St. Germain's darkest gift – would his love save her from the True Death?

Chelsea Quinn Yarbro

A Flame in Byzantium

US/52804-2 • $4.50
CAN/52805-0 • $5.50

Cover art from Chelsea Quinn Yarbro's novel *A Flame in Byzantium*, which features Atta Olivia Clemens.

which is easily accomplished by placing some of the soil in special shoes that have hollow heels. She will no longer need food and drink but will need to take blood every two weeks, mostly from a regular group of willing donors. She will have little need for sleep and will gain a great deal of strength, although not a superhuman amount. Unlike St. Germain, she will be able to enjoy normal sexual intercourse.

Eventually, Silius withdraws his protection of her family; her father and brothers are then killed and the family's possessions are confiscated. After Olivia learns that her mother has also died, she becomes emboldened and publicly opposes her husband, revealing the crimes he has committed. Unfortunately, he has anticipated her move and set plans in motion that will have her tried and condemned for various crimes, freeing him to take a fourth wife who will put him in line to assume the throne. Instead of being vindicated, Olivia is instead sentenced to be buried alive. Fortunately for her, her tomb is guarded for only three days and St. Germain rescues her. Unfortunately, they are not able to stay together for long because St. Germain has been ordered to leave Rome. Olivia remains in Rome and is finally vindicated when her ex-husband is exposed as the criminal he is and is cruelly executed.

She remains in Rome for some time, living quietly, but during the time of the Emperor Justinian she moves to Constantinople. Her further adventures are chronicled in a set of Yarbro novels, including *A Flame in Byzantium* (1987), *Crusader's Torch* (1988), and *A Candle for d'Artagnan* (1989). Olivia initially prospers in Constantinople, but she encounters trouble and is almost killed when she is sentenced to be punished by being thrown into the sea in a sack. She manages to escape the sack and is rescued by Niklos, one of her servants. She moves eastward and lives in Tyre in the Holy Land in the twelfth century as Islamic forces move west during the time of the Crusades. She makes her way back to Rome and by A.D. 1214 has settled again in St. Germain's old house. There she remains until Papal politics force her north to France in the seventeenth century. During the politically intriguing time of Cardinal Richelieu, she develops a relationship with the famous Musketeer d'Artagnan. That is the last that readers have seen of Olivia.

SOURCES:

Yarbro. Chelsea. *Blood Games*. New York: St. Martin's Press, 1979. Reprint, New York: Tor Books, 1989.

———. *A Candle for D'Artagnan*. New York: Tor Books, 1989.

———. *Crusader's Torch*. New York: Tor Books, 1988.

———. *A Flame in Byzantium*. New York: Tor Books, 1987. Reprint, New York: Tor Books, 1987.

Coker, Tom

Tom Coker, the muscular vampire created by Raphael Nieves, was introduced in the comic book mini-series *Cold Blooded*. Coker is a strong young man with a long dark hair, and he has a prominent tattoo of a Chinese beast at the base of his neck. As a young man, he adopts a life of freedom, traveling around the country as a hobo with his diminutive friend, Jerome Walsh, who keeps a journal of their travels. In 1921, they find themselves in Rotgut, Texas.

Hungry, Coker and Walsh are caught while trying to steal a chicken. Alexandro Garcia de la Pena, the owner of the chickens, is actually quite friendly to the pair and invites them to stay for a few days and work for their keep. Three days later, they are invited to a small party at de la Pena's home. Coker and Walsh are surprised to learn that de la Pena and the rest of his guests are vampires who intend to feed on the fresh blood the pair have to offer. de la Pena is actually an ancient vampire who traveled to the New World with Hernando Cortez. He feasted on the crew of the ship that brought him to America and for a period was hailed as a deity by a tribe of Central American people.

In the ensuing chaos at de la Pena's home, Walsh manages to fend off a female vampire with a crucifix. He then finds de la Pena feeding at Coker's neck. He fights off de la Pena, but Coker knows he has been infected by the vampire and begs Walsh to shoot and kill him, which he does. Walsh buries his friend and leaves town. Several days later, an angry Tom Coker, now very much a vampire, catches up with Walsh and demands to know why his friend left him behind.

Coker and Walsh manage to patch up their differences and resume their friendship, but only after Coker feeds off Walsh. In the 1970s, Walsh's brash nephew finds his uncle's journal and publishes it as a mass-market paperback called *The Vagabond Vampire*. Walsh hates his nephew for this betrayal, although he likes his nephew's daughter, Celia. It seems that the nephew and his wife have mistreated Celia, and she hates them as much as Walsh does. Stirred both by Walsh's resentment and Celia's anger, Coker kills the nephew and his wife and Walsh became Celia's guardian. Now that Celia is grown, he watches over her.

Coker is a nocturnal being. He enjoys the fear his victims feel because it adds spice to the taste of their blood. He is an alienated individual with a narrow range of emotions. Apart from Walsh and Celia, he thinks of humans as little more than cattle and moves through human society as an absurd chaotic force. He also has a short temper, and will brutally kill anyone who happens to be in his way when his hunger needs to be satiated.

SOURCES:

Nieves, Raphael, and Kyle Hotz. *Cold Blooded*. No. 1-3. Chicago: Arpad Publishing, 1993.

Nieves, Raphael, and Frank Gomez. *Cold Blooded: The Burning Kiss*. Chicago: Arpad Publishing, 1993.

Nieves, Raphael and Vincent Price. *Cold Blooded: The Slayer*. Chicago: Arpad Publishing, 1993.

Collins, Barnabas

In 1967, Barnabas Collins, the vampire character created by producer/director Dan Curtis and played by actor Jonathan Frid, is introduced into the story line of the failing daytime television soap opera *Dark Shadows*. He becomes the show's central character and saves it from early cancellation from ABC's afternoon schedule. As the show eventually reveals (beginning with episode 366), Barnabas is the son of Joshua Collins and nephew of wealthy family patriarch Jeremiah Collins in New England during the 1780s. At that time, the Collins family is hosting Andre du Prés and his daughter Josette (portrayed by Kathryn Leigh Scott), Barnabas's fiancée,

DAN CURTIS: LIVING IN THE SHADOW OF A VAMPIRE

While some people have a monkey on their back, producer-director Dan Curtis has a vampire. His name is Barnabas Collins. In the mid 1960s, the award winning Curtis had an idea for a daytime soap opera with a gothic twist. Thus, the New England adventures of the Collins family and governess Victoria Winters were born.

Dark Shadows went on the air on June 27, 1966. However, the show was plagued by low ratings so Curtis began experimenting with supernatural elements. Then in the winter of 1966–67, he added a vampire, the 200-year-old Barnabas Collins, who made his first appearance in April 1967. *Dark Shadows* went from a show about to be canceled to a hit. The show ran into 1971, had two movie spinoffs, and led to two further Curtis made-for-television vampire productions, *The*

Night Stalker (which led to a series) and a version of *Dracula* starring Jack Palance.

However by the end of the 1970s, Curtis had put horror and vampires behind him and gone mainstream. He spent the 1980s making made-for-television movies, including the successful *The Winds of War* (1983) and its sequel, *War and Remembrance* (1988-89), based on the books of Herman Wouk. Now he could get Barnabas Collins off his back.

However, the fans of *Dark Shadows* refused to go away and continued to beg for the show. Curtis did not (and still does not) want to be remembered for his vampire series, but finally relented in 1990 and sold a new, prime time *Dark Shadows* series to NBC. The series aired just as the Gulf War began and had trouble competing with its compelling images. The series died but not *Dark Shadows*, and not the calls he receives to remake the show again. Vampire fans hope he gives it another go.

who have arrived from their plantation in Martinique for the wedding of Josette and Barnabas. Josette is accompanied by her maid, **Angélique Bouchard** (Lara Parker), who is also a witch. Angélique, in her desire for everything her employers possess makes moves on Barnabas, but he refuses her advances. Angélique then turns on Josette, and through her witchcraft causes Josette to marry Barnabas's Uncle Jeremiah. Barnabas kills Jeremiah in a duel.

Eventually, Barnabas is tricked into marrying Angélique, but when he discovers her occult actions, he shoots her. Believing that she is dying, Angélique curses Barnabas with words that set the course of his future: "I set a curse on you, Barnabas Collins. You will never rest. And you will never be able to love. Whoever loves you will die. That is my curse, and you will live with it through all eternity." As her words die out, a vampire bat flies into the room and heads straight for Barnabas's throat. He dies from the attack only to arise as a vampire. He decides that Josette should join him in his vampiric existence, and begins to drain her of her blood. Before he can finish the transformation, however, Angélique's spirit lures Josette to a cliff where she falls to her death. Joshua Collins, having learned of his son's condition, locks and chains Barnabas in a secret room in the family mausoleum to stop the plague of his vampiric attacks.

Barnabas's background thus explains his initial appearance in episode 210. Collins's employee Willie Loomis, looking for a hidden treasure, discovers the secret room in the nearby mausoleum that contains the coffin in which Barnabas has been secured. Not realizing what he was doing, Willie releases Barnabas from his prison of

As vampire Barnabas Collins, Jonathan Frid brought a touch of evil to daytime television in 1967 on the gothic soap opera *Dark Shadows*.

many decades. Soon afterward, Barnabas presents himself at the door of Collinwood, the family estate, as the family's long-lost English cousin. He receives permission to take up residence in the Old House, the former family manor. But he needs blood and soon discovers Maggie Evans, (Kathryn Leigh Scott) who is the very image of Josette, his lost love. Barnabas vampirizes her in an attempt to bring her into his world. Barnabas's attacks upon Maggie lead to his meeting with Dr. Julia Hoffman (Grayson Hall), a blood specialist. Brought in to deal with Maggie's illness, she discovers Barnabas's nature. Rather than destroy him, she falls in love, and her infatuation leads her to develop an experimental serum to cure him.

Barnabas is in many ways a traditional vampire. He needs a regular injection of blood, which he obtains by biting the necks of his victims, preferably young females. He has prominent fangs and an aversion to sunlight and garlic. He is vulnerable to the stake and to decapitation. However, he possesses a history and a complex, even sympathetic, personality. Along with his blood lust, he has a moral sensitivity, an ability to show great passion and love, and is a victim of great suffering. In Angélique he has an enemy who keeps returning in various guises to thwart his plans for happiness. Barnabas is thus something very new to the vampire genre, and the television audiences of the time were most responsive. His adventures would continue for almost 800 more *Dark Shadows* episodes. In 1970, *Dark Shadows* creator/producer Curtis featured Barnabas in a full-length movie, *House of Dark Shadows*. (Barnabas died at the end, and thus he did not appear in the 1971 follow-up, *Night of Dark Shadows*).

In 1966, concurrently with initiation of the original television series, romance story writer Marilyn Ross (pseudonym of Daniel Ross) completed the first of thirty-three *Dark Shadows* novels. Although based upon the television series, beginning with the sixth volume, Ross leads Collins into a series of completely new adventures. The first issue of a comic book called *Dark Shadows* (from Gold Key), yields even further stories, as did a brief newspaper comic series (recently reprinted in book format). Barnabas inspired a wide variety of products, including a *Dark Shadows* board game, trading cards, Halloween costumes, jig-saw puzzles, and several model kits.

Over the decades, Barnabas and *Dark Shadows* has been kept alive by thousands of fans. In 1990, as the broad revival in interest was only beginning to manifest, Barnabas was given new life when NBC launched a prime time version of *Dark Shadows*. The early episodes covered the basic story line of the emergence of Barnabas Collins (portrayed by Ben Cross). However, the new series had to compete with coverage of the Gulf War and was canceled after only thirteen episodes. The new series did inspire a new set of Barnabas memorabilia and a new comic book that again extended Barnabas's adventures.

Collins is only the second modern vampire to gain a wide public following. Though there is little likelihood that a new *Dark Shadows* series will come to television, the continuation of *Dark Shadows* fan conventions and publications suggests that interest in Barnabas will remain for many years.

SOURCES:

Dark Shadows: The Comic Strip Book. Los Angeles: Pomegranate Press, 1996.

Scott, Kathryn Leigh. *The Dark Shadows Companion: Twenty-fifth Anniversary Collection*. New York: Pomegranate Press, 1990.

Stockel, Shirley, and Victoria Weidner. *A Guide to Collecting* Dark Shadows *Memorabilia*. Florissant, Mo.: Collinwood Chronicle, 1992.

Cortland, Ben

Ben Cortland is the vampire featured in Richard Matheson's cutting edge novel, *I Am Legend* (1954). Building upon the atomic paranoia of the decade, Matheson set his story in a postapocalyptic society some time in the early 1970s. Cortland is a typical suburbanite. His wife Freda is killed in the war and he is infected by a bacteria that creates an isotonic solution in the blood. The bacteria needs fresh blood to survive in the host body; without it, the bacteria will leave the old host and seek a new one. The old host's body will then rapidly decompose. The bacteria can be killed by garlic and solar radiation, which forces the host to sleep during the day and only come out after sunset. The bacteria causes canine teeth to grow and turns the host's flesh a grayish-white color.

Cortland, and other vampires like him, are extremely difficult to kill. He has survived numerous assaults and accidents, including gunshot wounds, knife wounds,

Ben Cross, shown here as Barnabas Collins in the 1990 version of *Dark Shadows*.

being hit by a car, and being crushed by a collapsed chimney. The bacteria creates a healing solution, almost glue-like in texture, that seals wounds quickly. A vampire can only be killed when a wound is kept open, which causes the bacteria to turn into a parasite that attacks its host. Thus a stake is the most effective weapon against vampires like Cortland.

The vampires face a problem because fresh blood is becoming scarce. The pudgy, bearded, dark-haired Cortland has located his own supply of fresh blood in the person of Robert Neville, who is not infected with the bacteria. Neville lives behind a barricade designed to keep Cortland out, but each night the vampire tries to lure him out into the open or attempts to make it past the barricade. After many evenings spent in this way, Cortland is attacked by a small group of humans who have developed a vaccine against the vampire germ. They literally cut Cortland apart with rifle and machine gun fire.

Since its appearance as a paperback novel, *I Am Legend* had been reprinted on numerous occasions, including a graphic art edition. It has also inspired two films: *Last Man on Earth* (1964), in which Giacomo Rosssi-Stuart portrayed Cortland; and *The Omega Man* (1971), in which the vampiric elements had been largely deleted. Anthony Zerbe portrayed the Cortland character, renamed Matthias.

SOURCES:

Matheson, Richard. *I Am Legend*. New York: Fawcett, 1954. Reprint, New York: Berkley, 1971.
Matheson, Richard, Elman Brown, and Steve Niles. *I Am Legend*. No. 1-4. Eclipse, 1991.

The Countess

The Countess (portrayed by Lauren Hutton), is the villainess in the comedy *Once Bitten* (1985). The 400-year-old vampire lives in a mansion in Hollywood, along with a personal servant and a group of minions. They are all nocturnal and sleep in more-or-less elaborate coffins. She is a somewhat traditional vampire, exposing fangs and long fingernails. She shows no reflection in mirrors. She is not repulsed by a cross (professing to be an atheist), but can be held at bay by fire. She has an aesthetic sense, especially enjoying the black roses she grows.

In the mid-1980s, she moves to Hollywood, where she (as *Andy Warhol's Dracula* before her) searches for a virgin. It is the week before Halloween and during the next seven days she must find such an individual and drink three times from him. That evening she goes to a Hollywood single's bar where she meets Mark Kendall (portrayed by Jim Carrey). Basically out of his environment, he has come to town out of his frustration with his girlfriend Robin who has refused him sex. Delighted with his youthful naivete, the Countess takes Mark home with her and proceeds to have her way with him. She bites him at a point near his artery on his inner thigh.

Mark remembers nothing of the evening, but begins to change. The next day, he orders a raw hamburger, takes a nap in his large trunk, turns pale, and beings to wear sunglasses. He dreams of the Countess.

Needing him again three days later, the Countess locates Mark in a clothing store while he is trying on a new pair of "black" pants. Although Robin is present

Before he was famous, Jim Carrey (right) was little more than a snack for the Countess in the comedy *Once Bitten*.

(she works in the store), the Countess succeeds in biting the virginal Mark again and getting away without Robin being aware of what has occurred. However, the Countess now sees Robin as significant competition. As she observes, "She's young, sweet, and she's pissing me off."

Several days later, on Halloween, the Countess shows up at the school costume party. By this time, Robin has figured out that the Countess, not Mark, is the real problem and that her attacks are responsible for Mark's weird behavior. To lure Mark to her estate for the final feeding, the Countess kidnaps Robin. When he arrives with friends in tow to rescue Robin, the Countess takes them prisoner and anticipates her third bite. Escaping momentarily, Robin and Mark are finally cornered in the coffin room. Robin, however, has come up with a solution. In the few seconds allotted to them, she ends Mark's virginity.

Midnight arrives. The Countess has lost her virgin and almost immediately loses her beauty and youthful appearance. Of no use to her, she leaves the young lovers with the assurance from her minions that there are other virgins in the world and that they will, somehow, somewhere, locate them and restore her.

Crainic, Anton

Anton Crainic (portrayed by Anthony Perkins) is a Transylvanian vampire being sought by Cathy Thatcher, his American daughter, in the 1989 made-for-television movie *Daughter of Darkness* (1989). Previously known as Constantine Cyprian, he is the last prince of an old Transylvanian family, the Cyprians. The public life of the family ended in the eighteenth century when its remaining members became vampires. Their castle was abandoned and they went underground. At a later time, a statue of Cyprian in a monk's hood was erected on the grounds of the well-preserved castle that in the twentieth century has become a tourist attraction.

Through the twentieth century, Cyprian and the family members have lived quietly in Bucharest, making allies with people who assist them with the hope of becoming immortal. They have devised a scheme to kidnap people and milk them over a period of time rather than trying to attack a new victim each evening. As the Ceausescu government with its extensive spy system permeates the society, the vampires have to change their identities frequently.

The story reveals the history of Crainic's daughter and the reason for her search. In the 1970s, Cyprian was known as Paul Alecsandri, a working man in Bucharest. He met a young American woman and unexpectedly impregnated her. Having been targeted by the secret police, he abandoned her shortly before the child was born and she returned to the United States to raise her daughter Cathy. When the woman died in 1976 her daughter decided to come to Romania to look for her father. Meanwhile, Alecsandri arranged for a hit-and-run accident and hasty pronouncement of his death. It was no problem to substitute a body for his, and a tombstone with his name on it was erected over his grave. He then assumed a new identity as Paul Crainic, a glass blower. He worked at his job in the evening.

As Cathy searches for her father, she finds Bucharest landmarks that had appeared in her dreams. She had seen the statue of the Cyprian castle, the graveyard with her father's tombstone, and the entrance to the glass-blowing shop. She finally makes contact with Crainic by first visiting the only address she has, a nightclub run by the vampires, and then by ferreting out the glass-blowing shop. Below the nightclub, the vampires keep a number of their victims confined.

As Thatcher discovers the truth about her family, Crainic is placed in an awkward position. Although he is the senior member of the vampires and their former prince, he recognizes that Cathy has become their hope for a future. Dying out, spending their life huddled in Bucharest cellars hiding from the light, the vampires want one of their number to impregnate Cathy with the hopes of her bearing a child vampire. Although Crainic recognizes the desire in his family, he wants to protect his daughter from them.

As the climax builds, the group of vampires accuse Crainic of being a traitor to the community. He is taken prisoner and placed in a room where over the next day the light would slowly burn him up. His daughter finally finds him and tries to free him while the other vampires are still asleep. She also brings kerosene to burn them out once she leaves with Crainic.

Anthony Perkins as Transylvanian vampire Anton Crainic in the made-for-television movie *Daughter of Darkness.*

The two cannot depart without a final confrontation with the vampire clan. They fight their way through the now-ablaze crowd, but one vampire makes it to the street. In his weakened condition from a day in the sun, Crainic's only option is to grab him and pull him into the flames. He kills the last vampire but commits suicide in the process. As the film closes, Cathy has lost her father, but not without meeting him and finding out the truth about her origin. She is now free, both physically and emotionally, to live the rest of her life.

Crosby, Linda

Linda Crosby, a contemporary teenage vampire, is featured in the comic book *Sweetmeats* written by Steve Tanner and Pete Venters. Crosby's life gets off to a difficult start when her mother dies while giving birth to her via caesarean section. Doctors are surprised to find that the mother's cause of death is internal lacerations, cause unknown. As Linda grows older, she experiences fainting spells and develops a rash if exposed to daylight. Abandoned by her father, she eventually winds up in a house of prostitution where clients pay huge sums of money to be with a child.

Among the first men to visit six-year-old Linda is a pedophile who happens to be a vampire. Before he can feed on her, however, she viciously kills him. As a result, she is placed in the isolation ward at a psychiatric hospital, where she stays for the next decade. Soon after she arrives at the hospital, an orderly (who is also a pedophile) tries to have sex with her and is killed the same way the man at the bordello was. From that time one, the staff at the hospital kept their distance and treated her with great caution.

When Linda is 16, a female physician named Dr. Page joins the staff. She takes an interest in Linda's case and begins to interview her on a regular basis. In the process, she reads through Linda's entire file and learns that it was really Linda's father who visited her at the bordello and was killed. Dr. Koenig, the director of the hospital, eventually becomes upset with Dr. Page because of the amount of time she is spending with Linda and pulls her from the case. He then tries to rape Linda himself with the usual results—he ends up dead.

Page is named acting director of the hospital. She realizes that Linda is a vampire. More importantly, she realizes that her earlier sympathy for the girl has turned into love. Linda feels the same way, easily ripping apart her the straightjacket in which she has been confined so that the two of them can physically express their love for each other. Dr. Page helps Linda finally escape the mental hospital by declaring her cured and releasing her.

SOURCES:
Tanner, Steve, and Pete Venters. *Sweetmeats*. Tundra Publishing, 1993. Reprinted in *Badblood*. New York: Heavy Metal Magazine/Metal Mammouth Inc., 1993.

Croydon, Charles

Charles Croydon, also known as Caleb Croft and Adrian Lockwood, is the primary vampire in the 1972 movie, *Grave of the Vampire*. Croydon was an English nobleman who became a vampire during the seventeenth century. Along with his wife Sarah, he migrates to America. There, he and Sarah are accused of being vampires after a number of murders were committed in New Salem, Massachusetts. Sarah was executed as a vampire in 1846, while Charles managed to escape and disappear from sight.

He is a fairly traditional vampire. He is a nocturnal being, although he does not necessarily need to sleep in a coffin. He has a set of fangs. He is a particularly violent vampire, frequently raping his victims and inflicting a fatal wound before he bites them.

After staying out of sight for a long period of time, he reappears in the twentieth century as Caleb Croft, a rapist and serial killer in Boston in the late 1930s. After one attack, he is trying to escape when he slips and falls onto the third rail of the mass transit track and is electrocuted. Pronounced dead, his body is shipped to California and placed in a crypt. After his "death," a book called *Mysteries of New England* is published that links the historic crimes of Charles Croydon to the modern crimes of Caleb Croft.

Three years after the Boston incident, Croft emerges from his crypt and begins a new rape and killing spree. Croft's first California victims are a couple who has parked next to the graveyard that held his crypt. He kills the man and drags the woman into an open grave and assaults her. She becomes pregnant after the rape and gives birth to a son. The baby refuses to nurse but does drink his mother's blood (thus surviving to manhood). Croft also brutally killed the policeman investigating the case.

Croft drops out of sight again after the rape. For the next two decades, he travels the country, changing locations frequently. At many of his stops, he takes a position as a college professor of folklore. At one of his teaching stops, he assumes the name Adrian Lockwood. One of his female students has read *Mysteries of New England* and makes the connection that Lockwood is really Croydon/Croft. She is fascinated by vampires and begs Lockwood to turn her into a creature of the night. Instead, he simply kills the naive young woman.

Soon after he kills the woman, he is visited by James Eastman, his son from the brutal rape committed years ago. Eastman has actually managed to live a fairly normal life—he is not a vampire, but his diet does consist of almost nothing but raw meat. He has been hunting his father for years and has craved a confrontation with him. When he finally finds him, he kills him with a stake to the heart. He pays a high price for his action, however, for as soon as his father is dead, James grows fangs and completes his transformation into a full-blown vampire.

Cutter, Valentine

Valentine Cutter, a 90-year-old vampire trapped in the abandoned subway tunnels below New York City, is the antagonist in J. R. Black's *The Undead Express* (1994). He is a rather traditional vampire with prominent fangs, vulnerable to the same dangers as other vampires, especially the sunlight. The story reveals Cutter had been a wealthy financier who made millions in the railroads. He had lived on 5th Avenue in New York at the beginning of twentieth century when, fascinated with the idea of an underground railroad, he invested in the new subway system for New York. In 1905, at a triumphal party for the opening of the subway, he encountered Barnabas, a thousand-year-old vampire who had found his way to New York. Cutter never returned to the surface.

Over the years, people wandered into the now-abandoned sections of the subway and became Cutter's victims. He turned some into vampires and became the leader of a cadre of the undead who survived off of rats and other small animals between the arrival of the human strays from above. The group was headquartered on an abandoned subway car, dubbed the Undead Express. Cutter's creator, not content with being trapped in the subway, at one point tried to climb out of the subway. He was killed in the sunlight.

Flash forward to the mid-1990s, when sixth-grader Zachery Kinkaid accidentally finds his way into that part of the subway inhabited by the vampires. He meets Cutter, who introduces him to the vampire world. Since he is the oldest vampire in the group, he can protect Zach from them. They develop a relationship and Cutter confides that he really does not like human blood at all, but prefers small animals. Zach takes Cutter for a walk around Manhattan in the middle of the night, and the philosophical vampire shares with Zach his basic premise, never trust anyone.

Later, Zach's best friend, Gabrielle, ventures into the subway to take pictures. Zach and his buddy J. R. go after her, sensing danger if she encounters the vampires. When they find her, she is already the vampires' prisoner, and they learn that Cutter has lied to him. Now ready to vampirize Zach, he has a proposition that might save the lives of the three. He proposes Zach throw the switch that will allow their subway car to enter the main subway lines currently in use, allowing them to attack people throughout the system. For some reason, none of the vampires can reach the switch, only a mortal can.

At Gabe's suggestion, Zach acquiesces and chooses line six. Everyone gets aboard the Undead Express and within seconds the vampires are free, speeding through the subway tunnels on their first ride. Then, just as suddenly they are plunged into the sunlight as the train emerges aboveground. Amid howls and screams, the vampires disintegrate in the rays of the sun. Cutter is the last to go. He makes no sounds of anger or protest, but quietly accepts his fate. There is even some hint that he has at last found a welcome release from his undead existence. Fortunately, for the three kids, the car comes to rest at a station before it crashes into another train.

Published as part of the Shadow Zone series of young adult novels, *The Undead Express* became a made-for-television movie in 1997.

SOURCES:

Black, J. R. *The Undead Express*. New York: Random House, 1994.

Czakyr

Czakyr is an ancient vampire who comes to the United States during the 1990s to escape the threatened extinction of his kind in Europe and who takes over the typical midwestern community of Allburg, U.S.A., in the 1992 film *Children of the Night*. Czakyr is a repulsive creature, reminiscent of **Graf Orlock** (*Nosferatu*, 1922), with pale white skin and a rat-like appearance. He has long, white hair, pointed ears, and prominent fangs. He talks infrequently, preferring to announce his presence with a snarl.

After arriving in America, Czakyr settles in to the flooded crypt of an abandoned church in Allburg. He captures a number of the town's children, brings them to his lair, and places them in suspended animation as a constant food supply. Not satisfied, he soon extends his dominion to include the entire town and calls his minions the children of the night. In the process Czakyr attracts several potent foes: Mark Gardner, a schoolteacher; Lucy, a high-school student, whose grandmother Czakyr has turned into a vampire; Cindy, Lucy's friend who has become a vampire; and Matty, the town drunk.

As the children of the night run wild, Lucy and Cindy go to the church to kill Czakyr by staking him in the heart. Simultaneously, Mark and Matty attack the hoard of vampires. The girls are no match for the ancient monster and are soon captured. Lucy escapes Czakyr's clutches temporarily by placing her cross necklace in his mouth. As he reacts to the burn, she slips from his arms. Mark arrives and is about to be dispatched, when Matty crashes into the wall of the church with his car. Atop the car is a cross illuminated with many lights. Czakyr burns in the light of the cross. His death frees all those who had been turned into vampires by his bite, and the next day they return to their normal human state, as if their brief vampiric careers had been a bad dream.

Czerner, Countess

The Countess Czerner, whose existence as a vampire is disclosed in the pages of the 1940s gothic novel *Dreadful Hollow*, is born to Count Czerner, a member of the Transylvanian nobility, and Magda, a lowly Gypsy woman. Magda is a dark-haired beauty, but also a vampire, who is eventually tracked and killed (by beheading and staking) by the local residents. Unfortunately, the female offspring of her family are carriers of the vampire blood taint, which she has passed to her daughter, Vera, and her granddaughter, Ana.

Countess Ana moves to rural England in the 1930s and, as World War II begins, resides in the Grange, an isolated mansion near the town of Tracy Meade Junction. Her youthful companion, Jillian Dale, finds her to retain the dark gypsy features of her grandmother. The aging Ana has black hair and eyes and long claw-like hands that set off her pale skin. In spite of her age, she has a noticeably prominent and perfect set of teeth.

Shortly after Jillian's arrival, a child from the village disappears without a trace. Almost immediately afterward, Jillian is denied access to the countess, and two guests arrive: Vera, the young "daughter" of the countess, and a Doctor Vostok, a physician from the countess's homeland. Vera appears as a younger version of the countess with the same hair, eyes, and teeth. Jillian notices that both women appear only after sunset but never at the same time. She also notices that the new countess wears Countess Ana's very distinctive earrings.

As the investigation of the boy's disappearance continues, it becomes evident that the two countesses are in fact the same person, the aging countess having been rejuvenated by the drinking of the missing boy's blood. Eventually, the boy's body is found, the Grange is destroyed by fire, and the countess is decapitated by her maid when the vampire countess attempts to feed off Jillian.

SOURCES:

Karlova, Irina. *Dreadful Hollow*. New York: Paperback Library, 1942.

Czuczron, Baron Lajos

Baron Lajos Czuczron, a Hungarian vampire of undetermined age, appears in Seabury Quinn's 1927 short story, "The Man Who Casts No Shadow." The baron is a tall, distinguished gentleman with swarthy skin, black hair, gray eyes, and a bushy mustache under a large nose. His most prominent feature, however, was a scar on his left cheek that ended where a white streak started through his hair. Little is known of the baron's background, except that he fought with the Serbians in 1913 during a war with the Turks. It is noted that he was a brave man in battle. On one occasion, after emptying his gun of bullets, he continued fighting hand to hand and bit one of the Turks, taking a chunk of flesh from his neck.

While his actual age is undetermined, he is at least 600 years old and is believed to be the product of a woman and her demon lover. He is rich, and, among Hungarians, has a reputation for cruelty. It is rumored that every hundred years he begins to show his age. As the hundredth anniversary of his becoming a vampire approaches, he needs the blood of a virgin, or he will simply drop dead. Otherwise, he is able to lead a rather normal life. Quinn's private-detective hero, Jules de Grandin, meets Czuczron at a reception in the 1920s. The Hungarian aristocrat is introduced to de Grandin as Count Czerny. de Grandin becomes suspicious when he shakes the count's hand and notices that the count has no palms, both sides of his hand being covered with hair. The detective also notices that when the count passes a mirror, he shows no reflection. He begins inquiries and finds a file on the Baron Czuczron.

Czuczron kidnaps the daughter of Mrs. Norman, hostess of the reception at which de Grandin had met Czuczron, and as de Grandin tracks him he receives reports of Czuczron's noticeable aging. When de Grandin finally tracks the vampire to his lair, the ancient being is completely white haired. Czuczron attacks the detective and is impaled on a rapier blade thrust into his mouth. He will not live another hundred years.

SOURCES:

Quinn, Seabury. "The Man Who Cast No Shadow." 1927. Reprinted in *Weird Vampire Tales: Thirty Blood-Chilling Stories from the Weird Fiction Pulps*. Edited by Robert Weinberg, Stefan R. Dziemianowicz, and Martin Greenberg. New York: Gramercy Books, 1992.

Dandridge, Jerry

Jerry Dandridge (portrayed by Chris Sarandon), the thousand-year-old vampire featured in the movie *Fright Night* (1985), is first noticed by high schooler Charlie Brewster when he moves into the house next door. His arrival is accompanied by a coffin being carried into the basement of his house and the discovery of the decapitated body of a murder victim by the police. Dandridge's vampirism is confirmed the following evening when Charlie, staring out of his bedroom window, notices his new neighbor's fangs as they are about to sink into a young woman.

Charlie moves to protect himself, but Dandridge is both too quick and too old. Since vampires cannot go where they are not invited, Charlie believes he is protected in his own house—that is, until Dandridge tricks Charlie's mother into inviting him in. When Dandridge turns up in his room, Charlie discovers that the vampire is very strong, does not reflect in mirrors, but is reeled by crosses. Dandridge also changes into a bestial form when enraged or about to feed. His fingers lengthen into claws, his eyes turn red, and his fangs protrude. In their initial encounter, Charlie fights him off by jabbing a wooden pencil into his hand.

Despite his age, Dandridge takes a personal interest in a high school senior and Charlie's girlfriend, Amy. He sees in her the image of a girl he knew many years ago. He decides to make her his vampiric companion. Along the way, he also turns Charlie's friend **Edward "Evil" Thompson** into a vampire. After Amy and Evil are bitten, Charlie has to move quickly—their condition can be reversed if he kills Dandridge before they live through a complete 24-hour cycle and feed. He enlists the aid of reluctant vampire hunter **Peter Vincent**, an actor and host of the horror movie television show *Fright Night*. Together, armed with crosses, stakes, and a pistol (for Dandridge's nonvampire house companion), they enter his lair.

To get to Dandridge, Charlie and Vincent have to kill both Evil and Dandridge's companion. Amy is neutralized. After a lengthy set of battles, the final confronta-

Chris Sarandon in *Fright Night* as Jerry Dandridge before...

tion occurs in the basement. In the ensuing fight, as Vincent stands defenseless against the vampire's fangs, Charlie rips the cover off the window, and the vampire dies in the blazing sunlight. Amy recovers from the initial bite and the teens return to their previous normal life.

The character of Jerry Dandridge was created by Tom Holland for the *Fright Night* screenplay. A novelization of the film appeared simultaneously with the movie's release. A comic book version of *Fright Night* (adapted by Joe Gentile) appeared in 1988 and turned into a series which extended the story sans Dandridge to 22 monthly issues. In *Fright Night II*, Dandridge's sister **Regine** comes to town to seek revenge.

SOURCES:

Fright Night. Nos. 1-22. Chicago: Now Comics, 1988–90.

Skipp, John and Craig Spector. *Fright Night.* New York: Tor Books, 1985.

Dave

Dave is the chauvinist vampire who originally brings together the group of female vampires who later emerge as the *Vamps* in the comic book series of the same name. Dave is a redneck from 1960s North Carolina when he meets poets Dee Franks and **Hugh Evans**, vampires who had removed themselves from the poetry scene in New York when their social circle began to notice that they were not aging.

When the story begins, Dee takes a liking to Dave because he is so different from the poets with whom she has been hanging out with in New York. Hugh soon grows jealous of their relationship and attacks Dave. To save his life, Dee gives Dave her blood and transforms him into a vampire. Dave enjoys the life and eventually begins to gather a small cadre of females he can lord over. In the early 1970s, he turns **Skeeter**, a Carolina belle whom he entices into the back seat of an old De Sota, into a vampire.

He later meets **Whipsnake**, an African American, and **Mink**, a pretty blonde actress. He finds **Screech**, a Chinese American, in a gothic nightclub, the Boneyard, and in 1990 seduces **Howler**, a down-and-out prostitute from Las Vegas. He operates as a pimp to the now-vampirized women and forces them to lure men to a selected location where the whole group feasts.

As a vampire, Dave is much stronger individually than any of his minions. All, however, have prominent fangs, are completely nocturnal, and vulnerable to sun-

...and after his transformation into a vampire.

light and a stake in the heart. They feed nightly, as soon as possible after awakening. One evening in 1994, the five women take advantage of Dave's vulnerability and weakened state after he gorged himself fully. They stake him, dismember him, and bury his various appendages in different locations. Liberated, they then take to the road on their motorcycles as the Vamps.

A short time later, Dave's body is discovered. The coroner in Wilson County, North Carolina, charged with conducting his autopsy, pulls the stake out of Dave's heart. To his surprise, Dave comes back to life, kills the coroner, and reassembles his own body. He is in contact telepathically with the Vamps, and immediately heads for New York with homicidal ideas foremost in his mind. Four of the Vamps obtain an amulet from a Santeria priestess that blocks Dave's direct contact with them, but the fifth, Howler, is vulnerable. She is trying to find her son who has been taken from her and sold in an adoption scheme involving a Las Vegas judge and a New York lawyer.

Dave catches up to Howler soon after she locates her son, and is about to kill her when the rest of the Vamps arrive to save her. Screech, standing at the window, shoots Dave with her crossbow. The arrow impales him, and together the Vamps dispose of his body in a more permanent manner.

SOURCES:
Vamps. Nos. 1-6. New York: DC Comics/Vertigo, 1995–96. *Vamps: Hollywood & Vein.* Nos. 1-6. New York: DC Comics, 1996.

David

David (portrayed by Keifer Sutherland) is the leader of a teenage vampire motorcycle gang in the film *The Lost Boys* (1987). A blonde, tough guy punk, David and the rest of the Lost Boys spend their nights finding victims and hanging out near the beach in the resort town of Santa Clara, California. The group spends its days tucked away from the sun in an abandoned resort that was destroyed in the San Francisco earthquake of 1906. As vampires, David and the others don't change into bats, but they do sleep hanging upside down from the rafters of the resort.

David and the Lost Boys have many traditional vampire attributes. They are nocturnal creatures but do not sleep in coffins. They have fangs, can levitate, and have no image in mirrors. When about to feed, their eyes turn yellow, garlic does not work on them, but holy water does. They heal very quickly from less than fatal wounds. While David appears to be the head vampire, he is in fact the second-in-command. The head vampire remains out of sight until very late in the film, when his secret is revealed.

The vampires have no trouble finding new victims because the resort town draws a large number of tourists and transients alike. One summer in the mid-1980s, the Emerson family moves to town. Older brother Michael (portrayed by Jason Patric) gets into trouble on the family's very first night in town when he finds himself attracted to Star, the only female in the Lost Boys group. Star is under David's control, and the only way Michael can get near her is to start hanging out with David and the gang. On one wild night, Michael parties with the group and drinks blood from a wine bottle, triggering vampiric changes in his body. He has to wear dark glasses after drinking the blood, can no longer eat normal food, and can spontaneously levitate.

Sam, Michael's younger brother, realizes what is happening to his sibling after he meets up with the Frog brothers, two local teens who fight vampires and work in the local comic book store (they have even published their own comic book called *Vampires Everywhere*). Sam knows that if he can find out who the real head vampire is, he and the Frog brothers can kill him, which will free his brother and Star from the vampire's curse since they are not full vampires yet. Sam and the Frog brothers kill David and several other the Lost Boys and finally unveil the real head vampire in the film's exciting conclusion. The film was also made into a book.

SOURCES:
Gardner, Craig Shaw. *The Lost Boys.* New York: Berkley, 1987. 220 pp.

Davis, Kate

Kate Davis, the lead character in the Australian movie *Thirst* (1987), is a modern young working woman making her way in the world. Without family—her mother died when she was a child—Davis establishes herself in the business world. She is looking forward to a happy life with her significant other when she runs into **The Brotherhood**, a community of modern vampires. Without her knowledge, they have been tracking her for some time and have slated her to marry one of their leading members, Mr. Hodge.

As she discovers, Davis is a descendent of the **Countess Elizabeth Bathory**, a picture of whom, complete with fangs, is shown to her. Her family name had been Dodkin but was changed in 1850 by her great-great-grandfather when he left Europe. Her family was characterized by a blood thirst that could be suppressed but not destroyed.

Once the Brotherhood kidnaps her and Davis becomes aware of who she is, she is told by group members that they wish to welcome her into their midst as a baroness and one of their leaders. She learns that the members of the Brotherhood do not think of themselves as vampires, but as a superior race. They have no supernatural abilities, but gain youthfulness and power from the consumption of human blood. Although they cannot shape shift or fly, they can walk freely in the daylight. Their eyes do turn red when they are about to feed.

The vampires of the Brotherhood have developed a sophisticated milking operation by which they take measured quantities of blood from donors who live in one of their "farms." Taken to one such farm, Davis is put through increasingly stressful situations with blood in the hopes of calling forth her own suppressed blood thirst. Although she fights it, the thirst eventually emerges, and she partakes in one of the group's rituals, during which they drink blood from a living body.

Davis is a reluctant vampire. Her human life still summons her, and she is repulsed by the thoughts of consuming blood. The tension of the decision she must make to freely join the Brotherhood and accept the marriage they have waiting for her looms.

de Lioncourt, Lestat

The vampire Lestat de Lioncourt has emerged as a second only to **Count Dracula** as the most influential character in vampire literature. Introduced in Anne Rice's *Interview with the Vampire* (1976), his full life story is told in the her novel *The Vampire Lestat* (1985). He then appears as the feature character and narrator of the subsequent volumes in the series known as *Vampire Chronicles: The Queen of the Damned* (1988), *The Tale of the Body Thief* (1992), and *Memnoch the Devil* (1994).

Lestat was born in 1760 in rural France, the seventh son of a marquis and his Italian wife, **Gabrielle.** He is one of the three sons who survives into adulthood. Bored with life at the family castle, but lacking the money to follow a proper profession suitable to his aristocratic birth, he is continually blocked in his career choices. He chooses a life in the monastery, and his father has his books taken away. He changes his mind and runs off with a theater group, but his brothers find him and bring him home. Eventually, his mother breaks down and gives him the money he

Tom Cruise won over even author Anne Rice in his riveting portrayal of the vampire Lestat de Lioncourt.

THE VAMPIRE GALLERY SALUTES: TOM CRUISE

What happens when you get millions of dollars to play a part and the popular author whose character you are going to bring to the screen rises up to denounce you in every media possible? If you're Tom Cruise, and you have chosen to take your acting career in a new direction in your quest to be the best, you buckle down and do the work. In the end, Cruise proved Anne Rice and all the other fans of the beloved Lestat de Lioncourt wrong.

Rice complained to any one who would listen that Cruise saw as too young, too American, and most of all, lacking in Lestat's main quality—androgyny (read: homosexuality). After all, Cruise had become a star playing some very manly roles beginning with *Risky Business* and continuing with the likes of *Top Gun*, *The Color of Money*, *A Few Good Men*, and *The Firm*. People tended to overlook his award-winning performance in *Born on the Fourth of July*.

Cruise stepped out of the limelight and nailed the part and transformed himself into Lestat, conquering the role at a shoot that was blanketed with tight security. In the end Rice admitted she was wrong and that Cruise had done what she had never believed he could. *Interview with the Vampire* was the first part in which Cruise portrayed a dark role. The film was completed and released in 1994 and went one to become one of the top grossing films of the year.

needs to escape the castle. He moves to Paris and begins a life on the stage. His career comes to an extremely sudden end when a vampire named **Magnus** attends one of his performances, is captivated by him, and selects him as his successor. Magnus, who lives in a tower outside Paris, is extremely wealthy but is not particularly happy as a vampire because his body was so old when he was changed into an immortal creature. He wants a young person to carry on his name and fortune.

Immediately after turning Lestat into a vampire, Magnus commits suicide, leaving Lestat with almost no understanding of his new state of being. Young and brash (Lestat is 20 or 21 when changed), immortal, and wealthy beyond belief, Lestat suddenly has the world at his feet but is uncertain what to do with it. A few months later, Gabrielle comes to Paris, dying of tuberculosis (then called consumption). She readily accepts Lestat's offer to join him in the nocturnal life.

Lestat and Gabrielle then encounter a coven of vampires led by **Armand** that follow an old set of rules passed on from a similar coven in Rome. They resent Lestat's seemingly carefree lifestyle, which is unusual for a vampire. Their confrontation with Lestat fails to change him and in fact leads to the group's dissolution. After listening to Armand's story and questioning him on the nature of reality, Lestat and Gabrielle conclude that he has nothing to teach them. They leave Paris and travel across Europe and around the Mediterranean. As they travel, Lestat leaves messages for the vampire **Marius,** Armand's maker. They settle in Cairo for a period during which time word is received that his surviving brothers have been killed in the French Revolution. The two then go their separate ways, Gabrielle travels to sub-Saharan Africa, while Lestat spends a period in the ground before traveling to Marius's sanctuary, where **Akasha** and **Enkil**, the original vampires, are kept.

Lestat de Lioncourt (Tom Cruise) and Louis de Pointe du Lac (Brad Pitt) dressed in their best finery in eighteenth century New Orleans in *Interview with the Vampire*.

From Marius, Lestat learns that vampires originated in ancient Egypt approximately 6,000 years ago when Akasha and Enkil were possessed by a spirit named **Amel**. All vampires since then have derived from Akasha and Enkil, who exist as living statues at Marius's sanctuary in the Greek Islands. While there, Lestat enters the shrine room for a private audience with the two primal vampires. He shares blood with Akasha and is almost killed when Enkil wakes up and attacks him. Marius intervenes and saves Lestat's life before sending him away. Lestat travels for a short time before settling in New Orleans later that same year.

In New Orleans, Lestat is drawn to **Louis de Pointe du Lac,** a morose young man with a strong death wish, which Lestat can sense. Louis feels guilty over his brother's death, which occurred after Louis refused to hand over the family fortune to him to fight a religious crusade against atheism. Lestat turns Louis into a vampire and is surprised when he sees that Louis resents the "gift" that Lestat has given him. Lestat is also frustrated by Louis' refusal to take human life to quench his thirst for blood.

Louis and Lestat's relationship is significantly changed, however, in 1784 when Lestat gives the "Dark Gift" to a five-year-old child named **Claudia**. Louis originally bit Claudia when his need for blood overwhelmed him, but it is Lestat who finishes the process of turning her into a vampire. Claudia takes to the vampiric life. She learns to hunt from Lestat and it is Louis whom she views as a father figure. The three live together for more than six decades, but Claudia harbors a growing resentment over the fact that her body has not matured even though her mind has. After she learns that Lestat is the one who actually turned her into a vampire, all of her anger focuses on him. She attempts to poison him with absinthe and then finishes the job with a knife. Louis throws Lestat's body in a nearby swamp and prepares to leave New Orleans with Claudia. Before they can leave, Lestat, not yet dead, rises from the swamp and makes his way back to the house. Louis sets Lestat on fire and burns the house down around him. As the inferno rages, Louis and Claudia catch a ship bound for Europe.

A wounded Lestat survives the fire and catches up with Louis and Claudia in Paris. He meets Armand and the new group of vampires he has assembled (the **Theatre des Vampires**) and tells them how Claudia and, to a lesser extent, Louis, have tried to kill him. Because it is forbidden in the vampire community for one vampire to kill another, Claudia is sentenced to death, along with a vampire named **Madeleine,** who serves as Claudia's surrogate mother. Armand, who is in love with Louis, frees him from the coffin that he is imprisoned in. Grief stricken, Louis warns Armand that he is about to exact his own revenge upon the Theatre des Vampires for killing Claudia. He burns down the vampires' theater, killing many of them. Armand escapes thanks to Louis' warning and takes out his anger on Lestat, throwing him off a high tower. Lestat, injured even worse than he was when he arrived, somehow makes it back to New Orleans, where he lives in seclusion and survives on the blood of small animals. In 1929, he settles into the ground for a long, healing sleep, where he remains until 1984.

Lestat is awakened by the music of a rock group, Satan's Night Out. He rises and introduces himself to the group. They hand him a copy of *Interview with the Vampire*, Louis' story of their life together. Reading the book motivates him. He changes the band's name to The Vampire Lestat and writes his own autobiography published under the same title. He throws himself into his new life as a performer, which causes many in the vampire community to resent him. Before long, he is a genuine rock and roll superstar, known round the world.

Lestat's music reaches the isolated frozen land where Marius has hidden Akasha and Enkil. In 1985, Akasha stirs in response to the music and kills Enkil before leaving the sanctuary. She has conceived a plan of world domination that involves killing most of the males in the world, both mortal and vampire. She plans a new Eden composed mostly of females. Through the remainder of the year, events move swiftly. The climatic events of Akasha's crusade come together at Halloween in 1985.

Lestat holds a huge concert in San Francisco that is attended by most of the vampires who have survived Akasha's initial killing spree. After the concert, she kidnaps Lestat and forces him to participate in the one of her massacres. Although a harrowing experience, Lestat learns a great deal about his own powers. Meanwhile, the surviving vampires gather in Sonoma County, California, where eventually Akasha and Lestat join them for a final confrontation. Akasha is killed and her power is transferred to the ancient vampire **Mekare.** After Akasha's demise, most of the vampires, including Lestat, travel to Miami, where Armand has constructed a large entertainment/shopping complex called Night Island. After a brief period of rest and relaxation, Lestat leaves for New Orleans.

There he meets **Jesse,** a young woman who was severely injured at his San Francisco concert and subsequently became a vampire. From her, he learns of **David Talbot,** the aging head of the occult research organization known as the Talamasca. He travels to London to meet Talbot, and the two form a close friendship, although Talbot refuses Lestat's offer of the Dark Gift. Lestat also meets the con man **Raglan James,** a strange and gifted human who has the power to exchange bodies with another person. He offers to temporarily switch bodies with Lestat so the vampire can see what it is like to live as a mortal. Against Talbot's advice, Lestat agrees to the exchange, only to discover that James has no intention of returning his newly acquired body or the vampiric powers that go with it. He steals a portion of Lestat's vast wealth and disappears. Lestat enlists Talbot to help him track James. They finally catch up with the body thief on a cruise ship and devise a scheme that will allow Lestat to get his body back. The plan has the added bonus of letting Talbot exchange his old body with the young body that James occupied before he met Lestat. Lestat finally forces the Dark Gift on the now youthful Talbot.

In his most recent adventures, Lestat travels to Heaven and Hell with Memnoch, known to most Westerners as The Devil, as his guide. The trip involves a discussion of the nature of evil, the purpose of Christ's incarnation and death on the cross, and the often bloody history of Christianity that followed. In the midst of this supernatural time-traveling adventure, Lestat witnesses Christ moving to his crucifixion on Golgotha. He sees Veronica use her veil to comfort him, and Christ's face miraculously appearing on it. He drinks Christ's blood and takes the veil and then flees. As he tries to escape back to Earth, Memnoch tries to stop him. In the process Lestat's left eye is pulled out of his head.

Lestat lands in Manhattan. Talbot listens to and records his story. Dora, a televangelist who is the daughter of one of Lestat's victims, steals the veil from him and displays it as a miraculous religious sign. Armand commits suicide by standing in sunlight as a testament to the veil's authenticity. Lestat is horrified that he has inadvertently given new life to Christianity.

Later in New Orleans, **Maharet,** Mekare's sister and also an ancient vampire, appears and gives him his missing eye, thus confirming his recent adventures as real. She also chains him so he will listen to Memnoch's final message. During his period of confinement, Talbot checks the facts in his original story. Finally freed from his chains, Lestat is still confused by what it all means, if in fact it means anything at all.

SOURCES:

Ramsland, Katherine. *The Vampire Companion: The Official Guide to Anne Rice's The Vampire Chronicles.* New York: Ballantine Books, 1993.

Rice, Anne. *Interview with the Vampire.* New York: Alfred a. Knopf, 1976. Reprint, New York: Ballantine, 1979.

———. *Memnoch the Devil*. New York: Alfred a. Knopf, 1994. Reprint, New York: Ballantine Books, 1995.

———. *The Queen of the Damned*. New York: Alfred a. Knopf, 1988. Reprint, New York: Ballantine Books, 1989.

———. *The Tale of the Body Thief*. New York: Alfred a. Knopf, 1992. Reprint, New York: Ballantine, May 1993.

———. *The Vampire Lestat*. New York: Alfred a. Knopf, 1985. Reprint, New York: Ballantine Books, 1986.

de Morrissey, David

David de Morrissey, a 400-year-old vampire, was introduced in Lori Herter's 1991 romance novel, *Obsession*. de Morrissey was born in 1582 in France. As a young man he ventures to England, where he studies with William Shakespeare. In 1616, he travels to Transylvania and meets with an unfortunate fate when he is turned into a vampire. He returns to England and eventually reveals his vampiric condition to his girlfriend Cecilia. She reacts with horror and commits suicide.

de Morrissey lives the eternal life of a vampire and lives in many places as the years pass. He visits America once in the nineteenth century but finds it too uncouth for his tastes. In the 1930s, however, with the Nazi menace spreading across Europe, he moves to America. He lives in New York until after World War II and then settles in Chicago, where he lives as a recluse in a large Victorian house. In twentieth-century America, he has finally realized his dream and become a playwright, authoring several dramas that have brought him critical acclaim.

His fame brings Veronica Ames into his life. She is a feature writer who hopes to do a profile on de Morrissey. She happens to know the playwright's attorney, who arranges a meeting and sets up an interview. The pair hits it off at the interview and develops a relationship. When enough time has passed that he feels he can trust her, de Morrissey shares his secret with Veronica. She is stunned, but handles the news much better than Cecilia had centuries before. Even though he loves her deeply and she loves him, de Morrissey is not sure she can handle the reality of his eternal existence. Instead of turning her into a vampire, he sends her away and tells her to come back in 10 years if she still loves him.

During the months and years that follow their parting, both de Morrissey and Veronica find other lovers. de Morrissey actually encounters several women because he uses sex as a means of controlling his blood lust. Their lives periodically intersect, however, and neither forgets the other. Many different stories unfold that test their love for each other, including de Morrissey being presented with the chance to become mortal again. The lovers' tale continued through three more books: *Possession*, *Confession*, and *Eternity*.

de Morrissey is a true romantic vampire—trim, handsome, and well-built. He has long brown hair, blue eyes, prominent fangs, and long fingers. He is a nocturnal creature and sleeps in a coffin on soil from his native land. Although he is not really a supernatural creature, he feels alienated from God, humanity, and the daylight world. He is unaffected by garlic or crosses. Surviving on blood stolen form local blood supplies, he does not eat normal food.

SOURCES:
Herter, Lori. *Confession*. New York: Berkley Books, 1992. ———. *Eternity*. New York: Berkley Books, 1993.
———. *Obsession*. New York: Berkley Books, 1991.
———. *Possession*. New York: Berkley Books, 1992.

de Pointe du Lac, Louis

Louis de Pointe du Lac, the lead character in Anne Rice's *Interview with the Vampire*, grows up on a plantation outside of New Orleans in the years immediately preceding the American Revolution. His family had received a French land grant and settled on two plantations on the Mississippi River. By the time he reaches his mid-twenties, he is the head of the household because his father has passed away. His brother has become a religious visionary, but Louis refuses to turn over the family's fortune to him so he can return to France to lead a crusade against atheism. The refusal leads to his brother's accidental death. Louis is so guilt-stricken that his desire to die attracts the attention of the vampire **Lestat de Lioncourt**. In 1791, at age 25, he is visited by Lestat.

Lestat drains him almost to the point of death and then allows him to drink from his arm. This lets Louis pass through death and into a vampiric state. As Lestat prepares to go to sleep in his coffin, he realizes that he does not have a coffin for Louis, who is forced to sleep on top of Lestat his first day as a vampire. Lestat tries to teach Louis to hunt, but Louis is repulsed by the idea of taking a human life. He is happy to learn that he can live off of animals. Lestat explains some of the other "rules" of being a vampire to Louis: Vampires have no problems with crosses or other religious objects. They have no power to change into other life forms or a mist. Stakes through the heart have no effect on them. Their senses, especially hearing and night vision, improve to a remarkable extent.

As unexplained deaths mount at Louis' family mansion due to Lestat's need for blood, the two vampires are forced to flee. Lestat burns the mansion before they move to New Orleans. Lestat enjoys life in the city, but Louis hates it and is forced to survive on rats. His moral problems with taking human life go hand in hand with the questions he has regarding his own salvation: Has he, in becoming a vampire, been damned? As he struggles with these issues, he is overcome by weakness when he sees a five-year-old girl begging her now-dead mother (dead due to the plague) to wake up. He pulls the girl close as if to comfort her and bites her, drinking her blood. Lestat looks on as Louis feeds.

Louis does not drain and kill the girl (who is named **Claudia**) and she is found and taken to a charity ward. There Lestat finds her and brings her back to the apartment that he and Louis share. Louis again drinks her blood, and then Lestat lets her drink some of his blood, turning her into a vampire. Lestat then presents Claudia as their child when he and Louis are out in public. Though Lestat made her a vampire, it is Louis who builds a relationship with her and becomes like a brother to her. She learns to hunt and feed from Lestat, but she sleeps in a coffin with Louis. Both think of Claudia as their little doll, and they dress her accordingly.

As the years pass, Louis is slow to appreciate that Claudia is growing into a woman, at least mentally. And as she matures, she questions the rightness of their making her an eternal child. She is so angry at Lestat for being the one who actually made her that she begins to plot his death. She apparently succeeds in killing him with poison and a knife, and talks Louis into helping her dispose of the body in a nearby swamp. With Lestat out of his life, Louis again reflects upon the theological questions that have troubled him. He goes to a cathedral, only to conclude that he is the only supernatural entity present. He goes to confession, only to have the priest question the truth of his fantastic statements and then condemn him as a devil.

Claudia suggests that they go to central Europe, where vampires are supposedly prevalent and they can find more of their own kind. However, it turns out that Lestat is not dead after all. He rises from the swamp and appears as they prepare to leave New Orleans. Louis sets Lestat afire and burns the house down around him, but he and Claudia leave and catch their ship to Europe before they confirm that Lestat is truly dead.

First they travel to Transylvania, and while there, they actually find a vampire. However, like other vampires they find, it is a mindless corpse and they kill it. The central European vampires have no information or companionship to offer them. Claudia then suggests that they go to Paris, where they can take advantage of their ability to speak French.

They have been in the city for several months when Louis is followed one evening by a person who turns out to be a vampire. His name is **Santiago,** and he has been sent with a message. Santiago and Louis fail to hit if off, however, and end up in a fight. Their battle is broken up by a third vampire, **Armand,** who delivers the message and invites Louis and Claudia to a performance by the **Theatre des Vampires,** which is a coven of vampires posing as a humans playing vampires on the stage.

After the performance, Louis has a chance to talk to Armand, who further destroys Louis' lingering theological hopes. He also finds Armand extremely attractive and sees that the feeling seems to be mutual. Claudia has no problem seeing the threat that Armand poses to her relationship with Louis and takes steps to ensure that she will not be alone. She finds a woman, **Madeleine,** who is quite willing to become Claudia's eternal mother. Claudia finally convinces Louis to transform Madeleine into a vampire, the first and only person he ever transforms.

Just as Claudia is getting used to her new life, the hard-to-kill Lestat appears in Paris and pleads his case to the other vampires, seeking justice and the punishment of Claudia and Louis, especially Claudia. Since many members of the coven did not care for the newcomers anyway, they are more than happy to seize all three of them. Claudia and Madeleine are killed, and Louis is locked in a coffin to suffer from thirst. Armand frees Louis, and in return, Louis warns Armand that he is planning to retaliate against the people who killed Claudia. He burns the theater, killing most of the vampires, and as it burns, he decapitates Santiago.

Afterward, he leaves Paris with Armand and they travel the world. They visit Egypt, travel across Europe and eventually land in the New York. They live together

Louis de Pointe du Lac (Brad Pitt) destroys the Theatre des Vampires in *Interview with the Vampire*.

in New York City for many years. Louis finally returns to New Orleans in the mid-1970s after Armand finally tells Louis that Lestat did not die in the theater fire in Paris, as Louis believed. He visits Lestat in New Orleans, has a final conversation with Armand, and then departs on his own. A short time later, he makes his way to San Francisco, where he meets a young writer named **Daniel Molloy**. He tells Molloy his life story and Molloy publishes the account as *Interview with the Vampire*, under the pseudonym Anne Rice.

In the years since the publication of *Interview with the Vampire*, Louis has led a quiet existence. He is reunited briefly with Lestat when Lestat launches his music career as the lead singer of a rock and roll band. He is spared when the original vampire, **Akasha,** begins killing off all of the vampires because Lestat loves him. He loses his usual reserved demeanor to challenge Akasha's right to interfere in the human world.

For author Rice, Louis is ever the reluctant vampire. He never fully accepts his condition, although he loses much of his resistance when he comes to the conclusion that little of the Catholic teaching he received when younger has any meaning in light of what he experienced as a vampire. He still abhors the thought of making anyone a vampire, especially after his experience with Madeleine. In one of his final appearances in the *Vampire Chronicles*, he meets Lestat, who has become human again. He refuses Lestat's request to once again make him a vampire.

SOURCES:

Ramsland, Katherine. *The Vampire Companion: The Official Guide to Anne Rice's The Vampire Chronicles.* New York: Ballantine Books, 1993.

Rice, Anne. *Interview with the Vampire.* New York: Alfred a. Knopf, 1976. Reprint, New York: Ballantine, 1979.

———. *The Queen of the Damned.* New York: Alfred a. Knopf, 1988. Reprint, New York: Ballantine Books, 1989.

———. *The Tale of the Body Thief.* New York: Alfred a. Knopf, 1992. Reprint, New York: Ballantine, May 1993.

———. *The Vampire Lestat.* New York: Alfred a. Knopf, 1985. Reprint, New York: Ballantine Books, 1986.

de Villenueva, Sebastion

The vampire appearing throughout a series of novels by Les Daniels, Sebastion de Villenueva originated in fifteenth-century Spain. According to the storyline, first presented in *The Black Castle* (1978), Sebastion participates in the seize of Malaga in 1487, part of the effort to drive the Moors from Spain. He is killed when a cannon explodes in his face. Carried from the battle, he dies some days later, and his body is returned to his castle in northeastern Spain and there entombed in a crypt. His brother, still a youth at the time of the siege, has become a monk and is eventually named inquisitor for his home territory.

In the days following his accident, Sebastion goes through a set of (undisclosed) "rituals" that make him a vampire. From the cannon, he retains a scar that runs down the left side of his face. He takes advantage of his brother's position and regularly visits the cells of the Inquisition where he feeds among the prisoners. For the first nine years of his vampiric life, he never takes a human life.

Sebastion is a vampire of the traditional **Count Dracula** mode, with the familiar variety of traditional powers and limitations. He can transform himself into a bat and fly or turn into a mist, a form in which he can pass through the smallest crack. He is subject to the second death—sunlight, fire, and/or a stake through the heart are fatal, and, of course, he needs to sleep on native soil.

At the end of *The Black Castle*, Sebastion dies in a fire he builds in front of his castle. However, his skull is not consumed in the flames, and once severed from his body rolls into the castle moat. It is later retrieved and taken to Mexico, where Sebastion is brought back to life to begin a new series of adventures. Aligned with an Aztec priestess, he ends his Mexican sojourn when she transforms him into pure spirit. He later reappears in revolutionary France (*Citizen Vampire*, 1981) when an alchemist brings him back from the spirit. Again, he returns to the spirit realm only to assume a body again in nineteenth-century England (*Yellow Fog*, 1986) and India (*No Blood Spilled*, 1991).

SOURCES:

Daniels, Les. *The Black Castle*. New York: Charles Scribners Sons, 1978. Reprint, New York: Berkley Books, 1979.

———— *Citizen Vampire*. New York: Charles Scribners Sons, 1981.

———— *No Blood Spilled*. New York: Tor Books, 1991.

———— *The Silver Skull*. New York: Charles Scribners Sons, 1970. Reprint, New York: Ace Books, 1983.

————. *Yellow Fog*. New York: TOR/Donald M. Grant, 1986. Revised, New York: Tor Books, 1988.

DeCobra, Gustav

Gustav DeCobra, a character created by Elliot S. Maggin, is one of several vampires encountered by comic book superhero **Batman** over his decades of fighting super villains. DeCobra makes his first appearance in *Detective Comics*, No. 455 (1976). As a young professor in the 1870s at Cornell Medical School, DeCobra advocates transplanting human hearts and begins conducting experiments to support his theories of how to perform such operations. The controversial nature of his work results in his dismissal, but he secretly continues his work. His ventures into graveyards at night to harvest hearts eventually lead to a face-to-face encounter with a vampire. As a result, DeCobra becomes one of the undead.

DeCobra, though a century old, appears as a young man with a resemblance to actor Christopher Lee. Like **Count Dracula** he dresses in formal clothes, complete with an opera cape. He has light brown hair with prominent sideburns and a vertical scar on the left side of his face that runs from his forehead to his cheek.

A hundred years after his transformation, DeCobra resides in a coffin in a secluded rural mansion near Gotham City. Bruce Wayne (the public persona of Batman) and his servant, Alfred, have car trouble in sight of DeCobra's residence. Inadvertently, Wayne awakens DeCobra and soon finds himself and Alfred under attack by the thirsty vampire. He holds off the initial attack with a hastily created cross. A few seconds later, Batman impales DeCobra with a wooden stake through his heart. Strangely, the stake has no effect on DeCobra. It seems the former Doctor DeCobra's research has proved successful: The vampire's heart is not where it should be in his body.

Batman quickly devises a plan. He engages the vampire in a fight, thus causing his heart to beat rapidly. Hopefully, Batman will then be able to locate it. In the ensuing fight, Batman can find no heartbeat or pulse on DeCobra, but he does notice the ticking of a large wall clock. Batman withdraws from the first fight to regroup. He realizes that DeCobra has developed the ability to remove his heart from his body and still remain alive. He then realizes that the loud ticking he heard from the wall clock was actually the beating of DeCobra's heart—his heart is hidden in the clock. He returns to resume the fight with DeCobra, and just as Batman is about to be killed, he grabs a bow and arrow and shoots the clock. The arrow impales the heart and DeCobra is finally killed.

SOURCES:
Maggin, Elliot S., and Mike Grell. "Heart of a Vampire." *Detective Comics,* No. 455. (January 1976).

des Essientes, M.

M. des Essientes is a Parisian vampire featured in Michael Talbot's novel, *The Delicate Dependency* (1982). He was born at the time of Charlemagne in the Rhone valley of France. He marries and settles down to a quiet life helping his parents in their vineyard. He helps them increase production by studying bees and pollination and applying his studies in a practical nature. He achieves local fame for his efforts, which leads to trouble. It seems the family vineyard is on land owned by a baron, and that baron has enemies. Those enemies—the Magyars —attack and destroy the baron's land.

A group of monks that call themselves the Illuminati ask des Essientes to come live with them in the Vosges Mountains. As it turns out, the monks are vampires and they initiate their new friend into the world of immortality. Their form of vampirism is like a viral infection, with the condition being transferred through the exchange of blood. Once infected, the new vampire grows a set of fangs to assist in feeding. des Essientes then turns one of his friends into a vampire, a falconer who lives with him and protects their residence with his trained falcons.

The Illuminati is part of an international fellowship of vampires. Among the prominent members of the Illuminati is **Lodovico.** In the twelfth century, traveling the land as a troubadour, Lodovico visits the monks' monastery. He invites des Esseintes to move to Paris as part of a secret group of vampires gathered on the Ile Saint-Louis and at Notre Dame cathedral. One result of this gathering of vampire intellectuals is the founding of the University of Paris.

des Essientes continues to reside on Ile Saint-Louis in a large residence that opens to the water way under the island's surface level. He is a nocturnal creature whose residence becomes a center of the vampire community in Paris each evening. The group has created alternative sources of blood and has no need to hunt humans. des Essientes becomes involved in a web of intrigue that has Lodovico and a man named Dr. John Gladstone at its center. Gladstone arrives at des Essientes' house in search of his daughter, who has been kidnaped by a vampire named **Niccolo Cavalanti,** a friend of Lodovico's. Lodovico is seeking Gladstone's cooperation and thinks he can gain it by kidnaping his daughter. Gladstone is taken prisoner by des Essientes, but he escapes and continues his quest, which eventually takes him to Lodovico's home in Italy.

SOURCES:

Talbot, Michael. *The Delicate Dependency*. New York: Avon, 1982.

Desire

Desire, a beautiful and seductive dark-haired vampiress, makes her single appearance in the 1982 movie *I, Desire* (also released as *Desire the Vampire*). Desire is of indeterminate age, but in the early 1980s, she is in the United States, moving from city to city. Before arriving in Los Angeles, she was in New Orleans, where a Roman Catholic priest came to know her for what she really was. When Desire leaves New Orleans, the priest leaves his parish and follows her to Hollywood, where she takes up life on the street as a prostitute. She feeds off of her clients, leaving them dead, drained of blood, and with two puncture wounds in the neck.

David, a law student who works in the morgue while finishing school, gradually realizes that a vampire is loose in Los Angeles. He faces off against Desire when she steals blood from the hospital where his girlfriend works as a nurse. Desire is a traditional vampire in many ways. She has prominent fangs that show even when her mouth is closed. She is strong, having entered the hospital by bending the iron security bars. She is a nocturnal creature who sleeps in a coffin on native soil. Her coffin is located in a secret room in her apartment. She wears a cape and is repelled by the cross.

David tracks the priest on the streets of Hollywood. The priest confirms that he is tracking a vampire and informs David of her supernatural aspects. Since Desire has seen a glimpse of hell, and knows what awaits her, she is strongly motivated to kill simply to lengthen her stay on earth. Her essential weakness is a righteous man. She has no power over a righteous man, a man who will not give in to her seductive appeal.

Eventually, David tracks Desire to her apartment, where the priest has proven his lack of righteousness. He has become a vampire. David stakes him. Desire tries to get to David, but as she lunges for him, he ducks. She plunges off the balcony to her death, since she lacks the power of flight or the ability to transform into a bat.

Desnoirs

Around 1950, a powerful Canadian Chippawa medicine man opposed to the movement of the lumber industry onto his people's traditional land, performs a secret ritual process that transforms his young daughter into a vampire. He releases the buxom vampiress in her abbreviated costume upon the lumberjacks who call her Desnoirs, literally translated from French as "from the dark." After she kills a number of the men, they corner her, stake her, and place her in an out building where they can keep an eye on her body.

All is well for many years until the arrival of Brandon Thorn. In 1967 Thorn, like many young men escaping the Vietnam War draft in the United States, comes to Canada and lands a job that takes him into the Chippawa forests where lumber is being cut. He becomes curious when he sees the building where Desnoirs's body is kept. When he breaks in, he finds that Desnoir is still there and still breathing. Using her mental powers, the vampiress forces Thorn to cut himself and give her blood. He removes the stake, and she fully returns to life. Desnoir shares blood with Thorn and transforms him into a vampire. Together, they begin to terrorize the lumberjacks again.

Desnoirs, Thorn, and the vampires they create are somewhat traditional. They are nocturnal and vulnerable to fire, sunlight, decapitation, and stakes in the heart. They need blood regularly. When receiving less than fatal wounds, they heal quickly. They sleep in the nude upside down like bats, with their toes serving as claws from which they hang.

In 1990, not having heard from his brother in nearly twenty-five years, Ray Thorn travels to Canada in search of him. Eventually, Ray finds Brandon and learns about his vampirism. After he resists Brandon's attempt to transform him into a vampire, Ray kills his brother and takes his body back to the United States. In her anger at losing her love, Desnoirs follows and seeks to kill Ray. In their initial confrontation, Ray succeeds in killing Desnoirs and her minions. Unfortunately, he is arrested, indicted, and convicted on six counts of murder. The ever resilient Desnoirs is subsequently revived by a group of young girls flirting with Satanism. They discover the location of her body and sacrifice one of their peers in order to revive her. Ray escapes from confinement while attending his father's funeral and goes in search of Desnoirs. In their final confrontation, both Desnoirs and Ray are destroyed.

SOURCES:

Polgardy, Ed, and Jim Balent. *From the Darkness*. Nos. 1–4. Newberry Park, Calif.: Adventure Comics, 1990–98.

———. *From the Darkness Book: Blood Vows*. Nos. 1–3. Valley Stream, N.Y.: Cry for Dawn Productions, 1992–93.

Diego y Rey, Lord Eduardo

Lord Eduardo Diego y Rey, the founder and leader of **The Conclave,** is a 400-year-old vampire featured in Garfield Reeves-Stevens novel *Bloodshift* (1981). During the first 200 years of his life, Lord Diego lived the same way most other vampires (they preferred the term *yber*) did—in rotting coffins and mausoleums, fearing each dawn and not knowing for sure that he would awake at dusk. Tired of living that way, he encountered several other intelligent *yber* and founded the Conclave, which became the ruling council of the *yber* community. It brought together all of the knowledge and wisdom of the vampire community, which previously had been handed down in a fragmentary way, usually by word of mouth from one *yber* to another.

The Conclave established sanctuaries where *yber* could exist without fear. It also set up a system of recruitment of new *yber* in which selected humans were chosen and served a period as a familiar. The familiar regularly provided blood for his or her mentor and took care of the mentor's affairs during the daylight hours. In return, at some point in the future, he or she would be allowed to experience the communion, the act by which an *yber* shared its strange white blood with a familiar, thus transforming him or her into a vampire. The Conclave also created and promoted a document called the Ways, which said that *yber* were supernatural creatures who were created by Satan. They were beyond the reach of the salvation offered by the church. The Conclave built its power on the supernaturalism articulated in the Ways. That supernaturalism set the rules for the Conclaves' ongoing conflict with the Jesuits, the Roman Catholic order that had the knowledge of the *yber* and how to destroy them.

Lord Diego and the *yber* are nontraditional vampires, although they live by the very traditional supernaturalism articulated in the Ways. *Yber* are not the undead. A person is transformed into an *yber* by having a large portion of his or her blood drained. This causes the person to slip into a state of shock, during which they receive some *yber* blood, which completes the transformation. Thus the *yber* remains a natural being. Their image shows up in mirrors. They cannot transform into other forms. The are relatively strong and have some heightened senses, including the ability to sense the presence of another vampire who approaches them. The *yber* have prominent fangs that can be filed down and capped if the individual has to interact with humans for a short period. Given the supernaturalism of the Ways, many vampires believe that they will be negatively affected by holy water and religious symbols. In fact, only those who believe that they will be affected actually are.

As head of the Conclave, Lord Diego has two primary challenges to his authority. First, one elder vampire, the oldest known to the *yber* community, refuses to acknowledge the Conclave's authority or the Ways. Known as the Father, he is supported by the large number of *yber* whom he brought to life. They refused to move against the Father.

Second is the more recent challenge posed by **Adrienne St. Clair.** She is part of a group of *yber* known as the Unbidden, who were created during World War II and who skipped the usual process of serving as a familiar before becoming a full-fledged vampire. Lord Diego is attracted to St. Clair and feels that eventually she will respond to him. Thus he protects her when most of the other Unbidden are killed. St. Clair is intelligent and looks at being a vampire from a scientific viewpoint, which makes her question the supernatural underpinnings of the Ways. She discovers many things about vampires that allow the *yber* community to improve their interactions with humans, such as realizing that *yber* don't have to automatically fall into the traditional deep vampire sleep when the morning comes. Her initial findings give Lord Diego important information that he uses to create a master plan for the Conclave to take over the world.

When St. Clair continues her research by adopting several scientists as familiars and pursuing her research outside of the *yber* community, Lord Diego realizes the danger she poses to him and orders her to stop. When she refuses, he orders her lover

Jeffrey killed. When even this doesn't stop her, he attempts to kill her. She flees to Canada, where he hires a contract killer to assassinate her. The killer, Granger Hilman, fails in his first attempt to kill her and actually becomes her ally. This happens only after he has killed all of her familiars, however, which causes her to travel to California and seek protection from the Father, her only chance for help.

After St. Clair arrives in California, Lord Diego manipulates the Jesuits into attacking the Father's mansion. It is his hope that the Jesuits will be blamed for the dastardly deed of killing the Father (and St. Clair). Diego will then rise up as their champion and use the Father's death as a rallying point from which he will consolidate the power of the Conclave. In one bold move, he would have eliminated the only two people who oppose him, and he would be free to impose his authority on the group. His plan is foiled, however, by the skilled killer Granger Hilman, with whom he ultimately met his fate.

SOURCES:

Reeves-Stevens, Garfield. *Bloodshift.*. Toronto: Virgo Press, 1981. Reprint, New York: Popular Library, 1990.

Dieudonné, Genevieve Sandrine de l'Isle

Genevieve Sandrine de l'Isle Dieudonné, a fifteenth century vampire, emerges as one of the central figures in the alternative history constructed by Kim Newman in his novel, *Anno Dracula* (1992). Newman presents the idea that **Count Dracula** traveled to England, as in the Bram Stoker novel, but instead of being defeated by **Abraham Van Helsing,** won his battle with the vampire hunter and went on to become the Prince consort of England. As a result, England became a haven for vampires. All of the famous fictional vampires from nineteenth century literature (**Lord Ruthven, Sir Francis Varney,** etc.) and many from the twentieth century (**Dr. Ravna, Graf Orlock,** etc.) appear in the novel.

Genevieve Dieudonné is a new vampire created for the novel by Newman. She was born in 1416, the daughter of a physician in rural France. She was given the "dark kiss" and turned into a vampire at the age of 16, a year after Joan of Arc was killed by the British. The time period makes her a contemporary of Gilles de Rais and a younger contemporary of Vlad Tepes. Chandagnac, the vampire who made her, had in turn been created by Melissa d'Aoques.

Most of the vampires in England were of Vlad Tepes' bloodline. Genevieve is from a different bloodline and possesses somewhat different characteristics. For example, for a few days each month she becomes lethargic and falls into a vampiric sleep. She does not sleep in a coffin, but on a blanket on the floor of a dark room. When she wakes up, her thirst for blood is strong and she must feed within a day or two. Because she is young, the sun does not seem to bother her. She is very strong, but cannot change shapes.

She lives in many places throughout her long life, including a period in China. In the late nineteenth century, she moves to England and takes a job at the Working Lads' Institute, helping the underprivileged in London's East End. She retains the appearance of a teenager. She is present when Jack the Ripper begins killing prostitutes, who are really all vampires trading sex for blood. The autopsies suggest that the Ripper is someone with some surgical training.

As a result of the slayings, Genevieve meets Charles Beauregard, a mortal and member of the mysterious Diogenes Club. Together they investigate the murders and track the assailant. The trail finally lead them to Dr. Jack Seward and Lord Godalming (two of the original characters in *Dracula*). For capturing the killers, they earn an audience with Queen Victoria and Count Dracula. Genevieve has become Beauregard's lover by this time and does not realize that she is caught up in a plot hatched by the Diogenes Club to end Dracula's rule in England. Beauregard carries a silver knife into the meeting and passes it to the Queen, who immediately commits suicide. Her act ends Dracula's hold on the country. In the ensuing chaos, Genevieve and Beauregard make their way out of the palace, she to a new life and identity and he to further adventures in the sequel to *Anno Dracula*, *The Bloody Red Baron* (1995).

SOURCES:

Newman, Kim. *Anno Dracula*. London: Simon and Schuster, 1992. Reprint, London: Pocket Books, 1993.

Dominguez, Don Sebastian Juan

Don Sebastian Juan Dominguez is a character featured in the role-playing game *Vampire: The Masquerade*, which involves the vampire clans knows as the Kindred and a ruling council known as **The Camarilla.** His story begins in 1828, when he owned a ranch near the then-small town of Los Angeles. On Christmas day, a ship wrecks in nearby San Pedro Bay. The locals take in the survivors and salvage the cargo. Don Sebastian opens his home to a survivor named Jack Turpin, who has recovered a large box from the ship. Unbeknownst to Don Sebastian, the box contains the body of Christopher Houghton, a vampire.

Houghton had been driven out of Boston and was on his way to China when the ship crashed. After waking and discovering that his plans have been thwarted, he goes into a rage and kills Turpin and the Dominguez family. Only Don Sebastian survives and escapes. Houghton eventually tracks down Don Sebastian and turns him into his ghoul servant. He decides that he wants show the vampires in Boston that they made a mistake when they kicked him out of the city by turning Los Angeles into a utopian city, much like ancient Carthage. He has Don Sebastian approach the governor of the state to aid in this vision. Houghton seems to lose sight of his vision, however, living a life of debauchery instead of working to create his utopian vision.

In 1879, Houghton suddenly realizes that he has strayed from his original path and undergoes a dramatic change. He returns to his vision to building a new Carthage that will be an artistic haven. On December 25, 1870, the forty-second anniversary of his shipwreck, he "Embraces" Don Sebastian and turns him into a vampire. He establishes the new vampire as the Prince of Los Angeles. Don Sebastian works with Houghton to turn Los Angeles into a metropolis that can support the cosmopolitan vampire community that Houghton envisioned in his earlier dreams for the city. In 1909, Houghton sees his first motion picture and becomes enthralled with the new art form. He uses his considerable wealth to bankroll a number of film studios.

As a vampire, Don Sebastian is undead but freely lives in the secularized modern world. Holy objects have no effect on him, nor does running water. A stake hurts him, but by itself is not fatal. Sunlight, fire, and decapitation are the main danger. Because he is undead, his heart does not beat and he does not need to breathe. In the presence of humans, he fakes respiration. He heals quickly of most wounds.

Don Sebastian rules with a light hand until 1927, when Alonzo de Portola attempts to overthrow his rule. Don Sebastian holds off the insurrection by simply making de Portola and his followers disappear. For the next generation, his only worry is the jealously he feels whenever Houghton becomes infatuated with another young movie star. This jealousy blinds him to the fact that a number of anarchists and loners are moving into Los Angeles and beginning to cause trouble.

In 1943, Jeremy McNeil, a vampire from New England, arrives in town. Houghton takes him in and becomes quite infatuated with him. Don Sebastian recognizes that McNeil is a threat to his position. McNeil feels that there should be no princes or hierarchies. Fearing that the young vampire will soon replace him, Don Sebastian waits until Houghton is out of the city and has McNeil beaten and orders him out of Los Angeles. Instead of leaving, McNeil plans a rebellion. On December 21, 1944, the rebellion begins with the systematic assassination of the city's elder vampires. Over the next 24 hours the battle rages.

During the course of the revolt, Don Sebastian is decapitated and killed. A story circulates that says that he was killed in a one-on-one battle with Salvador Garcia, McNeil's chief associate in the revolt. In fact, when Garcia entered Don Sebastian's house, he found that a great slaughter had already taken place and that Don Sebastian was dead, his head severed from his body. Garcia smeared himself with Don Sebastion's blood and announced that he had killed the prince. He did this as a bit of propaganda to send a warning to the Camarilla that a new prince would not be tolerated in Los Angeles.

In the wake of the revolt, McNeil declares the formation of the Anarch Free State of Los Angeles. The revolt spreads north to San Francisco and south to the border, making California unique in the world of the Kindred.

SOURCES:
Dudley, Noah. *Los Angeles by Night*. Stone Mountain, GA: White Wolf, 1994.

Donna Mia

Donna Mia, is a succubus demon who made her first appearance in the horror anthology comic book *Dark Fantasies*. While superficially appearing to be a vampire, she is in fact a succubus demon who has possessed the body of a young girl. As a woman, she was born in the winter of 1418 in Arba, Fruili, an impoverished part of Italy. As a demon, she was with the spirits cast out of heaven with Lucifer. After their fall, they split into two groups. Those who serve Lucifer are the devils. Those who reject Lucifer and want to repent are the demons. Lucifer forbade their attempted return to heaven and closed the doors leading out of hell. The demon who becomes Donna Mia found her way out of hell but has been unable to find her way back to heaven.

As Donna Mia, the demon appears as an attractive and seductive young woman with shoulder-length dark hair. She has a set of bat-like wings, cloven hoofs, and a tail, each of which make it difficult to move about in human society. She can change her shape to hide any two of the three, but not all three. Usually, she will hide the wings and feet, and tucks the tail between her legs. She has a set of pointed ears that are hidden under her hair. In the daylight, she dissolves into a mist, re-forming each night. As a succubus, she drains the life from her victims. Feeding is an intimate matter that almost always involves sex.

Donna Mia lives in Europe for many years, but in the early 1990s, she moves to the United States. The first person she meets in New York is a vampire who invites her to a party at the home of the vampire prince of New York. (Vampires in Europe and America are organized along aristocratic bloodlines.) Donna Mia, who prefers to dress in nothing at all under normal circumstances, wears a very revealing dress to the party. The evening is a disaster. The vampires are very condescending to her and treat her with contempt. She gets the last laugh, however. As morning arrives, she pulls the drapes down off the windows and lets the bright sunlight in, killing everyone at the party but her.

After the party, she is on her own with at least two enemies in hot pursuit. One is a "demolustrate," an inquisitor from a secret order that specializes in tracking down demons and disposing of them. The demolustrate tracks Donna Mia with a divining rod and comes armed with a hand of glory, a magical implement that will help him capture Donna Mia. She barely escaped their first encounter with the hunter. Her other pursuer is the entire vampire community. The head of that community wants her to stand trial for killing the prince of New York. She does not recognize the vampires' authority and does her best to evade them.

Donna Mia is the creation of Trevlin Utz. She first appeared in the second issue of *Dark Fantasies*. More recently, she has graduated to her own comic title.

SOURCES:
Dark Fantasies. No. 2. Richmond, VA: Dark Fantasy Productions. 1993.
Utz, Trevlin. *Donna Mia.* Richmond, VA: Dark Fantasy Production, 1995.
———. *Donna Mia.* No. 1–2. Urbana, IL: Avatar, 1997.
———. *Donna Mia Giant Size.* Urbana, IL: Avatar, 1997.

Doran

Doran, is a fifteenth-century vampire featured in the role-playing game *Vampire: The Masquerade*. He established the presence of **The Camarilla,** the worldwide body that governs vampires, in New Orleans. He is a member of the Ventrue Clan, from which most of the leaders of the Camarilla were drawn. The Ventrue are the most learned and sophisticated of the vampires and they blend in easily in human society.

Doran was made a vampire in 1471, his parent being Gaius Marcellus, a vampire who had been a Roman tribune before living quietly in France for many centuries. A student of philosophy, Doran turns his attention to studying the social structures within the vampire community. In the early 1600s, he moves to America. He is disappointed with life along the Eastern seaboard because he feels that the European nations that are colonizing America are corrupting it just as they corrupted their own homeland. In 1705 he migrates westward and settles in what was to become New Orleans. Shortly after his arrival, he is joined by one Simon de Cosa, a Spanish vampire. After de Cosa attacks Doran over a dispute in 1713, a long-lasting feud develops. After Doran gains control of Jean Baptiste le Moyne, Sieur de Bienville, the governor of the territory, de Cosa befriends other influential members of the community and forces Bienville from office in 1713. Bienville is replaced by de Cosa's servant, Antoine Cadillac, but their victory is short-lived because Bienville returns to power in 1716.

While de Cosa harasses Doran for the next half century, Doran remains firmly in power. Their power struggle goes on behind the scenes in New Orleans, but it plays a large part in the city's development. In 1763, as a result of the Seven Years War, Spain gains control of the territory. All of the government officials under Doran's control are removed from office. de Cosa seems to be in control, but his position is fragile, as is that of the small group of Spanish officials trying to control the restless French populous. Doran gains support from the growing vampire community in New Orleans (part of the larger vampire community known as the Kindred).

de Cosa is never able to consolidate his power, and after the French again take control of Louisiana in 1801, he flees the city and is never heard from again. French control quickly passes to the Americans, who purchase the Louisiana Territory in 1803. Doran suddenly finds himself caught in the middle of a struggle between two opposing groups of magicians. He aligns himself with the group that makes its headquarters in New Orleans as they battle their rural counterparts, the Technomancers. Doran believes the Technomancers are in Louisiana merely to steal the magical powers found there. The Technomancers finally attack in an attempt to take over the city. It turns out that the famous battle that human historians call the Battle of New Orleans was actually a fight between Doran and his allies and the Technomancers, which Doran's side won.

Doran is firmly in control after the battle, and for the next century he manages the city's growth in spite of the outside forces that at times seem to overwhelm it—cholera, the American Civil War, the Great Depression, and so on. With the post-World War II recovery bringing the city back to life, Doran announces his vision for the city, a new era in which mortals and vampires will be united. This idea runs counter to one of the key principles of the Camarilla called the Masquerade, which perpetuated the myth that vampires did not exist so that vampires would not be persecuted by humans. Doran knew there would be opposition to his plan, but he is unprepared for the overwhelming opposition. He is assassinated in 1955 and is succeeded by Marcel, who still rules the city today.

SOURCES:
Roskell, Patricia Ann. *New Orleans by Night*. Stone Mountain, GA: White Wolf, 1994.

Cover art from the comic book *Draculina*.

Draculina

Draculina is a young female vampiress who appears in the comic book that bears her name and serves as the hostess for the horror anthology comic book series, *Draculina's Cozy Coffin* (1994). Draculina is a midwestern girl who dreams of finding fame and fortune in Hollywood. Shortly after he 18th birthday, she loads up her car and heads for Los Angeles. Shortly after she arrives and before she can get settled, her car with all her worldly possessions in it is stolen. Broke and out of work, she is forced to take a part in a pornographic movie.

Shooting on the film is interrupted by the appearance of a stranger wearing formal evening wear and a cape. He kills the small movie crew and takes the terrified young girl to his home, a Hollywood mansion. There, he reveals to the girl that his name is Lewis and that she has been brought to his home to serve his personal pleasure. If she is obedient, they can live together for eternity. At that point, she realizes that Lewis is a vampire. As if to confirm her fears, he bites her and turns her into a vampire.

As that part of the story unfolds, a man named Wilson approaches the house with revenge on his mind. He enters the house and confronts Lewis and was followed into the house a few minutes later by the police. In the ensuing chaos, Lewis flees, leaving the girl laying on the floor. To convince the police that they are dealing with vampires, Wilson puts a drop of blood on Draculina's lips. Meanwhile, a policeman searching the house finds several women being held prisoner by Lewis. They appear to be half starved, and in fact they are—for blood. As soon as they are released, they attack the policemen and one by one drain their blood. Draculina joins in the carnage. Wilson attacks her with an ax, but she simply takes it from him and leaves. Thus, in the matter of just a few hours, the naive midwestern girl has been reborn as Draculina.

For the next part of her adventures, she goes on a killing spree and is about to face the police again when someone picks her up in a car and takes her to a mansion outside the city. There, the man who picked her up explains why he needs her. It seems that his wife died a year ago and he has been preserving her body ever since. In seeking a way to revive her, he comes across the idea of giving her a transfusion from a vampire. He convinces Draculina to give his wife a transfusion and it actually works—his wife comes back to life. Unfortunately, she was dead for so long that she just comes back as a mindless creature with no intellect or memory. Instead of rejoining her husband, she is tracked down and killed.

SOURCES:
Gallagher, Hugh, "Blood of the Bride." *Draculina*. No. 1. Centralia IL: Draculina Publishing, 1993.

Dracutwig

The story of Dracutwig, a young vampiress reminiscent of the 1960s model Twiggy, appears in the 1969 book *Dracutwig* by Mallory T. Knight (pseudonym of Bernard Hurwood). Dracutwig is born in Transylvania near the Carpathian Mountains in the winter of 1950–51, the offspring of **Count Dracula** and a beautiful villager, Charmaine Shakowsi. Two days before Dracutwig's birth, Dracula marries her mother, who dies during childbirth. Dracula names his daughter as he does because she is a new twig on a seemingly dead branch of his family tree. She grows up in his castle and sleeps in a coffin, although she outwardly appears quite normal.

Dracutwig grows into a beautiful young woman with long black hair. Though somewhat pale and, like Twiggy, very thin, the village boys fall in love with her. Dracula protects her, but, when she is eighteen, is too late to prevent Josef, one of the old vampires also living in his castle, from being the first to bite her. Josef pays with his undead life. Dracula then sends his daughter to London to attend Mrs. Ponsonby-Smythe's School for Young Ladies. He richly provides for her, but before school begins, she ventures into the city on a shopping spree that completely changes her life's course.

During her spree, she meets fashion photographer Harry Brockton. He was looking for a new image, and Dracutwig arrives to become the manifestation of that new image: the "Dead Look!" Within a month she is the top model in the Western world. Even Count Dracula finally hears of his daughter's new career and quietly ventures to London to see what is happening.

Brockton initiates his new world-class model to the joys of sex, but during their lovemaking, Dracutwig has a strange new urge. She turns and bites Harry on the neck. Luckily for him, she does not break his skin. He is a hemophiliac. The next day, however, changes in Dracutwig's life begin on a grand scale. Dracutwig notices that her image in a mirror is becoming blurry. Film from three days of shooting is messed up. Soon, her image disappears altogether from both mirrors and film. Concurrently, her urges to bite people and drink blood overcome her, and she begins to move about the London streets at night, seeking victims.

Slowly, Harry becomes aware that Dracutwig is a vampire, but decides to marry her despite that fact and over the strong objections of his wealthy mother. Harry's mother, who also figures out Dracutwig's true nature, finally becomes enraged to the point of attempting to kill Dracutwig. She breaks into her suite and shoots her. Since bullets do not kill vampires, Dracutwig was up and about the next day, as if nothing had happened. On the second try, Harry's mother uses a stake and is more successful.

As it turns out, Harry's mother has fallen victim to a plot by her son to gain control of the family fortune. Unfortunately, the mother does not figure out the scheme until she is confined to a hospital psychiatric ward, while Harry drives off with his latest infatuation, a young blonde, in a Rolls Royce. What Harry has not counted upon, however, was the presence of the large bat following him as he drives away.

SOURCES:
Knight, Mallory T. *Dracutwig*. New York: Award Books, 1969.

Dragosani, Boris

Boris Dragosani is a Russian agent who gets his wish and becomes a vampire in Brian Lumley's novel *Necroscope* (1988). He is the child of a Romanian couple who had sex on the grave of an ancient vampire named **Thibor Ferenczy.** The woman was a virgin, and her blood dripped into the ground and was absorbed by Ferenczy, who was trapped below and barely alive. As a child, Boris is drawn to Ferenczy's grave and is contacted by the vampire, who teaches the youth about his special abilities—he can read the thoughts of the dead through their entrails.

As an adult in the mid-1970s, Dragosani works for a secret Soviet agency that specializes in psychic espionage—ESP, "locators" who can track people anywhere on the globe, and other mental tricks. Dragosani's talent allows him to examine the internal organs of a dead body and read them for information. He has a counterpart in England, **Harry Keogh**, who is a necroscope—that is he can actually talk to the dead without "reading" their entrails. Dragosani is hated by the dead because the means by which he obtains information from them is seen as a horrible violation, whereas Keogh is beloved by the dead because he is the only person in the world who can hear their voices and talk to them.

Dragosani decided to travel to Romania to once again visit Ferenczy's grave. He has decided that he wants to be a vampire, to join the *vamphyri*, as the ancient race of vampires is called in Lumley's world. During his conversation with Ferenczy, he learns of his origins for the first time. Ferenczy then grants his wish, turning him into a vampire. A colleague from Russia who made the trip to Romania with him becomes Dragosani's first meal.

Dragosani's next assignment takes him to England, where he is supposed to kill the head of England's E-Branch, its own version of a psychic spy agency. By this time, Dragosani has discovered the downside of vampirism—the constant blood lust. He decides he doesn't want to be a vampire after all, so Ferenczy promises to help him return to human form if Dragosani will free the ancient vampire from his grave and

Original artwork from Daerick Gross from the *Necroscope* comic book series.

provide him with fresh blood. Dragosani complies, but the ungrateful Ferenczy attacks Dragosani as soon as he is freed from his grave. His attack fails—Dragosani kills Ferenczy. Angered, Ferenczy makes contact with Keogh through Keogh's "deadspeak" and tells him how to kill the upstart Dragosani.

Dragosani returns to his Russian headquarters, where he plans to use his powers to take over the world. Keogh foils his plans by traveling to Russia and then literally raising an army of the dead from the ancient battlefields in the Russian countryside. All of the dead near the Russian headquarters either hate Dragosani for the way he treats the dead or hate the Russians due to past battles and conflicts. In the fight both men were killed, Keogh by gunfire and Dragosani by a stake to the heart and decapitation. Keogh uses his powers to send Dragosani's spirit to live in the body of Thibor Ferenczy, banishing him from the Earth forever.

SOURCES:
Lumley, Brian. *Necroscope*. London: Grafton, 1988. Reprint, New York: Tor Books, 1988.

Drake, Mr.

Mr. Drake, the new guidance counselor at Bailey Elementary School in Bailey City, U. S. A., is, like **Mrs. Jeepers**, the school's new third-grade teacher, the object of speculation that he is a vampire. There is no denying he looks the part and, ultimately, his actions betray him. He appears suddenly one day in the schoolyard dressed in back, his outfit highlighted by a long leather coat. He has pale skin, pointy teeth, and slicked-back black hair. A Romanian, he speaks with a thick European accent, and his hands are cold to the touch. Although he can go out in the daytime, he prefers the dark and even keeps the lights turned off in his office.

Mr. Drake discovers that he is not hungry during the day and usually is able to wait until after dark to eat. His favorite meal is a midnight snack. On the other hand, he is constantly thirsty, and, from the various beverages available to him in the school, chooses to drink pink lemonade. While a few of the kids conclude that Mr. Drake is Dracula, others observe that Dracula doesn't drink lemonade.

When he leaves the school at the end of the day, Mr. Drake wears a cloak. He seems to keep to the shadows and winds up at the Clancy mansion, where Mrs. Jeepers lives. The school kids decide that he must sleep in the coffin in the mansion's basement. Finally, the kids decide to test Councilor Drake (whose initials C. D. suggest **Count Dracula**) with garlic potato chips and a mirror. The tests prove indecisive, and before they can run further tests, Mr. Drake is gone. It seems that since he had come to town, his allergies had intensified and he felt like he had to move on to a more favorable environment. But had he really moved because the kids were on to him? They will never know. In the meantime they still have their suspicions about Mrs. Jeepers, their third-grade teacher.

SOURCES:
Dadey, Debbie, and Marcia Thornton Jones. *Dracula Doesn't Drink Lemonade*. New York: Scholastic, 1995.

Drayven

Drayven is the original vampire, according to the comic book series *The Gothic Scrolls: Drayven*. Drayven is a Hebrew slave in ancient Egypt. He is discovered by Nepthys, leader of a race of demonic beings who are the result of sexual relations between Satan's fallen angels and human women. These offspring assume dominion over the desert areas of Earth, where they are worshiped as deities. They demand sacrifices and feed on the blood of the victims. Taken before the demonic Nepthys after being singled out for insubordination, Drayven is immediately enthralled by the goddess's beauty.

Nepthys feeds and is taken by the vitality she feels from him. She sees that a maiden, Kryla, is sent to him. Drayven and Kryla fall in love, but Nepthys possesses his love and through Kryla leads Drayven into a sharing of blood. As he is about to begin his new life, events are unfolding elsewhere. Moses has approached the Pharaoh and the Hebrews are leaving Egypt. Nepthys decides to abandon Egypt. She leaves Drayven bleeding in her chamber and drags off Kryla with her.

Having become an immortal vampire and having rejected God, Drayven now spends his nights in search of Kryla and a means to his own salvation. Early in his search he rejoins the Hebrews and becomes a general in his friend Joshua's conquering army. When Joshua discovers what has happened to Drayven, however, he banishes him.

In modern times, Drayven resides in Chicago. He has a vampire acquaintance, Searec, whom he met in the Middle Ages. Searac becomes a vampire by drinking from Drayven, and later together they search for the Holy Grail in the hope that drinking from it will cure them. Now, Searec masquerades as a socialite and runs a nightclub, the Red Grail. They fight over an unusual woman named Peace. Drayven finds that in her presence, her heightened vitality grants him at least some temporary release from the thirst that dominates his existence. He keeps her secluded to protect her. Searac believes Drayven protects her for his personal satisfaction.

The Gothic Scrolls are Drayven's accounts of his adventures throughout the centuries.

SOURCES:
Hernandez, David. *The Gothic Scrolls: Drayven*. Boca Raton, Fla.: Davdez Arts, Inc., 1997.

DuCharme, Janette

Janette DuCharme is one of the main vampires in the television movie/film *Forever Knight*. She is more than 1000 years old, although her exact origins are murky. She was born to noble blood, but her life turns sour when she is sold into prostitution, possibly by her husband. Her life at the brothel is horrible. She befriends Anna, another prostitute, only to watch as the brothel owner savagely beats her to death after she becomes pregnant. Later, she is attacked by two soldiers, whom she tries to flee. She thinks she is safe when she reaches a group of nuns, but a priest gives her back to the men. As one of the men tries to rape her, she bites him and flees. Fully expecting to be caught from behind, she stops to see if she is being followed. She is stunned when she sees that her attacker now lies dead on the ground, killed by a stranger in a black cloak.

The stranger is **Lucien LaCroix,** a vampire. He visits Janette at the brothel and offers her a way out of her pain and suffering. She accepts his offer and is transformed into a vampire by LaCroix. Her first act as a vampire is to kill Daviau, the brothel owner who killed Anna.

For the next 200 years, she travels with LaCroix until they meet a young soldier named Nicolas de Brabant (who much later in life takes the name **Nick Knight**). Janette seduces Nicolas and then hands him over to LaCroix, who turns him into a vampire. He and Janette begin an on again, off again affair that lasts for centuries. In the sixteenth century, they actually live together as husband and wife for more than 90 years. Janette, however, cannot stand such strong feelings of love and leaves. Nick and Janette remain in contact for the next few centuries.

In the 1940s, Nick, Lucien, and Janette reunite in London. Nick and Janette begin to live together again, and at the height of the Nazi blitz on London, they "adopt" a young boy named Daniel, which awakens Janette's maternal instincts. Nick, who is a reluctant vampire and hates to feed on or harm people, is afraid that Janette is going to turn the boy into a vampire, so he makes him leave. LaCroix tracks him down, however, and turns the child into a vampire. Nothing is known of Daniel after that point.

In the television series *Forever Knight*, Janette (portrayed by Deborah Duchene) lives in Toronto and owns a night club called The Raven, which is a popular hang-out for the local vampire community. Just when it seems that Janette is falling for Nick again, she abruptly sells the club to LaCroix and leaves town (and the show), Her return to the show was in the works when the show was canceled in 1996.

Duckula, Count

Count Duckula is a cartoon character that was introduced in the United Kingdom in the 1980s. A cross between **Count Dracula** and Donald Duck, he lives in modern-day Transylvania at Castle Duckula with his servants, Igor and Nanny. Although the latest in a long line of vampire ducks, and feared by the local villagers, Count Duckula is a vegetarian who prefers tomato juice to blood. He wears the requisite formal evening attire and opera cape, but he has no fangs. He sleeps in a magical coffin than can transport, not only him, but his entire castle to various parts of the world for his different adventures. He has an archenemy in Dr. Von Goosewing, the vampire hunter. The unfortunate count is in love with the doctor's niece, Vanna von Goosewing.

Count Duckula was brought to television in an animated cartoon series in the United Kingdom in 1988, a series later shown in America. His story was brought to comic books by Marvel Comics in 1988 in a *Count Duckula* comic that appeared bimonthly for fifteen issues.

SOURCES:

Count Duckula. Nos. 1–15. New York: Marvel Comics, 1988-91. Drake, Royston. *Duckula: The Vampire Strikes Back*. London: Carnival, 1990.

Duncan, Fred

In the children's book *A Vampire Named Fred*, Fred Duncan makes an unusual first impression on Hermie and Al, two young boys who help their new neighbors move into their home in a residential neighborhood at the edge of a small American town. They help Carl, a short thin man who had guided the movers, to unpack all the boxes. The last box, a long thin one, contains a man. He is asleep with his hands crossed over his chest. He wears a tuxedo. He sits up and speaks with a heavy accent. His skin is pale white and cold to the touch. He has a sharp nose, pale lips, and slicked-back hair. He is tall, like a basketball player.

Carl introduces the man to the boys as Fred. They recognize him as a vampire and are afraid. Fred quickly assuages their fears by explaining what is true and false about vampires. He tells them that he has had to face considerable prejudice because the movies give people false impressions of vampires. Over a glass of Perrier, he tells them, for example, that vampires have very sensitive skin and thus tend to go out at night, although with the proper clothing, they could go out in daylight.

That evening after dark, the boys come back to visit with Fred and Carl. Hermie is taken aback by the large bat, actually Fred, hanging from a large bird perch in the living room. Carl explains that Fred does not drink blood but prefers hamburgers, well done.

Fred has several very real problems. For example, cats do not like vampires, and very soon after Fred moves in, a host of cats show up around the house, arching their backs and howling. Al and Hermie take care of the problem by luring them away with catnip. A more serious problem for Fred is finding work. Bound to the evening, it is often difficult for a vampire to make a living. The young boys eventually come up with a solution: show business. With his ability to turn into a bat, the boys reasoned, Fred is in a perfect position to do a trained bat act. He and Carl try out the act at a children's birthday party. The children are delighted and Fred is hooked on performing. And in the process of moving and finding a job, Fred has solved another problem. He now has some new friends: Hermie and Al.

SOURCES:

Crider, Bill. *A Vampire Named Fred*. Lufkin, TX: Maggie Books, 1990.

Dupah

Dupah is a young vampire ready to move into adulthood in the low-budget comedy, *A Polish Vampire in Burbank* (1980). For young vampires, the crucial step is their first bite. Dupah has grown to manhood in his father's castle located in the mountainous region of Burbank, California. He sleeps in a coffin with his Frankenstein doll and wears his store-bought bat-covered pajamas. However, rather than going out at night to feed and participate in the other activities enjoyed by boys his age, Dupah is content to watch television all night. At the end of each evening, his father brings him food which he collects in a plastic bag after his own feeding.

Dupah's family members are traditional vampires. They sleep in coffins. They have to feed each evening, but their bite alone does not have the power to turn their victims into vampires. They are repelled by garlic and crosses. Papa is an aristocratic Eastern European and dresses formally in the same clothes each evening. Dupah wears more informal contemporary clothing.

Dupah has been slow to hunt because of his self-doubt—he believes his fangs are too short to penetrate a victim's skin. But Dupah's father is unsympathetic and grows impatient with his inhibited son. In an attempt to initiate him, he sends Dupah out with his older sister Yvonne to hunt on the streets of Burbank. On his second night out he finds a girlfriend, Delores Lane, who likes vampire movies. He is slow to make his move, but several nights later she invites him to a party. Just as he works himself up to make his move for the jugular, someone announces that dawn is approaching. Dupah barely makes it home and, like Cinderella, loses his shoe.

Delores finds his shoe the next day and brings it to the castle. Finding Dupah sleeping in his coffin, she thinks that he has gone to great pains to impress her. She is also offended that he has never put the bite on her. After she crawls into the coffin, Dupah finally loses his virginity. Delores returns to her home ready to make changes in her new vampiric life.

The two young lovers immediately experience some of the hard choices that come with their new life. Dupah's papa reminds him, for example, that vampires cannot be faithful and take blood from only one person. Yvonne, he notes, attacks two or more victims each evening. And then there is the problem of becoming infatuated with one's food and turning her into a vampire without telling her about the rules of the game. What ordinary people take for granted, like sunshine, are to young vampires, like Delores, absolutely fatal.

Delores falls victim to her own ignorance, and is consumed in the sun. She reestablishes contact with Dupah who now has a new choice thrust upon him. Now dead, Delores appears to Dupah as little more than a skeleton with hair, although her spirit is alive and well in the skeleton. Dupah must decide if he will go on living his vampire life or if he will sacrifice his own life and die (thus becoming a skeleton) so he can be with Delores. A true romantic at heart, there is no debate over what he will do.

Durward, Lady

Lady Durward, a different kind of psychic vampire, is the target of the vampire hunting team assembled in Hammer Films', *Captain Kronos: Vampire Hunter* (1974). Lady Durward is the widow of Hagen, the ninth Lord Durward, minor royalty in the small

Captain Kronos defeats Lady Durward using the reflective blade of his sword to shield himself from her hypnotic gaze.

nineteenth-century town of Durward, somewhere in Germany. She is a Karnstein by birth, and hence related to the vampire **Carmilla Karnstein.** A tall blonde with brilliant blue eyes, Lady Durward lives in a large mansion near the village which has taken its name from her family. She has two children, a son and daughter, both now young adults. In the seven years since the death of her husband, Lady Durward has been busy. Utilizing a combination of necromancy and vampirism, she works to regain her youth, attain immortality, and resurrect her husband, the best swordsman of his generation, to join her.

To accomplish her goal, Lady Durward becomes a recluse, seeing no one but her son. She wears a mask to cover the change that is gradually happening to her. She has become an accomplished practitioner of the dark arts, and as a vampire begins attacking the young women in the neighborhood. After drawing them to her with her hypnotic eyes, she sucks the women's youth and vitality with a kiss on the lips. The victims are left with the appearance of great age. A trickle of blood runs from the corner of their mouths. Although they wear crosses, the sacred symbols are useless if worn without the faith to execute their purpose.

Lady Durward also attacks Dr. Marcus, the local physician, although she bites him rather than immediately taking the youth remaining in him. He has assumed responsibility for the deaths of the young women in town and summons army-friend-turned-vampire-hunter **Captain Kronos** and his colleague, Professor Grost, to defeat Lady Durward.

Proving Lady Durward (as opposed to her daughter, Sarah, the other likely candidate) is the vampire involves the assistance of a young friend of Captain Kronos, who volunteers to be the vampire's next target. She is invited to stay over at the Durward mansion just as Lady Durward is culminating her work. She has attained the youthful appearance she sought and has brought her husband back to life. Captain Kronos uses all of his skill to defeat Lord Durward in a sword battle and then turns his weapon on Lady Durward. Her career ends impaled on the recently forged sword.

Edward

Edward, one of the main vampires in the role-playing game *Vampire: The Masquerade*, is the prince of the vampire community in Denver. In the eleventh century, he serves as a troubadour, accompanying William the Conqueror on his conquest of England. He is disgusted at the carnage and chaos of war, feelings that never really leave him as the centuries pass. He is somewhat obsessed with keeping the peace and quelling disorder before its gets out of hand. He is part of the Toreador Clan, the most sophisticated and artistic of the several vampire groups that form **The Camarilla,** the worldwide governing organization for the Kindred (as the vampire community is known). He is of medium height with dark, well-groomed hair, and he is always well dressed.

Edward has an intense love for music. In 1808, while in Austria for the opening of opera season, he meets a young Austrian soldier who shares his interest. When a group of human businessmen discover his vampire secret, they try to kill him and seize his fortune. Knowing he cannot defeat the men himself, he turns the soldier (whose name is Duke) into a vampire to help him fight. Together, they eliminate the men. Duke remains with Edward to this day.

After the incident, the vampire Prince of Vienna asks Edward and Duke to leave the city to avoid further trouble. They move on to Eastern Europe and settle in London toward the end of the century. Anticipating the start of World War I, they move to the United States in 1900 and travel West until they find a comfortable home in Denver. There are already Kindred living in the city, but too few to make organizing worth their while. In 1920, Edward and Don Alonzo de Vargas, the only two elder vampires, decide to organize. With Duke's support, Edward proposes that he become prince of Denver and share power with Duke and Don Alonzo in a ruling council. The three have ruled Denver ever since.

In his most recent adventure, Edward has to deal with a perceived threat to his power. He has been informed that a reclusive vampire named Jacob Prestor is conspiring to overthrow his rule. In fact that is not the case. Prestor is actually the famous scientist **Louis Pasteur,** who, in the world of the *Vampire* game, is now a vampire. Pasteur is really busy researching a "cure" for vampirism, but there are members of the vampire community who see this as a threat to their existence and thus want to stop him. For this reason, they spread the rumor that Jacob Prestor is trying to overthrow William. When he learns that William wants to kill him, Prestor creates a new group of vampires to protect him. He hates himself for turning these people into vampires, but he thinks he is close to discovering a cure and will be able to change them back to humans very soon. However, William moves swiftly to kill Prestor, and the new vampires are never changed back.

SOURCES:

Berry, Jeff. *Alien Hunger.* Stone Mountain, GA: White Wolf, n.d.

The Elder

The Elder is an ancient vampire assigned as the guardian of the original vampires **Akasha** and **Enkil** after they become immobile and cease to need blood. He is aware of the story of how vampires originated and the claim that the existence of all vampire depends upon the ancient, living statues that he guards. Tiring of his assignment, he decides that the ancient legend needs to be tested since several millenia have passed since the origin of vampires. He places the pair out in the direct sunlight. His actions immediately have a disastrous effect—every vampire in the world is burned, and many of the weaker ones are killed.

The vampire **Marius** is sent to Egypt to discover the reason behind the burning. He finds the Elder, learns the story of the origin of vampires, and realizes that the Elder must have placed Akasha and Enkil in the sun. Akasha asks Marius to take them out of Egypt and he agrees, relocating them to his island sanctuary in Greece. Enraged, the Elder tries to kill Marius but ends up being killed by Akasha.

SOURCES:

Ramsland, Katherine. *The Vampire Companion: The Official Guide to Anne Rice's The Vampire Chronicles.* New York: Ballantine Books, 1993.

Rice, Anne. *The Queen of the Damned.* New York: Alfred A. Knopf, 1988. Reprint, New York: Ballantine Books, 1989.

Ely, Duncan

Duncan Ely, the antagonist in Fred Mustard Stewart's *The Mephisto Waltz* (1969), is a Satanist in search of immortality and a continued life with his true love, his daughter Roxanne. When the story opens in the late 1960s, Ely is a successful concert pianist who is near death. A man in his seventies, he is white-haired, tall, and thin, and has large hands.

Some twenty years earlier, Ely's wife was killed in an accident. Her throat had been ripped out while the couple was on a ski vacation. The story notes that Duncan is the owner of a black Labrador named Robin, one of a series of similar dogs he has possessed over the years, each capable of such an act. Before she died, Ely's wife gave birth to a daughter who grew into a black-haired beauty. Roxanne was married briefly, but since her divorce seems content to devote her life to assisting her father.

Roxanne (Barbara Perkins) and Duncan Ely (Curt Jurgens) from *The Mephisto Waltz*.

As he ages, a wealthy Ely concocts a scheme to continue his life, career, and love affair with his daughter. He makes contact with His Infernal Majesty through a book, an 1835 reprint of a medieval black magic text, *The Book of Calls*. The process of survival requires his locating a new body into which his soul can move at the moment of death. His death must be intentional. He must be wearing the life mask of his victim and consume some of the victim's blood at the time of death (hence the vampiric aspect). He finally locates a new home for his soul in Myles Clarkson, a young writer Roxanne's age who has large hands similar to Ely's and who at one time contemplated becoming a concert pianist.

Ely's transformation is slowly discovered by Clarkson's wife who notes the personality change in her husband as he quickly assumes the career of the late Ely. Finally concluding that her husband is indeed dead, she concocts a scheme that allows her to have some element of revenge, ultimately thwart the late Ely's plans, and prevent her husband from divorcing her and marrying Roxanne.

Breaking into the Ely home, she knocks out Roxanne and steals the book, takes a sample of her blood, and removes her life mask from the wall. She then goes home

ANIMAL VAMPIRES

Its not just bats and wolves associated with vampires anymore. Other animals have found their place in the contemporary vampire explosion. Possibly the most popular animal vampire of all time is Bunnicula, the cute little rabbit that found a home with Chester the cat, Harold the dog, and the Monroe family in Deborah and James Howe's juvenile classic *Bunnicula* (1979) and its many sequels. Contrast the loveable Bunnicula with Zoltan, Count Dracula's attack dog who became a vampire in a novel (*Dracula's Dog* by Ken Johnson in 1977) and then a movie (*Zoltan...Hound of Dracula* in 1978).

Without discounting Zoltan, it was juvenile literature, not movies, that became the real home of animal vampires. Animals became a means of introducing children to vampire monsters, making them less scary and transforming them into objects of humor.

Through the 1980s, for example, Count Duckula, the Transylvanian vegetarian vampire, gave Bunnicula a run in the children's popularity race. In the end, however, it was the cat (always associated with vampires in Japan) who took over. More than half-dozen turned to cats for their vampire character, including one fine Japanese tale by Lensey Namioka, *Village of the Vampire Cat* (1981).

Winning the award as the most unusual vampires, animal or human, are the turkeys, who appeared in the 1972 film *Blood Freak* (a turkey in every sense of the word) and in Dian Curtis Regan's delightful juvenile novel, *Fangs-giving* (1996).

and, after consuming Roxanne's blood, commits suicide while wearing the life mask. Her former body is buried and, enjoying a new life as Roxanne, she emerges to confront Ely (in the body of her husband) of all that has occurred. His musical career will continue, but Roxanne is forever out of his reach.

SOURCES:
Stewart, Fred Mustard. *The Mephisto Waltz*. New York: Coward, McCann & Geohagen, 1969. Reprint, New York: Berkley, 1978.

Enkil

Enkil is the husband of **Akasha**, the original vampire in Anne Rice's *Vampire Chronicles*. As soon as she became a vampire, Akasha also turned Enkil into a vampire, making them a sort of ruling couple of the vampire community. He was originally a ruler in Egypt 6,000 years ago. As Akasha's husband, he assists her in helping to turn their people away from cannibalism. This angers the more conservative forces in Egyptian society.

The opposition forces would have been easily held in check if not for a seemingly random sequence of events that spell disaster for Enkil and Akasha. Akasha orders that two witches—the sisters **Mekare** and **Maharet**—be brought to her court to demonstrate their magic. During their "performance," they insult Akasha and Enkil. In addition, they make contact with a spirit named **Amel** who unleashes his poltergeist-like effects on the audience. Akasha is very angry with the two witches, and even though Enkil urges her to simply let them go on their way without punishment, she does not heed his words.

Akasha determines their punishment, but it is Enkil who actually reads the sentence in public. He orders Mekare and Maharet to be publicly raped by the Chief

Steward **Khayman.** Amel retaliates by attacking Khayman. Priests try to exorcise his dwelling but are unsuccessful. The conservative forces who oppose Akasha and favor a return to the old ways seize the opportunity to overthrow Enkil and the queen and attempt to assassinate them. As Akasha lays bleeding, her soul tries to escape her body. Amel seizes it and essentially takes over her soul. He then enters her body and fuses himself to it, thus creating a new entity, the vampire. Akasha shares her blood (and, as it turns out, the essence of Amel's spirit) with Enkil. Like Akasha, Enkil heals miraculously and the pair emerge as the original vampires.

When Mekare and Maharet are brought back before Enkil and Akasha, they explain what has happened and tell the couple that the only way to end Amel's possession is to destroy their own bodies. Akasha finds that solution unacceptable and Enkil again stands by meekly as Akasha orders Mekare's tongue cut out and Maharet's eyes plucked out. They escape execution when Khayman, who was the first person vampirized by Akasha, helps them escape and offers them the "Dark Gift" of vampirism.

In the first years following Amel's possession, Enkil and Akasha have an almost insatiable thirst for blood, which causes them to kill many, many people. They also create a number of new vampires and discover that as the number of vampires increases, their own hunger decreases. Eventually, they have no need for blood at all. Once they reach that point, they cease to move and become living statues and remain together for centuries. In his final form, Enkil has long black hair, and his hairless chest is bare. He wears a broad gold collar and a white linen kilt and many decorative rings on his fingers.

The pair attain legendary status in the vampire community as "Those who must be kept." They are preserved and protected by vampire guardians who, although they don't fully understand what is happening, know that the very existence of all vampires depends upon the well-being of the royal couple. This link to all vampires is made abundantly clear when, several millenia after they first become vampires, they are set out in the sun by a bored guardian. Almost immediately, every vampire in the world is burned. Many weaker vampires die from the incident. One vampire, **Marius,** is sent to Egypt to discover what has caused this scourge. He discovers just what the guardian, who is known as **The Elder,** has done. Akasha urges Marius to take them to Europe, which he does, becoming the new guardian in the process. Before they leave, Akasha kills the Elder. In their new home, Enkil and Akasha become impersonal observers of the world by occupying the minds of vampires and mortals alike and seeing what they see through their eyes.

Over the years, they are visited by a few outsiders. Maharet, one of the witches approaches Akasha and strikes her and then stabs her in the heart with a dagger. As a vampire, Maharet feels the wound in her own body and immediately understands that the core of Amel is alive in Akasha (and not Enkil) and that the life of all vampires resides within her. Anne Rice's most famous vampire, **Lestat de Lioncourt,** visits the couple's chamber once when visiting Marius. Akasha wakes up and embraces Lestat, sharing blood with him. Enkil suddenly awakens himself and separates them. He is about to kill Lestat when Marius appears and saves him.

Some years later, in 1985, Marius enters the shrine room and discovers that Akasha has killed Enkil. All that is left of his body is a clear, glasslike shell—he has been completely drained of blood. It seems that Akasha woke from her slumber when she heard the music made by Lestat's rock band, The Vampire Lestat. Akasha, rejuvenated, leaves the shrine room and begins an attempt to dominate the world that would change the face of the vampire community forever.

SOURCES:

Ramsland, Katherine. *The Vampire Companion: The Official Guide to Anne Rice's The Vampire Chronicles*. New York: Ballantine Books, 1993.

Rice, Anne. *The Queen of the Damned*. New York: Alfred A. Knopf, 1988. Reprint, New York: Ballantine Books, 1989.

———. *The Vampire Lestat*. New York: Alfred A. Knopf, 1985. Reprint, New York: Ballantine Books, 1986.

Eramus

Eramus is the vampire narrator of a collection of short stories by Ronald Chetwynd-Hayes called *The Monster Club* (1975). Of indeterminate age, Eramus first appears late one evening on a London street, where he attacks Chetwynd-Hayes. He bites him, but not deeply enough to turn him into a vampire. When Eramus learns his victim's identity, he apologizes, because Chetwynd-Hayes is his favorite writer. To show just how sorry he is, he invites the author to join him at the Monster Club, an underground hotspot where modern-day vampires and other creatures of the night gather to socialize. Eramus promises Chetwynd-Hayes that he will gather plenty of material for his new book at the club.

At the Monster Club, the author learns that the main menu item is blood. Eramus doesn't care for it, however, because he prefers to gather blood fresh from a victim. On the wall behind the table where the pair sit is a monster genealogy chart, which Eramus takes the time to explain to Chetwynd-Hayes. It seems the different types of monsters are easily distinguished by their dominant trait—vampires drink, werewolves hunt, ghouls rip a body apart and eat it, shaddies lick, maddies yawn, mocks blow, but shadmock only whistle. Eramus proceeds to tell Chetwynd-Hayes stories about the various monsters.

Eramus is a traditional vampire with fangs and a blood thirst. He defends monsters and the fact that they prey on humans, noting that the number of victims killed by monsters is minuscule when compared to the number of murders humans themselves commit. Crimes by monsters seem almost insignificant when held side-by-side with the many ingenious ways humans have discovered to destroy entire populations—guns, bombs, war, and fatal diseases. In the end, Eramus proposes that Chetwynd-Hayes be admitted to the club. He argues that the club cannot truly call itself the Monster Club without admitting a single human member to represent humanity's monstrous acts.

The Monster Club was brought to the screen in 1985, with Vincent Price assuming the role of the vampire. It was also turned into a comic book featuring artwork by stellar graphic artist John Bolton.

SOURCES:

Bolton, John. *John Bolton's Halls of Horror.* No. 1-2. Guerneville, CA: Eclipse Comics, 1985.
Chetwynd-Hayes, Ronald. *The Monster Club.* London: New English Library, 1975.

Evans, Hugh

Poet Hugh Evans, a centuries-old vampire, emerges as the ultimate source of the group of female vampires known as the Vamps, who lend their name to the comic book series of the same name. A contemporary of Shakespeare, as a young man he had encountered an ogre of a vampire who, because of its ugliness, had difficulty luring victims. He first broke Evans's back and then transformed him into a vampire very slowly so the damage never healed. He then used Evans to attract his meals. It was many years before Evans was able to get away from him.

In twentieth-century America, however, Evans has emerged as a minor poet in New York City. He finds a mate in fellow poet Dee Franks. During the 1960s, after several decades in New York, they leave the city, as their social circle realizes that neither vampire is aging. The pair head for the Deep South, where in North Carolina they encounter a redneck named **Dave**. Uncouth and very different from New York poets, Dave is a welcome relief for Dee, in particular, who is attracted to his raw energy. Evans grows jealous and one evening attacks Dave. Dee gives Dave some of her blood to save him, and he becomes a vampire.

Eventually, Evans and Franks move on to California. They leave Dave who has begun to build a harem. The five vampire girls turn on Dave, kill him, and emerge as the Vamps.

Meanwhile, Evans and Dee settle in California where they build a modest following as vampire poets. Fans come to their home and give blood while listening to them read. Then in 1996, they are caught up in the schemes of Lawrence Dai Szae to become a vampire. He kidnaps Evans and holds him in the basement of a house in San Francisco while demanding that he be made a vampire. Evans refuses.

Dissuaded, Dai Szae turns to a more elaborate plan. He promotes a vampire movie built around the story of rock star Rhys Campbell, who had survived an encounter with the Vamps in New York City. The story lures the Vamps to Los Angeles where one of their members, **Mink**, is hired to star in the vampire movie. Dai Szae reconnects with **Screech,** an old acquaintance who had originally met Dave some years ago while researching vampires for Dai Szae. While Dai Szae pursues Screech as an alternative to Evans's making him a vampire, Franks involves **Skeeter** and the remaining Vamps in the quest to locate Evans. They finally track him to San Francisco and rescue him while Screech finishes off Dai Szae. When Mink's career crashes (her image cannot be captured by film), the Vamps reassemble and head off for new adventures, while Evans and Dee pick up their poetry career where they left off.

SOURCES:

Vamps. Nos. 1–6. New York: DC Comics/Vertigo: 1995–96.
Vamps: Hollywood & Vein. Nos. 1–6. New York: DC Comics, 1996.

Fallon, Webb

Webb Fallon (portrayed by John Abbott), the 400-year-old vampire in the Republic film, *The Vampire's Ghost* (1945), was cursed with his nocturnal condition after wrongfully causing the death of a young woman. His one positive memory of his human life is an act of service performed for Queen Elizabeth at the time of battle with the Spanish Armada. She had honored him with a box inscribed 1588, Fallon's most prized possession. He keeps a small quantity of his native soil in it.

Fallon is of average appearance, his most distinguishing feature being his large hypnotic eyes with which he is able to bend people—especially any who threaten his existence—to his will. He is able to walk around in daylight, but prefers the dusk. In the world of colonial Africa, he has settled in the fictional village of Bakuna where he runs a local bar/nightclub. Townspeople admit their lack of knowledge of him, but also realize they live in a place where it is impolite to inquire about a person's past.

As the plot progresses, a series of deaths occur on the local plantation. All the bodies are found with two little marks on their necks, drained of blood. The white leadership in town, including plantation owner Roy Kendrick, turn to Fallon with hoping he might know the local underworld life and potentially lead them to the killer. The native Africans are the first to realize that Fallon is the vampire responsible for the deaths. He does not reflect in a mirror and a bullet fired at him passes through his body without apparent effect. The townsfolk decide to kill Fallon with a spear dipped in molten silver, but it only wounds him. With the assistance of an unsuspecting Kendrick whom Fallon has hypnotized, Fallon is healed by the moonlight.

Upon his recovery, Fallon turns his attention to Julie, Kendrick's fiancé, whom he has decided to transform into his vampire bride during a ceremony in a deserted jungle temple. Kendrick, freeing himself from Fallon's hypnotic spell, tracks the pair to the jungle hideaway with the aid of native drums. The arrogant Fallon had earlier informed Kendrick that the only way to finally dispatch a vampire is to burn him and scatter his ashes, a task Fallon is able to complete to bring the plot to its just conclusion.

Webb Fallon (John Abbott) from the film *The Vampire's Ghost*.

The Vampire's Ghost has been heralded as the only film based upon John Polidori's *The Vampyre*, the first vampire story published in 1819. However, except for the element of the healing moonlight, almost nothing of Polidori's story is included in the original story by Leigh Bracket upon which *The Vampire's Ghost* is based. Webb Fallon certainly bears little resemblance to **Lord Ruthven**, the antagonist in the book *The Vampire's Curse*.

Feodorovna, Tatiana

Tatiana Feodorovna, the second eldest child of Czar Nicolas II and Czarina Alexandra of Russia, appears as a vampire in Michael Romkey's 1989 novel, *I, Vampire*. Born in 1897, Tatiana is executed along with the rest of the Russian royal family by the Communists in 1918. Before her execution, she had been turned into a vampire by the infamous Rasputin, who had been using his vampiric powers to keep her brother Alexis alive. When Rasputin was taken away, he left Tatiana to care for her brother. Because she is a vampire, she survives the execution attempt. Her family does not.

As a vampire, Tatiana has silky white skin and cherry-red lips. Her fangs are retractable. She is known for her distinctive perfume, Cote's Jasmin de Corse. Over the years, she affiliates herself with **The Illuminati**, the guiding force in the vampire community, and becomes an activist fighting Caesar Borgia, a rogue vampire who is trying to take over the world.

In 1989, while in Chicago, she meets a human named **David Parker**, who she thinks has potential as a vampire. Parker, a lawyer whose professional life has been largely destroyed by changes in his personal life, begins a relationship with Tatiana without realizing that she is a vampire. Slowly he discovers who and what she is. She eventually turns him into a vampire, following the established pattern for introducing the vampire "virus" into a human being—biting him three times at two-week intervals. Although she does not follow procedure and gain the Illuminati's permission before turning Parker into a vampire, the group eventually accepts him.

While the drama with Parker is unfolding, Tatiana is heavily involved in fighting Borgia's latest evil scheme, which involves taking over western Europe using German World War I General von Baden, Jack the Ripper, and the British Prince Albert Victor. Tatiana and Parker work together to foil Borgia's plan.

SOURCES:
Romkey, Michael. *I, Vampire*. New York: Fawcett Gold Medal, 1990.

Ferenczy, Thibor

Thibor Ferenczy, the first of a number of ancient vampires in the *Necroscope* series of novels by Brian Lumley, first appears in *Necroscope* (1988), although his life story is primarily featured in *Necroscope II: Vamphyri!* (1988). Ferenczy was born and grew up in the fifteenth century Wallachia (Romania). As the young warrior Thibor the Wallach, he fights for Vladimir I, the ruler of Wallachia. He is so successful in the battle that Vladimir sends him to Ferenczy Castle to kill an old enemy, Faethor Ferenczy.

What Thibor does not know is that Faethor is not a man at all, but rather a 1000-year-old vampire, the latest in a long bloodline of creatures known as the *vamphyri*. He has grown weary of the world and wishes to pass his bloodline on to a worthy successor, which he deems Thibor to be. He leaves his lands and his devil's head banner to his new son, Thibor Ferenczy. Vamphyri can turn a person into a vampire by draining their blood, but that person is not a true vamphyri. To be one of the powerful ruling vampires, the successor must receive the vampire "egg" from his predecessor, which Thibor does. Initially unhappy with his fate, Thibor rises up and slays Faethor.

As a vampire, Thibor becomes a hideous creature with a bestial appearance and a mouth full of fang-like teeth. When aroused, he is no longer even recognizable as a a human. Within two weeks of killing Faethor, he returns to his home and reports to Vladimir I. He is loyal to his ruler and continues to serve as a warrior for Vladimir even in his new state, but eventually Vladimir turns on him and confines him to a tomb with silver and iron chains. There he remains until the twentieth century.

In the 1950s, a young Romanian couple enjoys a night of passion on the ground above Thibor's now-deeply buried grave. The woman is a virgin, and some of her blood seeps into the ground below her. Thibor absorbs the precious substance, connecting him to the woman, and when she bears a child as a result of that evening, the vampire has a special psychic connection to the infant boy. The child, **Baron Dragosani**, eventually makes his way to Thibor's grave and learns he can communicate with the vampire deep in the ground. The vampire teaches him that he has a rare skill—he is a necromancer who can read information and thoughts from dead bodies by studying their entrails.

When he is older, Dragosani puts his special skill to use for a secret branch of the Soviet government that specializes in the "psychic" espionage. At that point, Dragosani realizes that he wants to be a vampire like Thibor, who accommodates his "son's" wishes. It doesn't take Dragosani long to realize that he does not enjoy living as a vampire because he cannot stand the constant blood lust that he feels. He returns to Thibor and demands to be made human again. Again Thibor agrees, but tells Dragosani that to help him, he must be freed from his grave. Once free, Thibor turns on Dragosani and tries to kill him. He fails, and is killed himself when Dragosani shoots him with an arrow shot from a crossbow and then decapitates him. Dragosani moves quickly to try to use his abilities to "read" Thibor's corpse, but the old vampires body turns into dust almost immediately.

Thibor's physical death, of course, was not the end of him. He remained conscious and began to communicate with **Harry Keogh**, a British agent who was a necroscope, a person with the ability to speak with the dead. In the return for his promise to continue visiting with him, he shared the secret of killing Dragosani.

SOURCES:

Lumley, Brian. *Necroscope*. London: Grafton, 1988. Reprint, New York: Tor Books, 1988.

———. *Necroscope II*. Wamphyri. London: Grafton, 1988. Reprinted as, *Necroscope II. Vamphyri*. New York: Tor Books, 1989.

Ferguson, Carlotta

Carlotta Ferguson is possibly the most famous pseudovampire in literature thanks to her starring role in Arthur Conan Doyle's Sherlock Holmes short story, "The Sussex Vampire" (1924). Holmes is called to the village of Lamberley, south of Horshan, in Sussex, England. Holmes initial reaction to the idea of vampires becomes one of his more famous sayings: "Rubbish, Watson, rubbish! What have we to do with walking corpses who can only be held in their grave by stakes driven through their hearts? It's pure lunacy."

Robert Ferguson, Carlotta's husband, calls Holmes' attention to the facts in the case. His wife is from Peru, where he met her in connection with his business, which imported nitrates from her homeland. She is a seemingly gentle and quiet person, but recently she had shown a very different side to her nature. She attacked Ferguson's teenage son Jack (a child from his first marriage) on two separate occasions. The attacks on the disabled boy were seemingly unprovoked and quite vicious. More importantly, she has been found by the nurse leaning over their baby and biting his neck. When discovered, the child had an open wound and Carlotta's face was smeared with blood. The nurse covered up the first incident, but Ferguson himself witnesses a second incident. She refuses to explain her actions.

The solution to the case found Watson and Holmes unraveling some complex family relationships. It seems that the teenage son was extremely jealous of the new baby, whom his father doted on. Carlotta discovered that Jack was poisoning the baby, but rather than expose Jack, whom she knew his father loved deeply, she chose to try and suck the poison out of the child. This explains why she was caught with the child's blood on her lips. The poison had been injected with a quiver used to hunt birds. Thus Holmes is able to solve the mystery and preserve his strong belief that seemingly supernatural acts can always be explained.

"The Sussex Vampire" has been frequently reprinted and anthologized, and a graphic art version appeared in 1996. In 1992, "The Sussex Vampire" inspired a full-length made-for television movies, "The Last Vampire," which retained the main story line but introduced a prominent new character named **John Sinclair Stockton**.

SOURCES:

Doyle, Arthur Conan. "The Sussex Vampire." *Strand.* (Jan. 1924).

———. "The Sussex Vampire" in *The Annotated Sherlock Holmes II.* Edited by William S. Baring-Gould. New York: Clarkson N. Potter, 1967.

———. "The Sussex Vampire." Adapted by Warren Ellis and Craig Gilmore. Plymouth, MI: Caliber Comics, 1996. Graphic art version.

Fern

Fern is one of the two vampires featured in the low-budget film *Vampyres* (1974), now considered a classic of the genre by vampire fans. Fern and her lover, **Miriam**, are shot and killed as they lie in bed entwined in each others arms. A short time later, they emerge as vampires, with no real explanation given for how that change occurs. They continue to live in the house where they were shot and find their next meals

Marianne Morris as the vampire Fern in the film *Vampyres*.

by hitchhiking on nearby roads. During the day, they sleep in a nearby graveyard. Whoever is unfortunate enough to stop and pick them up gets invited back to their house, where he or she is killed and drained. The women then put the body back in the car and stage what appears to be a serious accident. Instead of biting, Fern prefers to open a wound on her victims with a knife, which allows her to drink freely.

Both Fern and Miriam are rather traditional vampires. They are totally nocturnal. They do not reflect in mirrors. They need a nightly supply of blood, and getting that blood is the major focus of their time spent awake each night. They prefer to seduce their primarily male victims with wine and conversation rather than simply attacking them.

Their life has become brutally monotonous until one evening when Fern is picked up by a young man named Ted. She immediately decides that she likes him. Later that evening, instead of attacking and killing him, she invites him to her bed. He awakens the next morning to find Fern gone and a cut on his arm. He ascribes the wound to his own carelessness while drunk. Later in the day he returns to the house, and after finding it strangely deserted, he falls asleep in his car. When Fern returns after darkness falls, she finds him there and invites him to come inside and join her, Miriam, and Rupert, a man Miriam was picked up by earlier.

Fern again makes love to Ted. She drinks a little from his wound, but still does not kill him. Instead, she helps Miriam finish off Rupert. They dispose of his body and return home to shower. They leave Ted at the house as dawn approaches. The next night, Ted and Fern make love for the third time. She is nearly trapped in the sunlight when she oversleeps and is caught in the bedroom as the sun begins to rise. Unable to make it back to the graveyard, Fern and Miriam spend the day in the basement of the house. Ted has finally realized what is happening to him, but he is barely conscious and is too weak to do anything about it. Fern and Miriam are in such a hurry to escape the light of the sun that they leave Ted to fend for himself.

Ted is awakened the next morning by an angry real estate agent, who suggests that Ted had better leave the premises right away. As he is preparing to leave, Ted overhears the salesman telling the prospective buyers that the house is supposedly haunted by two women who had been killed inside. Ted is left to wonder whether his experience had been real or all just a dream. Fern and Miriam are left to continue there nightly routine of wine, love, and blood.

The film was made into a fan book that includes pictures and stories about the movie in 1996.

SOURCES:
Greaves, Tim. *Vampyres*. Glen Carbon, IL: Draculina Publishing, 1996.

Fionguala, Ethelind

Ethelind Fionguala appears in the 1988 story "Ken's Mystery." A rare breed of Irish vampire, Ethelind lives in County Cork in the 1880s. She is about to marry a man named O'Connor, but on the night of her wedding is stolen by a group of vampires. Later that night, she is rescued by the Kern of Querin and becomes his wife. She does not live long and after her death is buried in an isolated grave.

During his visit to County Cork, a man by the name of Mr. Keningale is told of Ethelind and the house of the kern, although he never receives details of her life. On All Hallow's Eve, as he walks home from a dinner party, Keningale gets lost and finds himself standing before Ethelind's grave. There he finds a woman sitting on the tombstone wearing a calla, an old-style outer garb popular in Ireland that completely covers one's clothes. The woman had pulled up the hood so that her head and face would be obscured. She and Keningale talk and she shows him the way back to town. He gives her a ring and she agrees to come to his room and allow him to paint her portrait.

After he leaves the woman, he wanders by the kern's old house. As he stands before the house, he begins to ask himself questions about the mysterious woman at the grave. If he plays some music, he thinks to himself, he can almost imagine her appearing. He takes his banjo and begins to sing a love song. Suddenly, a young, beautiful, richly attired woman appears from the second-story window. She drops a key to Keningale and he unlocks the door and goes in the house. A cold but soft hand leads him through the darkness to a large room decorated in antique splendor. The pale-skinned woman is dressed in white with diamonds in her hair and on her bosom. Keningale recognizes her as a woman who has appeared in his dreams since childhood. Somehow he knows this is her one night of the year.

He kisses her cold lips. As he sings to her, her cold, pale skin becomes ruddy and warm. He becomes cold and bloodless. The form of Ethelind becomes brighter, but her image loses its distinctiveness. Eventually Keningale passes into unconsciousness, only to awaken the next morning with all the blood seemingly taken from him. Where did Ethelind go? That remains a mystery.

SOURCES:

Hawthorne, Julian. "Ken's Mystery." In Julian Hawthorne, *David Poindexter's Disappearance*.1888. Reprinted in Dalby, Richard, ed. *Dracula's Brood*. New York: Dorset Press, 1987.

Fitzroy, Henry

Henry Fitzroy, the illegitimate son of King Henry VIII of England, first appears in Tanya Huff's novel, *Blood Price* (1991). Raised in relative comfort, Fitzroy, is named Duke of Richmond and Somerset, Earl of Nottingham, and a Knight of the Grater. While enjoying his carefree existence, he meets Christina, a 200-year-old vampire, with whom he shares blood. He appears to die and is buried. It takes Christina three days to dig him out and assist him through the "time of frenzy," which accompanies the change. She also teaches him to feed without killing, but after a year she disappears from Fitzroy's life.

As a vampire, Fitzroy combines traditional traits with nontraditional ones. He is nocturnal, but he does not sleep in a coffin, merely a dark space. He does not eat or drink normal food and does not reflect in mirrors. He is not affected at all by crosses or holy water, and he has developed great strength. Since he was turned into a vampire, he ages much slower than he did as a human. As a result, by the late twentieth century, he appears to be only in his mid-20s.

After Christina leaves him, he make his way to Italy and settles in Venice, where he begins a relationship with Ginevra Treschi. He confides in her and tells her that he is a vampire. Suspected of associating with the devil, she is taken into custody by the Inquisition. Fitzroy is unable to prevent her torture and death, but he does take revenge on her killers. He remains in Europe until after World War I, when he moves to Canada. He eventually settles in Toronto, where he lives alone in a condominium. He makes his living writing romance novels under the name of Elizabeth Fitzroy.

In the early 1990s, a serial killer strikes Toronto who leaves distinctive marks on his victims and drains them of their blood. The murders are called the vampire killings by the press, and Fitzroy suspects a young vampire is in the midst of the frenzy for blood that accompanies the conversion from human to vampire. To protect himself, he begins to track the killer. He soon meets Vicki Nelson, a former police officer now working as a private detective who is investigating the murders. They join forces and are soon led into a realm of magic, where they must face a demonic force that is responsible for the killings. For the first time since Ginevra, Fitzroy allows himself to fall in love. He confides in Vicki, who admits that she loves him and returns his trust by letting him feed from her in an emergency. Fitzroy and Nelson's adventures continued in a series of novels throughout the 1990s.

SOURCES:

Huff, Tanya. *Blood Debt*. New York: DAW Books, 1997.
———. *Blood Lines*. New York: DAW Books, 1993.
———. *Blood Pact*. New York: DAW Books, 1993.
———. *Blood Price*. New York: DAW Books, 1991.
———. *Blood Trail*. New York: DAW Books, 1992.

Fleming, Jack

Jack Fleming, a reporter turned vampire, appears in a series of novels by P.N. "Pat" Elrod, the first of which, *Bloodlist* (1990), tells the story of his origins. Fleming was born in Cincinnati at the beginning of the century. As a young reporter in New York City, he is assigned to cover the 1931 opening of *Dracula*, the famous movie starring Bela Lugosi. While interviewing moviegoers, he meets an attractive young woman named Maureen. The two begin to date and he soon falls in love with her, even though he learns that she has a terrible secret—she is a vampire. After he learns that, the two of them share blood, but he shows no signs of being a vampire himself. Without warning, Maureen disappears from his life. For five years he searches for her, with no luck. He even places personal ads in newspapers, hoping that she will get in touch with him.

In 1936, he moves to Chicago. He arrives on a Monday and checks into a seedy motel. He receives a phone call that is designed to lure him away from the hotel, and when he next awakens, four days have passed of which he has no memory. He realizes immediately, however, that he has been murdered and that he is only awake because he is now a vampire. The blood he had shared with Maureen allowed him to survive the attack. As soon as he realizes his predicament, he begins to take steps to ensure his survival. He purchases a trunk to sleep in and travels in the trunk to his hometown of Cincinnati, where he gathers some of his native soil from his family homestead. He does not kill humans to survive, but rather gets his blood from cattle at a nearby stockyard. He feeds every other evening.

Fleming is a somewhat traditional vampire. He appears to be in his mid-20s. He has no aversion to crosses, garlic, or silver, but he does have fangs and does not reflect in the mirror. He cannot turn into a bat or wolf, but he does have some supernormal attributes. He can disappear and suddenly reappear, and he can travel through walls. Bullets and most other physical attacks cause no pain and have little effect on him; he also heals very quickly. A wooden stake can kill him. He is sensitive to daylight and sleeps in a totally dark space. Since he is dead, he only breathes when he talks and when he is in the presence of other humans and wants to pass as normal.

Fleming does not lose his sexuality, as many vampires do. He still hopes to find Maureen, but during the search for his killer or killers, he meets a woman named Bobbi and begins a relationship with her. He enjoys biting her and drinking her

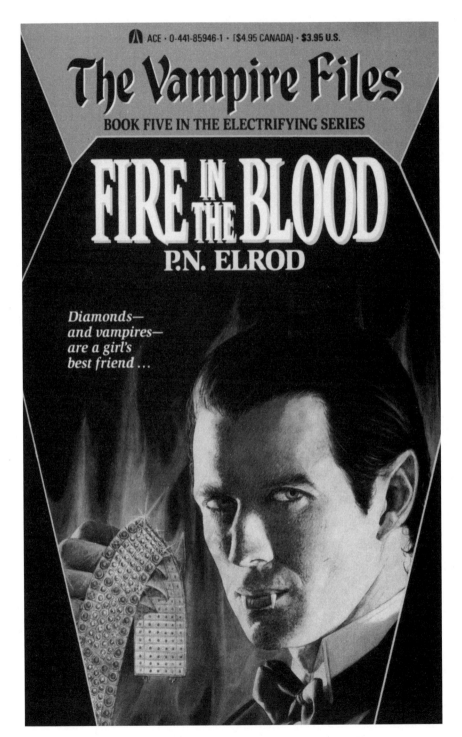

ACE · 0-441-85946-1 · [$4.95 CANADA] · $3.95 U.S.

The Vampire Files

BOOK FIVE IN THE ELECTRIFYING SERIES

FIRE IN THE BLOOD

P.N. ELROD

*Diamonds—
and vampires—
are a girl's
best friend …*

Cover art from P.N. Elrod's novel *Fire in the Blood*, which features reporter-turned-vampire Jack Fleming.

blood during sex, but is careful to always separate drinking during sex from his feeding for nourishment.

Soon after he returns to Chicago from Cincinnati, he returns to his hotel room and finds his bags of native soil missing. He decides to seek help in his quest to unravel the mystery of his death and enlists the help of private investigator Charles Escott. He and Escott become close friends, to the point where Fleming moves into Escott's house, where he lives in a specially constructed room in Escott's basement. He stops sleeping in the trunk and begins sleeping in a normal bed with a bag of his native soil beneath it. His room in the basement has a special emergency trapdoor that gives him access to the kitchen above. He also has his own rooms upstairs that he uses at night, and he has a typing room in the basement.

With his living arrangements set, he and Escott begin a series of adventures that are recounted in Elrod's subsequent novels. In one of them, he had a passing encounter with another vampire, **Jonathan Barrett,** who was changed into a vampire in a very similar fashion to Fleming back in the 1770s.

SOURCES:

Elrod, P. N. *Art in the Blood*. New York: Ace Books, 1991.

———. *Blood on the Water*. New York: Ace Books, 1992.

———. *Bloodcircle*. New York: Ace Books, 1990.

———. *Bloodlist*. New York: Ace Books, 1990.

———. *Fire in the Blood*. New York: Ace Books, 1991.

———. *Lifeblood*. New York: Ace Books, 1990.

Ford, Alexander Algernon

Alexander Algernon Ford is a 2100-year-old vampire featured in the low-budget film, *The Body Beneath* (1970), which was written and directed by Andy Milligan. Ford is the leader of a clan of vampires who date back to the first century B.C. The original Fords were buried on the site that in the nineteenth century became London's Highgate Cemetery. Every evening, the entire Ford clan comes to life in the cemetery. Alexander has been chosen as the family monarch because he is so level-headed and unbiased in making decisions that effect the entire clan.

Every 40 years the family goes through a period of renewal by fathering new bodies using the female mortal descendants of the Fords. However, the bloodline is deteriorating due to the many years of intermarriage. Alexander believes that if the present rate of deterioration continues, the Ford clan will die out in another century. He proposes that the entire family move to the United States because the Ford descendants that live in North America seem to have retained a strong bloodline.

With the exception of the oddity of how his clan is renewed, Alexander is a traditional vampire who lives in a nocturnal world, although he has the ability to withstand the negative effects of the sun temporarily. He avoids mirrors. He drinks from the necks of his victims.

As a last option prior to moving to America, Ford selects two young Ford women as possible candidates for raising a new generation. He invites them to his temporary residence, Carfax Abbey (which was **Count Dracula**'s main London residence in the 1931 Bela Lugosi movie), and holds them prisoner. After determining that they are unsatisfactory, he turns them over to the clan to be drained of blood and killed. In the end, Alexander leads the clan onto a chartered ship for America, where they plan to make a new home in Forest Lawn Cemetery in Los Angeles.

Frene, Frank

Frank Frene, a psychic vampire, is the subject of Algernon Blackwood's short story, "The Transfer" (1912). He lives in twentieth-century London where he is a successful businessman and well-known philanthropist. He is successful with everything he lays his hand to, but he is also a supreme artist at taking the fruits of others for his own advantage. He vampirizes everyone around him and leaves them tired, exhausted, and listless.

Frene has a married younger brother, with two kids. He lives in a suburban home with a large yard and garden. In his garden is a small patch that does not allow anything to grow in it. Frene's son Jaimie describes it as a dying part of nature.

One day the vampiric Frene brother comes to call. The family gathers in the garden, and suddenly the conversation is interrupted by Frene's being drawn to the bare spot. He walks to it and a struggle—invisible to most—begins. Eventually he steps in the middle of the patch and faints. He is carried inside and spends the rest of the day in a kind of delirious sleep.

From that day on he drops out of society—never again mentioned in the newspapers. His life becomes singularly ineffective. The psychic vampire had met his match.

SOURCES:

Blackwood, Algernon. "The Transfer." 1912. Reprinted in Ryan, Alan, ed. *The Penguin Book of Vampire Stories: Two Centuries of Great Stories with a Bite.* New York: Penguin Books, 1988.

Frost, Deacon

Deacon Frost, a vampire created by writer Marv Wolfman, makes his initial appearance in the thirteenth issue of Marvel Comic's most successful vampire series, *The Tomb of Dracula,* reappearing in subsequent issues until he is finally written out of the series in the late 1970s. Frost is a chemist in 1860s Germany. He begins to experiment with the blood of a recently deceased vampire with the hope of uncovering the secrets of immortality. However, in the process of turning an unwilling young woman into his laboratory guinea pig, he has a fight with her husband. During the fight, he accidentally injects himself with his own serum and becomes a vampire. Although a traditional vampire in many respects, Frost discovers he has the additional ability to create vampire clones of his victims after killing them.

After disappearing for many years, Frost emerges in mid-twentieth-century America. He has white hair, including a full beard and mustache, red eyes, and prominent fangs. He blends into society by taking on the persona of a doctor. As such, he is invited to the bedside of a black woman who is having a difficult labor.

BUT THEY'RE NOT VAMPIRES!

There are characters closely associated with the vampire world who are often thought of as vampires, at least in the eyes of young males. In reality, however, they are not vampires. Morticia Addams of *The Addams Family* is a prime example. She originated in the cartoons of Charles S. Addams and brought an element of the monstrous and bizarre to suburbia. Her long black hair and slinky black dress were suggestive of a bat, and it is easy to forgive audiences for expecting fangs to pop out in her mouth at any moment. Morticia proudly carries on the noble tradition of the vamp, moving with a grace and seductive manner that assured her husband Gomez would never stray. She is far closer to a witch than a vampire.

Much the same could be said of pop culture icon Elvira, who draws her image from a variety of earlier characters, including both Morticia and Vampirella. Unlike Morticia, Elvira lives in a world where vampires regularly pop in for visits, at least they do in her adventures in the *Elvira, Mistress of the Dark* comic book (Claypool, 1993 to the present). As a witch, Elvira has another connection to vampires. Her little witch's familiar, who is continually taking new forms, is a vampire pet.

Frost proceeds to vampirize her, although the baby she bears survives. He grows up to be known as **Blade the Vampire Slayer**, developing a set of wooden knives that he uses with great efficiency to fight vampires.

Frost reappears in 1971 when he attacks and transforms a private detective, **Hannibal King**, into a vampire. Like Blade, King seeks revenge on Frost for what he has done. Finally in 1976, Blade and King meet, and in spite of Blade's aversion to vampires of any kind, he teams with King to track Frost. Frost has become visible while developing a scheme to take over the world with his vampire clones.

After some months of searching, Blade and King track Frost to his underground lair. After overcoming a number of his minions, the duo finally locate Frost in his secret laboratory, where the white-haired vampire attempts to hold them off with a deadly solution of fungus. Together, Blade and King impale him, and both Frost and the fungus are consumed in a fire that Frost ignites as he collapses against his lab equipment.

SOURCES:

"The Final Glory of Deacon Frost." *The Tomb of Dracula.* No. 53. New York: Marvel Comics, Feb. 1977.

"To Kill a Vampire!" *The Tomb of Dracula.* No. 13. New York: Marvel Comics, Oct. 1973.

Fury, Michael

Michael Fury (portrayed by George Chakiris), the vampire hero of the film *Pale Blood* (1991) lives a solitary existence in contemporary Europe. A somewhat traditional vampire of indeterminate age, Fury is a handsome male in his forties who possesses some unusual abilities. He levitates and moves so swiftly that he seems to appear and disappear suddenly. He prefers young females as his food source and tends to bite them on the breast rather than on the neck during sex. He takes very little blood during each encounter and hence his victims do not die from loss of blood. He

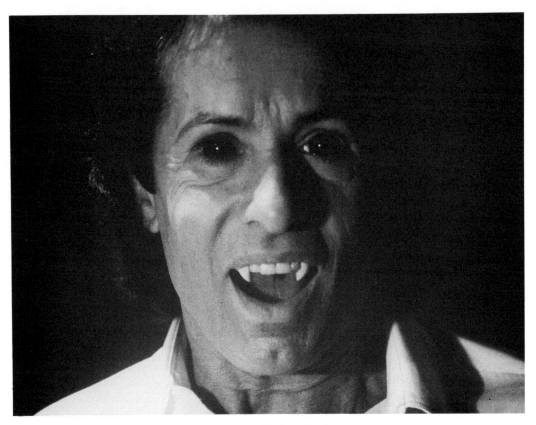

Michael Fury (George Chakiris) is the vampire hero in the film *Pale Blood.*

is hurt by sunlight and weakened by garlic. A modernized vampire, he carries a light-weight tentlike coffin in which to sleep during the daylight hours. He has learned to live among humans and obtains the blood he needs without killing, but unable to locate other creatures like himself, he is beset by loneliness.

Some hope emerges in early 1990s Los Angeles. A series of killings occur which, at least superficially, might indicate the work of another vampire. Three women have been found, each with puncture wounds and her blood drained. Secretly hoping to find a real vampire, Fury hires a private detective to help him track the killer.

As the murders continue, Fury relocates to Los Angeles. There he discovers that the detective he has hired, an attractive young woman, is both a vampire buff who would like to find a real vampire to fulfill her fantasies and a clairvoyant who can tap into the murders. He also encounters a film maker who has filmed the murder scene. Fury begins to personally investigate the murder scene and is captured on film utilizing some of his vampiric powers of swift movement.

As his investigation proceeds, Fury discovers the film maker has murdered the women and drained their blood. He then carefully places the bodies in bizarre settings that ensure widespread news coverage. Like Fury, he was searching for a real vampire to capture on film—this portrayal of an otherworldly creature would be his ticket to fame and fortune.

As Fury gets closer to confronting the film maker, the film maker traps Fury in a cell-like room that has been saturated with garlic juice. His confinement sets the stage for the final confrontation between the vampire, the ambitious serial killer, and the inquisitive detective. Without giving away the entire plot, Michael Fury does live to fight another day.

Futaine, The Cevalier Pierre

The Cevalier Pierre Futaine, one of the early aristocratic vampires to appear in the wake of Bela Lugosi's *Dracula* (1931), is the subject of Henry Kuttner's 1937 pulp fiction story, "I, the Vampire." Discovered by movie director Jack Hardy at a Satanist club in Paris, Futaine shows up in 1930s Hollywood as an actor soon to play the lead in a vampire movie *Red Thirst*. When introduced to movie director Mart Prescott at Hardy's cocktail party, Prescott notices some odd traits about Futaine: Although a handsome man, his hands are cold; his clean-shaven cheeks are heavily made up; and a deathly pallor lingers beneath the makeup. Oddly, Futaine's lips are not rouged, but are red as rubies. His eyes are black.

At the party, Prescott also encounters Hess Deming, whose wife died two days earlier of a mysterious illness the doctors called pernicious anemia. Although keeping conversation with his guests, Jack Hardy looks pale and wears a scarf around his neck. Complaining of a throat infection, he bears two little marks over the jugular, just like Deming's wife. Later Hardy confides to Prescott that Futaine put him under his power and forced Hardy to bring him to Hollywood. Futaine has made Hardy keep photographers away and ensure there are no mirrors on the movie set. Hardy also had a vault built below his own isolated canyon home in which he stays during daylight hours, the door of which can only be opened by a special key.

The next evening at the movie studio, a cameraman invites Prescott to see an early screen test for *Red Thirst*. Futaine appears on the film as a glowing oval fog. Prescott also observes the same neck wound on Jean Hubbard, the female character cast opposite Futaine. As Prescott comes to the reluctant conclusion that Futaine is indeed a vampire, news reaches him that Deming's wife awoke as she was being cremated, and was burned alive before her body could be retrieved.

Prescott confronts Futaine as he arises the next evening. Jean Hubbard is with him; he has just dined. Calling her Sonya, Futaine identifies her as the image of a woman he had been lovers with before he was turned into a vampire. He had made Sonya a vampire many years ago, but her body had been discovered and staked. He intended to share his blood with Jean that evening in an attempt to regain his lost love.

In a struggle, the vampire paralyzes Prescott with his hypnotic eyes. But Futaine is now in a self-made trap. Because he just confided his love of Sonya to Prescott and noted his regret of forcing the vampire's life upon her, he knows that only his own death will free Jane, the new Sonya. After dawn comes, Prescott awakes from his hypnotic trance and finds the key to the sleeping vampire's lair.

SOURCES:

Kuttner, Henry. "I, the Vampire." In *Weird Tales*. 1937. Reprinted in Weinberg, Robert, Stefan R. Dziemianowicz, and Martin H. Greenberg, *Weird Vampire Tales*. New York: Gramercy Books, 1992.

Gabrielle

Gabrielle is the mother of Anne Rice's most famous vampire, **Lestat de Lioncourt,** and is a continuing character in Rice's *Vampire Chronicles*. Born in Naples, she married a marquis in her youth and went to live with him at his castle in Auvergne, an isolated region of France. She bore him eight sons, three of whom survived to adulthood. The youngest was Lestat. Over the years, the blonde, blue-eyed woman tended to withdraw from her family. She had no real friends and disliked life in the castle.

As the *Vampire Chronicles* begin, she, like Lestat, is lonely and unhappy with the life in which they find themselves. She sympathizes with Lestat whenever his plans for leaving the castle are foiled and his dreams are crushed time and time again. Eventually, she secretly gives him the money he needs to leave the castle and move to Paris in 1779. By that time, her health is failing because she has developed tuberculosis (then called consumption), which at the time was incurable. She is sure that she will die soon, so she wants Lestat to have the chance to escape from the castle and see Paris that she never had.

Gabrielle does not die right away, however. Instead, she survives and travels to Paris herself the following year, where she is reunited with her son. By the time she reaches Lestat, she is near death. She recognizes immediately that something is different about her son, so he confides in her that he has become a vampire and is immortal. When he offers to turn her into a vampire so that she might live forever, she jumps at the opportunity. Her transformation to a vampire turns out to be one of the most erotic that Lestat will ever experience.

Gabrielle dislikes being called mother, so Lestat refers to her by her given name. She takes to the vampiric life quickly, and Lestat treats her as his equal. As she is adapting to her new life, she kills one victim and steals his clothes. From that point forward, she usually wore men's clothes because they were much more efficient to wear while hunting.

Gabrielle is with Lestat when he first meets **Armand** and his coven of vampires. Like Lestat, she knows little of the vampiric life and hopes that she can learn from Armand. When this hope proves fruitless, she and Lestat leave Paris and travel across Europe, spending some time in Cairo. Periodically, she disappears for days into the woods to commune with nature. When her remaining two sons are killed in the French Revolution, she finally leaves Lestat to go live in the African jungles. She urges Lestat to get rid of all of his possessions and come and live free as she does, but he chose another direction.

Gabrielle loses touch with Lestat for most of the nineteenth and twentieth centuries. In 1985, she meets him briefly in San Francisco and then stays for his final confrontation with **Akasha,** the original vampire who had arisen in an attempt to take over the world. After Akasha's death, Gabrielle accompanies the vampires who survived Akasha's purge to Armand's complex on Night Island, near Miami. She and Lestat separate again when he leaves for New Orleans, and so far, she has yet to reenter his life.

SOURCES:

Ramsland, Katherine. *The Vampire Companion: The Official Guide to Anne Rice's The Vampire Chronicles*. New York: Ballantine Books, 1993.

Rice, Anne. *The Queen of the Damned*. New York: Alfred a. Knopf, 1988. Reprint, New York: Ballantine Books, 1989.

———. *The Vampire Lestat*. New York: Alfred a. Knopf, 1985. Reprint, New York: Ballantine Books, 1986.

Geraldine

One of the very first vampires in English literature, Geraldine makes a brief but not insignificant appearance at the beginning of the nineteenth century in Samuel Taylor Coleridge's poem, *Christabel*, completed around 1800. Geraldine is never called a vampire and her origins are never revealed, but in the 1930s Arthur H. Nethercott made the definitive case concerning her vampiric nature as demonstrated in the opening scenes of the poem.

Geraldine is a richly clad woman first seen bathing in the moonlight when discovered by the youthful Christabel, who leads her to her father's castle. As she approaches the castle door where her benefactor resides, Geraldine faints, but after Christabel assists her across the threshold, she quickly revives. When she walks by the dog, it uncharacteristically lets out an angry moan. (It is commonly believed that vampires are revived by moonlight, cannot enter a house without an invitation, and have a negative effect upon animals.)

After walking her past the dog, Christabel shows Geraldine to a resting place. She opens a bottle of wine that they share. Then at Geraldine's suggestion, Christabel undresses, after which Geraldine partially disrobes, revealing her breast and half her side. Christabel responds by entering a trance-like state. Yet Geraldine neither speaks nor stirs:

> Ah! what a stricken look was hers!
> Deep from within she seems half-way
> To life some weight with sick assay,

And eyes the maid and seeks delay;
Then suddenly, as one defied,
Collects herself in the scorn and pride,
And lay down at the Maiden's side!

In a scene with obvious lesbian overtones, the two women lay together for an hour and again the animals are effected:

O Geraldine! One hour was thine!
Thou'st had thy will! By tairn and rill,
The night-birds all that hour were still.
But now they are jubilant anew,
From cliff and tower, tu-whoo! tu-whoo!

The next morning, Geraldine awakes refreshed with her lean, old, and foul body rejuvenated:

"That (so it seemed) her girded vests/Grew tight beneath
her heaving breasts."

Christabel, on the other hand, awakes with a sense of guilt and immediately goes to pray. She then leads Geraldine to an audience with her father, the lord of the castle. Geraldine immediately ingratiates herself to Lord Leoline while Christabel has a momentary flashback to her vision of Geraldine's foul body when she first disrobed. She attempts to have her father send Geraldine away, but he is already enraptured and in the end turns from his daughter and departs with Geraldine on his arm. Like her origins, her future is not revealed.

Christabel was composed in two parts, the first written and published in 1798. A second part was finished around 1800. Christabel thus preceded Southey's *Thalaba*, the first English-language poem to actually mention the vampire in its text.

SOURCES:

Nethercott, Arthur H. *The Road to Tryermaine: a Study of the History, Background, and Purposes of Coleridge's "Christabel."* Chicago: University of Chicago Press, 1939. Reprint, New York: Russell & Russell, 1962.

Gilcrease, Murphy

Murphy Gilcrease is the subject of the low-budget coming-of-age film, *Teen Vamp* (1988). Murphy Gilcrease is another nerdish teenager with a crush on the most beautiful girl in school, Connie Sutton. When he gets up enough courage to ask her out, she blows him off. To soothe his hurt feelings he decides to lose his virginity at the local whorehouse, where a lady vampire seduces Murphy for his rare prized possession, virgin blood. Without losing his virginity, he is bitten by the beautiful vampiress and within a few minutes is a vampire himself. He feeds later that night on a deer.

While feeding, Murphy develops fangs and elongated fingernails, but otherwise appears quite normal. Although the evening is his time to feed, he can move about in daylight and continues to attend classes. Soon news of his having become a vampire spreads. Bucky, the football hero, who also likes Connie, attacks him in the hall at school. To get away from him, Murphy disappears, but not before biting Bucky, who soon emerges as a vampire.

Vampirism also has its positive aspects for Murphy. He begins to lose some of his nerdish qualities, and Connie, who feels used by the arrogant Bucky, begins to pay attention to him. Murphy's mother and her minister are concerned, however, and the minister is among the first to figure out what Murphy—and a host of other students—has become.

Everyone concerned with the outbreak of vampirism among the youth, including Bucky's football coach, gather to resolve the vampire epidemic. As the vampires are about to be destroyed, unbeknownst to anyone, Murphy's best friend takes matters into his own hands. He goes back to the motel/brothel where Murphy had his original encounter and dispatches the vampire who originally bit him. Miraculously, as she dies, Murphy and everyone whom he infected suddenly lose their vampire attributes. As normal teenagers again, and the real question becomes, Will Murphy or Bucky now get the girl?

Gilda

Gilda is an African-American lesbian vampire featured in Jewelle Gomez's novel *The Gilda Stories* (1991). She was born a slave on a plantation in Mississippi in the 1830s. For the early part of the novel, she is simply a nameless slave girl. As a teenager, she kills a white man who tries to rape her. Escaping the plantation, she makes her way to New Orleans, where she is taken in by a white brothel owner named Gilda (from whom the girl will take her name in the future). Gilda just happens to be a 300-year-old vampire. The slave girl is given a place on the staff and is taught to read and write. Eventually, as she matures, she is invited to join Gilda and her assistant, Bird (a Native American), and become a vampire like them; she accepts. Gilda and Bird teach her to feed off humans. The vampires travel swiftly under cover of the night and take small amounts of blood from sleeping people. In return for the blood, they probe the mind of each victim and give them new dreams, new ideas, or positive energy to strengthen them as a gift. To them, this seems to be a fair exchange. Only on the rarest of occasions do they kill.

Gilda grows tired of life and passes everything to Bird and the slave girl, who takes her benefactor's name. After some years, Bird leaves to return to her tribe, and Gilda turns the brothel over to one of the prostitutes. Gilda moves to San Francisco with only a few possessions, including a cross given her by her mother, and finds the small vampire community that lives on the West Coast. She moves frequently throughout the twentieth century because she must hide the fact that she does not age. In the 1920s, she resides on a farm in Missouri, and in the 1950s, she operates a beauty parlor in Boston. While in Boston, she reunites with Bird and works with her to kill a vampire operating as a pimp in the black community. The pimp is difficult to kill, but they manage the feat by knocking him out with an overdose of heroin, removing his heart, and leaving him on a small boat to burn in the sun.

In New York City in 1971, she selects Julius, a man who works in a theater company with her, as her first vampire "child." To create a vampire, she must not just take blood, but share it. She does not mate with Julius, but she does begin a relationship with another vampire named Effie, with whom she moves to rural New Hampshire. There, she begins a life as a reclusive writer of romance novels.

The Gilda Stories then shifts into the middle of the twenty-first century. Pollution and poor land management are wreaking havoc on the human community. Vampires have to face their own problems—humans have realized that vampires are real, and a new breed of vampire hunters have sprung up to eradicate them. After living underground for several years, Gilda decides to join Bird in Peru, where a vampire sanctuary has been established. On the way to her new life, she is almost killed when some hunters catch her at the vulnerable point in her trip—crossing the running waters of the Panama Canal. She survives and is reunited with Bird at Machu Picchu in Peru.

In addition to having a problem crossing running water, Gilda must also have some of her native soil with her wherever she goes. She has a pad filled with the soil placed on her bed, and has more sewn into her clothes and put into the soles of her shoes. She has great strength and can move about in indirect sunlight. She does not eat normal food, but she does enjoy champagne.

SOURCES:
Gomez, Jewelle. *The Gilda Stories.* Ithaca, NY: Firebrand Books, 1991.

Gordell, Belec

The man by the name of Belec Gordell (portrayed by Francis Lederer) in the film *The Return of Dracula* (1958) is a vampire. There's a possibility he is **Count Dracula** himself, but he is definitely not Belec Gordell. Sometime in the 1950's, artist Gordell migrates to America and has the unfortunate circumstance of boarding the same train as a vampire who's decided to move to the United States from the Balkan Mountain region in Southeastern Europe. Soon after the train leaves the station, the vampire dines on Gordell's blood and assumes his identity, using his papers to pass through immigration and customs. He crosses the Atlantic on an ocean liner and boards another train headed to a small town in California where his "family," the Mayberrys (in reality Gordell's cousins) welcome him.

Gordell is a traditional Eastern European vampire. He is a nocturnal being who sleeps in a coffin. He reacts to crosses and his image never appears in mirrors or photographs. He easily changes into mist and various animal forms. Like other vampires who emulate Bela Lugosi's portrayal, he doesn't sport fangs but does leaves puncture wounds on the neck of his victims. Though he has no cape, he wears an overcoat as if it were a cape.

Gordell upsets the Mayberry family. They had been looking forward to establishing a comfortable relationship with their European cousin, instead they're saddled with this strange man. Not very personable in any case, he proves to be completely unavailable during the day and interested only in establishing his food supply after dark. Not exactly the perfect houseguest. His first victim is a young blind

Francis Lederer portrayed the suave, Dracula-like vampire Belec Gordell in the film *The Return of Dracula*.

woman who transforms into a vampire after his attack and becomes his minion. He also set his sights on his "cousin," Rachel Mayberry, a blonde teenager who dreams of becoming a dress designer.

Freely moving among the ignorant Californians, Gordell soon comes under the scrutiny of immigration officials and a policeman from his home country who are investigating a body found near the rail tracks. The immigration agent is killed by Gordell's minion, who is quickly traced to the mausoleum where she rests during the day.

Gordell does not fall to the investigators, however, but rather to Rachel and her boyfriend. He carries Rachel to the lair he's established in an abandoned mine. Her boyfriend soon arrives to save her, not really aware of what he faces. The vampire Gordell would generally quickly dispose of them but for the cross Rachel wears. Backing away from the cross, he falls into an open pit and is impaled on an old piece of lumber. His body quickly dissolves. One assumes the Mayberrys resume their daily lives, glad to be rid of their strange and mysterious "cousin" from Europe.

Green, Hess

The story of Hess Green is told in the film *Black Vampire* (1973), also released as *Ganja and Hess*. Dr. Hess Green is an African-American anthropologist who has been studying the Myrthian people, an ancient African culture whose records indicate that they had an addiction to blood. His colleague, Mr. George Matara, prior to committing suicide, stabbed Green three times with the Myrthian knife they had discovered, thus turning Green into an immortal vampire. Subsequently, Green's dreams were haunted by the images of the Myrthian queen who also protects him. He is unable to be killed.

Green is different from Eastern European vampires. He has no fangs, he moves about freely in daylight, and continues to eat a normal diet. He is also cold all the time, a sign of his undead condition. He drinks blood out of a cup rather than directly from a body. He has vowed not to take another life.

Several days after Matara disappears, his wife Ganja shows up looking for him. She moves into Green's house, and after the two develop a relationship, she learns the truth behind her husband's death. She accepts Green's explanation and Green, hoping for some enjoyment in his new life, makes her a vampire. She, unfortunately, does not have his reservations about killing and murders a person who has come to Green's house for dinner.

Now addicted to blood, Green decides he wants a way out of uncomfortable existence, and learns it can be reversed by coming under the shadow of the Christian cross. Green attends a revival meeting at an African-American church and is saved. Although freed, his body soon manifests the death he has already passed through. For him his death is a happy ending.

Gregory

Gregory is an ancient vampire who is featured in Patrick Whalen's novel, *Night Thirst* (1991). The 900-year-old vampire is a rarity: most people bitten by a vampire (which is all it takes to transform) either die or go mad due to the cravings caused by their blood thirst. Only a few move beyond that first stage, when they are called New Ones, to survive and thrive as Ancient Ones. Gregory survives the major European outbreak of vampirism, mistakenly recorded in history books as an outbreak of the plague, or Black Death. In reality, it was an outbreak of vampirism, and as the New Ones multiplied quickly, the epidemic took millions of lives.

When the epidemic ran its course and most vampires had died, the few remaining Ancient Ones were tracked down and immobilized. Their bodies were entombed in a church in France. Following World War I, given the lack of stability in Europe, the bodies were moved to a monastery on Chinook Island, off the coast of Washington state. Two monks were sent to guard the bodies, and all was well until 1981, when the two monks died in accidents. Unguarded, the monastery was left open to exploration by the growing population on the island. Around 1990, some college students discovered the tombs and in their ignorance released the vampires. The awakened vampires satiated their thirst on the students, who became New Ones.

Among the vampires awakened are Gregory and Clementina, his love of 500 years. They realize that a new outbreak of vampirism is spreading across the island and they try to contain it. They destroyed all the boats they can find, thus isolating the island. Except for a few people who barricade themselves in the island's lighthouse, all the people on the island become New Ones. In order to kill the vampires, one of the last human residents sets off an explosion in the nuclear power plant on the island. The radiation kills all but a few people: Gregory, one of the New Ones, and four humans from the lighthouse who make their escape in a boat that Gregory failed to destroy.

Eventually, three of the four humans are killed, The fourth, named **Braille,** is a former Green Beret trained in martial arts. He was bitten during their escape from the island and becomes a vampire. His self-discipline (gained from his martial arts training) allows him to survive the New One stage and become an Ancient One. The New One escapes to Seattle and launches a new epidemic of vampirism. Gregory settles in a small town, Stanwood, and tries to adjust to life in the twentieth century. However, as soon as he learns of the events in Seattle, he heads for the city.

As an Ancient One, Gregory is extremely strong. He has fangs, which extend when he is about to feed or is enraged. He is largely nocturnal, but can move about in the daytime as required. His bite transfers the vampiric condition, but he takes pains to kill his victims so they do not rise as New Ones.

Once in the city, he confronts Braille. They resolve their differences and unite to deal with the spread of vampirism. They go to the command headquarters established by the government and convince the Vice-President of the United States that vampires are taking over the city and that the only way to save the country, possibly the world, is to drop a nuclear weapon on Seattle. Both also decide that death is the best thing for each of them and try to commit suicide by entering the blast zone. They reach an area near the drop point and spend their last minutes talking to each other while sitting on a park bench.

Unfortunately, from their perspective, they are not allowed to die. Their bodies are quickly discovered and they are revived with a transfusion of fresh blood.

SOURCES:
Whalen, Patrick. *Night Thirst*. New York: Pocket Books, 1991.

Greystone, Christina

Vampire Christina Greystone is the subject of the comic book story, "The Vampiress Stalks the Castle This Night" (1974). Greystone lives in a castle–like mansion not far from New York City. She appears as a young woman in a seductive, low-cut black dress. She is nocturnal and spends her days in a coffin. Trapped in the present, she has little concern for the memory of her past. She looks like any other attractive young woman until excited or ready to feed, when her fangs appear.

After many years of undead life, she is visited one evening by a young couple with car trouble. They are both 17, and the girl is pregnant. While the boy steps into another room to use the phone, Greystone attacks the girl. She is able to use a cross to repel the attack, and the vampiress transforms into a bat and flies away. The bat flies at the young man, and in desperation, he grabs a flag staff and stakes the surprised vampiress. The couple depart the castle and say little about what has occurred, knowing that the authorities wouldn't believe them if they reported the incident.

SOURCES:

"The Vampiress Stalks the Castle This Night." *Vampirella* . No. 37. Warren Publishing Co., Oct. 1974.

Griffin, Deirdre

Deirdre Griffin is a beautiful, auburn-haired vampire who first appears in Karen E. Taylor's novel, *Blood Secrets* (1993). She was born early in the nineteenth century. She lives a fairly normal and happy life—at age 28, she is happily married and expecting her first child. Then one rainy evening, she is riding home in a carriage when it overturns. Her husband is killed and her child stillborn. To make matters horribly worse, as she lays in the wreckage, she is bitten by a vampire. Angered at what is happening to her, she bites back, exchanging blood with the creature. As a result, she becomes a vampire herself.

As a vampire, Griffin moves about frequently and takes on many different identities to hide the fact that she is immortal. In the U.S. Civil War, she serves as a nurse, entertaining some of the healthy young men about to go into battle and easing the pain and suffering of the wounded and dying as they return from battle. At least one picture of her from that period has survived. During World War II, as Doreen Gallagher, she works the night shift in a steel plant. In the 1960s, as Diane Gleason, she serves travelers as a waitress in Kansas. She also works as a prostitute named Dorothy Grey in the South before making a move to Manhattan, where she develops a successful business as a fashion designer.

While working in Kansas, she had met a vampire named Max Hunter who liked her and helped set up her business in New York. Max runs a night club called the Ballroom of Romance, where Griffin spends several evenings each week. Since she needs to feed about once every week under normal circumstances, the club is a perfect place for her to meet young men who serve as her next meal. She invites the men into a room in the rear of the club, drinks a small bit of their blood, and then plants a hypnotic suggestion telling the men to forget what has occurred. She requires only a small amount of blood, so she never kills any of the men, nor does she turn them into vampires.

In the early 1990s, her life is disrupted when a vampire killer began to attack and kill some of the men whom she has previously used as a food source. Their deaths are investigated by Mitch Greer, a New York policeman who meets Griffin and begins a relationship with her. Before the mystery can be solved, Max Hunter is killed and Griffin leaves the country, abandoning her business before the killer can strike her next. She moves to London, where she lives for two years. Her new life is interrupted by **The Cadre,** a vampire organization who holds her responsible for Hunter's death. They force her to come back to New York City by threatening Greer. When she returns, she resumes her relationship with Greer and solves her conflict

Cover art from Karen E. Taylor's novel *Bitter Blood*, which continues the saga of beautiful vampire Dierdre Griffin.

with the Cadre by discovering who Hunter's real killer is. She turns Greer into a vampire, and together they track down the rogue vampire who is responsible for Hunter's and many other deaths.

Griffin has primarily nontraditional vampire characteristics. She has amber eyes and almost translucent pale skin. Her fangs retract when she is not feeding. She tends to sleep during the day, and while the sun burns her skin, she heals quickly. Since she has never really died, her image does reflect in a mirror. Crosses have no effect on her, and she has no supernatural powers. However, all of her senses have been heightened, and her body seems to be attuned to the cycles of the sun and the moon. She rarely eats solid food, but enjoys fine wines, especially burgundy. She also smokes.

Griffin's adventures are continued in the sequels *Bitter Blood* (1994) and *Blood Ties* (1995).

SOURCES:

Taylor, Karen E. *Blood Ties*. New York: Zebra Books, 1995.
————. *The Vampire Legacy: Bitter Blood*. New York: Zebra Books, 1994.
————. *The Vampire Legacy: Blood Secrets*. New York: Zebra Books, 1993.

Grimes, Crispen

Crispen Grimes, the vampire antagonist in the NBC made-for-television movie *House of Frankenstein* (1997), is a vampire of unknown age. A researcher who traced the family history discovered for many centuries the family had reported there was only one male child per generation, that his mother had always died in childbirth, and he was sent away to school, only to return at the time of his father's death. The researcher concludes that Grimes has simply been reinventing himself.

A timeless and powerful creature, Grimes can transform himself into a demon-like monster, with cloven hoofs, who can fly. It is in this form that he usually feeds. The researcher believes that he was a fallen angel, a fact that would account for his grotesque appearance and his repulsion to holy objects. Although stakes generally kill a vampire, Grimes is so old and strong that stakes only slow him down. Fire is his ultimate nemesis.

In present-day Los Angeles, the setting for most of the movie, Grimes has risen to the position of Master Vampire and, as such, is in control of all the creatures of the night, particularly other vampires and werewolves. He owns a nightclub, the House of Frankenstein, a reflection of his desire to find the lost body of the creature created by Dr. Victor Frankenstein, whom he believes holds the secret to his undead existence. Finally, Frankenstein's body is located, brought back to Los Angeles from the icy north, and reanimated. Meanwhile, one of Grimes's werewolf minions kills a human, and inadvertently scratches another, turning her into a werewolf. Werewolf Grace has an affair with Vernon Coyle, the detective in charge of the investigation of the city's mysterious deaths.

Although the rest of the movie reveals more bloodshed and mayhem, the final confrontation occurs between Grimes and Coyle in the House of Frankenstein, where they fight over Grace, whom they both desire. As the club burns and the other

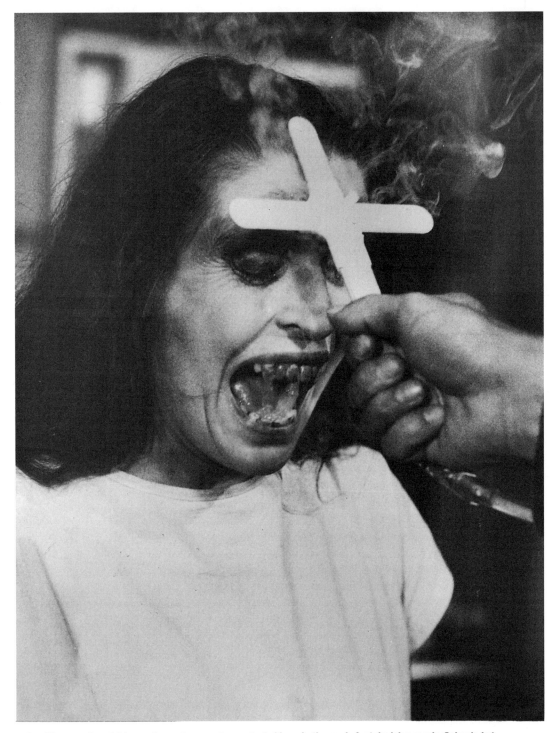

Crucifixes are harmful to most vampires, as demonstrated here in the made-for-television movie *Salem's Lot*.

vampires are destroyed, Grimes realizes he can kill Coyle, but gives up when it becomes clear that no matter who wins the fight, Grace can never love him. The final scene shows Grimes diving into the consuming flames. Is he dead? Since old vampires are notoriously difficult to dispose of, only Grimes himself knows for sure.

Grimwald, Lady Vanessa

Lady Vanessa Grimwald, a 200-year-old vampire, is the subject of the comic book story, "Death of the Party" (1978). Lady Vanessa is a young, attractive black-haired woman who resides in an otherwise abandoned mansion. It is to this mansion that Roland Parks comes one evening. He is planning to stay at the mansion for several days to finish a suspense thriller he's writing. He is counting on the mansion's eerie atmosphere to inspire him, as he has to get the completed manuscript to his publisher within a week.

Lady Vanessa manifests soon after he settles down to work. He finds her in the basement standing on the stairs near her recently opened coffin. She is about to relieve her thirst when Parks cuts a deal with her. If she refrains from attack until he finishes his novel, he will throw a party, invite a lot of people he dislikes for various reasons, and she can have her fill. Lady Vanessa is a cunning vampire, and she agrees to his proposal on the condition that he invite exactly 13 guests. He agrees.

As he works, Vanessa reads and comments favorably on his writing, something his wife has never done. He decides to add her to the guest list. Then with the manuscript completed and sent to the publisher, the Friday party is set to begin. Parks checks on the guests; all thirteen are present, including his wife and the Dowling twins. He mingles and watches as one by one they disappear. However, too late he discovers that only one of the Dowling twins is present. He had thought he saw them from across the room talking to Lady Vanessa. In fact, he had only seen one, but since the twin was reflecting in the mirror, it appears as though there were two people. He is one guest short.

At the end of the evening, Lady Vanessa comes to him. Parks is now the thirteenth guest. He tries to cut a new deal, but Lady Vanessa declines.

SOURCES:
"Death of the Party." *Ghostly Haunts*. No. 57. Charlton Comics, Mar. 1978.

Grinder

Grinder appears as a guest villain in the first two issues of the comic book, *Grimjack Casefiles*. Grinder is a young man in the fantasy world of Cynosure, a medieval city where the multiverse meets. In Cynosure the laws of physics can change from block to block and in crossing the street one has to be prepared to enter a new dimension. Law and order in the city is provided by **The Cadre**, an agency designed to deal with threats to Cynosure's safety. The Cadre arose out of the Demon Wars some 20 years ago and in the intervening years has become a powerful and somewhat tyrannical organization. In Cynosure and adjacent realms, remnants of the demon world continue to exist, and the traditional rules of vampirism tend to break down.

Among the residents of Cynosure is a soldier of fortune, Jahn Gaunt, better known by his nickname, Grim Jack. (For unknown reasons, the name is one word in the title of the comic book and two words in the text.) Grim Jack has an obvious Scottish background. At one point, Grim Jack is approached by an old friend, Mike "Cracker" Crocker, to locate the person who had turned him into vampire. The search leads him to **Miranda Mastenbrook** and then to her maker, Grinder, one of the leftovers from the Demon Wars. He resides in Pdwyr, a realm adjacent to Cynosure. He is the son of MaeThe Mathonwy, the lord of the land and Grim Jack's mentor.

In happier days, Jack had fallen in love with the lord's daughter, Rhian, and treated her brother, Gdeon, as his own kinsman. Grim Jack had vowed to protect their home, Kear Mathon, but was away when the demons overpowered it and killed everyone. He returned to bury their bodies. He missed one body, that of Gdeon, who was killed by vampires. Gdeon still has the body of the 15-year-old he had been when he was vampirized. The Cadre liked the idea of having a vampire among them as an assassin, and helped provide his cover at the youthful gatherings in the home of a man named Wolfingham, where he met and vampirized Miranda. When Cracker showed up to take Miranda home, Grinder followed, knocked him out, and turned him into a vampire. He also anticipated Grim Jack's eventually coming after him.

Grim Jack catches up with them, and after dispatching Miranda, tracks Grinder and Gdeon into Pdwyer to Kaer Mathon. As they are about to square off, Cracker shows up and attacks Grinder first. While watching the battle, Cadre forces arrive. Jack leaves Cracker to finish Grinder, and gives the Cadre forces his full attention. When free to return to the two battling vampires, he decapitates his old friend (who had asked to be killed earlier) and then Gdeon. He learned from his previous experience with Miranda that mere staking does little good. He stuffs their mouth with garlic and disposes of their bodies in a purifying fire. In this mythological world, this process is sufficient to prevent their return.

SOURCES:
"Buried Past." *Grimjack Casefiles.* First Publishing, Nov., Dec. 1990.

Harker, R. B.

R. B. Harker, the vampire villain in the film *Howling VI: The Freaks* (1990), appears in the small town of Canton Bluff as the head of a carnival, Harker's World of Wonder, which he describes as a sanctuary for the freaks of the world. Canton Bluff is in the midst of a drought which is driving many of its citizens away, and the carnival comes as a welcomed diversion.

Harker is a nocturnal creature of supernatural strength. Like many of his vampire associates, he sleeps in a box of his native earth. Appearing quite normal most of the time, he transforms into a batlike creature when he is ready to feed. The first person Harker entices his way and attacks is the town's female banker.

Placing himself in the route of the carnival is Ian Richards, the werewolf star of the *Howling* series. The back story involves Harker, who had attacked and killed Richards's family years ago, sparing only Ian who was cursed to turn into a werewolf at the full moon. Harker also possesses knowledge of a spell that can reverse the curse on command. Shortly after Harker sets up shop in Canton Bluff, one of his assistants observes Richards as a werewolf and reports him to Harker, who captures Richards as his newest exhibit.

After Harker takes Richards prisoner, the town sheriff learns of the many local deaths that seem to be associated with Harker's circus, and decides to investigate. He arrests Harker, only to watch him break the handcuffs easily. He kills the sheriff and leaves the body so that Richards emerges as the likely suspect. The townspeople turn into an angry mob after discovering the sheriff's body, mutilated and drained of blood. They load their guns with silver bullets provided and blessed by the local minister, and trek to the carnival for the final confrontation between Harker and the werewolf.

Cover art from the comic book *Embrace,* which feature loner vampire and heroine Josie Hart.

Harrison, Dr.

Dr. Harrison, psychotherapist and vampire, is an associate of the ancient vampire **Regine** in the film *Fright Night II* (1988). Following the destruction of vampire **Jerry Dandridge** in *Fright Night* (1985), Dr. Harrison is assigned to counsel Charlie Brewster, the high school student involved in the killing of Dandridge. Without revealing his own vampirism, he emphasizes to Brewster that there are no vampires, and maintains Brewster's experience can be accounted for as entirely misunderstood natural and psychological phenomena. As it becomes evident that Regine is a vampire, Harrison has to reinforce his perspective.

After Regine kidnaps Charlie to complete his transformation into a vampire, Charlie's new girlfriend Alex must save him. She has a problem, however, as vampire hunter **Peter Vincent** has been carried off to the state hospital after publicly attacking Regine and branding her a vampire. Alex knows Dr. Harrison and convinces him to go to the state hospital and help her free Vincent.

On the way to the hospital, they are stopped at a railroad crossing where Harrison reveals himself as a vampire and attacks Alex. Reacting quickly, she pulls a piece from a railroad tie to serve as a stake. The consummate professional, Harrison dies while making psychological reflections on his condition.

Hart, Josie

Josie Hart is the vampire rocker featured in the comic book *Embrace*. An orphan adopted by Virginia and Allen Hart, Josie Hart is a beautiful young girl, portrayed throughout the series as a loner afflicted with a disease that makes her allergic to sunlight. She finds her niche as the leader of a successful rock band. However, just as she and the band start to make it big with a hit song, several men attack her and kill several members of the band. In fleeing, she discovers she possesses the superpowers of strength and speed.

The attack jolts Hart's memory, who realizes she is, in fact, the last of an elder race of vampires. Her true relatives have all been destroyed by a new breed of vampires led by their master Tamlin. Distracting Tamlin from his effort to destroy Hart is Elijah, a rogue vampire who seeks vengeance on Tamlin's cohorts because they killed his lover and transformed him into a vampire. Tamlin tries to set a trap for both Hart and Elijah, but fails. As a result, Hart accepts her new life as Embrace the vampire and joins forces with Elijah against Tamlin and the new breed of vampires.

SOURCES :

Embrace. Hickory, NC: London Night Entertainment, 1996.
Embrace: Hunger of the Flesh. Nos. 1-3. Hickory, NC: London Night Entertainment, 1997.

Harte, Dennis

Dennis Harte, a vampire private investigator, is featured in the 1991–92 comic book miniseries *Harte of Darkness*. As Major Cherry, Harte fought in Vietnam. Isolated in

PLANTS AS VAMPIRES

It seems farfetched at first to think of a plant as a vampire, but in early vampire movies, there were scenes that compared the Venus flytrap to a vampire. Since a plant can be a carnivore, why can't it be a vampire?

While several B-movies with vampire plants have been made, the plant as vampire really took center stage in the 1960 Roger Corman surprise hit, *Little Shop of Horrors*. In it, Audrey (a cousin to the Venus flytrap) grows into a monstrous talking plant who bellows out the famous line

"Feed me!" His human assistant, Seymour, serves Audrey only the most deserving victims to satiate his blood lust. The public loved Audrey—the movie was remade in 1972 (as *Please Don't Eat my Mother*), turned into a Broadway musical in 1982, and then remade again in 1986 (with that version based on the play).

In *Night of the Dragon's Blood*, a novel that proposed that Adolf Hitler was a vampire, a Transylvanian plant was introduced that secreted a red, blood-like substance called dragon's blood that could kill vampires. It was used to defeat Hitler and his vampire soldiers.

the jungle in the early 1970s, he met Nguyen, a thousand-year-old vampire. Harte, as Major Cherry, was found dead and was buried. Two nights later he arose as a vampire, and worked his way back to the United States where he assumed the persona of Dennis Harte. In present-day Houston, Texas, Harte works primarily at night as an unlicensed private eye, who rarely finds the need to carry a gun.

As a vampire Harte conforms to traditional norms. Although raised a Roman Catholic he cannot enter a church or touch the cross. He has no reflection in mirrors nor an image on film (and hence cannot have a private eye photo ID). He cannot enter a building without an invitation, a minor hindrance to his investigative work. On the other hand, he can venture outside during the day for short periods of time, as long as he wears sunglasses, although his supernatural powers of strength and animal transformation are greatly diminished. Occasionally, his beast nature is forced to the surface, but he works on keeping it in check.

Harte befriends a Roman Catholic priest, Friar Julian Bennett, who is sympathetic to Harte's condition. Because Harte cannot enter a church, Friar Bennett meets Harte on occasion to act as his spiritual advisor. Harte has worked out methods of obtaining blood that keep him from taking life except on those rare life-and-death occasions when his bestial nature is aroused.

In Vietnam, Harte had a close war buddy named Grissom. Before he died, Grissom saved Harte's life. While working on a case of the disappearance of a young woman, Harte discovers that, like himself, Grissom had met Nguyen and became a vampire. Grissom resurfaces at the end of the 1980s in the United States as **Jack Steelgate**, a wealthy businessman. In Vietnam, he seemed to enjoy killing, and as a vampire he has little conscience about killing mortals. Steelgate wants his old buddy to join him, but Harte rejects his new lifestyle. Their confrontation becomes crucial for Harte's career.

SOURCES:
Harte of Darkness. Nos. 1-4. Westlake Village, CA: Eternity Comics, 1991–92.

Heather

Heather is an attractive young blonde who becomes a vampire at the strip club which lends its name to the low-budget thriller *Vamps* (1996). Heather is a modern vampire, unaffected by the supernatural trappings of the cross, holy water, or mirrors. Although she cannot turn into nonhuman form, she enjoys traditional vampiric characteristics and rituals, such as protruding fangs and sleeping in a coffin.

The start of the film presents our heroine as an all-American clean-cut beauty down on her luck. Heather has flunked out of school and is depressed, broke, and in need of a job. **Tasha**, the owner of Vamps, teaches Heather how to strip and hires her. What Heather does not realize is that Tasha and the two other strippers, **Randy** and **Tabitha**, are vampires.

The same night Heather is hired, a former acquaintance from high school, Shamus McConnell, shows up at Vamps. Shamus's best friend has brought him to the club to celebrate his birthday, but because Shamus is a priest he does not enjoy himself. Shamus encounters Heather, whom he remembers as his co-star in the high school play. Over the next few days they spend a lot of time together as Shamus contemplates his priestly vows. Eventually, Heather makes a pass, but Shamus refuses her affections.

Both Heather and Shamus are devastated by their parting. Heather tells her story to Tasha, who seizes the emotional opportunity to transform Heather into a vampire. First, she sends Randy to kill Shamus, then she bites Heather and mingles her saliva with Heather's blood. She leaves her asleep while she tracks down other men from her past who have wronged her and brings them back to Vamps. When Heather awakens, Tasha informs her of what has transpired. Heather is reluctant to drink the blood, although Tasha tells her that drinking is a necessary part of the transformation. She must drink the blood or die. When one of the men begins to scream profanities at Heather, all Heather's inhibitions leave her. The drinking is an ecstatic experience.

Meanwhile, Randy is not successful in killing Shamus, and in defending himself, Shamus stakes her. He then pursues Heather and finds her just as she is experiencing the rush of her first feeding. Tasha tells her to kill Shamus, but instead, she turns on Tasha and drains her. With Tasha and Randy dead, Heather inherits the club and with Tabitha runs Vamps as a growing business. With Shamus as the new bartender, it seems like time to hire some additional strippers.

Henzig, Lord of

The Lord of Henzig is an ancient vampire whose career is detailed in the short story, "The Undead Die" (1948). Centuries old and living in an abandoned castle somewhere in rural Europe, the lord sleeps in a coffin (containing native soil) in one of the castle's underground rooms. He dresses richly with jewels plainly visible on his shirt and rings on his clawlike hands. He is dark and strong, with prominent fangs. Each evening as he awakes, he feels the blood thirst and needs to feed as soon as possible. He takes his victims by biting them on their necks.

Approximately 300 years ago, he attacked a couple of 17 year olds, **Robert Warram** and his girlfriend Lisa, who had lost their way while exploring the castle ruins. He bit them and then placed their bodies in an earth-filled coffin to await their awakening the next evening. Through this process, he transformed them into vampires to join and serve him. He exercised his power over them, but he also taught them the secrets of surviving as vampires.

Henzig can transform into a bat, wolf, or other form, having mastered the means of controlling the very cell structure of the body. The ability to transform into a bat is among the first he taught his new minions. He can see in the dark, and communicates via telepathy, only one of the occult practices he passed on to his students.

His demise comes some years after turning Robert and Lisa. The two contact the Great Earth Elemental, a powerful godlike being who responds to their nightly prayers, a most unusual practice for creatures of the night, to return to mortality. He teaches them to contact the universal fields of force that would allow them to defeat and destroy Henzig. Over the next several years they learn to use the forces and to shield their own thoughts from Henzig as they become masters. The occasion for their showing their skill comes one spring when they have a disagreement with Henzig. He insists that the three feed together. The two refuse, and in the battle of invisible forces, Warram wills Henzig out of existence.

SOURCES:
Evans, E. Everett "The Undead Die." 1948.

Hitler, Adolf

Adolf Hitler, certainly one of the most reviled people in history, has even been the feature of a pair of vampire tales. Many people have speculated that he could have escaped the final siege of Berlin at the end of World War II and relocated to South America, but two authors have taken that premise one step further. In a story for the comic book series *Weird War Tales* (1980), Bob Haney suggested that Hitler might have made his escape as a vampire. In his novel *Night of the Dragon's Blood*, William Pridgen fully fleshed out the Hitler-as-vampire plot.

In Pridgen's book, Hitler orders the SS in 1944 to detain a woman named Countess Borca and bring her to Berlin. The Countess, who lived in a castle in Transylvania, is a vampire. When the Nazi defeat becomes inevitable, Hitler has the Countess turn him and hand-picked SS troops turned into vampires. The entire group of vampires then escapes from Berlin and moves to Brazil, where a jungle compound had been constructed. Hitler settles in to write his memoirs and make plans for the future. The SS troops busy themselves constructing a "blood factory" where human victims can be milked like cattle.

As vampires, Hitler and the troops are primarily nocturnal, but can freely move about in daylight with only slightly diminished strength. Normally they sleep in their coffins during the day. They are fully supernatural creatures who show no reflection in mirrors and react negatively to garlic. They can transform into a bat, which is how the SS troops keep watch over the compound each evening. They have

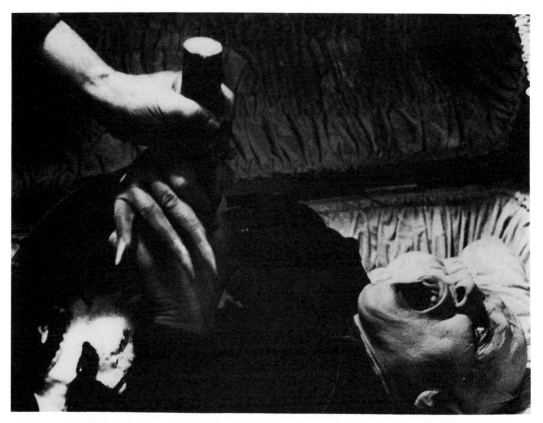

Not all vampires can be killed with a stake to the heart, but this one from the made-for-television movie
Salem's Lot **clearly can be.**

pale skin and retractable fangs, and all they have to do to turn a human into a vampire is bite the person once. Most victims are drained of their blood by the mechanical equipment of the factory and are never actually bitten. When all the blood is drained out of a body, the carcass is thrown into a nearby pool of piranhas.

In 1952, Hitler launches a new plan for conquering South America. His first step is to offer eternal life to the then-leaders of the various countries. From Argentina, Eva Peron comes to Hitler's headquarters as a personal representative of her husband Juan. Hitler does not wait for Eva to say yes or no to the proposal of eternal life—he simply turns her into a vampire immediately. When she does not return, Juan Peron replaces her with a look-alike.

One of Eva's former lovers, Hi Hickenlooper, realizes that the real Eva is missing and confronts Juan, who confesses the duplicity. Together, the men develop a plan to find Hitler and rescue Eva. Hickenlooper discovers a plant called the dragon's palm that grows in Transylvania and secretes a substance that is fatal to vampires. He travels to Brazil and boldly walks into Hitler's compound professing to be a follower. There, he offers the dragon palm plant to Hitler, telling him that it is the proper plant for vampires to grow on their compound. The Countess confirms the plant's Transylvanian origins. Hitler accepts Hickenlooper into his camp and turns him into a vampire.

Four months later, when the plants mature, Hi milks them and mixes the dragon's blood into the vampires' blood supply. Poisoning the blood is designed to coincide with a preplanned commando raid on the camp. The dragon's blood kills all the vampires except those who did not drink blood that evening, including Eva, Hi, the countess, and Hitler. With his troops dead, Hitler faces Hickenlooper in a final confrontation. The Fuhrer proves to be a tough opponent, but Hi prevails and gives Hitler a taste of his own medicine in the piranha pool.

SOURCES:
Haney, Bob. "Beyond Gotterdammerung." *Weird War Tales*. No. 90 (Aug. 1980).
Pridgen, William [Ronald L. Ecker]. *Night of the Dragon's Blood*. Palatka, FL: Hodge & Braddock, 1997.

Hofnstyne, Baron Hegyi Lipzig

Baron Hegyi Lipzig Hofnstyne is a traditional aristocratic Eastern European vampire who appears in the comic book story "The Lonely Vampire" (1975). He resides in a castle overlooking a remote Balkan valley. He has slicked-back black hair and some supernatural powers, such as the ability to transform into a bat. Vampire bats fly around the castle each evening—mutants of the baron's former victims who are searching for food that has become increasingly in short supply.

While the baron lives a lonely life in the castle, the residents of the valley have had enough of his vampirism. With the priest's leadership, they plan to leave, and gather at the border as the baron's soldiers block their exit. The baron, traveling to the village for dinner, finds it deserted and returns to the castle. The bats follow the people to the border, however, and attack. After being driven off with crossbows, they also return to the castle.

Looking out upon the returning bats, the baron realizes they are hungry, and that he is their only possible target. He knows he has to stay awake until dawn to avoid their attack, but he is so tired.

SOURCES:
"The Lonely Vampire." *Ghostly Haunts*. No. 43. Charlton Comics, Mar. 1975.

Howler

Howler is a member of a female vampire motorcycle group known as the Vamps, who lend their name to the comic book series of the same name. Howler, originally Jezz Davidson, is a redhead with a twin sister Jenny. She moves to Las Vegas in the late 1980s, and soon after turns to prostitution to make money to support herself and her child, Tommy. The courts intervene and take custody of the child. She later learns that she has become the victim of an elaborate adoption scheme involving the judge and a New York lawyer. They conspire to take children from poorer women and place them for adoption.

While working to get Tommy back, she meets **Dave**, a vampire who turns her into one of his minions. She is 24 when it is reported that she dies of an overdose. As Howler, she joins Dave's other girls, **Skeeter, Screech, Mink**, and **Whipsnake**. Together the five lure men to remote places where they and Dave feed. Dave is a harsh unappreciative taskmaster and after several years with him, the girls catch him at a weak point after he has gorged himself with blood. They stake him, dismember his body, and bury the parts in separate graves. They emerge as the Vamps and head far from Wilson County, North Carolina, where they had slain their maker.

Howler is the natural leader of the group, and she guides them to Las Vegas, where she hopes to find Tommy and place him in a safe home with Jenny. Along the way, the girls develop a system of feeding so that one of the group always protects them during the time of stupor following the ingestion of blood. Each morning they find a new place to rest away from the sun, their natural enemy, and awake each evening with the blood thirst upon them. As vampires, the Vamps are also vulnerable to religious symbols, if in the hands of a true believer, or wooden stakes in their hearts, but bullets have no effect upon them.

While the other girls enjoy Las Vegas, Howler pursues the judge who kidnapped Tommy. Once he tells her all she needs to know, she makes him her next victim. She then directs her compatriots to New York, where Whipsnake, an African American, had grown up. Now she pursues the lawyer who handled her son's adoption. She treats him very much like the judge, but learns from him the family to whom the child has been sold.

In the meantime, Dave's body has been found. When the coroner removes the stake, Dave revives, and reassembles his own body. Telepathically, he knows where the Vamps are, and heads for New York in search of them. The Vamps are aware of his encroachment, and obtain a magical amulet from a priestess of Santeria to throw Dave off their track by shielding their presence from him. Howler, however, still in pursuit of her son, is unprotected.

Howler locates Tommy and takes possession of him just as Dave arrives to attack her. The rest of the Vamps come to Howler's rescue, kill Dave with a crossbow, and dispose of him in a more permanent manner. The Vamps cover their trail and emerge stronger than ever, ready for new experiences and a new life on their own.

SOURCES:
Vamps. Nos. 1–6. New York: DC Comics/Vertigo, 1995–96.
Vamps: Hollywood & Vein. Nos. 1–6. New York: DC Comics, 1996.

Illyana

Illyana is the head of a Hollywood escort agency that lends its name to the low-budget thriller, *Blonde Heaven* (1995). Like most of the call girls at Blonde Heaven, Illyana is a vampire. Four-hundred years ago, she was invited into a vampire coven by her lover Vincent, himself a vampire of many centuries. Illyana became a vampire, but soon afterward, Vincent was killed. She has never found a replacement for him, and has lived alone for the last four centuries. Old and strong in vampiric ways, Illyana has the power to shape shift and has been known to adopt the form of a man to attract new recruits to the agency.

In *Blonde Heaven*, Illyana's position is challenged by Angie, the latest addition to the staff, who has sought escort work while looking for a job as an actress. She is slated to become a permanent member of the Blonde Haven vampire staff, but Illyana's plans are thwarted when Angie's old boyfriend teams with a vampire hunter to save her. While she loses out on obtaining Angie, Illyana discovers there are always others ready to sign up for a promising career.

Jacula

Jacula, the most famous of the many female vampires in Italian adult comics, lends her name to 327 comic books published between 1969 and 1982. As a young woman in Transylvania in 1835, Jacula is bitten and is subsequently turned into a vampire. She eventually becomes so proficient (for example, she learns to live unscathed in the sunlight), she is elected as the vampire queen. More often than not depicted in the buff, Jacula is helped by an aristocratic mortal lover, Carlo Verdier. At various times during her long career, she survives encounters with Frankenstein, Jack the Ripper, and the Marquis de Sade.

In the main Jacula story line, vampires are in league with the devil, who uses them as he attempts to locate Jesus Christ's grave to prove to the world that his resurrection is a myth.

Jacula was created by a group of comic artists known as Studio Giolitti. Though very successful, it finally succumbed to the protests of some Christian leaders and police harassment of its publishers (first Erregi, then Ediperiodici) and ceased publication, although reprints of 129 issues still ran through 1984. There was also a French edition. A well-known Italian Gothic music band calls itself Jacula.

SOURCES:
Jacula. No. 1–327. Milan: Erregi/Ediperiodici, 1969–82.

James, Raglan

Raglan James, vampire hunter turned vampire, is the title character in Anne Rice's *Tales of the Body Thief,* in which he has a brief, but traumatic encounter with the vampire **Lestat de Lioncourt.** Raglan was born around 1928 in India, but grew up in London, England. He attended Oxford University, but instead of following a career, he becomes an accomplished con man and thief. He is also a psychic, and, in many ways, a genius. His great accomplishment is discovering the means and developing the ability to actually take possession of other people's bodies—that is, he can place his soul or spirit into the physical shell of another persons body and make it his own. He was briefly a member of the Talamasca, the secretive occult research organization, but was fired for theft and unethical behavior.

Once, when James learned that he was dying of cancer, he took a job in a hospital and exchanged his body for that of a healthy young man. He is in that young, healthy body when he begins to track Lestat in the early 1990s. To demonstrate to Lestat that he has powers of his own, he reveals himself to the vampire on several occasions, proving he has the power to track him. Finally, he and Lestat meet, at which time James proposes that they exchange bodies, if only temporarily. Lestat is intrigued. Just once, he would like to remember what it is like to live as a mortal. Against the advice of his knowledgeable friend **David Talbot,** Lestat agrees to the exchange, much to his regret. James has no intention of giving the body back and immediately disappears. He attempts to steal all of Lestat's wealth and does manage to gain access to some 20 million dollars.

James makes it easy for Lestat and Talbot to follow him by leaving a string of murders in his wake. Talbot and Lestat track him to the luxury liner, Queen Elizabeth 2, in the Caribbean near the island of Curacao. They devise a plan to force James's spirit out of Lestat's body as he returns to his stateroom just before dawn. The plan works perfectly and even has an added bonus—not only does Lestat get his body back, but a second switch occurs when James occupies Talbot's aging body and Talbot switches into James's youthful one.

James even manages to use this last bit of bad luck to his advantage, however. Impersonating Talbot, James asks Lestat for the "Dark Gift" of vampirism. Lestat has wanted his friend to take the gift for years, but he had always refused. Now, excited that he has finally said yes, Lestat almost turns James into a vampire before realizing at the last minute that the switch had occurred. Lestat pushes James away, and a short time later he dies at a hospital, trapped in Talbot's body.

SOURCES:

Ramsland, Katherine. *The Vampire Companion: The Official Guide to Anne Rice's The Vampire Chronicles.* New York: Ballantine Books, 1993.

Rice, Anne. *The Tale of the Body Thief.* New York: Alfred A. Knopf, 1992. Reprint,: New York: Ballantine, 1993.

Jeepers, Mrs.

A would-be vampire with just enough controlled scariness to attract most third graders, Mrs. Jeepers appears in several digest novels: *Vampires Don't Wear Polka Dots,* and its sequels, *Dracula Doesn't Drink Lemonade* and *Mrs. Jeepers' Batty Vacation.* But the question seems to be, Is Mrs. Jeepers, the third-grade teacher at Bailey Elementary School in Bailey City, USA, a vampire? Some of the kids think so, but because she wears a bright pink dress with green polka dots her second day in class and Liza remarks, "...vampires don't wear polka dots," other students think she may just be eccentric.

Jack Palance made his mark portraying Count Dracula in a popular made-for-televison version of the classic tale.

She is short with red hair, and wears black-laced pointy-toed boots and a green broach that she occasionally rubs. The kids believe they've seen it glow. She also has a bat bracelet that was given to her by her husband. She is from Transylvania and speaks with a Romanian accent. And she moved into the Clancy estate that the kids believe is haunted with ghosts and vampires. Some kids witnessed the movers take a long thin box into the house; it could be a coffin.

As a new teacher, Mrs. Jeepers will have to sustain the antics of the class bully Eddie, whose fun level has dipped considerably since Mrs. Jeepers took control of the unruly class. To prove what he has come to believe, Eddie buys a book, *Vampires and Witches: The True Story*. After reading the chapter on vampires, Eddie brings garlic to class and scatters it around the room. Mrs. Jeepers spends the morning sneezing as if she has a bad cold. She recovers quickly after the custodian sweeps up during the noon hour.

The experiment doesn't prove anything to most of the kids, but Howie admits he is scared. After lunch Eddie starts his antics again—this time with spitballs. Mrs. Jeepers invites Eddie outside the classroom, and when he returns he is as white as a ghost. After school, he tells his curious classmates, "I'll only say this, you guys were right. Mrs. Jeepers is no ordinary teacher.... I know one thing, I'll never make her mad again." The kids never do find out if she is a vampire, but at least none of the students are bitten.

SOURCES:

Dadey, Debbie, and Marcia Thornton Jones. *Vampires Don't Wear Polka Dots.* New York: Scholastic, Inc., 1990.

————. *Dracula Doesn't Drink Lemonade.* New York: Scholastic, Inc., 1995.

————. *Mrs. Jeepers' Batty Vacation.* New York: Scholastic, Inc., 1997.

JERRY *see:* NERO, JERRY

Jesse

Jesse, a mortal descendant of the ancient vampire **Maharet,** first appeared in Anne Rice's *The Queen of the Damned* (1988). In 1950, her mother, Miriam Reeves was pregnant when she was killed in a car accident, the shock of which caused Jesse to be born on the spot as her mother lay dying. Miriam had been named for the mother of the twins Maharet and **Mekare,** the witches of ancient Palestine who became vampires some 6,000 years ago. Maharet was pregnant at the time she became a vampire and bore a child, also named Miriam, who became the progenitor of a large family now spread internationally among the peoples of the world. Miriam became a common family name that appeared again and again in the large family.

After the accident, Maharet claims the infant Jesse and places her with Maria and Matthew Godwin, members of her extended family in New York City. Maharet, who acts as archivist and historian for her huge family, stays in touch with Jesse through regular letters. Jesse has a normal childhood that is distinguished only by her psychic abilities. After high school she enters Columbia to study ancient languages, art, and anthropology. During class breaks she travels extensively and meets members of the family in other countries.

Following graduation, Jesse travels to Maharet's home in Sonoma, California, where she has her first brush with vampirism. **Mael,** a vampire staying with Maharet, becomes overly protective of her and wants to turn her into a vampire so that she will not be susceptible to the many diseases and accidents that seem to plague humans. At the last minute, Maharet intervenes and prevents him from doing so.

Jesse then moves to London. A tabloid article about her psychic abilities brings her to the attention of the Talamasca, a low-key international occult research society. She accepts the group's offer to join the staff. When **Daniel Molloy** publishes his book *Interview with the Vampire* in 1976, the Talamasca sends her to New Orleans to see if the story is true. She not only locates the house in which the vampires **Lestat de Lioncourt, Louis de Pointe du Lac,** and **Claudia** had lived, but also finds some of Claudia's possessions that had been hidden in a secret compartment in one of the walls of the house. She begins to get too involved in the case and is pulled off of it and sent to India.

After the publication of *The Vampire Lestat,* Jesse attends the huge concert by Lestat and his rock band in San Francisco. As she watches the show from the edge of

WHEN THE MUSE DEPARTS

Anne Rice, after five very successful novels featuring the vampire Lestat de Lioncourt, has announced that after *Memnoch the Devil* (1997), Lestat has left her. As she told her fans, "It was after I finished Memnoch that I felt Lestat walked off on me. He left me. He just left me. He said, 'Anne, no more for now.' And off he went. Also, if and when you read the book, you'll see why he left. Who could blame him? But the fact is, he left. And when he did, it was like the wind. I felt it. It happened. I couldn't control it. He just split on me.

So what does a writer do when a favorite character leaves? Rice announced that for the book signings for Memnoch, she was going to wear a wedding dress. Why a wedding dress? Possibly because she feels deserted, conflicted, and just as in love with Lestat as ever and the dress reminds Lestat that she is still his bride? Maybe because she never had a real wedding dress? Most likely, its because she just likes old fashioned beautiful white dresses! When you are at the top of your field, you can pretty much do what you want.

the stage, she realizes that Lestat is just like Mael and that both really are vampires. Swept away by the realization, she climbs on-stage and manages to taste some of Lestat's bloody sweat, which triggers an explosion of feelings inside her. The moment does not last, however, because another vampire in the show realizes she is part of the Talamasca and thinks she is a threat to Lestat. He attacks her, and in the ensuing melee, her neck is broken. Mael accompanies her to the hospital and gives her some of his vampire blood to help her heal faster. When Maharet arrives, she goes one step further, finally giving Jesse the "Dark Gift" and turning her into a vampire.

Jesse has little time to adjust to her new state when she is thrown into the midst of the Sonoma vampire community's battle with **Akasha,** the original vampire who is determined to rule the world. The group manages to defeat Akasha, and after her death, Jesse joins the others when they travel to the Night Island complex near Miami, Florida, that is owned by the vampire **Armand.**

During her years with the Talamasca, Jesse had been impressed with **David Talbot,** its leader. She even facilitated setting up a meeting between Lestat and Talbot, who became friends. Jesse remains friends with Talbot (who eventually becomes a vampire) through the years and stays in close contact with him.

SOURCES:

Ramsland, Katherine. *The Vampire Companion: The Official Guide to Anne Rice's The Vampire Chronicles.* New York: Ballantine Books, 1993.

Rice, Anne. *Memnoch the Devil.* New York: Alfred A. Knopf, 1994. Reprint, New York: Ballantine Books, 1995.

———. *The Queen of the Damned.* New York: Alfred A. Knopf, 1988. Reprint, New York: Ballantine Books, 1989.

Jonas, Father

Father Jonas, a vampire with the Darkling Disciples, encounters the extraterrestrial **Vampirella** when he unknowingly makes a victim of the uncle of **Adam Van Helsing,** a vampire hunter who has fallen in love with the beautiful young Vampirella.

Lily Jordan is the star of the graphic novel series, *Confessions of a Teenage Vampire*.

Father Jonas is a former priest who turns to the dark side and affiliates with an evil occult organization whose goal is no less than world domination. Their plans call for the incarnation of the basic elements of alchemy (earth, air, fire, and water) in human beings. Father Jonas is the first incarnation fire. The second, a female embodiment of the water element, has also been created.

The creation of each embodiment requires blood, which forces Father Jonas to cause an airplane crash in the Rocky Mountains. On the plane are Vampirella and Adam's uncle, Kurt Van Helsing, the brother of **Conrad Van Helsing.** Kurt is found with two bite marks on his neck and his blood drained. Conrad is initially convinced that Vampirella is the killer. After she convinces him that she is innocent, their search for the perpetrator leads them to the site of the crash. Father Jonas confesses that he and one of his minions have caused the crash and taken blood from three passengers, including Conrad's brother. In the ensuing confrontation, Father Jonas is pushed back with a cross and appears to catch fire and perish in the flames.

Vampirella and the Van Helsings head for New Orleans to search for the headquarters of the Darkling Disciples, which they find, as well as a revived Father Jonas. It turns out that Father Jonas did not die in the fire, but was badly burned. For his failure, the Darkling Disciples heal him but give him monster-like lower appendages in place of his human legs. Father Jonas captures Vampirella and is about to use her and her cohorts as sources of blood for the next part of his plan when Vampirella breaks free and brings him together with the woman embodying the water element. The resulting conflagration finally destroys Father Jonas and the Darkling Disciples for good.

SOURCES:

Englehart, Steve, and José Gonzalez. "Hell from on High." *Vampirella* 22 (1972). Reprinted in *Vampirella Transcending Time and Space.* New York: Harris Comics, 1992.

———. "The Witch Queen of Bayou Parish." *Vampirella* 23 (1972). Reprinted in *Vampirella Transcending Time and Space.* New York: Harris Comics, 1992.

Jordan, Lily

Lily Jordan, whose adventures appear in a series of graphic novels collectively titled *Confessions of a Teenage Vampire*, is a normal high school student in the small new England town of Lemachard. She has a variety of school friends and one enemy, Rosie Cartwright, the school bully. The petite blonde differs from most of her classmates, however, in that she has an interest in history, especially the history of her town, which was founded by **Philip Lemachard** in the 1600s. Lily knows about his life, his trip to France, and his subsequent disappearance. She is also fascinated with his mansion that still stands in town.

One day while walking home from school, Lily notices someone moving in the mansion. She wanders into the house and finds a man who looks strangely like Philip Lemachard. He introduces himself as Philip Lemachard the seventh. He takes a liking to Lily, gives her a tour of the mansion, and invites her back anytime.

Lily returns one day to discover Lemachard in a wild, frenzied state. He hastily gulps some green liquid and returns to normal. He then shares the truth with her. He is in fact the original Philip Lemachard, who had become a vampire in France and, after many years of feeding off humans, discovered a serum that took the blood thirst away so he no longer had to kill. However, Sang, the vampire who made him, likes the sport of killing and is out to destroy Lemachard for spreading the serum throughout the vampire community. Lemachard tells Lily their confrontation will take place very soon in town. While he believes that he will be defeated by the older, stronger Sang, Lemachard says he will try to defend himself.

He sends Lily away, but she returns just as the attack by Sang begins. She and Lemachard get trapped in a room, where Lemachard transforms her into a vampire to save her. As a newly transformed being, she immediately passes through the first stage of the vampire's life, the blood fire, a period of heightened sensory input and strength, thus escaping Sang for the moment.

When Lily recovers from the blood-fire symptoms she learns that Lemachard is dead. However, he left her his mansion and fortune. He also extracted a promise from her to never give into the thirst and only drink the serum. As long as she refuses to touch real blood, she can move about in the daytime and continue a somewhat normal life. As student by day, vampire by night, Lily prepares herself for the day when she must once again confront Sang.

SOURCES:

West, Terry, and Steve Ellis. *Confessions of a Teenage Vampire: The Turning.* New York: Scholastic, Inc., 1997.
———. *Confessions of a Teenage Vampire: Zombie Saturday Night.* New York: Scholastic, Inc., 1997.

Jorge, Count

Count Jorge is a conventional aristocratic Transylvanian vampire and subject of "Enter Freely of Your Own Will," a short story by Frank Hayes. As a young man, Jorge, is wandering around his father's land when he comes upon some peasant children being harassed by a bat. Following what he believes is his duty to those who live on his family's land, he fights it off, but is bitten in the process. Out of the encounter, he develops an intense blood lust.

He tries valiantly to find a cure. He takes blood from animals, but ultimately craves human blood. He kills some twelve people before finding help from a business associate of his father's. The man puts silver around one of the castle's dungeon rooms and coaxes Jorge into it. There he stays until he is cured.

In 1871, the castle is visited by a Mister Johnson who finds the count still alive. The count invites in his visitor, serves him food and drink, and tells him his story. The count, it seems, cured himself by starving to death. Now he is just a ghost who endlessly roams the castle. Upon finishing the account of his life, the count immediately fades away and leaves Mister Johnson to hurriedly abandon the haunted building.

SOURCES:

Hayes, Frank, and Pat Boyette. "Enter Freely and of Your Own Will." *Haunted* 21. (Carlton Comics, April 1975).

Judge Axel

Judge Axel appears in *A Return to Salem's Lot*, the 1987 made-for-television movie sequel to *Salem's Lot*, which had been made into a movie in 1979. (*Salem's Lot* is based on Stephen King's 1975 novel of the same name.) In the movie, Judge Axel is the leader of the vampire community that controls the small town of Salem's Lot, Maine, a decade after the town was targeted for domination by the vampire **Kurt Barlow.** Barlow's vampire children were largely destroyed by fire (see Stephen King's *Salem's Lot*), but by the late 1980s, the town has revived. The surviving residents have become vampires and have a new leader: Judge Axel. The elderly, white-haired judge lives in a house at the end of Main Street, where, next to his wife, Martha, he sleeps away the days in a coffin.

Axel and the vampires he controls represent an ancient race that came to the New World 300 years ago. Ever since, they have lived quietly in rural New England. Their vampire characteristics are somewhat traditional in that they are nocturnal (both sunlight and firelight can fatally burn them) and are repelled by sacred symbols (holy water burns their skin like acid). They are not, however, allergic to garlic, and their reflections show in mirrors.

It has been Judge Axel's plan to present a facade of normalcy to the surrounding rural community. During the day, the town is patrolled by a small group of docile and cooperative drones—humans conceived during a vampire's union with a human. The vampires have largely weaned themselves from human blood by raising cattle, which they use for their blood rather than their milk. Only occasionally do they attack humans.

Judge Axel conceives of a plan to document the vampires' world and, by portraying them as harmless eccentrics, assist with their seamless integration into human society. To help his cause, the judge lures anthropologist Joe Weber (Michael Moriarity)—known for his love of studying unique societies—into the vampire's midst. While Weber's teenage son falls for a pretty young vampire, Weber is coerced into conducting a study of the community. For a short time, Weber rationalizes to himself that perhaps the vampires are not all that bad. But the arrival of a former Nazi hunter, who has switched his career to tracking vampires, recalls Weber from his delusion.

Operating from a base inside the community's church, Weber and the Nazi hunter begin killing the vampires and their drones, but are unable to complete the task during the first day. When the vampire community awakens that night, the beleaguered pair survive a mass attack and simultaneously rescue Weber's son.

Axel was to be their first target, but when Weber arrives at his house, he discovers that the judge has chosen an alternate sleeping place. Weber eventually finds Axel in the schoolhouse but is unable to kill the elder vampire. Angered, Axel then tracks Weber to the blacksmith's shop. Not a vampire to be taken lightly, Axel changes into a beast-like creature and wages battle. The struggle ends when Weber is finally able to stake Axel while the Nazi hunter is finishing off the other vampires indirectly by destroying their coffins, thus denying them a place to sleep during the coming day.

Julian, Damon

Damon Julian, the leader of the vampire community in New Orleans in the 1850s, appears in George R. R. Martin's 1982 novel, *Fevre Dream*. Formerly known as Julian Lamont, he emerges as the leader of a group of vampires seeking a safer home. In the 1750s he charters a boat from Lisbon, Portugal, to New Orleans. For a century the vampires operate out of New Orleans and travel the Mississippi River. They find the slave culture allows them to operate freely without much fear of discovery.

Julian is not of the undead, but rather, he is a vampire by birth. His line originates in Poland. As a vampire, he is a different species from humans, but he's not a supernatural creature. He has no problem with mirrors, garlic, holy objects, wolfsbane, or silver. He is nocturnal and the sun will burn him after a short time. He does not sleep in a coffin.

In 1957 one of Julian's distant kin, **Captain Joshua Anton York,** arrives in New Orleans and presents a plan to save the vampire from his blood lust. He's discovered a blood substitute created with sheep's blood and a mixture of herbs. Rather than receive the news with happiness, Julian prefers the old ways and fights York. He eventually takes over his boat, named the *Fevre Dream*, and puts York under his control. He removes the human crew and sails the boat into an obscure bayou where it remains hidden throughout the Civil War. The war proves disastrous to the vampire community, and only a dozen are left under Julian's control.

While Julian remains headquartered on the boat, York's partner, Captain Abner Marsh, never gives up looking for his boat. In 1870, he finally tracks it down and rejoins York for a final confrontation with Julian aboard the *Fevre Dream*. In the battle, Julian is killed with a shotgun blast to the brain.

SOURCES:
Martin, George R. R. *Fevre Dream.* New York: Poseidon Press, 1982. Reprint, London: VGSF, 1989.

Karnstein, Carmilla

Carmilla Karnstein is the original female vampire in English prose fiction, and, as such, is one of the most influential vampire characters in literature. She first appeared in Sheridan Le Fanu's 1872 story collection, *In a Glass Darkly*. In the story, she is identical to a person otherwise known as Countess Mircalla Karnstein, a young woman of the late seventeenth century and descendent through her mother of the Karnsteins. The Karnstein family castle was in Styria.

Le Fanu's story unfolds in the mid-nineteenth century. The youthful Carmilla is traveling through rural Styria when her carriage breaks down. She is greeted warmly and taken in at a nearby castle owned by a retired Austrian civil servant and his 19-year-old daughter Laura. Laura is startled when she realizes that she recognizes Carmilla as the same woman who had appeared in her bedroom some 12 years earlier, before she and her father had moved to the castle. It seems that when Laura was but six years old, a woman had entered her bedroom and comforted the young child. Laura fell asleep in the woman's arms but suddenly awakened when she felt what seemed to be two needles entering her breast. She cried out, and the person Laura knew only as "the lady" slipped out of bed, onto the floor, and disappeared, possibly under the bed. Her nurse and a housekeeper came running into the room in response to Laura's cries, but they found no one there and noticed no marks on the girl's chest. Now, under the ruse of the broken-down carriage, Carmilla had returned to prey on Laura once again. She visits Laura in the form of a cat and a female phantom. In addition to recognizing her as "the lady" from her childhood, Laura also notices that Carmilla looks exactly like a 1698 portrait of the Countess Mircalla Karnstein.

As Carmilla begins to prey on Laura, an old friend of Laura's family arrives at the castle. The friend, General Spielsdorf, informs his hosts that his daughter has died and relates the strange account of her death. For some time, she had been wasting away, suffering from an illness that had no known natural causes. A physician then deduced

Poster art for the movie *The Vampire Lovers,* from Hammer Studios.

that the girl was actually the victim of a vampire, but the general does not believe the doctor. One night, however, he hides in his daughter's room and actually catches the vampire in the act. He is stunned to see that it is a young woman he knew by the name of Millarca (in her various guises, Carmilla always chooses a name that is an anagram of Carmilla). He tries to kill her with his sword, but she easily escapes.

Just as the general is finishing his tale, Carmilla enters the room. He immediately recognizes her as Millarca, but she escapes before the men can deal with her. A group then tracks her to the Karnstein castle some three miles away, where they find her resting in her grave. Her body is lifelike, and a faint heartbeat is detected. The casket floats in fresh blood. The men drive a stake through Carmilla's heart, which causes her to emit a "piercing shriek." The men finish the job by severing her head, burning her body, and scattering the ashes.

The vampire characteristics that Carmilla exhibited in Le Fanu's story were common to vampires of folklore and played an important part in shaping the characteristics exhibited by future fictional vampires, both male and female. She had become a vampire from the bite of another vampire. She was somewhat confined geographically to the area near her grave. While somewhat pale in complexion, she was quite capable of fitting into society without gathering unwanted attention. She had two needle-like teeth, but they were not visible at most times. She generally bit her victims in the neck or chest. Carmilla was primarily nocturnal, but was not totally confined to the darkness. She had superhuman strength and was able to undergo a transformation into various shapes, especially those of animals. Her favorite shape was that of a cat. She slept in a coffin that she could leave without disturbing any dirt covering the grave. Her bite neither turned the victim into a vampire nor killed him/her—rather, she fed over a period of time while the victim slowly withered away. Just as she was turned into a vampire by a bite, however, she could turn people into vampires if she so desired.

Carmilla's Influence: While earlier writers had written about the vampire-like *lamiai* and other female vampires who attacked their male lovers, Carmilla introduced the female revenant vampire to gothic literature. Carmilla would directly influence Bram Stoker's presentation of the vampire, especially his treatment of the female vampires (the **"Brides of Dracula"**) who attack Jonathan Harker early in *Dracula*. The influence of Carmilla was even more visible in "Dracula's Guest," the deleted chapter of *Dracula* later republished as a short story.

Through the twentieth century, "Carmilla" has had a vital existence on the motion picture screen. The story served loosely as the inspiration for *Vampyr*, Carl Theodore Dryer's 1931 classic, although the first movie based directly on "Carmilla" was the 1961 French film *Et Mourir de Plaisir* (*Blood and Roses*) directed by Roger Vadim and starring his wife, Annette Vadim, as the vampire. It was followed by *La Maldicion of the Karnsteins* (also known as *Terror in the Crypt*) the following year. Then at the beginning of the 1970s, in the wake of its many successful vampire movies, Hammer Films would turn to Carmilla and her family for three films—*Lust for a Vampire* (1970), *The Vampire Lovers* (1970), and *Twins of Evil* (1971). *The Vampire Lovers*, in fact, is perhaps the most faithful adaptation of Le Fanu's original story.

Ingrid Pitt as Carmilla in *The Vampire Lovers*.

The Hammer movies inspired other European efforts to bring Carmilla to the screen. The Spanish productions, *La Hija de Dracula* (*The Daughter of Dracula*) was released in 1972. It was followed by: *La Comtesse aux Seiens Nux* (1973), which was released under a variety of titles, including a highly edited version called *Erotikill* (1981); and *La Novia Ensangretada* (1974), which was released in the United States as *Till Death*

Do Us Part and *The Blood Spattered Bride*. Over the last 20 years, the story of Carmilla has inspired *The Evil of Dracula* (1975) and *Valerie* (1991), while television adaptations appeared in England in 1966, Spain in 1987, and the United States in 1989.

"Carmilla" was brought to the attention of a generation of comic book readers in 1968 by the Warren Publishing Company in *Creepy* (No. 19). Warren was one of the publishers that essentially ignored the Comics Code of 1954, which forbade including vampires in comic books. More recently, Malibu Comics released a six-part adult version of *Carmilla*. In 1972, the story was included on a record album, *Carmilla: A Vampire Tale*, released under the Vanguard label by the Etc. Company.

SOURCES:

Author's Note: A favorite of vampire anthologists, "Carmilla" has been reprinted numerous times. It is easily accessible in: Alan Ryan, ed. *Vampires: Two Centuries of Great Vampire Stories.* Garden City, NY: Doubleday & Company, 1971.

Glut, Donald F. *The Dracula Book.* Metuchen, NJ: Scarecrow Press, 1975.

Keesey, Pam. *Vamps: An Illustrated History of the Femme Fatale.* San Francisco: Cleis Press, 1997.

Le Fanu, Sheridan. *In a Glass Darkly.* 1872.

Katani, Baroness Clarimonde

Baroness Clarimonde Katani (Pai Dagermark) is a nineteenth century German vampire featured in the 1971 comedy, *The Vampire Happening* (originally released as *Gebissen Wind nur Nichts Happening der Vampire*). The story begins when Clarimonde, an Italian by birth, ignores her family's protests and is brought to Germany to become the Baroness von Rabenstein. Her life takes a nasty turn for the worst when she apparently dies under mysterious circumstances with two strange puncture wounds in her neck. Of course, she has really become a vampire.

Although she is one of the undead, Clarimonde remains trapped in her coffin in the basement of her castle until the 1970s. She is finally freed from her coffin just as her great granddaughter Elizabeth von Rabenstein arrives at the castle for a visit. In her home in America, Elizabeth is a famous movie star who appears under the stage name Betty Williams. It seems that Elizabeth is the spitting image of her great grandmother, with the exception of their hair—Elizabeth's is blonde, while Clarimonde's is dark. With Clarimonde awake and roaming the castle, the stage is set for comedy when the other inhabitants of the castle—Elizabeth's boyfriend and the elderly caretaker Joseph—repeatedly confuse the two women.

Joseph and the boyfriend realize that Clarimonde is a vampire and attempt to kill her. Unfortunately, thanks to the wigs that Elizabeth wears, they can never tell which woman is Clarimonde and which is Elizabeth in time to act. The audience is able to keep the two women straight by their nail polish—red for Elizabeth, black for Clarimonde—but the two hapless men never catch on. At one point, the boyfriend has an opportunity to end the confusion but refuses to drive the stake in because of Clarimonde's striking resemblance to Elizabeth.

Several nights after Clarimonde's awakening, all of the vampires in the area are scheduled to attend their annual gathering at nearby Castle Oxenstein. Elizabeth intercepts the invitation, and, not realizing that there is a vampire on the loose,

Meg Tilly as Carmilla Karnstein in a more recent adaptation of Sheridan Le Fanu's classic tale.

decides to attend. Joseph and the boyfriend follow her to the Castle (thinking it is Clarimonde) and plot to destroy the vampires by changing the castle's clock so the vampires would be trapped in the morning light. Their plan works—sort of. Most of the vampires are killed, but two survive—**Count Dracula,** who was the event's special guest, and Clarimonde. Thinking that he is shipping Elizabeth's dead body back to Hollywood, Joseph instead sends Clarimonde's very much alive body there instead, where she emerges and takes over the life of Betty Williams, feasting on her legion of fans.

The dark-haired Clarimonde is a traditional vampire. She is pale, possesses a prominent set of fangs, and reacts adversely to garlic and the cross. A nocturnal creature, she returns to her coffin each dawn and is vulnerable to sunlight and the stake.

Katrina

Katrina remembered as much for her sensual dancing as for her vampire attributes is the owner of the After Dark Club, a strip joint, in the 1986 movie *Vamp*. Katrina, a rare African American vampire in the movies, has a vague

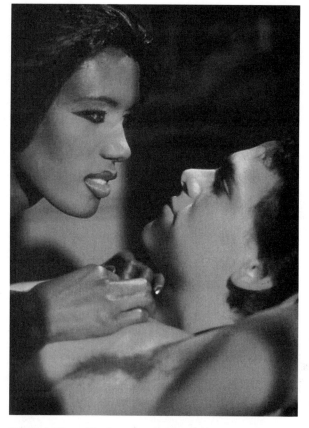

Katrina (portrayed by Grace Jones) prepares to dine on her latest victim in the film *Vamp*.

origin but appears to have been a queen in ancient Egypt. She rarely speaks, at times communicating orders to her minions simply by taking sudden retribution on those who disobey or fail her.

Her new home in an unnamed American city is disturbed one evening when three college freshmen from a nearby college come to town looking for a stripper for a fraternity party. While **A.J.** tries to cut a deal, Keith meets an old acquaintance who now works as a barmaid, and Duncan just enjoys the strippers. A.J. decides that Katrina (portrayed by Grace Jones) is the one he should lure back to the college. He asks to see her, but she, instead of responding to his proposition, begins to seduce him. Before they are very far along, Katrina changes. Her fingernails and toenails lengthen and fangs appear in her mouth. Her eyes lose their color, and she takes on a bestial appearance. Before A.J. can escape, she bites him. Her bite leads to A.J.'s very quick transformation.

Katrina and her minions are traditional vampires. They are nocturnal creatures, residing in coffins in a room below the club. They show no image in mirrors. They are vulnerable to stakes in the heart, fire, and sunlight. After Duncan is vampirized

Three of the female vampires/strippers who work at the After Dark Club in the film *Vamp*.

and killed, and Keith, the sole surviving member of the trio, is unable to get away, Keith goes on the attack. He dispatches a number of Katrina's minions by first burning their coffin room and the club, and then impaling them with arrows (it turns out that he is an accomplished archer).

Katrina, naturally, proves more difficult to kill. Shot in the mouth with an arrow and stabbed in the heart with a stake, she simply pulls out the intruding weapons. Unfortunately for her, however, by that time it is the end of a long night. The sun comes up, and, as a final desperate move, Keith lets in the light. Katrina burns into a heap of ashes and bones, but not before she musters just enough of her fading life to raise her middle finger at the victorious young man as he leaves her underground lair.

Kenyon, Countess Sarah

Countess Sarah Kenyon, a seventeenth-century British vampire, is the subject of F. G. Loring's 1900 short story, "The Tomb of Sarah." Countess Sarah is the last of the Kenyons and lives alone with her black Asiatic wolf in her castle near Bristol, England, at the beginning of the 1600s. Although she is a beautiful young woman, she has a bad reputation. The townspeople believe she sends her wolf out to seize babies, sheep, or other small game so she can devour the blood. In 1630, a woman who lost two babies confronts the countess and strangles her. She is entombed in a graveyard at Hagerstone. The tomb bears a strange inscription: "For the sake of the dead and the welfare of the living, let this sepulcher remain untouched and its occupant undisturbed until the coming of Christ."

The inscription is heeded until 1841 when renovation of the church requires the movement of the tomb approximately 10 feet. The lid is removed and a temporary cover placed over it. Inside the tomb lies a well-preserved body of a woman with a rope around her neck. The skin on the body is pale and wrinkled. That evening all the dogs in town seem to come alive with howling and barking. A big black dog, unknown in the town, is seen coming and going.

The next day, the woman appears alive, the color having returned to her cheeks and the wrinkles noticeably decreased. On the third day she leaves the tomb in a cloud of fog. Having discerned that she is a vampire, the rector and one of the workmen prepare for her return with garlic, a stake, and dog roses. Just as dawn is breaking Countess Sarah returns, and makes her way across the dog roses before the two men stake her. As the priest reads the burial service over her, a sense of peace seems to return to the beautiful vampiress, her fangs having disappeared. Soon she disintegrates into mere dust.

SOURCES:
Loring, F. G. "The Tomb of Sarah." *Pall Mall Magazine.* London, 1900. Reprinted in Shepard, Les, ed. *The Dracula Book of Great Vampire Stories.* New York: Jove, 1978.

Keogh, Harry

Harry Keogh is the main character in a series of novels by Brian Lumley, beginning with *Necroscope* (1988). He is the character in the title: a necroscope, or person who has the ability to communicate with the dead. His talent makes him a dangerous weapon in humankind's battle against vampires. He is the son of a fortune teller, who

Cover art from the comic book version of Brian Lumley's *Necroscope,* which features Harry Keogh.

possessed strong psychic abilities of her own. From her, he inherited his strange talent, which puzzled him at first but grew stronger as he became a young man. In the 1970s, he was recruited to join a secret group called the E-Branch, which specializes in psychic intelligence gathering and monitoring. The Russians have their own version of E-Branch, and the two are always in conflict.

After he joins E-Branch, he learns that his step-father, Victor Skukshin, is really a Russian spy. He could recognize people who had ESP talents, and was sent to spy on British ESPers. He spotted Keogh's mother because of her talent, married her, and then killed her so he could inherit her fortune. He remained in England after he killed her. Keogh eventually learns of his betrayal by speaking with his dead mother in the spot that she drowned.

Keogh is recruited by Sir Keenan Gromley, the head of the E-branch. Gromley has no real psychic talent of his own—he is simply a "spotter," who can identify people who have psychic ability (much like Keogh's step-father). Gromley is killed by a Russian agent **Boris Dragosani,** a truly evil man who can also speak with the dead, but in a horrible way. Whereas Keogh is welcomed by the dead as a friend, Dragosani is hated. Instead of talking with the dead, he forces them to give up their secrets by reading their entrails with his hands, essentially squeezing their very thoughts out of their lungs, their hearts. What he really does is torture the dead until they can stand it no more and are forced to talk to him. After he kills Gromley, he puts the older man through the horrible process to learn more about E-Branch.

Dragosani also has other plans. He wants to become a vampire, and to do so, he releases an ancient vampire names **Thibor Ferenczy** from his grave in Romania. Ferenczy repays Dragosani for releasing him by granting his wish and turning him into a vampire. In return, Dragosani tricks Ferenczy and kills him. Needless to say, this angers Ferenczy. To retaliate, he contacts Harry Keogh using deadspeak and gives Keogh the information he needs to find and defeat Dragosani. In return, Keogh promises to visit Ferenczy so he will not be lonely in death.

To defeat Dragosani, Keogh must travel to Russia to the headquarters of their psychic branch. Harry does not have to do this the conventional way, however. In his time spent talking to the dead, he has had many long conversations with a mathematician named Mobius, who invented something called the Mobius Strip. The Strip flattens out three dimensions to two, and two to one, which means it should theoretically be possible for a person to travel anywhere in the known universe in the blink of an eye. Keogh is able to master this amazing power, which is at the heart of the entire *Necroscope* series.

Using his power, Keogh travels to Russia in an instant. Once there, he uses his deadspeak to communicate with the thousands of dead soldiers who lie buried in the area of the Russian E-Branch. He convinces them to rise up out of their graves and fight Dragosani, who is the enemy of the dead. They do, and they defeat Dragosani and his forces. In the final confrontation, Keogh kills Dragosani by staking and decapitating him; he is later killed himself. Once dead, Harry exists as a an energized spirit being who eventually reincarnates in the body of his own son.

In his new body, Harry's battles with vampires continued in Lumley's lengthy novels. Not only does Harry fight vampires on our Earth, but he also battles them on a similar planet that exists in a parallel universe. The gate to that universe is discovered deep in the Ural Mountains in Russia, and it turns out that the alternate world is filled with a hideous and powerful form of vampire known as a the *wamphyri*. In fact, it is likely that vampires on Earth descend from the vampires on Starside/Sunside, that at some point in ancient history, a *wamphyri* from that world traveled through the gate and flourished on Earth. Harry, as his son, actually ends up living in the alternate world, where he is known as a the Dweller and is worshiped by the people there. He also fathers twin sons, Nathan and Nestor, who figure prominently in their own series of Lumley novels. Nathan battles vampires, while Nestor actually becomes a *wamphyri* lord. As a The Dweller, Keogh himself is eventually infected with vampirism and becomes the creature he most hated in the world.

Vampires in Lumley's world are heinous creatures, a different species from humans altogether. They have a bestial appearance and are clearly monsters who cannot live in human society.

SOURCES:

Lumley, Brian. *Necroscope*. London: Grafton, 1988. Reprint, New York: Tor Books, 1988.

———. *Necroscope: The Lost Years*. New York: Tor Books, 1995.

———. *Necroscope II. Wamphyri*. London: Grafton, 1988. Reprinted as a *Necroscope II. Vamphyri*. New York: Tor Books, 1989.

———. *Necroscope III. The Source*. London: Grafton, 1989. Reprint, : New York: Tor Books, 1989.

Khayman

Khayman is the first person to receive the "Dark Gift" of vampirism from **Akasha** and **Enkil,** the original vampires in Anne Rice's *The Queen of the Damned.* In ancient Egypt, nearly 6,000 years ago, he was the Chief Steward to the court of Akasha and Enkil, who were the king and queen of Egypt. In the novel, Akasha has an interest in witchcraft and the supernatural and orders Khayman to locate two witches of Palestine named **Mekare** and **Maharet** and bring them to the queen. He does as he is ordered, although he tries to befriend the witches and make their stay in Egypt as comfortable as possible. Unfortunately, the pair anger Akasha and Enkil by unleashing the power of the spirit **Amel.** Khayman is ordered to punish them by raping them in front of the royal court. In the process, he impregnates Maharet.

The rape enrages Amel, who wreaks havoc on Khayman, inhabiting his spirit and destroying his house. Attempts to exorcise the spirit fail. Akasha and Enkil attempt to reason with Amel, but are unsuccessful. They meet with further troubles when their opponents, angered by the attack of the spirit, attempt to assassinate them. Near death, Amel seizes the opportunity to shift his spirit from Khayman to Akasha and Enkil, turning them into vampires who crave blood in the process. Khayman actually gives Akasha a knife to cut herself so she can share her blood with Enkil. At Akasha's request, Khayman brings Mekare and Maharet back to the royal court, where they explain to Akasha what has happened. They are punished for their actions—Mekare has her tongue cut out and Maharet's eyes are removed and they are imprisoned.

From Maharet Akasha has learned that the intense blood thirst that she and Enkil are experiencing will lessen with the creation of each new vampire. Thus, Akasha turns against Khayman and turns him into a vampire. This act of betrayal finally ends his loyalty to the queen. He travels to the prison where Mekare and Maharet are held and turns Mekare into a vampire; she then turns Maharet into one as well. This gives them additional powers to use against Akasha. He helps them escape from prison, but when the women are soon recaptured, he manages to evade the captors and make his own escape. He turns several other people in Egypt into vampires and then leaves to roam the world, making stops in Miletus, Athens, and even Troy.

After many centuries of living as a loner with no connection to the larger vampire community, Khayman resurfaces in the mid-1980s and meets some of the new vampires who have appeared in America. He has changed over the centuries. He survived a terrible episode that caused all vampires in the world to be burned when Akasha, the original vampire, was left to burn in the sunlight. As a result of that episode, he has very tough skin that is immune to the destructive rays of the sun. He no longer experiences a blood thirst, but when he does drink fresh blood, it refreshes him and enhances his powers.

The lonely Khayman attempts to make contact with some of the new vampires and in the process discovers that his powers have become greatly enhanced—he can now kill another vampire telepathically with his mind. However, this is not his intent. He affirms his love for the other vampires and is shocked when Akasha goes on a killing spree that is designed to kill most of the men (vampires and humans) in the world. He is able to witness some of Akasha's killings in his mind, which causes him briefly to wonder if he is the true killer. However, he dismisses that idea and realizes that Akasha has returned and is at work. The two meet briefly, but go their separate ways. Khayman flies off to join the vampire **Lestat de Lioncourt** to prepare for the final confrontation with Akasha.

He travels to San Francisco and attends a rock concert by Lestat and his band, The Vampire Lestat. There, he meets other new vampires and is reunited with Maharet. He speaks with **David Talbot** and Aaron Lightner from the Talamasca, an occult research group. He is strongly attracted to **Mael** and **Armand,** but they do not respond to his advances. He joins several old vampires—including **Louis de Pointe du Lac, Gabrielle,** and Maharet—for the gathering of vampires that follows Lestat's concert. Thus, he is one of the vampires present in Sonoma, California when Akasha arrives to continue her plan of world domination. Khayman sits with Lestat and voices his opposition to all that Akasha intends.

When Akasha is killed, Khayman joins the other surviving vampires at Night Island, Armand's complex in Miami. There, **Daniel Molloy** (of *Interview with the Vampire* fame) listens to his stories of the past. Khayman is seen for the last time drifting out to sea on Armand's boat, watching the stars and contemplating his existence.

SOURCES:

Ramsland, Katherine. *The Vampire Companion: The Official Guide to Anne Rice's The Vampire Chronicles.* New York: Ballantine Books, 1993.

Rice, Anne. *The Queen of the Damned.* New York: Alfred A. Knopf, 1988. Reprint, New York: Ballantine Books, 1989.

Killer

Killer, a lesser vampire who appears in Anne Rice's novel *Queen of the Damned* (1988), is a member of the Fang Gang, a group of vampires who ride motorcycles and listen to vampire **Lestat de Lioncourt**'s music as they dance in graveyards. He is noteworthy in part as the one who bites and then gives his blood to **Baby Jenks,** another character in the novel, thus turning her into a vampire. His vampiric existence is cut short by the massive killing of vampires carried out by **Akasha,** the original vampire, in 1985.

SOURCES:

Ramsland, Katherine. *The Vampire Companion: The Official Guide to Anne Rice's The Vampire Chronicles.* New York: Ballantine Books, 1993.

Rice, Anne. *The Queen of the Damned.* New York: Alfred A. Knopf, 1988. Reprint, New York: Ballantine Books, 1989.

Kimble, Grace

Grace Kimble, the female vampire who stars in the comic book series *Vigil*, is a policewoman in a large metropolitan police department in California. Her father, a former assistant director of the FBI, refused to let her join the agency, however, she defied him by getting her college degree in criminal psychology, becoming an expert in martial arts, and joining a police department. After finishing at the head of her class at the Police Academy, she appears to have a promising career ahead of her.

One evening while working her regular beat, she comes across a vampire killing a woman. She shoots him several times, but the bullets do not stop him. In a subsequent encounter, both she and her partner, MacArthur Douglas, are killed by the vampire. Douglas is buried, and arises from his grave to take his first meal from a dog passing through the graveyard. Grace awakens in the morgue where her corpse has been taken. Unwilling to kill to survive, she steals her needed blood from the local blood bank. Reunited, the crime-fighting pair plot to destroy the vampire who infected them.

As the duo lay their plans, the vampire suddenly attacks, and in the process of dispatching him, Douglas is permanently killed. As a vampire, Kimble is confined to the night. She is exceptionally strong, and her aging stops, although she lacks any ability to fly or shape shift. She concludes that there is nothing particularly supernatural involved in vampirism, as it is a physical condition passed along in the vampire's blood. She turns to a virologist for a possible cure while resuming her duties as a cop, reassigned to the night shift.

A turning point for the vampire cop occurs when she goes after Rupert Michaels, a late-night talk-show host who doubles as a vampire leading a group of debauched vampires. Michaels plots to kill Kimble, but in the process she confronts him on the stage where his show is broadcast. In the dark she decapitates him and kills a number of his vampire associates. Unfortunately, when the lights come on, movie star Gregory Tonell is standing on stage amid the bodies. Authorities assume Tonell is the killer, so he leaves for Mexico with Kimble to sort out his future.

The period in Mexico sets the stage for Kimble and Tonell's life together. In the continuing series of adventures, she tries to seek a cure for her condition. Tonell tries to clear his name, but it proves impossible. Thus he fakes his death and eventually becomes a vampire. The pair of nocturnal bloodsuckers make their way in the world.

As a character, Vigil first appeared in a weekly comic strip creator Mike Iverson wrote for his college newspaper. Arvin Loudermilk took over the character and recreated her for the comic book series originally published by Innovation Comics. Through the mid-1990s, the story continued in a number of miniseries from Millennium Publications, and more recently it has appeared in a series from Duality Press.

SOURCES:

Vigil: Desert Foxes. No. 1–2. Narragansett, RI: Millennium Publications, 1995.

Vigil: Eruption. No. 1–2. Narragansett, RI: Millennium Publications, 1994.

Vigil, Fall from Grace. No. 1–2. Wheeling, WV: Innovation Corporation, 1992.

Vigil, The Golden Parts. Wheeling, WV: Innovation Corporation, 1992.

Vigil, Kukulkan. Wheeling, WV: Innovation Corporation, 1993.

Vigil, Rebirth. No. 1–2. Narragansett, RI: Millennium Publications, 1994.

Vigil: Road Trips. Narragansett, RI: Millennium Publications, 1996.

Vigil: Scattershots. No. 1–2. Phoenix, AZ: Duality Press, 1997.

Vigil: Vamporum Animaturi. Narragansett, RI: Millennium Publications, 1994.

Cover art from the comic book series *Vigil*, which features the adventures of Grace Kimble.

King of the Vampires

The King of the Vampires, a character created by writer Garth Ennis, appears in a series of stories in the DC comic book *Hellblazer*. Portrayed as the first vampire on Earth, the King of the Vampires originates in the prehistoric past. He is there as the first human walks on the African Savannah, and that first human becomes the King of the Vampire's first victim. The King is there throughout human history. He bites the necks of Roman senators and their wives. He has a field day during World War I, walking the battle fields and feeding. At one such field, the Somme, the King runs into William Constantine, an American sergeant, who happens upon the King as he is feeding on one of the sergeant's men. The King kills Constantine.

The King of the Vampires rules over an underworld court that includes a large number of minions who spend much of their time making plans for forays into the surface world to feed off of the humans. The King's thoroughly modern vampires are confined to the night but find garlic, running water, and stakes in the heart to be minor nuisances. Holy objects only affect a vampire stupid enough to believe in them. These vampires are characterized by their supernatural strength, their teleporting powers that take them instantly to any place in the universe, and their ability to charm people to do their will. Feeding is a whole new reality, better than sex. These vampires have teeth sharper than razor blades, and, to them, the blood they consume tastes better than the best wine. And it is all forever.

In the mid-1990s, the King wanders through London, where he and his companions find no lack of victims. Here he encounters John Constantine, a magus (master of magic) and general man of mystery. He has previously encountered Constantine, a descendent of William Constantine, whom the King killed 80 years earlier. Constantine recognizes the King for who he is and turns down the King's offer to join his realm. Constantine is concerned about the many human victims who would be negatively affected by his action. In the meantime, however, Constantine enters of a low period in his life. His own morose meditations on the nature of society and other negative qualities have cost him his relationship with his long-time female companion Kit. He now drifts around London among the street people.

When the King finds Constantine on the street, he seemed in no condition to provide any meaningful opposition. The King decides to toy with him. However, upon drinking Constantine's blood, the King has an immediate negative reaction. It's demon blood, and to him it is poison. As the King lay on the ground unable to rise, Constantine uses his remaining strength to drag him into the sun. Constantine watches as the King of the Vampires burns to nothing. The reign of the once-immortal King ends.

SOURCES:

Ennis, Garth, and Steve Dillon. "Down All the Days." *Hellblazer,* No. 68 (DC Vertigo, August 1993).

————. "Rough Trade." *Hellblazer,* No. 69 (DC Vertigo, September 1993).

Ennis, Garth, and William Simpson. "Remarkable Lives." *Hellblazer.* No. 50 (DC Vertigo, February 1992).

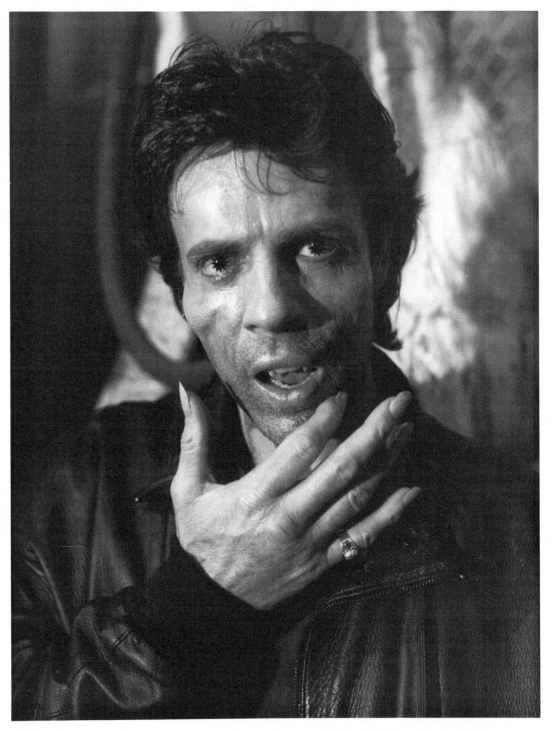

Rick Springfield was the original Nick Knight when the vampire cop made his debut in *Forever Knight* in 1989.

Klopotkin, Count Yorgi

Count Yorgi Klopotkin is the subject of an anonymous short story, "The Cousins," published in text format in 1976 in the comic book *Haunted*. The count is 410 years old and lives alone (his servants have long since departed) in a castle somewhere in the Balkans. He has prominent fangs and can transform into a bat. He has an impressive wine cellar, but does not drink—wine, that is.

One summer in the mid-1970s, the count learns that he has cousins in California. He invites them to stay at his castle for the summer. The cousins, Garry and Lucia Hilguth, and their daughter, Nadia, like to travel and they enjoy hunting. The prospect of visiting the Balkans settles their plans for the upcoming summer.

The Hilguths are overjoyed upon their arrival at the castle. When they are welcomed by a large bat flying above them in the court yard, they realize that they can start hunting immediately, and they react quickly. Taking their weapons from their car, they shoot the bat with a crossbow and unwittingly kill their cousin, the count. Unfortunately, it turns out that the Hilguths have also prematurely ended their summer sojourn in the Balkans. The villagers who live nearby know the prophecy that when the last of the Klopotkins dies, the castle will fall. They watch it tumble, also burying the Hilguths under tons of stone, and know that their vampire problem has at last been solved.

Knight, Nick

Nick Knight, a centuries old vampire who is working in modern-day Toronto as a police detective, is one of the more popular vampires of the 1990s. He has actually had two different incarnations, both on television. The first was in a made-for-television movie called *Nick Knight* that originally aired on August 20, 1989. Actor Rick Springfield played Knight, a 400-year-old vampire who had lived in many places under many different names throughout his long existence. His older vampire acquaintances know him as Jean Pierre from his days in Paris. In the movie, he is working the night shift for the Los Angeles Police Department. He is assigned to investigate a series of murders in which the victims have been drained of their blood. One of the murders occurs in a museum, where a goblet used to drink blood in an ancient ceremony has been stolen.

In the movie, we learn what type of vampire Knight is. He is totally nocturnal, and not only must he stay out of the sun, but he has a strong reaction to garlic and crosses. Wooden stakes can destroy him, but bullets hardly slow him, and he heals quickly. When angry or about to feed, his face takes on a bestial appearance. He is very strong, fast, and can fly. Most importantly, Knight is unhappy with his condition. He does not feed on humans and is striving to regain his human nature. He survives on bottled blood that he keeps in his refrigerator. He can turn someone into a vampire by sharing his blood, but he has rarely exercised that option. His one human confidante is L.A. coroner Dr. Jack Brittington, who is trying to help him return to normal.

Knight recognizes that the murders may have been committed by **Lucien LaCroix,** his old enemy. LaCroix, who originally made Knight a vampire, has a vested interest in not allowing him to become human again. He regularly appears to thwart Knight's attempts to reach his goal. While investigating the museum murder, Knight meets archeologist Alyce Hunter, who becomes his human confidante. She discovers that the goblet that was stolen was used in a ceremony to cure vampirism. Knight's murder investigation leads him not to LaCroix, but to Jack Fenner, a blood-mobile attendant with a grudge against transients, who was the real murderer. LaCroix had actually committed only one murder—that committed in the museum during the theft of the cup. In his efforts to stop Knight, LaCroix first destroys the cup and later kills Alyce, draining her blood. Enraged, Knight destroys LaCroix.

Knight reappeared in 1992 in the new television series *Forever Knight.* While Knight retained most of his characteristics from the movie, there were a few changes. The action shifted from Los Angeles to Toronto, and Knight had aged four centuries; his birth date as a vampire now set in 1228. His real name was changed from Jean-Pierre (mentioned in passing in the earlier movie) to Nicolas de Brabant. The story of his past was gradually revealed through flashbacks as the series proceeded. In the opening episode, Nicolas (portrayed by Geraint Wyn Davies) is a knight in the Crusades who awakens to find himself turned into a vampire by LaCroix (portrayed by Nigel Bennett). He had previously been seduced by **Janette DuCharme** (portrayed by Deborah Duchene), a female vampire. Nicolas, Jannette, and Lucien live together for many years until Nick renounces their vampiric evil and begins to search for a way to become human again. These early years are told through flashbacks that appear throughout the series.

In the series, Knight works as a Toronto policeman on the graveyard shift. His sole confidante is **Dr. Natalie Lambert,** a forensic pathologist who knows Nick is a vampire and who is working on a means to transform him back into a human being. LaCroix, who died at both the end of the movie and the end of the two-part premier of the television series, is mysteriously brought back to life (his resurrection from a flaming stake is never explained) and is working in Toronto as a late-night radio announcer. Janette is the manager of the Raven, a nightclub where the local vampires hang out. The television show gained a dedicated following before it was canceled in February, 1996 after just three seasons on the air.

SOURCES:

Strauss, Jon. "Forever Knight." *Epi-log* 36 (November 1993): 4-11.
———. "Forever Knight." *Epi-log* 37 (December 1993): 29-35, 62.

LaCroix, Lucien

Lucien LaCroix is an evil vampire who continually interferes with **Nick Knight**'s attempts to regain his humanity in the *Forever Knight* television series. Like Knight, LaCroix makes his first appearance in the made-for-television movie, *Nick Knight* (1989). The movie naturally centers on Knight, originally known as Jean-Pierre, whom LaCroix (portrayed by Michael Nader) had turned into a vampire some 400 years previously. After a period during which the two work as a team, Jean-Pierre rejects the life of constant killing and breaks from LaCroix. He begins a search for his lost mortality and tries to make amends through his actions for all of the evil he has committed. The spiteful LaCroix continually foils Jean-Pierre's attempts to regain his mortality.

Among his many adventures, Knight participates in an 1889 archeological dig. His target is one of a pair of goblets reportedly used in a ritual to cure vampirism, and he manages to find one. Nearly 100 years later, in the 1980s, he is working as a policeman in Los Angeles. One evening he is called to a museum after a watchman is killed and drained of his blood. He later learns that LaCroix is in Los Angeles; he bit the watchman and stole the matching goblet, a part of the museum's collection.

To make his presence known to Knight, LaCroix takes a job as a radio announcer using the nickname the Nightcrawler. When Knight tracks him down, he offers him a choice, the goblet or the life of Alyce Hunter, a staff person at the museum. As Knight tries to protect Hunter, LaCroix destroys the goblet. In the ensuing fight, Knight kills LaCroix by impaling him.

In 1992, the characters from *Nick Knight* were given new life in a television series, *Forever Knight*. The story line underwent several important revisions, including a change of location from Los Angeles to Toronto. Nick, whose real name is now Nicolas de Brabant, is a young soldier who returns from the crusades in the year 1228. He spends the evening with a young woman, **Janette DuCharme,** and wakes to find himself a vampire, having been transformed by LaCroix (now portrayed by Nigel Bennett).

In spite of Nicolas' desire to recover his lost mortality, LaCroix, Janette, and Nicolas have numerous adventures over the centuries and LaCroix repeatedly appears to remind Nick what he really is. On occasion people beg Nick to be made into vampires, and when he refuses, LaCroix steps in and transforms them. The ambiguity of the centuries-old relationship between Nick and LaCroix is demonstrated during the Civil War when Nick first meets the Enforcers, a vampire organization dedicated to keeping the existence of vampires unknown. As a Union officer during the conflict, one of the Enforcers targets Nick for possible elimination. LaCroix saves him.

Generally though, LaCroix plays the role of Nick Knight's nemesis. For example, in 1916 in San Francisco, Knight decides to test the powers of acupuncture to make him normal. While he lays covered with needles, LaCroix kills the owner of the acupuncture shop. Later, in 1966, Knight is in East Germany searching for the *Aberat*, a book with spells that are rumored to cure vampirism. LaCroix finds the book first, and as Knight watches helplessly, it is consumed by flames.

LaCroix is a fairly traditional vampire. He is nocturnal, though he does not need a coffin for his bed. He is repelled by the cross and garlic. He has some supernatural abilities, particularly the ability to fly and superhuman strength. He greatest vulnerability is sunlight. When he is about to feed, his face assumes a bestial quality and his eyes change color.

LaCroix remained a continuing character through the four season of *Forever Knight*, and also appears in a new set of books based on the series.

SOURCES:
Garrett, Susan M. *Forever Knight: Intimations of Immortality.* New York: Boulevard Books, 1997.
Sizemore, Susan. *Forever Knight: A Stirring of Dust.* New York: Boulevard Books, 1997.
Strauss, Jon. "Forever Knight." *Epi-log* 36 (November 1993) 4-11.
———. "Forever Knight." *Epi-log.* 37 (December 1993): 29-35, 62.

Lake Fujimi, The Vampire of

The unnamed vampire who haunts the region around Lake Fujimi, Japan, is the subject of the film by director Michio Yamamoto, *Lake of Dracula* (1971). The film tells the tale of a family that lives near the lake, having moved their from Europe in the early twentieth century. No one in the family is a vampire at the start of the story, but there were incidents of vampirism in the family's past. The story primarily focuses on the grandson of the man who originally built the family estate on Lake Fujimi. The story is set in the 1950s and then shifts to the 1970s.

The 25-year-old grandson seems to be fine when he suddenly manifests the traits of a vampire and attacks his piano teacher. Just as he finishes attacking the teacher, a child in search of her lost dog wanders through the front door of the teacher's house and witnesses the bloody murder. She clearly sees the vampire's face, and he would have killed her, but the vampire's father pulls her away and saves her from his son. The father recognizes that his son is a vampire and locks him away, where he soon dies. However, 18 years later, at the beginning of the 1970s, he is reborn and begins

The Vampire of Lake Fujimi in the film *Lake of Dracula* is modeled after Christopher Lee's portrayal of Count Dracula, as shown here in the film *Dracula A.D.*

attacking the people who live around the lake. He targets the child who had seen him 20 years earlier, who is now a young woman who lives with her sister near the lake.

The vampire in the film is a traditional vampire in the mold of Christopher Lee's **Count Dracula,** upon whom he was partially modeled. He dresses in a black suit with a white turtleneck shirt and wears a cape. He has prominent fangs and red eyes that become yellow when he is ready to feed. He is very strong and is a nocturnal creature who sleeps in a coffin. He is vulnerable to both fire and a stake to the heart. He bites his victims on the left side of their neck leaving two puncture wounds. His bite does not kill immediately, and his victims become his slaves whom he can summon telepathically.

The young woman watches in terror as one by one, the people around her are turned into vampires. She seeks help from a physician friend, who figures out that a vampire is on the loose. The woman and the doctor locate the house where the vampire hides and confront him. They are no match for the vampire's superhuman strength, but the vampire slips off a balcony and is impaled and killed. After the vampire dies, all the people he had bitten return to normal.

Latham, Benjamin

Benjamin Latham is the protagonist of the John Russo film *Heartstoppers* (1992). Latham is a physician in rural western Pennsylvania at the time of the Revolutionary War. To conduct scientific experiments, he needs to draw blood from patients. The equipment he uses to do that is very primitive, and when several neighbors witness him using it, they conclude that he is up to no good and must be a vampire. He is tried, convicted, and hung. His body is staked and enclosed in iron shackles, and a garlic necklace is placed around his throat. He is buried at a crossroads, which, according to folklore, is another way to combat a vampire.

Over the course of the next two centuries, his body dissolves, as does the garlic and stake. While he was not a vampire at the time of his execution, he actually becomes one 200 years later. His body reconstitutes itself, and at the beginning of the 1990s, he is reborn when a bulldozer working at a construction site uncovers his grave. He is a nontraditional vampire. He has the usual bloodlust, but lacks fangs. He is very strong, though, so he uses his strength to knock his victims out and then opens a wound in their arm or leg to drink their blood. His saliva is poisonous to the average person.

Latham lives in present-day Pittsburgh. He understands almost immediately that he has become a vampire, and the idea of living on earth as a monster causes him great anguish. He seeks help from a Catholic priest but receives no solace. He finally finds a degree of happiness when he meets a young woman who makes his miserable existence a little easier to bear, although the bloodlust is always there.

Lavud, Count

Count Lavud (German Robles), a Hungarian vampire living in Mexico, is the subject of the important 1957 Mexican movie, *El Vampiro (The Vampire)*. Count Lavud moves from Bukonia, Hungary, to Sierra Negra, Mexico, in the mid-1940s, soon after World War II. There he develops a reputation among the local townspeople for walking around at night and wearing a cape. The townspeople also notice that area once again is experiencing a rash of vampire attacks, much like it did nearly 100 years earlier.

Lavud is a traditional Eastern European vampire. He dresses in formal evening clothes and is completely nocturnal, sleeping in a coffin on soil from his native town in Hungary during the day. He has no reflection in mirrors and can teleport from one location to another. Most importantly, he has a prominent set of fangs, making him the first vampire to ever show his fangs on-screen.

Lavud has come to Mexico to avenge his brother, Karol Count Luvad, who had come to Mexico in the early 1800s and established an estate, the Sycamores. He too was a vampire who fed off the local population, and eventually his secret was discovered. He was killed by a stake through the heart on January 19, 1840. His estate fell into the hands of the Gladdington family. Count Lavud intends to regain the Sycamores from the Gladdingtons by any means necessary.

The Gladdingtons—Ambrose and his unmarried sisters Mary and Eloise—refuse to give up the estate. Frustrated for nearly a decade, the Count finally vampirizes Eloise (accomplished with two separate bites to the neck) and plans a particularly tortured death for Mary, whom he hates. He has Eloise poison her sister in such a way that she appears dead. His plan is that she will be buried alive, only to awaken in her coffin and suffer a horrible, slow death. She uncovers the plot and tells her maid, arranging to be rescued from her tomb soon after everyone leaves her gravesite.

Lavud hopes that Mary's death will finally give him access to the Sycamores, but her place in the family is immediately taken by her strong-willed niece Martha, who inherited Mary's share of the estate. Martha opposes selling the run-down property to Lavud (who calls himself Mr. Duval) and soon discovers that he is really a vampire, as is her Aunt Eloise. She is assisted by a doctor who helped Mary before her "death." and by Mary herself, who has revealed to Martha that she is really alive and hiding in an area below the house.

Lavud, unaware of Mary's survival, but quite aware that Martha has discovered his secret, decides he cannot take the time to change Martha into a vampire and instead has Eloise poison her. He then kidnaps her, which forces Mary to reveal that she is still alive. Mary and the doctor face off with Lavud in a final encounter. The doctor fights off Lavud long enough to hear the rooster's crow, signaling dawn. The doctor then rescues Martha while Lavud rushes to the safety of his coffin. He is not safe, however, as Mary follows him and kills him with the traditional stake through the heart.

In *El Vampiro's* sequel, *The Vampire's Coffin* (1959), the doctor takes Lavud's body to his laboratory, where an ignorant lab assistant removes the stake from his the vampire's heart. This bring's Lavud, and also Eloise, back to life and forces the doctor to fight them once again.

Lazaro Ruiz Cortinez, Don

Don Lazaro Ruiz Cortinez, today a powerful rural Costa Rican landowner described in Michael Romkey's *The Vampire Virus* (1997), has an interesting history as an age-old vampire. Originally born in Medellin, Spain, in 1485, Lazaro is the youngest of five children. His mother was the daughter of an apothecary and his father a civil servant of peasant background. His parents were able to provide him with good schooling that launched his career in the priesthood. His hometown is also the birthplace of Hernado Cortes, the New World explorer, and in 1511, Lazaro traveled to America with his fellow townsman.

Once in Mexico, he left Cortes to travel to what is presently Costa Rica in search of a golden city, known as the secluded home of the ancient Zona people. As a result of this invasion of their territory, all of the members of the expedition except Lazaro were killed, but not before they spread measles among the population. So many died that their civilization was wiped out. Their city, situated in the hidden valley of Zonatitucan, survived, although even today is unknown to the rest of the world.

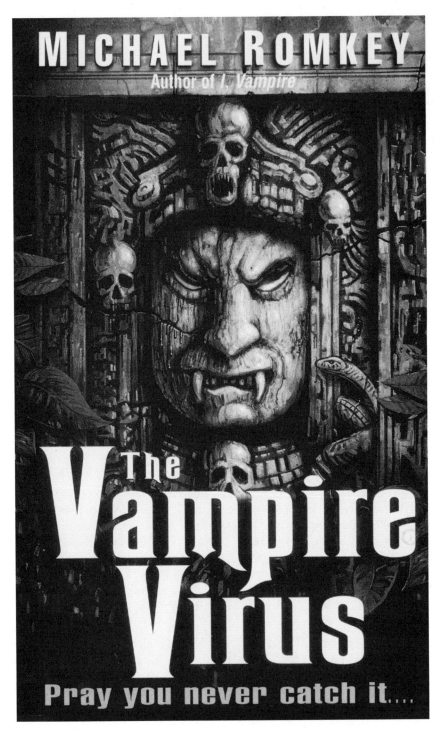

Cover art from Michael Romkey's book *The Vampire Virus*, featuring Don Lazaro Ruiz Cortinez.

After the death of the great majority of the population, Lazaro did not die, but became a vampire from the three bites of a tiny vampire bat. Because vampirism is a disease passed from the bats, three successive infestations are needed to free the virus in the body, thus the number of vampires is relatively small.

In his newly created form, Lazaro emerges as the ruling force in the area, but has no supernatural powers such as the ability to fly or transform into nonhuman form. He needs to have human blood every fortnight in order to survive (animal blood is no substitute), but he soon learns that he doesn't need to kill anyone to obtain it. As a vampire, he is confined to the night, and besides sunlight is vulnerable to fires, explosions, and decapitation. Vampirism does not cause death, and so Lazaro's body is warm to the touch and he does not stink of decay.

Today, 400 years after his vampiric transformation, he retains his youthful appearance as a man in his mid-thirties. He is handsome, with olive skin, long dark black hair, and dark hypnotic eyes. He lives as the virtual despot over the remaining Zona people. Although up until now he has enjoyed a relatively peaceful existence, Lazaro's world is becoming undone as he is invaded by a variety of outside forces, beginning with an archeologist who begins work on the abandoned city. When she dies in the rain forest, an autopsy reveals a deadly new virus. Dr. Bailey Harrison, a physician who comes to Costa Rica to investigate the virus, does not understand that she is studying the virus that causes vampirism, although she soon discovers that the local bats carry the virus.

Ludwig von Beethoven, the famous composer, has also come to pay a visit, as he survived the years since his recorded death as a vampire. He is the representative of a vampire brotherhood, and is vitally interested in the success of Harrison's research. The havoc surrounding these events—Lazaro's mixed feelings about having his haven opened to the outside world, the attacks of a young Zona who has ambitions of taking Lazaro's place, and Beethoven's presence—are further complicated by Lazaro falling in love with the beautiful doctor. In the end, the world's encroachment is the significant change agent in Lazaro's life and he must find a new way to live.

Both Harrison and Lazaro are comforted by their exotic setting, but trust that Lazaro's wealth can provide some solace and the means of restructuring their lives together elsewhere.

SOURCES:
Romkey, Michael. *The Vampire Virus*. New York: Fawcett Gold Medal, 1998.

Lee, Count Magnus

Count Magnus Lee is the 10,000-year-old vampire who has established himself as a feudal lord in the fantasy world of the distant future in the full-length animated film, *Vampire Hunter D* (1985). It is A.D. 12,090 and the old vampire rules the land dominated by his mountaintop castle. The local villagers live in fear of him, his several vampire family members, and his supernatural minions. While they have some sophisticated weaponry that has survived the devolution of civilization, he is beyond any harm it can inflict.

Lee rules as a medieval authoritarian monarch, only his arrogant daughter approaching him as an equal. His long life has produced an overriding boredom, and he at time roams the land of the villagers for momentary diversion. He is taken aback by the crosses they wear, but his werewolf helpers snatch them away.

On one of his forays into the land, he meets pretty young farm girl Doris Lang, and samples her blood. It is the sweetest he has had in some time. Upon his return to the castle he formulates a plan to make Doris his bride and use her for entertainment. He assures his jealous daughter that she will be discarded after a season and not come to possess a permanent place in the vampire family.

In the meantime, Doris has engaged the service of a vampire hunter known only as **D** to destroy Lee. Lee moves quickly to organize a wedding service. Before D can act, Lee kidnaps Doris, believing his minions can take care of the nuisance vampire hunter. However, D proves a formidable foe. He, in fact, is a dhampire, the product of a vampire's mating with a mortal woman, and thus possesses many vampire traits, including their extraordinary strength. Not stopped by the minions, he makes his way to the castle hall in time to confront Lee before he can complete the wedding ceremony and consummate his marriage.

Lemachard, Philip

Three-hundred-year-old Philip Lemachard makes his appearance in the graphic novel *Confessions of a Teenage Vampire: The Turning* (1997). The founder of the seventeenth-century New England town that bears his name, Lemachard is a hero to all the townspeople who know nothing of the dark side of his existence. He is remembered for withstanding British tyranny and healing his neighbors with his knowledge of alchemy. However, after founding the community and making some money, he went to France for a vacation and was never heard of again. Actually, while in France he encountered an old vampire, Sang, who transformed him into a creature of the night.

For some time, he and Sang wandered Europe, but eventually the guilt of constantly killing people overtook him and he went to work on a serum that would suppress a vampire's thirst. By taking the serum, a vampire never needs to attack or kill anyone again. Lemachard created a successful formula and was able to offer the solution to other vampires in the hopes of civilizing them. While most accepted it, Sang rejected it, as he did not want to become civilized.

For the last 100 years, Lemachard and Sang have fought, but Lemachard's present-day New England hometown brings them together for a final confrontation. Because Sang is older and stronger, Lemachard believes that he will be defeated. As the day of confrontation approaches, Lemachard befriends **Lily Jordan,** a high school student fascinated with the town's history and founder.

Lily learns of Lemachard's secret existence and, unable to stay away, shows up at his old mansion just in time for the battle. To save Lily, Lemachard transforms her into a vampire, but elicits a promise that she will never drink blood, only his serum.

He also knows that in the immediate aftermath of transformation the new vampire experiences blood fire, a period of sensory overload. With the heightened strength gained during this transition, she should be able to escape Sang. A short time later, Lemachard is killed at the hands of Sang. In the last days of his life, he left his wealth and estate to Lily, who he hoped one day would find a means of destroying Sang and regaining her own humanity.

SOURCES:

West, Terry, and Steve Ellis. *Confessions of a Teenage Vampire: The Turning.* New York: Scholastic, Inc., 1997.

LESTAT *see:* DE LIONCOURT, LESTAT

Levé, Ralph

Ralph Levé, the musician who becomes a rock star in the comedy *Rockula* (1990), is 400 years old, and for most of those years has lived with a curse. In the seventeenth century, he fell in love with a 22-year-old woman. Unfortunately, she was the girl-friend of a peg-legged pirate. As the pair were about to elope, the pirate appeared. Having lost his sword, he attacked with a hambone. The girl was killed, and Ralph ran away. Ever since that event, every 22 years the three are reunited and history repeats itself: Ralph meets and falls in love with a reincarnation of the girl; on Halloween Ralph runs away; and the pirate kills the girl. In spite of his cowardliness, Ralph loves the girl and as a result is now the world's oldest virgin.

Ralph is a somewhat traditional vampire. He has fangs and can with effort turn into a bat. He is negatively affected by the sunlight, but can get by with a super sun-block lotion. He can fly, but is not good at it. Garlic does not affect him, and he faints at the sight of blood. He lives with his mother Phoebe, a promiscuous vampire who often embarrasses him. He has a peculiar relationship to mirrors. His alter ego lives behind the mirror and Ralph has regular conversations with his twin, who complains of being trapped in a world in which everything is backward.

Like clockwork, the 22-year cycle is ready to reach its culminating point. True to form, two weeks before Halloween Ralph meets his love Mona. This time she is a singer with a rock band. To be close to her, he creates a rock band, with Bo Didley playing backup and billing himself as Rockula, complete with a stylized black bat costume. He is an immediate hit.

For the Halloween confrontation, Stanley, Mona's ex-boyfriend-used-car-sales-man, comes dressed as a pirate complete with peg leg and hambone. Predictably, Ralph finally rises to the occasion and fights Stanley and finds true love with Mona.

Lichtenstein, Dr.

Dr. Lichtenstein is a vampire hunter who appears in the 1980s graphic art series **Cit-izen Nocturne.** He is an older man with white hair and glasses living in the Ger-

Cowardly vampire Ralph Levé (portrayed by Dean Cameron) tries his hand at music with the help of the Sax Man.

Angie Everhart, shown here with co-star Dennis Miller, starred as the vampire Lilith in the film *Tales from the Crypt Presents Bordello of Blood*.

man-speaking areas of Central Europe. In the late 1980s, assisted by his younger colleague Axel, he tracks **Rovena Venisette,** who the doctor figures is first in the blood line of the vampires he has discovered. It is the doctor's goal to wipe out the plague of vampirism.

Lichtenstein arms himself with crosses, a rope of garlic, and an axe. His assistant, Axel, carries a crossbow. The doctor also develops a serum that serves as a blood substitute. (Some years ago, he faced the possibility of becoming a vampire and developed the serum as a preventative for future encounters.)

In his quest for Rovena, Lichtenstein tracks down **Max Morrisey,** who was transformed by Rovena several years ago. Lichtenstein wants information as to Rovena's whereabouts, but Morissey convinces him that they must work together. So, as a team they go to Castle Venisette in Austria. Morrisey succeeds in killing Rovena, but in the process, the distrusting Lichtenstein believes that Morrisey has betrayed him. He catches Morrisey from behind and decapitates him with his axe. With all the vampires apparently killed, Lichtenstein leaves the castle. Meanwhile, **Angus Bender,** a vampire Lichtenstein has overlooked, puts Morrisey's head back in place and pushes him into the pool of Rovena's blood, which has the potential of reviving Morrisey. The story ends with Morrisey's fate undetermined.

SOURCES:

Allred, M. Dalton, and Laura Allred. *Graphique Musique*. No. 1–3. Eugene, Oreg.: Slave Labor Graphics, 1988–90. Reprinted as *Citizen Nocturne*. Brave New Words, 1992.

Lilith

Lilith, a popular name for a female vampire, returns in the film *Tales from the Crypt Presents Bordello of Blood* (1996). The mother of all vampires has spent 400 years confined to her casket placed in a long-buried cave in an unnamed Latin American country. The only knowledge of Lilith's existence is possessed by a dwarf who has a treasure map showing the cavern's location. He also possesses the large key with blood inside it, the only means of controlling Lilith once reawakened.

When finally discovered, Lilith's corpse has decayed beyond recognition. The dwarf, however, has found her heart which he places inside her body cavity. After a few minutes Lilith slowly comes back to life, and as might be expected, is extremely thirsty. She satisfies her need at the expense of several of the dwarf's helpers.

Having retained her appearance as a beautiful and sensual young redhead in her early thirties, Lilith and the dwarf go into business on the edge of an American city. Running a bordello in a large old mansion that doubles as the McCutcheon Mortuary during the day, Lilith provides a variety of services for her male clientele, who in turn provide food for the bordello's employees. She and her partner have a side business selling the victims' cars. Lilith frequently interrupts the client's service, noting that it is the house's prerogative for one of the girls to start with a client, but for her to personally complete the process.

In many respects, Lilith is a traditional vampire. As such, she would explode if exposed to sunlight, be consumed in a fire, and or be burned by holy water. She has a long tongue and fangs for the penetration of the jugular. Her victims retain two bite marks over a period of time after being initially attacked. Just her bite transforms humans into vampires, and through her business establishment the number of vampires is slowly growing. However, many of her victims are killed following their use as food. Lilith reaches into their rib cage and withdraws their still-beating heart upon which she enjoys munching.

A nocturnal creature, Lilith takes comfort in the perfect cover the bordello provides for her activities. Although a few have figured out that she is a vampire, she controls the troublesome investigators by turning them into tonight's dinner.

Lilith, The Daughter of Count Dracula

Lilith, the daughter of **Count Dracula,** is a Marvel Comics character created by Marv Wolfman and introduced in the June 1974 issue of *Giant-Size Chillers*, which picked up and expanded the story of Dracula from Marvel's very successful *The Tomb* *of Dracula*. Her name is, at least in part, suggested by Lilith, the vampire-like creature from Hebrew folklore.

Lilith's story begins in Belfast, Ireland, where young Angel O'Hara and her new husband are breaking the news of their marriage and her pregnancy to her father. He loses his temper and hits the young man, who is killed by the blow. As she reacts to the event, for a moment Angel wishes her father dead. As her anger rises, a misty light floats into the house and moves into Angel. Suddenly she is transformed into Lilith, who has invaded and taken over her body. The red-headed, green-eyed Angel now stands before her father as a dark-haired, red-eyed Lilith. She is dressed in a skin-tight black suit with a cape and a stylized bat image on her forehead. Her immediate reaction is to feed, and Angel's father is the food supply before her.

In the Marvel universe, Lilith is the daughter of the fourteenth-century wife of Vlad the Impaler. Kicked out of the palace by Vlad, the mother turned the baby girl over to a gypsy woman and then committed suicide. Vlad later killed the gypsy's husband and son. In revenge, the woman, a witch, turned the child into a vampire, but with a uniqueness: She would be able to walk in the daylight and the cross would not affect her. Also, when she died, her soul would move on to take over a new body. Her purpose in life would be to destroy her father. At one point, in the nineteenth century, she and her father agree to go their separate ways and never see each other again. They do not meet again until the 1940s, at which time **Quincey Harker** slays her. Again revived, she returns in the 1970s at which time she suggests that she and her father join forces and jointly rule the world. Dracula rejects the proposal.

Nothing more is heard of Lilith until the Fall 1977 issue of *Marvel Preview* (No. 12), which reveals that Lilith/Angel has moved to New York and is living with a man, Martin Gold. As Angel, her pregnancy is beginning to show, but as Lilith she ventures out to feed. Her story continues in the November 1978 issue of *The Tomb of Dracula* (No. 67). Dracula has moved to New York. Intuiting the presence of his daughter, he follows her to Gold's apartment. He has at this time lost his vampiric powers and has come to get his daughter to bite him again. She not only turns him down, she attacks him but carefully avoids biting him. As he swears his revenge, she calls the animals and the weather to torment him.

At this point, Dracula is near the end of the first phase of his Marvel career. In 1979 he faces his last battles, recovers his vampiric powers, and returns to the leadership of the undead, only to be killed by Quincey Harker. Dracula is never ultimately killed, of course, and is revived again in time to appear in the new series *The Tomb of Dracula*, begun as an adult-oriented magazine without Comics Code approval. In the June 1980 issue (No. 5), Lilith returns and seeks the aid of Viktor Benzel to help her kill Dracula. He carries out a magical process that separates Angel and Lilith, so Lilith can travel to Castle Dracula and confront her father. Although she is able to use the powerful tools of the cross and holy water against him, in the final moment she cannot bring herself to murder her father.

After her encounter with Dracula, she adopts the name Lilith Drake and settles in the south of France. In 1983 (in No. 62 of *Doctor Strange*), Dr. Stephen Strange, the sorcerer, works a magical spell called the Montesi Formula to destroy Dracula, Lilith, and supposedly all the vampires throughout the world. Lilith dies knowing that her father is dead also.

SOURCES:

Doctor Strange. No. 62. New York: Marvel Comics, Dec. 1983.
Giant-Size Chillers. Vol. 1. New York: Marvel Comics, 1974.
"Lilith." *The Official Handbook of the Marvel Universe* 2, 18 (Oct. 1987): 23-24.
Marvel Preview. No. 12. New York: Marvel Comics, 1977.
The Tomb of Dracula. No. 1–70. New York: Marvel Comics, 1971–79.

Little Dracula

Little Dracula, the son of **Count Dracula,** the ruler of the Undead Empire of Transylvania, is the title character in the 1992 comic book miniseries that bears his name. The three-part series follows the humorous format that dominates the presentation of vampires to children. There is no actual biting shown, although in the demise of certain characters, such as the vampire huntress, it is strongly suggested.

Little Dracula resides at Castle Dracula with his family, which includes his father the Count, his mother, and sister Millicent. He has finally come of age, and his father sends him to the local village dressed in his formal evening clothes, complete with opera cape and tennis shoes. He is fast on his feet and can fly. The fanged young vampire, accompanied by Handy, a detached hand reminiscent of Thing from the Addams Family, heads for the village, where his first encounter is a disaster. He attacks two mannequins. Disheartened, he returns home.

Upon arriving home, he discovers his parents have been staked while sleeping in their coffins. Little Dracula's Granny suggests that all is not lost. If the person who performed this act can be found within two weeks, and if that person will pull out the stakes, then Count Dracula and his wife will be revived. Little Dracula takes it upon himself to locate his parents' killer, and he and Handy head for town. From the local news, they learn that the killer is a vampire hunter and they follow him to Paris.

On the train to Paris, they have their first encounter with the vampire hunter, who turns out to be a novice actress attempting to make a name for herself. She tries to kill Little Dracula, but he escapes and finds her on stage in Paris. His attempt to get to her is briefly interrupted by the Phantom of the Opera, Jr., but he finally tracks her to the Tincannes Film Festival.

The vampire huntress had signed a film contract with David Lynchpin, the famous director. Lynchpin is taken by Little Dracula's ability to transform into a bat and hires him for his movie, *Death of Dracula*, which chronicles the vampire huntress's story. He then convinces him to shoot the movie at Castle Dracula. In order to get the huntress to pull out the stakes, Little Dracula piles firewood around his parents' coffins to disguise the stakes and their bodies. When the huntress needs some stakes as stage props, she inadvertently pulls the two stakes out the of the vampires' bodies. Count Dracula and his wife chase her off the grounds. Lynchpin abandons the movie, and Little Dracula is happy as the castle returns to it normal unearthly routine.

SOURCES:
Little Dracula. No. 1–3. Santa Monica, CA: Harvey Comics, 1992.

Lodovico

Lodovico, an ancient vampire, is the main character in Michael Talbot's book *The Delicate Dependency*. His age is indeterminate, but he was alive at the time of Constantine and is pictured on the Arch of Constantine. He was later a friend of the Borgias and to this day has a residence at Massa Marittina, a village not far from Florence, Italy. He is described as tall with dark hair and hypnotic eyes. He is handsome and androgynous. He favors vampires living together with humans, coexisting peacefully.

In the twelfth century he traveled through Europe as a troubadour visiting the group of vampires known as the Illuminati. Because vampires lived so long, the members of the group had the opportunity to develop both their aesthetic senses and their intellectual abilities to a very high level. During his travels in Europe, he invited a number of vampires to form a small community in Paris centered on the new Notre Dame cathedral. A new human intellectual community sprang up in the wake of the vampire group and became the founding core of the University of Paris. Eight centuries after Lodovico founded the Paris vampire group, his colleague **M. des Essientes** still serves as its leader.

As one of the elder vampires, Lodovico makes the group's concerns his concerns, always looking out for its well-being. He studies world events and monitors anything that can potentially harm the vampire community and the stable life it has developed in the human world. Thus he is attracted to the work of Dr. John Gladstone in London. Gladstone, who serves on the staff of Ridgewood University Hospital, has isolated a strain of flu for which there is no cure. If released, it would do untold damage to humanity. Lodovico wants the virus destroyed. To achieve that goal, he dispatches an associate, **Niccolo Cavalanti** to meet the doctor.

Lodovico wants to both destroy the virus and attain Gladstone's cooperation. He is forced to kidnap Gladstone's daughter, an event that leads the doctor to track his daughter, first to the vampire community in France and then to Lodovico's estate in Italy. Along the way, Lodovico lurks in the background, monitoring the doctor's progress and placing obstacles (in the form of illusions) in his path, testing his resolve and leading him to a final confrontation.

SOURCES:
Talbot, Michael. *The Delicate Dependency.* New York: Avon, 1982.

Lothos

Lothos, the nemesis of **Buffy Summers,** is the 1,200-year-old leader of a cadre of vampires who has continually tried to establish a dominion for himself in the human world. He is a rather traditional vampire, confined to darkness. He is pale, has prominent fangs, levitates freely, and possesses extraordinary strength, although he can be countered by someone trained in the martial arts. He manifests no ability (or desire) to transform into nonhuman form. He is vulnerable to a stake in the heart and the acidlike effects of holy water. He entertains himself by playing the violin.

Over the years Lothos's efforts have been countered by a succession of slayers, all female, all designated by a birthmark on their left shoulder. The latest incarnation of the Slayer is Buffy, a young cheerleader living in the Los Angeles area. Lothos came to Los Angeles in the late 1980s hoping to establish himself in the city. As he begins to lose the young vampires he and his close associate are creating, he is led to Buffy who has just begun her training as the Slayer.

Angered, he lays his plans to attack her during an upcoming high school dance. The appearance of his minions at the dance leads to an inevitable free-for-all and the concluding one-on-one fight between Lothos and Buffy. Buffy finally dispatches him with a hastily improvised stake which she drives into his heart with a well-aimed kick. Lothos dies, voicing his surprise and consternation with the immortal exclamation, "Oops!"

Lothos first appears in the film *Buffy the Vampire Slayer* (1992), and the simultaneously released novelization by Ritchie Tankersley Cusick.

SOURCES:
Cusick, Ritchie Tankersley. Based on the screenplay by Joss Whedon. *Buffy the Vampire Slayer.* New York: Archway/Pocket Books, 1992.

LOUIS *see:* DE POINTE DU LAC, LOUIS

Lucard, Adam

Adam Lucard, the handsome, young, dark-haired, college lecturer at Columbia University in New York City by day, is in fact the product of the union of **Count Dracula** (hence his name) and Dracula's cousin. Having found his last living relative, Dracula wished to produce a child. The mother consented if Dracula would stay away from the child, and after his birth went to great lengths to get him away from the castle. She secretly arranged for the baby's transport to America before she committed suicide.

At one point when Adam was a young boy, Dracula tracked him to his new home. His grandmother temporarily fought him off and escaped with Adam. She had given him instructions to always wear the amulet his mother had given him, and to always sleep with a cross resting on his chest. She hid him away to sleep until he was found, and then, like his mother, killed herself to break Dracula's trail to the boy. He was found by another couple who read care giving instructions in a book they found with Adam, and finished raising him. By 1975, he seemed to have a life ahead of him, although he had to hurry home each evening by nightfall and use the cross to combat his growing blood thirst.

Lucard finds professional success, but his process of keeping his blood thirst under control and leading a normal life is disturbed one evening by one of his ambitious students, who breaks into his apartment. When she ignorantly removes the cross that rests on his sleeping body, Lucard immediately awakens, overtaken by thirst. He drains the student, transforms into a bat, and flies around the city further satiating his thirst. He adopts the image of his father, complete with fangs and a cape.

When he awakens the next morning, he finds the drained body lying next to his bed. He stakes it, thus preventing it from turning into a vampire, and vows never to repeat last night's events. Adam Lucard appears in a single issue of the comic book *Fright*, in a story that was originally designed to set up a character for a series of adventures that never emerged.

SOURCES:

"And Unto Dracula was Born a Son." *Fright.* No. 1. Atlas Comics, Aug. 1975.

Luna

While several female vampires have appeared in films in supporting roles (or as vamps) over the history of the cinema, Luna (portrayed by Carol Borland) was the first female vampire to be cast in a starring role. As such, she appears in the 1935 Tod Browning film, *Mark of the Vampire,* a remake of Browning's earlier silent movie, *London After Midnight.* Along with **Count Mora** (portrayed by Bela Lugosi), Luna became the most famous pseudo-vampire in the cinema.

Luna was the daughter of the Czechoslovakian Count Mora and resided with him in a nineteenth-century rural castle. Legend has it that he murdered her, and then committed suicide. Since suicide was a popular means of becoming a vampire in Eastern European lore, Luna and her father were believed to have joined the

Sex sells in the graphic novel series *Vamperotica: Red Reign,* **which features the adventures of Luxura.**

undead and to regularly roam the lands around the castle, ready to kill anyone who would move into their now-deserted home.

Ignoring the local superstition, Sir Karell Borotyn and his daughter move into the castle, and shortly afterward Borotyn is murdered. Some think he was killed by the vampires, as the body was found drained of blood with two wounds on the neck. Investigators are brought in from Prague to find the guilty party, but their investigations are distracted by reports of villagers who claim that they have actually seen Count Mora and Luna walking around the castle. According to the reports, Count Mora is in formal wear, and Luna in white diaphanous night clothes. She has a pale, colorless face and her long hair reaches to her waist. She stands by as Count Mora attacks Borotyn's daughter.

Like Mora, Luna never speaks as she wanders through the grounds frightening all who come in contact with her. Only at the end of the film, after the real and mundane murderer is revealed, does the audience hear her speak in response to Mora, as the actors are divesting themselves of the trappings of their costumes. The plot reveals the actors were hired by the local authorities to portray the former castle residents for the purpose of helping ferret out the true killer.

SOURCES:

Mank, Gregory W. "Carol Borland." In *Carol Borland, Countess Dracula*. Anescon, NJ: MagicImage Film Books, 1994.

Luxura

Luxura, the glamorous vampire and central character in the comic book *Vamperotica*, is an old and powerful being who resides in a vast underground complex somewhere in contemporary America. Luxura is tall with long talon-like fingers. Her distinguishing feature is the luxurious hair that adorns her head. A buxom beauty, she dresses in a scarlet bikini-like outfit, complete with knee-high boots, multiple arm bracelets, and skull adornments on the shoulders and knees.

Luxura is a traditional supernatural vampire. She frequently transforms into an animal, and, acquiring bat wings, flies freely. As an old vampire, she has acquired wealth and status in the vampire world. Her underground complex provides a variety of exits into the surface world of humans, including Studio V, a nightclub she owns. Her collection of bottled blood includes samples from a wide variety of individuals, many drawn from her dispatched enemies, lining the wall of one room. The samples are kept hot and liquid, as fresh as when first drawn. When she wishes to recall an incident, she can sample the blood of the relevant participant in the past event.

Luxura's pleasures include the drawing of a victim's blood as it has been enriched with emotions, especially fear or passion. She is also the frequent target of younger vampires who would like to feed off her storehouse of power. So far, none have succeeded in quenching their thirst with her blood. In the present, an issue with an old lover, one who still has the ability to arouse the heights of passion within her, dominates Luxura's relationships. **Pontius Vanthor** has posed the vision of the Red Reign. He suggests that the Kith (the vampire community) come out of

Cover art from "The Insurgents Ball," part of the popular *Vamperotica: Red Reign* series.

its underground life and take over the world. Humankind would be enslaved and treated like cattle.

While Luxura is inflamed by Vanthor, she is opposed to his plans which she believes can only lead to disaster. Instead she lives by the three edicts that have come to govern Kith life: Sustain the blood source (humans); regulate the Kith (through the vampire police force, the Red Militia); and maintain discretion. Soon after learning of the plans for Red Reign, Luxura meets the rogue vampire called the **Blood Hunter,** and he serves as the catalyst in her becoming an active agent in countering Vanthor's plans.

Creator Kirk Lindo introduced Luxura in the first issue of *Vamperotica* (1994), the lead product of Brainstorm Comics, and she continues her adventures in the comic and in several spin-off titles.

SOURCES:

"Badlands." *Vamperotica.* No. 24. Brainstorm Comics, Feb. 1997.
"The Blood Is the Life." *Vamperotica.* No. 4. Brainstorm Comics, Mar. 1995.
"Blood of the Damned." *Vamperotica.* No. 18. Brainstorm Comics, Sept. 1996.
"Certain Death." *Vamperotica.* No. 28. Brainstorm Comics, June 1997.
"Damned If I Do." *Vamperotica.* No. 20. Brainstorm Comics, Oct. 1996.
"Deadly Desire." *Vamperotica.* No. 1. Brainstorm Comics, 1994.
"Death Devours All Lovely Things." *Vamperotica.* No. 22. Brainstorm Comics, Dec. 1996.
"Hunter's Blood." *Vamperotica.* No. 17. Brainstorm Comics, July 1996.
"The Hunting Time." *Vamperotica.* No. 25. Brainstorm Comics, Mar. 1997.
"Immortal Markings." *Vamperotica.* No. 23. Brainstorm Comics, Jan. 1997.
"The Insurgents Ball." *Vamperotica.* No. 31. Brainstorm Comics, Sept. 1997.
"Last Rights." *Vamperotica.* No. 21. Brainstorm Comics, Nov. 1996.
"Queen of Ages." *Vamperotica.* No. 26–27. Brainstorm Comics, April, May 1997.
"Wages of Sin." *Vamperotica.* No. 3. Brainstorm Comics, Dec. 1994.
"War of the Worlds." *Vamperotica.* No. 29–30. Brainstorm Comics, July, Aug. 1997.

Lyall, Andrew

Andrew Lyall, a vampire who moves through the gay community on America's west coast, was introduced in two short stories in Jeffrey N. McMahan's anthology, *Somewhere in the Night* (1989). Two-years later, his adventures continued in the novel, *Vampires Anonymous.*

Lyall is a young, fair-haired, handsome man who was turned into a vampire in the early 1980s. He needs blood to live, but he does not want his victims to become vampires like him. To prevent this, he doesn't bite his victims. Instead, he carries a switchblade knife with a long sharp blade that he uses to decapitate them; he then drains them of their blood. The local police think they have a serial killer on their hands and have dubbed him the Sleepy Hollow Killer.

Andrew is a somewhat traditional vampire. He has fangs. He is nocturnal and sleeps in a coffin. He can transform into a bat. Crosses, cold running water, and sunlight adversely affect him. He does not reflect in a mirror. He does not kill often and has learned that drinking a lot of strawberry margaritas seems to suppress his thirst

Cover art from Jeffery N. McMahan's novel, *Vampires Anonymous,* **which features the exploits of Andrew Lyall.**

for blood. He is managing to survive quite well and even has an active social and sexual life, but it seems that someone has discovered his secret. The bodies of several of his victims have been found with mismatched heads, indicating that someone has followed him and switched the heads after he leaves the scene. That someone turns out to be a gay teenager named Kevin Barker.

Six years after his turning, a riot developed in the gay area of the town when police turned on the small community. Andrew was present in a bar when the police arrived and was instrumental in calling on the cop to turn against his comrades. To reclaim his situation among his fellow police officers, Eddie Cramer is determined to find the Sleepy Hollow Killer. His quest led him to Stephen Verruckt, a bartender in a gay bar who had developed a dislike for Andrew.

The four men's lives come together on a bluff above the ocean. There, Stephen Verruckt has hatched a plan to lure Andrew there so he can kill him. He has tied the teenager, Kevin, to a tree branch, along with three heads he has taken from Andrew's victims. Andrew falls for the bait, and when he appears, Stephen tries to kill him. He fails, and flees by jumping into the ocean. Andrew frees Kevin, who simply walks home. Eddie finds Stephen, who leads him to a murder site where there is a the body of a boy matched with the wrong head. They also discover Kevin in his apartment with another body and head. Kevin gives evidence that makes it appear that Stephen is the Sleepy Hollow Killer, never even mentioning Andrew's name. Stephen is then convicted as the Sleepy Hollow Killer and sent to a facility for the criminally insane. Stephen is cleared and released, however, when the Sleepy Hollow killings continue even after Stephen is incarcerated. Upon his release, he joins with Eddie to help him hunt down Andrew, who is on the run on the west coast.

During his travels, Andrew develops a long-term relationship with Pablo Salduna. Salduna is a member of Vampires Anonymous, a group modeled on Alcoholics Anonymous that is designed to help vampires end their violence and lose their dependency on blood. Andrew is in conflict, however, as he is also attracted to another group of vampires led by Kane Davies. Davies' group believes that vampires should be vampires and revels in the traditional and very manly ways of the vampire community. When Pablo is staked and decapitated, Andrew finds himself attracted even more to Kane.

The tension between Kane and the VA, and the increasingly determined search for Andrew by Steven and Eddie provides the dynamics for the next phase of Andrew's life. The tensions would have to be resolved, and not every one would live, before Andrew could take up a normal life, as much as a gay vampire could possess anything resembling a normal existence.

SOURCES:
McMahan, Jeffrey N. *Somewhere in the Night.* Boston: Alyson Publications, 1989.
———. *Vampires Anonymous.* Boston: Alyson Publications, 1991.

Mackenzie, Nathaniel

Nathaniel Mackenzie, mercenary, adventurer, and vampire, is a friend of fellow adventurer Jack Frost, who lends his name to a 1980s comic book series published by Amazing Comics. While traveling in a small German town, Mackenzie is arrested by the town constable, whose daughter Mackenzie had been attempting to date. The overprotective constable throws Mackenzie into a cell with another person the townspeople refer to as "the animal." Several days later, Mackenzie wakes up to discover that the animal has bitten him. They fight and Mackenzie kills the animal with the only weapon he has available: a wooden spoon. As he is dying, the animal thanks Mackenzie. Mackenzie soon develops a thirst for blood and realizes that he is now a vampire.

After being released from the German jail, Mackenzie returns home to his wife, Nancy, and tries to keep his true nature a secret. His secret doesn't last, however, and Mackenzie leaves home soon after Nancy discovers what he has become, though not before he bites her several times. Nancy contacts Frost and shows him her bite wounds. After hearing nothing from or about her husband for some time, Nancy gives him up for dead, until she sees a story in the newspaper about a young girl who is found with her throat ripped out and her blood drained. A coin that belonged to Mackenzie is discovered near the dead girl's body.

Frost tracks his former friend to the sewers of New York City. Based on his initial encounter with Mackenzie, Frost concludes that Mackenzie is in fact a vampire and must be stopped. He consults a knowledgeable friend who advises him of the weapons that are most effective against vampires holy water and other sacred objects, wooden stakes, and sunlight. Returning to the sewer, Frost finds a note directing him to Wildwood Cemetery. When Frost arrives at the graveyard, Mackenzie is on top of a cross-shaped monument. Obviously, sacred objects do not affect him. When Mackenzie attacks, Frost stakes him, and that seems to be the end of the vampire.

When Frost returns home, however, he finds Mackenzie waiting for him. He listens to his friend's story and then finishes him off with his trusty pistol, which he has loaded with wooden bullets. He now waits with his crossbow and arrows for Nancy, who had died several days ago while Frost was pursuing her husband.

SOURCES:

Van Hook, Kevin, and Lee Harmon. "Behold Tomorrow." *Jack Frost* 1 (Amazing Comics, 1987).
———. "Dancing on My Grave." *Jack Frost* 2 (Amazing Comics, 1987).

Madeleine

In Anne Rice's *Interview with the Vampire* (1976), Madeleine is a doll-maker in Paris who is "adopted" by **Claudia,** the vampire who is forever trapped in the body of a five-year-old child. Claudia is brought to Paris by her soul mate and trusted companion, **Louis de Pointe du Lac** after the two of them have apparently killed their vampire companion **Lestat de Lioncourt.** After the two of them settle in Paris, Claudia becomes restless when she realizes that Louis has fallen in love with a Parisian vampire named **Armand.** Afraid she is losing Louis and will be left alone, Claudia finds Madeleine and brings her to Louis so he can turn her into a vampire and serve as Claudia's "mother."

Madeleine is beautiful, with dark red hair, violet eyes, and pale skin. She is despondent because her own child has died; she carries her picture in a locket and uses her face on the dolls she makes. When Claudia offers her a chance to once again have a child, this time for all eternity, she leaps at the opportunity. Louis is reluctant to convert Madeleine, because he has never turned any human into a vampire, but eventually Claudia manipulates the guilt he feels for the role he played in her own conversion to a vampire (a vampire that would be forever trapped in a child's body).

Madeleine feeds voraciously. Louis believes she has gone mad and has completely lost touch with reality. Claudia is happy, however. Madeleine burns her doll shop and uses her skills to make furniture for Claudia that is custom-made for her small size. Sitting in her special chair, Claudia almost appears to be an adult.

All is not well, however. The group of vampires led by Armand, the **Theatre des Vampires,** wants to kill Claudia because of her attempt on Lestat's life, which is a violation of their vampire code. Armand warns Louis to get Claudia and Madeleine out of town as soon as possible, but Louis does not act fast enough. The vampires from the Theatre, led by **Santiago,** come and take Claudia and Madeleine. While Louis is locked away in a coffin, Claudia and Madeleine are placed in an open air-shaft that is exposed to the daylight sun. Wrapped in each others arms, they die together when they are consumed by the rays of the morning sun.

SOURCES:

Ramsland, Katherine. *The Vampire Companion: The Official Guide to Anne Rice's The Vampire Chronicles.* New York: Ballantine Books, 1993.

Rice, Anne. *Interview with the Vampire.* New York: Alfred A. Knopf, 1976. Reprint, New York: Ballantine, 1979.

The vampire Mae (portrayed by Jenny Wright) from the film *Near Dark*.

Mae

Mae (portrayed by Jenny Wright) is a member of the vampire clan that wanders through rural Oklahoma and Texas in the film *Near Dark* (1987). A beautiful blonde vampire, Mae is relatively new to nocturnal life (she was transformed four years ago), and stands in contrast to Jesse, the group's leader, who is a Civil War veteran. Nevertheless, Mae is very strong and fast. Her hearing and sight have greatly improved. However, she is confined to the night, the sun being her worst enemy. Animals, sensing what she has become, do not like her. Although the clan members don't eat food, they do enjoy smoking tobacco.

The vampires of Mae's clan are amoral. Killing is a necessary part of life, and they do so without remorse. To cover their actions, they must be sure that after feeding their victims are completely dead, and they go to great lengths to hide the nature of their victims' deaths. To further prevent discovery, they have adopted a nomadic existence. They live out of leisure vans and motels.

Mae (Jenny Wright) and Caleb, the young vampire lovers from the film *Near Dark.*

In contrast to her fellow vampires, Mae has retained some of her humanity, and occasionally shows love and compassion. When she bites Caleb, a naive young man out for a night on the town, she enjoys his company. Because she fails to kill him before dawn, he must be introduced into the clan, who are disgruntled about welcoming an additional member. Mae agrees to see him through the transition. Unfortunately, Caleb has an aversion to killing. He can only feed from Mae after she consumes her evening meal.

Each evening the clan sets up situations to provide Caleb with the opportunity to learn to kill. One evening they walk into a roadside tavern and kill everyone, but Caleb still refuses to join them. His reluctance to acquiesce to a vampiric lifestyle is also hindered by his family, a father and little sister, who are unaware of his situation and seek to retrieve him.

Caleb's family succeeds in finding him, and he goes home with them. He is healed of his near-vampiric condition by their love. The clan, however, will not let him go that easy. They capture his sister, and Mae must choose between her love for Caleb and life with her fellow vampires. In the final confrontation, the clan's enemy is the sun. Mae is badly burned, but makes her way to Caleb's farm where he shares his blood and his love with her. Mae is freed of her vampiric condition presumably to lead a normal life.

Mael

Mael, a Celtic vampire who become a continuing character in Anne Rice's *The Vampire Chronicles,* is a Druid priest who recruits **Marius** to the vampiric life. Mael approaches Marius, a Roman whose mother is Celtic, in the city of Massilia in Gaul. Mael is not yet a vampire when he first meets Marius; he is simply a recruiter. Mael is very tall, with long blond hair, a narrow face, gleaming eyes, strong jaw, and hawk-like nose. He wears pre-Roman Celtic dress. When he meets Marius, Marius notes that he looks young and innocent in many ways, but in other ways seems old beyond his years.

Mael tells Marius that he has come on a mission from his gods and he invites (forces is probably closer to the truth) Marius to accept his invitation to become one of them. Marius understands that the invitation is a death sentence. Mael instructs Marius in the process and meaning of becoming a god, but Marius does not fully understand until the moment comes when he is face to face with the vampire who will offer him the "Dark Gift." The vampire who performs the act is an old vampire who has survived an event called "the burning" that nearly killed all the vampires in the world. (The burning occurred when the original vampires, **Akasha** and **Enkil,** were placed directly in the sun; vampires around the world felt their pain and many died.)

Soon afterward, Mael encounters another old vampire and is finally given the "Dark Gift" himself. In the process of becoming a vampire, he loses his Druid faith and becomes a wandering rogue vampire for the next few centuries. Until the mid-1980s, his only appearance occurs when he visits Marius in Venice shortly before the latter's house is burned down.

In the 1980s, he becomes an associate of **Maharet,** one of the early vampires from ancient Egypt. He also becomes the protector of her mortal descendent **Jesse.** She finds him friendly but eerie, and finds it impossible to look at him. He drives her to Maharet's home in Sonoma County in California, where occasionally he reads poetry to her or plays the piano. She begins to understand that there is something very different about him—for example, he never appears until after dark. She finally realizes that he is not human at all, although she does not understand what he is.

Mael becomes very protective of Jesse. To make sure that she never falls victim to one of the many threats to mortal life, he decides to turn her into a vampire. He is just beginning the process when Maharet intervenes and stops him.

In 1985, Mael attends the rock concert put on by **Lestat de Lioncourt** and his band, The Vampire Lestat. Most of the vampires from California are at the concert, along with many others, in anticipation of a final confrontation with Akasha. It seems that the original vampire seeks world domination and is attempting to kill most of the males in the world, vampire and human.

During the concert, Jesse's neck is broken. Mael goes to the hospital and donates his blood, knowing that his vampire blood will speed the healing process. Maharet arrives and completes the process of transforming Jesse into a vampire. All three are present a short time later in Sonoma when Akasha engages them (and the other vampires who were at the concert) in a final battle. She loses and is killed. Following Akasha's death. Mael joins a group of vampires who gather at a complex called Night Island in Miami, Florida that is owned by the ancient vampire **Armand.**

Mael makes his final appearance in the *Chronicles* after Lestat returns from a visit to heaven and hell that he undertook with Memnoch the Devil (as told in the Rice book of the same name). Lestat returns with Veronica's veil, the veil supposedly imprinted with the face of Christ just prior to the crucifixion. Mael travels to Manhattan to see the veil, and, just as Armand had before him, attests to the veil's authenticity by allowing himself to be burned by the sun on the steps of St. Patrick's Cathedral.

SOURCES:

Ramsland, Katherine. *The Vampire Companion: The Official Guide to Anne Rice's The Vampire Chronicles.* New York: Ballantine Books, 1993.

Rice, Anne. *Memnoch the Devil.* New York: Alfred A. Knopf, 1994. Reprint, New York: Ballantine Books, 1995.

————. *The Queen of the Damned.* New York: Alfred A. Knopf, 1988. Reprint, New York: Ballantine Books, 1989.

————. *The Tale of the Body Thief.* New York: Alfred A. Knopf, 1992. Reprint, New York: Ballantine, May 1993.

————. *The Vampire Lestat.* New York: Alfred A. Knopf, 1985. Reprint, New York: Ballantine Books, 1986.

Magnus

Lestat de Lioncourt, the main vampire in Anne Rice's *The Vampire Chronicles*, first spots Magnus in the audience at a theater in Paris where Lestat is working as an actor. At the time, Lestat was an aspiring and talented young actor who was completely caught up in his career and the travel and success it would bring. But Magnus's face almost makes him forget what he is doing on stage. It is white, like a mask. One minute, it glows, the next, it is gone.

At the time that Lestat first sees him, Magnus is more than three centuries old. He has prominent fangs, colorless skin, and black and silver hair. His fingers are noticeably long. He is very powerful and has the ability to fly. He has grown wealthy over the years and keeps his fortune in a tower outside of Paris that also serves as his lair.

Some time after that first night at the theater, he appears in Lestat's room at three o'clock in the morning. He calls Lestat "Wolfkiller." He grabs the half-naked Lestat and carries him to a rooftop high above the city. There Magnus professes his love for Lestat and bites him for the first time, sending Lestat into a state of ecstasy. Lestat awakens in a high tower several miles from Paris. Magnus tells Lestat that he has been chosen by him to receive the "Dark Gift" of vampirism. Magnus himself had been turned into a vampire after he had already aged as a human and felt that

Lestat would enjoy the experience much more as a young man and would make the perfect vampire.

Magnus turns Lestat and then prepares to take his own life—he is tired of living as a vampire in such an old body. He prepares a bonfire that will be his funeral pyre, and Lestat realizes that he is about to be left as a new vampire without a teacher to show him how to survive. Magnus brushes aside Lestat's pleas and gives him a few simple instructions just before he leaps into the flames. He warns Lestat to scatter his ashes, otherwise Magnus might come back in a more hideous form, and if he did, he would take his anger out on Lestat. The young vampire quickly accepts his fate and the riches which have been left to him. Among his first acts after dressing in Magnus's fine clothes is to take his first drink from a human (Magnus's old servant).

The character of Magnus was partially inspired by Count Magnus, the subject of a short story by M.R. James. His story is told in Rice's novel, *The Vampire Lestat*.

SOURCES:

Ramsland, Katherine. *The Vampire Companion: The Official Guide to Anne Rice's The Vampire Chronicles.* New York: Ballantine Books, 1993.

Rice, Anne. *The Vampire Lestat.* New York: Alfred A. Knopf, 1985. Reprint, New York: Ballantine Books, 1986.

Maharet

Maharet is an ancient vampire who emerges as a central character in Anne Rice's *The Queen of the Damned* (1988) and in other volumes of *The Vampire Chronicles*. Initially, she is not a vampire, but a witch. Her mother is **Miriam,** and her twin sister is named **Mekare** (she is also a witch). The twins share a distinguishing head of flaming red hair, which they inherited from their mother. Some 6,000 years ago, the pair resided in Palestine among the caves of Mount Carmel. Their people were cannibals who consumed the flesh of the dead, believing that although the spirit had departed, some residue of power remained in the body. The tribe also believed that it was a sign of respect to eat the bodies, especially for the children of the deceased. They were 16 when **Akasha** and **Enkil** became joint rulers of the Nile Valley.

The twins were well-known in their tribe for being able to consult a powerful spirit. They also had the power to bring rain, and it was this rain-making ability that caused their fame to spreading far and wide, even to Egypt. When Akasha and Enkil learn of the girls' abilities, they invite them to an audience with the royal court. Advised by both their mother and the spirit they conversed with that danger awaited them, they refuse the invitation. However, the queen is not to be denied. Maharet and her sister are captured and taken to Egypt. Along the way, them are befriended by **Khayman,** the Chief Steward of the royal court.

During their first audience with the king and queen, Mekare angrily denounces the deaths that occurred just so Akasha could bring them to Egypt. Maharet tries to silence her headstrong sister, to no avail. When they are next brought before the queen, the spirit that they converse with, **Amel,** becomes uncontrollable and wreaks havoc, causing the queen to question her own belief in her goddess. Amel goes so far as to attack the queen. An angry Enkil orders that Maharet and her sister be publicly

Louis Jordan is one of the many actors who made a name for himself portraying Count Dracula. He is shown here in a scene from the BBC production of *Dracula*.

raped in front of the court as their punishment; he orders an unwilling, but obedient, Khayman to carry out the punishment. They are allowed to return home after the rape, and Maharet has a child as a result of the rape. She names her Miriam, after her mother.

Meanwhile, the events at the royal court cause the Egyptians to turn against Akasha and Enkil. Just when it appears that they have been killed, Amel enters both of them and turns them into the very first vampires. This spares their lives but creates a blood lust that nearly drives them insane. The sisters are brought back to the court and asked to explain what has happened. They tell the queen exactly what has occurred, and for their trouble, they are punished again. Maharet has her eyes poked out, and Mekare's tongue is cut off. Khayman grabs Maharet's eyes and shoves them into her mouth; she immediately swallows them.

The girls are locked up in prison, where they are visited by Khayman. It seems that Khayman has been turned into a vampire by Akasha and Enkil, the first human turned by the pair. Angered by their actions, he decides to help the sisters seek their revenge by offering the "Dark Gift" of vampirism to Mekare, who promptly turns her sister. They girls flee the prison but are captured and entombed in stone coffins that are set adrift on the ocean, Maharet from the eastern shore of Egypt and Mekare from the western.

After 10 days, Maharet's coffin sinks and she escapes when the water loosens the seal. She discovers that if she takes the eyes of her victims, she can see again. She begins to search for her sister. During her search (although not until several millennia have passed), she hears the story of "those who must be kept," a pair of ancient vampires. She realizes that the pair must be Akasha and Enkil. It seems that as more and more vampires roamed the Earth, the royal couple's need for blood kept diminishing, until they finally ceased to move and became little more than living statues.

Maharet learns that Akasha and Enkil are kept in a shrine at the home of a vampire named **Marius.** Still bent on revenge, Maharet sneaks into the chamber where Akasha and Enkil are kept and plunges a knife into the queen's heart. Akasha's heart stops beating for just a moment before it begins to heal itself. However, in that moment, Maharet feels the repercussions in her own body, feeling just what Akasha feels. She becomes dizzy and feels a sense of being disconnected, feels the first hint of real death. In an instant, she understands that the life force of all vampires resides within Akasha, and that if she were to die, all vampires would die. As much as she hated Akasha, the queen of the damned had to be protected if vampires were to survive.

As time passes, most vampires must move frequently or "go to ground" to avoid raising suspicions over their always-youthful appearance. Maharet overcomes this obstacle by devising a clever story. Over the centuries, her daughter Miriam has had children, and those children have had many children of their own, spreading the family to all corners of the world. Maharet's story says that there is a branch of the family that is designated as the family record-keeper, and in each generation, one member of that branch is named Maharet and given the task of maintaining the records. Of course, each generation, that person is really the original Maharet herself. In addition to keeping her out of the ground, this ploy also keeps her from going insane or losing large blocks of memory, which are also common occurrences in the vampire community.

At a later point in *The Vampire Chronicles*, Akasha awakens and sets out on a plan of world domination. She forces a final confrontation with a group of vampires in Sonoma County, California, a group that includes Maharet. Things are not going well for the vampires when Mekare shows up in the nick of time to offer her assistance. She pushes Akasha into a glass wall, which severs the queen's head. Maharet then quickly gathers up Akasha's brain and heart and passes them to Mekare, who consumes them, thus becoming the new keeper of the vampire life force.

In what feels like anticlimactic action, Maharet also appears in a later volume of *The Vampire Chronicles* and visits with **David Talbot,** the person who helped the famous vampire **Lestat de Lioncourt** reclaim his vampire body from **Raglan James** (as told in *Tale of the Body Thief*). Lestat made Talbot a vampire in return. Maharet shows Talbot all the records she has accumulated over the centuries and later serves as Lestat's messenger when he wants to get in touch with Talbot.

After Lestat's trip to heaven and hell (as told in *Memnoch the Devil*), during which he loses an eye, it is Maharet who returns it to him. She also locks Lestat up so he will not do damage while recovering from the effects of his journey to the beyond. While Lestat is confined, she helps Talbot write an account of the journey. In the end she frees Lestat for further adventures in as-yet unwritten chapters in *The Vampire Chronicles*.

SOURCES:

Ramsland, Katherine. *The Vampire Companion: The Official Guide to Anne Rice's The Vampire Chronicles.* New York: Ballantine Books, 1993.

Rice, Anne. *Memnoch the Devil.* New York: Alfred A. Knopf, 1994. Reprint, New York: Ballantine Books, 1995.

————. *The Queen of the Damned.* New York: Alfred A. Knopf, 1988. Reprint, New York: Ballantine Books, 1989.

————. *The Vampire Lestat.* New York: Alfred A. Knopf, 1985. Reprint, New York: Ballantine Books, 1986.

Malt Liquela, Count Demonte

Count Demonte Malt Liquela, the subject of the 1997 low-budget cinematic farce *Limp Fangs*, is a traditional Transylvanian aristocratic vampire. He sleeps in a coffin filled with native soil. He wears the same tuxedo and cape night-after-night, but the resemblance seems to end there. For example, Demonte is not Romanian, but an African–American. And instead of two fangs, he has only one located in the center of his mouth. In previous centuries, Demonte had lived in a castle in Transylvania, but some decades ago he was inescapably sealed in his crypt. As the twentieth century comes to an end, his castle is being leveled and a shopping center put up in its place. In the midst of the construction process, he is awakened when a sticky foul-tasting yellow liquid drips on his coffin and face. (One of the construction workers has relieved himself above ground on the spot just above the count's resting place).

Count Malt Liquela awakens to a very different world than the one from which he came. Vampires are not feared. Rather, they are worshiped by young women as celebrities. A prime example is Count Falstaff, an old friend of Demonte's who is now the famous leader of a popular rock band. Count Falstaff also heads the Bloodsuckers Coalition, an organization that credits itself with turning vampires into celebrities. In television interviews, Falstaff portrays his vampire life as one continuing party.

In his attempt to come to terms with this new world, Demonte has a major problem. Soon after awakening, he selects a victim from which to quench his thirst. Rather than being horrified and scared, the victim thinks Demonte is cool. Rather than reluctantly succumbing to his hypnotism, she willingly jumps at him and brings him home to meet her parents. Surprisingly, Demonte finds that his single prominent fang has become limp, and he can't seem to stiffen it to take the blood he needs from his more-than-willing victims. To deal with his problem, Demonte seeks out his old friend Falstaff. Falstaff wants to help, but is more concerned that Demonte might destroy the new image of vampire virility that he has worked so hard to create. Falstaff reacts by sending some women to Demonte who he thinks might help, but he also alerts some mercenary friends. It might become necessary to eliminate the count.

Since Demonte is not helped by the surrogates sent by Falstaff, the mercenary squad goes after him. Suddenly, he is back in a familiar world in which his life is threatened by vampire hunters. Then, a women he approaches shows fear and screams at his approach. That is all the curing Demonte needs. His fang responds immediately and is hard again. Demonte has solved his own problem and is now ready to join his fellow vampires and celebrate his new status in the modern world.

Man-Bat

Man-Bat is one of the vampire-like characters introduced into comic books in the 1970s by DC Comics after changes were made to the strict guidelines of created in 1954 when the Comics Code was issued. One of the main tenets of the code was the banning of vampires. Created by Frank Robins, Man-Bat made his initial appearance in *Detective Comics* No. 400 (Spring 1970). The original story concerns Kirk Langstrom, a expert on nocturnal mammals at the museum in Gotham City, the home of superhero **Batman.** Langstrom is obsessed with the idea of besting Batman in some way. In seeking to accomplish his goal, he concocts a serum made from the glands of bats. The serum gives him a natural sonar power and the super-sensitive hearing ability associated with bats. However, there is an unwanted side effect—he begins to transform into a giant bat-like creature.

Langstrom is still trying to find some way out of his predicament when thieves break into the museum. Batman responds to the break-in and is about to be defeated by the criminals when Man-Bat shows up to help. Batman and Man-Bat have their next meeting when Man-Bat attempts to steal drugs that he hopes will reverse his condition. He desperately needs the drugs because he is trapped in his bat form with his marriage to his fiancé Francine fast approaching. When at first he can't get the drugs, Francine, in an act of love, drinks some of the bat serum and turns into a bat-like creature herself. With Batman's help, however, the couple receive the antidote they need and return to human form. It appears that Langstom's Man-Bat adventures are over, but of course that is not the case.

In *Detective Comics* No. 429, Francine is bitten by a vampire bat and becomes a vampire she-bat. Batman believed that Langstrom has gone on a murderous rampage, but it is really Francine in her vampire form. Batman finally tracks Francine to her home and confronts the couple. Kirk has been totally unaware of his wife's nocturnal activities. She is saved by a total blood transfusion. Langstrom shows Batman how he has continued his research and can now turn into Man-Bat at will with the help of a pill. He decides to join Batman in fighting crime and earns a large reward that leaves him independently wealthy.

At the end of 1975, Man-Bat received his own mini-series of comic books for the first time. The initial issue of DC Comics's *Man-Bat* appeared in December 1975. In this series, Langstrom is called upon to battle super-criminal Baron Tyme, who has discovered a means to control Francine and use her to commit crimes. Tyme's intervention reactivates Francine's vampirism. After that series, Man-Bat became a continuing character in the *Batman Family* comic books and made sporadic appearances in both *Detective Comics* and *Batman*, most recently in issues No. 536 to 538 (November 1996 to January 1997). On very rare occasions, he interacts with other DC characters such as Superman (*DC Comics Presents* No. 335 in 1981). Additional Man-Bat mini-series appeared in 1984, 1995, and 1996.

SOURCES:
Conway, Gerry and Steve Ditko. *Man-Bat.* No. 1–2. New York: DC Comics, 1975–76.
Delano, James and John Bolton. *Batman-Man-Bat.* No. 1–3. New York: DC Comics, 1995.
Dixon, Chuck and Flint Henry. *Man-Bat.* No. 1–3. New York: DC Comics, 1996.
Robbins, Frank and Neal Adams. *Man-Bat.* New York: DC Comics, 1984.

Marie

Marie (portrayed by Anne Parillaud), the beautiful and seductive female vampire in the film *Innocent Blood* (1992) is of indeterminate origin or age, although she is not so old that she has become bored with life. She is also experienced enough to have developed some essential rules: She never plays with her food and she always finishes her food after dining (so that no evidence of her having been the cause of her food's demise remains). Without fangs, she is a messy eater who bites into her victim's neck. When the feeding is over, her face is covered with blood. She carries a sack containing a towel for cleaning herself after supper.

The action of the film takes place in present-day Pittsburgh. Having recently lost her lover, Marie is sad and lonely. A finicky eater, she is hungry, not having fed in a week. Reading about some gangsters in the newspaper, she decides to "dine Italian." Along the way, it becomes evident that she has an aversion to garlic and light, but not to religious objects. Fire and sunlight are her real enemies and she must get out of the sunlight or quickly perish.

Circumstances prevent Marie from properly finishing her gangster meal, and the person whose blood she has consumed is transformed into a vampire as well. The new vampire, Sally (short for Salvatore) the Shark, has no rules, and dines indiscriminately. Marie feels an obligation to kill him. In the process of tracking Sally she demonstrates her strength and speed, but not the ability to transform into an animal.

In order to defeat Sally, she makes common cause with a young policeman. They must quickly learn to trust each other as they spend a day hidden away in a motel

The hypnotic gaze of the beautiful vampire Marie (portrayed by Anne Parillaud) from the film *Innocent Blood*.

room. Trust turns to lust and lust to love. As a vampire, Marie is far from asexual. When she feeds, or when she becomes sexually aroused, her eyes change color and become phosphorescent.

Marius

Marius, an ancient vampire in Anne Rice's *The Vampire Chronicles*, was introduced in *The Vampire Lestat* (1985) and continued as a major character in *The Queen of the Damned* (1988). He grew up in a wealthy Roman household as the illegitimate son of a Roman senator and a Celtic mother. He was allowed to do what he wanted with his life and given the money to do finance any endeavor. He decides to become a scholar and chronicler and travels extensively. He has blue eyes and blond hair, and often wears red velvet.

He is in a tavern in the city of Massilia during his 40th year when he is accosted by **Mael,** a Druid who says he has been sent to make Marius a god. Mael instructs Marius in the process and meaning of becoming a god, but Marius does not fully understand until he is taken prisoner at a Samhain feast and comes face to face with the vampire who will offer him the "Dark Gift." The vampire who performs the act is an old vampire who has survived an event called "the burning" that nearly killed all the vampires in the world. The wretched creature instructs Marius to go to Egypt and find out why he and other vampires had been burned.

Marius does as he is told and locates a community of vampires in Alexandria, all of whom were burnt. Among them is **The Elder,** who has been assigned to guard **Akasha** and **Enkil,** the two original vampires who had become nothing more than living statues. It turns out that it was The Elder who caused "the burning" when he tired of his guardian's role and moved Akasha and Enkil out into the sun. When they were burned, so were all of the vampires around the world. Many perished, but the stronger ones survived.

From the group in Alexandria, Marius also learns the story of the origin of vampirism and just how the fate of all vampires is tied to Akasha and Enkil. He then has an audience with Akasha, who asks him to take them out of Egypt. He complies with her wishes by stealing two antique mummy cases and disguising Akasha and Enkil as mummies, smuggling them out of Egypt. To assist Marius, Akasha allows him to drink from her. He travels with their bodies for a period until he settled into a fortress on one of the Greek isles in the Aegean and creates a sanctuary.

In the fifteenth century, Marius meets a young man named **Armand.** Marius finds him in a brothel in Constantinople, where he had been sold into slavery. He falls in love with Armand and brings him to Venice, where Marius is living the life of a nobleman and artist. He paints a picture of the young boy called, *The Temptation of Amadeo*. When Armand is 17, Marius offers him the Dark Gift and turns him into a vampire in the hope that the two can have a long relationship.

While this was happening, Marius made an enemy in **Santino,** an Italian vampire who leads a satanic coven and does not like Marius's attempt to live and move among mortals. Some six months after Marius turns Armand, Santino leads an attack on Marius's Venetian home and burns it to the ground.

Marius's next significant role in *The Vampire Chronicles* involves **Lestat de Lioncourt.** While seeking more knowledge about the vampiric condition, Lestat had met Armand in Paris. Armand told him about Marius, and believed that the older vampire would have much to teach Lestat. Lestat's search for Marius lasts a decade, and in the end, it is Marius who finds Lestat. He takes the young vampire to the Greek sanctuary where Akasha and Enkil are kept. He tells Lestat his life story and the story of the original vampires. He gives Lestat a brief tour of the shrine where the ancient pair are kept, and later Lestat returns to the chamber on his own accord. He awakens Akasha and drinks some of her blood. Enkil also wakes up and is about to kill Lestat when Marius intervenes. He sends Lestat away, although he promises to always be available if Lestat should ever need him. Lestat promises not to reveal the sanctuary's location.

At some point during the twentieth century, Marius moves Akasha and Enkil to a remote location in the frozen northland. After Lestat becomes a rock musician,

Marius plays his music for the royal pair. Akasha responds to the music by waking up, killing Enkil, and leaving the shrine, although not before thanking Marius for the fine job he has done as their protector. She begins her plan for world domination.

Akasha destroys his house, leaving it open to the elements, and Marius is buried in the ice and snow. Two vampires, **Pandora** and Santino (ironically the same Santino who had burned his house down in Venice several centuries earlier), discover the wreckage and pull Marius out of the snow. Subsequently, they all join those vampires who oppose Akasha and kill her before she can take over the world. After her death, Marius advises Lestat to drop his plans to write about her. Lestat had already figured this out on his own. After this final encounter with Akasha, Marius has drifted into obscurity and made only cameo appearances in later volumes of *The Vampire Chronicles* (at least those published before 1997).

SOURCES:

Ramsland, Katherine. *The Vampire Companion: The Official Guide to Anne Rice's The Vampire Chronicles.* New York: Ballantine Books, 1993.

Rice, Anne. *The Queen of the Damned.* New York: Alfred A. Knopf, 1988. Reprint, New York: Ballantine Books, 1989.

———. *The Vampire Lestat.* New York: Alfred A. Knopf, 1985. Reprint, New York: Ballantine Books, 1986.

Marks, Chastity

Chastity Marks, a leading vampire in the supernatural world of Chaos! Comics, emerges in post-apocalyptic New York City after its destruction by Evil Ernie. Chastity is born and grows up in Toledo, Ohio, the 18-year-old daughter of an alcoholic father who runs a hair salon. She is into drama and rock. He is into disco and popular fashion. In 1976 she runs away from home after her father forcefully cuts her hair and gives her a Farrah Fawcett hairdo. Her money gets her to England. Broke, she takes a job in a dress shop and is introduced to the punk rock scene. Tying up with a member of a band, she takes a second job as the band's roadie. One night shortly thereafter, she encounters a vampire. She fights him off, but not before he bites her.

Chastity awakens the next morning in the home of a woman who calls herself the Countess. She introduces Chastity to the embrace and explains that Chastity is now a vampire. Chastity is thirsty, and her life of being beaten down by her father wells up within her. Her fangs emerge. After she feeds, she feels for the first time that she is in control. She loves it.

Chastity enters the world of vampires at a critical moment. Someone is killing the vampire Lords of Europe. As a vampire, Chastity is different. She cannot be detected by other vampires. The Countess turns her into an assassin in order to discover who the killer is. She soon discovers, however, that there is no killer. Rather the Countess is trying to destroy the peace between Europe's vampires. Chastity frees herself from the Countess by exposing the plot.

Chastity returns to the band, which is ready to leave on their American tour. Chastity accompanies them prepared to enter fully into their nocturnal world. But first, she must take care of some unfinished business in Toledo. She visits her father one last time and gives him a haircut, a Mohawk. That taken care of, it appears that Chastity's future is made. She is happy as a vampire powerful and in control and for the next 20 years, she enjoys life as an eternal young adult. She grows even more powerful by taking blood from older vampires. New York is her playground, but she has not at this point encountered Evil Ernie.

In the supernatural Chaos! story line, Evil Ernie is a serial killer whose destructive powers have been greatly enhanced by Lady Death. His first great rampage leads to the assassination of the President of the United States and the destruction of much of Washington, D.C. The government's attempts to kill him backfire, and Manhattan is largely destroyed by violence and fire. At the time that Manhattan is turned into a lifeless hush, Chastity is residing there. Only she and creatures of the night like her survive. Summoned by the other vampires who have lost their human comeliness in the fire, Chastity is asked to be their instrument of death. Will she kill them, and then take revenge on Ernie?

The challenge of taking on Ernie is just what Chastity wanted. Killing humans is simply feeding. It is too easy. It used none of her skills, not to mention her supernatural strength and speed. In their first encounter, Chastity learns that Evil Ernie is not easy to kill, but then neither is she. Their battle ends as dawn approaches and Chastity must get out of the sunlight. Out of their first encounter, Chastity realizes that she has much in common with her target victim. He is a killer, like her, and in her eyes, he's cute. But Ernie rejects her advances, and in the ongoing Chaos! world, Chastity decides her role: to figure out how to kill Ernie and do it.

SOURCES:

Chaos! Bible. Scottsdale, Ariz.: Chaos! Comics, 1995.
Chastity. Nos 1–4. Scottsdale, Ariz.: Chaos! Comics, 1997.
Evil Ernie. Nos 1–5. Scottsdale, Ariz.: Chaos! Comics, 1996.

Marlowe, Dr. Wendall

Dr. Wendall Marlowe (Paul Naschy) is the Dracula-like vampire in the low-budget Spanish film, *Gran Amore del Cionde Dracula* (1972), released in English as *Dracula's Great Love* and as *Dracula's Virgin Lovers*. Marlowe lives in a former sanitarium in Borgo Pass, which he purchased after the doctor who had run it had left in scandal over the high rate of deaths among his patients. He quickly claims his first victim after moving in by attacking one of the men who delivers his coffin.

Shortly after he moves in, he is visited by a group of young women and their male escorts. The group was touring the region when their coach broke down with night approaching. Marlowe allows the group to stay while they attempt to find a way to repair the wheel to the coach. As might be expected of a vampire, Marlowe disappears each day. At night, he vampirizes the women of the party one after another.

Marlowe is a traditional aristocratic Transylvanian vampire who is modeled on **Count Dracula** (in fact, as we learn, he may possess Dracula's spirit). He wears a cape with evening dress, and is nocturnal and sleeps in a coffin. He has hypnotic eyes and can levitate. His image does not reflect in mirrors, and he is repelled by the cross.

In his library there is a book called *The Memoirs of Professor Van Helsing*. The book describes how Dracula's spirit is immortal and will repeatedly return in a new form after each current bodily existence is ended. In his earthly life, he always seeks a virgin who will fall in love with him and whose blood he can use to awaken his daughter Rodna. Marlowe is clearly the spirit of Dracula reborn.

In the group of female visitors from the coach Marlowe finds Karen, a virgin who does fall in love with him. He plans to use her in a ceremony at the next full moon to revive Rodna, but in the meantime he falls in love with her. Instead of draining her blood, he tosses his daughter's coffin into the nearby lake and plans to spend his life with his new love. His hopes are dashed, however, when Karen learns that he is a vampire and is disgusted by him. In spite of her love, she cannot live with a vampire. In response, Marlowe commits suicide by staking himself.

Martin (portrayed by John Amplas), the title character of the 1976 film by George Romero, believes he is a vampire.

Martin

Martin (portrayed by John Amplas), the title character from the 1976 film and subsequent novelization, is a disturbed youth with a blood fetish who believes he is vampire. He lives in an extended family (primarily with his older cousin Tata Cudo) who perpetuates that belief. According to Cudo, Martin, surname Matthias, was born in 1892, the son of Rudy Matthias and an Elena Balressa. He was one of nine born into the family with the sign of vampirism (and there are a variety of signs that mark a baby as a future vampire in Polish folklore). Martin accepts the notion that he was 84 years old at the time he moved to Pittsburgh to live with his cousin and work as a delivery boy for him.

Whether Martin was an 84-year-old anomaly or simply a disturbed youth in a disturbed family, he is decidedly nonsupernatural in his vampirism. He lacks fangs (not a part of Eastern European folklore) and is not affected by mirrors, garlic, or religious symbols. The sun irritates his eyes, but it does not burn his flesh. He has no

Older cousin Tata Cudo dispatches his young cousin Martin, who thinks he is a vampire. From the 1976 film *Martin*.

extraordinary strength or hypnotic ability. To the contrary, he has to pick the lock or find some ordinary means of entry into the residences of his victims. Unable to hypnotize his victims, he used a syringe to drug them, and then opens a vein in their arm (not the neck) from which he drinks.

Martin is a sexually dysfunctional loner who generally feeds on young females. After putting his victim to sleep, he strips and joins her in bed, his substitute for normal sex. He is a messy feeder, but cleans up afterward, leaving his victim to appear to have committed suicide by slashing her wrists. After the killings, Martin calls a local late-night talk show host who finds him a humorous and harmless weirdo.

Martin's nemesis is Cudo. A pious Roman Catholic, Cudo promises to allow Martin to live undisturbed in his house until such time as Martin kills someone in Pittsburgh. Making a last-ditch effort to save him, Cudo surrounds himself with traditional protective artifacts and brings in an elderly Catholic priest to do an exorcism on Martin, who dismisses the acts as empty superstition. In the end, Cudo learns of one of Martin's several killings and immediately dispatches his surprised cousin with a stake through the heart, a death-dealing act whether the victim is a vampire or not. He then buries the corpse in an unmarked grave in his backyard. He covers the grave with seeds (folklore dictates that a vampire must count all the seeds before rising and attacking his family) and a cross.

SOURCES:

Romero, George, and Susan Sparrow. *Martin.* New York: Stein & Day, 1977. Reprint, New York: Day Books, 1980.

Mastenbrook, Miranda

Miranda Mastenbrook is a young woman in the fantasy world of Cynosure, a city where the "multiverse" meets. In Cynosure, the laws of physics change from block to block, and by crossing the street, one might be entering a new dimension. In Cynosure, the rules of vampirism, like other paranormal processes, tend to break down. Law and order in the city is provided by the Cadre, an agency designed to deal with threats to Cynosure's safety.

Miranda is a young teenager whose well-to-do merchant father lives in a suburban area. She manifests her teenage rebelliousness by joining the local ghoul scene and dressing in what is termed demon-chic. The ghouls party at the residence of a man named Wolfingham. At one of the parties she meets **Grinder,** a young man seemingly near her own age who turns out to be a vampire. Her father hires Mike "Cracker" Crocker to bring her home. After retrieving Miranda from Grinder, Cracker makes a pass at the beautiful Miranda, only to discover that she, too, is a vampire. He stakes her, but while trying to figure out what to tell her father, he is hit on the head and wakes up as a vampire himself.

Cracker approaches an old friend and soldier of fortune, John Gaunt, better known by his nickname, Grimjack. Cracker asks Grimjack to locate the person who turned him into a vampire. Grimjack's search leads him to Miranda Mastenbrook.

Grimjack arms himself with garlic dust and silver knives and heads for Wolfingham's. In spite of the stake she had received from Cracker, Miranda is very much alive (or, more precisely, undead). Grimjack blows garlic dust in her face to prevent her from changing shape, but she gets away. Later when he picks up her trail with a magic medallion, he finds her at home acting as if nothing had happened.

Grimjack uses a silver coin to force her to reveal herself as a vampire, and in front of her startled father, she transforms into a large bat-like creature. Grimjack then kills her, but remembering her resiliency, decapitates her, puts garlic in her mouth, and incinerates her in the bathtub. He washes her ashes down the drain. Miranda Mastenbrook is destroyed, but Grimjack now has to deal with the one who had created her.

Miranda Mastenbrook appears as a guest villain in the first two issues of the comic book *Grimjack Casefiles.*

SOURCES:

Ostrander, John, and Tim Truman. "Buried Past." *Grimjack Casefiles,* Parts 1 & 2. (First Publishing: November and December 1990).

The Master of Rampling Gate

The Master of Rampling Gate is a vampire created by author Anne Rice apart from her five-volume *Vampire Chronicles*. The story was published in an edited form in *Redbook* magazine (1984), but a more complete version of the text appears in the graphic novel published by Innovation Books (1991).

The story's main character was born in the fourteenth century in the village of Knorwood, England. As a young man, he explored an old, reputedly haunted structure near the village. He found it inhabited by a vampire who took blood from him. Two years later, the plague hit the village. When the young man became sick, he found his way back to the vampire's haunted structure and was given the Dark Gift (being turned into a vampire). Over the centuries the town of Knorwood disappears and forests reclaim the land. Only the young vampire remains.

Four hundred years later, the Rampling family moves into the neighborhood and builds Rampling Gate, their mansion, on the same spot formerly occupied by the ancient structure. The new village of Rampling emerges where Knorwood had once been. The vampire, known as the Master of Rampling Gate, makes himself known to the various residents of the house and in his own words, "subjugates them." In 1888, the last resident dies. He has two children whom he raised apart from the house, and with his dying words asks his son to tear it down, although he does not say why. His children, Richard and **Julie Rampling,** visit the mansion to determine if they should follow their father's admonition.

The Master makes himself known to Julie, first seemingly as an intruder. Julie recognizes him as having the same face as a man she saw in London when she was six years old. Finally, he introduces himself and tells Julie his story, and in the process explains why he does not want the house torn down. Julie is open to his invitation to make her a vampire and his request that she introduce him to the modern world. She accepts the Dark Gift and immediately makes arrangements with her brother to have the mansion transferred to her name so he has an excuse not to carry out his father's last wish. Leaving Richard to enjoy the house as long as he wishes, Julie and the Master travel to London to begin their new life and relationship.

SOURCES:

Ramsland, Katherine. *The Vampire Companion: The Official Guide to Anne Rice's The Vampire Chronicles.* New York: Ballantine Books, 1993.

Rice, Anne. "The Master of Rampling Gate." *Redbook* (February 1984). Rev. ed. *The Master of Rampling Gate.* Adapted by James Schlosser and illustrated by Colleen Doran. Wheeling, WV: Innovation Books, 1991.

Maximillian

Maximillian, one of a small group of African-American vampires, is portrayed by comedian Eddie Murphy in the film *Vampire in Brooklyn* (1995). According to the mythology of the movie, vampires originated in Egypt, but at some point dispersed—some to Transylvania, and some to the islands of the Bermuda Triangle. They lived happily in the Caribbean until this century, when they were destroyed, except for Maximillian, who is the last of his kind.

Maximillian travels to Brooklyn in search of a mate, whom he finds in the form of Rita (Angela Bassett), a young woman who is half vampire. Eager to preserve his blood line, he needs to locate her before the next full moon.

Reminiscent of Frank Langella's *Dracula* (1979), Maximillian's first appearance is as a wolf on board the ship to Brooklyn. He leaves the crew dead, their throats cut and drained of blood. Then as Maximillian he appears out of a misty fog to confront two local street hoods, displaying an array of his superhuman skills. He recruits their would-be victim as his Renfield. Giving Julius (Kadeem Hardison) a few drops of blood, he transforms him into his ghoul, the person to handle his affairs during the daylight hours. The immediate concern is a place to keep the coffin in which Max sleeps. Julius proceeds to develop a taste for bugs.

Maximillian turns out to be a very traditional vampire. He is negatively affected by religious symbols, mirrors, and garlic, and a stake in the heart would kill him. He has strange, hypnotic eyes, although they are yellow, not red. Having

Suave and sophisticated vampire Maximillian (portrayed by Eddie Murphy) from the film *Vampire in Brooklyn.*

established himself in Brooklyn, Maximillian turns to the process of seducing Rita, who turns out to be a detective. He bites her and allows her vampire heritage, complete with new fangs. Slowly she becomes aware of the truth of her heritage, her blood thirst arises, and she must choose between her humanity and vampirism. Maximillian's fate is sealed by her decision.

Meinster, Baron

The brief career of Baron Meinster, a traditional Transylvanian vampire and disciple of **Count Dracula,** is detailed in Hammer Films', *The Brides of Dracula* (1960). Meinster is a traditional vampire in keeping with the myth developed in the previous Hammer Films movie, *Horror of Dracula* (1958), starring Christopher Lee as Dracula. He has prominent fangs, does not reflect in a mirror, and is repulsed by holy water and the cross. He has hypnotic eyes, which he uses to full advantage in seducing his favorite food, young women. His single bite transforms his victims into vampires. His power is confined to the night, and he sleeps in a coffin during the day. He can transform into a bat, and is quite vulnerable to fire, daylight, or the well-placed stake.

Vampire Maximillian (Eddie Murphy, seated) holds the hand of Rita (Angela Bassett), whom he hopes to marry.

Meinster first appears as a young man in his twenties, his vampire career having been cut short due to the demise of his human mother. As a boy Meinster had kept company with some unsavory companions, one of which turned him into a vampire. Seeing the damage he was causing to human life, his mother had him chained up and confined to one wing of the Meinster Castle, an ominous dwelling that stands on a hill above the village of Bartstein, Transylvania.

Shortly after Dracula's death in the 1890s, Bartstein is visited by a beautiful young woman, Mme. Marianne Danielle, passing through on her way to assume a teaching post at a school in a nearby town. Stranded in Bartstein, she accepts the invitation of the Baroness Meinster to stay in the castle. While there, she sees the young baron and, not understanding what she is doing, steals the key to his bonds and frees him. The baron immediately turns on his mother and vampirizes her. Later, he seduces Marianne into becoming his bride.

The next day, Bartstein is also visited by Dr. Abraham von Helsing, who has been

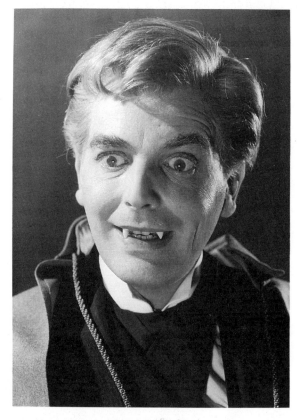

David Peel as Baron Meinster in *The Brides of Dracula*.

summoned by the local priest. von Helsing understands vampirism to be the survival of an ancient Pagan cult. His first confrontation with the vampire ends in his fighting him off with a cross. The baron attacks von Helsing, who fights off the vampire's advances with holy water. The young baron is disfigured as if acid has been thrown in his face. Reeling from his wounds, he is caught by von Helsing in the shadow of a windmill— the arms of which cast a crosslike shadow on the surprised baron.

Mekare

Mekare is an ancient vampire who emerges as a central character in Anne Rice's *The Queen of the Damned* (1988) and in other volumes of *The Vampire Chronicles*. Initially, she is not a vampire, but a witch. Her mother is **Miriam,** and her twin sister is named **Maharet** (she is also a witch). The twins share a distinguishing head of flaming red hair, which they inherited from their mother. Some 6,000 years ago, the pair resided in Palestine among the caves of Mount Carmel. Their people were cannibals who consumed the flesh of the dead, believing that although the spirit had departed, some residue of power remained in the body. The tribe also believed that it was a sign of respect to eat the bodies, especially for the children of the deceased. They were 16 when **Akasha** and **Enkil** became joint rulers of the Nile Valley.

The twins were well-known in their tribe for being able to consult a powerful spirit. They also had the power to bring rain, and it was this rain-making ability that caused their fame to spreading far and wide, even to Egypt. When Akasha and Enkil learn of the girls' abilities, they invite them to an audience with the royal court. Advised by both their mother and the spirit they conversed with that danger awaited them, they refuse the invitation. However, the queen is not to be denied. Maharet and her sister are captured and taken to Egypt. Along the way, they are befriended by **Khayman,** the Chief Steward of the royal court.

Questioned by the royal couple, they tell of spirit contacts and miracles. Mekare takes the lead in responding. She is enraged by the fact that Akasha and Enkil's troops killed many people just to bring the twins to Egypt. This impudence angers the queen. During the twins' second audience with the queen, the girls anger her even more when the powerful spirit they converse with, **Amel,** becomes poltergeist-like and wreaks havoc. Additionally, Amel's actions destroy the queen's own belief in her goddess. Amel actually attacks Akasha, which leads Enkil to order that the girls be punished by being publicly raped in front of the royal court. A reluctant, but obedient, Khayman is forced to carry out the punishment. Afterwards, the pair is released and allowed to return home.

Amel stays in Egypt. After Akasha and Enkil are attacked by their own people and lie near death, Amel invades both of their bodies and turns them into the first vampires. Unable to explain their enormous blood thirst or to understand what has happened to them, Akasha and Enkil bring Mekare and Maharet back to the court to help them understand. The girls bluntly tell the queen exactly what has occurred, and for their trouble, they are punished again. Mekare has her tongue cut off, and Maharet has her eyes poked out. Before her tongue is cut out, Mekare prophecies that she will survive long enough into the future to become the instrument of the queen's downfall.

The girls are locked up in prison, where they are visited by Khayman. It seems that Khayman has been turned into a vampire by Akasha and Enkil, the first human turned by the pair. Angered by their actions, he decides to help the sisters seek their revenge by offering the "Dark Gift" of vampirism to Mekare, who promptly turns her sister. They girls flee the prison but are captured and entombed in stone coffins that are set adrift on the ocean, Mekare from the western shore of Egypt and Maharet from the eastern.

Little is known of what happens to Mekare over the next several millennia. Her sister searches for her, but to no avail. There is some indication that she was in Peru for a while. However, in the mid-1980s, Mekare resurfaces. At the same time that Akasha awakens and attempts to achieve world domination, Mekare causes many, many people to have a dream about a pair of red-headed twins and the queen, Akasha. Unfortunately, those who receive the dream do not understand it.

Akasha begins to slaughter all the male vampires in the world, which is part of her plan. A group of survivors gathers in Sonoma, California, where Akasha soon arrives to force a final confrontation. It appears that the vampires will lose, but Mekare appears in the nick of time and pushes Akasha into a glass wall, which severs the queen's head. Maharet then quickly gathers up Akasha's brain and heart and passes them to Mekare, who consumes them, thus becoming the new keeper of the vampire life force.

In the ongoing world of *The Vampire Chronicles*, Mekare is still alive. She has been taken to a safe location and is known to all vampires as the "one who must be protected."

SOURCES:

Ramsland, Katherine. *The Vampire Companion: The Official Guide to Anne Rice's The Vampire Chronicles*. New York: Ballantine Books, 1993.

Rice, Anne. *The Queen of the Damned*. New York: Alfred A. Knopf, 1988. Reprint, New York: Ballantine Books, 1989.

Metternich, Paul

Paul Metternich is a 70-year-old Viennese neurologist and vampire hunter who appears in Sydney Holer's 1935 novel, *The Vampire*. Metternich is tall, with a full beard and gold-rimmed glasses. The story opens in 1935 as Metternich is investigating some cases of possible vampirism in continental Europe. He is pulled away from those cases when he is summoned to London by his former student, Dr. Martin Kent.

In London, Metternich finds two cases of interest. Kent specifically asks him to consult on the case of Sonia Rodney, the daughter of Lord Rodney. She has reported that her will has been taken over by a **Baron Alexis Ziska,** an Eastern European nobleman. She had initially been attracted to the baron, and he expressed his desire to marry her, but something had gone wrong. The second case that Metternich investigates involves Elizabeth Platting, a young woman who has been found suffering from a loss of blood and two puncture wounds on her neck.

Metternich explains to Kent and the other affected parties that vampires are rare, but nonetheless real. He uses the research of famous vampire scholar Montague Summers to prove his point. Metternich tells the others that a vampire is a bloodsucking ghost inhabiting a human host. Such creatures can call upon the powers of Satan and are very strong. They can be identified by their extended canine teeth.

When Kent and Metternich compare notes about the Rodney case, their observations lead them to Ziska. The two know they must prove that Ziska is the vampire if they are to stop the attacks on Sonia Rodney. Metternich, operating from an apartment on Welbeck Street, finds a few additional allies, and together the men track Ziska to his lair, which is in the basement of his country's embassy. Metternich carries a crucifix and a long-bladed sword-stick with him to do battle. He first attacks the baron with holy water, which locks the baron in human form and prevents his escape. He then impales Ziska with the sword. His work done, he returns to Vienna.

SOURCES:

Horler, Sidney. *The Vampire*. London: Hutchinson & Co., 1935. Reprint, New York: Bookfinger, 1974.

Frank Langella restored the image of Count Dracula as a very sexual being in the 1979 film version of *Dracula*.

Mezgar, Bela

Is Bela Mezgar a vampire? That's the question posed by three suspecting teens in the small town of Barkley, Pennsylvania, in the junior novel, *The Case of the Visiting Vampire* (1986). Bela Mezgar is a tall, thin Romanian of indeterminate age who comes to Barkley to star in a local drama production, *The Castle of Count Dracula*. He looks the part. His black hair is combed straight back, his skin is cold and clammy to the touch, and his eyes are hypnotic.

Led by would-be monster hunter J. Huntley English, M.H., pals Verna Wilkes and Raymond Almond investigate the visiting actor and give him the traditional vampire tests. He stays away from garlic, refuses to meet one of them for lunch (which would require his going out in daylight), and steps back from a cross stuck in his face. Then there is the coffin in the basement of the theater, which scares the trio senseless when they see a hand slowly emerge from underneath its lid.

Soon the kids discover that Mezgar is an artist in residence at nearby Chatham College in Pittsburgh. They follow him to the home of Sonya Hanson, the person on the drama committee who had arranged his appearance. Hanson also arranged his invitation to the college. Although the kids confront him, Mezgar can explain everything, including his being startled at the sudden appearance of the cross. He confides he came to America to escape Ceausescu's Romania, and arrangements are being made for him to elude surveillance by the country's secret police during the Dracula drama. When Mezgar makes his escape at the end of the play's run, young monster hunter Huntley gets some credit for his part in the affair, but realizes he will have to look elsewhere for a real vampire.

SOURCES:
Stevenson, Drew. *The Case of the Visiting Vampire.* New York: Dodd, Mead and Co., 1986.

Mikhailovich, Count

Count Mikhailovich, a traditional aristocratic Transylvanian vampire, is the subject of Joe Gill's short story "The Vampire Lives!" Mikhailovich is five centuries old. He resides in a castle, sleeps in a coffin, and wears a cape, though otherwise his clothing is less formal. He has fangs, but under most circumstances they are not noticeable. The villagers who reside near the castle refuse to enter the count's dwelling place. In the early 1970s, a graduate student named Anton Marguy arrives to conduct a study of the castle. The only person he can find to give him a tour is a disagreeable man named Mikhail.

Anton is out to prove definitively that vampires do not exist and that there is nothing to what he labels the "vampire myth." However, he gives in to the fright of his girlfriend, Alicia, and cuts short his tour on the first day. Following dinner, Anton and Alicia retire to their separate rooms. Shortly after going to bed, the sleeping Alicia is visited by the count, who turns out to have been their tour guide. Though awakened by her screams, Anton is unable to prevent Alicia's kidnaping by the count.

Anton's belief in the myth of vampires is shaken when he arrives at the count's castle and empties his pistol into the count to no effect. His neck is saved from the count's teeth by the opportune fall of a wooden beam from the aging ceiling that impales and kills the count. However, before Anton had arrived at the castle, the count had his way with Alicia. Now, Anton and his thesis must contend with his stricken girlfriend.

SOURCES:
Gill, Joe, and Pat Boyette. "The Vampire Lives!" *Haunted* 13. (Carlton Comics, July 1973).

Mink

Mink is one of a group of female vampires who collectively have given their name to the DC Comics series *Vamps*. Mink is a pretty, young blonde who aspires to an acting career. She is also concerned about her looks and upset that she cannot see herself in a mirror. As a vampire, the only time she can see her reflection is briefly in the eyes of her next victim. She has fangs, is completely nocturnal, and needs to feed daily.

At some point in the 1980s, she encounters **Dave,** a vampire who turns her into a vampire and makes her one of his minions. She is joined by four other women: **Howler, Whipsnake, Screech,** and **Skeeter.** Dave uses the women to help him handle his tiresome daily task of finding food. The women lure men to an agreed-upon spot, where Dave is waiting. Then, they all dine.

In 1990, Mink joins her sisters in attacking Dave at his most vulnerable moment, just after he has fed and is in an unresponsive stupor. Together, the five stake him, dismember him, and bury his body parts in different graves. Following that communal act, they emerge as the Vamps. They then straddle their motorcycles and hit the road. Howler, their natural leader, and the only one still concerned with a matter from her pre-vampiric existence, directs them to Las Vegas. While there, Mink visits the gaming rooms. She likes to win and finds that the heightened senses she now possesses as a vampire aid her greatly in that regard. She also picks up a young man who runs one of the roulette tables to join her for her first meal in Sin City.

Mink accompanies the other Vamps to New York but really comes into her own in Hollywood in 1996, when she decides to resume her acting career and manipulates producer Harris Silver to hire her to star in his new vampire flick. The film is actually based on an encounter between Skeeter and a rock musician during their New York stay. Skeeter had left him in the middle of feeding, and he recovered. The movie is shot in the evening, and as the filming progresses, Mink fills her imagination with grand delusions of her future life as a star. Her plans fall apart at a private screening, when it turns out that all of her scenes in the movie are blank. It turns out that not only does Mink's image not show up in mirrors, but it cannot be captured on film either. After a temper tantrum, she calms down and leaves Hollywood with her sisters for their next adventure.

SOURCES:
Lee, Elaine, and William Simpson. *Vamps,* No. 1–6. New York: DC/Vertigo, 1995–96.
————. *Vamps: Hollywood & Vein,* No. 1–6. New York: DC Comics, 1996.

Miriam (portrayed by Anulka) and Fern (portrayed by Marianne Morris) as the lesbian vampires in the film *Vampyres.*

Miriam

Miriam is one of the two vampires featured in the low-budget film *Vampyres* (1974). A young blonde, she is shot and killed as she and **Fern,** her lover, lay entwined in each others arms. A short time later, the pair emerge as vampires, a circumstance that the film leaves unexplained. Since the time of the two women's deaths, the local townspeople have spread rumors that the women still haunt the house in which they were killed.

Both Miriam and Fern are rather traditional vampires. They are totally nocturnal. They do not reflect in mirrors. They need a nightly supply of blood, and obtaining that substance is their main activity each night. Most of their victims are men, who they usually seduce using wine and good conversation instead of simply attacking them. Unlike Fern, who tends to use a knife to cut open her victim's body, Miriam is more traditional and uses her teeth.

The monotonous routine of Miriam's and Fern's life is disrupted by Fern's attachment to Ted, a hitchhiker she picks up near their house. Fern is infatuated with Ted and refuses to drain his blood enough to kill him. After the two women spend several evenings with Ted, Miriam is also somewhat jealous that Fern prefers him to her. On their third evening with Ted, the two both drink from him and then make love next to his unconscious body. That day the women sleep in the basement, and Miriam happens to keep one eye open, which allows her to spot an intruder. When night falls, she leads Fern to the intruder's caravan, where they attack the intruder and feast on her and her husband. As the movie ends, it appears that life will go on unchanged for the vampire pair, since no one will buy the house because of the local rumors.

SOURCES:

Greaves, Tim. *Vampyres*. Glen Carbon, IL: Draculina Publishing, 1996.

Miyu, Vampire Princess

Vampire Princess Miyu, a contemporary Japanese vampire, looks and occasionally acts like a girl in her early teens. Originally appearing in Japanese *manga* (comic books), she has become the subject of a television series (later released on video) and, in the mid-1990s, an American comic book series. Her name in Japanese, Kyuuketsuki Hime Miyu, is literally translated as "Bloodsucking Demon Princess Beautiful Evening." She was born in post-World War II Japan, where she lived a relatively normal life until puberty. However, when she is 13, a demon named Larva is sent to destroy her. Miyu fights off the attack when she discovers that she has the blood thirst and makes Larva her first victim and servant. Larva also became the clue to her own origin.

Miyu is part of the supernatural world's vampire clan. In the mythological past, most of the gods and demons (the *shinma*) abandoned the Earth to human beings. They now reside in a nether dimension called simply the Dark (or the Night). However, one clan decided to return to Earth. The leaders of the *shinma* gave the vampire clan two tasks: to guard the gateway to the Dark and to hunt down the members of the recalcitrant *shinma* clan and banish them back to the Dark. Miyu, the current guardian (or sentinel), is a member of the vampire clan living on Earth to secure the sleep of those who lie below. To accomplish her task, Miyu's aging is halted. She operates as an ageless and amoral creature. She hunts the *shinma* but must also select people from which to obtain her own nourishment. She has been given sufficient power to execute her duties as well as immunity to the traditional dangers for vampires (sunlight, religious symbols, etc.).

Himiko, a spiritualist who investigates alleged supernatural occurrences and performs exorcisms (for a fee), encounters Miyu during one of her adventures hunting the *shinma*. While investigating the trance-like state of a young girl named Aiko, Himiko is unable to exorcise whatever is possessing the girl. She refuses her fee, but her interest is piqued. Upon further investigation, she discovers that the girl's parents have been dead for some time. While Himiko is in the process of trying to unravel the case, Miyu arrives and saves the girl. It turns out that the girl was possessed by Raen, one of the *shinma*. Miyu defeats the demon and Aiko returns to normal. Himiko befriends Miyu and becomes an ally who Miyu relies on in her long-term battle with the demonic forces.

In 1997, *Telebi Tokyo* (TV Tokyo) launched a 25-episode TV series featuring Miyu. The first American comic series appeared in 1995, and a second series two years later.

SOURCES:

Kakinouchi, Narumi. *New Vampire Miyu.* Translated by Kuni Kamura. Fredericksburg, VA: Studio Ironcat, 1997–98.

————. *Vampire Miyu.* No. 1–6. San Antonio, TX: Antarctic Press, 1995–96.

Modoc

Modoc is the 265-year-old vampire mentor in the comedy *My Best Friend Is a Vampire* (1988). His current assignment involves **Jeremy Capello,** a high-school student who has suddenly begun to change after a late-night encounter with Nora, a beautiful young vampiress. Modoc appears in Jeremy's bedroom to assist him into his new life as a vampire. His toughest job is actually convincing his new pupil that he really *is* a vampire. Only the undeniable changes he is undergoing finally force Jeremy to accept his new identity. In one of their early conversations, Modoc gives Jeremy the address of an all-night butcher shop where he can purchase pig's blood. Fortunately, when his fangs pop out and the blood lust overtakes him in the midst of a first date, Jeremy stops himself from biting her and heads for the butcher shop.

Modoc is a patient teacher who has mastered the art of staying alive. He gives Jeremy the vampire's manual, *Vampirism, A Practical Guide to an Alternative Lifestyle*, and tries to convince Jeremy to think of himself as a member of a misunderstood minority group that only needs some respect and understanding. Vampires can live off of animal blood and thus have no need to kill off their peer group. And since they age only one year each decade, they have time to enjoy life. Also, like Jeremy, Modoc is a living vampire. Having never died, he can go out in the daylight, although like all vampires, he may prefer the darkness. As the initial phase of his mentoring comes to an end, he gives Jeremy the keys to his BMW, and a warning about the local vampire hunter: **Professor Leopold McCarthy** is totally misguided, but nevertheless dangerous.

Modoc hangs around to watch over Jeremy as McCarthy launches an attack on him. When the two finally come face to face in the local graveyard, Modoc reappears with a group of beautiful young vampires and a final solution to the McCarthy problem. Humane vampire that he is, he invites the would-be vampire hunter to become a vampire himself. With the newly recruited vampire in tow, Modoc leaves Jeremy and is off to his next assignment.

Molloy, Daniel

Daniel Molloy is the interviewer in Anne Rice's famous *Interview with the Vampire* (1976), and he eventually becomes a vampire himself. He was portrayed by Christian Slater in the movie version of the book. He is tall and slender with ashen hair and violet eyes. At the time of the interview with **Louis de Pointe du Lac,** he is in his early twenties. After hearing Louis' story, he begs Louis to turn him into a vampire. Louis is enraged that Molloy seems to have missed the whole point of his tale and would actually desire such a life after what he has just heard. Louis bites Molloy, but does not draw much blood and does not turn him into a vampire. When Molloy wakes up from the attack, he sets out on a search to find Louis or one of his vampire colleagues. He heads to New Orleans to begin his search.

He transcribes the tapes from the interview and publishes them as the book *Interview with the Vampire* under the pseudonym Anne Rice. He then meets **Armand,** the vampire Louis had feelings for at the **Theatre des Vampires** in Paris. They develop a relationship that at first is nothing more than Armand occasionally showing up to learn about the twentieth century from Molloy and Molloy thirsting for the "Dark Gift" that would make him a vampire. Armand is a bright pupil and uses Molloy's teachings to quickly make a fortune. He shares all of his possession with Daniel, except the Dark Gift. Armand does give Daniel an amulet that contains a vial of his blood. If he is ever in danger from other vampires, he is to break the vial and drink it. The vampires would feel Armand's power and stay away.

While Armand regularly takes blood from Daniel, his refusal to finish the job and make him a vampire is a source of constant conflict. Daniel leaves him and his life degenerates. Daniel is 32 (12 years have passed since he wrote *Interview with the Vampire*) when Armand relocates his desperate former lover. Armand realizes that the only way to keep Molloy from dying is to finally turn him into a vampire.

The timing is right for other reasons. Around the world, vampires are being killed, and the entire community is facing its largest threat ever. **Akasha,** the original vampire and the life force behind all vampires, is attempting to dominate the world by killing off all males, vampire and human. Armand does not know this yet, however. It is actually Daniel, who has the power of clairvoyance, who perceives that Akasha is behind the evil. It is in the face of this threat, plus Daniel's impending death, that causes Armand to finally offer the Dark Gift. It is the only time in his very long life that Armand has turned anyone into a vampire.

SOURCES:

Ramsland, Katherine. *The Vampire Companion: The Official Guide to Anne Rice's The Vampire Chronicles.* New York: Ballantine Books, 1993.

Rice, Anne. *Interview with the Vampire.* New York: Alfred A. Knopf, 1976. Reprint, New York: Ballantine, 1979.

———. *The Queen of the Damned.* New York: Alfred A. Knopf, 1988. Reprint, New York: Ballantine Books, 1989.

———. *The Vampire Lestat.* New York: Alfred A. Knopf, 1985. Reprint, New York: Ballantine Books, 1986.

The Monk

One of the first vampires to appear in comic books is also the first vampire encountered by **Batman.** In 1939, the Monk made his initial appearance in *Detective Comics* (No. 31), just five months after Batman's initial appearance in *Detective Comics* (No. 27). The Monk is a rather unattractive old man of indeterminate age who lives in a castle in Transylvania. In public he wears a bright red robe and a hood that covers his face. The hood has two slits for his eyes, above which there is a gold skull and crossbones. He sleeps in a coffin. He has the power to transform into a wolf, but his primary asset is his clairvoyant hypnotic ability, by which he is able to control his minions, primarily a woman named Dala, and to call his victims to him.

Batman initially learns of the Monk one evening when he finds his girlfriend, Julie Madison, wandering the streets in a trance-like state. Bruce takes Julie to a doctor, who recommends an ocean voyage to recover from the effects of the hypnotism. Thus begins a series of encounters between Batman and the Monk that lead him from the cruise ship to the Monk's stronghold in Paris, and eventually to his castle in Transylvania.

Once at the castle, Batman must overcome the Monk's hypnotic power and the wolves he calls to his assistance. He survives the first night, which ends with his finding a silver statue. During the day, he makes some silver bullets and, drawing no distinctions between werewolves and vampires, simply shoots the Monk and his assistant Dala.

The initial death should have confined the Monk to literary history, but the character was revived for a five-part storyline in *Batman* and *Detective Comics* in 1982.

SOURCES:

"Batman Versus the Vampire." *Detective Comics.* No. 31–32. Oct., Nov. 1939. Reprinted in *The Greatest Batman Stories Ever Told.* New York: DC Comics, 1989.

"Blood Sport." *Batman.* No. 349. July 1982. "The Millionaire Contract." *Detective Comics.* No. 518. Sept. 1982.

"The Monster in the Mirror." *Detective Comics.* No. 517. Aug. 1982.

"Nightmare in Crimson." *Batman.* No. 350. New York: DC Comics, Aug. 1982.

"What Stalks the Gotham Night?" *Batman.* No. 351. New York: DC Comics, July/Sept. 1982.

Mora, Count

After successfully playing **Count Dracula,** Bela Lugosi portrayed an Eastern European aristocratic vampire, Count Mora, in the classic *The Mark of the Vampire* (1935). The character who became Count Mora originally appeared in the silent

Bela Lugosi as the classic, aristocratic European vampire Count Mora, shown here with his daughter Luna.

movie, *London After Midnight*, with Lon Chaney portraying the pseudo-vampire. Tod Browning, who originally wrote and directed *London After Midnight*, directed its remake with Lugosi. Lugosi had assumed the title role in *Dracula* in 1931 after Chaney, who had been slated by Browning for the part, died of cancer.

Legend has it that Count Mora, who lived in a castle in rural Czechoslovakia during the nineteenth century, reportedly killed his daughter **Luna** and then committed suicide. Because such an act leads to the vampiric state in Eastern European folklore, the pair are doomed to walk the grounds as vampires. Ignoring local superstitions, Sir Karell Borotyn and his daughter move into the castle. When Borotyn is discovered dead with two marks in his neck and his body drained of blood, vampirism is immediately suggested as the cause. Townspeople report seeing Count Mora and his daughter (portrayed by Carrol Borland) walking quietly around the castle grounds. In the face of the reports, it is suggested that Ms. Borotyn needs protection, and a short time later Count Mora manifests and attacks her. Black-

The menacing Bela Lugosi as Count Mora in *Mark of the Vampire*.

thorne, commonly used in Eastern European countries as a protection from vampires, is placed around the castle to keep Count Mora away.

The end of the story reveals the real killer, who attempted to cover his actions by evoking the specter of the vampire. Count Mora and Luna acknowledge that they are actors who were hired by the town's local investigators to assist in drawing out the real killer.

Morbius, Michael

Michael Morbius first appeared in comic books in 1971. He was the first original vampire introduced after the revision of the Comics Code, the set of standards passed by the comics industry in 1954 in an attempt to self-regulate itself by limiting the amount of violence and gore that could appear. Vampires were among the supernatural creatures who were banned by the code.

In the world of comic books, Morbius was an outstanding biologist who had won the Nobel Prize for his work. Just as he is engaged to be married, however, he contracts a rare blood disease and becomes ill. He begins to work on a cure and creates a serum from vampire bat blood; he treats himself with the serum and with electric shocks. His radical treatments finally stop the effects of the disease, but they also create a number of unwanted side effects. He grows fangs and develops an intense thirst for blood, which causes him to vampirize his best friend. He also develops certain superpowers, including the increased strength that many vampires experience. He also finds it easy to fly, since his bones have become hollow.

Beginning with an encounter with Spider-Man in *Amazing Spider-Man* (No. 101, 1971), he squares off against various Marvel superheroes. He is able to survive battles with the Bestial Lizard and the Human Torch and then challenges the X-Team in *Marvel Team-Up* (No. 3 and 4). After defeating Iceman and the Avenging Angel, he is bested by Cyclops. In the X-Men laboratory he is treated by the X-Team scientist Professor X, but the professor's treatment with an experimental enzyme only confirms Morbius's status as the "Living Vampire." Morbius escapes from the X-Team to continue his many adventures, in most of which he fights villains who are more evil than himself. He is constantly searching for ways to meet his need for blood without killing innocent people. Periodically he finds time to search for a possible cure for his condition.

In 1973 Morbius appeared in the new Marvel magazine-size comic, *Vampire Tales*, the first issue of which appeared in the fall. Then, in February 1974, Morbius also became the featured character of *Fear* (No. 19). For the next few years, Morbius stories appeared simultaneously in the two comics. *Vampire Tales* published 11 issues through June 1975, while *Fear* concluded its Morbius story thread with issue No. 31 in December 1975. In 1976 his adventures continued when he appeared in *Marvel Two-in-One* (No. 15) to fight The Thing. He also squared off against **Blade the Vampire Slayer** in *Marvel Preview* (No. 8).

Morbius finally found a cure for his condition in 1980 in *Spectacular Spider-Man* (No. 38). In that story, Morbius drinks some of Spider-Man's radioactive blood and then is struck by lightning, which for some reason drains him of his vampiric powers. He subsequently devises a serum that returns him to a normal human life. He is brought to trial for the multiple murders he had committed as a vampire, but he is acquitted by reason of insanity. This seemed to be the end of the Michael Morbius character, especially after Marvel killed off all its vampire characters in December 1983. The characters were killed off when Dr. Stephen Strange invented a magical spell called the Montesi Formula that destroyed all vampires. However, a door was left open for Morbius's return—since he was a human and was no longer a vampire in 1983, he did not perish with the rest of Marvel's vampires.

Thus the stage was set for Morbius's return. After many years in oblivion, Morbius the Living Vampire made a dramatic reappearance in *Dr. Strange: Sorcerer Supreme* (No. 10) in November 1989. After living normally for several years, he decides to take a vacation to New Orleans. There, he meets a beautiful woman named Marie. He goes home with her and discovers that she is actually Marie Laveau, a woman known for keeping herself young by using the blood of vampires. Since there were no more true vampires in the world, she was aging again. She forces

Morbius to undergo an intense but nonfatal electric shock, which reverses the shock he had received years earlier and again turns him into a vampire. He then has to battle Dr. Strange, who, while attempting to save his brother, weakens the Montesi Formula and allows the vampires to return to Earth (*Dr. Strange: Sorcerer Supreme*, No. 14, February 1990).

In September 1992, with vampires returning and supernatural evil on the rise, Morbius joins old Marvel heroes such as Ghost Rider and **Blade the Vampire Slayer** to form the Midnight Sons, a group assembled to fight the new wave of evil arising as the Montesi Formula weakens. His adventures, recounted in his own comic book, *Morbius, the Living Vampire*, begin with his fight against the union of evil entities led by Lilith, Queen of Evil and Mother of Demons. While a number of Morbius's colleagues are destroyed in the fight, he survives and continues to battle evil today as a reluctant vampire with a conscience and a thirst for blood.

SOURCES:

Benton, Mike. *Horror Comics: The Illustrated History.* Dallas, TX: Taylor Publishing Company, 1991.

Fear. No. 20–31. New York: Marvel Comics, 1973–1974.

Ghost Rider and the Midnight Sons Magazine. No. 1- . New York: Marvel Comics, 1993.

Marvel Preview. Marvel Comics. No. 8. New York: Marvel Comics, Fall 1976.

Morbius, The Living Vampire. No. 1–32 . New York: Marvel Comics, 1992–95.

Morgan, Michelle

Michelle Morgan is the beautiful young vampire who makes her first appearance in the direct-to-video thriller *Subspecies* (1990), and becomes a central character in the two sequels: *Bloodlust: Subspecies II* (1993) and *Bloodlust: Subspecies III* (1995).

Michelle is the victim of centuries-old **Radu**'s attempt to gain the blood stone from his father, King Vladimir. Radu kills his father and takes the magical object, which drips the blood of the saints. With the blood stone, vampire Vladimir had been able to live at peace with his mortal neighbors. However, Radu views it primarily as a means of augmenting his already considerable powers.

Just as Radu is reentering the family estate, Castle Vladislav, Michelle and two other graduate students arrive in Romania to study Transylvanian folklore. Intrigued by the castle, they pay a closer visit, and their arrival calls Radu's attention to their presence. One by one he attacks them, turning them into vampires with his bite. In the meantime, Radu's brother Stefan arrives on the scene, discovers his father's corpse, and makes plans to kill Radu. In the conflict that culminates in Stefan staking and decapitating Radu, both coed-vampires are killed. Michelle joins the handsome Stefan in the vampiric life.

As the story progresses, it's clear that Stefan and Michelle did not count on Radu's power of rejuvenation. With the assistance of some demonic helpers, Radu is able to revive and kill Stefan as he lays in his coffin. In his lust for Michelle, he delays killing her and thus allows her to escape to Bucharest, taking the blood stone with her. While Radu determines how best to pursue her, she calls her sister Rebecca to her side and begins to learn what a vampire's life entails. Unlike Radu, whose appearance keeps him from human company, Michelle retains her beauty and easily moves

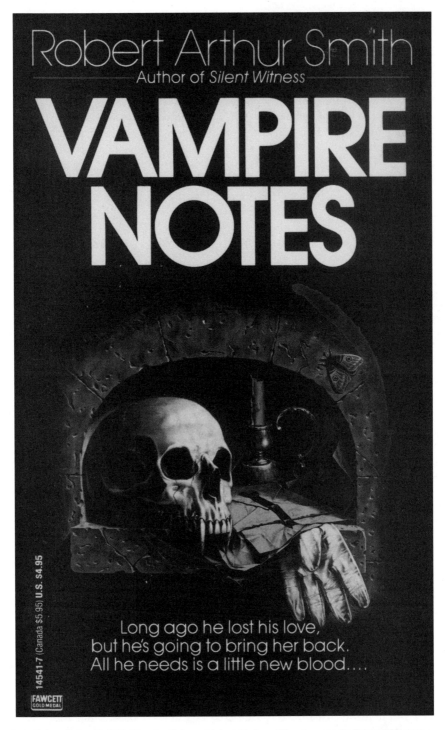

Cover art from Robert Arthur Smith's *Vampire Notes,* which reclusive millionaire vampire Edward Mornay.

through the nightlife of Bucharest. She also finds a coffin in a museum, where she sleeps during the day.

Inevitably, she has to confront Radu, who has teamed up with his sorceress mother, now a horribly disfigured hag. In their first major confrontation, Michelle and Rebecca are successful in staking Radu and setting his mother on fire. However, both recover and come after Michelle and her bewildered sister, who only slowly is grasping the nature of the creatures with whom she has become involved.

In their second confrontation, Radu captures Michelle and imprisons her within the castle. Hoping to win her over as a mate, he begins to teach her about vampiric life. He shows her his resting place deep in the castle and teaches her about feeding. Together they hunt among the local villagers. Michelle bides her time with Radu while Rebecca finds help from the local calvary: a learned scholar, a young man from the American Embassy, a CIA fighting specialist, and a Bucharest policeman. Together, armed with a revolver loaded with silver bullets, they go to Castle Vladislav to rescue Michelle, thus setting up the climatic confrontation in the film.

In the end, they take Michelle away in a body bag, which shields her from the sun's light. In the process, they throw the blood stone away in order to divert the pursuing Radu, earlier slowed by his reception of a clip of silver bullets. Michelle's friends discover her condition, and now they must work out a way to keep her alive, surviving in her vampiric state, while not losing her moral and loving relationship with humanity.

Mornay, Edward

Edward Mornay, the reclusive millionaire vampire in Robert Arthur Smith's *Vampire Notes* (1989), lives in Santa Monica, California, where he has lived since the 1980s. Mornay is approximately five feet, eight inches tall and strongly built. Complaining of a skin condition brought on by the sun, he appears only after dark. He is pale and bloodless with a strange, delicate—almost feminine— facial beauty. His fingers are noticeably long and his hands cold to the touch. He does not eat or drink human food. He has forsaken his private existence, and instead is in the process of building a new theater and commissioning a producer to stage a play he has written.

Mornay's play is autobiographical. Its plot concerns the love affair between himself, born Philippe de Tarcenay, the son of a French royal family who resided at Mornecy in the Jura in the early nineteenth century, and Rosalie Beauchemin, his true love. The story reveals that Rosalie was the ward of her cousin Justin, who intended to marry her to a fellow nobleman who could bring him influence in Paris. De Tarcenay had somewhat forsaken his royalist upbringing and joined Napoleon's army. He was wounded at Waterloo and left without support following the return of royalists to power. Justin had him arrested and charged with plotting to assassinate the new king. De Tarcenay escaped from custody and ran away with Rosalie. However, Justin caught up with them and, according to the script, the couple decided to commit suicide by jumping off a cliff.

De Tarcenay had hoped their suicide pact, the event with which the play ends, would turn both he and Rosalie into vampires, the fate of true suicides. In fact, he arose a short time later as a vampire. He assumed the name Edmond Mornay, but there was no Rosalie. He assumed that her body had floated away in the river below the cliff and remained lodged in some underground hollow, beneath a bank. He knew she was a vampire, possibly traumatized by death and now existing in a state of suspended animation. His search for her body had been fruitless.

Over the years, Mornay became obsessed with finding Rosalie. He had a small museum of Rosalie's possessions, some of which he loaned to the actress who was playing her part. The play was a means of summoning her into wakefulness and to his side.

As the theater nears completion and the play begins production, a variety of events cause producer George Hargreaves to learn of Mornay's vampiric life. The actors, who normally attempt to assume the role of the characters they portray, found themselves in a state approaching possession as they rehearsed. And Santa Monica is facing a serial killer, dubbed the "Gentleman Slasher," who leaves a corpse behind every few days.

Eventually, Hargreaves confronts Mornay, and seemingly kills him with a sword through the heart. However, Mornay does not die, and once again Hargreaves has to face the angry vampire, this time in the presence of an equally angry resurrected Rosalie. Their encounter comes to a fiery conclusion in the theater, where Mornay has to contend with the romantic and distorted account of the events surrounding de Tarcenay's and Rosalie's death.

SOURCES:

Smith, Robert Arthur. *Vampire Notes.* New York: Fawcett Gold Medal, 1989.

Morrisey, Max

Max Morrisey's creator, graphic artist M. Dalton Allred, refers to his vampire character by an appropriate title: "Citizen Nocturne." Morrisey is transformed into a vampire in the mid-1980s by 200-year-old vampiress **Rovena Venisette.** They meet one evening at the Rockoplast, a night spot in Kaiserlautern, Germany. Nothing happens that first evening, as Morrisey's wife is with him. But several days later, while on a trip to Belgium, Rovena shows up, seduces him, and bites him. He returns home with a pressing thirst and bites Merete, his wife. Subsequently, he leaves his job as a broadcaster, joins the United States Air Force, and now earns his living as a graphic artist.

Morrisey is a traditional vampire. He is hobbled by garlic and pushed away with a cross. He is subject to a stake in the heart, fire, sunlight, and decapitation. He is strong but cannot fly. He has prominent fangs. He is distinguished by his conscience and his love for his wife, both retained from his human days.

Two years after his transformation, he returns to Kaiserlautern to find Rovena. His wife is in limbo. She has never drunk blood, and Morrisey hopes that if he can get to Rovena, his wife can be brought back to normal. However, before he can locate Rovena, he is found by **Dr. Lichtenstein** and his cohort, Axel, both vampire hunters. They have tracked Morrisey in the belief that he can lead them to Rovena. They make a deal to track her together.

Morrisey figures out that Rovena is in her castle at Chiemsee, a small town not far from Salzburg. Joining them for the trip is Morrisey's wife, Merete, and **Angus Bender,** a six-year-old boy transformed into a vampire 56 years ago. Angus hopes that by killing Rovena, he will begin to age again.

After all arrive at the castle, Rovena takes Merete prisoner and offers Morrisey a choice of seeing her transformation completed or watching her die. In fact, she wants Morrisey as her eternal companion and to achieve that end takes him to her bed. He seizes the opportunity and kills her. Lichtenstein, however, doesn't trust his vampire partner and decapitates Morrisey, leaving his body in Rovena's castle to rot. Lichtenstein fails to account for Angus, however, who remains behind in the castle when everyone else leaves. He puts Morrisey's head back in place and pushes the body into the pool of blood that Rovena has accumulated from previous killings. As Lichtenstein moves away from the castle contemplating his future, Morrisey seems to be pulling himself together.

Morrisey first appears as a character in 1989 in the comic book *Graphique Musique.*

SOURCES:

Allred, M. Dalton, and Laura Allred. *Graphique Musique.* No. 1–3. Eugene, OR: Slave Labor Graphics, 1988–90. Reprinted as *Citizen Nocturne.* Brave New Words, 1992.

Mortella

Mortella is the lamia (i.e., female vampire) featured as a villain in the DC comic book series *The Warlord.* Travis Walton, the Warlord, lives in a timeless mythological sword-and-sorcery world. He is traveling on mammoths through the frozen lands of the East when he and his traveling companions learn of Mortella.

Many centuries ago Mortella wreaked havoc in the towns and villages of Skartaris. She appears as a young woman with pale skin and long black hair. She wears a skimpy red outfit with a gold necklace and cape. Her amulet emits power that allows her to raise the dead. Although the people she resurrects can be dispatched relatively easily with a stake, Mortella is herself immortal. At one point, however, she is overcome and staked. Not ultimately killed or destroyed, she is at least laid to rest, and to prevent further trouble, her body is carried to the frozen lands of the East. A shaman is placed in charge of seeing that she never rises again. Her amulet is buried elsewhere and a tree grows over the spot.

As Walton passes through the land, one of his party, ignorant of what he was doing, discovers Mortella's corpse and removes the stake. He is immediately bitten and turned into her minion. She then moves to retrieve her amulet. Within a short time she kills or captures all of the Warlord's party. Given a second chance to fight her, Walton impales her. She merely pulls out the stake. He finally figures out that the amulet is the only weapon truly effective against her. He grabs it, and when he turns it on her, it saps her power. Defeated, she transforms into a bat with her remaining strength and flies away. She is rendered essentially powerless as long as her amulet is kept away from her.

SOURCES:

Fleisher, Michael, and Ron Randall. "The Cold Night of the Undead." *Warlord* 108 (August 1986).

————. "The Revenge of the Vampire." *Warlord* 109 (September 1986).

Murray, Cousin

Cousin Murray makes his appearance in the junior novel *A Vampire Named Murray* (1995). He suddenly appears one day at the Brooklyn, New York, home of the Kaufmans, announcing that he is their cousin from the obscure land of Vulgaria, the smallest country in the world. He wears formal clothes set off with a white bow tie, a black cape, white gloves, and a baseball cap from Miami. The Kaufman twins, Kelly and Kevin, bond with him immediately, and after some initial reluctance the Kaufmans invite Murray to stay in the room in the attic. There he sets up his white-satin-lined coffin and his secret stash of V-8 juice.

Murray's appearance is distinguished by his red lips, fangs, and pointed beard. He is a centuries-old vampire, although he never says exactly how many centuries old. Unlike typical vampires, Cousin Murray is allergic to blood (especially his own) and is, in fact, a strict vegetarian. His favorite food substance is V-8 juice (and other red fluids) and he carries a briefcase full of juice cans around with him to ensure a hearty supply. He uses his fangs to punch holes in the cans. He never eats sweets, for every vampire knows sugar causes tooth decay.

Mr. Kaufman decides that if Murray is going to stay, he needs a job, so he assigns him to the mailroom of his clothing manufacturing company. However, his Vulgarian clothes immediately catch the attention of Kaufman's designer, who suggests that plummeting sales could be reversed with a new line of evening clothes based on Murray's attire. As host of the popular "Murray Look," Cousin Murray is a walking fashion statement. Meanwhile, he seems to have found his calling in life, as a stand-up comedian for children. They love his appearance, his manner, and his corny jokes.

As the plot continues, Murray's family in Vulgaria are repulsed by the idea of the "Murray Look" and urge Murray to return to his homeland. Since Murray is reluctant to leave New York, they confront him while he is entertaining children in a local hospital. Their presence causes a scene grand enough to persuade Murray's family to return home and allow him to go on with his life in America.

SOURCES:

Miller, Judi. *A Vampire Named Murray.* New York: Bantam, 1991.

Nadja

Nadja, the daughter of **Count Dracula,** appears in the independent film *Nadja* (1995). Some 200 years ago, Count Dracula fell in love with a simple Romanian peasant girl, one of his rare relationships with a human. She resided near the shores of the Black Sea in the shadows of the Carpathian Mountains. She became pregnant by Dracula and bore him two children, the twins Nadja and Edgar. Unfortunately, she died in childbirth. Grief-stricken, Dracula withdrew even more than he had previously. He was a distant father, giving his children little warmth or time.

Nadja grows up to be a vampire. By the beginning of the 1990s, she has moved to New York City, where she lives with her slave Renfield. Though they rarely see each other, her brother and father also live in the city. They are opposed by Van Helsing, a descendent of **Abraham Van Helsing.** He tracks down Dracula and stakes him, for which he is promptly arrested by the police. Nadja, using her hypnotic powers, goes to the morgue and reclaims the body. She removes the stake from the heart and has her father's body cremated. She keeps the ashes.

Shortly after her father's death, she meets a woman in a coffee shop. They go back to her apartment and she seduces the woman. The woman turns out to be married to Van Helsing's nephew. Through her, Van Helsing is finally able to find Nadja and kill her by decapitating her and burning her body. However, before that happens she transfers her consciousness and her spirit to one of her victims and continues to live through her.

Nero, Jerry

Jerry Nero, a pot-smoking vampire living in San Francisco, was introduced in the *Tales of Jerry*, a series of underground comic books written and drawn by Jane O. Oliver, beginning in 1978. In San Francisco, Jerry appears to be a young man with

DESTROYING THE VAMPIRE— WITH STYLE

What's a writer to do? Justice demands that most bloodsuckers meet their end. With 50 vampire novels coming out every year, there are only so many ways to dispatch a vampire utilizing the all too familiar traditional means: a stake in the heart, fire, or sunlight. For whatever reason, writers have come to prefer the purely modern anti-vampire tool, sunlight, as the means of death (sunlight wasn't introduced until 1920 by F.W Murnau in his silent classic *Nosferatu*). Even when the noble vampire decides to commit suicide, he or she almost always chooses the light of the sun to end his or her eternal agony. Despite the seeming sameness of vampire deaths, a few writers and movie makers have risen to the challenge and gone beyond the norm.

Blacula was staked with style. Upon his reawakening in *Scream, Blacula, Scream*, he became involved in voodoo and was killed when a priestess drove a stake into the Blacula voodoo doll. In a similar manner, Gustav DeCobra placed his foul vampire's heart in a grandfather clock, where its beat could harmonize with the clock's ticking. Thus, he survived when Batman impaled him, but not for long. Batman solved the puzzle and used a bow and arrow to shoot the heart where it was hidden in the clock, killing DeCobra.

The cross is a traditional defense against vampires because it is the most easily utilized tool of the sacred world, but their are others. In *Fright Night II*, Belle, the shape-changing vampire minion of Regine, learns that the hard way when he turns into a panther. He leaps at vampire hunter Peter Vincent, who promptly wraps him in a sacred altar cloth. Surrounded by the holy material, he dies instantly.

Adolph Hitler, who appeared as a vampire in the novel *Night of the Dragon's Blood*, met a unique end. Bullets didn't stop him, and he survived other seemingly fatal wounds, but he finally succumbed when he was pushed into a swimming pool that was filled with piranha.

long hair, basically a typical California hippy. In reality, Jerry was born on February 13, A.D. 1200 as Lorenzo de Ponte Nero, the son and heir of Duke Paolo de Ponte Nero. As Lorenzo, he experiences a fairly normal childhood for that time period and is trained to be a knight. However, his life is unfulfilled because women avoid him as a result of a prophecy that was once foretold about him: "Death he shall not see, a living man he shall not be."

One evening, on his way home from a tournament, he encounters a beautiful young woman, Lady Montini, who asks him to be her champion. Smitten by the first woman to show an interest in him, he does not realize that she is a vampire. She attacks Lorenzo and his family, turning the young man into a vampire, killing his father, and driving his mother Eugenie to suicide. Somehow he manages to kill Lady Montini after she kills his father. With the death of his parents, he inherits his father's title. He remains in Italy for several centuries, at first trying to discover a way out of his condition. His desire to be human again even leads him on a pilgrimage to the Holy Land and a journey to the underworld; nothing helps. In his travels, he does have several interesting encounters, befriending another young vampire named Vlad, who is of course the legendary **Count Dracula,** and fighting alongside Caesar Borgia.

Lorenzo moves to the New World in 1799 when he travels to New Orleans, where he meets a vampire named Lansat and his associate Lazlo. He remains in America, eventually takes the name Jerry Nero, and settles in San Francisco, where most of his story takes place. His best friend is Mort Mindblown, a mortal, and he also associates with a small circle of vampires who also live in the city. For a brief period he plays guitar in a band called the Undead. In the mid 1980s, a researcher who wants to study vampires obtains a clip of his hair and clones a second Jerry. The experiences of Jerry and his clone are told in a series of loosely connected graphic art short stories.

Jerry is a traditional vampire. He has prominent fangs, He reacts adversely to garlic, holy water, and crosses. He has great strength and can change into various animal forms or into mist. His image does not register on film or in a mirror, and he casts no shadow. He is nocturnal and sleeps in a coffin. Jerry actually seems to fit right into the San Francisco counterculture by meditating and smoking pot. His story seems to have ended in 1993 with the death of creator Jane Oliver. Several people have vowed to continue Jerry's story, but as of 1998, none had done so.

SOURCES:
Oliver, Jane O. *Tales of Jerry.* No. 1–14. San Francisco: Karma Comix Production, 1978–1993.

Nocturna

Nocturna (portrayed by Nai Bonet) is the star of a 1979 low-budget comedy of the same name. In the film, she is the granddaughter of **Count Dracula.** After 126 years of life, the youthful vampire decides that it is time to have her own life, especially in light of the fact that the Dracula family has fallen on hard times. In the Transylvania she grew up in, royalty, especially vampire royalty, were no longer appreciated. Castle Dracula had been turned into Hotel Transylvania and was overrun with staff and guests. Count Dracula (John Carradine) was feeling his age and each evening as he arose from his coffin, he had to fish his false fangs from the glass in which they soaked.

Bored, Nocturna develops a relationship with Jimmy, a musician with a disco group who is staying at the hotel. He invites her to his room to hear a record the group had cut, and, against her father's advice about hanging around with mortals, she decides to return to the United States with him.

Not having told Jimmy that she is a vampire, she does not stay at his apartment. She connects with the thriving vampire community that lives in the city and they offer her a free coffin. She also attends a meeting of Blood Suckers of America, the local vampire organization that helps vampires deal with the problems they face living in a modern, urban world. The main problem is that too many pollutants are getting into the blood stream of the city's population, which of course is their food. They also have to develop creative means of avoiding the violence that traditionally accompanies their feeding. The meeting ends when a policeman overhears their discussion and all the vampires turn into bats and fly away.

Nocturna is thrilled with the nightlife in New York. When she writes a letter to her grandfather and tells him what fun she is having, he becomes alarmed and comes to New York to take her back home. However, once there, he finds an obstinate daughter who lives with the hope that her love will make her normal so she can live as a mortal.

Nai Bonet as Nocturna, the female vampire from the 1979 low-budget comedy of the same name.

Nothing

Nothing, a contemporary punk vampire, is the central character in Poppy Z. Brite's 1992 novel, *Lost Souls*. He was born in the mid-1970s. His father is Zillah, a 100-year-old vampire. While partying with his cohorts Twig and Molochai at a bar in the French Quarter of New Orleans run by an even older vampire, Christian, Zillah meets a teenaged girl named Jessy, who is infatuated with vampires. Jessy approaches the trio, and Zillah ends up taking her to bed in Christian's meager living quarters above the bar. Zillah disappears after impregnating Jessy, and the fair-haired Nothing arrives nine months later. As was common to vampires in Brite's fantasy world, Jessy dies while delivering her first-born. Christian takes the baby to Maryland and leaves him with a family to be raised as one of their own.

Growing up in Maryland, Nothing gravitates to the high school's fringe crowd, which thrives on sex, drugs, and weird music. Even there, though, he does not feel like he really belongs. Thus he leaves home and heads for the small town of Missing Mile, North Carolina, drawn there by a cassette tape of music he likes. Along the way he drinks his first blood, from a biker who picked him up as he hitchhiked south. Then, coincidentally, he is picked up by Zillah, Molochai, and Twig. The three vampires have no idea who Nothing is, but they agree to take him to Missing Mile. They actually plan to just toy with their passenger before feeding on him, but they quickly realize he is different. They are especially impressed when he readily drinks down the wine-blood mixture they share with him. Instead of becoming a victim, Nothing becomes Zillah's lover.

In Missing Mile, they meet up with Christian, who has moved there and become a bartender. When the 383-year-old vampire meets Nothing and learns his unusual name, he confirms his lineage by repeating the brief message he wrote on the note that he left with the baby when he dropped him off in Maryland. By this time, the Nothing and the other four vampires have become entangled in a conflict with the rock band that had recorded the song that drew Nothing to Missing Mile. The group decides to leave the conflict behind them (so they think) and head back to New Orleans, where they rent the very room where Nothing had been born.

Nothing's enjoyment of New Orleans is short-lived. Soon after settling in, he goes out exploring the city and meets Jessy's father. Refusing to admit that Nothing is his grandchild, the old man tries to kill him. Zillah saves Nothing by killing the old man, but when he and Nothing drink the man's blood, they become ill because the man was dying of cancer. Thus they are not at their best when they are attacked by the members of the band from Missing Mile, who they thought they had left behind. The band breaks into the poorly guarded room where the vampires sleep and manage to kill Zillah and Christian. Molochai, Twig, and Nothing escape, and Molochai and Twig decide to make Nothing their new leader. In the death of his father, Nothing finally becomes somebody.

Zillah and the other vampires are nontraditional creatures. They don't have real fangs, but they file their teeth to give them sharp points for biting. They are not

A bored Nocturna (portrayed by Nai Bonet) helps her aging grandfather—Count Dracula.

supernatural, nor are they repulsed by religious symbols. They also cannot shapeshift. They can eat normal food, but they prefer alcoholic beverages. They were not the true undead, but rather they are of a different race than humans. Zillah is sensitive to sunlight, but Nothing, just coming into his vampiric existence, is only mildly bothered. He wears sunglasses to combat his discomfort.

SOURCES:

Brite, Poppy Z. *Lost Souls.* New York: Asylum, 1992. Reprint, New York: Dell, 1992.

Opoltscheska, Duchess

The Duchess Opoltscheska, a displaced member of an Eastern European aristocratic family, lives in the small Belgian city of Saint-Guitton during the 1920s. In the years after World War I, she takes an interest in the city's old cemetery, which has been unused since the beginning of the century. She offers to buy the land from the impoverished town if the town agrees to two conditions. First, she would construct a mausoleum for herself on the land, and no one else could be buried in the cemetery after her. Second, the grounds would need to be protected by three guardians, two of whom would be the duchess's former servants. The servants would hire and supervise the third guardian. After the city accepts her modest conditions and generous offer, her palatial mausoleum is constructed, and the wall around the cemetery is raised to three times its previous height.

The duchess dies soon after the mausoleum is completed. The caretakers immediately take charge of the cemetery and, over the next eight years, hire a series of drifters to assist them. The duchess, glassy eyed, white-haired, and possessed of a toothy grin and claw-like fingers, walks the cemetery at midnight each evening. She visits the caretakers' cottage and feeds off of their latest transient assistant. She is cold to the touch. She lies on top of her victims, bites their necks, and sucks their blood. The victims would wake having experienced it all as a dream, but wondering about the neck wound that would not heal.

The duchess exists this way for eight years, until one of the hirelings, having found the graves of the previous assistants, figures out what is happening. The next time the duchess attacks, the assistant kills her in a most unorthodox manner by shooting her with a revolver.

Orlock, Graf

The vampire Graf Orlock (also known as Count Orlock; variations on his last name include Orlok, Orlac, or Orloc) first appears in the 1922 German silent film *Nosferatu, Eine Symphonie des Garuens*. *Nosferatu* was an attempt to adapt the story of Bram Stoker's *Dracula* to the screen, but in such a way that the book, still very much in copyright, would be disguised. Director Frederich W. Murnau changed the title, the setting, and the names of all of the leading characters of the novel. He also offered a very different image of **Count Dracula** from the one that was later used in the *Dracula* stage play of the 1920s and the famous Bela Lugosi film made in 1931. His image of Dracula/Graf Orlock veered in the direction of the traditional monster, a creature which clearly was not human in any way.

In the movie, the leading characters regularly consult a book called *The Book of Vampires*. From that they learn that the first vampire was born in 1443. Four hundred years later, one of the earliest vampires (perhaps even the very first one) decides to move from his castle in rural Transylvania to Bremen, Germany. To that end, he contacts a real estate agent named Knock, who sends one of his employees, Waldemar Hutter, to Transylvania with the sales agreement. When he first appears, with a cap covering his bald head and ears, the full horror of Orlock's appearance is not yet evident. It soon will be.

Murnau's interpretation of Dracula presents Orlock as a rodent-like creature with a bald head, large pointed ears, bushy eyebrows, a hawk-like nose, and fangs in the center of his mouth rather than extended canine teeth. He has extremely long, claw-like fingers. Except when he is about to attack, his hands remain at his side and he walks with slow, deliberate steps. Unlike Dracula, he casts a shadow and his image is reflected in glass. There is an aura of the supernatural about him as doors mysteriously open and close and he appears and disappears at will. There is also the hint of death in his prominent eyes, each of which has a black circle around it. Orlock sleeps in a coffin with Transylvanian dirt, the unconsecrated soil assisting in the preservation of his powers. He has hypnotic powers with both humans and animals, especially rats.

After working out the transfer of property, Orlock leaves Hutter behind and catches a ship bound for Bremen. Along the way, he kills all of the sailors on the ship. Landing in Bremen, he disembarks along which the hundreds of rats who have made the journey with him. A short time later, an outbreak of the plague was reported. (There actually was an outbreak of plague in Bremen in 1838.) Again from *The Book of Vampires*, Hutter's wife, Ellen, learns that the way to kill a vampire is the sacrifice of a pure woman. She must offer herself willingly, allow the vampire to feed, and keep him until dawn.

Graf Orlock also differed from Dracula in that he was a totally nocturnal creature. He did not have the power to move about in the daytime—the sunlight was deadly. Although Dracula's powers were somewhat limited in the daytime, and he preferred the evening, Dracula had no problem moving around London in the daylight. However, by making him a nocturnal creature, Murnau invented a new way to kill a vampire—expose him to the daylight. Orlock is destroyed when he steps in front of an open window and disintegrates.

Murnau changed Dracula, but not enough to keep Stoker's widow from suing for copyright infringement. She won her case, and most copies of the film were destroyed as part of the settlement. Those that survived were not shown again in public until the 1960s. Thus it is difficult to assess *Nosferatu*'s impact prior to its rerelease. In 1944, **Armand Tesla,** the Dracula-like vampire portrayed by Bela Lugosi in *The Return of the Vampire,* burned up in the sunlight. Far more than *Nosferatu,* that movie seemed to have effectively introduced the idea of a totally nocturnal vampire being destroyed by the sunlight. While its early impact cannot be measured, Graf Orlock has emerged as a significantly influential figure in the development of the vampire in the last generation. The idea that sunlight kills a vampire has become a standard insight concerning vampires, and numerous movies, books, and short stories have chosen the sunlight as the deadly force that brings down the vampire.

The frightening vampire Graf Orlock from the 1922 silent film *Nosferatu.*

THE RETURN OF ORLOCK: Because of the lengthy legal proceedings during Florence Stoker's life, it was not until the 1960s that copies of *Nosferatu* began to circulate. However, enough was known about its plot that it possibly affected the ending of Hammer Films' first Dracula production, *Horror of Dracula* (1958), in which Van Helsing kills Dracula by pulling a cover from a window to let in the morning sun. The character Graf Orlock did not reappear until 1979, when *Nosferatu: the Vampyre,* a new version of the old film, was made with Klaus Kinski assuming the title role. The new movie was written, produced, and directed by Werner Herzog. It keeps the distinctive portions of the original *Nosferatu* storyline, but it more clearly acknowledges that it was based on *Dracula,* in part by using the names of the characters in Stoker's novel.

Nosferatu: the Vampyre was one of four important vampire movies released in 1979. Two others were for the big screen: *Love at First Bite,* the Dracula spoof with George Hamilton, and *Dracula* (1979), starring Frank Langella (and in which Dracula was killed by the sunlight). The last one was a made-for-television adaptation of Stephen King's *'Salem's Lot.* It included a Graf Orlock-like vampire, **Kurt Barlow.**

Orlock did not appear again until 1991, when three different comic book companies, each trying to capitalize on the renewed interest in vampires, issued comic

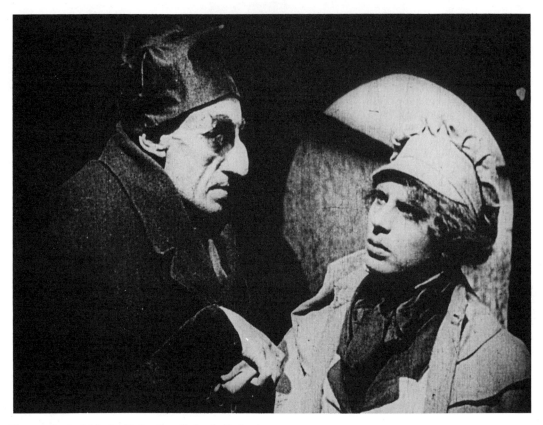

The vampire Graf Orlock with Jonathan Harker in *Nosferatu*.

books inspired by Orlock. The first of these, issued by Tome Press in 1991, was a straight adaptation of the 1922 movie. *Nosferatu* (1991), issued by Dark Horse Comics, is the translation of an apocalyptic vampire tale by French writer Philip Druillet that features an Orlock-like character. There is little obvious connection to *Dracula* in Druillet's work, which was also translated into German.

Also in 1991, Millennium Publications issued a four-part series called *Nosferatu* in which author Mark Ellis provided a complete story of Graf Orlock's existence quite apart from the *Dracula* legend and brought Orlock's menace into the present. In Ellis's tale, Graf Orlock is an eleventh-century nobleman whose estate is in the Carpathians. He becomes a vampire, but he is eventually killed and his body is sealed in the castle. Returning from the Crusades, an English knight stops at the castle. His squire frees Orlock, who is once again able to move about freely in human society. The knight, William Longsword, is bitten by Orlock and turned into a vampire. The series tracks Orlock throughout history as he perpetuates his evil, causing wars and bringing down plagues. Longsword, who has spent the centuries tracking down and fighting Orlock, finally catches up with him in contemporary Brooklyn, where a group of plague victims has been discovered. The story ends in a final conflagration in which Orlock is killed, but not before he passes on his undead condition.

SOURCES:

Ellis, Mark. *Nosferatu: Plague of Terror.* No. 1–4. St. Paul, MN: Millennium Comics, 1991–92.

Druillet, Philip. *Nosferatu.* Milwaukee, OR: Dark Horse Comics, 1991.

Monette, Paul. *Nosferatu: the Vampyre.* New York: Avon Books, 1979.

Nosferatu: A Symphony of Shadows, a Symphony of Shudders. No. 1–2. Plymouth, MI: Tome Press, 1991.

Skal, David J. *Hollywood Gothic.* New York: W. W. Norton & Company, 1990.

Orlok, Byron

Byron Orlok (portrayed by Robert Vaughn), named for **Graf Orlock** from the classic Dracula movie, *Nosferatu* (1922), is the antagonist in the 1989 horror spoof, *Transylvania Twist.* Byron Orlok is the younger brother of Marinus Orlok, who lives in a castle near Handsburg, Transylvania. They are descended from an illustrious family of rogues, although Byron is the black sheep of the present generation. He tortured animals as a child and was an even bigger trouble-maker as a teenager. As a result, Marinus banned him from the castle. Byron spent the next 50 years of his life looking for *The Book of Ulthar*, a textbook of magical spells.

When Marinus is reported dead, friends and family gather at the castle, including Byron. Also on hand are Marinus's daughter Marissa, young librarian Dexter Ward, and Marinus's old friend, vampire hunter **Victor Van Helsing.** It seems that Ward is there strictly on business—20 years earlier Marinus checked *The Book of Ulthar* out of the library at Arkham, Massachusetts (note the sly references to H.P. Lovecraft) and never returned it. The group is met by a castle attendant and three vampire brides.

The Book of Ulthar was written by an ancient sorcerer who had cast a spell that banished the Evil One to the outer realms. In the book is a counter-spell that will release the Evil One if the spell is ever spoken out loud. Byron is intent upon reading the incantation, but is staked just in time to prevent the return of the Evil One. However, in the meantime Van Helsing falls victim to the three vampire women and discovers that being a bloodsucker isn't such a bad life after all.

Klaus Kinski resurrected the terrifying vampire Graf Orlock in the 1979 remake of *Nosferatu.*

Pandemonium, Santanico

Santanico Pandemonium, a leader among the community of vampires in Quentin Tarantino's book (later made into a film) *From Dusk to Dawn* (1995), is a dancer at the Titty Twister, a sleazy bar just across the Mexican border. Outwardly a nightspot catering to bikers and truckers, the Titty Twister is actually run by a group of vampires who live off of both the blood and possessions of the patrons.

Santanico is a sensual and seductive Latino, with long dark hair and dark eyes. Her costume is a bikini ornamented with a hair piece and a large albino snake. Introduced as the "Epitome of Evil" and the "Mistress of the Macabre" her sensuous dance draws in the predominantly male audience like moths to a flame.

Of indeterminate age, her end comes the night that Seth and Richie Gecko arrive. The Gecko brothers are robbers and killers on the run. They agree to meet their contact, who offers them sanctuary at the Titty Twister, and once they arrive they feel safe. Richie is completely taken by Santanico's dance, especially when she jumps on their table, and begins a sensual dance exchange with her body, Richie, and a bottle of whiskey.

Richie might simply have had a delightful sensual experience had it not been for his wounded hand. However, in a fight with another patron, the wound is opened and blood flows. Santanico is now the one entranced. Suddenly, she morphes into a lizardlike bat creature with prominent fangs and bites Richie. A single bite from her snakelike fangs are enough to turn her victim into a creature of the night.

Seth pulls his revolver and shoots Santanico. She drops off Richie as if dead. Suddenly, vampires of all kinds—dancers, bartenders, bouncers—appear everywhere, and all the patrons are caught up in the fight. The bullets but a momentary nuisance, Santanico comes back to life and turns her attention to Seth as he lies on the floor. Seth

A scene from the film version of Quentin Tarantino's *From Dusk til Dawn,* which featured the stripper/vampire Santanico Pandemonium.

turns his gun on the chandelier above Santanico and shoots the supports that keep it in place. Santanico is impaled by the sharp points of the chandelier.

SOURCES:
Tarantino, Quentin. *From Dusk to Dawn.* New York: Miramax Books, 1995.

Pandora

The vampire Pandora is a lesser character in Anne Rice's *Vampire Chronicles*, the several novels that have become key words in the revival of interest in vampires in the 1990s. She is beautiful, tall, and brown-haired. When the vampire **Marius** meets her, she is a Greek courtesan. The two immediately fall in love, but Pandora seems to have an underlying motive. She claims that she was once a vampire who was destroyed at the time the original vampires, **Akasha** and **Enkil,** were placed in the sun in an attempt to kill them. She perished, but has since reincarnated as a mortal. She talks Marius into turning her into a vampire.

Marius is the guardian of the original vampires, and he is at his sanctuary on one of the Greek islands when he transforms Pandora. He also allows her to drink some of Akasha's blood. Subsequently, they stay together for 200 years, and she assists him in caring for "those who must be kept." However, their relationship eventually comes to an end, and over the next centuries he sees her only twice, including a brief meeting in Dresden, East Germany.

The last time they meet, Pandora tracks Marius to his secret sanctuary some days after Akasha has awakened and begun her campaign to take over the world. Marius has been buried in the ice and snow, and with fellow vampire **Santino**'s help, Pandora rescues him to join the confederation of vampires who stand against Akasha. After Akasha's death, many of the vampires go to vampire **Armand**'s estate on Night Island, near Miami. Marius tries to rebuild a relationship with Pandora, but is unsuccessful.

Vampire **Lestat de Lioncourt** concludes that of those at the final confrontation with Akasha, Pandora is the only one who seems unable to recover. He believes earlier in life she had been wounded psychologically, and the trauma of Akasha's death affected her more deeply than it should have. She leaves the others' company in a depressed state.

SOURCES:

Ramsland, Katherine. *The Vampire Companion: The Official Guide to Anne Rice's The Vampire Chronicles.* New York: Ballantine Books, 1993.

Rice, Anne. *Pandora.* New York: Alfred A. Knopf, 1998.

———.*The Queen of the Damned.* New York: Alfred A. Knopf, 1988. Reprint, New York: Ballantine Books, 1989.

———. *The Vampire Lestat.* New York: Alfred A. Knopf, 1985. Reprint, New York: Ballantine Books, 1986.

Parker, David

David Parker, the subject of Michael Romkey's 1990 novel, *I, Vampire*, was born in 1959, the son of a wealthy Chicago real estate developer. Pressed by his father into a law career, he forsakes his music talents to attend Harvard and the University of Chicago Law School. He marries Clarice Luce, the daughter of a lawyer, and takes a position in her father's law firm. Their marriage does not work out, however, and in the end he is asked to leave the firm.

In 1989, as his marriage is disintegrating, he attends the opera and sees a stunning woman dressed all in white. Several day later, while sitting alone in a hotel lounge, the woman reappears and introduces herself as **Tatiana Feodorovna.** They begin a relationship that is invigorating for Parker, but strange nonetheless. Tatiana always appears after dark and never stays past dawn. Curious, Parker follows her home to a house on Chicago's Gold Coast. He finally puts all the pieces together and realizes that Tatiana is a vampire and is in fact the sole surviving daughter of Nicolas Romanov, the last czar of Russia.

She initiates the process of turning Parker into a vampire by drinking his blood and introducing the vampire virus into his system. He does not die but does undergo a tremendous physical change as the virus alters his genetic material at the cellular level. During the next two weeks, he consumes only water and discovers that the sun now hurts his eyes. To make Parker's genetic transformation complete, Tatiana reintroduces the virus to his body two weeks after the initial bite and then again two weeks after that second attack. The final genetic changes occur after the third infection.

As a new vampire, Parker does not become immortal, but his life span is greatly enhanced. He needs to feed every two weeks and for that purpose develops fangs that are retractable when not in use. He does not have to kill his victims to feed off of them. His image does reflect in mirrors. Only able to come out at night, he has heightened senses, especially hearing, and the opportunity to develop his intellect. As a vampire, he is sexually sterile. Death can only come from a massive trauma to the body

Parker is separated from Tatiana after the final bite that makes him a vampire. He has to learn to feed by himself, and in the process the blood lust overcomes him and he kills for the first and only time. He makes the decision that the blood lust will not dictate his actions and decides to leave Chicago, first moving to Las Vegas and then on to Paris. He is eventually introduced to the mystical and near-mythical group the Illuminati, who help him learn the true sweep of vampire history. The Illuminati is the guiding force in the vampire community, but it faces opposition from an evil conspiracy led by Caesar Borgia and his sister Lucretia. The siblings are plotting to take over the world, and Parker becomes deeply entangled in the intrigue. The Borgias are aided in their attempt to take over western Europe (the first part of their plan) by General Von Baden, one of the founders of the Nazi Party, and Jack the Ripper, who the book claims is really British Prince Albert Victor. Parker does not have to fight the Borgias alone however—he is aided by an interesting assortment of historical figures himself, including Rasputin and the composer Wolfgang Mozart. All are vampires.

SOURCES:

Romkey, Michael. *I, Vampire.* New York: Fawcett Gold Medal, 1990.

Pasteur, Louis

Louis Pasteur, the scientist credited with proposing the existence of microbes as the immediate cause of disease, was born in 1822 in France. After graduation from the Ecole Normale Superieure in 1847, he began his illustrious research career while serving as a professor of chemistry at several different universities. His accomplishments included inventing the process of pasteurizing milk and the discovery of the process of immunization. In 1887 he became director of the Pasteur Institute. That much, of course, is historical fact. To those who play the game *Vampire: The Masquerade*, however, Louis Pasteur has had another productive life as a vampire.

In 1890 he encounters Georges. Pasteur is interested in what appeared to be Georges natural immunity to disease. Georges hopes that the great scientist can cure him of his condition: vampirism. Pasteur hires Georges as a lab assistant, and together they begin what would turn out to be the final research project of his life. Their first success is the development of a serum that induces vampirism in a subject. Because his health is failing and he does not want to leave his research unfinished, Pasteur takes the serum himself and becomes a vampire. He "dies" on September 28, 1895 and is buried as an honored citizen of France.

Pasteur, of course, rises from his grave and begins a new life searching for the answer to vampirism. His research brings him to the attention of an elder vampire named Thaddeus, who is threatened by the possibility that Pasteur might succeed. He works secretly to destroy the vampire scientist, fearful that any direct action will attract the attention of even older, more powerful vampires. Finally, in the 1990s, Pasteur relocates to Denver, Colorado, where he assumes the name Jacob Prestor. Thaddeus then visits William, the prince of the vampires in the city, and convinces him that the reclusive Pasteur/Prestor is actually leading a conspiracy to overthrow the present ruling council of the Kindred.

Nancy Perkins (portrayed by Sandra Harrison) is the teen vampire star of the film *Blood of Dracula.*

Pasteur learns that William is intent on destroying him. To protect himself, he uses the serum to create a number of new vampires to act as his bodyguards. He doesn't want to take this step, but he is convinced that his breakthrough is near and that the men will not have to remain as vampires for very long. However, William kills Pasteur before he has time to teach the vampires how to live in their new nocturnal existence. After William kills Pasteur, he realizes that he has been tricked by Thaddeus into committing the deed. Thaddeus, of course, has already moved on.

SOURCES:
Berry, Jeff. *Alien Hunger.* Stone Mountain, GA: White Wolf, n.d.

Perkins, Nancy

Nancy Perkins (portrayed by Sandra Harrison), the teen vampire in the horror film *Blood of Dracula* (1957), provides an exploration of vampire as Neanderthal man. Her mother having recently died, Nancy is placed at Sherwood Boarding School by her just remarried father. As she acts out her frustration and anger over her mother's death, her attitude is brought to the attention of the chemistry teacher, Ms. Blanding, who believes she has found a way of unleashing a great, albeit destructive, power over the earth. This power, latent in every human being, is so horrible that, once recognized, the world would be forced into peace.

Attracted by Nancy's strong will and intense emotions, Blanding recruits her for an experiment. She hypnotizes her, ostensibly to heal an acid burn. While healing the burn, Blanding utilizes a magic amulet with powers to heal and destroy, along with a posthypnotic suggestion, to place Nancy under her control.

That evening a student is killed. Two wounds are found on her neck above the jugular vein and the blood is drained. The police are baffled, except for one officer whose suggestion of vampires is dismissed. The next evening, while the girls are in the cemetery on a scavenger hunt, Nancy transforms into a Neanderthal-like creature with two prominent fangs. She quickly dispatches one of the girls and her boyfriend, and just as quickly returns to her normal appearance in time to join the others in discovering the bodies.

During the day, she becomes upset over the surge of power and the urge to kill that seems to erupt in her, which surfaces when she almost attacks her boyfriend. She confronts Blanding and demands that Blanding release her. Blanding refuses, overjoyed at Nancy's actions, which substantiate her hypothesis. In the ensuing cat fight, both are killed, Nancy being impaled on a piece of broken furniture.

Peron, Eva

Eva Peron, the beautiful first lady of Argentina in the years after World War II, has been immortalized on stage and screen many times, but William Pridgen's novel, *Night of the Dragon's Blood* (1997), is probably the first time she has appeared as a vampire. In the novel, she has an American lover named Hi Hickenlooper during the war. She leaves him in 1944 to marry Juan Peron, who of course becomes president of the country. Hickenlooper truly loved Peron and never forgets her. He travels to Buenos Aires in 1952 to mourn her death and is startled when he thinks he sees her walking into the bar where they had first met. He goes to the public viewing of Peron's body and there he is able to confirm that the corpse on display is not Eva Peron. He confronts Juan Peron with his finding and learns that Eva was sent to Brazil to negotiate with **Adolf Hitler,** who had managed to escape Germany. She never returns from her trip to his jungle headquarters.

Hi travels to Brazil in search of Eva and discovers why she never returned—Hitler is now a vampire, as are the crack SS troops guarding the compound. It seems that when Hitler escaped from Germany, he took with him Countess Borca from Transylvania, who was really a vampire. She was happy to turn Hitler and his troops into creatures of the night. When Eva arrives at the compound, Hitler has the Countess bite her and turn her into a vampire. As a vampire, her skin becomes very pale, although she can move about in the sunlight. She is a fairly traditional vampire in that she sleeps in a coffin, is allergic to garlic, and no longer shows a reflection in mirrors. She also has retractable fangs that only appear when she is ready to feed. She gets her fresh blood from a kind of "milking" facility that Hitler has set up to drain the local peasants of their blood.

With the assistance of Juan Peron, who desperately wants his wife back, Hickenlooper launches a plan to rescue her. A plant called dragon's blood, which secretes a substance fatal to vampires, has been discovered in Transylvania. Armed with a handful of seeds, Hickenlooper travels to the compound and volunteers to join the SS troops. He is placed in charge of growing plants that are appropriate for vampires. Of course, he is turned into a vampire as a well.

Four months of intrigue follow while the plant matures. Finally, Hickenlooper is able to milk the plant and slip the dragon's blood into the blood supply used by every vampire in the compound. Almost all of the vampires are killed immediately. A few, however, including Hitler, the Countess, Eva, and Hi, do not drink the mixture. Hi and Eva then team up to kill Hitler, after which they make their escape. Instead of returning to Juan, Eva stays with Hi, and the two move to America, where they find a cure for their vampiric condition. As for Peron in Argentina, the rest of his life is documented in the history books.

SOURCES:

Pridgen, William (pseudonym of Ronald L. Ecker). *Night of the Dragon's Blood*. Palatka, FL: Hodge & Braddock, 1997.

Perne, Alisa

Alisa Perne is the youthful vampire in the continuing series of young adult novels, *The Last Vampire*. Hip 1990s Alisa is an extremely wealthy teenager who believes she is the last vampire alive. Standing five feet, two inches tall and muscular, Alisa appears to be 18 years old, although she can pass for either a high school senior or a young adult. She lives in Beverly Hills, California, but changes her identity quickly as circumstances demand.

As a vampire, she has some gold flakes in her eyes, a faint transparency to her skin, and a graceful movement about her body. She needs blood weekly, at least. After a month she becomes obsessed, but has gone as long as six months without it. She can take animal blood, if necessary, but it is unsatisfying. She also eats and digests human food. When she bites, the victim feels extremes of pleasure. A drop of her own blood heals the bite marks quickly, and the victim hardly remembers the encounter.

An older vampire, she is not greatly affected by the sun (although she prefers the night), holy objects, or garlic. She is very strong and fast, is the master of most martial arts systems, and possesses acute hearing and sight. She is immune to disease and regenerates quickly from any wounds, without scarring.

Like most modern-day vampires, she has a history. She was born by the name of Sita in ancient India over 5,000 years ago. She was but a child when a disease hit her village. Her friend Amba, eight months pregnant, was among the victims. However, instead of cremating her body, a priest took her body for a magical operation. He invoked the presence of a demon, a yakshini, into Amba. When the demon took possession, he cut a deal to have the plague removed. The demon departed, seemingly, but the child Amba was carrying suddenly showed signs of life. Cut from her body, the male child was named **Yaksha.** Yaksha grew into a handsome, intelligent young man with black hair, blue eyes, and a beguiling smile.

Meanwhile Sita had married Rama, a young man of the village, and borne a daughter. One evening Yaksha appeared to her and offered her a choice. He could drink her blood and kill her, or she could depart with him, become a vampire, and be his eternal mate. In either case she would never see her husband and child again. She chose to survive. Noting the ecstasy of the experience, she shared blood with Yaksha and joined the roving band of vampires he had already made.

The decisive event for Sita was Yaksha's challenge to battle the God-man Krishna. He lost and Krishna inflicted a high price. He set Yaksha to destroy all of the vampires he had previously made. He then made Sita promise to make no more vampires, and in return, she would be protected by his grace. Yaksha left on his mission, and Sita concluded that he had finally accomplished his task. She had heard that he had been killed during the Middle Ages, hence she was the last vampire.

However, Alisa's current existence in Beverly Hills as a high school student is disturbed by the return of Yaksha, not yet dead, who still has to complete his mission. Alisa is the last vampire he has to kill. Her task becomes assisting the nearly invulnerable Yaksha to die, while preventing his killing her. The solution to that dilemma sets the stage for a series of adventures throughout the novels, during which she breaks her promise to Krishna and makes new vampires, spends time as a mortal, and bears a new daughter, Kalika, who is even more powerful than her mother.

SOURCES:

Pike, Christopher. *The Last Vampire*. New York: Archway/Pocket Books, 1994.

———. *The Last Vampire 2: Black Blood*. New York: Archway/Pocket Books, 1994.

———. *The Last Vampire 3: Red Dice*. New York: Archway/Pocket Books, 1995.

———. *The Last Vampire 4: Phantom*. New York: Archway/Pocket Books, 1996.

———. *The Last Vampire 5: Evil Thirst*. New York: Archway/Pocket Books, 1996.

———. *The Last Vampire 6: Creatures of Forever*. New York: Archway/Pocket Books, 1996.

Principal's Wife

Though never named, the wife of the principal of a prestigious girl's school in rural Japan emerges as the key vampire in the 1975 Japanese film, *Evil of Dracula*. Vampirism had come to the area some 200 years ago when a white man was shipwrecked off the coast. He was a Christian and was tortured and forced to convert to the local religion. He renounced Christianity and spat on the cross. For those actions he was cursed and turned into a vampire. His first victim was a 15-year-old girl. After she was victimized, the villagers realized what was happening and killed the man and the girl and buried their bodies.

The movie then tells how, a century later, the pair comes back to life and begins to attack each person who takes over as principal of the girl's school, which was founded at the end of the nineteenth century. Each successive principal and his wife

Cover art from *Sheila Trent: Vampire Hunter*.

are turned into vampires. People noted the changes that came over each man and his wife after they had been at the school for some time. They would stop socializing and refuse to come out until after dark. Their skin went pale and their fingernails lengthened.

In the mid-1970s, a new psychology professor named Dr. Shiraki comes to the school. He arrives to find that the current principal's wife has just been killed in a car accident. Her body is in the basement of the school in a coffin. The principal asks Shiraki to become his successor.

His first night in the school, Shiraki sees a beautiful young woman walking around in a blue negligee with a wound on her breast. She attacks him, displaying an impressive set of fangs in the process. He later discovers that the woman is a student who had disappeared from the school some time earlier.

With the help of the school's doctor, Shiraki begins to understand that vampires are responsible for the strange occurrences at the school. Specifically, two vampires—the principal and his wife. The couple has transformed one of the schoolgirls into a vampire and has now targeted Shiraki. They hope that Shiraki and the girl will become mates so that the two older vampires can leave the school and live peacefully. Shiraki has other ideas and manages to kill the principal and his wife in a final confrontation with them, although it is not easy. Things that would kill an ordinary human or even the average vampire only slow the couple down. However, when he finally stakes them, they age rapidly before his eyes and then crumble to dust.

Purgatori

Purgatori is a demonic vampire who makes her first appearance in the March 1995 issue of the Chaos! Comics publication, *Lady Death*. She was born in ancient Egypt as a young slave girl named Sakkara. One day, the queen of Egypt, a lesbian, sees her and takes her to the palace, where she becomes a favorite in the queen's harem. However, everything changes when the queen is forced to marry the ruler of a neighboring land to gain military power to quell the unrest in her own land. Before he will marry her, the other ruler demands that the queen kill all the women in her harem. She complies, and only Sakkara manages to survive.

She escapes and makes her way to a meeting with a vampire named Kath, who is supposed to grant her immortality. She shares blood with Kath, who senses the blood of fallen angels flowing in her veins. He knows that she will be a truly unique vampire, and in fact, she emerges as the vampire creature Purgatori. A purely supernatural being, she has reddish skin, two horns, prominent fangs, and a set of bat-like wings.

Enraged at the queen's betrayal, she travels to the royal wedding and attacks the wedding party, turning several guest into vampires in the process. The new vampires become her mortal enemies. At a later date, she summons Lucifer and asks him to take her sexually. As he draws near, she unexpectedly bites him and tastes his blood. Outraged at her impudence, he banishes her to Necropolis, the city of the dead.

There, she seeks out Lady Death in the hopes that the Lady will allow her to drink her blood. Much like Lucifer, Lady Death is outraged by the audacity of Purgatori's request and banishes her back to Earth, where she is destined to walk the planet as a a lowly vampire.

Her return to Earth triggers a series of adventures detailed in other graphic novels in the series. She of course has further run-ins with Kath, as a well as battles with Jade and Kabala, two of her enemies from the wedding.

SOURCES:

Pulido, Brian. *Evil Ernie: Straight to Hell*. No. 1-5. Phoenix, AZ: Chaos! Comics, 1995-96.

———. *Lady Death*. No. 1-4. Phoenix, AZ: Chaos! Comics, 1995.

———. *Purgatori: Dracula Gambit*. Phoenix, AZ: Chaos! Comics, 1996.

Pulido, Brian, and Jim Balant. *Purgatori: The Vampires Myth*. No. 1-3. Phoenix, AZ: Chaos! Comics, 1996.

Pulido, Brian, Jim Balant, and Paul Pelletier. "Purgatori." *Chaos! Quarterly!* Phoenix, AZ: Chaos! Comics, 1995.

Quay, Sabella

Sabella Quay, a resident of the nova Mars colony at some point in the future, makes her appearance in Tanith Lee's 1980 novel, *Sabella, or the Blood Stone*. She grew up in Easterly, the daughter of an ore-blaster who was killed when she was only two years old. At the age of 11, she finds a smooth plum-sized stone with a ring at one end. Three years later, she kills the boy with whom she has her first sexual experience. It becomes a watershed experience as she comes to understand that she really is not human. She begins to menstruate earlier, but it soon ceases. She starts to wear the blood stone constantly at about the same time her mother moves the family from Easterly to Hammerhead Plateau.

Sabella is petite and beautiful, weighing 107 pounds with flowing, long black hair. While away from her secluded residence she generally wears sunglasses. Not of the undead, she is nocturnal because her blood, less opaque than human blood, is vulnerable to the rays of the sun. She does not enter a vampiric sleep nor does she sleep in a coffin. Not having a supernatural existence, she casts a shadow and reflects in mirrors. She can be killed in much the same way as her human neighbors. She has learned not to kill the men with whom she has sex and after moving to Hammerhead Plateau takes blood primarily from the deer in the nearby countryside.

At one point her mother dies of a heart attack. At a later point her Aunt Cassi dies. As her aunt has figured out that Sabella is a vampire, she leaves her niece a jeweled crucifix as part of her inheritance. For the time being, she lives on Hammerhead with her lover Jace, from whom she takes blood and whom she allows to dominate her, realizing that the victim has to be stronger than the oppressor, or he dies.

SOURCES:

Lee, Tanith. *Sabella, or the Blood Stone.* New York: Daw Books, 1980. Reprint, London: Unwin, 1987.

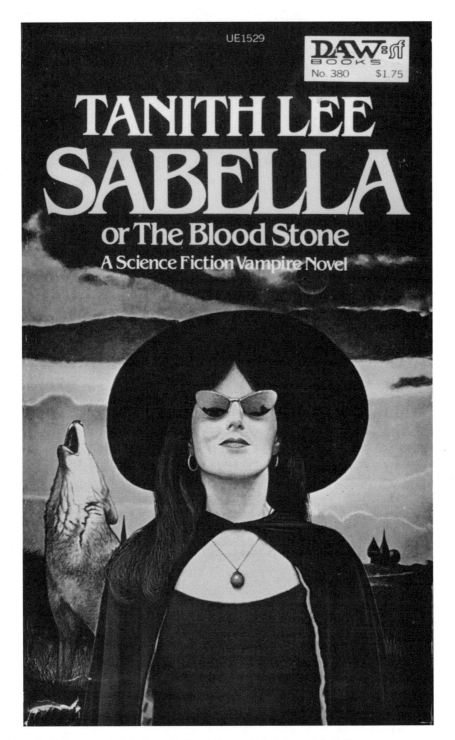

Cover art from Tanith Lee's novel, *Sabella, or the Blood Stone,* which features Sabella Quay.

Quesne, Marshall

Marshall Quesne (portrayed by Humphrey Bogart) is a medical doctor who is turned into a vampire in the film *The Return of Dr. X* (1939). Dr. X, full name Maurice Xavier, was born in 1897. He becomes a brilliant doctor but also commits a particularly heinous murder. Tried and convicted, he is executed in the electric chair in 1937. That should have been the end of the story, but Dr. Francis Flegg, a New York City physician and researcher at a large hospital, has other plans. He steals Xavier's body and uses a new technique he has discovered to revive him. The revitalized Dr. X, now known as Dr. Quesne (pronounced "cane") assists Dr. Flegg in his continuing research as a hematologist.

Quesne looks like Dr. Xavier with short dark hair. However, he now has a pasty complexion and has developed a white streak in his hair. His hand is cold to the touch. He is a completely modern vampire without a single supernatural attribute. He is not adversely affected at all by traditional vampire repellents such as garlic, sunlight, mirrors, and holy objects.

Flegg discovers that Dr. Quesne has a serious problem—his body cannot create new blood. He needs regular infusions of new blood to survive. Francis tries to create a blood substitute but is only partially successful. Quesne's blood type is quite rare, so the pool of available donors is quite rare.

When the blood supply runs short, Quesne kills one of Flegg's patients who has the same blood type and drains her blood. The woman just happens to be a famous actress, and Flegg has to act quickly to hide the crime. He discovers her body and quickly revives her, turning her into a vampire also. However, a reporter has already

Humphrey Bogart portrayed vampire Marshall Quesne in the film *The Return of Doctor X*.

seen the woman's dead body, so he begins to investigate Flegg. Flegg keeps the actress alive through transfusions, but he cannot stop Quesne from killing again.

Quesne's background is finally uncovered by the reporter as he searches through old newspaper files. Before he can go to the police, however, Quesne kidnaps a nurse known to be his blood type and heads for the site in New Jersey where he had committed the murder that sent him to the electric chair. Fortunately, the police arrive just in time to save the girl and kill Quesne. Because he is not a supernatural creature, it takes only bullets to end his life.

Radkoff, Victor Dr.

Dr. Victor Radkoff, hypnotherapist, psychoanalyst, and motivational speaker in the film *Vampire at Midnight* (1988), is killing people in Los Angeles and drinking their blood. Unknown to his clients and the many people who attend his lectures, Radkoff lives as a vampire. He sleeps all day and conducts all of his business at night. He does not sleep in a coffin, but on an elevated platform. He has fangs that show when he opens his mouth. Radkoff uses his work to attract potential victims, whom he hypnotizes and then gives a necklace with a single heart-shaped stone to as a visible sign that ties them together.

Radkoff has a nemesis in Roger Sutter, a no-nonsense officer with the Los Angeles Police Department. Assigned to the murders, he slowly comes to the conclusion that he is facing a vampire, and that his girlfriend is on Radkoff's hit list. She is a young pianist who is attracted to Radkoff in the hopes that he can help her with her career. She has been blocked in her skill development. Radkoff hypnotizes her and gives her a necklace.

Carelessness in retrieving one of the necklaces becomes the means of Sutter's finally tying the otherwise unrelated victims together. Sutter's understanding of the mundane is finally sustained when the vampire he is chasing turns out to be merely a common, if kinky, serial killer. Radkoff has artificial fangs and lives in a fantasy world as a vampire. He carries a knife hidden in his sleeve to dispatch his victims. Having discovered the truth, Sutter must now track him down and arrest him. Given Radkoff's ability as a hypnotist, confining him is no simple feat.

Radu

Radu is the evil vampire in the *Subspecies* series of movies, the first vampire movies out of post-Ceausescu Romania. Radu first appears in the film *Subspecies* (1990) and his further adventures are recounted in two sequels, *Bloodlust: Subspecies II* (1993) and *Bloodlust: Subspecies III* (1995), and in four issues of the *Subspecies* comic book.

Poster art for *Vampire at Midnight,* which featured the villian Dr. Victor Radkoff.

The son of King Vladimir, an old Transylvanian vampire, Vladimir has two sons: Radu, the elder and the product of his coupling with a sorceress, under whose spell he had fallen; and Stefan, a product of his love with a mortal. As Radu grows to manhood, Vladimir sees him as an evil person and banishes his son and his mother from the family castle.

Radu is a Nosferatu-like vampire with white skin, elongated fingers, red lips, and prominent rodentlike fangs. He is unable to move incognito into human society, as is Stefan. He is strong and extremely fast. He can transform himself into other forms and fly. However, he is bound to the night, and secretly sleeps deep in Castle Vladislav during the day. He is vulnerable to fire and impalement, although he is very hard to kill.

It is now the 1990s, and Radu has returned to the castle. He seeks the blood stone, Vladimir's most precious possession. Several centuries ago, he had learned that the Pope possessed the object which dripped the blood of the saints of the ages. A gypsy stole it and gave it to Vladimir. In the blood stone, Vladimir has a blood source which allows him to live in peace with his nonvampire neighbors. He fears, with some basis, that in Radu's hands, the blood stone will be used to augment his evil and end the placid community relationships. Vladimir has his son imprisoned, but he escapes with the assistance of some demonic helpers, the subspecies. He then kills the king with a knife and steals the blood stone.

Radu's attention is drawn to three woman, graduate students studying vampire folklore among the people who reside near Castle Vladislav. His plans to vampirize them are blocked by Stefan who has discovered his father's body. With the aid of a local confidant, Stefan assembles weapons—a blackthorn spear, oak stakes, an axe, and a shotgun filled with rosary beads—to pursue his brother.

In their confrontation, Radu is dispatched, staked, and decapitated. Unfortunately, two of the women have been killed. Michelle, the third, has fallen in love with Stefan, who transforms her into a vampire. However, they had not counted on the subspecies who emerge to assist the fallen Radu. While Stefan and Michelle sleep, they reattach Radu's head and remove the stake. The revived Radu kills Stefan. Before he can dispatch the beautiful Michelle, however, she awakens, takes the blood stone, and escapes to Bucharest.

While Michelle becomes acclimated to vampiric life, Radu visits his mother, who lives quietly in Bucharest. He promises her the blood stone, but wants Michelle for a plaything. She gives him some instructions for disposing of the bodies of Michelle's friends and tells him to wait until the full moon to move against her.

Radu is now set to claim the blood stone and Michelle. In their first encounter, aided by her sister Rebecca, Michelle is successful in again impaling Radu and in setting his mother on fire. However, it is not so easy to dispose of the resilient Radu. He comes back to capture Michelle and the blood stone, and Rebecca must call upon all of the local powers—a learned scholar, an American counsel, a Bucharest policeman—to assist her. In a confrontation inside Castle Vladislav, Michelle empties a clip of silver bullets into Radu. He is slowed but not stopped and pursues the group who have coaxed Michelle to join them. In his attempt to at least regain the blood stone, he is lured into the dawning rays of the sun only to be consumed in flames. Again he appears to have been ultimately dispatched, but the subspecies find the blood stone which had been tossed over the castle wall. Thus, hope for Radu's revival remains at the end of the first film, setting the stage for more Radu adventures in the *Subspecies* sequels.

SOURCES:

Subspecies. No. 1–4. Malibu, CA: Eternity, 1991.

Rakosi, Bela

Bela Rakosi is a traditional Eastern European aristocratic vampire patterned to a large extent after Bela Lugosi 's interpretation of **Count Dracula** in the 1931 movie *Dracula*. He first appears in the 1972 series of the Italian comic book *Zagor Gigante* (No. 85) in a story spread over three issues. Having emigrated from his native Hungary to the American West, Rakosi encounters Zagor, a hero figure of the American frontier. Zagor discovers the richly furnished wagon in which Rakosi's coffin travels; nearby is the body of a man with two puncture wounds in his neck. Eventually the coffin is unloaded at an isolated mansion and a short time later Zagor and his companions meet Rakosi for the first time.

Like Dracula, Rakosi dresses formally, with a cape. He has fangs. A totally nocturnal creature, he sleeps in a coffin, doesn't show a reflection in mirrors and is repelled by the cross. He can also transform into a bat. Slowly Zagor figures out that Rakosi is a vampire and waits for him when he returns to his coffin as dawn approaches. Rakosi is killed when the sunlight hits him.

In 1981, an old servant of Rakosi magically recalls the vampire to life. Rakosi spreads terror in the imaginary Western city of Bergville until he is again destroyed by Zagor.

Both Zagor and Bela Rakosi were created by Guido Nolitta (pseudonym of Sergio Bonelli). The three "Zagor Contro il Vampiro" ("Zagor vs. the Vampire") issues were authored by Nolitta and drawn by Gallieno Ferri. The original account of Zagor's encounter with Rakosi was collected in 1995 in a single hardcover volume.

SOURCES:

Castelli, Alfredo, and Gallieno Ferri, "Il ritorno del vampiro." *Zagor Gigante*. No. 238–240. Milan: 1981.

Nolitta, Guido, and Gallieno Ferri, "Alba Tragica" *Zagor Gigante*. No. 87. Milan: Sept. 1972.

———. "Angoscia!" *Zagor Gigante*. No. 85. Milan: July 1972.

———. "Zagor contro il vampiro." *Zagor Gigante*. No. 86. August 1972.

———. *Zagor contro il vampiro*. Milan: Mondadori, 1995.

Rampling, Julie

Julie Rampling is the mistress of Rampling Gate, a mansion in rural England, in Anne Rice 's short story "The Master of Rampling Gate" (1984). Julie was born around 1867 at Rampling Gate, the family mansion located a short distance from the town of Rampling, some five hours by train from Victoria Station in London, but, along with her brother Richard, was brought to London where she grew up. She has one prominent memory from her childhood. She was six years old when on a train at Victoria Station, she saw the face of a handsome young man in the window. Her enraged father reacted. He labeled the man an unspeakable horror. For her, the face became the ideal of masculine beauty. As Julie grows to womanhood and becomes a poet and writer, her memory lingers.

In 1888 her father dies, and upon his deathbed makes a final request to Richard that he demolish the house. Reluctant to follow through on the request, Richard and Julie move back to Rampling Gate, and as their pleasant days pass they are more and more convinced that they should not destroy the mansion. Then one evening, Julie sees an intruder who turns out to possess the same face she had seen 15 years earlier. When they meet again, he tells her his story of having been raised in the fourteenth century and of his having become a vampire to escape the plague. He has lived in the house and the structure that preceded it for all the intervening centuries. He considers himself the **Master of Rampling Gate** and has subjugated all the Ramplings who have lived in the house over the last four centuries.

Julie is open to his invitation to make her a vampire and his request that she introduce him to the modern world. She accepts the Dark Gift (being turned into a vampire) and immediately makes arrangements with her brother to have the mansion transferred to her name so he has an excuse not to carry out his father's last wish. Leaving Richard to enjoy the house as long as he wishes, Julie and the Master travel to London to begin their new life and relationship.

SOURCES:

Ramsland, Katherine. *The Vampire Companion: The Official Guide to Anne Rice's The Vampire Chronicles.* New York: Ballantine Books, 1993.

Rice, Anne. "The Master of Rampling Gate." *Redbook* (February 1984). Rev. ed. *The Master of Rampling Gate.* Adapted by James Schlosser and illustrated by Colleen Doran. Wheeling, WV: Innovation Books, 1991.

Randy

Randy is a strip club dancer and vampire who works at Vamps, the club featured in the 1996 low-budget film of the same name. The dark-haired beauty spends an average evening dancing for the clientele of lonely men who flock to Vamps, but after work hours, picks one of the club's patrons with whom she spends the rest of the evening. Randy is a spontaneous creature and will on occasion take a particularly obnoxious (and sexist) patron out for sex and a snack. She lives in an apartment above the club with Tabitha, another Vamps dancer.

Like the other vampires at Vamps, Randy is a modern vampire who has lost most of the supernatural traits generally ascribed to them. She can be seen in the mirrors that decorate the walls of the club. Holy water and crosses leave her unmoved. She is young, but has the potential of great age, as long as she does not run into any physical problems such as decapitation or a stake in the heart. She is strong and keeps up her strength with nightly feeds.

At one point, as **Tasha**, the club owner, is about to transform the new dancer **Heather** into a vampire, she sends Randy to kill Heather's boyfriend Shamus.

Horror legends Boris Karloff and John Carradine came together in the horror classic, *House of Frankenstein*. Here Karloff stakes Carradine, who played a Count Dracula-like character named Count Latos.

Shamus is a vampire/horror-movie aficionado who knows the legends and has a few memorabilia from the movies. As Randy attacks, he tries the traditional approach to ward her off, but she does not respond to a cross or holy water. Finally, in desperation, as Randy is about to kill him, he grabs an old movie prop, a bathroom plunger, one end of which has been sharpened as a stake. He holds it in front of him and Randy impales herself as she charges at her quick-thinking target.

Ravna, Dr.

Victorian German nobleman Dr. Ravna is featured in the film *The Kiss of the Vampire* (1962). A vampire of indeterminate age and origin, Ravna appears to be middle-aged. He resides in a chateau in an isolated area of Bavaria with his son Carl and daughter Sabina. He is a traditional vampire in that he has fangs and is repelled by garlic and religious symbols. He is able to move about in daytime, but avoids the direct sunlight. His greatest asset is his hypnotic power.

The story begins after Ravna has gathered several dozen minions, beautiful young women to whom he is especially attracted, and organized them into a cult. He holds the local villagers captive through fear, and is opposed by Professor Zimmer, who has lost a daughter to Ravna.

The opportunity to abolish Ravna is occasioned by the village's arrival of a honeymooning couple from England, Gerald and Marianne Harcourt. They have lost their way and run out of gas. Because there is no gas in the village, they have to wait while some is brought from a distant city. Ravna takes an immediate liking to Marianne and invites the couple to a party he is giving. At the party, his children separate the couple, and while Gerald drinks the champagne, Ravna drinks from Marianne's neck.

Cast out of the chateau *sans* wife, Gerald unites forces with Zimmer, who plans to fight the cult with magic. He performs a magical ritual called the "Invocation of the Forces of Evil," designed to force evil to destroy itself. As the ritual is completed, the chateau is attacked by a group of vampire bats who kill all of its inhabitants. Fortunately, Gerald rescues Marianne just in time, and she escapes the chateau's fate.

Ravnos, Countess Tanya

Countess Tanya Ravnos, the aristocratic vampiress who lives in a nineteenth-century Gothic fantasy world in a castle near the small European town of Kleinenberg, is featured in the continuing comic book series, *Gothic Nights*. Created by writer David Barbour and artist Timothy Vigil, Countess Ravnos makes her first appearance in the second issue of the graphic art anthology series *Raw Media Mags* (1992) but emerges with her own series from Rebel Studios in 1995.

Two hundred years ago, she was a servant girl who, along with her sister, were given to a cruel countess. She was spotted by the king, a vampire who bit her, and she eventually took the place of her abusive countess. Ravnos is a traditional vampire, and a sexually active one. Sexual activity inflames her blood lust, although in any case she feeds each evening. She has no reflection in a mirror and can easily transform into a bat to roam across her lands.

Countess Ravnos lives quietly in her castle. Her servants supply her with food each evening, which does not endear her to the people who live in the surrounding lands. Her lover Anton is a werewolf who each month at the full moon joins the local pack to hunt. However, at the latest full moon, the local authorities act. They capture Anton, crucify him, and mutilate his body. The angry Ravnos revenges herself on the burgomaster's son.

In this world of emerging science, Ravnos has one possible means of reuniting herself with her lover. She carries his body to Dr. Frankenstein and demands that he reanimate him. The reanimation process is successful, but she failed to tell Frankenstein that his subject is a werewolf. At the next full moon, the reanimated lycanthrope goes wild and has to be killed again. The countess sheds tears of blood as she realizes that she must face her future without Anton.

SOURCES:
"Gothic Nights." *Raw Media Mags*. Pt. 1, No. 2. Pt. 2, No. 4. 1992, 1994.
Gothic Nights. No. 1– . Sacramento, CA: Rebel Studios, 1995– .

Redfern, Delos

Delos Redfern is a vampire king featured in the Night World fantasy realm of the young adult novel, *Black Dawn* (1997). Delos lives in a castle in the Dark Kingdom, a mysterious hidden location founded by Delos's grandfather in the mountains of Washington State, a realm cut off from the mundane world by a heavy mist. There has been no contact between the Dark Kingdom and the outside world for over 500 years, until recently when some of the Dark Kingdom witches ventured into the outer world and captured a group of teenage mortals, now enslaved as their prisoners in the abysmal castle.

The story reveals that three years ago, Tormentil, the king who had ruled for many years, died, and his son Delos succeeded him. Delos is now 17 years old. He has dark hair, yellow eyes with dark lashes, and translucent white fangs. He has an unusual ability as the possessor of the blue fire, a powerful, destructive force that he can release through his arm.

The people of the Dark Kingdom have lived with a prophecy: The world of humans is about to come to an end and the Night people will rule again. To prevent this millennial disaster, four powers (one of whom is Delos) will meet as the end time approaches. If they work in unison, the disaster can be prevented.

Over the course of the story, Delos must face the plot of a group of witches who look forward to humanity's destruction. Aiding him is Maggie Neely, a teenager who finds her way to the Dark Kingdom after her brother is taken prisoner by one of the evil witches. Like Delos, she discovers she has a role to play in the land's prophecy.

SOURCES:
Smith, Lisa Jane. *Night World: Black Dawn.* New York: Archway/Pocket Books, 1997.

Reed, Richmond

Richmond Reed, an old vampire portrayed by John Carradine in the film *Vampire Hookers* (1978), had some 136 years ago established himself in a cemetery near an unnamed Asian city. He is the resident of an elaborate set of underground rooms, the entrance being disguised as a tomb. Venturing infrequently from the graveyard, Reed is assisted by three vampire women who, although many decades old, appear as young girls. They visit the local bars each evening where they offer their bodies to the many sailors out on the town looking for a good time.

Reed is a somewhat traditional vampire. He sleeps in a coffin, is repulsed by garlic and crosses, and is vulnerable to a wooden stake in the heart. Of cultured breeding, he enjoys quoting Shakespeare to his victims. He has a human servant, Pavel, who above all else wants to become a vampire and in his spare time imitates what he believes to be proper vampire behavior.

After his many years of successful existence, Reed meets his downfall when his chief girl, Cherish, lures an American sailor to their underground lair. His buddies refuse to give up looking for him and eventually discover Reed's underground center. Reed is killed in a traditional manner with a stake.

Regine

Regine, the brother of vampire Jerry Dandridge in the 1985 movie *Fright Night*, comes to town seeking revenge for his death in the sequel, *Fright Night II* (1988). Charlie Brewster, the high school student who first spotted Jerry, has gone through three years of psychological counseling with **Dr. Harrison** and is all but convinced that there are no such things as vampires. **Peter Vincent**, the reluctant vampire hunter, has gone back to hosting horror movies on his television show, *Fright Night*. Then, one evening after visiting Vincent, Charlie sees Regine move into the Hotel Elegante, the resident hotel in which Vincent resides.

Regine is a long-haired seductive beauty, who, like her brother Jerry, appears young, though she is 1000 years old. She is accompanied by three minions: Louis, a werewolf; **Belle**, a vampire; and Bozworth, a bug-eating Renfield figure who drives her limousine. Regine begins her attack by going to Charlie's college dorm and taking some of his blood. It is her plan to turn him into a vampire and then torture him forever. Like her brother, Regine does not reflect in mirrors, is repelled by crosses and holy water, and can change into an animal or mist. She sleeps in a coffin.

Since he has been convinced that vampires do not exist, Charlie pushes aside his thoughts about Regine until a college friend goes into her apartment. Charlie watches as his friend is vampirized. Later, Charlie and Vincent go to Regine's apartment only to discover a party. Charlie's friend appears to be fine, but Vincent notices that Regine and Belle do not reflect in the mirror in his cigarette case. Meanwhile, Charlie's doubts come back to the fore.

The next evening, Vincent discovers that he has been fired from his job on the television show and replaced by performance artist Regine, who uses her vampiric abilities to produce spectacular special effects. Vincent attacks her on the air and is carried off to the state hospital. With Vincent out of the way, Regine takes Charlie to her apartment to complete his transformation. Charlie's girlfriend, a psychology major, springs Vincent from the hospital and takes him to Regine's apartment, where they grab Charlie and begin the process of eliminating Regine's minions one by one. The have holy water, a spear gun, and an altar cloth from the local parish church.

In the end, they square off against the elder vampire herself. She retreats to the basement, where she corners Charlie and his girlfriend. Fortunately, dawn approaches and Vincent is able to use a broken mirror to reflect sunlight onto the enraged Regine. She, like her brother before her, is consumed in flames.

A comic book version of *Fright Night II* (adapted by Matthew Costello) appeared in 1988.

SOURCES:

Fright Night II. Chicago: Now Comics, 1988.

Renauld, Thurman

Thurman Renauld, a vampire of indeterminate age, is the subject of the 1954 short story "The Secret of Thurman Renauld." A modern vampire, he can move about in

The vampiress Regine from *Fright Night II* prepares for her next meal.

the daytime, is married, and is living a somewhat normal suburban life in 1950s America. His wife, Marla, is fearful, however, as every full moon Renauld becomes terrified. She thinks he is going insane and consults Dr. Lenox Wingard, a psychiatrist. Wingard is sure that all of Renauld's fears are the results of repressed memories in his unconscious psyche.

DOING IT HIS WAY: QUENTIN TARANTINO AS A VAMPIRE

Not everyone likes vampire movies and it takes a different breed of actor to pull off the portrayal of the creatures. Quentin Tarantino (b. 1963) fits the bill. Tarantino got his start in motion pictures by going to the cinema with his mother. She liked the movies enough to name him after a character in a Burt Reynolds' flick. Young Quent furthered his education by working in a video store in Manhattan Beach, California, a position which provided ample opportunity to watch and critically assess a wide variety of movies, new and old. Then at the age of 22, he started making his own movies. With a few acting classes under his belt, he composed a fake resume and began to peddle himself and his work. His first break was the sale of a script, *Natural Born Killers*, which he sold for $50,000, enough to bankroll his movie: *Reservoir Dogs*, released in 1992. The movie earned him a fragile reputation as a creative outsider ready to make his mark on the movie industry. That fragile reputation was firmly established with the release in 1994 of the highly acclaimed *Pulp Fiction*.

In 1995 Tarantino collaborated with friend Robert Rodriguez to produce a different kind of vampire movie, *From Dusk Till Dawn*. In this film, evil is an absurd chaotic force that comes out of nowhere to suddenly disrupt—and even end—one's life. Evil is the violence of a psychotic serial killer who enters the life of a convenience store clerk or a minister and his teen children on a vacation. Then it is a singer/dancer, Santanico Pandemonium, who suddenly becomes a vampire and with her minions turns on the serial killer and his companions.

For Tarantino and Rodriguez, evil's effect is immediate. Bullets kill in seconds and even a minimal vampire bite transforms the victim in a matter of minutes. No need for the formality of exchanging blood or a night in the grave. Otherwise peaceful people emerge with a bloodthirst that completely alters their understanding of needs. Many audiences just can't relate to the overwhelming reality that violence represents, nor laugh as Tarantino delivers his message in a package of dark humor.

Renauld consents to become Wingard's patient. He tries to explain his situation. He has dreams of a creature with blood dripping from its mouth. A month into the sessions, Marla disappears. He believes that she has finally left him, but he continues to go to Wingard. The psychiatrist tracks the problem to a fear of cemeteries and plans to take Renauld to a cemetery at the next full moon. As planned, they arrive at the Vista del Mar Cemetery, where members of the Renauld family are buried.

Renauld then takes charge of the session and shows the doctor the real source of his anxiety. It is an empty grave marked "Thurman Renauld." Renauld explains to the doctor that he really is a vampire and must feed monthly at the time of the full moon, or else he will return to the grave forever. Since Renauld wishes to continue his earthly existence, the doctor is forced to cancel all of his future appointments.

"The Secret Fear of Thurman Renauld" originally appeared in the horror anthology comic book *The Beyond* in 1954. The author is unknown, but Lou Cameron brings the story to life in his artwork. *The Beyond* was reprinted in a colorized version by Marcus David in 1987.

SOURCES:

Cameron, Lou. "The Secret Fear of Thurman Renauld." *The Beyond* 26 (April 1954). Reprinted in *Halloween Horror* 1 (Eclipse Comics, Oct. 1987).

Rentlow, Jeremy

Handsome young vampire Jeremy Rentlow is the antagonist in the novel *The Vampire Curse* (1971). He is a 24-year-old artist with dark wavy hair who resides at Rentlow's Retreat, an estate mansion near Tumlee, Massachusetts. He was adopted by the Rentlows as a young boy, and as he grew to adulthood, used his abilities to create a number of statues that now grace the estate. However, his maturing has also been associated with a series of strange deaths.

The first death occurred 10 years ago, when May Argon, the sister of housekeeper Mrs. Foxhall, mysteriously died. Then, more recently, Sarah Calvert was found dead. Sarah, her brother Rory, Jeremy, and his sister Estrella grew up together. Both Sarah and Estrella had sat with Jeremy for a sculpture.

Flash forward to the early 1970s, when 18-year-old Tenna Haliday falls under Jeremy's spell. Her divorced mother has just remarried and sends her to live with her aunt, Jane Rentlow. Not long after she arrives, Jeremy persuades her to sit for him. Rory and Mrs. Foxhall both warn her to stay away, but she feels compelled to see him. For three weeks she sits for him as her image slowly emerges out of the hunk of marble. However, in her last session, which lasts for three hours, she comes away completely depleted. She notices that her throat hurts and she has a small wound there. She visits the town doctor who confirms she has an anemic condition, as she has lost a lot of blood.

Tenna is able to push Jeremy away for a few days, but he has announced that they are engaged to be married. Tenna slowly concludes that Jeremy is a vampire, although a most nontraditional one. He walks around in daylight and uses the sun to highlight Tenna's features as he sculpts. He does not sleep in a coffin or avoid mirrors. He does not seem to need a regular supply of blood, although he appears to be taking it when available. He shows no supernatural abilities, he simply loves beauty. Is he a vampire, or just a very disturbed young man? Although the answer to this question is never revealed, Jeremy allows the wave of the rocky shore to engulf him—bringing whatever existence he had to a timely end.

SOURCES:
Winston, Donna. *The Vampire Curse*. New York: Warner Books, 1971.

Robespiere

Robespiere is a 160-year-old vampire from Hungary who makes his appearance in the low-budget film, *I Married a Vampire* (1987). During his long life he has been many things—a Shakespearean actor, a philosopher and, as he is currently billed, a historian. His sister Olivia lives in a house in an American city and works at a menial job at a computer company. At work, Olivia meets Viola and invites her home to meet her brother.

Viola is the complete victim. Since moving to the city, the first time she has been away from her controlling parents, she is taken advantage of by a series of men from her landlord to her lawyer and her boss. However, before her first evening with

Robespiere and his sister is over, she figures out that he might be a vampire. While Olivia leaves for a visit to her homeland, Viola accepts Robespiere's invitation for tea and chess.

Robespiere is handsome, enjoys silent movies, and likes to talk philosophy. He claims to have known his favorite, the nineteenth-century German philosopher Ludwig Freuerbach. He believes that death is an important marker is one's life, and as a vampire, he lives for a long time, but not forever. He is not a traditional supernatural vampire. He does not transform into an animal and has no negative reaction to garlic and holy objects. However, he is strong and goes for the throat of his victims.

Robespiere's blood lust hits him at midnight each evening. The first time Viola sees what he refers to as his illness, he sends her away. However, she seems to have nowhere to go and nothing else to lose. She offers him her life, and love is born. Robespiere gives her the first lessons in not being a victim which begins in a change of image—a new dress and hairstyle. He then joins his wife in visiting each of the men who has taken advantage of her and gives each of them a taste of his form of revenge. Before the young lovers start to build their new life together, there is a final confrontation with Viola's parents to whom Robespiere teaches a new level of sensitivity to their daughter's needs.

Robey, Drake

Drake Robey, a vampire gunfighter, appears in the first vampire western, Universal's film *Curse of the Undead* (1959). Drake Robey is the Americanized name taken in the late-nineteenth century by Drago Robles (1826-1859), the son of a wealthy California landowner whose family had in years past received a grant of land from the Spanish king. That land has become a ranch owned by Dr. John Carter.

As a young man, Drago marries. Unfortunately, while Drago is away on a trip to Spain, his brother, Roberto, seduces his wife. Upon his return, Drago kills his brother. Later, after Drago's death, and as a result of his fratricide, Drago becomes a vampire. His father tries to kill him by driving a silver knife into his corpse and pinning him to his casket. However, the knife does not kill him.

Robey is a somewhat traditional vampire. He dresses in black, though a cowboy outfit has replaced the tuxedo favored by European royalty. He is largely a nocturnal creature but has the ability to move about in the daylight. He sleeps in a coffin in a nearby mausoleum. He is repelled by the cross, and he drinks whisky and smokes cigars.

A generation later, Drago returns to his land and begins attacking the young women in town. Drago also attacks and kills Dr. Carter, the ranch owner. Drago's reappearance comes at a time when the Carter family is battling a neighbor over water and land boundaries. After her brother is killed in a gunfight, Delores Carter hires Robey to kill the man responsible. Instead, Robey attacks Delores and begins to take her blood, but stops when he falls in love with her.

As the deaths continue, the town's preacher finally figures out who and what Robey is and calls him out. The two face each other in a gunfight. Robey is not fast, but has always relied upon the fact that bullets do not harm him. However, Robey does not count on the preacher having fashioned a bullet out of the small cross he wears as a lapel pen, which he received at the time of his ordination. Shot by the preacher, Robey dissolves into dust as the crowd, including Delores, watches.

Roissey, Nicole

Nicole Roissey makes her appearance the comic book series, *Hero Alliance* (1991). Also known as Misty, Nicole is a shapely young blonde who attempts to join the Hero Alliance, a coalition of superheroes that has banded together to stop crime in the urban world. In the early 1990s, Nicole had been a college student working part-time as a research assistant at Lindelman Research. The laboratory in which she worked was studying biological death, pseudo bacteria, and reanimation. The laboratory housed a number of experimental animals and supplies of blood. Nicole was killed one evening in an accident, and survived the incident as a vampire.

A moral person, Misty turns on the criminal element as her food. On occasion, in her enthusiasm, she commits murder. One such incident leads to her contact with Victor, head of the Hero Alliance. He attempts to integrate her into the Alliance because she has a number of attractive superpowers such as shape shifting and extraordinary strength, but because she had been less than honest in disclosing her true state, it is difficult for Victor to accept her. Very quickly her behavior, including her lying, deception, and execution of people out of her need to quench her thirst, prove unacceptable.

After Victor discovers that she is a vampire, she tries to escape by turning into a mist. One of the superheroes, Vicki, transforms into a large container in which she scoops up the cloud of mist. Victor takes the responsibility of flying off into the dawning light and exposing the young vampire to the death-dealing rays of the sun. Nicole's career ends as quickly as it began.

SOURCES:
"Promises to Keep." *Hero Alliance.* No. 17. Innovation, Nov. 1991.

Rollins, Katherine

Prostitute-turned-vampire Katherine Rollins is the subject of newspaperman **Carl Kolchak**'s attention in an episode entitled "Vampire" (1973) of the television series, *The Night Stalker*. The original made-for-television movie, *The Night Stalker* (1972), introduces **Janos Skorzeny**, a vampire who roams Las Vegas and bites a number of women, one of whom gets away. Katherine Rollins, a high-priced prostitute, is reported missing at the same time Kolchak and the police are concerned with Skorzeny. About 25 years old, Rollins is short and pretty, with long dark hair.

In the television episode, Kolchak moves on to Chicago after the Skorzeny affair and hears about some killings in Los Angeles which call to mind the vampire slayings

Marilyn Chamber's portrayed Rose, the very unorthodox vampire in David Cronenberg's splatter-fest, *Rabid*.

in Las Vegas. On another story assignment, Kolchak heads for the City of Angels, where Rollins continues to operate as a prostitute who takes her victims from her client list. Like Skorzeny, she has fangs, is nocturnal, and is vulnerable to crosses, fire, and daylight. After a series of attempts, Kolchak finally tracks Rollins to the Hollywood Hills where he traps her in a ring of fire made by pouring a circle of gasoline on the ground. In the midst of the ring is a large, flaming cross, which subdues Rollins long enough for Kolchak to stake her. With Rollins dead, the Los Angeles Police Department threatens Kolchak with a murder charge if he tries to print the story.

Rose

Among the most unorthodox of vampires, Rose (portrayed by Marilyn Chambers) makes her appearance in David Cronenberg 's splatter classic *Rabid* (1977) as a perfectly normal pretty young woman living in Montreal in the mid-1970s. An accident on a motor bike one fall day changes her world, as she is taken to a nearby hospital where doctors perform skin graft operations using some experimental techniques they are developing. Her recovery is slow.

Finally, one evening she awakens and calls the doctor into her room. Partly responding to his own lustful feelings, he agrees to her request to be held. As they embrace, a penile object comes out of a strange opening that has developed under Rose's arm. With its needlelike point, the new appendage penetrates the doctor and sucks his blood. When he is found later, he complains of numbness to one side of his body and has no memory of what occurred. In spite of all the blood lost, the doctors think he might have had a stroke.

Feeling strong after the encounter, Rose begins to attack others somewhat uncontrollably. She takes little blood, but upon awakening from the experience, her victims begin to foam at the mouth and turn into mad people with homicidal urges. The rabies-like disease they have been infected with slowly spreads through Montreal. Unaware of the consequences of her actions, Rose continues to bite people as the city is placed under marshal law and the World Health Organization declares an epidemic emergency. Police are ordered to kill any people they see infected.

Rose is likened to Typhoid Mary, a carrier of the disease who is immune to it. Blood has become her only food. Although her boyfriend Hart Read informs her of what she has become, she doesn't believe him. As she takes another victim, this time she watches to see what happens. While phoning Hart to explain what she has done, her victim awakens, and Rose becomes just another victim of the epidemic.

Rozokov, Dimitri

Dimitri Rozokov, a 500-year-old vampire living in Canada, is introduced to the world in the novel *The Night Inside: A Vampire Thriller* (1993). Born in Russia in 1459, Rozokov migrates to Germany where, as a young man, he begins to dabble in necromancy. He calls up a vampire, who takes him as her next victim. After several days' experience of life as a vampire, his guilt overtakes him and he shows the parish priest where the vampire rests. The priest kills her in the traditional manner, by staking her, placing garlic in her mouth, and decapitating the corpse. Rozokov overcomes his guilt in the months and years ahead, but in order to keep his presence hidden from mortals, he decides not to kill recklessly or needlessly.

In 1865 Rozokov relocates to Paris when he meets vampire Jean-Pierre, the only other vampire he has ever encountered. They take an apartment together and soon have a young woman, Roxanne, living with them. One day Rozokov comes home to find the apartment in flames. Both Roxanne and Jean-Pierre are dead.

With hopes for a brighter future, Rozokov leaves Europe and settles in Toronto. There, in the 1890s, he becomes the target of Ambrose Delaney Dale, an occult researcher. He has tracked Rozokov to the inner city, where he has been feeding off prostitutes. At one point, Rozokov simply decides to go to sleep. He chooses an abandoned warehouse, and sleeps for almost 100 years.

Rozokov is middle-aged when he awakens. He now has pale skin and black eyes. He is very strong and has long fingers, but not inordinately so. Gone are many of the traditional vampire characteristics he once possessed. He does not sleep in a coffin and his image is reflected in mirrors. He is not negatively affected by religious symbols, and does not transform into a bat or mist.

Immediately after awakening, Rozokov attacks several men who have occupied the warehouse. He is captured and imprisoned and forced to participate in pornographic snuff films. His captors bring women in and allow him to feed only enough to stay alive and minimally active. One of the women, **Ardeth Alexander**, concocts a scheme to escape. She allows Rozokov to drain her, which leads to her death. Buried without being staked, she comes back to life as a vampire and attacks the people who have been holding Rozokov captive.

Together the two move to Toronto. Learning to exist under their new conditions, Rozokov as a twentieth-century being and Alexander as a vampire, seems to provide all of the stimulus the couple needs. However, Rozokov soon becomes aware that he is being tracked by Althea Dale, Ambrose's ancestor. Dale has AIDS and hopes that the vampire's blood will cure her. She also has a considerable amount of money that she is using to fund a sophisticated hematology research laboratory—the likes of which could use a sampling of Rozokov's blood. Dale's plans end in a fiery conflagration, and Rozokov is free to pursue his dream of living a quiet life somewhere in his chosen homeland.

SOURCES:

Baker, Nancy. *Blood and Chrysanthemums: A Vampire Novel.* New York: Viking, 1994.

———. *The Night Inside: A Vampire Thriller.* New York: Viking, 1993. Reprinted as *Kiss of the Vampire.* Greenwich, CT: Fawcett Columbine, 1995.

Ruthven, Lord

The original vampire of prose fiction, Lord Ruthven (pronounced *rí-ven*) made his initial appearance in "The Vampyre" (1819), a short story by John Polidori that was originally attributed to **Lord Byron**. Like Lord Byron, Ruthven was a nobleman, which helped begin the tradition of presenting the vampire as a member of European nobility. That tradition was made most famous, of course, years later in the form of Bram Stoker's **Count Dracula**.

Lord Ruthven, a mysterious stranger of uncertain age and parentage, infiltrates London society and makes friends with a young man named Aubrey. In comparison to other people, Ruthven is rather pale and somewhat cold in his demeanor, but he is a favorite of the ladies. He freely loans money to people to use at the gaming tables, but those who accept his generosity generally lose the money and are led further into debt and eventual degradation.

Ruthven travels to Rome with Aubrey. There, Aubrey becomes upset with Ruthven when he tries to seduce the young daughter of an acquaintance. Unable to stop Ruthven, Aubrey leaves and travels on to Greece by himself. In Greece he meets and is attracted to an innkeeper's daughter named Ianthe. She is the person who first introduces Aubrey to the legend of the vampire. Just as Aubrey is fully falling in love with Ianthe, Ruthven re-enters the picture. A short time later, Ianthe is attacked and killed by a vampire. Aubrey, of course, knows about vampires but fails to make the connection between Ruthven and the attack on Ianthe. He and Ruthven leave the small town and continue their travels around Greece.

As they journey across country, they are attacked by bandits. Ruthven is seemingly killed in the attack, but before he dies, he makes Aubrey swear to conceal the matter of his death, as well as any crimes he might have committed, for the period of a year and a day. The bandits carry his body to a nearby site, where it will be exposed to the moon's light. As Aubrey makes his return to London, he begins to realize that Lord Ruthven seems to destroy anyone upon whom he showers favors, especially the women who become his lovers. This disturbs Aubrey.

Upon Aubrey's return to London, Ruthven causes Aubrey even more distress when he reappears and reminds him of the oath he had taken in Greece. This causes Aubrey to suffer a nervous breakdown. Ruthven seizes the opportunity to ingratiate himself with Aubrey's sister. The two hit it off and actually announce their engagement. Aubrey, because of his oath, feels that he is powerless to stop the wedding. The marriage takes place on the day the oath runs out, but by then it is too late. Ruthven has killed his sister and disappeared, off to work evil in some other corner of the world.

Polidori developed Lord Ruthven from elements of the European folklore which had become well-known across Europe after the vampire epidemics of the previous century. In his introduction, Polidori refers specifically to the Arnold Paole vampire scare and the survey of vampirism written by Dom Augustine Calmet. And while the vampire had been the subject of some German and British poems, Polidori, as noted by Carol Senf, took the crude entity of European folklore and transformed it into a complex and interesting fictional character, the first vampire in English fiction. No longer was the vampire simply a mindless demonic force unleashed on humankind, but rather he was a real person (albeit a resurrected one), capable of moving unnoticed in human society and picking and choosing victims. He was not an impersonal evil entity, but a moral degenerate dominated by evil motives, and a subject about whom negative moral judgments were proper.

Polidori used a story fragment started by Lord Byron in Switzerland in 1816 but never completed as the basic outline of his story. Byron's story concerned two friends who traveled from England to Greece, where one died. Before the one friend died, he extracted an oath from his companion. Polidori's reliance on Byron's story, in spite of its not mentioning vampires, is obvious. Polidori, who split from Byron, also seems to have directed "The Vampyre," at his former friend, modeling the vampire on the pale-complected Lord Byron. Like Byron, Ruthven was most attractive to women and had numerous affairs. Additionally, the name Ruthven came from Lady Caroline Lamb's *Glenarvon*, a piece she wrote satirizing Byron.

"The Vampyre" was widely reviewed and greatly affected the new generation of romantic writers. For example, playwright Charles Nodier was asked to review it and wrote the preface to the French edition. Then his friend Cyprien Bérard wrote a two-volume sequel to the story, *Lord Ruthwen ou les Vampires*, which appeared early in 1820. Because it was published anonymously, many ascribed the sequel to Nodier. However, Nodier wrote his own version of the Ruthven story and called it *Le Vampire*; it was the first vampire drama and opened on the Paris stage in the summer of

1820. Nodier's story made a crucial alteration in Polidori's original, in that Ruthven was forced to face the fatal consequences of his evil life. That change was to stay with the story in subsequent retellings of Lord Ruthven's tale. Within two months, James R. Planché brought Lord Ruthven to the London stage in *The Vampire, or, the Bride of the Isles*. Meanwhile back in Paris, Lord Ruthven appeared in four other vampire plays—two serious melodrama, two comedic—before the year was out. He made his debut in Germany in 1829 in an opera, *Der Vampyr*, by Heinrich August Marschner.

Lord Ruthven made his last appearance on the Parisian stage in 1852 in Alexander Dumas' final work before he left Paris and retired to Belgium. After Dumas' play, the Lord Ruthven character seems to have gone into retirement, only to be succeeded by the likes of **Sir Francis Varney** (also known as Varney the Vampire), **Carmilla Karnstein**, and Count Dracula. It was not until 1945 that Lord Ruthven would be rediscovered, when he served as the initial inspiration for a movie, *The Vampire's Ghost*, produced by Republic Pictures. However, by the time the script was developed, the story line bore little resemblance to "The Vampyre," and its leading character, **Webb Fallon**, had only the vaguest likeness to Lord Ruthven. Lord Ruthven then made a brief appearance when *Vampire Tales*, the Marvel comic book, adapted "The Vampyre" in its initial issue in 1973.

The most recent revival of Lord Ruthven, a new version of Marschner's opera, appeared on BBC television in 1992. In *Der Vampyr: A Soap Opera*, Ruthven was now a modern Londoner and his name had been change to Ripley the Vampyr.

SOURCES:
Goulart, Ron. "The Vampire." *Vampire Tales* No. 1 (1973): 35–48.

Sackville-Bagg, Rudolph

Rudolph Sackville-Bagg, popularly known as the "Little Vampire," is the subject of an ongoing series of young adult novels by German author Angela Sommer-Bodenburg. Translated into multiple languages, including English, French, Italian, Spanish, and Portuguese, they have become the most popular vampire-themed juvenile books ever published.

Rudolph Sackville-Bagg first appears in *Die Kleine Vampir* (translated into English as *My Friend the Vampire*). Like juvenile vampires in general, he is a somewhat sympathetic character, at worst a somewhat mischievous boy, with the primary elements of horror hovering in the background. He was born more than 150 years ago but became a vampire as a child and thus remains in his diminutive body. His family had come from Viscri (or Weisskirch), a small town in Transylvania near Sibiu that had been settled by Siebenburger Sachens (Germans) seven centuries ago. At one point, the Turks destroyed the town fort, and the vampires moved their coffins into the basement of the church. They tired of the regular ringing of the bells disturbing their sleep during the day and moved to Germany.

Rudolph is part of a large family, which includes his younger sister Anna, his older brother Gregory the Gruesome, his father Frederick the Frightful, his mother Thelma the Thirsty, grandmother Sabina the Sinister (the first vampire in the family), grandfather William the Wild and, the most bloodthirsty in the family, Aunt Dorothy. In Germany the family lived in an underground crypt area of a cemetery. In the early 1990s, the night watchman staked one of their family, Rudolph's Uncle Theodore, and all are now cautious in their movements.

The record of Rudolph's modern adventures begins with his sudden appearance one Saturday at the window of Tony Noodleman, a young boy whose parents have gone out for the evening. He has fangs and wears a cape, and sleeps in a coffin at the local cemetery. He brings a cape to Tony, which allows his new friend to fly about just like him. After they get to know each other, they experience a wide variety of adventures. In one of the early novels, *The Vampire Moves In*, Rudolph moves into the Noodleman's storage unit in the basement of their apartment building after being kicked out by his parents for fraternizing with humans. His presence soon creates a major problem, not the least of which is the terrible stench radiating from his coffin. For a brief period in the mid-1990s, Rudolph's family moves back to Transylvania (in *The Little Vampire Meets Count Dracula*) and the Noodlemans visit Rudolph's homeland on vacation. While there, he meets the infamous **Count Dracula**.

By 1998, more than 15 volumes of the adventures of the Little Vampire had been translated and published in English, and additional titles appear to be forthcoming.

SOURCES:

Sommer-Bodenburg, Angela. *The Little Vampire and the Christmas Surprise*. New York: Simon & Schuster.

———. *The Little Vampire and the Mystery Patient*. New York: Simon & Schuster, 1992.

———. *The Little Vampire and the School Trip*. New York: Simon & Schuster, 1994.

———. *The Little Vampire and the Wicked Plot*. New York: Simon & Schuster, 1993.

———. *The Little Vampire in Danger*. New York: Simon & Schuster, 1991.

———. *The Little Vampire in Despair*. New York: Simon & Schuster, 1992.

———. *The Little Vampire in the Lion's Den*. New York: Simon & Schuster, 1993.

———. *The Little Vampire in the Vale of Doom*. New York: Simon & Schuster, 1991.

———. *The Little Vampire Gets a Surprise*. New York: Simon & Schuster, 1993.

———. *The Little Vampire Learns to Be Brave*. New York: Simon & Schuster, 1993.

———. *The Little Vampire Meets Count Dracula*. Hemel Hempstead, Herts., UK: McDonald Young Books, 1995.

———. *The Little Vampire Strikes Back*. New York: Simon & Schuster, 1991.

———. *My Friend the Vampire*. New York: E. P. Dutton, 1982. Reprint, New York: Minstrel/Pocket Books, 1986.

———. *The Vampire in Love*. Reprint, New York: Minstrel/Pocket Books, 1993.

———. *The Vampire Moves In*. New York: E. P. Dutton, 1982. Reprint, New York: Minstrel/Pocket Books, 1986.

———. *The Vampire on the Farm*. New York: E. P. Dutton, 1990. Reprint, New York: Minstrel/Pocket Books, 1990.

———. *The Vampire Takes a Trip*. New York: Dial Press, 1985. Reprint, New York: E. P. Dutton, 1985.

St. Clair, Adrienne

Adrienne St. Clair, a rogue vampire who defies the authority of **the Conclave**, is featured in Garfield Reeves-Stevens' novel, *Bloodshift* (1981). A young British nurse during World War II, she is trapped behind enemy lines in France in 1944. She hides in the root cellar of a barn, unaware that it is inhabited by an *yber* (or vampire). He immediately feeds from her, but shortly thereafter German soldiers arrive. He is killed, and in the process, his white blood drips on the lips of St. Clair, who is transformed into an *yber*. She survives the next weeks by taking blood from the recently dead on the nearby battlefield. There she meets Jeffrey, another *yber*, who becomes her mentor and, eventually, her lover.

After the war, she is introduced to the Conclave, the *yber's* ruling council. It has assumed the authority to grant permission to make new *yber*. They select future *yber* and make for them familiars, human servants who assist the nocturnal *yber* during

THE VAMPIRE GALLERY SALUTES: CHELSEA QUINN YARBRO

Chelsea Quinn Yarbro stands out among the small group of authors who redefined vampire lore in the 1970s. Through her character St. Germain, Yarbro explores the life of a multi-millennia-old creature who retains important elements of his humanity, including a strong moral code. But what life style can sustain a vampire century after century—and lead neither to boredom nor madness? As a gentleman scholar, St. Germain discovers the way. He stays out of petty politics unless his direct self-interest is at stake, but, like Superman, frequently intervenes in the lives of people around him when they are unjustly suffering.

A native of California, Yarbro went to work in her father's business after college. When the business failed, her family's personal tragedy turned into a boon for the literary world as she tried her hand at writing. Like many of her colleagues, she started with short stories and explored many different genres, from mystery to fantasy to science fiction. Her first award came in 1973 from the Mystery Writers of America; her first novel, *Time of the Fourth Horseman* (1976), was a suspense story. She probably could have made it in mystery, suspense or any other genre, but vampire fans can be glad she ultimately chose horror in general—and vampires in particular.

Part of Yarbro's insight comes from the fact that she is an occultist. She concludes that the generally accepted vampire tradition is in fact, wrong. If one removes the traditional religious overlay, the vampire becomes an entity who shares a somewhat enjoyable (if kinky) sex life, and bestows a conditional immortality. She also began to explore the vampire's lifestyle, asking herself what a vampire would do with his or her very long life. Rather than build a life around a series of monotonous attacks on its neighbors, she concludes the vampire would most likely cultivate a life of scholarship and culture. She was a bit ahead of her time: as early as 1971 she tried to sell a book with a vampire hero, but no one was buying. She finally sold the idea to St. Martin's Press in the late 1970s, and St. Germain made vampire history.

the daylight hours. However, as soon as the war ended, the Conclave had to deal with a number of new *yber* like St. Clair, who were created during the war and apart from any apprenticeship. She is one of the few of the Unbidden, as these new *yber* are termed, who survived. The rest have been executed.

St. Clair is approximately 30 when she is transformed. Within hours, her canine teeth drop out and fangs grow in. Over the next months, her major organs fuse. While not appearing to age, changes continue to occur, and new abilities appear. She is a nontraditional vampire. Having never died, like other *yber*, she does not have many of the attributes commonly ascribed to the undead. Her image appears in mirrors. She is unaffected by holy water or religious symbols. She can be killed by sunlight, decapitation, or by massive damage to her heart (such as that provided by the traditional stake, an explosion, or multiple gunshots).

St. Clair brings her medical and scientific knowledge to her new situation. Not particularly attuned to the Conclave's perspective that vampires are basically supernatural products of Satan, she begins to search for a more mundane explanation. With Jeffrey and a select group of fellow *yber*, she moves into some deep caves in France where many discoveries had been made. While vampires can be destroyed in the sunlight, for example, they find there is no need for them to fall into the vampiric sleep during the daytime if they are otherwise protected.

She becomes convinced that vampirism is best understood as a disease, and begins a systematic search for its cause. In that effort she begins to recruit nonvampire scientists, who become her familiars. The Conclave, especially its leader, **Lord Eduardo Diego y Rey,** who sided with St. Clair in her initial review as an Unbidden *yber*, forbids further research. The Conclave sees that while her early research had been helpful, it had reached a point where it threatened the basis of its authority.

The Conclave orders Jeffrey's death as a message to her, but she responds by fleeing to Canada. She tries to continue her research on developing a blood substitute with Dr. Christopher Leung. The Conclave pursues her and kills him. She flees to California to an independent elder vampire known as the Father. Many centuries old, and the oldest vampire known to members of the Conclave, he refuses to acknowledge its authority. Using the power he has as the creator and mentor of many of the *yber*, he stands apart and offers his protection to any *yber* who rejects the Conclave's hegemony.

St. Clair's arrival in North America makes her the focus of a number of larger forces. Medical researchers working for the United States government need her as they have discovered humanity is going through a massive evolutionary change. The change can be halted by some as yet unknown substance in the *yber* blood that is the agent that will prevent humans from going the way of the dinosaur in the very near future. Her research, and the mundane explanation of vampirism it provides, threatens the long-term authority of the Conclave and is interfering with Lord Diego's immediate plans for world conquest. Her seeking the protection of the Father, however, provides Lord Diego the opportunity to manipulate the *yber*'s old enemies, the Jesuits, into attacking the Father and finally destroying his challenge to the Conclave's authority.

Having reached the Father's sanctuary in Naciamento, a small town near San Luis Obispo, California, she finds herself in a pitched battle between the Jesuit vampire hunters, United States government operatives, the Conclave's forces, and the Father's allies. At stake is the catastrophe facing humanity and St. Clair's research. Her hope is finally placed in the hands of an unlikely hero, Granger Helman, a contract killer hired by the Conclave to kill St. Clair, who ends up as her friend and confidant instead.

SOURCES:

Reeves-Stevens, Garfield. *Bloodshift*. Toronto: Virgo Press, 1981. Reprint, New York: Popular Library, 1990.

St. Germain

St. Germain, a 4,000-year-old vampire, is the major character in a series of novels by Chelsea Quinn Yarbro. Yarbro based Germain on a real historical figure, the Count de St. Germain, an alchemist who lived in eighteenth century France. The real Count was a cultured gentleman who composed music and spoke multiple languages. A prince from Transylvania, his real name was apparently Francis Ragoczy. He was rich, earning his money in international trade, possibly jewels. The few details of his life that are known suggest that he was of medium height, always wore black and white, rarely ate in public (even at his own parties), claimed extraordinary powers (including his assertion that he was several thousand years old), and encouraged an aura of mystery about the details of his life. In these few details of the real St. Germain, Yarbro found those qualities that meshed with her evolving image of what a vampire should be. In making the fictional St. Germain her protagonist, she did not have to change any of the facts that were known about the real St. Germain; she simply had to add the vampire myth.

In the late 1970s, when she was first creating the St. Germain character, Yarbro was studying and consciously reworking the **Count Dracula** myth that had developed throughout the twentieth century. By logically approaching the idea of how a vampire could really exist in the world as we knew it, she was forced to abandon many of the traditional ideas about vampires. For example, she removed the overlay of medieval Christianity that often went hand-in-hand with the vampire myth, which served to remove the automatically "evil" stigma associated with vampires. She saw vampires as extremely sexual creatures, who, in biting their victims, shared a moment of sexual bliss with them. With his bite, a vampire had the ability to grant a degree of immortality to the person he or she was biting.

Yarbro also decided that the vampire would have to be very intelligent to survive in a hostile environment. That intelligence would also help the vampire avoid the boredom that could result from eternal life and help him or her find creative and entertaining ways to pass the centuries. Finally, Yarbro differed from traditional vampire scholarship in regards to the importance of blood. To her, the nourishment provided by the blood was not the most significant part of the vampire's bite; rather, the essence of vampirism was the very act itself and the intimacy and contact with life that it provided. Thus the bite become a sexual act.

St. Germain makes his debut in *Hotel Transylvania* (1978). His origin is never fully revealed, but parts of his history are spelled out in each novel he appears in. He was born some 4,000 years ago in what is today Transylvania of Proto-Etruscan stock. The religion of his people featured a vampire god and priests who were also vampires. Because he was born in the winter (the "nighttime" of the year in agricultural societies), he was initiated into the priesthood. Some details of this priesthood are provided in the 1981 novel *Path of the Eclipse*. St. Germain was initiated into the priesthood, but before he could assume his position he was captured by a rival clan and taken into slavery. He served very successfully in his captors' army, but his only reward for his valor was execution. He survived his execution only because his killers did not know that to fully destroy one of the vampires, you had to either burn the creature or sever his spine, i.e., cut off his head.

Having survived that execution attempt, St. Germain began his long existence. When we meet him in *Hotel Transylvania*, he is living in eighteenth century France. The book is essentially a historical romance detailing the love affair of the alchemist/vampire St. Germain and Madelaine de Montalia. Their happiness is shattered when a coven of devil worshipers takes Madelaine to serve its evil purposes. It seems that Madelaine's father had struck a deal with the cult and promised his daughter in exchange for its help.

Cover art from Chelsea Quinn Yarbro's novel, *Hotel Transylvania,* which features St. Germain.

Throughout the early chapters of *Hotel Transylvania*, St. Germain slowly reveals to Madelaine the nature of his existence. Alert readers will be tipped off to St. Germain's condition in the very first chapter, when he repeats one of Dracula's most famous lines. When offered a glass of wine, Germain simply says, "I do not drink wine." He tells Madelaine that he is many centuries old, and that he needs only small quantities of blood to survive (often as little as half a pint, which is about a wineglass full). Contrary to popular belief, he is not adversely affected by sacred objects, such as crosses. He can walk freely on consecrated ground. He *is* negatively affected by running water and sunlight, but he counteracts this by drawing strength from soil from his native land cleverly hidden in the hollow heels of his shoes. The shoes allow him to walk freely in the daylight, although he remains primarily a nocturnal creature. The main super-human ability he does have is enormous strength, which he demonstrates when he defeats the devil-worshiping cult and saves Madelaine.

St. Germain does possess human emotions, but he has learned to stay out of the affairs of humans whenever possible. He does, however, fall in love on occasion, as he did with Madelaine. When this happens, Yarbro takes the opportunity to show readers just how different his form of sexuality is. While Germain can participate in most sexual activities, he suffers from a form of impotence. However, for both him and his partners, his bite is a more than adequate replacement for sexual intercourse and is an intensely erotic act. Interestingly, satisfying sexual relations can occur only between a vampire and an ordinary human. Two vampires are unable to bite and satisfy each other—the act holds no arousal. Thus, if an affair between a vampire and human progresses to the point where the human becomes a vampire (by either drinking St. Germain's blood or being bitten and drained repeatedly by him), the affair would come to an end. The two vampires could and often did remain friends, but their love affair ceased to be.

In her second and third novels, Yarbro again placed St. Germain in historically significant time periods and showed what his life was like amidst periods of great social change. In *The Palace* (1979) he is living in fifteenth century Florence, Italy, and in *Blood Games* (1980), in Rome during the time of Nero. In each of these, St. Germain encounters life and death experiences that force him to contemplate the reality and the meaning of "true death," that is, being burned or having his spine severed. Also central to these novels is the introduction of **Atta Olivia Clemens**, his friend through the centuries. She first appears in *The Palace*, but her story is told in *Blood Games*. It seems that her husband had forced her to have sexual relations with many other men while he watched and fed his own voyeuristic desires. When she meets St. Germain, they become lovers and he arranges for her to escape her husband's power and become a vampire. She of course becomes one of his closest allies. Olivia's exploits are more fully detailed in three other Yarbro novels devoted to her—*A Flame in Byzantium* (1987), *Crusader's Torch* (1988), and *A Candle for d'Artagnan* (1989).

In the most recent St. Germain novels, the vampire hero is brought forward into more modern times, first in Nazi Germany (*Tempting Fate*, 1982) and then in various other settings (*The Saint Germain Chronicles*, 1983).

SOURCES:

Yarbro, Chelsea Quinn. *Blood Games*. New York: St. Martin's Press, 1980.

———. *A Candle for D'Artagnan*. New York: Tor Books, 1989.

———. *Crusader's Torch*. New York: Tor Books, 1988.

———. *A Flame in Byzantium*. New York: Tor Books, 1987.

———. *Hotel Transylvania*. New York: St. Martin's Press, 1978.

———. *The Palace*. New York: St. Martin's Press, 1979.

———. *Path of the Eclipse*. New York: St. Martin's Press, 1981. Reprint. New York: New American Library, 1982.

———. *The Saint Germain Chronicles*. New York: Pocket Books, 1983.

———. *Tempting Fate*. New York: St. Martin's Press, 1982.

Sanders, Count Damien Vincent

Count Damien Vincent Sanders (portrayed by Kevin Glover) is the subject of the low-budget comedy, *Love Bites* (1993). Count Damien is 347 years old, and during his long life has lost much of his concern for his physical surroundings. He sleeps in a coffin in a small, rather rundown house in West Hollywood, California. He is assisted by his bug-eating servant Mansfield. In most ways, Count Damien is a rather traditional Eastern European aristocratic vampire, except that, after several centuries of undead life and one-night stands, he has grown bored. He takes his blood from blood banks and has little sexual interest. He dresses formally, is cold to the touch, and burns in the sun. As vampires go, he has effective hypnotic skills.

One evening, Jake Hunter, a young would-be vampire slayer, enters his home, ready to make his reputation by killing the count. His activity is interrupted by the appearance of a young man, a hustler whom the count has hired as a companion for the evening for the unattractive Mansfield. When the count does appear, Jake finds him very different from what he expected. He is strongly attracted to him and finds his feelings returned. For the first time in his undead existence, the count falls in love.

When Jake runs away, the count is distraught. He destroys his coffin and wanders off into the night. He is attacked by a group of anti-gays who occasionally prowl West Hollywood, and returns home in a disheveled condition. Jake is waiting for him, but dawn is imminent and the vampire has no place to sleep. Jake gives him a love bite and they walk hopefully out into the dawn together. Maybe the love bond will cure the count of his vampiric condition.

Santiago

Santiago, one of the vampires in the **Theatre des Vampires,** appears in Anne Rice's *Interview with the Vampire* (1976). Santiago first appears after **Louis de Pointe du Lac** and **Claudia** have arrived in Paris and are walking the streets one night. Louis senses that he is being followed by someone who is trying to mimic their footsteps exactly. That someone turns out to be Santiago, who is tall with a pale face and long black hair. He is dressed just like Louis, who calls him a trickster for imitating his steps and manner. They scuffle until the older vampire **Armand** interrupts them. Armand gives Louis a card to the Theatre des Vampires. He still does not know who Santiago was.

Louis attends the performance the next evening and is formally introduced to Armand, who tells him that it was Santiago who followed them the night before and scuffled with him. After a long discussion with Armand, he leaves and is again accosted by Santiago, who asks him for more details about Lestat, whom Louis had mentioned while talking to Armand. Just then, Armand interrupts the late night encounter again and warns Louis to answer none of Santiago's questions.

Santiago also has a conversation with Claudia. He tells her that there is one serious crime for which the vampires in the Theatre would always hunt down the perpetrator—one vampire killing another vampire. Santiago suspects that Claudia and Louis have killed Lestat, which in fact they have attempted back in New Orleans, before sailing for Paris. His suspicions are confirmed when Lestat actually appears, alive, in Paris. Santiago is the leader of a group of vampires from the Theatre who take custody of Louis, Claudia, and Claudia's surrogate mother, **Madeleine.** He orders Louis to be locked in a coffin and places Claudia and Madeleine in an open airshaft where they are consumed in the fiery rays of the morning sun. Louis escapes, but not in time to save them. In revenge, he sets fire to the Theatre and kills Santiago by decapitating him with a scythe. Santiago's body is burned up in the ensuing blaze.

SOURCES:

Ramsland, Katherine. *The Vampire Companion: The Official Guide to Anne Rice's The Vampire Chronicles.* New York: Ballantine Books, 1993.

Rice, Anne. *Interview with the Vampire.* New York: Alfred A. Knopf, 1976. Reprint, New York: Ballantine, 1979.

Santino

Santino, the Italian vampire in Anne Rice's *The Vampire Lestat,* is made a vampire in the twelfth century, during the time of the Black Death. During his first years as a vampire he envisions the vampire as being a creature so mysterious and powerful that its very existence confuses and challenges the human belief system about God. Like the Black Death, he anticipates the vampire's presence will make human's doubt God's existence. He becomes the leader of the vampires of Rome and organizes them into a coven.

A natural leader, Santino lays down the Great Rules for the vampire community:

1. Each coven must have its leader and only the leader can order the making of a new vampire.

2. The Dark Gift (or the ability to turn someone into a vampire) must not be given to the crippled, the maimed, children, or those who otherwise cannot survive on their own.

3. The older, more powerful vampires should not turn people into vampires. Their power should remain in reserve and not be passed to the newly made.

4. No vampire should destroy another, except a coven leader, who has the power of life and death over his own coven.

5. No vampire should reveal his true nature to a mortal and allow that mortal to live.

There are rumors that Santino went mad and that his coven dissolved. At one point vampire **Lestat de Lioncourt** meets members of a Roman coven who know nothing of Santino. However, after dropping out of sight for several centuries, Santino reappears in 1985 and accompanies fellow vampire **Pandora** as she heads north to rescue **Marius**, guardian of the original vampires, who had been buried in the ice and snow after **Akasha,** the original vampire, left her sanctuary and began her campaign of world domination.

SOURCES:

Ramsland, Katherine. *The Vampire Companion: The Official Guide to Anne Rice's The Vampire Chronicles.* New York: Ballantine Books, 1993.

Rice, Anne. *The Queen of the Damned.* New York: Alfred A. Knopf, 1988. Reprint, New York: Ballantine Books, 1989.

————. *The Vampire Lestat.* New York: Alfred A. Knopf, 1985. Reprint, New York: Ballantine Books, 1986.

Sarah

Sarah appears in Seabury Quinn's short story, "The Man Who Cast No Shadow" (1927), but bears a strange resemblance to **Countess Sarah Kenyon**, the vampire in the story by F. G. Loring, "The Tomb of Sarah" (1900).

Sarah, an obscure woman buried several centuries ago in a church graveyard in New Jersey, is discovered to be a vampire by private detective Jules de Grandin while he is searching for another vampire, **Count Lajos Czuczron.** According to the story, in colonial days many believed the young woman was a murderer and a witch. She was accused of killing several children who died of mysterious circumstances. Finally, one woman who had lost a child strangled her. She was buried in the church's graveyard, her grave was surrounded by wild garlic bushes, and a strange inscription was placed on her tomb:

> Let none disturb her deathlesse sleepe
> Abote ye tombe wilde garlick keepe
> For is shee wake much woe will boast
> Prayse Father sonne & Holie Goast.

In the 1920s, the Hungarian vampire **Count Czuczron** has the garlic bushes removed from Sarah's grave. Sarah emerges and takes as her first victim Guy Eckhart, the house guest of one of de Grandin's acquaintances. When de Grandin examines the young man, he notices a large red patch on his chest, similar to that created from a vacuum cup being held to the skin for some time. In the center of the red patch are a number of tiny puncture wounds in two arcs, like a pair of parentheses.

Sarah is seen by the maid, a slim young black-eyed woman, who is found with, oddly enough, a rope around her neck. With his hypothesis confirmed, de Grandin returns to the church and drives a long stake into the grave. A moan comes from out of the grave. He removes the stake and shows those with him that the end is covered with blood. He then drives the stake in again and leaves it there. Nothing is ever heard again of Sarah roaming about.

SOURCES:

Quinn, Seabury. "The Man Who Cast No Shadow," 1927. Reprinted in Weinberg, Robert, Stefan R. Dziemianowicz, and Martin Greenberg, eds. *Weird Vampire Tales: 30 Blood-Chilling Stories from the Weird Fiction Pulps*. New York: Gramercy Books, 1992.

Screech

Screech is a member of a female vampire motorcycle group known as the Vamps, who lend their name to the comic book series of the same name. Of Chinese heritage, Screech grew up in Northern California in the 1970s. Under her birth name, Lai Lan, she becomes an artist who works on a computer. She meets fellow Chinese-American Lawrence Dai Szae, who develops an obsession with vampires. He asks her to search the computer for any references to real, contemporary vampires. Their search leads them to a nightclub, the Boneyard, where Lai Lan is accosted by a real vampire, a redneck named **Dave**, who plans on adding her to his growing group of young females he keeps as his minions.

As Screech, Lai Lan travels with Dave for several years, until 1994, when one evening in North Carolina the group, which includes **Howler, Skeeter, Whipsnake**, and **Mink**, catches Dave at his most vulnerable moment, just after he has gorged himself on blood, and kills him. They put a stake in his heart, dismember him, and bury his body parts in separate locations. In that shared act, they emerge as the Vamps and hit the road on their motorcycles.

Not having a real agenda, the women follow Howler to Las Vegas. As somewhat traditional vampires, they are nocturnal, and have to find a safe sleeping place each dawn, usually by burrowing underground. They awake with a blood thirst, and feeding becomes the first item on the evening's agenda. To prevent their vulnerability, one of the women delays feeding until the other four have passed through their period of post-dining stupor. As vampires, they have fangs, can be killed with a stake in the heart, and do not reflect in mirrors. The only place they can see their reflection is in the eyes of their next victim.

In Las Vegas Screech finds locating victims almost too easy, and she joins the girls as they travel across country to New York to assist Howler in her quest for her son, who has been put up for adoption. In New York, Howler heads off on her personal business, while Screech and the others explore the city. They become aware that Dave has somehow been resurrected and is on his way to capture them. Although Whipsnake finds a magical means of diverting him from the group, Dave is able to hone in on Howler. The Vamps reassemble at the home where her son Tommy has been placed, and Screech kills Dave with a crossbow. Afterward they dispose of Dave in a permanent manner.

Their next adventure leads the Vamps to Hollywood, where Mink tries to recover her lost acting career. They encounter Dai Szae, who has concocted an elaborate scheme to become a vampire, including luring a rock singer to Hollywood to

Winona Ryder as Mina Murray and Gary Oldman as Count Dracula in *Bram Stoker's Dracula*.

participate in a vampire film. Although Dai Szae woos Screech with gifts of ready victims, she tires of his feeding her and goes back to hunting her own food.

Ultimately, she turns him into a vampire only to discover that he had arranged for her to be killed—an ill-fated plan that Screech thwarts. After it is discovered that Mink's image does not show on film any more than it does in a mirror, it is time for the Vamps to put down their Hollywood dreams and take to the road again.

SOURCES:

Vamps. No. 1–6. New York: DC/Vertigo, 1995–96.
Vamps: Hollywood & Vein. No. 1–6. New York: DC Comics, 1996.

Seth

Seth is one of a string of female vampires who visits earth from outer space in the low-budget horror film, *Caress of the Vampire* (1977). The original vampires, all extraterrestrial, arrived on earth many centuries ago. They are very strong and very seductive. They each possess a prominent set of fangs and need a regular ingestion of blood. As sexual creatures, they often engage a partner in sex to set up a feeding.

In the mid-1990s, Seth moves into a residential area of an American city. She has long dark hair and a pierced tongue. She has a vampire roommate Angie. Their relatively small spaceship is kept in the garage of the apartment. Both Seth and Angie prowl the streets for possible victims, who are attacked and drained in a traditional manner.

Seth has set her sights on the new neighbor, a buxom woman who is quite open to a relationship with a female. Meanwhile, the police are investigating the series of "vampire" murders that have hit the community. One attack initiated by Seth was caught on an amateur video, the viewing of which dispelled any hesitancy to ascribe the murder to a vampire assault. The next evening, the officers spot Seth walking the streets and begin a pursuit that leads them to the spaceship. Seth beats a hasty retreat far beyond the police's jurisdiction. Although gone, she will soon be replaced by one of her extraterrestrial sisters.

Shade, Scarlett

Scarlett Shade, the sexy writer of vampire novels, is the subject of the novel, *Shade* (1994). Her unhappy childhood was punctuated by her mother's death during childbirth and her father's sexual abuse. She overcame her upbringing, however, and became a successful writer. She created two successful vampire characters, Count Downe and Countess Showery, who appear as continuing characters in her books. Her fans identify with the characters and at conventions carry their infatuation with Shade's characters and work to the point of committing suicide.

As a young woman, Shade was turned into a vampire by a 100-year-old vampiress named Jeanne who befriended her and taught her how to survive. Shade has red hair and blue eyes. She tends to wear tight-fitting clothes that show off her physical endowments. As a vampire, she has fangs and can transform into mist and move about. She can also move about in daylight, but prefers the evening. As a writer of vampire novels, she pretends to act like a vampire to perpetuate her image. Thus she carries her coffin with her without arousing suspicion. She does not need her coffin to sleep, and is content with a small amount of native soil and a dark room. Holy symbols do not affect her.

Shade has a very special relationship to mirrors. Prior to becoming a vampire, she reasoned that, for a supernatural being, mirrors can serve as a transportation system, as they reflect the soul and the desires held inside of individuals. After becoming a vampire, she discovers she guessed correctly, and thus can enter the lives of those fans who agree with the philosophy of her novels and identify with her characters. She has a psychic connection with their lust and can feed off of it and use it to gain information for her future novels. As part of her everyday outfit, she wears an antique mirror necklace.

The fact that people have committed suicide out of their attempts to be like Shade's characters serves the vampire well. She can take her victim's blood and then leave them as if they have committed suicide. Unfortunately, her bite communicates the vampiric condition. Her victims arise, but without training do not succeed as vampires. They exist in a state similar to limbo. At the end of the story, one of her fans, Philip Ottoman, figures out that Shade is in fact a vampire and is killing fans at the conventions. He sets out to kill her, with stake in hand, and succeeds.

SOURCES:
Darke, David. *Shade*. New York: Zebra, 1994.

Sinistre, Count Armand

French vampire Count Armand Sinistre is the leader of a vampire community in the film *Devils of Darkness* (1965). As a human, he was born in Brittany in 1588, but early in the next century is buried alive for his crimes. He returns as a vampire and among his early acts claims a gypsy woman, Tanya, on her wedding day as his own bride and eternal mate. He establishes himself in a nearby cave and emerges at night as the leader of a small group of vampires that hold a small Breton village in fear. Much of his power is derived from a talisman he possesses that pictures a serpent and a bat.

Count Sinistre is a traditional aristocratic vampire. He appears to be in his thirties. Although nocturnal, he can operate in the daytime as needed, and sleeps in a crypt. He has supernatural powers and can, for example, transform into a bat and fly. He is particularly vulnerable to the cross. The group he heads operates as a coven and works magic. They dress in red robes with hoods.

In the mid-1960s, Sinistre's hold on the village is shaken by the arrival of several British guests at the local inn. Two young men are attacked and killed while exploring the caves where Sinistre sleeps. Sinistre also attacks Ann Forest, the sister of one of the men, but in the process drops his talisman. The talisman is found by Forest's boyfriend, Paul Baxter, who takes it with him to England.

Sinistre mobilizes his coven to recover the talisman. In England, he seduces and kidnaps a young woman loosely connected to Baxter and holds her as ransom in

Count Armand Sinistre leads his group of vampires in a ritualistic ceremony in the film *Devils of Darkness*.

order to force Baxter, who has since learned of the talisman's power, to return the missing object. However, Sinistre likes the girl and decides to initiate her into the coven to replace his present bride. Baxter breaks up the ceremony and rescues the girl. Chasing Baxter, Sinistre runs into the light of the rising sun and is caught in the shadow of a cross. He quickly burns.

Skeeter

Skeeter is a member of a female vampire motorcycle group known as the Vamps, who lend their name to the comic book series of the same name. A brown-haired beauty with a southern drawl, she grew up in the Carolinas where she met **Dave**, a redneck vampire who turned her one night in the early 1970s. She is the first of the five young females he gathers as his minions, and together with **Mink**, **Whipsnake**, **Screech**, and **Howler**, she lures men to the location where Dave waits to join the evening meal. In 1994, she rises up with her vampire sisters and kills Dave, dismembering him and scattering the body parts. Taking to the road on motorcycles, they emerge as the Vamps.

Skeeter follows Howler, the group's leader, to Las Vegas, and from there the Vamps venture to New York City to assist Howler in her quest for her son, who has been put up for adoption. While there, Skeeter becomes attracted to rock singer Rhys Campbell. She is in the midst of feeding off him when the rest of the group gets the psychic impression that Dave has somehow been resurrected. Leaving Campbell as an unfinished meal, the group disposes of Dave in a more permanent manner and then departs for Hollywood so that Mink can resurrect her lost acting career.

In the process of discovering Hollywood, the other women become involved in an elaborate plot concocted by the wealthy Lawrence Dai Szae, an old friend of Screech's. Dai Szae wants to become a vampire, and arranges for Rhys Campbell, who lives to write about his encounter with the Vamps, to come to California and make a movie about his experience.

After Mink lands the star role in Campbell's movie, he and Skeeter reconnect. She tries to console him when she learns he is half-vampire, and impotent, although she does not finish the transformation. She also tells him her version of the vampire origin myth, which she claims has been passed to her: The first vampire was a baby who grew in his mother's womb, and became blood crazed while still in the womb. He stayed there for thirteen months. Having drained his mother, he used his teeth to break out of his mother's womb and he attached himself to her sister. He bit her and she then turned on the child and drank its blood. The child merely laughed, as he had made the first vampire. From that night, the woman drank from her victims and the infant from the woman. He sunk his fangs into her breast like a nursing baby and let her do all the work.

In California, Skeeter also meets Dee Frank, a vampire she knew back in North Carolina. She had originally turned Dave, but was now in trouble. Her longtime mate, poet **Hugh Evans**, has disappeared. As it turns out, the kidnaping of Evans is part of Dai Szae's plot. Skeeter gets Campbell and the other Vamps involved, and together they locate and rescue Evans. In the meantime Mink's movie career comes crashing down when it is discovered that her image does not show on film. The Vamps leave Hollywood and hit the road for better horizons.

SOURCES:
Vamps. No. 1–6. New York: DC/Vertigo, 1995–96.
Vamps: Hollywood & Vein. No. 1–6. New York: DC Comics, 1996.

Skorzeny, Janos

A traditional Eastern European aristocratic vampire, Count Janos Skorzeny appears in *The Night Stalker*, the acclaimed made-for-television movie and subsequent novelization of Richard Matheson's screenplay. Skorzeny was born in 1900 in Craesti, near the town of Cluj, Transylvania, in what is now Romania. He grew up on his father's ancestral estate. At the age of 16, and in spite of wartime restrictions, he was sent by his father, Count Leo Vlad Skorzeny, to England to continue his education at Grimpen Academy in West Riding. During his school years, there were reports of mysterious deaths of cattle and sheep, and no less than five young girls disappeared, but their loss was attributed to the nearby moors and never connected to Skorzeny.

When the movie opens, Count Skorzeny has returned to his father's estate. His father dies and he inherits a fortune. There are also a number of mysterious deaths and disappearances in the immediate area during this time. In 1923, Skorzeny closes his castle and begins traveling. He is seen at different places in Germany throughout most of the 1930s, resurfaces in Paris during the years immediately preceding World War II, and spends the war years in England. After the war he attains British citizenship under the name Paul Blasco, claiming a nonexistent university degree from Heidelberg. He remains in England for several years, conducting hematology experiments, and then moves to Canada in 1948, where he stays for the next 20 years. Wherever he travels, there are reports of unusual deaths and robberies of blood banks.

It is not until 1970, when he travels to Las Vegas, that the records of the count's life are assembled and the story of the series of murders/disappearances put together. He attracts the attention of a newspaper reporter, **Carl Kolchak**, the Night Stalker, and Kolchak begins his marginal career tracking down stories of supernatural crimes and occurrences with the Skorzeny case. Kolchak observes and documents the count's tendencies, including his preference to sleep in a white pine coffin that contains his native earth. He does not show his image in mirrors, and, like most traditional vampires, is repelled by holy water and crosses. Kolchak especially notes his very bad case of halitosis, which he fights with an array of mouthwashes. He also has a makeup kit for creating disguises.

During his time in Las Vegas, Skorzeny kills several women and kidnaps others so he can feed them glucose and regularly milk them for their blood. One of the women he bites, **Katherine Rollins**, survives, and Kolchak would come to track her killings in Los Angeles several years later.

SOURCES:

Rice, Jeff. *The Night Stalker.* New York: Pocket Books, 1974. Reprinted as *The Kolchak Papers 1: The Night Stalker.* Massapequa Park, NY: Cinemaker, 1993.

Steelgate, Jack

Jack Steelgate, the antagonist of **Dennis Harte** in the comic book miniseries *Harte of Darkness*, had become a vampire in Vietnam. As an American soldier named Grissom, he had fought beside Colonel Cherry (later to become private investigator Dennis Harte). After Cherry had been killed (and later resurrected as a vampire), the two had been separated. Harte heard that Grissom had been killed. Actually, he had encountered Nguyen, the same 1,000-year-old vampire that had bitten Cherry/Harte, who had, like him, become a vampire.

Upon his return to the United States, Grissom assumes a new identity and life. A traditional vampire, he cannot enter a church and is repulsed by sacred objects such as the cross. He has no reflection in mirrors and leaves no image on film (and hence has to choose an occupation that does not require a photo ID). He cannot enter a building without an invitation, but can venture out in the day for short periods if he wears sunglasses. During the day, he does not have access to his full powers (strength, ability to transform into an animal). He has a beast nature that he enjoys releasing occasionally.

In 1990, as Jack Steelgate, Grissom becomes a multimillionaire and opens an office in Houston, where Harte works quietly as a private investigator. He has conceived a scheme of creating an empire of vampires and sets about organizing a vampire community in Texas. In the course of his building his vampire organization, Houston becomes the scene of a number of unexplained deaths and disappearances. Harte is hired to find Danielle Cassidy, a young woman who disappeared. His work on her case brings him into contact with his old buddy, from whom he learns about Nguyen. Steelgate invites Harte to join him, and in order to overcome the amoral millionaire and complete his assignment, Harte allows his own bestial nature to come out.

SOURCES:
Harte of Darkness. No. 1–4. Westlake Village, CA: Eternity Comics, 1991–92.

Stockton, John Sinclair

John Sinclair Stockton is the pseudovampire who becomes the object of Sherlock Holmes' investigation in *The Last Vampire* (1992), the made-for-television movie version of Arthur Conan Doyle's short story "The Sussex Vampire." Stockton does not appear in the original short story, which focuses upon **Carlotta Ferguson**, but as the mysterious resident of the Victorian village of Lamberley, he becomes the center of interest of the movie version of this tale.

A middle-aged gentleman, Stockton moves to the village after a lifetime of travel, study, and writing. He has authored one book, *The Religions of Peru.* Not a very personable individual, he becomes the object of community prejudice, especially after it is discovered that he is a descendant of the Sinclairs, a family that had once been a wealthy and powerful force in the community, but were burned out a century ago after village gossip had targeted them as vampires. It is noted by the local townspeople that Stockton seems to live a nocturnal existence and never attends church.

Stockton becomes a matter of interest to Sherlock Holmes following the death of two Lamberley residents: the blacksmith who quarreled with Stockton and died suddenly after some words with him; and Riccardo, the infant son of Bob Ferguson and his Peruvian wife Carlotta who died following the evening Stockton attended their home as a dinner guest. Although neither death manifested signs of criminal activity, Holmes believes his investigation might prevent a crime against Stockton.

Stockton has a natural affinity for members of Bob Ferguson's family. He gives violin lessons to his oldest son Jack, a troubled boy who feels emotionally alienated after his mother's death and father's second marriage. Stockton can speak Spanish and lived for awhile in Peru, which Carlotta finds engaging. Ferguson, lacking the skills to deal with the crisis in his own family, becomes jealous and enraged at Stockton. One evening after an angry exchange with Ferguson, Stockton has an accident with his carriage and is killed.

Incidents following Stockton's death merely fuel speculation that he is a vampire. Ferguson's maid Delores is attacked and left with two puncture wounds on her neck. Carlotta is found sucking blood from Delores's wounds. Jack is killed when, thinking himself a vampire with the ability to fly, he dons a cape and jumps from a building. The villagers exhume Stockton's body from consecrated ground and take it to the ruins of the Sinclair home. They burn his possessions. Ferguson makes a stake and drives it into Stockton's corpse in an effort to put an end to the town's disturbing events.

Holmes finally discovers the source of the events in Jack's mental malaise. Thinking himself a vampire, he had attacked Delores with a sharp stick covered with poison. Carlotta, figuring out what he had done, tried to suck the poison from the wound. No one thought to ask her what she was doing, but merely assumed that Stockton had turned her into a vampire. While unable to prevent the deaths of Stockton or Jack, in solving the puzzle Holmes is able to quell the villagers' fear and bring some degree of peace to the Ferguson home.

Stone, John Alucard

John Alucard Stone is a Miami businessman in the independent, low-budget film, *A Taste of Blood* (1966). Stone receives a package from London that contains two bottles of very strange slivowitz, the plum brandy of Transylvania. The usually clear liquor is blood red. He is told to drink a toast to his ancestor. Stone is the last descendant of **Count Dracula** and, as his great-grandson, has inherited all of his property, including the Carfax estate outside London.

Stone begins to take some of the slivowitz each evening and slowly changes into the likeness of his ancestor. His wife Helena and friends notice that he is becoming nocturnal. He never goes to the office and starts to withdraw from Helena. His hands become cold and clammy to the touch, and he turns from Helena's cross-shaped necklace.

Stone is then summoned to England, and while there he murders three people, Philip Harker, Wayne Seward, and Lord Gold, each the great-grandson of one of the descendants of the six people who tracked and killed Dracula in the 1890s. Each, like Dracula, is stabbed in the heart. Stone is also given a ring that allows him to hypnotize people.

By the time Stone returns to Miami, his transformation into a vampire is complete. He now has plans to bite his wife three times and complete her transformation by sharing his blood with her. But first he flies to Houston, Texas, and kills Sherry Morris, the descendant of vampire hunter Quincey Morris. By the time he returns to Miami, **Dr. Howard Helsing**, the descendant of the great vampire hunter **Abraham Van Helsing**, has arrived on the scene to explain Stone's behavior. He and Dr. Hank Tyson, Stone's best friend, track the entranced Helena to the secret location where Stone has placed his coffin. Here, as dawn approaches, Helsing forces Stone into his coffin with a cross held before his face and then stakes him. Helena awakes, and again all is well in South Florida.

Talbot, David

David Talbot is a friend of the vampire **Lestat de Lioncourt** and is also the former Superior General of the The Talamasca, a very old semi-secret organization operating in the world of Anne Rice's *The Vampire Chronicles*. Created in the eighth century A.D., the Talamasca has observed and documented a wide variety of supernatural (or what today is termed paranormal) activity, including vampirism, and has a special collection of items that reputed "vampires" have left behind.

Talbot, a resident of London, headed the Talmasca in the decade following World War II. Shortly after he was introduced to the storyline of the *Chronicles* (in the third volume, *The Queen of the Damned*), he invited the vampire **Jesse** to affiliate with the organization. In 1985, he sent her on a mission to New Orleans to see if a book that was recently published called *Interview with the Vampire* was really true. The book claimed to be the true account of an eighteenth-century New Orleans vampire. In New Orleans, Jesse was able to locate the house in which vampires Lestat, **Louis de Pointe du Lac,** and **Claudia** had lived. More importantly, she found several items that Claudia had hidden in a secret compartment in a wall in the house. Talbot pulls Jesse off the case just as she begins to get emotionally involved in it.

Talbot meets Lestat for the first time when Jesse sets up a meeting of the two. This happens shortly after the vampire queen **Akasha** has been foiled in her attempt at world domination and killed. Lestat is somewhat fascinated with the Talamasca and toys with the idea letting the group offically study him. He travels to England to meet with Talbot, and, after he gets to know him and forms a friendship with him, offers him the "Dark Gift" of vampirism. Talbot, already 74 years old, declines, but becomes even further entangled in Lestat's life in another volume of the *Chronicles*, *Tale of the Body Thief*.

In that book, Lestat switches bodies with a mysterious character named **Raglan James,** who has the power to switch bodies with another person. Talbot expresses his

Jane Talbot (portrayed by Coleen Gray) ages rapidly when her secret, youth-giving formula begins to fail.

disdain for the idea, but Lestat decides to give it a try because he wants to remember what it feels like to be mortal. Unfortunately, as soon as James gets into Lestat's body, he decides to keep the body, steal Lestat's assets, and leave Lestat in his mortal state. Talbot agrees to help Lestat and mobilizes the resources of the Talamasca. He helps track James to a tour boat in the Caribbean. There, Talbot and Lestat trick James and force him out of Lestat's body. Something unexpected happens, however. When James is knocked out of Lestat's body, he jumps into Talbot's body instead of back into his own. Talbot, meanwhile, is forced into James' youthful body, while Lestat reclaims his own. Happy with his new, young, and strong body, Talbot now readily accepts Lestat's offer of the Dark Gift.

Talbot overlooks the fact that, by associating with Lestat, he broke two of his own rules—don't get involved with the subject of a study, and don't talk to (much less become!) a vampire. After assuming James' body and becoming a vampire, Talbot retires from the Talamasca. Thus he is available to be with Lestat when the latter returns from his later adventures in heaven and hell (as told in *Memnoch the Devil*), and helps to record Lestat's accounts of his travels. He is briefly tempted to follow fellow vampire **Armand**'s example and fly into the sun so he can die and go to god, but refrains after Lestat talks to him. Several years later, he travels to Rome and convinces the vampire **Pandora** to tell him the story of her life.

SOURCES:

Ramsland, Katherine. *The Vampire Companion: The Official Guide to Anne Rice's The Vampire Chronicles*. New York: Ballantine Books, 1993.

Rice, Anne. *Memnoch the Devil*. New York: Alfred A. Knopf, 1994. 354 pp. Rept.: New York: Ballantine Books, 1995.

Talbot, Jane

As the middle-aged alcoholic wife of physician Paul Talbot, Jane Talbot (portrayed by Coleen Gray) is the vampire-like character featured in the film *The Leech Woman* (1959). When the film opens, Talbot is losing her beauty and her husband has become inattentive. One day in his office, she agrees to a divorce, and soon after encounters an old black woman who tells her that she is the one that she has seen in her "dreams of blood."

Later, the old woman tells Dr. Talbot of her ability to live to the age of 152 through a substance from her African homeland. She gives him the last of the substance to test, and then tells him that there is an additional substance that returns youth. Talbot gives her money to return to her tribe, and then, with his wife, follows her to Africa.

With a guide, the Talbots make their way to the Nado village and witness the old woman become youthful again. The woman explains that the youthful appearance remains for a short time only, and is given to the aging members of the tribe as a last gift. Unfortunately, the additional ingredient is fluid from the participant's pineal gland, the extraction of which causes the person's death. The woman also informs the Talbots and their guide that they cannot leave the village and will be killed to protect the secret from the outside world.

Talbot agrees to participate in the process, selecting her husband as the pineal fluid donor. She is overwhelmed with the change and develops a compulsion to be young, reminiscent of **Elizabeth Bathory**. She and the guide escape with the youth-giving substance. She arrives in Los Angeles (having killed a person in New York to obtain his pineal fluid) as her young niece, Terry Howard, and begins the process of seducing her young lawyer. To keep her youth, she picks up a victim in a local bar and kills him in his car. The similarity of the victim's wound to that of her victim in New York leads the police to her. By this time, the elixir is working for a shorter and shorter period of time, and each time it wears off, she is measurably older than before. The last batch, made with the pineal gland fluid of the lawyer's fiancée, does not work at all. In her despair, Talbot finally commits suicide.

Tasha

Tasha is the seductive vampire owner of a strip club that lends its name to the film *Vamps* (1996). Like most establishments of this nature, Vamps caters to lonely men—the perfect venue for Tasha and her vampire employees to find their next meal. Tasha, an attractive redhead, is actually several hundred years old. Her family had faithfully served a queen who turned out to be a vampire. As a reward for their loyalty and service, the queen made Tasha (or Natasha) a vampire.

As the owner of Vamps, Tasha has quarters in the basement where she keeps her satin-lined coffin. She is a modern nonsupernatural vampire. While she can live indefinitely, she cannot turn into a bat, and is not repulsed by crosses or holy water. Unlike traditional vampires, her image appears in mirrors. She has fangs that emerge when she feeds, and she is vulnerable to physical attack.

Tasha is assisted at Vamps by two young stripper vampires, Randy and Tabitha, but is ready to bring a fourth girl into their group. She appears in the form of **Heather**, a down-on-her-luck student who has flunked out of college and is broke. Tasha trains her to strip and hires her for the club. In spite of her beauty, she has a history of being manipulated and rejected by men—the latest of whom is a priest, Shamus McConnell, with whom Heather has fallen in love. Tasha uses her emotional low as the opportunity to transform her into a vampire.

Tasha sends Randy to kill Shamus, and she attacks and kidnaps one of Heather's former boyfriends. She then bites Heather and mingles her saliva with her blood. When Heather awakens, she must complete the process by feeding, or else die. Although fearful, when her former acquaintance attacks her with profanities, she overcomes her inhibitions. However, the crisis arises when Shamus appears on the scene to tell her that he really loves her. Having to choose between him and Tasha, Heather turns on Tasha and drains her. As Shamus has already killed Randy in the heat of the battle, only Heather and Tabitha are left to run Vamps.

The Temptress

The Temptress, a succubus demon operating in a contemporary African-American community, is the villainous force in the film, *Def by Temptation* (1990). The succubus chooses to manifest through a young woman residing in a Manhattan apartment. She is seductive and aggressive, her only notable physical attribute being her long gold fingernails. Fangs appear as she is ready to attack. She operates out of the local bar, where a continuous line of men come in to pick up a woman for the evening. Avoiding any kissing, she invites them to her home, and as they relax in her bed, attacks them. Only a few of the men notice that all the mirrors in the apartment are covered.

The larger purpose of the succubus is to keep morality in check through the use of her sexuality. In the modern world, the succubus meets her real challenge in Joel, a young divinity student, who has come to New York from the South to sort out his doubts about his calling. Victory for the succubus comes whenever she destroys innocence, and the naive Joel is the last of an ancestral line of ministers. Because he has a deeply ingrained set of morals, he does not react as most men to the Temptress's enticements, although in the end he is able to encounter the evil head-on. He destroys the present incarnation of the succubus with the light of the cross, and she is sent back to hell, at least temporarily. Of course, she always has other young women through whom she can manifest.

Tesla, Armand

For another dark role, Bela Lugosi dons his vampire's cape, not as **Count Dracula,** but as Armand Tesla, the undead Romanian scholar of the film *The Return of the Vampire* (1944). Tesla is a distinguished gentleman of the early eighteenth century who, prior to his physical death in 1744, studied the occult and vampirism deeply and wrote a learned text on the subject. In the twentieth century, when the storyline takes place, he has made his way to England, and during World War I plagues London with his attacks. His survival is aided by Andreas, a drone whom he has turned into a wolfman.

Tesla is almost identical to the Count Dracula of the 1931 Universal picture. The hypnotic-eyed creature wears formal clothes, complete with opera cape. He sleeps in a coffin on his native soil. He can be driven off with a cross and, of course, can be killed with a stake in the heart and revived by removing the stake. Despite Tesla's similarities to the original Count, *The Return of the Vampire* is important for establishing the vampire as a purely nocturnal creature (which the classic 1922 German film *Nosferatu* did somewhat successfully). Like **Graf Orlock,** Tesla cannot venture out in the daytime.

Tesla's nemesis is Lady Jane Ainsley, a woman whose daughter is attacked by Tesla. With the help of Professor Walter Sanders, Ainsley tracks Tesla and stakes him in 1918. They place his body in an unmarked grave and continue on with their lives. All is well until 1944, when a treatise written by the now-deceased Sanders falls into the hands of Scotland Yard. One of their inspectors is determined to open the grave and possibly charge Ainsley with murder, although the Germans thwart his plans by bombing the graveyard. Tesla's coffin is opened and two ignorant clean-up workers pull the stake from his heart. The revived Tesla places Andreas under his control and finds a new resting place.

Bela Lugosi once again plays the part of a vampire, this time appearing as Armand Tesla in the 1944 film,
The Return of the Vampire.

After his revival in 1944, Tesla assumes the identity of Dr. James Bruckner, and as such is welcomed by Ainsley into her home and laboratory. He plans to steal her daughter Nicky and take her to Romania. Ainsley, trying to convince the Scotland Yard detective that Tesla is in fact a vampire returned from the grave, tracks him until the Germans interfere again. Told by Ainsley that he does not have to be Tesla's servant, Andreas turns on Tesla with a cross, but as the bombs drop, Tesla is knocked unconscious. Andreas carries him outside where the sun finishes him off in one of the more memorable scenes in the early cycle of Dracula movies.

Thompson, Edward "Evil"

Edward "Evil" Thompson is the knowledgeable but skeptical friend of Charlie Brewster in the film *Fright Night* (1985). Something of a nerd, he tells Charlie all about vampires while ridiculing his belief at every turn. He participates in a scheme with Charlie's girlfriend Amy and television horror movie host **Peter Vincent** to prove that his new neighbor, **Jerry Dandridge**, is not a vampire. However, after Dandridge sets out to attack all of Charlie's friends who are aware of his existence, Evil is the first to fall. He is stopped in an alley and turned into a vampire. He then assists Dandridge in the kidnaping of Charlie's girlfriend Amy.

Like all of the *Fright Night* vampires, he is repelled by crosses and displays prominent fangs. He transforms when enraged or about to feed. When he reveals himself and attacks Vincent, the scared actor pushes a cross in his forehead. It burns a scar into the skin it touches. Hurt, Evil leaves immediately.

While Charlie and Vincent plan an all-out assault on Dandridge, Evil goes into Charlie's house looking for his mother. She is away at her work on the night shift so he climbs in bed, where Vincent finds him. He changes into a wolf and attacks. Cornered, Vincent finds a makeshift stake and impales the wolf as he jumps for the throat. Evil dies, and Vincent reluctantly returns to Dandridge's house.

SOURCES:
Fright Night. No. 1–2. Chicago: Now Comics, 1988.
Skipp, John, and Craig Spector. *Fright Night.* New York: Tor Books, 1985.

Tibor, Baron

One of the new vampire characters to emerge in the wake of changes to the Comic Code that had banned vampires from comic books through the 1960s, Baron Tibor became a recurring character the Gold Key series, *The Occult Files of Doctor Spector.* In the series, Doctor Spector, the narrator, is an occult investigator who tells of his encounter with the Transylvanian nobleman in the first issue.

Baron Tibor, like **Count Dracula,** had terrorized the countryside near his castle for 300 years. He was a strong nocturnal being who slept in a coffin on native soil, and could transform into a bat or into mist. The villagers caught up with him in the early 1930s, however, staked him in the heart, and buried him in a secret grave.

Forty years later, a group who wants to become his disciples and hopes that he will turn them into vampires discovers the grave. They bring a black horse to the graveyard and dig up the grave over which the horse refuses to walk. Once the coffin is opened, the group remove the stake and Tibor comes back to life. However, upon awakening, he is not the same vampire he once was. During the 40 years, he had drifted among the evil dead in the netherworld. He had vowed that should he ever return to earthly life,

BLOODY BAD GIRLS

Comic books have always been a world dominated by boys. They buy them, they read them and most of their stars are men: strong, handsome, self-assured. With the prominent exception of Wonder Woman, it is rare when a strong female character carries a series. However, as the 1990s draw to a close, the male-dominated comics are beginning to change. Suddenly, mid decade, several score of strong female characters emerged in popular new comic book series. They are called the bad girls, beautiful women—feminine to the core—filling male roles, operating as one would expect a male to operate, complete with testosterone.

A vampire, Vampirella, was the original bad girl (though some could argue that Barbarella, upon whom she was modeled, was the first). Vampirella is an extraterrestrial hero whose need for blood is provided via serum, thus eliminating her continual need to attack unworthy humans as a means of fulfilling her next meal. Once the marketability of bad girls was recognized, vampires became a natural. Brian Ulido created one of the early bad girls, Lady Death, and went on to give us Purgatori and Chastity—and he does not seem to be finished yet. There are other bad girls as well: Lady Vampré haunts modern Los Angeles, and Luxera dominates a vast underground empire while resisting the influence of two rogue vampires, the Blood Hunter and Pontius Vanthor. Most recently Luxera has been joined by her grandchild Bethany, only half vampire, but all woman.

he would spend his time making amends for all the deaths he had caused. Alive and thirsty, his vow wars against his immediate need for blood, and comes in direct conflict with the cult of would-be followers who now clamor for his attention.

Dr. Spector arrives at the castle in the nick of time with a solution. He has discovered a serum that will relieve Tibor of his thirst. Tibor welcomes Spector's solution, and together they see to the destruction of the group of wannabe vampires. As a former vampire, Tibor has a number of ventures that challenge his resolve, including the break-in of his castle by thieves. Unfortunately for the robbers they steal his chandelier, where every day the local bat community gathers as a sleeping place.

Eventually, however, the serum loses its potency, and Tibor returns to his vampiric state. Rather than call Dr. Spector, he travels to America, in part because he is called by an immortal disembodied brain who is looking for an immortal body into which he can be transplanted. Spector is able to quell Tibor's thirst temporarily with some synthetic blood, but in the end, after destroying the brain, Tibor ends his existence by impaling himself.

SOURCES:
"The Brain of Xorkon." *The Occult Files of Doctor Spector.* No. 15. Aug. 1975. "Cult of the Vampire." *The Occult Files of Doctor Spector.* No 1. 1972. Reprinted in *The Occult Files of Doctor Spector.* No. 25, 1973.
"Of Bats and Men." *The Occult Files of Doctor Spector.* No. 11. Dec. 1974.
"She Who Serves the Dark Gods." *The Occult Files of Doctor Spector.* No. 9. Aug. 1974.

Trapp, Philip

Philip Trapp, the psychotic vampire hunter in the novel *Blood Work* (1994), is an albino born to insensitive parents in Philadelphia, who mercilessly kid him about his pale skin and white hair. When he is about five, his father takes him to an amusement park. The day climaxes with a trip to "Dracula's Castle," where Trapp is told to put the stake in the fake **Count Dracula**'s heart. He does and, much to the surprise of his father, is given a medal for his bravery. When his father hugs him, it is the first sign confirming the boy's new self-image.

As he grows older, he identifies himself as special, set apart to kill vampires. He watches for signs. One comes when his sight is threatened by a milk-colored substance replacing the small amount of color in his eyes. Later, as he learns more about vampires, a dream confirms that he is among the unique ones chosen to lead a lonely life killing vampires.

As an adult, Trapp learns of porphyria, a disease that gives its victims some of the symptoms of vampirism. They are light sensitive, have deformed teeth, and hate garlic. Blood seems to help them. There is no medical cure. Trapp knows that people inflicted with porphyria are really vampires, and as a hospital lab technician, he is in the perfect position to permanently cure the afflicted with a silver dagger in their hearts.

He begins his killing in 1985. He kidnaps victims, buries them in the woods where he and his father had hunted deer, and takes some of their body parts. He saves the hearts, which he impales with a silver knife, and feeds the liver and kidneys to his rottweiler. He then begins tracking down relatives whom he understands are also infected with the taint of vampirism.

His killing is interrupted by Dr. Elizabeth Broward, who treats porphyria victims, and widower Zack James, who happens to discover the shallow grave in which Trapp had buried some of his victims. Trapp comes to see Broward as the Queen of the Vampires, whom he must kill at all costs. As Broward and James close in on him, he targets Broward.

SOURCES:

Zachary, Fay. *Blood Work*. New York: Berkley Books, **1994**.

Tsepes, Stephen

Stephen Tsepes is a 300-year-old vampire featured in two films of the late 1980s, *Graveyard Shift* (1987) and *The Understudy: Graveyard Shift II* (1988). He appears as a young man in his twenties who establishes himself in an apartment in the city and takes a job as a cab driver during the graveyard shift. A thoroughly modern vampire, he is unaffected by crosses or garlic, and his image shows in a mirror. He sleeps in the nude in an ornate coffin. He is very strong and quickly recovers from bullets, but is vulnerable to a stake in the heart, decapitation, and sunlight. Over the decades, he has considered ending it all, but never seems to have the courage.

Stephen is drawn to young women who are in a death cycle, and these become the victims he turns into vampires. They feed off others and periodically return to Stephen for him to feed off them. He feeds from their breast rather than their neck. Routine changes for Stephen when he meets Michelle Hayden, a video producer dying of a terminal disease. Recognizing her marriage is little more than an inconvenience, he invites Michelle to his apartment, something he has never done with any of the other women, and they explore the possibilities of love in a coffin. She arouses a passion in him that he has not experienced before, which is passed on to the other vampires he has created. The passion releases in the others in the form of a series of savage killings.

Michelle's husband Eric is jealous of the new man in his wife's life and shares his concern with a friend who is somewhat knowledgeable of vampirism. Eric, his friend, Michelle, Stephen, and all of the vampire women gather at Michelle's studio one evening for a final confrontation. As a result, Stephen is staked, and Eric's friend and all the women are killed. The police arrive just as Eric is about to stake his wife. He is arrested, and she survives to adopt a new life as a cab driver during the graveyard shift.

Stephen is dead, but resurfaces in the film's sequel In the sequel, he begins to appear as a spirit to a young actress Camilla, who is starring in a vampire movie. He now needs a new body and slowly talks Camilla into helping him. She kills the male star of the movie and, with the blood, Stephen is able to reappear in the actor's body. He takes over the role in the movie, in which he portrays a vampire pool shark. One by one, Stephen moves in on the other women working on the film. Rather than feeding from their breast, however, he primarily feeds from a cut made between their thumb and forefinger.

Camilla's fiancé discovers Stephen's identity and challenges him to a game of pool, the symbol of what in past centuries would have been a duel. The challenge moves to a more violent level as others become involved, and eventually Stephen wins the game. Ultimately, Stephen is destroyed when the curtain is pulled off the window and rays of morning light stream in. However, Camilla has already taken up her new life visiting pool halls looking for a means to quench her thirst.

Tummelier, Peter Augustus

Peter Augustus Tummelier, the vampire featured in David Martin's 1994 novel, *Tap Tap*, was born and grew up on Hambriento Island, Florida, a fairly wealthy community. His best friend as a boy is Roscoe Bird, the son of a man who runs a small fishing charter service for residents and tourists on the island. As boys, the two fantasize about buying a boat and sailing around the world. During these years, Roscoe's father commits suicide, reportedly as a result of some of the wealthy residents turning on him and ruining his business.

Peter has an older brother, Richard. The two siblings entertain themselves during their youthful years by holding seances. They conjure a spirit whom they called Tap Tap, the spirit of a martyred priest who died on the island centuries ago. Richard has mental problems though, and the family sends him to a hospital in Europe. As an adult, Peter is a rather short five feet six inches, with thick eyebrows, black eyes, a long thin nose, and a widow's peak. He retains a love for rock and roll music and is wealthy enough to drive a black Mercedes with a bright red interior.

In the years after the three leave the island, Roscoe settles in Washington, D.C. with his wife Marianne and loses contact with Tummelier. Tummelier in the meantime meets an old vampire who introduces him into "The Life." Life as a vampire has not tarnished his boyhood fantasy of a trip around the world with Roscoe on their own boat. He plans his reentry into the life of his boyhood friend by killing and drinking the blood of Philip Burton, the man who had caused the suicide of Roscoe's father 20 years ago, and his wife. He comes to Washington and contacts Roscoe directly.

Roscoe's reluctance to leave his present life leads Peter to attempt to curry favor by killing other people Roscoe dislikes, which makes Roscoe the primary suspect for a police department that does not believe in vampires. Before Tummelier is brought down, he is weakened by drinking tainted blood. He kidnaps Marianne, which leads to a final confrontation with Roscoe, but before being brought down by some severe body trauma, he passes on "The Life" to the captive Marianne.

SOURCES:

Martin, David Lozell. *Tap Tap*. New York: Random House, 1993. Reprint, New York: St. Martin's Paperbacks, 1996.

Vampire

Vampire, a seventeenth-century nobleman bitten and turned into a vampire by **Count Dracula**, is a major character in the children's comic book miniseries, *Monster in My Pocket*. Once transformed, Vampire is stricken with the blood thirst. Blessed with Old World charm and continental reserve, he becomes the charismatic leader of a group of "good" monsters. But his charm completely deserts him when a beautiful woman appears, and he will risk much to tap her blood.

In the recent past Vampire faced the evil Warlock, who wished to lead the monsters in an all-out attack on humanity. Vampire proposed that the two gather their followings and allow them to decide. Two weeks later the world's monsters gathered at a volcanic peak. Suddenly there was a blinding light and then complete darkness. When light returned, a wall surrounded the monsters. When they broke through the wall, they found themselves all shrunk to the size of a child's toy. They were in Los Angeles.

Vampire has the ability to fly and to transform into a bat or mist. His main asset is his personal magnetism, which allows him to compel others to do his will. However, his powers have been diminished in his diminutive state. As the leader of the dozen monsters, he suggests that they find a place and means of recovering their natural size. They find a human friend in Jack Miles, who resides in Burbank, a Los Angeles suburb, and their search for a formula to resolve their situation leads to a variety of adventures.

The storyline of *Monster in my Pocket* was later revised for children's television. In this version, all "evil" monsters, Vampire, Frankenstein's monster, Medusa, and Swamp Thing, escape the place where they have been confined. However, both they and their monster captors are shrunk. They now seek to regain their size while fighting their former jailers, the "good" monsters, led by the Invisible Man. The series was also released on video.

SOURCES:

Monster in My Pocket. No. 1–4. Santa Monica, CA: Harvey Comics, 1991.

CORMAN'S CLASSIC: *DANCE OF THE DAMNED*

Roger Corman is known around Hollywood for making quickie, low-budget flicks, most genre-based, each guaranteed to make a profit, none destined for greatness. In the process, Corman has inadvertently launched the careers of a number of talented actors, most notably Jack Nicholson, who made his debut in *Little Shop of Horrors* in 1960. In 1988 Corman gave a creative young female writer, Katt Shea Ruben, the opportunity to put her first motion picture together. She wrote the script and directed her modest film, *Dance of the Damned*. It had only two characters of note, one of whom never reveals his name; he is just identified simply as "The Vampire."

Corman has been responsible for a number of vampire movies over the years, including several noteworthy efforts, including *Not of this Earth* (1957), the first sci-fi vampire movie. Unlike the others, *Dance of the Damned* (1988), emerged as one of the great vampire movies of all time. Far from the common vampire who considers humans in much the same light as humans considers cows, "The Vampire" has an unusual problem, he is an outsider without the sun—and without the community of other outsiders. *Dance of the Damned* explores the brief relationship (six hours) established by "The Vampire" with his next meal, in this case a young woman in despair over the direction her life has taken. As the pair share their unhappiness with each other, the desire for life and the need for food takes over and, and as the dawn approaches, each must make life-affirming decisions if they are to survive past the dawn.

Little seen when it first was issued, *Dance of the Damned* now has a cult fans who eventually got the opportunity to view it.

The Vampire
(*The Dance of the Damned*)

Known only as the Vampire, he is the central character in the classic vampire film *The Dance of Damned* (1988). According to the myth of storyline, vampires are not supernatural, they are members of a separate species. They are born, not made, and have no way of turning humans into vampires. This vampire was born several centuries ago. As a young boy, his family had been trapped in a barn that was set on fire. His mother saved him by pushing him into the earth and using her body to cover him from the flames as he dug deeper. He slept for 100 years and when he arose was scarred and disfigured. He survived on rodents and other small animals.

As the young boy grows and tries to integrate into vampire society, the other vampires shun him, as they only appreciate beauty. Thus, he grows up as an outcast living on the edge of human culture. Over the course of time, taking human blood heals him, and he grows into what appears to be a handsome young adult. Cut off from his own people, he is alone, but now lives in a richly furnished home in Santa Monica, California. It is constructed to prevent unauthorized entry and exit.

Like most traditional vampires, the Vampire has fangs, hypnotic eyes, and long fingernails. He is very strong and fast, his hearing is acute, and his vision is like looking through a red filter. He does not get diseases, and bullets affect him only momentarily. He is vulnerable only to fire and sunlight; thus he is totally nocturnal. He is not the undead, and he does not sleep in a coffin.

After several centuries of life, he is lonely and curious about the sunlit world. It is also his night to feed, and if he misses his feeding he will die. From among the human herd, he selects Jodi, a young woman, as his victim. He perceives that she has a wish to die, but he also wants to communicate with her. He promises to wait until the last minute (6:00 A.M.) before taking her life, but in the meantime, he wants her to tell him about the daylight and assuage his loneliness. He takes her to see her young son, who is being kept from her by her estranged husband, and she takes him to the Santa Monica Pier and puts him under one of the spotlights to give him a taste of sunlight.

As dawn approaches, Jodi's survival instinct takes over. She struggles to find an escape route from the house into the sunlight that is just outside. As the vampire stands outside the door, she barricades herself in the bathroom and opens a window, at least partially. She leaves the Vampire with a choice as to whether or not to enter the sunlit bathroom.

Vampirella

Vampirella, the sexy extraterrestrial vampire, in second only to **Count Dracula** when it comes to successful vampires in the comic book world. She first appeared in the self-titled premier issue in 1969 and appeared in 112 issues through the 1970s before she disappeared. Then, at the beginning of the 1990s, Harris Comics purchased the rights to Vampirella from Warren Publication. Harris has since published 50 new issues of Vampirella, primarily in a number of mini-series featuring different authors and artists.

Perhaps because many authors have been used on the Vampirella series, there are several versions of how Vampirella came to Earth from her home planet of Drakulon. The various retellings are all unique and have little in common, other than the fact that Vampirella is an alien who moves to Earth at some point. Here are the variations of the origins of Vampirella:

ORIGINS, 1975 VERSION: In the early comic books, her origins were described very superficially. All the reader knew is that she was from a planet on which blood was like water on Earth—it flowed in rivers and streams. However, the supply of blood was being threatened by the double suns around which Drakulon whirled. It was not until issue 46 that her biography was filled in. Vampirella had grown up on Drakulon and was engaged to a young man, Tristan. Like other vampires, she exhaled carbon monoxide. Over the centuries, the carbon monoxide in the atmosphere had broken down the protective layer of creatone that surrounded the planet and protected the residents from the most harmful rays of the twin suns. The planet was now dying. Vampirella is able to escape when a space ship from earth arrives. She discovers that the crewmen of the ship have life-giving blood running through their veins, and she survives the trip to Earth by killing them one by one.

ORIGINS, 1988 VERSION: In the first issue of *Vampirella* from Harris Comics, the vampire's life was traced to her pre-Drakulon days. In this version, Vampirella first lived in ancient Egypt as the infamous Cleopatra. As Cleopatra, she was summoned

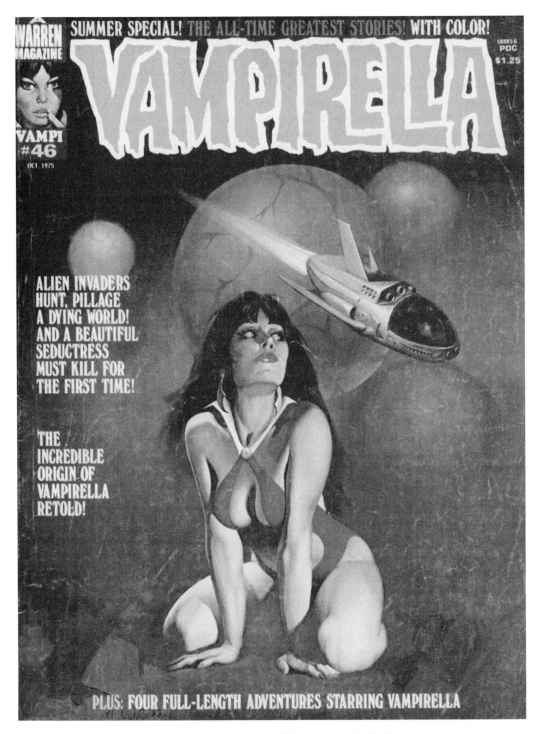

Cover art from the October, 1975 issue of *Vampirella*. now published by Harris Publications, Inc.

to the temple of her husband (and brother) Ptolemy to consummate their marriage. Ptolemy was also a vampire. As soon as she entered his temple, she was grabbed and shackled to a large column. Out of a crypt in front of the column, the vampire-king arose and bit Cleopatra. What followed was the life of Cleopatra as we know it from the history books—her enchanting and seductive ways, her brief affair with her true love, Mark Antony, and its tragic ending. After Mark Anthony died, she entered the vampire temple set upon killing Ptolemy. Having staked him and killed him, the god Amun-Ra appeared and rewarded her by allowing her to reincarnate on the planet Drakulon. To make this happen, she quickly committed suicide via the poisonous snake brought to her by her loyal slave Pendragon (whom, in another twist in the Vampirella universe, she would work for in a storyline set in the 1970s).

ORIGINS, 1995 VERSION: In the 1995 series, *Vengeance of Vampirella*, her extraterrestrial origin was replaced by a mythological one. This story involved Lilith, the first wife of Adam in Hebrew folklore, who sought to earn forgiveness from the God of Order. After her creation, she rejected Adam and was expelled from Eden. In her rage, she hated God and her hatred took on form as the lilin (a demon-like being), who in turn spread evil in the world God created. She finally decided to renounce evil and return to the light and forced her way back into the Garden of Eden, which had been neglected since Adam and Eve had been expelled.

In Eden, Lilith initiated the plan for her own redemption, which began with caring for the garden. She then created the twins Magdelene and Madek and sent them into the world to undo the evil that had resulted from her own hatred. The plan backfired and the twins merely created more evil. She then created Vampirella to defeat the twins and then take on the enormous job of battling all the evil in the world. Before going into the world, she was trained to master the dark side that resided within her, which she had inherited from Lilith.

ORIGINS, 1996 VERSION:. In the made-for-television movie, *Vampirella*, her origins took on a more sinister, science fiction angle. This story began in the ancient times on Drakulon, when people would attack each other and drain their victim's blood. As society evolved, this behavior became unacceptable. Then, approximately 3,000 years ago, a man named Vlad formed a small cult that plotted a revolution against Drakulon's leaders. Vlad was arrested and was supposed to be tried for his crimes. However, during his appearance before Drakulon's council, a rescue team arrived and saved Vlad while killing the members of the council. Vlad himself drank the blood of Vampirella's father. The killers then fled to Earth.

Determined to bring her father's killers to justice, Vampirella followed them to Earth on a returning Mars probe. The journey took 3,000 years. Once on Earth, she joined forces with **Adam Van Helsing,** the head of a vampire eradication agency. Together they would track down Vlad and his minions.

VAMPIRELLA ON EARTH: Vampirella arrived on earth in 1969. She is a huntress for the blood within humans. She is strong and needs a daily dose of blood. She is not bound by the darkness, but freely moves about in the daytime in her skimpy costume. Early on, she is involved in an airplane crash, after which she is found by a doctor who runs a rural clinic. He falls in love with her and she comes to trust him. Most importantly, he creates a synthesized blood substitute that frees Vampirella from her need to attack humans. Unfortunately, the doctor's nurse is a disciple of Chaos, an evil force, and becomes jealous of the doctor's feelings for Vampirella. She carries with her *The Crimson Chronicles*, the bible of the Chaos followers, and below the clinic is a temple where Chaos worshipers gather. Here Vampirella has her first encounter with Chaos; she is taken prisoner by his followers.

Meanwhile, two experts in the ways of evil supernaturalism, **Conrad Van Helsing** and his son Adam, are investigating the plane crash in which Vampirella was involved. Conrad's brother was also on the plane, and his body was found drained of blood. Armed with pictures of the four people on the flight whose bodies were not found, the somewhat psychic Conrad identifies Vampirella as something out of the ordinary and concludes that she had killed his brother. The pair track down Vampirella, who is still being held prisoner by the leader of the Chaos cult, who wants to force Vampirella to make him a vampire. After the Van Helsings arrived, he also takes them prisoner.

While Conrad is unconscious, Vampirella tells her story to Adam, who becomes convinced she is not guilty. Vampirella finally breaks free of her chains, and, since she has been starved while she was held captive, is about to feed from Adam. Just then Conrad wakes up, and what he sees only confirms his suspicions about Vampirella's true nature. Vampirella and Adam escape at that point and go their separate ways, but before they part, Adam willingly lets her feed from him. He does not turn into a vampire because that is not the way that Vampirella transmits vampirism.

Vampirella then finds a job as the assistant to an aging magician and alcoholic, Pendragon. Their first tour takes them to the Caribbean, where they are shipwrecked on an island. There they encounter a man attempting to find a serum to cure his wife of werewolfism. He takes Vampirella prisoner to use her as a guinea pig. Meanwhile, Adam shows up and together they extricate themselves from the situation.

Conrad had also come to the Island to look for Adam, and he is taken prisoner by the followers of Chaos, who are also present. Pendragon, Adam, and Vampirella conspire to free him. Once they escape, Conrad's opinion of Vampirella begins to change. It changes completely when Vampirella helps him track down his brother's real killers, who turn out to be a group of Chaos followers from New Orleans. This cements the bond between Conrad, Adam, Vampirella, and Pendragon, and the four would have numerous adventures through the 1970s.

After issue number 112 (February 1983), the Warren Vampirella series came to an end. After several years of lying dormant, Vampirella was brought back for the 1990s by Harris Comics. In the most recent adventure of the four friends, they battle the forces of Chaos in the subways of New York City. Conrad is taken prisoner, and Vampirella goes after him. Adam leaves, stunned by the events that have unfolded. The three do not meet for the next decade. During that time, Chaos's minions establish themselves in Washington, D.C., while Adam becomes a United States Senator, and Conrad remains a prisoner. Vampirella is in a state of amnesia and thinks she is Ms. Normandy, the head of a girl's school in Washington.

The catalyst for Vampirella's awakening, and the occasion of a new mini-series, *Vampirella: Morning in America* (Harris, 1991), is the appearance of an old enemy, Ethan Shroud. He initially holds Conrad prisoner and abducts and vampirizes one of the girls at Vampirella's school. Later, he returns the body of the now deceased Conrad to Adam. Conrad is briefly resurrected, and the old team of Vampirella, Pendragon, and the Van Helsings reunites to defeat the various evil powers that had become focused on the nation's capitol. Having smashed the conspiracy and killed Shroud, the elderly Conrad ends his earthly life, and Adam, Pendragon, and Vampirella begin the task of dealing with the remaining forces of Chaos.

The three would operate together for the next few years until Vampirella encounters Nyx, who kills both her and Adam, the latter permanently. Adam's death in *Vengeance of Vampirella* (No. 25) coincides with the new story of her origin that was put forth in 1995 that changes her nature from that of an extraterrestrial being to a supernatural one (the Lilith story). New Vampirella adventures continue to appear.

SOURCES:

Author's Note: Several hundred issues of comic books featuring Vampirella have appeared. For a complete list through 1997, see Vampirella: A Collector's Checklist, *available from the Transylvanian Society of Dracula. The original stories in the Warren issues of Vampirella are now rare and expensive, but have been reprinted in the Harris series Vampirella Classic.*

Busiak, Kurt, and Louis la Chance. *Vampirella: Morning in America.* No. 1–4. New York: Harris Comics/Dark Horse, 1991.

Goodwin, Archie, and José Gonzales. *Vampirella Classic.* No. 1–5. New York: Harris Comics, 1995.

Lewis, Budd, Jose Gonzalez, "The Origin of Vampirella." *Vampirella.* No. 46. Warren, Oct. 1975. Reprinted several times in Vampirella collections.

Loew, Flaxman, and Jose Ortiz. "The Vampire of the Nile." *Vampirella.* No. 113. New York: Harris Comics, 1988: 17–28.

Melton, J. Gordon. *Vampirella: A Collector's Checklist.* Santa Barbara, CA: Transylvanian Society of Dracula, 1998.

Sniegoski, Tom, et al. *Vengeance of Vampirella.* No. 1–25. New York: Harris Comics, 1994–1996.

Vampré, Lady

Lady Vampré is the featured character in a series of comic books from Blackout Comics. She was born in April 1843 as Elizabeth Blessing White. Although her mother died during childbirth and her father died when she was 14, Elizabeth nevertheless grew into a beautiful young woman in rural Virginia as the Civil War began.

When the story begins in June 1862, Elizabeth has just married Sergeant Michael Courtney, a Confederate soldier home on leave after having fought at Shiloh. Elizabeth's wedding evening is interrupted when a vampire breaks into her bedroom and kills her husband. She is kidnaped and turned over to an old vampire named Baraclaw, who moves across the lines of war and dines on soldiers. Because Elizabeth reminds him of his lost love, Angelique Vampré, Baraclaw turns Elizabeth and takes her as his mistress, and so begins her existence as Lady Vampré. Baraclaw moves in the top echelon of society and exercises some power in the government. Realizing that his influence is ending in Washington, he decides to turn on President Lincoln. He follows Lincoln to the Ford Theater, and as he is about to bite the president John Wilkes Booth moves to assassinate Baraclaw. He succeeds in shooting the

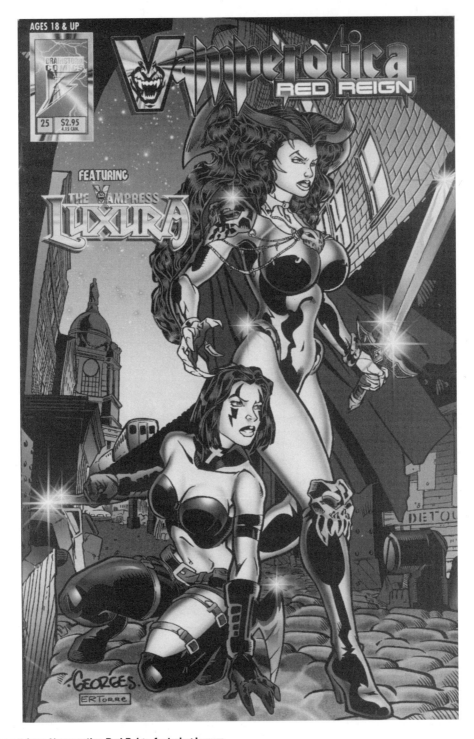

Cover art from *Vamperotica Red Reign*, featuring Luxura.

vampire, but in the process kills Lincoln. Although the bullets only wound Baraclaw, his temporary disability frees Lady Vampré. She escapes before Baraclaw can reassert his control over her.

Over the next century, she survives on animals, while only occasionally needing human blood. She tries to feed on criminals and those who have harmed others, but finds she cannot be their judge and executioner. She is always hungry. Then, in Florence, Italy, in 1966, she finds her way into a church and meets a nun, the long-lost Angelique who had freed herself from Baraclaw. She assures Lady Vampré that just as she has freed herself from Baraclaw, so too can Lady Vampré keeps free from taking human life and survive on the blood of lesser animals. In the succeeding decades, Lady Vampré affirms her humanness, in spite of her confinement to the night.

In present-day Los Angeles, Lady Vampré meets another vampire, named Savanna, who declares her rituals can free vampires from their confinement to the night. She forces Lady Vampré to assist her. The magic kills Savanna and many of the other vampires who participate in the process, but not Lady Vampré. She remains alive to wrestle with the two sides of her nature that fight for dominance.

SOURCES:

Bad Girls of Blackout. No. 0–1. Freehold, NJ: Blackout Comics, 1995.
Bad Girls of Blackout Annual. Freehold, NJ: Blackout Comics, 1995.
The Death of Lady Vampré. Freehold, NJ: Black Out Comics, 1995.
Lady Vampré: Pleasures of the Flesh. Freehold, NJ: Blackout Comics, 1996.

Vanthor, Pontius

Pontius Vanthor, the antagonist of **Luxura** in the *Vamperotica* comic book series, is an old and powerful vampire and the former lover of Luxura. He dresses in a costume that befits his status, a skintight bodysuit, large belt adorned with a large set of fangs that surround his genital area, and a cape held in place with a skull. Vanthor makes his first appearance in the story "Something Wicked" in *Vamperotica* (1994) and has remained a continuing character in the series, often spoken of even when he does not visually appear.

Although rumored dead, Vanthor has recently reappeared to inform Luxura, also a powerful ancient vampire, of his crusade to establish the Red Reign. He calls for the vampires to come out of their underground world and run wild over the earth, eventually establishing themselves in power and treating humanity as cattle. While enjoying the passion that Vanthor arouses in her, Luxura believes that his plan is perverted. Unfortunately, before the Red Militia, the vampire police, can move against him, he has gained many followers and become powerful.

Luxura initially rejects Vanthor's offer to join forces with him, in spite of the knowledge that in so doing she would become a reigning queen in the New Order, and he leaves her to ponder the future. She now wages a continuous war to stop Vanthor's upsetting the stable life the vampire community has achieved in the modern world.

Vanthor has made a second enemy, the **Blood Hunter**, a rogue vampire whose girlfriend was killed by some of Vanthor's followers. In that same encounter, the

Blood Hunter had been transformed into a vampire and has since dedicated his existence to fighting the Red Reign by killing Vanthor's followers. In the process he is gaining the power and expertise so that eventually he can go against Vanthor himself. To ensure the Blood Hunter's death, Vanthor gives a magical sword to his lieutenant Dreaddoom.

Vanthor also faces another enemy, Icarus, a satellite armed with a laser. Making common cause with a Dr. Sharon Reed, the Blood Hunter plans to use Icarus against Vanthor. While the Blood Hunter fights Dreaddoom, Reed arms and aims Icarus at Vanthor's headquarters in the Light Eye Corporation Building. As the laser destroys the building, the Blood Hunter defeats Dreaddoom and comes away with the sword as a new weapon in his arsenal.

SOURCES:

"Baptism." *Vamperotica.* No. 6. Brainstorm Comics, Aug. 1995.
"Search and Destroy." *Vamperotica.* No. 25. Brainstorm Comics, Mar. 1997.
"Something Wicked." *Vamperotica.* No. 2. Brainstorm Comics, 1994.

Vardelek, Count

Count Vardelek, a Hungarian nobleman, makes his appearance just three years before **Count Dracula**, as the villain in Stanislaus Eric's "The Sad Story of a Vampire" (1894). Vardelek is described as an attractive man with a fair complexion and long, wavy hair. He is tall with long slender hands. His nose is long and there is a sadness in his green eyes. By no means a nocturnal creature, Vardelek arrives in Strygia by train. Here, like **Carmilla Karnstein** before him, he is stranded and invited to stay with the family in the local castle. Trusted by the Wronskis, he becomes the friend of the youngest family member, a boy named Gabriel.

Vardelek takes an immediate liking to Gabriel, and the first time they meet he takes the boy's hand and seems to gage his pulse. The usually shy Gabriel also likes Vardelek. Over the next few days, Vardelek seems to appear younger and more vital, and Gabriel appears to lose his vitality. When Vardelek leaves the castle, he returns somewhat older looking, but soon regains his youth. Gabriel becomes focused on Vardelek and rushes to greet him upon his return. Over the next few days, Gabriel grows weak with a wasting illness that has no accompanying physical manifestations. He finally dies and Vardelek disappears.

SOURCES:

Eric, Stanislaus. "The Sad Story of a Vampire." In *Studies of Death: Romantic Tales*. London, 1894. Reprinted in Shepard, Leslie. *The Dracula Book of Great Vampire Stories*. Secaucus, NJ: Citadel Press, 1977.

Varney, Sir Francis

Sir Francis Varney is the central character in a series of "penny dreadful" novels originally published in weekly installments over the span of several years in the mid-1840s. The installments were later collected into a book, *Varney the Vampire* (1847), the first full-length, English-language vampire novel. Because he was the first in the genre, Varney has had immense influence in the establishment and subsequent development of the literary vampire.

In the serial he is described as possessing white skin, as if he is bloodless. He has long, fang-like teeth, long fingernails, and shining, metallic eyes. Immediately after feasting, his skin takes on a reddish color. Like **Lord Ruthven,** the vampire in John Polidori's original vampire tale "The Vampyre," Varney has great strength, can walk around freely in the sunlight, and only needs blood occasionally (not nightly). His bite does not pass along his vampiric condition to his victim. He can be wounded, and even killed, but he will revive once his body repairs any damage done to it. Varney is first presented as an entirely evil character, but later in the tale he takes on a more complex nature and shows himself to be an honorable individual with feelings like any other person.

Varney's story opens with his attack upon the young and attractive Flora Bannerworth. Having entered her bedroom, he bites her and begins to drink the gushing blood. Interrupted by members of the family during his repast, Varney is shot but manages to escape. His initial attack leaves two puncture marks in Flora's neck. Henry Bannerworth quickly concludes that Flora has been attacked by a "vampyre" (the common spelling throughout the novel). From a book he had read on Norway, he knows that vampyres attempt to drink blood to revive their own body. In addition, they tend to feed on evenings just prior to the emergence of the full moon; this is due to the fact that the moonlight has curative powers for the vampyre, so that if he is injured, the rays of the full moon will revive him. In fact, it is the light of the moon that allows Varney to recover from the gunshot wounds he received. The importance given to the moon's light throughout the novel further emphasizes Varney's link to and evolution from Lord Ruthven, who was also healed by the moon.

The first half of *Varney the Vampire* traces Varney's increasingly complex relationship with the Bannerworth family and their close friends and associates. Despite the fact that he bit their daughter, the Bannerworth's are actually sympathetic towards Varney once they learn of the his condition and his virtuous nature. When they further learn that Varney has a connection to one of their ancestors, they actually become his protectors when a mob sets out to destroy him.

After completing his interaction with the Bannerworths, Varney moves on to a series of increasingly brief encounters with various people; the storyline of the novel actually becomes quite repetitive. Over and over, Varney attempts to establish himself in a new social setting, bites someone, and is found out and hunted, which causes him to flee for his life. Varney's big problem is that he is singularly inept at attacking people (he almost always chooses young women) and is repeatedly caught when people respond to his victims' cries.

While bits and pieces of Varney's history are recounted throughout the novel, the reader has to be patient and wait until nearly the end of the story to learn Varney's entire history, including the tale of how he became a vampire. It seems that Varney's real name was Mortimer. He lived in London during the time that Cromwell had Charles I beheaded in 1649 and proclaimed the Commonwealth.

Mortimer sided with the British crown against Cromwell, and helped members of the royal family escape to Holland, for which he was handsomely rewarded. At some point around 1657, he was caught helping someone escape. Chaos ensues, and in a moment of passion, Mortimer strikes his son, accidentally killing the young man. The last thing he remembered after that was a flash of light and being struck to the ground with great force.

Mortimer was knocked unconscious, and when he recovered, he was lying on the ground next to a recently opened grave. A voice that came seemingly out of thin air told him that he was being punished for killing his son, and that henceforth he would be cursed among men and known as Varney the Vampyre. He later discovered that he had been shot by Cromwell's men and two years had passed since he lost consciousness. In the meantime, Cromwell had been deposed and the crown restored. His former house had been burned, but the money he had buried under the floor was still there. With it he was able to make a new beginning. He slowly learned the rules of his new vampiric nature.

Varney the Vampire was issued anonymously, and for many years the authorship was in question. Montague Summers, whose books on the vampire have had immense influence, believed the author to be Thomas Prest, who had written *Sweeny Todd,* the single most successful penny dreadful. However, in 1963 Louis James, looking through the scrapbooks of James Malcolm Rymer, found conclusive evidence that Rymer had authored Varney. Rymer had emerged in the 1830s as an editor and in 1841 published his first novel, *The Monk.* It seems that his difficult financial condition forced him reluctantly into popular fiction, which was looked down upon.

Varney the Vampyre: or, The Feast of Blood originally appeared in 109 weekly installments. The entire manuscript was then collected and printed as a single volume of more than 800 pages. It was the first vampire fiction in English since Polidori's work and the stage dramas it inspired. Varney thus served as an important transitional character between the original literary vampires of the early nineteenth century (**Christabel, Lord Ruthven**) and the more fully matured characters who came later (**Carmilla Karnstein** and **Count Dracula**).

In the twentieth century *Varney the Vampire* has had a checkered publishing history. Because it was actually a poorly written novel, copies were not saved and the book became a rare volume. While many vampire writers made reference to it, few had seen a copy and fewer still had taken the time to work their way through it. After being unavailable for many decades, reprints were finally published in 1970 and 1972. The audience for the reprints was somewhat limited, however, so the book has since gone out of print once again.

SOURCES:

Louis, James. *Fiction for the Working Man,* 1830-1850. London: Oxford University Press, 1963.

Rymer, James Malcolm. *Varney the Vampyre; or, The Feast of Blood.* London: F. Lloyd, 1847. Reprint edited by Devendra P. Varna. New York: Arno Press, 1970. Reprint edited by E.F. Bleiler. New York: Dover Publications, 1972.

Velcro, Vincent

Vincent Velcro, the vampire component of the U. S. Army special forces unit known as the Creature Commandos, appears in a set of short stories throughout the 1980s in the comic book anthology, *Weird War Tales*. Introduced in an early issue of *Weird War Tales* (1980), Velcro and the Creature Commandos appear in more than 15 subsequent issues over the next several years. According to the tale, Velcro was born in 1911 in New York City. Orphaned early in life, he grew up on the streets. His youthful experience bred a streak of bravery into him, along with an equally prominent anti-authoritarianism. After joining the army, he rose to the rank of sergeant. His career was cut short by his arrest and sentence to 30 years in the brig for striking (and crippling) an officer.

After World War I begins, Velcro is given an alternative to spending three decades behind bars: He can join Project M (the "M" standing for monster). Over several months he is given an experimental serum and vampire bat blood. He develops many of the attributes of a classical vampire and soon needs regular ingestion of blood to survive.

Velcro has many of the attributes of a traditional vampire. He dresses in black, has slicked-back black hair (cut in a manner to give the appearance of horns), and wears a shirt with a high collar. He has prominent fangs and can change into a bat and fly about. Having arrived at his state through chemical change, he is not undead. Thus, he can operate in the daytime and his image appears in mirrors.

Velcro is united with Warren Griffith, a werewolf, and Lucky Taylor, who stepped on a land mine and has been reconstructed into a Frankenstein figure. Under their leader, Lieutenant Matthew Shrieve, they constitute the Creature Commandos. They are sent to Europe as a secret weapon to be used against the Germans (although they also serve in the Pacific and north Africa), where Velcro is free to feed on the enemy. Before the war is over the Creature Commandos are joined by a female, Dr. Medusa. Together, the Creature Commandos share a series of adventures.

SOURCES:

"The Children's Crusade." *Weird War Tales*. No. 102. New York: DC Comics, Aug. 1981.

"The Creature Commandos." *Weird War Tales*. No. 93. New York, DC Comics, Nov. 1980.

"The Creature Commandos vs. The Faceless Enemy." *Weird War Tales*. No. 97. New York: DC Comics, Mar. 1981.

"Death Smiles Thrice." *Weird War Tales*. No. 121. New York: DC Comics, Mar. 1983.

"The Doomsday Robots."*Weird War Tales*. No. 111. New York: DC Comics, May 1982.

"Heroes Come in Small Sizes." *Weird War Tales*. No. 118. New York: DC Comics, Dec. 1982.

"Roses Are Red—but Blood Is Redder!" *Weird War Tales*. Pt. 1., No. 109. Pt. 2., No. 110. New York: DC Comics, Mar., Apr., 1982.

"The War at Home." *Weird War Tales*. No. 105. DC Comics, Nov. 1981.

"You Can't Pin a Medal on a Robot." *Weird War Tales*. New York: DC Comics, No. 115, Sept. 1982.

Venessa

Venessa, the true wife of **Count Dracula**, is the subject of the film *Dracula's Widow* (1989). Of indeterminate age, Venessa (portrayed by Sylvia Kristel) is an attractive

Sylvia Kristel portrays Count Dracula's wife Venessa in the film *Dracula's Widow*.

seductress who in past centuries was married to Count Dracula. She is the only survivor of the events of 1893 that killed her husband and all the other residents of Castle Dracula. However, her whereabouts in the intervening years are somewhat confused. She is unaware of her husband's death at the hands of **Abraham Van Helsing** and seems to have been confined to her coffin until it was shipped to America. However, when awakened, she is dressed in a rather drab contemporary gray business suit.

As the storyline progresses, Venessa's body is accidentally sent to the Hollywood Wax Museum, where she emerges into a new, unfamiliar world. Once she realizes she is in present-day America, her only goals are to survive (with regular intakes of blood) and find her way back to Transylvania. She bites Raymond Everett, the owner of the wax museum, and makes him her unwilling minion, much to the consternation of his girlfriend Jenny Harker. He is unable to strike the blow when he has an initial opportunity to kill her, and later learns that the way to erase the effects of his slowly changing condition is to turn on Venessa.

Venessa is a nocturnal creature. During the day she sleeps in a coffin with native soil. She is very strong, and can change into a bat to fly about and into a wolflike beast to feed. She has prominent fangs, which she likes to flash as she snarls at people. She is repelled by the cross, but is most vulnerable to a stake in the heart.

Venessa insists that Raymond take her back to her husband in Transylvania. Raymond informs her that her husband is dead, having been destroyed by Van Helsing a century ago. At first she doesn't believe him, but her nightly feedings manifest her rage and frustration. She invites herself into a Satanic coven and savagely kills 16 people as they are in the midst of sacrificing a young woman. She also learns that Van Helsing's grandson is alive and living in Los Angeles. She approaches him and he confirms Count Dracula's death and his grandfather's role in bringing his death about. He pushes Venessa away with a large crucifix, but stumbles and drops his protection. She bites him and leaves him to rise as a vampire.

As more and more bodies show up dead, the police have a difficult time accepting the fact that the series of vicious killings they are investigating are caused by a vampire. Eventually, after his partner is killed, the chief investigator is convinced. In the morgue, he is given a vivid demonstration by Van Helsing, who stakes one of the corpses that briefly comes back to life as the stake is driven in.

In the end, Everett is arrested, and Venessa is cornered by the police inspector and Jenny Harker. Jenny throws a stake to Everett, who impales Venessa. She dissolves away, leaving only a messy spot on the floor.

Venisette, Rovena

Rovena Venisette is a 200-year-old comic book vampiress who resides in the Castle Venisette in Chiemsee, a small town near Salzburg, Germany. She is beautiful and seductive, and has over the years grown strong. She has a number of vampire minions, but usually kills her own victims. She likes to hang them up and allow the blood to run over her body as she drinks. She collects the blood in a pool in which she likes to swim. Although it is not fresh blood, it is nevertheless refreshing. A traditional creature of the night, she is subject to death by decapitation, fire, sunlight, and the stake. She is repelled by garlic and the cross. Her bite begins a transformation process that is completed when the victim feeds, not necessarily from her.

Venisette has an enemy in **Max Morrisey,** whom she transformed in the mid-1980s, when the story takes place. In his thirst, he bit his wife. Because she has not yet fed, Morrisey hopes that by killing Venisette his wife will return to her normal, human state. Venisette is also tracked by **Dr. Lichtenstein**, a vampire hunter who has joined Morrisey in his quest to kill Venisette. Rovena captures Morrisey's wife and offers him a choice of seeing her transformation completed or watching her die. Venisette, in her desire to have Morrisey join her as her eternal companion, leads him to bed. She dies in flames as Morrisey sets the bed on fire.

Her death frees Morissey's wife, but Lichtenstein double-crosses Morrisey and decapitates him. The vampire hunter leaves his body to rot away in the castle, but another vampire pushes him in the pool of blood and puts his head back in place.

SOURCES:

Graphique Musique. No. 1–3. Eugene, OR: Slave Labor Graphics, 1988–90. Reprinted as *Citizen Nocturne.* Brave New Words, 1992.

Victor, Son of Dracula

Victor's story is told in the French film, *Dracula Pere et Fils* (1976), released in the United States as *Dracula and Son.* When the film begins, **Count Dracula** has waited 400 years for a bride, and at last meets the woman of his dreams when, in 1784, Marsha arrives in Transylvania at Castle Dracula. Nine months later she bears a son, Victor. In the twentieth century, Transylvania is transferred to Romania, and after World War II becomes subject to the Communist rule out of Bucharest. Eventually, the Communists claim the castle and, following the death of a servant with a cross made of a hammer and sickle, Dracula and Victor decide to leave Transylvania for Paris.

Along the way, they are separated. Dracula finds his way to London, but Victor makes it to Paris. He is now 189 years old, but looks like a young adult. He is a traditional vampire who sleeps in a coffin, lives out of the reach of the sun, and has fangs. He wants to be a normal human being and cannot stand the taste or smell of blood.

While Victor is making his way in Paris, Dracula is discovered in London as someone who happens to look strangely like actor Christopher Lee, and is hired to play himself in a movie. He becomes a star and goes to Paris on location. Here he is reunited with his son, but they have an increasing number of conflicts, not the least being their attraction to the same woman, Nicole, who looks very much like Marsha. Out of his love, Victor discovers that he has become human. He can exist in daylight, and his reflection can be seen in the mirror.

To keep Nicole from his father, Victor takes Nicole away, but Dracula follows. He will not relent, and finally, as dawn breaks, Nicole pulls the curtain from the window and Dracula fries in the morning light. She and Victor are now free to live and love. But what of the next generation? Will they revert to family tradition?

Viroslav, Count Alexander

Count Alexander Viroslav is a 500-year-old Bulgarian nobleman who resides in a castle near the village of Boleslaus in easternmost Bulgaria, near the Romanian border, in the novel *The Kiss* (1996). Transformed into a vampire by the supernatural being the Black Prince, the count has a number of traditional vampiric powers. He can change into a bat and fly; he has heightened senses, especially hearing; and his image is not visible in a mirror. A nocturnal creature, he sleeps in a coffin. Viroslav is also vulnerable to sunlight, fire, and the stake, the traditional enemies of the vampire.

When the novel opens at the beginning of the 1700s the count meets Maria, his future wife, in Budapest. A Russian who has fled her homeland, she is in love with Gregor, a young man from a wealthy family whom she met in Krakow, Poland. The count falls in love with her, turns her into a vampire, and forces Gregor to be her servant. For the next two centuries, the three make their life in the Viroslav castle. They have a stable relationship with the local villagers.

The downfall of Viroslav and his world begins with the arrival of Rebecca Brittan and Richard Anderson, a young couple fleeing Nazi Germany. They are dropped off at Boleslaus when they run out of money. The countess picks up the stranded pair and invites them to the castle as her guests. The count and countess proceed to wine and dine the couple, but also attack them both sexually and vampirically. The novel reveals the sexual parameters of their encounter: vampires can make love, but not reach orgasm. A new vampire can be made only during the sex act. At the point of climax, while his fangs penetrate the victim's neck, the vampire shares his body fluids, both saliva and semen. Only a male vampire can initiate the change that will lead a victim to become a vampire. The vampire can share his or her body fluids in such a way as to transmit a limited immortality to a human without making the victim a vampire, as in the case of Gregor.

The arrival of the American couple is quickly followed by the appearance of a small cadre of Nazis led by an officer who had been spurned by Rebecca. It is his intent to take the couple back to Germany. He walks into the castle unaware of what awaits him, including the fact that Rebecca has become a vampire. The final confrontation, complete with the appearance of the Black Prince, signals the end of the present count and countess and the establishment of a new regime in Castle Viroslav.

SOURCES:

Reines, Kathryn. *The Kiss*. New York: Avon, 1996.

von Beethoven, Ludwig

Following an illustrious career as a composer, Ludwig von Beethoven died in 1827; or at least that's what the history books would have us believe. According to Michael Romkey's *The Vampire Papers*, however, Beethoven became a vampire and still lives, though his ability to move about freely in public has been limited by his fame. Consequently, he operates under the pseudonym Gregor Samsa, a name he picked up from the main character in Franz Kafka's story "The Metamorphosis." Beethoven's progenitor was a Carpathian vampire who bit Beethoven the requisite three times, thus passing the virus which causes the vampire mutation.

Beethoven has become a member of and agent for the Illuminati, a fraternity of vampires dedicated to cultivating harmony and wisdom in the world. The Illuminati keep careful control of the vampire population: Its members do not create new vampires without the organization's approval. (This means they can bite victims for blood, but refrain from multiple bites, which passes the virus that causes mutation.) As an Illuminati agent, Beethoven is sent to rural Costa Rica to the estate of **Don Lazaro Ruiz Cortinez**, a wealthy landowner and vampire. There, in the bat-infested rain forest, a doctor from the United States Centers for Disease Control is researching a new virus. Although the doctor has not tied the virus to vampirism, the Illuminati see great potential in the research for discovering the cause of and cure for their condition. Beethoven is sent to insure the doctor's safety and success.

Beethoven is a traditional vampire in many ways. He has fangs, is confined to the dark hours, and must have blood at least fortnightly. (Animal blood cannot substitute for human blood.) As a member of the Illuminati, he has learned that killing victims is unnecessary. A vampire bite produces moments of extreme ecstasy for the victim, and the vampire has the power to erase any memory of the encounter. The wounds heal very quickly, so that in most cases there is no trace of the bite by the time the victim awakes.

SOURCES:
Romkey, Michael. *The Vampire Virus*. New York: Fawcett Gold Medal, 1998.

von Kaldenstein, Count Ludwig

Count Ludwig von Kaldenstein is the subject of the short story "The Vampire of Kaldenstein" (1938). The tall, pale count has lived in the family castle in southern Bavaria for more than 300 years (the last known burial in the castle having occurred in 1645). He has red eyes, black hair, and long pointed hands and fingernails. He sleeps in a vault in the castle by day, but in the evening can be seen on the turret or flying around in the form of a bat. He doesn't cast a shadow, is repelled by sacred objects, and never drinks wine. He is inflamed by blood.

Occasionally, a traveler would stumble upon the castle and gain entrance. During the years after World War II, the local priest would go into the castle with a small chest containing the sacramental host and rescue the person. In 1933, a young man on a walking tour ignores the advice of the locals and visits the castle. The count welcomes him into his home, but later the young man finds himself entrapped within its walls. He is introduced to two of the count's relatives, including Count Feodor von Kaldenstein, who supposedly died in 1645. They carry on a conversation as to what part of his body they will bite.

Fortunately, the priest arrives just in time, and is able to drive the vampires back into their coffins. He then places a crucifix on each and sprinkles them with holy water. The priest's actions seem effective for the count's deceased relatives, but for the count the solution is merely temporary. The next evening he is seen walking on the turret of his castle.

SOURCES:

Cowles, Frederick. "The Vampire of Kaldenstein." In Frederick Cowles, *The Night Wind Howles*. 1938. Reprinted in Parry, Michael, ed. *The Rivals of Dracula*. London: Corgi, 1977.

von Klatka, Count Azzo

Count Azzo von Klatka is the vampire of an anonymous novelette originally published in German in the middle of the nineteenth century and then translated and published in English in 1860 as "The Mysterious Stranger." As the story goes, von Klatka was a fifteenth-century knight who resided in a castle in the Carpathian Mountains, one of the many owned by Germans who had been given strategic lands by the Hungarians. They served as a first line of defense for the Hungarians now threatened by the Turks. However, he turned his home into a den of iniquity. He took any of the local maidens who caught his fancy and kept them in his castle, and he had traitorous dealings with the Turks. Finally, the local residents rose in revolt, stormed the castle, and killed the knight. They planted an oak tree at the spot where he fell. Because he was of noble birth, rather than being destroyed his body was placed in the nearby church.

Von Klatka's fate is that he survived as a vampire who rests by day in his church crypt. In the years that follow, he is seen periodically by the locals who believe that the areas around the oak tree and the castle are haunted. In the century after the knight's death, the castle had not been reoccupied and fell into a state of disarray. The "ghost" who shows himself on moonlit nights is tall and well built. He wears a broad-brimmed hat and carries a sword.

Early in the sixteenth century the lands that include the castle are inherited by the Knight of Fahlenburg who, accompanied by his daughter Franziska, his niece Bertha, and Franziska's suitor Baron Franz von Kronstein, journey from his home in Austria to take possession of his property. Von Klatka assists the new owners on their journey by calling off a group of wolves who are about to attack their party. Intrigued by the "mysterious stranger" who aids them and learning of the stories surrounding the castle, Franziska and the baron visit the ruins and linger at the church into the early evening when von Klatka finally shows himself. Franziska invites him to the castle, but von Klatka declines, telling her that he only comes out in the evening.

Over the course of the story, von Klatka becomes a regular visitor at the Knight of Fahlenburg's estate. Almost at once the Lady Franziska begins to sleep late in the morning, appearing fatigued, and has a painful wound, a red streak, on her neck that does not heal. She also has dreams of a mist coming into her room and kissing her on her neck. The family welcomes the arrival of Woislam, a knight who had fought in Turkey. Concerned about Franziska's illness, he proposes a solution. He takes the young lady to the chapel, and while he prays she drives three large nails into von Klatka's coffin. She then applies some of the liquid that runs out of the coffin to her neck wound. Only afterward does Woislam inform everyone that von Klatka is a vampire. It was part of the remedy that the victim be the one to drive the nails into the coffin. From that day forward, Azzo von Klatka is never seen again.

SOURCES:

"The Mysterious Stranger." In *Odds and Ends*, 1860. Reprinted in, Parry, Michael, ed. *Rivals of Dracula*. London: Corgi, 1977.

von Krolock, Count

Count von Krolock (portrayed by Ferdy Mayne) is the villain who becomes the target of vampire slayers **Professor Ambronsius** and his assistant Alfred in the comedy *The Fearless Vampire Hunters* (1967). Von Krolock is a traditional aristocratic Transylvanian vampire who resides in a castle near a small village in what appears to be the eighteenth century. He is tall, dressed in black with a scarlet-lined cape, and possesses prominent fangs and red-tinged eyes. His reflection cannot be seen in a mirror.

A nocturnal creature, von Krolock sleeps in a coffin. Also living with him at the castle are his vampire son and a number of vampire minions. The latter sleep in stone crypts that fill the castle's central courtyard. Ultimately, von Krolock is a Satanist who thinks of himself as the other vampires' pastor, and they as his congregation. They are slowly growing in numbers and once a year they have a grand ball to celebrate their timeless state.

The small realm ruled by von Krolock is invaded by elderly-scholar-turned-vampire-hunter Professor Ambronsius, and Alfred, his only student, while on a larger vampire-searching tour of central Europe. They arrive in the nearby village on the evening before the annual ball. Prior to their retirement for the night, they are introduced to Sarah, the lovely young daughter of the innkeeper. Alfred is immediately infatuated with her. However, a few minutes later, von Krolock breaks into the inn, bites Sarah, and takes her with him back to the castle. Alfred follows them to the castle, and Ambronsius joins him the next day.

They explore the empty castle together, and watch the following evening as it comes to life. Unfortunately, Alfred loses their bag of weapons and they are unable to harm von Krolock or the other vampires. Planning to add them to the night's dinner menu, von Krolock locks them up. Eventually they escape, taking Sarah with them as they depart. In the process, Sarah completes her transformation into a vampire and bites Alfred. Inadvertently, von Krolock, through Sarah, utilizes Ambronsius as his instrument for spreading vampirism from Transylvania to the rest of the world.

von Lock, Adam

Adam von Lock is featured in the comic book *Vapor Loch: Diary of a Man's Lost Soul* (1994). The son of a nineteenth-century scientist who died a laughingstock of his peers for searching for a means of controlling time, von Lock continues his father's research. His research takes him to Transylvania where he discovers the tomb of Prince Vladimir Tepes (**Count Dracula**). The casket has an encrypted message that he deciphers. It contains the formula for immortality. In his subsequent travels he assembles the implements necessary for the formula, including Cleopatra's pyramid-shaped incense box, the golden chalice used at Jesus's Last Supper, Vladimir's skull, and the innocent blood from a wicked woman.

In order to obtain the last necessary item for the formula, Adam lures a prostitute to his lab where he drains her blood. He plunges Vladimir's skull in the blood, the drippings of which are caught in the chalice. The blood is poured into the incense box. Finally, Adam breathes in the vapors coming from Cleopatra's box. He then inscribes a star of David on his chest with the remaining blood. The initial process is complete, although he is now a vampire with a need for more blood. In obtaining it, von Lock has the power to turn into a bat and fly about.

Von Lock's new life is soon challenged by Simeon, the son of Dracula, also a vampire, who resents his stealing the head of his father. They meet for battle at von Lock's father's grave site, which is interrupted by a group of supernatural beings who describe themselves as the beings who stand behind all the legends and stories of gods and demons. Simeon has been their champion, but they are going to give von Lock a chance to unseat him. They announce that they will return in a month. Von Lock prepares himself in part by drinking more blood for its strength. His final act before the battle is to drink from his girlfriend with the promise that he will bring her back to life. He wins, but is now faced with the problem of reordering his life and bringing life back to his dead love.

SOURCES:
Sky Comics Presents Monthly. No. 1. Florence, KY: Sky Comics, July 1992.
Vapor Loch: Diary of a Man's Lost Soul. Florence, KY: Sky Comics, 1994.

Voytek, Anton

Anton Voytek, a thirteenth-century Hungarian prince residing in present-day San Francisco, makes his appearance in the made-for-television movie *Vampire* (1972). Portrayed by Richard Lynch, Voytek appears as a handsome young man with an aristocratic bearing, hypnotic eyes, and a taste for beautiful women. He always wears an opera cape. Because of his long blonde hair, he is known as the golden vampire.

He moved to San Francisco to escape the Nazi holocaust. His wealth allowed him to purchase an abandoned mansion formerly owned by the Highdecker family. To his new home he shipped his priceless collection of art, which was placed in the mansion's subbasement. However, before he could establish himself in his new home, he met a priest who learned his secret. As a result of their encounter, the priest is killed and both Voytek and his paintings are buried.

Most of the movie takes place 40 years later, when the apparently abandoned mansion is pulled down and the site prepared for a new church. The process of clearing the land frees Voytek and he quickly moves to recover his art collection, if not his land. In this endeavor he enlists the aid of an art expert. Once the collection is found and assessed, it is soon discovered that all of the pieces were reported stolen over the centuries. The art expert turns Voytek in for possession of stolen property. After breaking out of jail, Voytek revenges himself on the art dealer by killing his wife.

Voytek must now contend with the art dealer, who is assisted by an old police-man who happened to be a friend of the deceased priest. From some old books they have become aware who Voytek is and that he has some points of vulnerability—he sleeps in a coffin, is hurt by crosses and holy water, and can be burned in sunlight. With their knowledge and the policeman's detective ability, the pair set out to find Voytek and destroy him by locating his several coffins (each of which has some soil from his homeland) and rendering them useless by leaving a cross in each. Inevitably, they are brought face to face with their evil antagonist and must confront him in a more direct manner.

Warram, Robert

Robert Warram is the subject of the short story "The Undead Die" (1948). The story begins a number of centuries ago when, as a young boy of 17, Warram lives in rural Europe managing a herd of oxen. He and his girlfriend Lisa, with whom he is very much in love, venture out in the fields one day and decide to explore an abandoned castle, in the basement of which they find a number of crypts. They become lost, and as evening approaches and they try to leave the castle, they only become more confused.

Suddenly, someone appears before them, offering to show them the way out. Rather than leading them to the entrance to the ruins, the person turns out to be the **Lord of Henzig**, a vampire. He bites them and immediately places their bodies in earth-filled coffins. The next evening he awakens them, completing the process of turning them into his vampire minions. He teaches them to transform their bodies into bats and other animal forms.

Over the years, Henzig strips the couple of most of their human and moral elements, and all that remains is their love for each other. While Henzig proves to be a harsh taskmaster, he also leaves the two to attend to other matters, and it is during those times that they develop their own life. They awake with the blood thirst upon them, and usually feed quickly. They discover the gnomes, elves, and other supernatural life forms in their surroundings, and learn they can live off animals and do not have to attack humans. Finally, they make contact with the Great Earth Elemental, a powerful godlike being who teaches them that there is a means of getting revenge on Henzig. They master the universal fields of force and are able to will Henzig out of existence.

For the next 300 years, Warram and Lisa lead an idyllic life. They sleep in adjacent coffins in the abandoned castle. They remain very much in love, and each dusk and dawn Warram awakens and sleeps with Lisa's name on his lips. Then one day a storm passes through the area and Warram awakes to discover that a tree has been uprooted and has fallen on the crumbling castle. A branch has impaled Lisa. Feeling he has no life apart from her, Warram places wood around their coffins and sets them afire. He dies with Lisa's name on his lips.

SOURCES:

Evans, E. Everett. "The Undead Die." In *Weird Tales*, 1948. Reprinted in Parry, Michael, ed. *The Rivals of Dracula*. London: Corgi, 1977.

Westenra, Lucy

Lucy Westenra is the most prominent female vampire in Bram Stoker's definitive vampire novel *Dracula*. While **Count Dracula** hovers in the background, Lucy's story dominates the central half of the novel. Lucy, more than any other character, demonstrates the true threat posed by Dracula—to the civilized world in general, and British womanhood in particular. Lucy is a vivacious and desirable young woman, what every man yearns to possess, a hearty mother for the next generation. She becomes an ugly, unclean, perverted monster who abuses the very children she has been destined to nurture.

Lucy makes her initial appearance in the fifth chapter where her correspondence with her long-time friend Mina Murray is recorded. While Stoker never describes her in great physical detail, she is obviously an attractive young woman in her twenties, the object of affection for three young men: Arthur Holmwood, to whom she eventually becomes engaged, Dr. John Seward, and Quincey P. Morris. In the meantime, she lives with her mother.

As the story opens, on July 24, Lucy and her mother are vacationing at Whitby, a resort town on the coast of northern England. Mina, of similar age to Lucy, joins them for the vacation and the three women retire to the home at the Crescent where they will stay for the next weeks. On July 26, Mina notes that Lucy is walking in her sleep. On August 8, a sudden storm hits Whitby during which the *Demeter*, the ship upon which Dracula came to England, wrecks on shore. On August 11, at 3 A.M., Mina discovers Lucy has left her bed, and she goes in search of her. She finds Lucy on the East Cliff in their favorite seat. As she makes her way to Lucy she sees "something, long and black, bending over her." When she calls out, the "something" looks up and Mina sees Dracula's white face and red eyes. After she helps Lucy home, she notices two tiny marks on Lucy's neck. Over the next few days Lucy grows more and more fatigued, and the wounds on her neck do not heal. Lucy's transformation into a vampire has begun.

Through August, Lucy seems to get better, and Mina, having finally heard from her true love, Jonathan Harker, on August 19, leaves for Budapest to join him. Lucy returns to London where Holmwood joins her, and they make plans to marry on September 28. However, her condition worsens, and he calls Dr. Seward in to examine her. Unable to figure out what is wrong with Lucy, Seward calls in **Abraham Van Helsing**, an expert in obscure diseases, as a consultant. She seems to improve, but then turns pale and loses all of her strength. Van Helsing prescribes a blood transfusion. As they are about to perform the procedure, her fiance Holmwood arrives and they use his blood. Later a second transfusion is taken from Seward and then, without offering an explanation, Van Helsing surrounds Lucy with garlic.

Dracula returns on September 17 to continue Lucy's transformation into a full vampire; at some point, not described by Stoker, Lucy drinks from him. (The necessity of sharing blood with the vampire as part of the process in creating a vampire is described later in the novel during Dracula's attack on Lucy's friend, Mina.) Morris is next in line to supply the blood needed to preserve her life, but by this time it is already too late—the transformation has progressed too far to reverse. Lucy dies and is laid to rest in the family crypt. Van Helsing immediately wants to treat the body as a vampire, but Holmwood (who by this time has inherited his father's title as Lord Godalming) strongly opposes any mutilation of the body. He asserts his role as widower; though they had not officially married, he considers Lucy his wife. In his opinion, the transfusion served to marry them and they were married in the sight of God.

While the men rest in indecision, reports surface of missing children who later are found and tell of being with a "boofer lady," child talk for "beautiful lady." Van Helsing persuades the men to institute a watch at Lucy's tomb. They view her empty coffin and after some time see her walking around. In the end they corner her in her coffin and any doubts they might have as to what she has become are lost. Arthur assumes his responsibility and drives the stake through her chest. At this point, it is noted that the harsh, fiendish expression which had characterized Lucy's appearance at the time of her death departs, and her normal face of sweetness and purity returns. Van Helsing finishes the process of slaying the vampire by cutting off her head and filling her mouth with garlic.

As *Dracula* was brought to the stage and screen in the 1920s, the character of Lucy was significantly altered, usually by elevating her status as Dracula's victim with a corresponding de-emphasis upon the reality of her vampiric existence. She disappeared completely from *Nosferatu, Eine Symphonie des Garuens* (1922), the first attempt to bring *Dracula* to the screen, and in Hamilton Deane's *Dracula* play. She returned in John Balderston's revision of Deane's play for the American stage, but as Lucy Seward, the daughter of a much older Dr. Seward. Both Mina and Lucy returned for the 1931 films, in both the English and Spanish versions. In *Horror of Dracula* (1958), Lucy has transformed into Arthur Holmwood's sister and Jonathan Harker's fiance. She is given strong parts in the Jack Palance version of *Dracula* (1973) and was central to Frank Langella's *Dracula* (1979). Her story as a vampire is most completely captured by Francis Ford Coppola in *Bram Stoker's Dracula* (1992).

Weyland, Dr. Edward

Dr. Edward Weyland, the ancient vampire who lives in America in the 1970s, is the subject of Suzy McKee Charnas's influential novel, *The Vampire Tapestry* (1980). In Charnas's myth, the vampire is a separate species, possibly as old as humans. According to her lore, over the millennia the vampire has shared the earth with other living creatures, living quietly on the edge of the human community. Considered the

A female vampire from the film *Count Yorga, Vampire*.

greatest of the earth's predators, he feeds on humans, and is thus at the top of the food chain. Because animal blood does not provide necessary nutrition, the vampire must obtain his nourishment from human blood.

The myth explains that throughout most of human history, the vampire has been bound to a village or small town. Living on small quantities of blood, he would not kill his victims, but periodically withdraw in order to protect himself and allow the village to replenish its blood. Throughout the years he would withdraw to a safe location where he would sleep (enter a state of suspended animation) for several generations, during which any memory of his attacks would be lost. When awake, he would live a singular existence, not wishing to breed competitors for the limited food supply. During his sleep, he would forget the details of his previous waking life, and upon awakening have to quickly adjust to the new situation he encounters. As society has increased its pace, the task of adjusting has become more difficult. Now, his bite does not produce a new vampire. The vampire does not have fangs; rather, he has a needlelike device in the tongue that secretes an anticlogging substance, allowing the vampire to feed from a small wound.

One such long-lived vampire reappears in the modern world. He assumes the identity as anthropologist Edward Weyland, a name he takes from a New England churchyard. In the 1970s he moves from a college in the South to take charge of a dream laboratory at a Cayslin College Center for the Study of Man. He is tall, gray-haired, and drives a Mercedes. He can move about in the daylight, but prefers the evening hours. Although he enjoys a job where a steady supply of victims are his, he soon discovers that a public life in the modern world, even the relatively obscure existence as a college instructor, is difficult to sustain. Beginning with a young female employee at the college, Dr. Weyland's identity as a vampire is discovered. The young woman shoots him, and others try to manipulate or harm him in various ways.

Although Dr. Weyland is able to recover from the shooting incident, escape some people who want to make money by putting him on display, and land another position as an anthropologist at a college in New Mexico, he cannot keep up the charade of his present life. He finally decides it is time for a sleep, and as the novel ends is somewhere in an obscure cave awaiting his next awakening.

SOURCES:

Barr, Marleen S. *Suzy McKee Charnas*. Mercer Island, WA: Starmont House, 1986.

Charnas, Suzy McKee. *The Vampire Tapestry*. New York: Simon & Schuster, 1980. Reprint, Albuquerque, NM: Living Branch Press, 1993.

Whipsnake

Whipsnake is one of a group of female vampires who lend their name to the comic book series *Vamps*. An African American, she is raised in the Washington Heights section of New York City, the youngest of seven sisters. Her father treats her like the son he never had and she learns a number of things necessary for survival on the streets. Her mother died giving birth to her, and she finds a substitute in Masoalena, who is a practitioner of Santeria, a magical African religion. Then as a young woman she meets **Dave**, a redneck vampire, at a neighborhood disco. He makes her one of his small group of minions. She finds a new sisterhood in **Mink, Skeeter, Screech,** and **Howler**, the rest of the members of Dave's group.

Like the other Vamps, Whipsnake is a rather traditional vampire. She has fangs and is totally nocturnal. She must get out of the sunlight, preferably underground, each dawn. She awakens with the blood thirst and feeds daily. Her image does not show in mirrors, and the only place it can be seen is in the eyes of her next victim. She is repelled by holy objects if held by a true believer. She is a child of her time, however, and dresses in contemporary, if skimpy, clothes rather than all black.

In the mid-1990s she joins her sisters in killing the unbearable Dave. They stake him, dismember his body, and scatter the parts. She leaves North Carolina with the group of sister vampires, and they emerge as the Vamps. They visit Las Vegas and then New York following Howler's search for her missing son. In New York they learn that Dave has somehow reassembled himself and is coming after them. Whipsnake takes Screech, Mink, and Skeeter with her to see Masoalena who works some of her magic. She constructs an amulet to block Dave's telepathic connection with them. Unfortunately, he is still connected with Howler and thus the four head for the home where they believe her son to be. They arrive in time to kill Dave once and for all.

Together again, the Vamps head for Hollywood where Mink wants to pick up her lost acting career. While Mink brushes up on acting, Whipsnake joins the effort to locate and rescue vampire poet Hugh Evans. After Mink's career comes crashing down because her image does not show on film, the Vamps head off for other adventures.

SOURCES:
Vamps. No. 1–6. New York: DC Comics/Vertigo, 1995–96.
Vamps: Hollywood & Vein. No. 1–6. New York: DC Comics, 1996.

Wingate, Simon

Simon Wingate, a Canadian vampire residing in Milgate, Ontario, some 50 miles from Sault Ste. Marie, is the subject of the romantic novel *Red Wine of Rapture* (1973). Born in the 1860s, Wingate is from an eastern European family who are victims of a hereditary curse, a sporadically reoccurring disease known as vampirism. For Wingate, the symptoms begin to manifest in his twenties when he has several bouts with nausea and weakness for which the doctors can find no organic cause. While family papers document the disease being passed down through the family, there were no traces of it through the nineteenth century. Wingate overhears his parents discussing the family illness and the papers describing it, but before they agree to talk to him about the details, they are killed in an accident.

Over the next few years, Wingate's symptoms come and go. Along with his brother Matthew, Wingate spends his time managing the family fortune. Then one day, when mountain climbing with a friend, he cuts his finger. Without thinking, he sticks his finger in his mouth and discovers that the blood has an amazing, reviving effect. Wingate then drinks from the cut on his friend's neck, and receives new strength in both mind and body, as well as a feeling of ecstasy.

Upon his return home, he reads the family history, which confirms his experience. Fortunately, he is wealthy and can obtain blood without the necessity of hunting and killing. In order to meet his blood supply, which involves regular ingestion, he imprisons a number of people in the basement of his mansion. Because the novel establishes vampirism as a hereditary disease, Wingate is a nontraditional vampire. He is not part of the undead, and so is not immortal, but potentially can live a long time. His image appears in mirrors. He is somewhat nocturnal, but not confined to the evening.

After discovering the truth of his brother's condition, Matthew is scandalized. He changes his name and becomes a recluse. He eventually marries Amy Volney and has a son, Davey. Unfortunately, Amy dies when Davey is two years old. As a youth, Davey begins showing all the symptoms of the disease.

When the majority of the novel's storyline takes place in the early 1970s, Wingate is a young man in his twenties. He meets Fiona Niesen, a young woman who has left home to discover the world, and soon transforms her into a vampire. Within weeks, her twin sister Fern shows up in the town of Milgate looking for Fiona. She accepts Wingate's invitation to stay at his house and assists him in his work, which includes research on blood diseases and vampirism. She finds herself falling in love with Wingate, but then discovers that her sister has become a vampire. Wingate tells Fern his whole story and she realizes that she is trapped in Wingate's house. He also explains that the house is booby-trapped and will blow up if he believes that his story will get out and scandalize him and his nephew, Davey.

Unbeknownst to Wingate, Davey overhears the conversation, and refuses to accept his condition and the harm that his survival would cause others. He arranges for Fern to escape, and as she leaves the booby-traps are set off, destroying Wingate and Fiona. Matthew dies in his ninety-ninth year, several years after the explosion at his brother's mansion. He leaves his entire fortune to the study of blood diseases.

SOURCES:
Worth, Margaret. *Red Wine of Rapture*. New York: Avon, 1973.

Winters, Jeff

Jeff Winters is the central character in the low-budget horror film *Kingdom of the Vampire* (1991). His 90 years of existence is belied by his appearance as a young adult still living at home with his vampire mother. Jeff's mother is a cranky woman feeling her age. While she tells Jeff that they come from a noble lineage now depleted by the action of ungrateful humans, she knows her hunting days are drawing to a close. She is feeling her age and must be content with the occasional young person or animal that for whatever reason comes to the house. She leaves the bodies and bloody mess in the kitchen for her son to clean up. All Jeff wants is to be normal, as evidenced by his job at the local convenience store and his new girlfriend.

A number of disappearances and several bodies that have been found in the community cause the sheriff to recall a similar time in his youth when bodies were being found. The sheriff and the townspeople kill a man named Dupre, claiming he was a vampire.

As Halloween quickly approaches, Jeff's mother is looking forward to propitiating the deity they acknowledge, including the vampirizing of Jeff's girlfriend. On Halloween, the principles (including Dupre's widow and child, who have returned to town) end up at the site in the woods, where it is time for the sheriff to resolve the details of the events from his youth, the girl to be saved, and Jeff to finally grow up.

Wulfe, Klaus Johann

Klaus Johann Wulfe, a 600-year-old German vampire, is the featured character in several of Wendy Snow Lang's comic book mini-series, collectively known as *Night's Children*. Klaus originally appeared in 1991 in the original *Night's Children* series along with his friends Julie and Billy. He was born in 1431, the son of Josef and Lotte Wulfe. His father teaches him coppersmithing and then sends him to the monastery to gain some scholarly and spiritual training. He spends two harsh years with the monks and returns home to marry the daughter of the local blacksmith. His wife dies a year later.

Klaus seeks solace from a local widow. His scandalized father urges him to move to the German settlement in Sibiu, Transylvania, where his brother lives. He finds work in a gunpowder factory. Klaus marries a Saxon girl and they have a daughter, Heidi, two years later. His wife is pregnant for the second time when Prince Vlad Tsepes (the historical **Count Dracula**) moves against the German community at Sibiu. Klaus's family is impaled and he is sent to Turkey as part of the tribute Vlad pays to keep the Turks at bay.

In Turkey he becomes the personal slave of Fatima, a woman who claims to be 800 years old and the surviving daughter of the prophet Muhammad. She's lying— she's not Fatima, but she is a vampire and more than a century old. However, her behavior angers Muyhiddim, the nephew of the sultan, and he has her killed. As she dies, Klaus, who had been bitten by Fatima, drinks of her blood and becomes a vampire, as does his friend Demi. Klaus escapes but is captured by Muyhiddim, who takes him to Romania (Wallachia) as his slave. He is in Muyhiddim's tent just south of Tirgovioste, the Wallachian capital, on June 17, 1462, when Dracula's army attacks. Klaus finds his brother Otto, an officer in Dracula's army, and with his help finally puts the Turks behind him.

Some of his exploits over the centuries are known. He joins the trek to California in the 1850s. He is in London in the 1880s. He is involved in the infamous Jack the Ripper case when it turns out that Jack is really a vampire named Vassily whom Demi had converted during a dalliance in Paris. Klaus tracks and destroys the Ripper. It is also during this time he meets Julia again, whom he turns into a vampire. Julia remains with him as his companion. Today Klaus and Julia live on the edge of urban society with a small group of friends and interact with a community of other vampires, some of whom he has known for a century or more. He and Julia take Billy, a former drug addict, into their nocturnal existence, in effect saving him from death by turning him. They retain their youthful appearance, not having aged since they turned, and are sexually active with a variety of partners. Klaus also carries with him the painful memories of the people he left behind when he was a mortal and remorse for the people he has killed through the centuries. He suppresses most of his feelings as a means of emotionally surviving.

SOURCES:

Snow-Lang, Wendy. *Night's Children.* No. 1–4. Albany, NY: FantaCo Enterprises. 1991.

———. *Night's Children: Double Indemnity.* Albany, NY: FantaCo Enterprises, 1992.

———. *Night's Children: Liaisons.* Kingston, RI: Millennium.

———. *Night's Children: Origins.* Kingston, RI: Millennium, 1994.

———. *Night's Children: Red Trails West.* No. 1–2. Kingston, RI: Millennium, 1994–95.

———. *Night's Children: The Vampire.* No. 1–2. Kingston, RI: Millennium, 1995.

———. *Night's Children: Vampyr!* No. 1–3. Albany, NY: FantaCo Enterprises, 1992–93.

———. *Night's Children: Vampyr!* No. 4. Kingston, RI: Millennium Publications, 1994.

Yaksha

Yaksha is the original vampire in *The Last Vampire*, the continuing series of young adult novels that bear that name. He was born under extraordinary circumstances more than 5,000 years ago in what is now India. A disease had spread through the village and, in desperation, a priest took the book of one of the recently deceased for a black magic ritual. The body of Amba, who had perished while eight months pregnant, was taken to a secluded place where, in the presence of a few of the villagers, the priest invoked the presence of a demon spirit, a yakshini. The yakshini came forth and briefly inhabited the body. However, after the ceremony, it was noticed that the child inside the corpse was moving, and the men ripped it out of the body. They named it Yaksha, a leaving of the yakshini, and gave it to a barren village woman to raise.

Nothing is said to the other villagers about the strange circumstances of Yaksha's birth, and he grows to manhood as an accepted member of the community. He is handsome, with black hair and blue eyes. His is intelligent, well behaved, and possesses a beguiling smile. However, one thing sets him apart: he grows at an extraordinary pace and by his ninth year already appears to be an adult.

About this time, men begin to disappear from the village. Only the ones present at Yaksha's birth realize they are the ones who are being taken by Yaksha. Among those present was Sita, who had been Yaksha's friend while growing up, but is now married with a daughter. One evening, Yaksha comes to her, and tells her that he is a vampire. He presents Sita with a choice: she can die, or join his small band of followers, the men who had disappeared, and be his eternal mate. She chooses to survive as a vampire, which means never seeing her husband or daughter again.

As Yaksha leads his followers around the countryside, people soon realize that death follows in their wake. Eventually he is led to Vrendabn where he hears of an extraordinary being named Krishna. Yaksha challenges Krishna to battle. Krishna accepts the suggested battle of flutes. Both men enter a pit filled with serpents, with

Poster art from the 1970 film *Count Yorga, Vampire*.

the understanding that the winner will be the one who can beguile the snake to stay away from him. Yaksha loses. Krishna calls off the snake before Yaksha is killed, but the price of freedom is high. Yaksha has to kill all of the vampires he was responsible for making, with the understanding that Sita will be the last one he kills. Krishna, in turn, makes a bargain with Sita: she is not to make any more vampires and she can only exist under Krishna's grace. Yaksha and Sita separate, as he pursues his mission and she makes her way in the world.

In the 1990s, Sita lives as **Alisa Perne**, a high school senior in Beverly Hills. She believes herself to be the last existing vampire, Yaksha having killed all of the others and then himself having died in the Middle Ages. However, Yaksha reappears and informs her that he has one last task to complete before he finally perishes: he must kill her. Neither of the two vampires is easy to kill, and so Alisa arranges for their mutual death. She rigs a set of high explosives in her mansion, although unbeknownst to Yaksha, she leaves herself a means of escape. In the explosion, Yaksha is killed and Alisa wounded. She disposes of his body.

Yaksha is not completely destroyed. His body is found by a young streetwise kid, Eddie Fender, who drinks his blood and inherits his strength and wisdom. As he begins to make additional vampires, Alisa discovers that she is not the last vampire. She is forced to recover Yaksha's body and then go head to head against Eddie. Yaksha now continues through the strength and heightened powers he has passed to his creation.

SOURCES:

Pike, Christopher. *The Last Vampire*. New York: Archway/Pocket Books, 1994.
———. *The Last Vampire 2: Black Blood*. New York: Archway/Pocket Books, 1994.
———. *The Last Vampire 3: Red Dice*. New York: Archway/Pocket Books, 1995.
———. *The Last Vampire 4: Phantom*. New York: Archway/Pocket Books, 1996.
———. *The Last Vampire 5: Evil Thirst*. New York: Archway/Pocket Books, 1996.
———. *The Last Vampire 6: Creatures of Forever*. New York: Archway/Pocket Books, 1996.

Yorga, Count

One of the first vampires to enter modern urban society, Count Yorga first appears in Robert Kelljan's film *Count Yorga, Vampire* (1970). He is a traditional eastern European vampire who travels from his native Bulgaria to 1960s Los Angeles where the film takes place. He is old, although of indeterminate age, and has gathered several widows throughout the centuries. He is a nocturnal being who can see in the dark and likes to sleep in a coffin. Like most traditional vampires, he has fangs and is repelled by a cross. He possesses the power to draw his victims to him with hypnosis, and his single bite is sufficient to turn a victim into a vampire.

Upon his arrival in Los Angeles, he establishes himself in a large old house and sets about the task of building companionship through creating a harem of young vampire women. He draws potential victims to him by opening a business as a medium. His victims sleep in the throne room he has established in the basement of his residence.

Among the count's initial victims are Donna Darnell, the daughter of his first victim, and her friend Erica. He kills Erica's lover, but Michael, Donna's boyfriend,

Robert Quarry as Count Yorga in *Count Yorga, Vampire.*

figures out that Yorga may possibly be a vampire and consults vampire expert Dr. Hayes. Michael destroys Yorga's plans with a makeshift stake (a broomstick) through his emotionless heart. However, the stake proves to be only a temporary setback, and Yorga recovers and moves to San Francisco where he initiates the same plan.

The rest of the story focuses on Yorga's newly created modest cadre of vampires. Yorga befriends Cynthia Nelson and lures her in as an unsuspecting member of his group. Eventually Cynthia's fiance calls the police, and while they are dealing with the harem, he pursues Yorga and plants a knife in his heart. Yorga is dead, but his lineage lives on. The fiance becomes a vampire and puts the bite on the lovely Cynthia.

SOURCES:

Gross, Edward. "Robert Quarry, Count Yorga, Rises Again." In Gross, Edward and Marc Shapiro. *The Vampire Interview Book.* East Meadow, NY: Image Publishing, 1991.

York, Captain Joshua Anton

Captain Joshua Anton York is the owner of a river boat on the Mississippi in the 1850s that gave its name to the 1982 George R. R. Martin novel *Fevre Dream.* His family comes from Poland and are hereditary vampires. York was born in France in 1785; his family was recognized as members of the lesser nobility. His mother dies during his difficult birth and Joshua is but four when his father is arrested during the French Revolution. After his father's decapitation (which ends his life as a vampire), he takes to the streets of Paris and becomes a capable thief. His blood lust emerges at the age of 10, after he has been shot, and from that time forward he needs to feed at least once a month. As a young man he moves to England and becomes a wealthy man.

York finally settles in rural Scotland and turns his attention to alternative methods of dealing with his condition. Around 1812 he decides to research the differences between vampire and human blood. Over a three year period, he creates a mixture based on sheep's blood and a variety of herbs that serves as a substitute for real blood and controls his blood lust. The creation of the substitute means he no longer has to attack or kill humans in order to survive.

He is also finally able to locate other members of his family who had relocated to the Carpathian Mountains. In 1826 he travels to Transylvania to share what he has discovered about the blood substitute and is welcomed as the "bloodmaster," a legendary savior who has been predicted to arise among his people. Hoping to save the entire community of vampires, many of whom had been killed in various purges over the centuries, he discovers that one group had previously left Portugal for New Orleans.

In the 1850s, he moves to the Mississippi River Valley, contacts Captain Abner Marsh, the owner of a small shipping company named for the Fevre (now Galena) River, and gives him the money to build a new boat to navigate the Mississippi. Meanwhile, York researches possible signs of his vampire cousins by collecting stories of unusual deaths from the newspapers. Once the *Fevre Dream* is functional, he heads for New Orleans where he encounters the leader of the vampire community, **Damon Julian.**

Julian is unreceptive to York's offer to provide the blood substitute and thus end the vampire's killing ways; he temporarily puts York under his control. The *Fevre Dream* is renamed the *Ozimandius* (from Shelley's poem). Marsh and the crew are put off the boat and it disappears during the Civil War. As it turns out, James simply hid the boat in an out-of-the-way bayou. Marsh finds it there in 1879 and again teams with York for a final confrontation with Julian.

York is clean shaven with light blonde hair, grey eyes with very dark pupils, pale skin, and feminine hands. He is a vampire by birth and, like others of his kind, is nocturnal, but can stand short periods in daylight. He will burn after an hour, but can quickly heal with an ingestion of blood or his blood substitute. He had no problem with silver, wolfsbane, or sacred symbols. He cannot change shape and does not grow hair. He does not sleep in a coffin and can easily cross running water.

SOURCES:
Martin, George R. R. *Fevre Dream.* New York: Poseidon Press, 1982. Reprint, London: VGSF, 1989.

Zachery

Zachery, the vampire turned vampire hunter in the film *Vampire Journals* (1996), is a nocturnal creature with a mortal's heart. He is on a mission of revenge against the vampire who turned him into a creature of the night and killed Rebecca, his true love, and all of the spawn related to her. He was transformed approximately a century ago by a female vamp named Serena with whom he had a brief dalliance. Through this century, he has killed hundreds of vampires with the Sword of Laertes, a weapon he carries with him. He finally arrives in post-Ceausescu Bucharest where a group of vampires are ruled by their master Ash.

Zachery is a traditional vampire, with pale skin and prominent fangs. He is strong and fast, and can transform into a bat and fly. Like his peers, he can be caught in the passion of feeding at which time he is distracted and vulnerable. He hates killing, and drinks only to survive. He does not have the strength to look upon the face of his victims and rarely takes enough blood to kill them. He counts on that momentary vulnerability in other vampires and uses it to get close to them for the kill. They are vulnerable to the sword either impaling them or decapitating them.

In the process of hunting Ash, he steps between Ash and his latest infatuation, a young American pianist, Sofia Christopher. Ash is enraptured with her and invites her to give a private performance at his nightclub, Club Muse, which is managed by his minions. After the concert, Ash takes Sofia to his room and bites her for the first time. He does not transform her immediately as he first wants her to acknowledge his masterhood. In the meantime, Zachery tries to figure out a means to get to her.

Just before he turns Sofia, Ash invites Zachery into his abode. After taking his sword, he offers him a deal. He would give Zachery sanctuary for one evening, supply him with free food, and allow him to see Sofia. In return he must leave town forever. Zachery agrees. While Zachery is feeding on the young woman Ash put at his disposal, Ash brings Sofia into the room. It is all he needs to finally convince her she has no hope. She accepts her fate and Ash shares his blood with her.

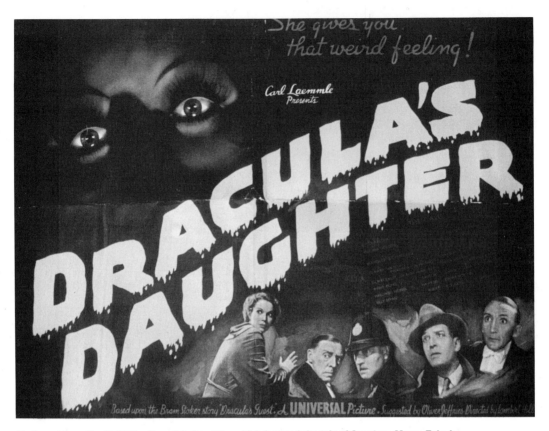

Poster art from the 1936 film *Dracula'a Daughter,* which featured the tale of Countess Marya Zaleska.

Zachery, however, feels that Ash has made their deal null and void, and he attacks him as he is turning Sofia. The wounded Ash is slow to respond when Sofia leaves with Zachery. Before he leaves the building, and as dawn is approaching, Zachery and Ash have their final confrontation. Zachery is able to use the dawn and push Ash into the morning's rays. He is destroyed, and he then pushes Sofia into a dark space to begin her education in the rules of survival as a creature of the night. Having disposed of Ash and again in possession of his sword, Zachery is free to continue his vendetta against the larger vampire community.

Zaleska, Countess Marya

Countess Marya Zaleska, the first of **Count Dracula**'s offspring, makes her debut in the film *Dracula's Daughter* (1936), the sequel to the infamous *Dracula* (1931) starring Bela Lugosi. Although presenting some discontinuity with the original story set in the 1890s (the film is set in the 1930s, for example), *Dracula's Daughter* is worth watching as the only true sequel to *Dracula*.

Countess Marya Zaleska (portrayed by Gloria Holden) is apparently powerless to stop her servant Sandor (portrayed by Irving Pinchel) from placing Count Dracula's ring on her finger.

When the film begins, the 100-year-old vampire emerges from obscurity after the death of Dracula at the hands of vampire hunter **Abraham Van Helsing**. Tall, dark, and dressed in black, she walks into the police station where the body is being kept temporarily and, using a large ring, hypnotizes the police officer in charge. She then burns the body with the hope that her father's death will free her from his influence.

In spite of this ritual, she remains a creature of the night, sleeping in a coffin. Although she shows no fangs, she leaves two puncture wounds in the necks of her victims. She feeds several times a week. At a party she meets psychiatrist Jeffrey Garth, a friend of Van Helsing. Convinced of the power of his profession, Garth tells Zaleska that treatment can cure any obsession if the will to overcome the condition is present in the patient. Not yet aware that she is a vampire, Garth encourages her to face her condition and deal with it.

Slowly Garth accepts the fact that Countess Zaleska is a vampire, a fact confirmed by her phobia about mirrors and her hesitation to change. Instead of continuing therapy, Zaleska decides that she will take Garth with her to Transylvania as her eternal mate. In order to accomplish her goals, she kidnaps his secretary and holds her for ransom; the price for her release being his decision to stay with her. Unfortunately for Zaleska, she has made her servant jealous, evidently promising him eternal existence as well. In his anger and disappointment over her choosing Garth, he shoots Zaleska with a well-aimed arrow in the heart. Fortunately for Garth, the local police arrive in time to save him from a similar fate.

Zane

Zane, the son of detective **Merrick Chapman**, is the featured antagonist in the novel *Rulers of Darkness 2* (1991). Zane is a 500-year-old vampire-like entity known as a hemophage, a human possessed of a unique gene that imparts vampire-like qualities. Not being a supernatural creature, he does not display the supernatural attributes often associated with vampires (for example, his image appears in mirrors, he is not repelled by religious symbols, he cannot transform into nonhuman forms). He possesses great strength and heals quickly from any wounds. His primary ability involves regulating the flow of blood in humans, thus he can put a potential victim to sleep and take blood without either harming the person or making his activities known. Like all hemophages, Zane is nocturnal.

At the age of 12, Zane developed leukemia. In order to save him, his father shared his blood. Zane became the only one of his many children who subsequently became a hemophage. However, over the centuries, Zane has discovered that he likes killing people, and becomes a serial killer in later life. He also develops a hatred of his father and thus taunts him by committing his crimes in Washington, D.C., where his father works as a police officer.

In the mid-1990s, Zane conceives a plan. He goes six months without blood. The dieting turns his hair white and ages his appearance to the extent that his father cannot recognize him. He then begins to commit murders that his father would recognize as being caused by a hemophage. Unplanned, at the site of one of the murders, he leaves some minute drops of his own blood that are recognized by his father's current girlfriend, hematologist Kate O'Keefe, as unique.

As he invades his father's world, Zane also discovers that one of O'Keefe's youthful patients is dying of leukemia. He gives her blood and she begins to turn into a hemophage. He also makes the mistake of taking some blood which quickly brings him back to his normal appearance and thus recognizable to his father, who eventually brings him to justice by confining him to an underground chamber where Chapman had imprisoned other renegade hemophages.

Ten years later Zane escapes confinement and contacts his daughter and Jean Hrluska, an intern at Adams Memorial Hospital. He leaves a body drained of blood as a signal of his nearness. As other murders occur, Hrluska is arrested but escapes to confront Zane, a meeting that will again bring Chapman back into his son's life.

SOURCES:

Spruill, Steven. *Daughter of Darkness.* New York: Doubleday, 1997.
———. *Rulers of Darkness.* New York: St. Martin's Press, 1995.

Ziska, Baron Alexis

Baron Alexis Ziska, an aristocratic eastern European vampire, is the subject of the novel *The Vampire* (1935). Of indeterminate age, he comes from the fictional land of Sovrania. Reminiscent of **Count Dracula,** he has black hair, hypnotic eyes, and a mustache, and his extended canine teeth can be seen when he opens his mouth. He appears to be in his late thirties. Like most traditional vampires, Ziska is repelled by the cross and holy water. He can transform into a bat and into mist. A Satanist who enhanced his powers with black magic rites, Ziska is not affected by most weapons, although he is vulnerable to a stake made of steel.

Simultaneous to his arrival in London in the mid-1930s, five of London's best-known society beauties disappear. These cases are then tied to the disappearance of Elizabeth Platting, a woman who ends up in a city hospital with two puncture wounds on her neck. In London, Ziska sets his sights on Sonia Rodney, the daughter of Lord Rodney. She reports that she feels he is trying to control her hypnotically, and has been somewhat successful. Lord Rodney calls a nerve specialist, Dr. Martin Kent, into the case, and he in turn commands the assistance of **Dr. Paul Metternich,** who has been tracking Ziska on the continent.

While Metternich is relating Ziska's vampiric profile to his current seduction over Rodney, Ziska announces that he is engaged to the young woman. He takes her prisoner, and the team assembled by Metternich finally track him to his lair in the Savronian embassy where, after an initial attack with holy water designed to hold Ziska in human form, Metternich impales him with a sword. As the climatic scene concludes, the aged Ziska crumbles to dust.

SOURCES:

Horler, Sydney. *The Vampire*. London: Hutchinson & Co., 1935. Reprint, New York: Bookfinger, 1974.

Vampire Groups
and Clans

The Brotherhood

The Brotherhood is the name taken by the community of vampires in the Australian film *Thirst* (1987). These vampires are not supernatural creatures but are a superior race that is able to live largely unnoticed amid humans. In the late twentieth century, there are approximately 70,000 members of the Brotherhood all over the world. Although they are vampires, a term they dislike and eschew as much as possible, the Brotherhood are modern post-scientific vampires. Their activities are not limited to the night, but they lack supernatural abilities such as flying and shape shifting. They also lack super strength, though they claim that the consumption of blood grants them youthfulness and personal power.

Throughout this century, these modern vampires have developed a thoroughly scientific approach to their peculiar dietary needs. They have established a network of blood farms that appear to be mundane research facilities. Inside each facility, a number of human donors reside and, unwittingly, are milked like cows. The donors' blood is distributed throughout the Brotherhood and relieves the necessity of attacking people and risking unwanted attention.

As an acknowledgment of their heritage, the Brotherhood gathers periodically for ritual celebrations, the highlight of which is the creation of a vampire from a live human donor. As they prepare to feed on the living person, their eyes become red and fangs appear, the only signs of their difference from humans.

The Cadre

The Cadre is an ancient ruling body of the vampire community that appears in Karen Taylor's novel *The Vampire Legacy: Bitter Blood* (1994). The Cadre is composed of the leaders of the various vampire "houses," or families, each founded by a prominent vampire. Currently, there are eight houses represented in The Cadre.

While not a governing body, The Cadre has the authority to act when a member of one of the houses is harmed or gets out of line. The Cadre's word is law. It can order punishments and can move against any who attempt to override its judgment.

In the early 1990s, Max Hunter, one of their prominent members of the group is murdered. Cadre members at first think that a mortal, New York policeman Mitch Greer, is the murderer. It turns out, however, that Greer's lover **Dierdre Griffin** is actually an independent vampire not affiliated with any of the houses, and it is she who is responsible for Hunter's death. Griffin goes before The Cadre and explains why she killed Hunter. The group feels that she was justified in her actions, and she is not punished. However, she agrees to perform one service for the organization if it calls upon her. The opportunity for her to perform that task arises quickly when a vampire goes wild in New York and begins killing humans and vampires alike. The Cadre had strict rules against killing one of its own, so it turns to Griffin to kill the rogue vampire. Since she is not affiliated with The Cadre, she is granted a special dispensation to kill the other vampire. The Cadre also appears in Taylor's 1995 book *Blood Ties*.

SOURCES:

Taylor, Karen E. *Blood Ties*. New York: Zebra Books, 1995.
———— *The Vampire Legacy: Bitter Blood*. New York: Zebra Books, 1994.

The Camarilla

The Camarilla is a worldwide organization of vampires founded in the fifteenth century to protect the vampire community from the actions of the Inquisition. Understanding what The Camarilla is and how it operates is integral to the popular role-playing game called *Vampire: The Masquerade*, which was created by Mark Rein-Hagen and initially published in 1991.

In the game, vampires originated as a separate species in ancient times. The original vampire was **Caine** (the biblical character who in Genesis killed his brother and was afflicted with an unspecified curse). *Vampire* suggests that the curse was eternal life and a craving for blood. After wandering in the wilderness for many years, he resumed life among the mortals and founded a city. There he had a number of children and grandchildren, so-called Second Generation and Third Generation vampires who also carried the curse. When a Fourth Generation rebels against their elders, the city is destroyed and the surviving vampires are scattered, destined to appear periodically as a secret force throughout history. The majority of vampires alive in the world today are Sixth Generation, and they face pressure to create no more vampires since it is believed that the blood thins and vampire powers are diminished with each subsequent generation.

Beginning in 1435, the Inquisition was able to capture and kill many of "the Kindred," as the vampires were called. It stamped out entire bloodlines by putting them to "true" death by fire. Prior to this attack, vampires had lived openly (albeit discretely) among humans, but the Inquisition drove the survivors completely underground. In 1486, a global convocation of vampires was held, during which a secret worldwide network was established. It established the law of The Masquerade, an attempt to convince the world that all vampires were dead, or, better still, they never existed. The Masquerade demanded that all vampires make a reasonable effort at secrecy. Then, as a group the vampire community initiated efforts to convince the world that they had never existed.

The vampires used humans to help with this subterfuge. The accumulated wisdom of the near-immortal vampires was turned over to intelligent mortals, who then used that wisdom to spurt the development of science and logic while suppressing superstition. This of course helped to crush any belief in vampires. In today's world, The Masquerade is under attack. It is threatened by a new mysticism that has arisen through a combination of forces—mind-altering psychedelic drugs, new music, and the popularity of "fictional" vampires in modern popular culture. Those affected by the new mysticism are ready to believe in the existence of vampires. Another problem is the generation gap between those vampires who created the Masquerade and understand its necessity and newer vampires (those created in the last century). The elders think that the brashness of their younger brethren is calling too much unwelcome attention to the vampire community.

In *Vampire*, the elder vampires have more powers than newer ones. For both old and young, the stake is painful, but by itself it is not fatal. Sunlight, fire, and decapitation are the main dangers that vampires face. Holy objects have no effect, nor does running water. Vampires have sharpened senses that aid them in hunting, including the power to impose their will on mortals. The elder vampires can change shapes, but most of the newer ones cannot.

New vampires can be created by first having their blood drained and then receiving some of the vampire's blood, though the new vampire has slightly less power than that of the vampire who created him/her. Vampires no longer breathe, though they can fake respiration. The heart no longer beats, so any blood consumed spreads through the body by osmosis rather than through the old artery/vein system. The blood carries all the oxygen the vampire needs to survive. Vampires heal quickly of most wounds. Being staked produces a form of paralysis.

The vampire exists in the shadows of the world of mortals. The worldwide vampire society exists as a parallel society beside that of mortals, whom are largely unaware of the existence of the vampire community. The vampires are organized into territorial clans ruled by princes. Every major city of the world supports a vampire community and vampires who enter a new city have to present themselves to the powers that are established there. To simply begin hunting is considered a violation of the vampiric order. Typical of city leadership is **Doran,** the original prince of New Orleans, and **Edward,** the contemporary prince of Denver. Atypical is Los Angeles, where Prince **Don Sebastian Juan Dominguez** was overthrown in 1944 and a series of Anarch Free States have been established from San Diego to San Francisco. Several famous people have become vampires and now constitute part of the *Vampire* mythos. Typical of these celebrity figures is **Louis Pasteur.**

Vampire primarily exists as a live action role-playing game. A card game version, *Jyhad,* which had continued the entire *Vampire* world view, appeared in 1994. The work of The Camarilla has been described in the more than 70 books published by White Wolf Game Studio.

SOURCES:

Berry, Jeff. *Alien Hunger.* Stone Mountain, GA: White Wolf, n.d.

Chupp, Sam, and Andrew Greenberg. *The Book of Nod.* Stone Mountain, GA: White Wolf, 1993.

Dudley, Noah. *Los Angeles by Night.* Stone Mountain, GA: White Wolf, 1994.

Greenberg, Daniel. *Who's Who among Vampires: Children of the Inquisition.* Stone Mountain, GA: White Wolf, 1992.

McCubbin, Chris W. *Vampire the Masquerade Companion.* N.p.: Steve Jackson Games, 1994.

Rein-Hagen, Mark, Andrew Greenberg, and Steve Crow. *Mind's Eye Theatre: The Masquerade Story Book.* Stone Mountain, GA: White Wolf, 1993.

———. *Mind's Eye Theatre: The Masquerade Character Book.* Stone Mountain, GA: White Wolf, 1993.

Rein-Hagen, Mark, et al. *Book of the Damned.* Stone Mountain, GA: White Wolf, 1993.

———. *Vampire: The Masquerade.* Stone Mountain, GA: White Wolf, 1991. Roskell, Patricia Ann. *New Orleans by Night.* Stone Mountain, GA: White Wolf, 1994.

Church of Eternal Life

The Church of Eternal Life is a vampire church that appears in the novels of Laurell K. Hamilton, beginning with *Guilty Pleasure* (1993). In the world of the near future, vampires have come out of hiding and have been afforded legal status as the result of a Supreme Court ruling in the case of *Addison v. Clark*. As a result, vampires now interact with humans and have even formed their own business districts. Hamilton's novels are all set in St. Louis, Missouri, where the vampire community thrives in an area known as Riverfront. Along with the spread of vampires has come a surge in new occupations, such as professional vampire killer. The protagonist of Hamilton's novels is just such a killer—**Anita Blake** hunts down vampires who have gone rogue and operate outside the law.

The Church of Eternal Life is located just outside of the Riverfront community. It wants to be identified with the vampire community, but not necessarily with the lifestyle followed by most vampires. The church offers humans a literal entrance into eternal life—it offers to change them into vampires. As an organization that does not believe in God or the supernatural, its building is decorated with an abstract color scheme void of any religious symbols.

The Roman Catholic church has rejected the idea of humans becoming vampires and considers the voluntary vampirism offered by the Church of Eternal Life to be a form of suicide. The church has a broad following, however, and each evening humans gather at the church to meet and be counseled by real vampires. Counselors try to communicate the pros and cons of a nocturnal existence tied to the drinking of blood.

SOURCES:

Hamilton, Laurell K. *Guilty Pleasures.* New York: Ace Books, 1993.

Clans, Vampire

Vampire clans are the dominant groups that comprise the popular role-playing game *Vampire: The Masquerade.* The game, which has exploded in popularity in the 1990s, includes a complete myth detailing the origin and organization of the world of the vampires, who are known as the Kindred. According to legend, vampires were created when the biblical Caine (or Cain) slew his brother Abel and was cursed with immortal life and the blood thirst. Ancient records kept by the vampire community continue Caine's story beyond that which is told in the Bible. Caine wandered the Middle East for a period of time and then settled down and founded a city (the name is unknown). There, he created three new vampires who constitute the Second Generation (generations are numbered in *The Masquerade* to designate how many layers removed a person is from Caine). Those three in turn created a number of vampires who constituted the Third Generation.

As vampires spread, Caine forbade the creation of further vampires, possibly because the food supply was diminishing. However, Caine's city was wiped out by a flood and he departed from his children. His whereabouts or fate since that time are unknown. Freed from his rule, the vampires of the Third Generation created many more children, who formed the Fourth Generation. This proved to be a mistake, however, because the younger vampires rebelled and slew their elders. Only a few of the Third Generation survived, while the Fourth Generation went on to build a new city, which might have been the famous Babylon of history.

After many centuries, the Fourth Generation fell victim to a popular uprising by mortals, and their city was destroyed. They scattered around the world and created the Fifth Generation. Today, all of the vampires of the Third through Fifth Generation have become recluses. The vampires continued to create new generations, however, and the Sixth through the Thirteenth Generations live in the major cities of the world side-by-side with humans. In the fifteenth century, for their own protection, many of those newer vampires organized into a large group that is known as **The Camarilla.**

The bloodline of every vampire can be traced back to one of the vampires of the Third Generation. Each bloodline is unique and is distinguished by a set of distinctive traits—sometimes physical, but more often by personality traits or differences in social standing. There are seven major clans that constitute The Camarilla. They are:

BRUJAHS: The youthful rebels of the vampire world. They are forever searching for new ways to express their individuality and tend to choose roles that are on the fringe of society—punks, bikers, anarchists, etc. They are the most uncontrollable of the vampires, and their clan is the most loosely organized.

GANGREL: They are wanderers, rootless travelers who are forever on the move. They are not opposed to the larger organized vampire world so much as they have no need for it. Gypsies are the mortal children of the Gangrel's founder.

MALKAVIANS: The Malkavians are all a little insane, as they come too close to grasping the nature of reality and have descended into chaos as a result. Such insanity can lead to wisdom and in turn generate power. It also leads to a love of pranks—status is often assigned among Malkavians based on the quality of the elegant pranks they play against one another, other vampires, or humans.

NOSFERATU: The most physically unique of the clans, the Nosferatu were recreated in the image of **Count Graf Orlock** of the 1922 film *Nosferatu.* The Nosferatu generally choose the twisted members of society (psychically or psychologically) as new recruits for their clan. Shortly after receiving the cursed gift, new vampires undergo a most painful transformation as body features alter into the rodent-like features common to clan members. The Nosferatu tend to keep to themselves.

TOREADOR: Often described as hedonists, but more accurately described as lovers of beauty. They tend to be regal, proud, and elitist. They love art and will often select artists as new vampires so their art will not be lost by death. The clan constantly struggles to find truth and beauty, although that does not necessarily imply "good" as it might in the human community.

TREMERE: This clan is the best organized of the groups. They are manipulative, intelligent, aggressive, and determined. They use the other clans in order to prosper. International leaders of the Tremere are located in Vienna and from there manage the clan worldwide. It is rumored that they possess the secrets of blood magic.

VENTRUE: The most human of the vampires. They possess good taste and like to live a comfortable life of leisure. They tend to remember and prize the time period when they became vampires. They also like to mingle with the elite members of human society. They have strong ties to members of their bloodline and cannot refuse a call for assistance.

Beside these seven most prominent vampire clans, there are other, smaller ones, including the Assamite and Giovanni. There are also the Caitiff, or clanless, vampires, who were usually abandoned by the one who made them a vampire.

When playing Vampire: The Masquerade (and Jyhad, the card game based on it), the action revolves around the political intrigue and skirmishes between the various clans. The idea of the Kindred, The Camarilla, and vampire clans originated with Mark Rein-Hagen, the creator of Vampire: The Masquerade. The game has played a very important role in sparking new interest in vampires and in popularizing the idea that they are social creatures that live in a community, albeit a community that is separate from humans.

SOURCES:

Brown, Steve. *Clanbook: Toreador.* Stone Mountain, GA: White Wolf, 1994.

Crow, Steve. *Clanbook: Brujah, a Past of Treachery/a Future of Flames.* Stone Mountain, GA: White Wolf, 1992.

Freeman, Brad. *Clanbook Gangrel: From the Forests of Mystery.* Stone Mountain, GA: White Wolf, 1993.

Grame, Davis. *Clanbook: Assamite.* Stone Mountain, GA: White Wolf, 1995.

Greenberg, Andrew, et al. *Clanbook: Ventrue.* Stone Mountain, GA: White Wolf, 1994.

Greenberg, Daniel. *Clanbook Malkavian: Method in the Madness.* Stone Mountain, GA: White Wolf, 1993.

Hatch, Robert. *Clanbook: Nosferatu.* Stone Mountain, GA: White Wolf, 1993.

———. *Clanbook: Tzimisce.* Clarkston, GA: White Wolf, 1996.

Herder, Keith. *Clanbook: Tembere.* Stone Mountain, GA: White Wolf, 1994.

Rein-Hagen, Mark, et al. *Book of the Damned.* Stone Mountain, GA: White Wolf, 1993.

———. *Vampire: The Masquerade.* Stone Mountain, GA: White Wolf, 1991.

The Conclave

The Conclave is a vampiric ruling council that appears in Garfield Reeves-Stevens novel *Bloodshift* (1981). It has provided the vampire community with stability for more than 250 years. The Conclave was founded in part to do battle with the Roman Catholic Church. It seems that the Jesuits have battled vampires since their order was founded in the sixteenth century, using a secret cadre of members called the Seventh Grade to identify and kill vampires. However, since the founding of The Conclave, the odds have evened out with the Jesuits and the battle with them has been contained.

The Conclave established its headquarters in Geneva. It brought together the wisdom of the vampire (who refer to themselves as the *yber*) community, whose members had slowly learned to survive on the fringe of the human community. Intent on its own survival, The Conclave promulgated the Ways, its understanding of the nature of vampires and a system by which to live that would be for the good of all. The Ways assumed that vampires were a product of Satan and that vampires were creatures outside the realm of God. It manipulated this supernatural perspective to keep control of the vampire community. For example, no new vampire could be created unless the conclave approved.

Under The Conclave's rule, the vampire community had prospered. It had consolidated its wealth and provided an identity for those vampires who had to interact with the human community. It also manipulated situations to draw the attention of the authorities away from the group. Among those used by The Conclave were individuals who became famous as real vampires: French soldier Victor Bertrand (1849), German serial killer Fritz Haarman (1920s), and British serial killer George Haight (1940s).

Cover art from the comic book *Deadbeats,* a modern tale of young vampires in Mystic Grove, Connecticut.

At the time of its founding, one senior vampire, the Father, refused to acknowledge The Conclave's authority. He had been the mentor of many vampires and he offered sanctuary to any vampires who rejected The Conclave's authority. The Father resided in the town of Naciamento, California, not far from San Luis Obispo.

As the novel shifts from the history of the group to the present day, it is revealed that The Conclave is experiencing a crisis. One vampire, **Adrienne St. Clair,** has been researching the nature of vampirism and has concluded that the Ways are based upon a fictitious understanding of the *yber*. Vampirism is really a natural phenomenon, possibly best understood as a viral infection. The supernaturalism of the Ways is all nonsense and is being perpetuated merely to keep The Conclave in power. After making some important discoveries, St. Clair begins to involve nonvampire researchers in her work. Conclave leaders, especially **Lord Eduardo Diego y Rey,** demand that she stop prying into vampirism, but she refuses. Since her mentor and lover Jeffrey has been killed by The Conclave, she flees to North America, ultimately joining forces with the Father.

St. Clair is unaware that her research is beginning to interfere with Lord Diego's plans for world conquest. However, he decides to use her flight to the Father as an opportunity to have the Father and the *yber* under his protection destroyed. If the Father was dead, Diego would be free to consolidate his power over the entire *yber* community. The fate of the community would hinge upon the confrontation between the Jesuits (who were to be blamed for the Father's death), St. Clair, and Lord Diego.

SOURCES:

Reeves-Stevens, Garfield. *Bloodshift*. Toronto: Virgo Press, 1981. Reprint, New York: Popular Library, 1990.

Deadbeats

The Deadbeats are a small group of vampires who are the subject of a continuing series of comic books from Claypool Comics called simply, *Deadbeats*. The story is set in the early 1990s near the town of Mystic Grove, Connecticut. The original Deadbeats consisted of four individuals—Coleen, Mickey, Dodger and Martine—who had been together for centuries. As early as 1494, they made an appearance in Granada, Spain, where they attacked and destroyed a large family. Shortly after they settle in Mystic Grove, they turn a local boy, Michael-Evan Southland into a vampire. Southland, the son of the town's mayor, not only joins the group but becomes its leader. He is more commonly known as Southie. Among his first acts is to change Brittany Bov, a spoiled local prom queen, into his vampire "soulmate."

The Deadbeats are rather traditional vampires. They are nocturnal, have fangs, and can transform into bats and fly. When they fly in their human form, they sprout wings. They react to the cross and to fire. They are the undead, and feel cold to the touch. Vampirism is passed by their bite, and unless mortally wounded, their victims will return as vampires in three days. The group's understanding of vampire history is that the original vampires created themselves through a sheer act of will, the ultimate turning from God.

Cover art from Richard Howell's *Deadbeats*.

Opposing the Deadbeats is, on the one hand, a parapsychologist and vampirologist, Dr. V.V. Ralston, head of Manderly Mental Hospital, and, on the other hand, King Hermano, the king of the vampires, who has also taken up residence near Mystic Grove. For a period, Ralston is assisted by vampire hunter Dakota Kane, who captures Mickey and turns him over to the doctor, who subjects him to an experiment aimed at returning him to his human existence. Mickey is killed in the process. As the Deadbeats continue their attacks on Mystic Grove, Ralston and Kane gain a number of supporters.

They gain an unexpected ally in King Hermano, who is secretly on a mission to change the image of vampires as degenerate parasites. He believes that vampires can take their rightful place as the superior race. The Deadbeats have defied his authority for centuries, and they represent an obstacle to his plan. He moves against Southie and the remaining Deadbeats and essentially destroys the group, sending Brittany to hell in the process. Southie follow her and is eventually able to rescue her and bring her back. Southie, loyal only to Brittany, breaks away from the remaining Deadbeats.

SOURCES:

Howell, Richard. *Deadbeats*. Leonia, NJ: Claypool Comics, 1993. Ongoing series.

Knight Club

Among the most unusual structures in the vampire community stands the Knight Club, a facility on the island of Puerto Rico used by the vampire community in its own self-policing. Serving as warden in the "vampire stockade" is Lance Knight, a former vampire hunter turned vampire. In the year 2001, Veronica Reverence, the leading character in the *Avenue X* comic stories of Brenda Black, is summoned to the Knight Club to be held accountable for the death of Pagan, a female vampire. Pagan had been seriously burned and asked Veronica to take her out of her misery and kill her. Veronica considers it a mercy killing; the vampire authorities see it as murder.

The Knight Club is to all outward appearances a night club whose floor show is a popular attraction to nonvampiric Puerto Ricans and the hotspot for the rich and famous who visit the island. As part of their punishment, the vampires confined to the building are forced to entertain the mortals.

In the *Avenue X* world, vampires are essentially nocturnal creatures. They are not killed by sunlight, but it weakens their hypnotic and telepathic powers and drains their strength, especially with newly made vampires like Veronica. They are also supersensitive to noise, and as they have had to adapt to the modern world they have learned to wear special silver earplugs that block much of the debilitating sounds of industrial society. Their body temperature is low and cold to the touch. They have fangs that facilitate attacks and blood sucking.

Vampires confined to the club are sentenced to an indefinite stay. Those vampires whose crime are serious enough to be sentenced to this unique prison have only one means of terminating their stay—to escape. There are the normal barriers, such as locks and guards, which don't normally present a problem for the average vampire. But prisoners are given short rations of blood that only sustain them and keep them hungry and in a weakened state. They are also not permitted to wear earplugs, and exits are blocked by noisemakers, the most effective barrier to their escape. Despite these obstacles, Veronica finally ends her sentence by escaping through an opening created by the earth's movement when an earthquake hits the island.

Avenue X originated as a radio drama series on WBAI in New York in 1990. In the mid-1990s, the story pitting the Knight Club and the vampire community against the resourceful Veronica Reverence appeared in several issues of the *Avenue* X comic book.

SOURCES:

Avenue X. Nos. 2, 3. Brooklyn, NY: Purple Spiral Comics. 1994–95.

Nightstalkers

In 1983, Marvel Comics killed all of the vampires in the Marvel Universe, an event which seemed to coincide with a relative lack of interest in vampires in the culture. The mechanism for destroying the entire vampire population was the magical operation conducted by the occult expert Dr. Stephen Strange called the Montesi Formula. However, by the end of the decade, the Montesi Formula had weakened, and a few vampires reappeared. The official recognition that the vampires were returning came in 1992, and the return of the vampires created the need for the Nightstalkers.

Lilith, the ancient Hebrew demon, is leading an invasion of the evil supernatural into the Marvel Universe, an alternative normal world inhabited primarily by superheroes and supervillains. The latter have unusual abilities, but as a whole their super powers are quite natural. Dealing with the supernatural requires heroes specially equipped, including occult adepts such as Dr. Strange and knowledgeable people such as those who make up the Darkhold, another anti-dark world group. The Nightstalkers bring together the anti-vampire experts **Frank Drake, Hannibal King,** and **Blade the Vampire Slayer.** The three, all characters created in the early 1970s by outstanding comic writer Marv Wolfman for *The Tomb of Dracula* series are brought together as a detective agency operating in Boston. The fact that Hannibal King is himself a vampire makes for tension within the group when they are not overwhelmed by the more important danger posed by Lilith's presence. Their adventures are recounted in their own comic book, *Nightstalkers,* the first issue of which appeared in November 1992. They also appear as guests in other Marvel titles, especially *Midnight Sons Unlimited.* However, in spite of drawing a relatively large audience, Marvel withdrew its commitment to horror and in 1994 discontinued all of the *Midnight Sons* series. In the final issue (April 1994), Hannibal King and Frank Drake were killed. Blade survived and was given his own series which lasted for another year until it was discontinued during a major reorganization of the entire Marvel Comics corporate enterprise.

As a footnote, in the world of vampires, death is never final and in 1998, the deceased Hannibal King was resurrected and reappeared as a detective operating against vampires in New York City.

SOURCES:
Midnight Sons Unlimited. No. 1–9. New York: Marvel Comics, 1992–1995
Nightstalkers. No. 1–18. New York: Marvel Comics, 1992–1994.

Societas Argenti Viae Eternitata (SAVE)

The Societas Argenti Viae Eternitata (The Eternal Society of the Silver Way), or SAVE, is an organization dedicated to the prevention of evil spawned from the Unknown as defined in the supernatural universe of the *Chill* role-playing game. According to game lore, SAVE was founded in 1844 in Dublin, Ireland, derived from the research begun in 1789 by Dr. Alfredo Fernandez Ruiz in the use of the Art (psychic powers). Originally named the Societas Albae Viae Eternitata (The Eternal Society of the White Way), the name was changed in 1985 to avoid any hint that the organization was racist. Founder Dr. Charles O'Boylan brought together a group of scientists who felt that data involving human intercourse with the unknown was being overlooked by established scientists.

O'Boylan concluded that there was an Unknown world consisting of two factions, one good, one bad, engaged in constant warfare. From this noncorporeal world, constructive energies poured forth to humankind, but it was also the home of a disciplined source of evil that regularly intruded upon humanity's realm. SAVE was founded to collect data on this evil Unknown, and funded some early expeditions in this regard. Although SAVE's members contacted that evil Unknown, they either destroyed or were destroyed by it. No hard evidence was obtained. In light of this observation, SAVE became a secret organization that contacts only those people who have previously encountered the Unknown.

The game reveals SAVE's history, which includes their first encounter with vampires in 1868 when an expedition in southern Bulgaria succeeded in immobilizing a vampire with a stake in the heart. They subsequently found that there were many vampires in the Balkan region. As the organization grew, it documented vampires from around the world (as well as other traditional monsters). Among the vampire types it has identified are the Alpine vampire, the Rakshasa (India) vampire, the African-American vampire, the Meso-American vampire, the vampire ninja (Japan), the Oriental vampire, and the Macedonian vampire. Each vampire type has it own characteristics and accordingly is vulnerable in various ways. It is also SAVE's opinion that both **Count Dracula** and **Elizabeth Bathory** are still alive and active.

SAVE has several hundred envoys in the United States and approximately 4,000 worldwide. In recent years, the organization has lost about 105 of its envoys annually. However, recruitment has kept pace with losses. International headquarters are currently located in Paris.

SOURCES:

Ladyman, David, with Jeff R. Leason and Louis J. Prosperi. *Chill.* Niles, IL: Mayfair Games, 1990.

Sanchez, Gali, and Michael Williams. *Vampires.* Delavan, WI: Pacesetter, 1985.

Southern Coalition Against Vampires

The Southern Coalition Against Vampires is a modern vampire-hunting organization whose activities are revealed in the film *Blood Ties* (1992). Their members, located primarily in Southern California, include people fanatically dedicated to ridding the world of vampires. According to the film's myth, vampires are traditional supernatural creatures of a different species. They do not live forever, but apart from accidents, live to be about 125 years old. They heal quickly, and are stronger than the average human by only a small percentage. They have come to the United States where they have assimilated as much as possible with the culture. Eschewing the term vampire, they call themselves Carpathians. Their patriarch, Eli Gilaran, is a wealthy land developer in Long Beach, California.

The Coalition emerges as more than a nuisance to the Carpathians in the early 1990s when they catch up with and kill a Carpathian couple who has moved to rural Texas. The Coalition stakes the couple and burns down their house, and shoots their son whom they track back to Long Beach. The anger of the Carpathians over what occurs is focused when Celia, an attractive member of the Long Beach family, is kidnapped, and Gilaran grants permission for the family to go after the Coalition. They wipe it out and dispose of the bodies in the ocean.

Theatre des Vampires

The Theatre of the Vampires (or Theatre des Vampires) is the center of the Parisian vampire coven introduced in Anne Rice's *Interview with the Vampire*, although the story of the origin of the Theatre is left for the sequel, *The Vampire Lestat*. The Theatre refers both to the building itself and the coven of vampires that performs and lives there. Located on the boulevard du Temple (a real street in Paris), the building had been Renard's House of Thespians. When **Lestat de Lioncourt** arrives in Paris in 1789, he finds his way to the theater, and begins what he thinks will be a career on stage. However, soon afterward, Lestat has his forced encounter with the vampire **Magnus** who turns him into a vampire and leaves him his wealth.

After setting himself up in rich surroundings, Lestat returns to the theater for a reunion with his former colleagues. He also encounters the coven of vampires led by **Armand,** with whom he comes into immediate conflict. The coven exists as a group with a system of rules and regulations, while Lestat makes his own rules. The Theatre seeks to destroy Lestat, but he finally gets through to them and frees them from the superstitious beliefs that are anchored in the past. In his anger at the coven's turning away from his leadership, Armand turns on them and kills all but four. Among the remaining four is a female, Eleni, who Lestat likes and to whom he presents the theater after he has purchased it. The four begin a new life as actors and, when Lestat refuses Armand's wish for the two to leave Paris together, he also joins the theater group.

Over the years, new vampires replace those that Armand killed and a new order evolves. Each evening the group plays to the avid theater-going public of Paris, who are unaware that much of what they see is more real than it appears. And in 1862, when Lestat's American "children," **Louis de Pointe du Lac** and **Claudia,** make their way to Paris, they soon discover the vampire community and the theater.

On their first evening at the theater, Louis and Claudia see a performance that includes the ravishing and feasting upon a young woman who had been kidnapped earlier in the evening. They soon take up life in Paris on the edge of the older community. Some of the vampires, however, learn that Claudia and Louis have attempted to kill Lestat, their benefactor, in direct contradiction to their prime directive. In return, they execute Claudia and **Madeleine,** the woman whom she adopted as a surrogate mother. Armand saves Louis, a fatal mistake, as Louis in his anger attacks the coven and burns the Theatre. Most of the vampires are killed as the Theatre is consumed in the flames. Armand, however, survives, because Louis warned him that he was going to seek his revenge.

The Theatre of the Vampires has an immense effect upon Lestat's personality. The love of performing he discovers there never leaves him, and is an underlying factor when he returns to the stage as a rock musician in the 1980s.

SOURCES:

Ramsland, Katherine. *The Vampire Companion:The Official Guide to Anne Rice's The Vampire Chronicles.* New York: Ballantine Books, 1995.

Rice, Anne. *Interview with the Vampire.* New York: Alfred A. Knopf, 1976.

———. *The Vampire Lestat.* New York: Alfred A. Knopf, 1988.

Vampire Hunters and Vampire Associates

Adam

Adam, the first human, emerges as a master vampire hunter in the alternative reality Earth of the comic book *Vampyre Wars* (1993). Adam lives in exile from Eden, cursed with immortality and doomed to watch the foibles of humanity generation after generation. His first wife **Lilith** angrily left him and was exiled to the airy void. She became the first vampire. In this mythical world, a large urban industrial (and polluted) complex has developed called Pluto, named for the underworld in Greek mythology. Here supernatural creatures such as vampires and werewolves (Lilith's lineage) are very real.

Pluto has been divided into various sectors, including V-only sectors where only vampires are allowed. Dwelling in the city are a number of vampires who became famous in the standard vampiric universe, including **Lord Ruthven, Sir Francis Varney,** and **Frank Frene**. Sir Francis has become a prosperous industrialist who developed and marketed Plasma 999, a synthetic blood that lacks taste but is otherwise available to keep vampires from attacking humans. The wealthiest and cleanest part of the city is termed Paradisio.

At one point, Adam is contacted by the mayor's office to deal with a problem. An alarming number of abductions of humans have occurred on the edge of Paradisio—whose residents are the wealthiest and have the purest blood. Adam contacts Sir Francis and together they track the kidnaping to Frank Frene, a rival industrialist who has begun a blood factory milking humans. He hopes eventually to market a better-tasting and cheaper product than Varney's Plasma 999. Frene's arguments that his plan will ultimately reduce the actual number of vampire attacks on people does not persuade Adam to allow him to continue.

Frene attacks Adam with the Horla, the psychic vampire first described by Guy de Maupassant in his short story "The Horla." The Horla feeds from the minds of its victims, but was defeated by the long and painful memories carried by the immortal

Jack MacGowran as Professor Ambronsius in
The Fearless Vampire Killers.

Adam. With the Horla out of the way, Sir Francis and Adam are free to rescue the kidnaped humans and destroy Frene's plant. For the moment all is well in Pluto.

SOURCES:
Vampyre Wars: The Blood Factory. South Bend, IN: Acid Rain Studios, 1993.

Ambronsius, Professor

Professor Ambronsius (Jack MacGowran), along with his assistant Alfred (Roman Polanski), are the subjects of the comedy, *The Fearless Vampire Killers; Or, Pardon Me, Your Teeth Are in My Neck*(1967). *The Fearless Vampire Killers* was also released as *Dance of the Vampires* in England.

Ambronsius is an elderly scholar, who, although a brilliant thinker, loses his teaching job because he devotes himself to studying vampires. In his early career, he wrote one book, *The Bat: Its Mysteries*, but spent the latter years of his life (perhaps in the eighteenth century) traveling through central Europe with Alfred, looking for vampires to destroy.

As Ambronsius's career is coming to an end, he and his traveling companion find their way to a small town in Transylvania. Given a room in the local inn, they meet Sarah, the innkeeper's daughter. Alfred is completely smitten with her, but before their first evening is complete, she is captured by the local vampire, **Count von Krolock,** and taken to his nearby castle. The fearless vampire hunters seize the moment of opportunity to rescue Sarah.

At the castle, they learn that the count leads a Satanic coven of vampire minions. Unfortunately, they are helpless to attack as Alfred lost their bag of weapons, and so the duo is limited to rescuing Sarah. The count has already bitten her once and plans to incorporate her into his fellowship that evening. The evening activities include a dance party at which everyone will dress formally and frolic to the latest tunes out of Vienna. Ambronsius and Alfred move among the vampires in order to contact Sarah and take her from the dance floor. However, their presence is noticed, as the three are the only ones to appear in the large mirror near the exit.

After a chase through the castle, they make their escape. Ambronsius is relieved, and Alfred is ecstatic to be seated in the sleigh next to his new love. Unfortunately, Sarah is in the process of completing her transformation into a vampire, and as Ambronsius drives away, oblivious to what is occurring a few feet behind him,

Vampire Count von Krolock (portrayed by Ferdy Mayne) sleeps in his coffin in *The Fearless Vampire Killers.*

Sarah attacks Alfred. Ambronsius does not live long enough to learn that his activity at the castle led to the spreading of vampirism from its confines in Transylvania to the rest of the world.

Blade the Vampire Slayer

In April 1971, Marvel Comics introduced *The Tomb of Dracula*. This publication carried the story of **Count Dracula** into the 1970s and brought together descendants of characters in Bram Stoker's novel to fight the revived vampire. During the course of this long-running series, author Marv Wolfman introduced several new characters to the vampire universe, the most enduring of whom is Blade the Vampire Slayer.

Blade, an African-American, is the modern incarnation of an ancient warrior, equipped to fight his adversaries with a set of teakwood knives. He initially appears in the July 1973 issue of *The Tomb of Dracula* (#10), where, on the London docks, he proceeds to kill several members of Dracula's legion. Their deaths lead Blade to **Quincey Harker** and **Dr. Rachel Van Helsing,** descendants of characters in Stoker's novel. The ensuing action takes Blade to the ship *Michelle*, over which Dracula has assumed control. Blade's initial confrontation with the legendary vampire ends in a draw, and Dracula escapes as the ship explodes. Blade returns two issues later to help Harker and **Frank Drake** (a descendant of Dracula's) find Harker's daughter, Edith, who has been kidnaped by Dracula.

Blade's origins are revealed in the series' October 1973 issue (#13). At the time of his birth, Blade's mother is visited by Deacon Frost, a physician who turns out to be a vampire. Frost kills Blade's mother, inspiring Blade to dedicate his life to hunting down her killer. His search grows into an enmity toward all vampires and leads him to the recently revived Dracula.

Blade frequently reappears throughout the 70 issues of *The Tomb of Dracula* series. (He also makes a guest appearance in the Fall 1976 issue of *Marvel Preview* (#8).) Eventually, the battle between Blade and Dracula draws to a seeming conclusion when Blade plunges one of his knives into Dracula's heart, and the vampire apparently dies. A group of others steals Dracula's body and removes the knife, however, allowing him to live. Later, Dracula finds Blade and bites him, but Blade is unaffected by the bite. It turns out that the presence of the vampire Deacon Frost at Blade's birth has rendered Blade immune to the vampire virus. In the June 1976 issue (#48), after many adventures, Blade teams with **Hannibal King,** another character created by Wolfman for the *The Tomb of Dracula* series. It seems that King also carries the scars of an encounter with Deacon Frost in his past. Together, he and Blade track Frost to his lair and destroy him.

Vampires are banished from Marvel Comics in 1983, courtesy of some black magic by Marvel's master of the occult arts, Dr. Strange, who invokes the Montesi Formula. By the end of the 1980s, that formula is being weakened, which allows a new assault upon the mortal world by the forces of supernatural evil. These forces are led by Lilith (the ancient Hebrew demoness, not Dracula's daughter). In the meantime, Blade practically disappears. He finds new employment in 1991, however, when he joins the story line for a revived *Tomb of Dracula* (1991–1992) by Epic Comics (a subsidiary of Marvel). In 1992 Blade joins the Midnight Sons, Marvel's assemblage of occult-oriented characters created to deal with Lilith's new supernatural invasion.

With the Midnight Sons, Blade is given a new image, similar to Marvel's other super heroes, and his weapons system is upgraded. Blade and his old acquaintances Frank Drake and Hannibal King unite as a private investigating team in a series called *The Nightstalkers*. The adventures of the Nightstalkers continue until early 1994, when both Drake and King are killed in a war with the supernatural forces of evil. Blade survives to continue the fight in his own new comic book series, *Blade, the Vampire Hunter*, which lasts for 10 issues. In 1998 a movie was released starring Wesley Snipes as Blade.

SOURCES:

Blade, the Vampire Hunter, nos. 1–10. New York: Marvel Comics, 1994–1995

The Nightstalkers, nos. 1–18. New York: Marvel Comics, 1992–1994.

The Tomb of Dracula. 4 vols. New York: Epic Comics, 1991.

The Tomb of Dracula. 70 vols. New York: Marvel Comics, 1971–1979.

Blake, Anita

Anita Blake, animator of deceased persons and vampire hunter, has been the subject of six novels by Laurell K. Hamilton, beginning with *Guilty Pleasures* (1993). The novels are set in St. Louis, Missouri in the near future. Vampires, zombies, and werewolves inhabit the world, and the United States has become the first country to recognize the existence of vampires and give them some legal status. Blake works for Animators, Inc., a business that specializes in reanimating the dead.

Blake's mother died when she was eight, and her father remarried. At age 13, she discovered her ability to bring the dead back to life when her dog died. She simply wished that the dog was still alive, and, the next morning, the dog showed up in her bedroom as a doggie zombie. Needless to say, the incident stunned her stepmother. Her more knowledgeable and open-minded father took the teenager to see her maternal Grandmother Flores, who practiced voodoo. The grandmother decided that Blake should not be further trained in voodoo, but should be given enough knowledge to control her abilities. Blake resumes a fairly normal life and later attended college and received a degree in biology. Her plans for graduate school were cut short when the owner of Animators, Inc. offered her a job using her peculiar skills. It seems that there was a market for her talent because a number of people seemed to need information that only a recently deceased person could offer. Animators, Inc. would temporarily reanimate the deceased person for a fee. The Catholic Church of course frowned on such activities, so Blake was excommunicated and decided to join the Episcopal church.

Blake's job description and life change when the U.S. Supreme Court rules in the landmark case *Addison v. Clark* that vampires must be given legal recognition. In addition to her reanimation duties, Blake is now responsible for hunting down rogue vampires who kill humans. She had one bad encounter with a vampire in the past, which left her with a broken arm and collar bone and a cross-shaped scar on her left arm where she was branded. She becomes known as The Executioner and is known and respected in the vampire community, which just wants to live peacefully with humans.

In St. Louis, the vampire community is highly visible. There is a **Church of Eternal Life,** where humans who want to become vampires can meet with vampires who will counsel them and offer them a literal fulfillment of their dreams. A vampire commercial district exists along the Mississippi River in an area known as the Riverfront. It has become a popular tourist attraction.

The leader of the vampire community is Jean-Claude, the master vampire of St. Louis. He owns a nightclub called The Laughing Corpse and lusts after Blake, whom he has bitten (and thus marked) on two occasions. He desperately wants Blake to become his lover, but she consistently refuses his advances. He becomes quite jealous of Richard, a werewolf who Blake is seriously dating.

Blake's many adventures as animator, vampire killer, and human who lives comfortably alongside the creatures of the supernatural world are well-documented in a

Cover art from the comic book *Bloodhunter*, part of the *Vamperotica* series.

series of novels that includes *The Laughing Corpse* (1994), *Circus of the Damned* (1995), *The Lunatic Cafe* (1996), *Bloody Bones* (1997), and *The Killing Dance* (1997).

SOURCES:

Hamilton, Laurell K. *Bloody Bones*. New York: Ace Books, 1996.

———. *Circus of the Damned*. New York: Ace Books, 1995.

———. *Guilty Pleasures*. New York: Ace Books, 1993.

———. *The Killing Dance*. New York: Ace Books, 1997.

———. *The Laughing Corpse*. New York: Ace Books, 1994. Reprint, London: New American Library, 1994.

———. *The Lunatic Cafe*. New York: Ace Books, 1996.

Blood Hunter

Blood Hunter is one of the continuing characters in the *Vamperotica* comic books. As a young man during the 1990s, Brandon Alexander is very much in love. His relationship is destroyed, however, when he and his fiancée are attacked by a group of vampires. His fiancée is killed, and Brandon, having bitten one of his attackers, is transformed into a vampire. Caught unprepared by his ensuing blood lust, Brandon attacks and kills his sister. Distraught, he attempts suicide by setting himself on fire, but his body heals itself in a few days. Soon after, he meets another vampire, Dougan, who teaches him the ways of the kith. Brandon learns the three basic laws of the kith: (1) protect the blood source (humans); (2) do not make new vampires without approval of the kith (a rule regulated by the kith police, known as the blood militia); and (3) maintain discretion concerning the existence of the kith. Noting that there is no law against killing the kith, Brandon formulates a plan to become the vengeful warrior vampire Blood Hunter and kill every vampire he can, including, in the end, himself.

After deciding what he must do, Blood Hunter kills Dougan and begins his seemingly impossible mission. Blood Hunter soon crosses paths with a powerful senior vampire named **Pontius Vanthor,** who has plans of his own. Vanthor has masterminded a scheme to free vampires from their historic underground existence by establishing a vampiric government under which vampires would live openly during a period of freedom to be known as the Red Reign. Humans would be treated merely as a food source—cattle to be milked. As Vanthor and his minions work to realize their plan, Blood Hunter works to thwart them.

Blood Hunter's wardrobe includes a red and blue body suit, cape, and utility belt. His cape and belt are held in place by fanged-skulls. His face is framed by a stylized set of fangs. He carries a silver-bladed sword and a pistol loaded with silver bullets. Blood Hunter can smell kith but has the ability to mask his own body odor. Each dawn he enters a waking sleep, during which his body is comatose, but his mind is alert. He is exceptionally strong and a master of fighting skills. He can fly and transform into mist or animal creatures. He lives in a secret manor that he reaches through an elaborate labyrinth of underground pipes.

Blood Hunter has a radio talk show, "Jugular Vein," that he hosts under the stage name Elan Vitae. Many of Vanthor's minions tune in, and the show becomes a means of contacting his vampire victims.

Blood Hunter is methodical in his killing until he meets **Luxura.** Luxura comes to control him and occasionally calls upon him to rid her of nuisances. Eventually, Blood Hunter cuts a deal with Luxura: She agrees to release her control over him (though keeping access to his thoughts), and he agrees to refrain from killing any vampires loyal to the house of Luxura until all others have been killed. Despite the agreement, Blood Hunter becomes completely enraptured with the beautiful vampiress. Like her, he has powerful sexual needs.

Blood Hunter, a character created by Kirk Lindo, made his first appearance in *Vamperotica 2* (1994) and has become a continuing character in its pages. In 1996, he was featured in a single issue of his own comic book, *Bloodhunter.*

SOURCES:

Lindo, Kirk. *Bloodhunter* Fayetteville, N.C.: Brainstorm Comics, 1996.

———. "Wages of Sin." *Vamperotica.* No. 3. December 1994.

———. "The Blood Is the Life." *Vamperotica.* No. 4. March 1995.

Lindo, Kirk, and Lachland Pelle. "Tortured Hunter." *Vamperotica.* No. 2. August 1994.

Lindo, Kirk, Dan Membiela, and Don Kramer. "Search and Destroy." *Vamperotica.* No. 25. March 1997.

———. "Fire in the Sky." *Vamperotica.* No. 26. July 1997.

Lindo, Kirk, Dan Membiela, and Henry Martinez. "Hunters Blood, Part 1." *Vamperotica.* No. 17. July 1996.

———. "Hunter's Blood, Part 2." *Vamperotica.* No. 18. September 1996.

———. "Hunter's Blood, Part 3." *Vamperotica.* No. 19. September 1996.

Membiela, Dan, and Don Kramer. "Kith Killer, Part 1." *Vamperotica.* No. 29. July 1997.

———. "Kith Killer, Part 2." *Vamperotica.* No. 30. August 1997.

Pabon, Gustavo & Adam Pekraker. Baptism, Part 1." *Vamperotica.* No. 6. August 1995.

———. "Baptism, Part 2." *Vamperotica.* No. 7. September 1995.

CAPTAIN KRONOS *see:* KRONOS, CAPTAIN

D

D, the mysterious vampire hunter of the full-length animated feature film *Vampire Hunter D* (1985), is a dhampire, the offspring of a vampire and a mortal woman. In this case the woman is a village girl in a feudal land of the distant future. In 12,090 CE, the earth is ruled by vampires and their supernatural minions, werewolves and demonic beings of various kinds. Civilization has devolved into feudal village life. Although some sophisticated weaponry and electronic gadgets have survived, they are of little consequence against the vampires.

D roams the land killing vampires. He is dressed in dark clothes that hide most of his features. His age is difficult to assess. His main weapon is a large samurai sword. He rides atop a cyborg horse. Like a vampire, he has great strength, heals quickly, and possesses a set of prominent fangs. As he moves through the land, he meets Doris Lang, a pretty young maiden who has been bitten by the local vampire lord, **Count Magnus Lee.** He accepts her offer of room, board, and more intimate companionship in return for his killing Lee.

As D is preparing to enter Lee's castle and confront him, the vampire moves to kidnap Doris. He plans to marry her, transform her into a vampire, and allow her to brighten his bored 10,000-year-old life for a season. D enters the castle to rescue her. He is fully aware that Lee expects him and that he will have to initially deal with all of his minions. The fiercest of the creatures are three snake women who entwine D and begin to sap his life force. D abides them long enough for Lee to believe that they can handle the vampire hunter. When Lee leaves him to his death, D breaks free of the snake women's hold and quickly dispatches them. He then engages the large, ancient vampire, intent upon destroying him and his vampire family.

Vampire Hunter D is one of the classic highlights of 1980s Japanimation.

Drake, Frank

Frank Drake, the great-grandson of **Count Dracula,** makes his first appearance in the very first issue of Marvel Comics long-running series, *The Tomb of Dracula*. His father dies in the later 1960,s and over the next three years Frank squanders his inheritance. All he has left is Castle Dracula in Transylvania. He decides to travel to the castle in 1971 to inspect his property and investigate the possibility of turning it into a tourist attraction. During the visit, one of his friends who accompanied him on the trip finds Dracula's tomb, and, in his ignorance, awakens him. Dracula attacks and turns Drake's fiancée (who had also made the trip) into a vampire.

Drake sells the castle and brings Dracula's coffin to London. That act ensures that Dracula and Drake's vampirized fiancée will follow him. Drake's career as a vampire hunter begins when he is forced to stake his former love. Dracula escapes and lives to fight another day.

In London, Drake meets **Dr. Rachel Van Helsing,** the great-granddaughter of **Abraham Van Helsing.** She is carrying on the family tradition of vampire hunting

Rupert Giles (second from the left) serves as Buffy's mentor on the television show *Buffy the Vampire Slayer*.

and introduces Drake to **Quincey Harker,** a descendant of Jonathan Harker, who helped Abraham kill Dracula back in the 1890s. Together the three wage a war against Dracula and his minions. Occasionally they are joined by the vampire hunter known as **Blade the Vampire Slayer.**

After several years of fighting Dracula, Drake experiences an identity crisis and leaves the others to engage in a period of self-reflection. He meets and begins an affair with Chastity Jones. They wind up in Brazil on a trip, and Drake is forced to fight when he has to defeat a group of zombies. This fight gives him a new sense of direction in his life. He returns to the vampire-fighting team, which has moved to Boston to follow Dracula, who has also moved there. After his return, Rachel Van Helsing professes her love, but before they can explore their new love, the whole group is taken prisoner by the evil Dr. Sun, who is also trying to kill Dracula. Dr. Sun eventually succeeds and kills Dracula. This presents a dilemma for Drake and the others—their nemesis Dracula is now dead, but it appears that Dr. Sun is an even greater evil. The vampire hunters are actually forced to bring Dracula back to life to help them defeat Dr. Sun.

The temporary partnership with Dracula doesn't mean the group has given up its goal of killing the king of vampires. In fact, Quincey Harker manages to do just that in 1979. With Dracula dead, Drake and Rachel lose their common bond and drift apart. He eventually meets a woman named Marlene, marries her, and settles down to a fairly quiet life during the 1980s. He is thrust back into the fight against vampires in 1991, however, when Dracula reappears and goes after Drake by attacking his wife Marlene. Drake rejoins forces with Blade, and together the two battle and defeat Dracula once again. The battle takes its toll on Blade, however, as he ends up in a straightjacket in a mental hospital.

In 1994, Drake is reunited with Blade and Hannibal King. Together they form the Nightstalkers, a vampire-hunting detective agency that aligns itself with a larger group that is fighting the influx of supernatural evil led by Lilith and her minions. The Nightstalkers battle Lilith for two years, but the results are disastrous—both Drake and King are killed. Blade survives and continues to fight vampires.

SOURCES:

Nightstalkers. No. 1–18. New York: Marvel Comics, 1992–1994.

Wolfman, Marv, and Gene Colan. *The Tomb of Dracula.* No. 1–70. New York: Marvel Comics, 1972–79.

———. *The Tomb of Dracula.* No. 1–4. New York: Marvel Comics, 1991–92 .

Giles, Rupert

Rupert Giles (portrayed by Anthony Stewart Head) is the Watcher, the person who guides, trains and chronicles the work of the chosen one, the woman who in each generation is selected as the Slayer, the vampire killer. In the case of Giles, the Slayer to whom he is assigned is **Buffy Summers,** a teenager at Sunnydale High School in a Los Angeles suburb, and the subject of a hit television series, *Buffy the Vampire Slayer,* which began on the Warner Brothers Network in 1997. Prior to their meeting, in the 1992 movie of the same name, Buffy was a student at Hemery High

School in Los Angeles, where she worked with another Watcher named Merrick, who was killed. Buffy killed her major vampire opponent, **Lothos,** but in the process of her vampire slaying, burned down the school gym and was expelled as a result.

A learned gentleman, Giles has the perfect cover for his true career as the Watcher in his role as the librarian at Sunnydale High. There he keeps his collection of old books that come in handy for research as Buffy encounters different incursions from the evil supernatural. He initially encounters his new ward when she comes into the library looking for a textbook. He offers her a book on vampires, which she rejects. However, as she becomes aware of the situation in Sunnydale (her classmates are becoming the victims of a large group of vampires led by the Master), she is forced to pay attention to Giles' warning about an imminent upheaval in the cosmos focused upon the staid little town.

Slowly (through the first episode), Giles becomes the fatherly center of a group of Buffy's classmates who are in on her secret identity. One of these, Willow (portrayed by Allyson Hannigan), is a computer wiz who searches for information on the Internet to supplement Giles' old books. A true bibliophile, Giles does not like computers because they lack the smell of good information sources like books. Though really a trainer and observer, Giles is often swept into the battle and uses his knowledge and inner strength to deal with the supernatural creatures himself. When, for example, Buffy is finally dealing with the Master, Giles is left in the library to deal with a tentacled monster, which finally retreats only when the Master is killed.

As the learned elder authority, Giles completes the figure of the vampire hunter traditionally embodied in **Abraham Van Helsing,** who is both the fatherly figure for a cadre of younger people trying to stop **Count Dracula** and an active vampire slayer himself.

SOURCES:

"Buffy the Vampire Slayer." *Spectrum* 13 (May 1998): 8-23.

Cusick, Ricky. *Buffy the Vampire Slayer: The Harvest.* New York: Archway/Pocket Books, 1997.

Cover, Arthur Byron. *Buffy the Vampire Slayer: Night of the Living Brain.* New York: Archway/Pocket Books, 1998.

Golden, Christopher, and Nancy Holder. *Buffy the Vampire Slayer: Halloween Rain.* New York: Archway/Pocket Books, 1997.

Vornholt, John. *Coyote Moon.* New York: Archway/Pocket Books, 1998

Glass, Carrie

Carrie Glass (portrayed by Michelle Owens), cop, vampire hunter, vampire, is featured in the film *Midnight Kiss* (1993). A young police officer, Glass is attractive with long dark hair; she works with her ex-husband in homicide. Their current case is very complex, involving a serial killer who targets young women. Curiously, each victim is found with bite marks and drained of blood. One night outside of her apartment, Glass becomes a target of this killer herself. Face to face with the killer—a young, blond-haired vampire who sports an earring with a cross on it—she fights for her survival. During their struggle, he bites her arm, but she pulls his earring off and the pain distracts the killer long enough for her to escape, with her blood intact.

That night, odd things begin to happen and she spends a fitful night, tossing and turning in her bed as she fights nightmares. She notices that light hurts her eyes and she gains a new strength. But most of all, she craves blood.

Even more determined to catch the killer, Glass acts as a decoy in the hopes that the vampire killer will be attracted once more. She has a fairly good picture of the young man she is seeking to lure into the open, a combination of her description and that of another woman who also escaped his clutches. He's brash and over-confident, with the ability to change his appearance somewhat, but she knows his earlobe will bear the scars of their encounter.

The ruse works and Glass and her partner eventually track the vampire down. Ultimately he's impaled with a knife and consumed by fire. As a result of his death, Glass loses her vampiric traits and resumes her former life and job as a police officer, a little older and a little wiser.

Harker, Quincey

Quincey Harker, the son of Jonathan Harker, is briefly mentioned at the end of Bram Stoker's original novel, *Dracula,* and emerges as a major character in 1973 in Marvel Comics' series *The Tomb of Dracula* (No. 7). An elderly man bound in a wheelchair and a former banker, Harker becomes the head of a vampire-hunting team that includes at various times **Dr. Rachel Van Helsing, Frank Drake,** and **Blade the Vampire Slayer.** Their present collaboration is occasioned by Drake's involvement in the recent awakening of **Count Dracula** during a visit to Dracula's Castle in Transylvania.

Harker's dedication to fighting Dracula finds its roots years earlier when he studied with **Abraham Van Helsing.** A highlight of Harker's ongoing battle is Dracula's attack on his young wife Elizabeth at the opera. During the same incident, Harker loses his legs after Dracula tosses him from their box. An anguished Harker must kill his wife after Dracula drains her. (Earlier, Harker suggests that he lost his legs while attempting to destroy a vampire coven.) During this phase of his fight with Dracula, Dracula also attacks his daughter Edith, and in a parallel to his wife, Harker is forced to stake and kill her.

After losing his legs, the bearded Harker becomes fascinated with anti-vampire gadgets and installs many on his motorized wheelchair. He also booby traps his home. When Dracula comes looking for documents in his possession that suggest the vampire is gradually losing his powers, Harker attacks him with wooden-tipped darts, a table in the shape of the cross, and arrows. Dracula escapes only because he captures Rachel and holds her for ransom.

Harker's final confrontation with Dracula occurs in 1979 near Castle Dracula. Their meeting is up-close and personal, and both perish. Harker stabs Dracula with a silver spoke from his chair and completes the job with a silver knife. Thirty seconds later, the explosives he has set in his chair explode, and he and Dracula are both buried under tons of stone. Harker disappears from the Marvel Universe, though a decade later Dracula arises to fight again. The remaining members of Harker's vampire-fighting team disperse after his demise, and following Dracula's return must carry on without Harker's assistance.

SOURCES:

Wolfman, Marv, and Colan, Gene. *The Tomb of Dracula*. Nos. 1–70. New York: Marvel Comics, 1972–79.

Helsing, Dr. Howard

Dr. Howard Helsing, the great-grandson of vampire hunter **Abraham Van Helsing,** arises to his ancestor's role in the low-budget film, *A Taste of Blood* (1966). A learned man, Dr. Helsing is an analyst attached to Hamburg University and has written a set of notable papers on delusions, hallucinations, and aberrations. He has been alerted to **Count Dracula**'s possible return by the deaths of Philip Harker, Wayne Seward, and Count Gold, all, like him, descendants of the six people who tracked and killed Count Dracula in the 1890s. In this case Dracula is represented by **John Alucard Stone,** the great-grandson and only descendant of the vampire.

Stone has been made aware of his ancestry and is slowly turning into a vampire. Helsing narrowly escapes an initial attempt to kill him in Hamburg, Germany. A short time later Helsing visits Miami, where Stone resides, hoping to save not only his life, but that of Stone's wife, Helena, and friends. He shares his knowledge of Dracula with Stone's best friend, Dr. Hank Tyson, who has prior knowledge of Helsing from having read his papers. After Sherry Morris, the descendant of Draculatracker Quincey Morris, is killed, Tyson becomes a believer. Together they track Stone, first to the warehouse where he stored everything he had brought back from England (including Dracula's coffin), and then to his secret lair where he summoned Helena. To vampirize Helena, Stone would need to bite her three times and then give her some of his vampire blood.

During the final confrontation, Helsing uses a cross to force Stone into his coffin, and as dawn approaches, Helsing stakes him. As soon as Stone perishes, Helena is released from her entranced state produced by his earlier bites.

King, Hannibal

Hannibal King, private investigator and vampire, is introduced in Marvel Comics' *The Tomb of Dracula* (1974). He is turned into a creature of the night by 100-year-old vampire **Deacon Frost,** whom he has been unable to locate over the years. One evening he is hired by Adrienne Walters to track the vampire that killed her husband. The case leads him to an initial encounter with **Count Dracula,** and eventually he meets **Blade the Vampire Slayer,** whose mother had been attacked by Frost. Blade temporarily puts aside his mission to kill all vampires and joins forces with King to kill Frost.

King appears infrequently in the Marvel Comics stories over the next few years, until the end of 1983, when all of the vampires in the Marvel universe, especially those from *The Tomb of Dracula* series, are killed by a magical spell, the Montesi Formula, performed by occultist Dr. Strange (*Doctor Strange*, 1983). Although the other vampires are destroyed, King experiences a return to normal life. At the beginning of the 1990s, the Montesi Formula weakens, and King turns into a vampire again. At the same time, the world is facing a new onslaught from the world of supernatural evil led by Lilith, Queen of Evil and Mother of Demons, a sorceress of obscure origin (not to be confused with **Lilith, Daughter of Dracula** and her minions).

King unites with Blade and **Frank Drake,** a descendant of Count Dracula who has been fighting vampires most of his adult life, to oppose Lilith and her minions. As the Nightstalkers, they operate as a detective/investigation agency in Boston, Massachusetts. They live on the edge of reality where the occult and supernatural are a constant and immediate experience. During this period, King's legitimacy is continually questioned, and King and his partners are frequently at each other's throats, except when an immediate attack makes their cooperation mandatory.

King and Drake are apparently killed in a 1994 story that portrays a final confrontation with Lilith. Blade survives to continue his battle with Dracula and Lilith, which is still a theme of present comic stories. In 1998, King also returns. Having apparently survived his earlier destruction, when we last see him he is living in a small New York apartment and carrying on the good fight.

SOURCES:

Nightstalkers. Nos. 1–18. New York: Marvel Comics, 1992–94.
"The Lone Cold Killer!" *Journey into Mystery.* No. 520. New York: Marvel Comics, May 1998.
The Tomb of Dracula. Nos. 25–54. New York: Marvel Comics, 1974–77.

Kolchak, Carl

The grandson of immigrants to the United States, Carl is born Karel Kolchak, but changes his name since everyone seems to misspell it. His Romanian grandfather tells him stories of the creatures of the night, including the real **Count Dracula,** Vlad the Impaler. In 1948, Kolchak graduates from Columbia University with a B.A. in Journalism and then goes on to serve his required two years in the army at the time of the Korean War. He is left with a trick knee.

In 1970, Carl Kolchak is simply another reporter for the *Las Vegas Daily News* when some strange killings begin to occur in the city. The victims, young women, are left bloodless, the only sign of struggle being two wound marks on their throats. Kolchak initially thinks that someone is imitating killings in old vampire movies. Slowly, as the facts focus suspicion on **Janos Skorzeny,** Kolchak comes to believe that there is a real vampire loose in the city. Kolchak helps put together a biography of Skorzeny that verifies his age, his career of deception, and the strange killings that occur wherever he happens to reside.

Kolchak is an ambitious reporter, determined to work on a big city newspaper. He sees the vampire story as his ticket to New York or some other major city. In the

Darren McGavin starred as vampire hunter Carl Kolchak in *The Night Stalker.*

end, he tracks Skorzeny to his house and the police see enough to verify Kolchak's hypothesis. However, the newspaper decides to suppress the vampire angle on the story and portrays Skorzeny as a serial killer. Instead of a position with the *New York Times*, Kolchak winds up on the staff of the *Independent News* service in Chicago, and numerous adventures follow. Among them, while on assignment in Los Angeles in 1973, Kolchak encounters **Katherine Rollins,** one of the vampires created by Skorzeny in Las Vegas. As with Skorzeny, Kolchak tracks the vampire and, as police watch, stakes it. And again, the authorities suppress the story. The police leverage the killing's appearance as a homicide rather than a vampire killing, and threaten to indict Kolchak for murder if he prints his account of the story.

The Night Stalker (1972), a made-for-television movie and the highest-rated movie of its type at the time, introduced Kolchak to the public and led to a television series the following year. Jeff Rice authored two books based on the movie and series.

SOURCES:

Rice, Jeff. *The Night Stalker.* New York: Pocket Books, 1974. Reprinted as *The Kolchak Papers 1: The Night Stalker.* Massapequa Park, N.Y.: Cinemaker, 1993.

———. *The Night Strangler.* New York: Pocket Books, 1974.

Kronos, Captain

Captain Kronos (portrayed by Horst Janson), a nineteenth-century Prussian vampire hunter, is a member of the Imperial Guard who returns from war to discover that his wife and daughter have fallen victim to a vampire. He is forced to stake both of them, the two people he loved most in the world. From that moment he dedicates his life to ridding the world of vampires and teams with Professor Hieronymus Grost to that end. He also serves as the protector of his assistant, a hunchback who is the frequent target of thoughtless persons and an extremely knowledgeable vampire aficionado.

Captain Kronos himself is a tall, handsome, blonde man who rides a black horse. He is an excellent swordsman and travels the country with an arsenal of weapons, from stakes and ropes to garlic and dead toads, in search of his bounty. As a means of detecting vampires, Kronos buries a toad where he thinks a vampire might reside. If an actual vampire passes the covered toad, it invariably sheds some of its eternal energy and brings the toad back to life.

Typical of his many adventures, Kronos is summoned to the town of Durward by his former Army colleague, Dr. Marcus, a physician. The town has been plagued by a series of attacks upon young women. When found, the young women appear old and seem to have died from old age. Each victim is found with a trickle of blood coming out of her mouth. Most of the victims are wearing crosses.

Professor Grost recognizes the agent as a different kind of vampire; one who takes youth and energy rather than blood. In all likelihood, he theorizes, the victims are hypnotized by the vampire and have little faith in the crosses they are wearing. Death is caused by the vampire's kiss.

A break in the case comes after their friend Dr. Marcus is bitten by a vampire. Recognizing that he is infected, Dr. Marcus submits to his friend to be killed. Kronos and Grost try to stake him, hang him, and burn him with fire, but nothing works. Inadvertently, they discover that he is vulnerable to steel. Kronos quickly forges a steel sword to use on his old friend. Kronos's toad test suggests that Sarah Durward, daughter of **Lady Durward,** head of the local leading family, is their likely vampire suspect.

Using a young woman as a decoy, they finally flush out the vampire, who turns out to be Lady Durward herself. In the past seven years since the death of her husband, Lady Durward—a Karnstein, hence a relative of **Carmilla Karnstein**—has worked to regain her youth, attain immortality, and bring her dead husband back to life, at which she has succeeded. During his life, Lord Durward had been a champion swordsman, and Kronos is called upon to show his own skills with his new sword. After dispatching the resurrected Lord, Kronos turns upon the Lady, leaving both the Durwards for others to bury, as he and the professor ride off to their next case.

Captain Kronos (Horst Janson) appears in the 1974 Hammer movie, *Captain Kronos: Vampire Hunter.* A projected series of Captain Kronos adventures never materialized.

Horst Janson portrayed the vampire hunter Captain Kronos in the film *Captain Kronos: Vampire Hunter*.

Lambert, Dr. Natalie

Any vampire trying to kick the blood habit and return to the world of normals needs help from mortal confidants. **Barnabas Collins,** for example, confided in Dr. Julia Hoffman, who helped him to change, at least temporarily. Detective **Nick Knight,** star of the television series *Forever Knight,* found his confidant in Dr. Natalie Lambert (portrayed by Catherine Disher). Lambert is a forensic pathologist who provides the crucial data in the original episode of the series, which concerns a vampire killer stalking Toronto. She notes the difference between the method by which a guard in a museum is killed and that of a series of homeless men who had been killed on the street.

While Lambert regularly offers her forensic expertise to push along storylines, her real task is as Nick's intimate. When for example, he goes home after an emotional moment to satiate himself with a bottle of blood, Lambert is the one who appears to comfort and counsel. Nick is plainly acting like a junkie who cannot break the habit, and Lambert's advice is usually some variation of going cold turkey. However, while vampirism can be likened to drug addiction, it is not the same. If one simply stops taking drugs, eventually the craving ceases. If a vampire like Nick withdraws from blood, he will weaken and die. Nick continually tests his condition by doing such things as swallowing garlic pills and attempting to pick up a cross.

Nick and Lambert originally met when, on her 28th birthday, a badly burned man was brought into her laboratory to be autopsied. As she watched, the corpse came back to life and healed itself. The newly revived Nick then told Lambert his story. She responded with understanding rather than fright and offered to help him become human again. Their new relationship is put to the test when Nick seems to interfere with Lambert's love life, but as it turns out, her new boyfriend is a serial killer.

Lambert's commitment to returning Nick's mortality is put to the test in the episode "I Will Repay" (originally aired September 15, 1992), in which Lambert's brother lay dying in the hospital, the victim of a gunshot wound. His killer had been let free on a technicality. Nick recalls a previous incident where he saved someone from dying by changing them into a vampire. Lambert begs Nick to save her brother. When he refuses, Lambert angrily withdraws, overcome with grief.

Nick's refusal to help Lambert's brother is due to the consequences of his previous attempts to play God. Although Lambert has visions of her brother becoming like Nick, a vampire, but one who can control his cravings and not kill, Nick remembers the new vampire he made had struck back in revenge and become a vicious killer. In the end, Nick goes against his better judgment and gives in to his feelings for Lambert saves her brother. As before, he turns on the man who shot him, and then in his new bloodlust, he kills all of his henchmen and an innocent victim. Nick has to undo the damage he has created by killing Lambert's brother.

Unfortunately, Lambert was one of the victims of the changes in *Forever Knight* at the beginning of the third season, when a new cast of regulars were introduced, much to the chagrin of fans. Her last action is to assist Nick by uncovering a murder in a death that seemed on first examination to be a suicide ("Love You to Death," May 2, 1993).

SOURCES:

Strauss, Jon. "Forever Knight." *Epi-log*. No. 36. November 1993: 4-11.
Strauss, Jon. "Forever Knight." *Epi-log*. No. 37. December 1993: 29-35, 62.

McCarthy, Professor Leopold

Professor Leopold McCarthy (portrayed by David Warner) is the incompetent Van Helsing figure in the comedy, *My Best Friend Is a Vampire* (1988). Set in late 1980s Houston, Texas, the film features the middle-aged McCarthy, a historian by training, who has researched vampires, has studied the many evil deeds they have done over the centuries, and is convinced that vampirism is evil. He is also aware that a single bite by a vampire is all that is necessary to create a new vampire. Given that a vampire must feed every evening, McCarthy calculates that it would take only a few years for vampires to begin to overrun humanity. His fear of vampires dominating the world fuels his work as a vampire hunter.

To assist his hunting endeavors, McCarthy has set up a workshop to manufacture antivampire paraphernalia, including a crossbow that shoots wooden stakes and a revolver with silver bullets. He drives a white van in which he carries his anti-vampire kit. He also has an assistant, Grimsdyke, a bungling incompetent who scares easily and cannot bring himself to kill, even if the victim is a vampire.

One such bungling occurs with a new vampire in town. When naive high school student **Jeremy Capello** delivers groceries one afternoon to Nora, the new resident of the dilapidated old Gardner mansion, he is unaware that she is a vampire. However, when he returns that evening to pay Nora a late-night visit with the hopes of ending a period of sexual inactivity, McCarthy and Grimsdyke are watching. The pair break in upon Nora and Jeremy, although not before Jeremy is bitten. The vampire hunters try to kill Nora, but succeed only in torching the house.

After Jeremy leaves Nora's, Grimsdyke confuses him with his best friend Ralph, and instead of kidnaping Jeremy, it is Ralph they inadvertently capture. The vampire-fighting duo head for the chapel at the local cemetery to give Ralph (whom they think is an unholy vampire) a proper death in a consecrated space. Before they can finish, however, Jeremy arrives. He convinces McCarthy that he has made a mistake. If he kills Ralph, he will face a charge of first-degree murder. McCarthy decides to free Ralph, and in the process discovers that Jeremy is a real vampire.

In the climatic scene, McCarthy is about to kill Jeremy when **Modoc,** who has been training Jeremy to be a vampire, arrives. McCarthy shoots him with the silver bullets, but Modoc points out that silver bullets are for werewolves and therefore have little effect on him. In order to thwart McCarthy's plans, Modoc calls forth a group of beautiful young vampires, even the seductive Nora whom McCarthy believed he had destroyed, and they attack McCarthy and transform him into a vampire. He suddenly has a whole new perspective on vampirism. As McCarthy leaves with his new friends, Grimsdyke totally freaks out and runs in the other direction. The audience is left with the feeling that his vampire-hunting days (or evenings) have come to a dramatic end.

One Eyebrow Priest

The One Eyebrow Priest (portrayed by Lam Chin Ying), so-named because his bushy eyebrows meet in the middle and seem to form one large eyebrow, is a Taoist priest (or *sifu*) whose real name is Master Lau. He is a vampire hunter extraordinaire in modern China. He was introduced in the Hong Kong-produced film, *Mr. Vampire* (1985), the same movie that introduced the famous Chinese hopping vampires. He also appears in a number of sequels. A middle-aged man, the Priest runs a mortuary, where he specializes in the proper burial of people to prevent any post-death problems. He has in his employ several bungling assistants.

Vampires in Hong Kong are distinctive when compared to traditional vampires. They cannot walk, they hop. They have little flexibility in their body, apart from some limited (and potentially lethal) movement from their arms. They are held in check by a magical talisman written in red ink on rice paper and stuck to their forehead. Their pursuit can be temporarily stopped by holding one's breath. They are most effectively destroyed by fire, but a potion made of ink, rice, and blood can also hold them in check. They are very strong, but can be defeated in a fight by an accomplished martial arts expert.

In his first adventure, Master Lau is asked to rebury a man's father who was improperly placed in the ground and is believed to be responsible for his son's recent monetary losses. After the body is removed from the ground, it is housed in the mortuary. The father comes to life and attacks his son, killing him and turning him into a vampire. Lau has to kill both vampires, protect his late client's daughter from a vampire attack, and deal with the incompetent policeman who is courting the daughter and suspects Master Lau of the crime. He also has to cure his assistant, who is infected from his brief encounter with the vampire.

After handling this complex situation, Master Lau returns for a number of sequels (*Mr. Vampire II, Mr. Vampire III, One Eyebrow Priest*) that made hopping vampires and Chinese vampire hunters a popular part of modern vampire lore.

Rotmann, Doktor

Doktor Rotmann, a most unusual vampire killer, is the subject of the short story "The Fearless Vampire Killer," which appears in the first issue of the graphic novel horror anthology, *Halloween Terror* (1990). An older man with a full white beard and mustache, Doktor Rotmann is heavyset and wears a hat and overcoat. Rotmann travels around nineteenth-century Germany executing vampires—his method of operation amply illustrated in his visit to the small town of Grunwald.

For the past six months the town has been under attack by a vampire, and approximately 30 people are dead. Rotmann arrives in the village as evening begins. Not wishing to lose any advantage his sudden appearance on the scene might cause, he turns down the town's immediate hospitality and ventures to a place where the local vampire is known to have been. Standing alone, with only a hammer and a stake, he calls out to the creature of the night.

The vampire is initially amused by the apparently defenseless old man. However, the old man proves amazingly quick and agile and soon has the vampire pinned. As he drives the stake in, he smiles and lets his victim see his fangs. Dr. Rotmann is also a vampire who travels the country eliminating the competition. He is handsomely paid, and when he returns to the village, his assistant has dinner waiting on the table for him.

SOURCES:
"The Fearless Vampire Killer." *Halloween Terror.* No. 1. Malibu Graphics/Eternity, Sept. 1990.

Summers, Buffy

A cheerleader at Hemery High School in the Los Angeles area in the early 1990s, Buffy Summers is confronted with the unwelcome news that she is the chosen one, her generation's Vampire Slayer. As a Vampire Slayer, Buffy's purpose in life is fighting the vampires who are terrorizing humankind. While initially rejecting her role and the changes it demands her to make to her adolescent lifestyle of shopping, cheerleading, and socializing, Buffy quickly connects with Merrick, the man destined to be her trainer. It seems that Merrick knows all about her weird dreams of encountering enigmatic creatures in historical settings. He claims that they are in fact memories of real events that Buffy has experienced in previous lives. He also claims to have been present when these events occurred.

Once Merrick gains Buffy's interest and trust, he informs her of her role as one of the Order of Slayers. He tells her that each Slayer has a birthmark on her left shoulder and that Slayers are reincarnated, spending each of their lives stopping the spread of vampirism. It turns out that **Lothos,** a 1,200-year-old vampire has come to Los Angeles with a plan to resurrect an army of vampires for his own purposes. Buffy is called upon to help thwart him. Merrick leads Buffy to the local cemetery, where some of Lothos's first victims are due to emerge from their graves. The ensuing confrontation with the newly emerged vampires convinces Buffy that all Merrick has told her is true. Nonetheless, a part of Buffy still wants a typical teenage life—a life in which nothing is more important than the upcoming high school dance, which she has helped to plan.

In the meantime, aware of the importance of her role, Buffy spends her afternoons training to be the Slayer and her evenings dispatching Lothos's minions (staking being the preferred method). She also meets a new boyfriend, Pike, who has lost his best friend to Lothos. Eventually, Buffy's nocturnal slaying activities catch the attention of Lothos, who strikes back by killing her mentor, Merrick. Having figured out that Buffy is the latest incarnation of the Slayer and the primary

Buffy the Vampire Slayer (here portrayed by Kristy Swanson in the movie version) dispatches another teenage bloodsucker.

obstacle to his plans to create a legion of vampires in Los Angeles, Lothos plots to kill her as well. He gathers his group of followers for an attack upon Buffy's up-coming high school dance.

During the dance, Buffy finally has the opportunity to square-off against Lothos, and, in the end, she uses her martial arts skills to defeat him. During the fight, she makes a stake from a broken chair and drives it home with a well-placed kick. With Lothos out of the way, it appears that Buffy will finish high school and resume her vampire slaying as an adult, but things change when a television network wants to turn a successful movie into a televsion series, which is just what happened with *Buffy*. In 1997, the new television version of *Buffy the Vampire Slayer* made its debut on the Warner Brothers network. The show picks up some time after Buffy's encounter with Lothos—it turns out she was blamed for burning down the gym at Hemery High that night (which she did, to destroy vampires) and had to transfer. As the show opens, she is settled into her new high school in a suburb called Sunnydale.

Buffy (and her still ignorant mother) hopes to finally resume a normal life, but such is not the case. She is bothered by dreams, and, more importantly, understands

Sarah Michelle Gellar is the new Buffy in the television version of *Buffy the Vampire Slayer.*

that the wave of deaths and disappearances that have struck her classmates is the work of vampires. She then meets **Rupert Giles**, the school librarian, who offers her a book on vampires. Slowly she again comes to terms with her chosen status.

Her first task is to handle the Master, a vampire king who is set to re-enter the world of humans from which he has been banished. Each century, there is one moment called the harvest when he can draw strength from the feeding of a selected minion, a vessel. On the evening in question, his vessel Luke takes over the local teen club and begins to feed. Fortunately Buffy, having been warned by a mysterious young man named **Angel** that "Tonight is the Harvest" arrives just in time to save everyone. The Master's first plan is thwarted, but he is not finished.

Shortly thereafter, Angel again intervenes and relates a prophecy which indicates that on the following evening, Buffy will fight the Master and lose. The next evening, at the school dance, Buffy and the Master fight. He wins round one, but she revives and finally kills him as the first season comes to a close.

Buffy begins the new year somewhat more accepting of her purpose in life, but now has a new object of her attention—Angel. Though he appears to be only a few years older than Buffy, he is in fact a 240-year-old vampire. Once a vicious killer, he encountered some Gypsies who punished him by restoring his soul. Vampires, it appears, are different in that they have no soul, hence no conscience. Angel is different and can no longer kill. One could not conjure a more perfect boyfriend for the unique human than a unique vampire. Their relationship grows through the school year and eventually culminates when they declare their love for each other and have sex. As a result of that moment of bliss, Angel loses his soul again and reverts to his former vicious nature. Now, Buffy, still in love, knows she must kill Angel, and Angel, having lost his soul, still remembers their love. Thus the tension is set for future confrontations. and in the meantime, Buffy has to foil the various plots of Spike and Drusilla, old vampire friends of Angel who have come to town to cause trouble while they try to kill the Slayer.

Buffy the Vampire Slayer was the product of the imagination of writer/producer Joss Whedon. The Slayer was originally portrayed by Kristy Swanson in the 1992 movie, and was immortalized in *Buffy the Vampire Slayer*, a novelization of the movie by Ritchie Cusick. In the subsequent television series, Sarah Michelle Geller portrays Buffy and leads the cadre of friends who together fight the vampires. Unlike the movie, which got very mixed reviews, the series has become a hit.

SOURCES:

"Buffy the Vampire Slayer." *Spectrum*. No. 13. May 1998: 8-23.

Cusick, Ritchie Tankersley. *Buffy the Vampire Slayer*. New York: Archway/Pocket Books, 1992. Novelization based on the screenplay by Joss Whedon.

———. *Buffy the Vampire Slayer: The Harvest*. New York: Archway/Pocket Books, 1997.

Cover, Arthur Byron. *Buffy the Vampire Slayer: Night of the Living Brain*. New York: Archway/Pocket Books, 1998.

Golden, Christopher, and Nancy Holder. *Buffy the Vampire Slayer: Halloween Rain*. New York: Archway/Pocket Books, 1997.

Vornholt, John. *Coyote Moon*. New York: Archway/Pocket Books, 1998

Trent, Sheila

Sheila Trent, a vampire who operates as a private investigator, first appears in the comic book *Sheila Trent: Vampire Hunter* (1996). She is a young woman with long red hair. A somewhat traditional vampire, she lives in an apartment with her kitten.

Not much is known about her, although the first story reveals her history: Formerly a Chicago policewoman, Trent leaves the force to become a free-lance investigator. One evening a man comes into her office and hires her to find out who is following him. She initially checks the waterfront where she finds the bodies of three muggers who have been drained of all moisture. Suddenly, the man in black who has been following her client appears. A vampire, he bites her and then turns to a second victim. He leaves both bodies partially drained. Trent recovers and approaches the second victim. Attracted to the open wound on her neck, she suddenly finds herself sucking the blood. The immediate feeling of ecstasy is followed by intense guilt as she realizes what she has done.

As a vampire, Trent adopts a new image with clothing from a fetish shop and in a series of stories joins the nighttime underground of the city to search for the one who made her.

SOURCES:

Sheila Trent: Vampire Hunter. Glen Carbon, IL: Draculina Publishing, 1996.

Van Helsing, Abraham

A major character in Bram Stoker's *Dracula*, Abraham Van Helsing is introduced as the wise, elder scholar who brings enlightenment to the confusing and threatening situation in which the group of other characters, all in their twenties, have become enmeshed. Van Helsing, a resident of Amsterdam, was originally called to England by Dr. John Seward, who describes him as an "old friend and master" as well as an expert in obscure diseases. Van Helsing is a philosopher, metaphysician, and advanced scientist.

His first task is to examine the ailing **Lucy Westenra**. He finds nothing with the exception of a blood loss, yet she isn't suffering from anemia. He returns to Amsterdam. In less than a week, after Lucy's condition takes a decided turn for the worse, he returns. He prescribes an immediate transfusion. He then notices two unusual marks on Lucy's neck. Again he returns to Amsterdam to consult his books. Upon his return a few days later, Lucy receives a second transfusion. By this time he has figured out the cause of Lucy's problem, though he does not share his knowledge with Dr. Seward. He merely takes steps to keep the vampire away from Lucy by surrounding her with garlic. She improves markedly and Van Helsing returns home once again.

Lucy loses the lifesaving garlic several days later, and **Count Dracula** returns to her bedroom to attack her once more. This time nothing, not even a third transfusion, can save her. Quincey P. Morris raises the possibility of vampires. After her death, Van Helsing takes the lead in organizing the men, particularly Lucy's fiance, Arthur Holmwood, to treat Lucy's corpse as a vampire. He instructs them to observe her movements after she is placed in her crypt; after observation, there is no doubt that she has joined the undead. While Holmwood pounds the stake into Lucy's heart, Van Helsing reads the prayer for the dead from a prayer book, after which he and Seward decapitate the corpse and fill the mouth with garlic.

After Lucy's death, Van Helsing turns to the task of learning all he can about Dracula. His goal is to discover his hiding places and eventually destroy him. In a meeting with all the principals, he receives their commitment to join the fight under his leadership. At this gathering (Chapter 18), he lays out, in a most systematic fashion, the theory of vampires (only partially revealed earlier), emphasizing their diverse powers and the manner by which they may be killed. He thus trains the men and sets them to the task at hand. Meanwhile, Mina Murray (by this time married to Jonathan Harker) is showing signs of Dracula's attack. She is growing pale and fatigued, but Van Helsing and the others are slow to recognize what is occurring. Van Helsing finally realizes, while talking to the madman R. N. Renfield, that Mina is under attack, and immediately leads Seward, Holmwood, and Morris to the Harker house, where they find Mina drinking from Dracula's chest. Van Helsing drives the vampire off with a crucifix and a eucharistic wafer (consecrated wafers are believed by Roman Catholic Christians to be the very body of Christ). To protect Mina he holds the wafer to Mina's forehead only to have it burn its imprint there—much like a branding iron.

Mina, who previously stepped aside to let the men engage Dracula, now becomes an active participant in the fight. She invites Van Helsing to hypnotize her and thus tap into her psychic tie to Dracula. In this manner, Van Helsing, who led the destruction of Dracula's boxes of earth, which he needs to survive, discovers that the vampire has left England and returned to Transylvania. He accompanies Mina and the men on the chase to catch Dracula. During the last leg of the journey, the group splits into three pairs. Van Helsing travels with Mina and they are the first to arrive at Castle Dracula. He draws a circle around her with the eucharistic wafers and enters the castle. He kills the three vampire brides who reside there, sanitizes Dracula's crypt, and finishes by treating the castle's entrances so no vampire can use them in the future.

Returning to Mina, he takes her some distance from the castle entrance where they are protected from the wolves while waiting for the remaining four slayers to converge for the final confrontation. Once all arrive, he holds a rifle on the Gypsies as Morris and Harker approach the box in which Dracula rests and watches as the pair kill Dracula.

VAN HELSING IN OTHER MEDIA: As *Dracula* was brought to stage and screen, Van Helsing assumed a key role, the plot often being simplified to a personal battle between Dracula and Van Helsing as the representatives of evil and good respectively. Interestingly, Hamilton Deane, who wrote the original *Dracula* play for his theater company chose to assume the role of Van Helsing rather than Dracula. However, it has been Peter Cushing, who played the part in several of the Hammer Films motion pictures, who is most often identified with the role of Van Helsing. He not only played Van Helsing at various times, but also portrayed several of the twentieth century descendants who continued his fight against vampiric evil.

Count Dracula (portrayed by Gary Oldman) was ultimately destroyed by Abraham Van Helsing in *Bram Stoker's Dracula.*

In both the movies and the world of comic books, descendants of Van Helsing have flourished. Cushing played Van Helsing's grandson in Hammer's *Dracula A.D. 1972.* Other descendants have been portrayed by Richard Benjamin in *Love at First Bite* (1979) and Bruce Campbell in *Sundown: The Vampire in Retreat* (1988). Marvel Comics invented **Dr. Rachel Van Helsing**, a granddaughter who continues the search and destroy mission against Dracula on the pages of *The Tomb of Dracula* through the 1970s. Recently, **Conrad** and **Adam Van Helsing** emerged on the pages of *Vampirella* as vampire hunters.

Several people have been identified as possible models for Van Helsing, including the author "Abraham" Stoker himself. Some have suggested Arminius Vambery, mentioned in chapter 18 as a friend of Van Helsing's. Vambery was a real person, a former professor at the University of Budapest, and the probable source of Stoker's initial knowledge of Vlad the Impaler, a historical model for Count Dracula. In *The Essential Dracula*, editors Raymond McNally and Radu Florescu suggest Max Muller, the famous Orientalist at Oxford University, as a possibility. They also suggest that Dr. Martin Hasselius, the fictional narrator in Sheridan Le Fanu's *In a Glass Darkly*, might also have inspired the character Van Helsing.

SOURCES:

Stoker, Bram. *The Essential Dracula.* Edited by Raymond McNally and Radu Florescu. New York: Mayflower Books, 1979.

Van Helsing, Adam

Adam Van Helsing, vampire hunter and associate of the extraterrestrial vampire **Vampirella,** is introduced in the short story "Who Serves the Cause of Chaos?" in the comic book *Vampirella* (1970). He is the son of **Conrad Van Helsing,** a descendent of **Abraham Van Helsing,** who tracks **Count Dracula** in the Bram Stoker novel. The series begins when the body of Conrad's brother, Kurt Van Helsing, is found in the wreckage of a plane. His blood has been drained and the only wounds are two fang marks on his neck. Being an expert on vampires and the supernatural, and motivated by the fact that his wife and now his brother have become victims of the undead, Conrad begins a search for his brother's murderer.

Unfortunately, Conrad is blind and must to some extent rely upon Adam for assistance. However, Conrad has some clairvoyant powers to compensate for his handicap, and obtains pictures of the four people whose bodies are missing from the wreck. He quickly scans them and picks up on Vampirella's complete alien nature. He jumps to the conclusion that she has to be the one responsible for his brother's death. When Adam and Conrad catch up with Vampirella, she is the prisoner of the demonic god Chaos, who wants Vampirella to transform him into a vampire. Conrad and Adam are also taken prisoner. While Conrad lays unconscious, Vampirella has the opportunity to tell her story to Adam and convince him that she is not the one who murdered Kurt. He believes her, but Conrad does not.

After they escape Chaos's possession, Adam continues to search for Vampirella and finds her on a Caribbean island where she had been shipwrecked and his air-

Mina Murray (here portrayed by Winona Ryder in *Bram Stoker's Dracula*) was ultimately saved by vampire hunter Abraham Van Helsing.

plane crashed. Before he catches up with her, however, he is taken prisoner by a biochemist whose wife has become a werewolf. The scientist had been experimenting with various compounds to cure her, using humans as guinea pigs. Vampirella and her new associate, the stage magician Pendragon, rescue Adam.

Adam accompanies Vampirella to the island republic of Cote de Soleil. They soon discover that Conrad arrived on the island and was taken prisoner. As Vampirella ventures off to scout the prison, Adam is shot and arrested. Vampirella shares her blood (which she considers a most intimate ritual) and saves him. She rescues Conrad from the voodooists who captured him, and finds a temporary truce with Adam's father while he recovers. In the light of the events on Cote de Soleil, Adam, Vampirella, and Pendragon join together to fight Chaos. Conrad refrains from joining them, still unable to fully trust Vampirella. Over the next year, Conrad, with Vampirella's help, discovers who actually killed his brother and drops many of his suspicions of her, and through the 1970s comics the four share numerous adventures.

In the last issue of the Warren Comics *Vampirella* series in 1983, Conrad is taken prisoner by the agents of Chaos and held to keep Vampirella and Adam in check. Vampirella goes after him, and that is the last Adam sees of either for almost a decade. In the meantime, the forces of Chaos settle in Washington and infiltrate the structures of human society. Adam continues on to a political career and eventually is elected to the Senate. Finally, in a 1991 issue of *Vampirella: Morning in America*, his questions regarding the whereabouts of his father and Vampirella are answered. His father's dead body is returned to him, and Vampirella, who has been suffering from amnesia, recovers her memory. Again, Adam, Vampirella, and Pendragon unite to defeat Chaos's agents.

For the next few years, Adam and Vampirella work together. However, in 1996 as the end of the *Vengeance of Vampirella* series, Vampirella and Adam encounter supervillian Nyx. She kills both Vampirella and Adam, and Adam is never resurrected for any future storylines.

SOURCES:
Author's Note: Several hundred issues of comic books featuring Vampirella have appeared. For a complete list through 1997, see Vampirella: A Collector's Checklist, *available from the*

Transylvanian Society of Dracula. The original stories in the Warren issues of Vampirella *are now rare and expensive, but have been reprinted in the Harris series* Vampirella Classic.

Melton, J. Gordon. *Vampirella: A Collector's Checklist.* Santa Barbara, CA: Transylvanian Society of Dracula, 1998.

Vampirella Classic. No. 1–5. New York: Harris Comics, 1995. Reprints of original stories from the Warren Comics series.

Vampirella: Morning in America. No. 1–4. New York: Harris Comics/Dark Horse, 1991.

Vengeance of Vampirella. No. 1–25. New York: Harris Comics, 1994–96.

Van Helsing, Conrad

Conrad Van Helsing, a descendent of vampire hunter **Abraham Van Helsing** and a scholar of the supernatural in general and vampires in particular, is introduced in the short story "Who Serves the Cause of Chaos?" in the comic book *Vampirella* (1970). When the series begins, the body of his brother, Kurt Van Helsing, is found in the wreckage of a plane. His blood has been drained and the only wounds are two fang marks on his neck. Motivated by the fact that his wife and now his brother have become victims of the undead, Conrad launches a hunt for his brother's murderer.

Conrad has one obstacle to his quest: he is blind. He compensates with his psychic abilities, and with the help of his son and assistant **Adam Van Helsing,** obtains pictures of the four people whose bodies are missing from the wreck. He quickly scans them and picks up on **Vampirella**'s completely alien nature. He jumps to the conclusion that she has to be the one responsible for his brother's death. When Conrad and Adam catch up with Vampirella, she is prisoner of the demonic god Chaos who wants Vampirella to transform him into a vampire. Conrad and Adam are also taken prisoner, and in the process, while Conrad lays unconscious, Vampirella has the opportunity to tell her story to Adam and convinces him that she is not the one who murdered Kurt. Conrad, having missed her monologue, does not believe she is innocent.

After Vampirella escapes from Chaos, she accepts a job as the assistant of the stage magician Pendragon and they leave to entertain tourists in the Caribbean. After a series of misadventures, Adam accompanies Vampirella to the island republic of Cote de Soleil. They soon discover that Conrad arrived on the island and was taken prisoner by a group of voodoo worshipers who tried to convince him to assist with their invocation of Chaos in order to retain their rulership of the island. Conrad refuses, and Adam and Vampirella show up in time to save him.

Conrad is still wary of Vampirella and refuses to join the pact that Adam makes with Vampirella and Pendragon to fight Chaos's organization. Later, however, when their opposition to Chaos leads them to the real murderers of Conrad's brother, a renegade priest, **Father Jonas,** and the Dark Disciples, Conrad is able put aside many of his doubts about Vampirella.

Throughout the 1970s stories, Conrad shares numerous adventures with his son, Vampirella, and Pendragon. In the last issue of the Warren Comics *Vampirella* series in 1983, Conrad is taken prisoner by the agents of Chaos and held to keep Vampirella and Adam in check. He dies in captivity and his body is sent to Adam, who has become a senator. He is briefly resurrected to join Vampirella to wrestle control of Washington from Chaos's minions who have moved in during the years of Conrad's captivity, but dies permanently as the fight reaches its climatic ending.

SOURCES:

Author's Note: Several hundred issues of comic books featuring Vampirella have appeared. For a complete list through 1997, see Vampirella: A Collector's Checklist, *available from the Transylvanian Society of Dracula. The original stories in the Warren issues of* Vampirella *are now rare and expensive, but have been reprinted in the Harris series* Vampirella Classic.

Melton, J. Gordon. *Vampirella: A Collector's Checklist.* Santa Barbara, CA: Transylvanian Society of Dracula, 1998.

Vampirella Classic. Nos. 1–5. New York: Harris Comics, 1995. Reprints of original stories from the Warren Comics series.

Vampirella: Morning in America. Nos. 1–4. New York: Harris Comics/Dark Horse, 1991.

Van Helsing, Dr. Rachel

Dr. Rachel Van Helsing, the great-granddaughter of vampire hunter **Abraham Van Helsing,** carries on the family's vampire hunting career in the long-running *The Tomb of Dracula* comic book series. Soon after **Frank Drake,** the modern descendent of **Count Dracula,** has his initial encounter with the lord of the vampires, Rachel encounters him in his sorrow over the loss of his fiancee and stops him from committing suicide. She introduces him to her colleague Taj, an Indian vampire hunter, and to the world of vampire hunting. She then introduces Drake to **Quincey Harker** and together they form a vampire hunting team with a special mission to stop Dracula.

In carrying on the fight, Rachel is attacked by a swarm of vampire bats and her face is scarred. Later, she is taken prisoner by Dracula and held for ransom when Dracula invades Harker's home. Harker has to free Dracula in return for Rachel's safety. After Drake returns from a brief departure, she and Drake acknowledge their love for each other and begin an affair that lasts until Dracula is dispatched by Harker in 1979. Afterward, they drift apart, confirming the basis of their relationship as the battle with the vampire. Having lost her entire purpose for living, Rachel becomes petty and spiteful. Drake finally leaves her, and hears later that she has been killed. Indeed, she does not return to fight Dracula when he returns in 1991.

SOURCES:

The Tomb of Dracula. Nos. 1–70. New York: Marvel Comics, 1972–79.

The Tomb of Dracula. New Series. Nos. 1–4. New York: Marvel Comics, 1991–92.

Van Helsing, Professor

Professor Van Helsing (portrayed by Peter Cushing), the grandson of vampire hunter Lawrence Van Helsing, appears in Hammer Films' *Dracula A.D. 1972*(1972). His grandfather, who authored a book on **Count Dracula,** died fighting the Transylvanian vampire. Not blessed with immortality or the ability to make magical returns, Lawrence had to be satisfied with passing on his knowledge of the occult to his descendants. Although he has not directly encountered Dracula (portrayed by Christopher Lee) as his ancestors have, as a London university professor Van Helsing continues the family tradition of seriously studying of the occult.

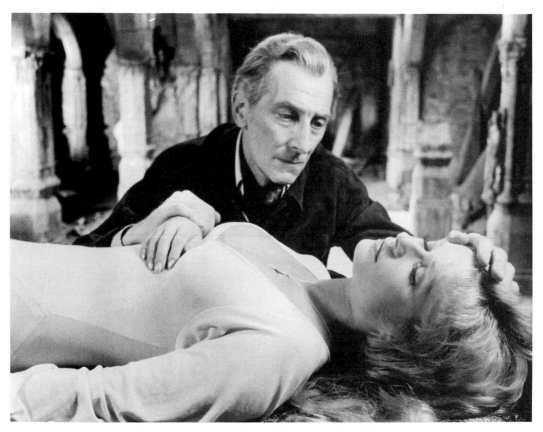

The legendary Peter Cushing as Professor Van Helsing in the film *Dracula A.D. 1972*.

Van Helsing is the guardian of his young-adult granddaughter Jessica Van Helsing. Jessica's friends hang out at a local pub. Among the group is a young man known as Johnny Alucard, who is playing around with Satanism. Unbeknownst to the rest of the group, he also possesses Dracula's ring and some ashes that had been recovered from Dracula's corpse in 1872. He plans to resurrect Dracula with the hopes of becoming immortal himself.

Van Helsing develops some initial concern about the group with whom Jessica is associating, especially after he figures out that Alucard is Dracula spelled backward. His concern heightens after Jessica disappears, and he learns that she has been picked to become the bride of Dracula. He gathers his antivampire weapons and heads for the abandoned church that the group uses for its rituals, where he finds Dracula behind the altar and the ritual ready to be consummated. Van Helsing wins the first round of the attack by plunging a silver dagger into Dracula, however, Jessica, under Dracula's hypnotic control, pulls it out. Dracula then chases Van Helsing to the graveyard outside, and as Van Helsing arrives at an area he has previously prepared, he throws holy water in Dracula's face. Dracula falls onto a stake sticking out of the ground and quickly disintegrates. The centuries-old battle between Dracula and the Van Helsings is finished, at least for the moment.

Van Helsing, Victor

Victor Van Helsing (Ace Mask), a vampire hunter distantly related to vampire hunter **Abraham Van Helsing,** appears in the horror spoof *Transylvania Twist* (1989). As a child, he is delighted when he receives a vampire hunting kit, and he eagerly begins using it. However, it is taken away from him when he stakes one of his classmates, who happens to be a vampire. As a teenager, he dates Betty Lou, a millennia-old vampire, whom he kills one night with holy water when they go out on a date. In keeping with his aggressive youth, as an adult Van Helsing decides to dedicate his life to eradicating the world of vampires.

Van Helsing befriends Marinus Orlok, a Transylvanian nobleman with vampiric tendencies. Orlok lives in a castle with three beautiful young vampire brides. Van Helsing breaks off his relationship with Marinus because of a disagreement over *The Book of Ulthar*, which Marinus hopes to use to release magical spells and invoke the Evil One.

In the later 1980s, Marinus is reported dead. Van Helsing is named the executor of the estate, and he travels to Transylvania to carry out his duties. The trip also

Horror movie host and vampire hunter Peter Vincent (portrayed by Roddy McDowall) holds off vampire (Chris Sarandon) with a crucifix in *Fright Night*.

gives him the opportunity to destroy a few more vampires along the way. At the castle he meets Marinus's evil brother,**Byron Orlok,** who is also searching for the book, Marinus's daughter Marissa, a singer, and Dexter Ward, a librarian who is searching for the book. It turns out that Marinus had found the book in the Arkham, Massachusetts, library and checked it out 20 years ago. It was long overdue.

In the process of settling Marinus's affairs, Van Helsing encounters the three vampire brides who reside at the castle. While Marissa and Dexter settle the matter of the book and dispatch the evil Byron, the women turn their attention to Van Helsing, whom they turn into a vampire. He would later declare that even though he had become a vampire, he was still a good person. He joins the three women to form a rock band, with the hopes of singing backup for Marissa's next video.

Vincent, Peter

Peter Vincent is the reluctant vampire hunter brought to life by actor Roddy McDowell in the film *Fright Night* (1985). A typecast horror actor who had played a

Peter Vincent shows a vampire (Stephen Geoffreys) the damage a cross can cause in *Fright Night*.

fearless vampire killer in several movies, Vincent had been reduced to reliving his movie persona as the host of the horror movie television show *Fright Night*. Following his encounter with vampire Jerry Dandridge, the teenage Charlie Brewster contacts Vincent, assuming he is the only person who can help him. Vincent rebuffs Brewster's initial approach to get involved—his only experience with vampires limited to Hollywood drama—but comes around when offered money. Only after a vampire attacks him does Vincent admit that all of his vampire hunter skills are a fraud and that he is just a scared actor.

Vincent has to overcome his fear, however, when Charlie's girlfriend Amy is kidnaped and the two become her only hope. Vincent gathers all of his traditional vampire-fighting equipment—crosses, wooden stakes, and other props from his days of movie glory—along with one really serious weapon, a pistol. Together, he and Charlie enter the den of vampires, which now includes the recently vampirized Amy. Scared, but affirming his courage with every step, Vincent moves through the dark house. As the first vampire in the form of a wolf leaps at the discombobulated vampire hunter, Vincent somehow finds a broken table leg and impales the creature. The surprised and successful Vincent, with newly discovered courage, is now ready to face Dandridge.

Vincent and Charlie find Dandridge in his coffin in the basement. As Vincent starts to drive the stake into the heart, Dandridge awakens and attacks him. In the ensuing fight, as Vincent stands defenseless against the vampire's fangs, Charlie rips the cover off the window, and the vampire dies in the blazing sunlight. With Dandridge dead, Amy reverts back to her normal self and Vincent returns to his television show.

In the sequel, *Fright Night II* (1988), the traumatized Charlie has been seeing a psychiatrist who tries to convince him that vampires are unreal and his experience was a mirage. After several years, Charlie is ready to accept that verdict, only to have another vampire, **Regine**, move in next door. When Charlie learns she has come to avenge the death of her brother, he calls the reluctant Vincent to the scene. Although he carries fond memories of his one moment of moral courage, he is reluctant to believe that more vampires exist and to place himself in danger should that be the case. His courage returns only after he reports for work to discover that Regine has replaced him as host for *Fright Night*. When he confronts her on the set, and publicly accuses her of being a vampire, he is thrown into a mental hospital.

As the plot thickens, Regine kidnaps Charlie and prepares to slowly turn him into a vampire. Now it is up to Charlie's girlfriend to first free Vincent and then assist the angry actor in rescuing Charlie. Once out of the hospital Vincent stops at a church for holy water and at home again to assemble all the props from his movie days. He is prepared to meet the vampire again, and again rises to the challenge. At the sequel's conclusion, its is Vincent who wields the ultimately effective weapon, a mirror reflecting the dawn's early light.

The character of Peter Vincent was created by Tom Holland for the screenplays of *Fright Night* and *Fright Night II*. A novelization of the film appeared simultaneously with the first movie's release. A comic book version of both *Fright Night* (adapted by Joe Gentile) and *Fright Night II* (adapted by Matthew Costello) appeared in 1988. The comic books turned into a series that extended the story to 22 monthly issues through 1990, and sprang several sequels.

SOURCES:

Skipp, John, and Craig Spector. *Fright Night*. New York: Tor Books, 1985.
Fright Night. Nos. 1–22. Chicago: Now Comics, 1988–90.
Fright Night II. Chicago: Now Comics, 1988.
Fright Night Halloween Annual. Chicago: Now Comics, 1993.

PHOTO AND
ILLUSTRATION CREDITS

Photos and illustrations used in *The Vampire Gallery* were reprinted with permission from the following sources:

Book and Comic Book Covers

Julian, San, illustrator. From a jacket of *A Flame in Byzantium*, by Chelsea Quinn Yarbro. Tor Books, 1987. Reproduced by permission.

Anne Rice's 'Queen of the Damned', vol. 1, issue 2 for cover art by Daerick Gross. Reproduced by permission of the illustrator.

Bethany the Vampfire, February, 1998 for a cover by Holly Golightly. Copyright (c) 1998 Holly Golightly. Reproduced by permission.

Cover of *Bitter Blood*, by Karen E. Taylor. Zebra Books, 1994. Reproduced by permission.

Cover of *Bloodhunter*, October, 1996 on page. (c) 1996 Kirk Lindo. Reproduced by permission.

Ellis, Steven A., and Stew Noack, illustrators. From a cover of *Confessions of a Teenage Vampire: The Turning*, by Terry M. West and Steve Ellis. Scholastic Inc., 1997. Illustrations copyright (c) 1997 by Steve Ellis. Reproduced by permission.

Cover of *Count Boris Bolescu and the Transylvanian Tango*, by Ann Jungman. Young Corgi Books, 1991. Reproduced by permission.

Deadbeats, June, 1993 for a cover by Richard Howell. (c) 1993 Claypool Comics and Richard Howell. Reproduced by permission.

Deadbeats, November, 1997 for a cover by Richard Howell. (c) 1997 Claypool Comics and Richard Howell. Reproduced by permission.

Draculina, n. 1, 1993 for a cover by Hugh Gallagher. (c) 1993 Hugh Gallagher. Reproduced by permission.

Embrace, December, 1996. (c) 1996 Everette Hartsoe. Reproduced by permission.

Fire in the Blood, by P. N. Elrod. Ace Books, 1991. Reproduced by permission of The Berkley Publishing Group, a member of Penguin Putnam Inc.

Cover of *Hotel Transylvania: A Novel of Historical Love*, by Chelsea Quinn Yarbro. St. Martin's Press, 1978. Reproduced by permission.

Necroscope, October, 1992 for a cover by Bob Eggleton. (c) 1992 Malibu Comics Entertainment, Inc. Reproduced by permission of the illustrator.

Necroscope, vol. 1, issue 1for splash page art by Daerick Gross. Reproduced by permission of the illustrator.

Cover of *Rulers of Darkness*, by Steven Spruill. St. Martin's Press, 1995. Reproduced by permission.

Smith, George, illustrator. From a cover of *Sabella; or The Blood Stone*, by Tanith Lee. DAW Books Inc., 1980. Reproduced by permission.

Sheila Trent: Vampire Hunter, n. 2, 1996. (c) 1996 Hugh Gallagher. Reproduced by permission.

Vamperotica Red Reign, October, 1997. Copyright (c) 1997 Brainstorm Comics, Inc. Reproduced by permission.

Vamperotica Red Reign, March, 1997. Copyright (c) 1997 Brainstorm Comics, Inc. Reproduced by permission.

Vamperotica Red Reign, September, 1997. Copyright (c) 1997 Brainstorm Comics, Inc. Reproduced by permission.

Vampirella, n. 46, October, 1975. (c) 1998 by Harris Publications, Inc. Reproduced by permission of Harris Publications, Inc.

Vampirella Vs. Pantha Showcase, January, 1997. (c) 1998 by Harris Publications, Inc. Reproduced by permission of Harris Publications, Inc.

Riley, Kelly, illustrator. From a cover of *Vampires Anonymous*, by Jeffrey N. McMahan. Alyson Publications, Inc., 1991. Cover art (c) 1991 by Kelly Riley. Reproduced by permission.

Cover of *Vampire Notes*, by Robert Arthur Smith. Fawcett Gold Medal, 1990. Reproduced by permission of Random House, Inc.

Cover of *Vampire Virus*, by Michael Romkey. Fawcett Gold Medal, 1998. Reproduced by permission of Random House, Inc.

Vigil: Eruption II, October, 1996 for a cover by Mike Iverson. (c) 1996 Arvin Loudermilk and Mike Iverson. Reproduced by permission of the illustrator.

Photographs and Movie Poster Art

Kobal Collection: 3, 9, 20, 30, 46, 53, 63, 65, 74, 98, 119, 122, 124, 130, 152, 157, 164, 168, 176, 184, 190, 199, 207, 221, 244, 261, 262, 271, 275, 276, 279, 281, 287, 292, 304, 311, 316, 378, 420, 425, 446, 447, 454, 460, 462, 468, 472, 477, 479, 480

David del Valle Archive: 4, 12, 14, 41, 53, 64, 66, 104, 106, 108, 110, 118, 218, 220, 222, 232, 236, 245, 266, 280, 284, 293, 306, 312, 314, 342, 367, 398, 410, 418, 424, 467, 474

INDEX

This index lists all nonfiction and fiction personal names, publication titles, short stories, films, television shows, plays, and songs that are listed in the text of The Vampire Gallery. The page number of the main entry for every vampire, vampire hunter or associate, and vampire group or clan is highlighted in bold.